THE AGE OF MILTON

BACKGROUNDS TO SEVENTEENTH-CENTURY LITERATURE

edited by C. A. PATRIDES *and*
RAYMOND B. WADDINGTON

THE AGE
OF MILTON

Backgrounds
to seventeenth-
century literature

C. A. PATRIDES
RAYMOND B. WADDINGTON

editors

THE AGE
OF MILTON

*Backgrounds
to seventeenth-
century literature*

MANCHESTER UNIVERSITY PRESS

BARNES & NOBLE BOOKS

© C. A. Patrides and R. B. Waddington 1980

Published by
Manchester University Press
Oxford Road, Manchester M13 9PL

First published in the USA 1980 by
Barnes & Noble Books
81 Adams Drive
Totowa, New Jersey 07512

British Library cataloguing in publication data

The age of Milton
   1. English literature—Early modern, 1500–1700
   –History and criticism.
   I. Patrides, Constantinos A.
   II. Waddington, Raymond B.
   820'.9'003   PR421

   UK ISBN 0–7190–0770–4
            0–7190–0816–6 (paperback)
   US ISBN 0–389–20051–4
            0–389–20052–2 (paperback)

1 8 4 4 0 3

Text set in 9/11½ pt VIP Palatino, printed and bound
in Great Britain at The Pitman Press, Bath

Contents

Illustrations

Between pp. 294–295

1. Richard Haydocke, title page for his translation of Giovanni Paolo Lomazzo, *A Tracte containing the Artes of curious Paintinge Caruinge Buildinge* (Oxford, 1598). Reproduced by courtesy of the Trustees of the British Library.
2. *Tomb of Sir Francis Bacon,* St Michael's, St Albans, Herts. Photo courtesy of the National Monuments Record.
3. Palladio, Convent of the Carità, Venice. Detail: Atrium. From Palladio, *I Quattro Libri dell'Architettura* (Venice, 1570). Courtesy of the Royal Institute of British Architects, London.
4. Etienne Dupérac, *Vestigij del Tempio della pace* [Basilica of Maxentius]. Folio 5 of the series of 1575. Reproduced by courtesy of the Trustees of the British Library.
5. Inigo Jones, *St Paul's Church,* Covent Garden. Engraving by Wenceslaus Hollar. Reproduced by courtesy of the Trustees of the British Library.
6. Inigo Jones, *Porch of St Paul's Cathedral,* London. Engraving by Wenceslaus Hollar. Reproduced by courtesy of the Trustees of the British Library.
7. *Whitehall as seen from the Thames* (*c.* 1640). Engraving by Wenceslaus Hollar. Reproduced by courtesy of the Trustees of the British Library.
8. Van Dyck, *Inigo Jones.* Engraving by Robert van Voerst for van Dyck's *Centum Icones.* Reproduced by courtesy of the Trustees of the British Library.
9. Rubens, *Fall of the Rebel Angels.* Engraving (after Rubens) by Lucas Vorsterman. Reproduced by courtesy of the Trustees of the British Library.
10. Rubens, *Peace and War.* National Gallery, London. Reproduced by courtesy of the Trustees, the National Gallery, London.
11. Rubens, *Apotheosis of James I,* centre panel, Banqueting House ceiling, Whitehall, London. Crown copyright; reproduced with permission of the Controller of Her Majesty's Stationery Office.
12. Van Dyck, *Lord John and Lord Bernard Stuart.* From the collection at Broadlands, Romsey, the home of Lord Mountbatten, which is open to the public from April to September.

The contributors

G. E. AYLMER, Master of St Peter's College, Oxford.

KENNETH CHARLTON, Professor of the History of Education, King's College, London.

PHILIPP P. FEHL, Professor of the History of Art, University of Illinois at Champaign.

PETER LE HURAY, University Lecturer in Music, St Catherine's College, Cambridge.

SAMUEL I. MINTZ, Professor of English, The City College of the City University of New York.

C. A. PATRIDES, Professor of English Literature, University of Michigan at Ann Arbor.

THEODORE K. RABB, Professor of History, Princeton University.

P. M. RATTANSI, Professor of the History and Philosophy of Science, University College, London.

THOMAS O. SLOANE, Professor of Rhetoric, University of California at Berkeley.

RAYMOND B. WADDINGTON, Professor of English, University of Wisconsin—Madison.

AUSTIN WOOLRYCH, Professor of History, University of Lancaster.

To the reader

The eleven chapters of the present volume, and the comprehensive bibliographies appended to it, provide varieties of contextualism for a fuller comprehension of the poetry and prose of Milton and his contemporaries. Our intention is to enrich those texts through a deployment of a diversity of interdisciplinary methods and perspectives. The erstwhile exclusiveness in attending to literature at the expense of its various backgrounds—or indeed vice versa—has rightly been arrested through a widespread and ever-increasing awareness that we must be fully cognisant of the responsiveness of Milton and his contemporaries to their interlocked social, political and cultural contexts. Convinced as we are of the validity of such an approach, we have collected in the ensuing pages new and authoritative studies of the manifold dimensions of the seventeenth century in the political domain as in the social and the educational, in the scientific as in the philosophical and the theological—and finally in the artistic inclusive of literature, music and the arts.

Our primary audience was conceived to be advanced undergraduate and postgraduate students of English literature. At the same time, our expectation was that other students of the period—those in the arts, the historical disciplines, and some of the social sciences—would find here much of singular usefulness to them. Nor did we disregard the possibility that teachers would wish to review largely familiar terrain, or to apprise themselves of the state of scholarship within adjacent disciplines.

Our title is not intended to proclaim that the seventeenth century was dominated by Milton in the way that the sixteenth was in every conceivable sense the Age of Erasmus. By 'the Age of Milton' we mean to confirm his self-evident stature within it, not only in that he is the period's foremost English poet and that his activities directly touched virtually every topic addressed in this volume, but in that his work reflects the period's spirit most comprehensively.

ABBREVIATIONS

Milton is principally if not exclusively quoted from *The Works of John Milton*, gen. ed. Frank A. Patterson (New York: Columbia University Press, 1931–40), 20 vols.—hereinafter abbreviated as *CE*.

The abbreviations 'P' and 'S' designate throughout Primary and Secondary sources respectively. Their appearance in the text and in the notes, always followed by a number, refers to the numbered entries in the two bibliographies on pp. 373–427.

ACKNOWLEDGEMENTS

We should like to acknowledge the encouragement, constructive observations and general advice of Professors G. E. Aylmer, Richard Dunn, Robert Kingdon, Richard McKeon, John Wallace, Joseph A. Wittreich, and our colleagues in our respective universities. We are also grateful to the Newberry Library in Chicago for support in the form of a fellowship, and to the same institution as well as to the British Library and the university libraries at Ann Arbor, at Madison, and at York, for the use of their facilities and the exemplary helpfulness of their staffs; and to the Departments of English in the last-named three universities for bearing some of the financial burden involved in the preparation of our typescript.

Acknowledgement is also gratefully made to the institutions which have given permission to reproduce the illustrations whose sources are as follows: the Trustees of the British Library, the National Monuments Record, the Royal Institute of British Architects, the Trustees of the National Gallery, H.M. Queen Elizabeth II and the late Earl Mountbatten of Burma.

York, Madison, Athens, London, Chicago and Ann Arbor   C. A. P.
                                                              R. B. W.

G. E. AYLMER

1

The historical background

The 'Age of Milton' is among the most eventful and complicated in English history. And in order to understand what happened within a particular span of time, in this case from 1603 to 1660, it is helpful to look back a little before and forward a little after. All dividing dates in history are arbitrary, although some are more hallowed by precedent than others. 1603 saw the accession of the Stuart dynasty, and hence the union of the crowns of England and Scotland; 1660 saw that dynasty's restoration after the only interval so far in Britain of republican rule. These dates have been much used too by generations of textbook writers and teachers, organisers of school and university syllabi and examiners. In this chapter an attempt will be made better to understand the reigns of James and Charles I and the regimes of the Commonwealth and the Cromwellian Protectorate by setting them in a slightly longer chronological perspective, approximately from the Spanish Armada in 1588 to the 1670s, between the deaths of Milton (1674) and of Hobbes (1679).

ELIZABETH I

The last years of Elizabeth I's long reign saw the Tudor State subjected to very severe, perhaps unparalleled stress and strain. England was at war with the greatest naval and military power of the Christian world, the Spain of Philip II. From 1580 onwards his empire included Portugal and its Asian and African possessions as well as the Habsburg territories in Iberia, Italy, the Low Countries, part of south-eastern France, large areas of central and south America, the Caribbean islands and the Philippines. The war was waged on the oceans, in the West Indian archipelago, in the Netherlands, at times in France and in Ireland. There the Spaniards gave such help as they could to the last great movement of resistance by the Gaelic Irish against English conquest and colonisation. For the Dutch and for the English, as for their opponents the native Irish, it was in part a war of religion, certainly a war of national survival; for Spain too it was a war of religion, also a defensive attempt to preserve her empire, and to repel English aggression in the New World and in the Netherlands. By the mid-1590s the costs of war were becoming prohibitive to both sides, and it was clear that neither was likely to win a decisive victory, although hopes and fears to the contrary prevented this from being generally recognised much before the early seventeenth century.

After an earlier period of insecurity, Queen Elizabeth I and her Ministers—notably William Cecil Lord Burghley—had ruled successfully over a relatively peaceful and united country, particularly during the middle part of the reign. But they had practised caution and frugality rather than reform, especially in matters to do with taxation and Crown finance. Meanwhile the religious divisions remained, and in some ways intensified as the reign went on. The great Puritan campaign, conducted jointly by clergy and laymen, many of them Members of Parliament, and even with 'fellow travellers' in the Queen's Council, was finally defeated in the years 1589–92. At the same time the Puritans lost their most powerful protectors in high places: Francis Walsingham, the senior Secretary of State, and Robert Dudley Earl of Leicester, the Queen's premier favourite. And the last three Parliaments of the reign were relatively quiescent in religion compared to those of the 1560s–80s. Despite Puritan opposition to the practices and beliefs of high-church bishops and other divines, there was indeed no outright attack on episcopacy and the Prayer Book from the 1590s to the 1630s. But there was plenty else to darken the great Queen's last years. The Roman Catholic minority suffered bitter persecution and their missionary priests risked execution as traitors; in this as in other respects both Parliament and the Council were more consistently and militantly Protestant than Elizabeth herself. Inside the government and the administrative system, corruption and factional fighting were rampant. The monetary inflation, if modest in pace compared to that of our own time, had a dislocating effect on a relatively static, pre-industrial society. As a result of this, the Crown, the Church, sections of the landowning class and the mass of the people, especially those who were dependent on wages, became worse off; other landowners, and wide sections of those in the upper and middle ranks of society—lawyers, merchants, tradesmen, yeomen and tenant farmers—held their own or actually grew richer. This tendency lasted, approximately, from the middle of Henry VIII's reign until into Charles I's. It was accompanied, and some historians now think partly caused, by population growth, particularly from the 1570s to the 1620s. This too was gradual by twentieth-century standards, but resulted in a labour surplus—hence the severe lag of wages behind prices—also pressure on land and other resources. The mid-1590s saw short-term economic troubles on top of these long-run developments: two or three very bad harvests brought large numbers of the poor to the brink of starvation, and London was only saved from mass famine by grain specially imported from the Baltic.

At this time Ireland was more of an outlet than America for England's surplus population. Whereas thousands settled in the southern Irish province of Munster, their very existence to be threatened by the O'Neill rebellion of the 1590s which spread there from Ulster, the only serious attempt to found an English colony across the ocean—on the coast of what is now North Carolina—was undertaken from 1584 to 1587 under Ralegh's patronage. Ill planned and led, and inadequately sustained, it had totally disappeared by 1589.[1] Despite the destruction of the Armada and some other English victories, the war with Spain was far from being uniformly glorious and successful. By the later 1590s most of England's great sea commanders, Drake, Hawkins, Frobisher and Grenville, were dead. So too were most of Elizabeth's original councillors and confidants. The rivalry between her new and last favourite, Robert Devereux second Earl of Essex, and Robert Cecil, Burghley's younger son and the heir apparent to his father's political influence and authority, together with the problem of succession to the throne itself that loomed ahead as the Queen aged visibly, threatened to tear the country apart; once more the spectre appeared of foreign intervention and civil war. In so far as she addressed herself to the matter at all, Elizabeth must have expected and intended her successor to be her cousin, James VI of Scotland. But she never nominated him publicly and probably did not even do so on her deathbed. Whereas in the early part of her reign the Queen's refusal either to marry or to name a successor had been a successful gamble on her own survival, now thirty years later neither course was realistic.

At home the power struggle intensified, with armed conflict a real possibility. Recalled in disgrace from Ireland—or rather anticipating recall by a dash to court—for having not merely failed to defeat O'Neill but for having entered into unauthorised negotiations with him instead, Essex was stripped of office and favour and thus faced imminent financial ruin. What might have been the last great baronial or 'bastard feudal' rebellion fizzled out like a damp squib in the abortive fiasco of the 'Essex revolt' in February 1601. Failure led the Earl and several of his fellow conspirators inexorably to the block; others to prison, exile, or disgrace. This left Robert Cecil and his allies in almost complete control of the government, and with a near monopoly of royal favour and patronage. The Queen's sureness of political touch may indeed still be seen in the so-called 'golden speech' to members of the Commons in her last Parliament in the same year, when she appeared to give way on the issue of monopoly patents and promised to rectify legitimate popular grievances, while defending her prerogative successfully. But the underlying problems, of inconclusive war, financial overstrain, inflation, religious and perhaps dynastic conflicts ahead, all remained unsolved. Nor did Elizabeth grow more generous in distributing honours and rewards as she grew older, but rather the reverse. She created virtually no new peers and very few new knights in her latter years. With the process of natural demographic shrinkage (families not replacing themselves in the male line) this meant that the hereditary aristocracy was actually beginning to die out. Yet there were many of the newly rich and influential with unsatisfied ambitions and aspirations: Ministers of State, financiers and royal creditors, successful speculators in privateering, naval and military commanders, top career lawyers. The Queen's wholly laudable frugality was degenerating into pathological meanness. Yet her instinct to restrict naval and military expenditure and to fight a limited war for limited objectives was entirely sound. Otherwise good money would simply be poured after bad.

Meanwhile the international scene was changing, both for the better and for the worse. After rejoining the Roman Church, Henry ('Paris is worth a mass') IV had made peace with Spain, sensibly abandoning his Dutch and English allies. Philip II, the last great Habsburg monarch, himself died in the same year, leaving—as it turned out—a quite inadequate successor. And by the time the Spaniards did eventually get an army ashore in Ireland, Essex had been succeeded by Charles Blount Lord Mountjoy, the ablest commander Elizabeth ever sent there. Moreover, because the Spaniards landed in the far south at Kinsale, O'Neill and his allies had to abandon their successful guerrilla base in Ulster and march the length of the country in order to join up with the besieged Spaniards. Having arrived outside Kinsale they were easily and overwhelmingly defeated in the only large, 'set piece' field action of the whole war. By the last weeks of the Queen's life, O'Neill was negotiating surrender terms with Mountjoy, who unlike the luckless Essex had the Queen's permission to treat with the rebel Earl of Tyrone—as he was in English eyes. Mountjoy concealed news of the Queen's illness and then of her death from the Irish leader until the treaty was safely signed and Tyrone's allegiance re-accepted. Spain's new rulers too, having been fought to a draw on land with the Dutch and with the English at sea, were now ready to consider peace terms. An end to the war would help English trade, even if it limited the scope for privateering and freebooting attacks on Spain's empire. The union of England, Scotland and Ireland under a single ruler for the first time in their history should have reduced military costs and helped trade. Perhaps too in a male-dominated culture people were tired of a woman ruler; no adult king had reigned in England for fifty-six years. When James succeeded he was already an experienced and, by contemporary standards, successful monarch. He came in unopposed, indeed on a great tide of enthusiasm, and hence with great opportunities. What, then, went wrong, and why?

JAMES VI AND I

The short answer is that James's reign was by no means a total failure, still less was it an unmitigated disaster. Too often biographers and textbook writers have portrayed the king as a slobbering pedant, lazy, prodigal and careless, sinking latterly into premature homosexual senility.[2] A compromise peace was soon made with Spain, and Britain was kept out of open involvement in foreign war until the last year of the King's reign, for a period of twenty years—no mean achievement. And she was then only drawn into the renewed European conflict against James's own better judgement. Overseas trade expanded, at least for the first ten years or so of restored peace. Internally, despite the various plots of the early years, the reign saw order and tranquillity preserved without excessively severe repression. The number of those imprisoned or executed for religious and political deviance was small. After the Gunpowder conspirators, only two religious radicals and the ex-Elizabethan favourite and war hero, Sir Walter Ralegh, were actually executed; one other person, an obscure clergyman, died in prison after being sentenced to death. Generally, James took a more temporising position in ecclesiastical affairs than either his predecessor or his successor. Expulsions of Puritan ministers after the failure of the Hampton Court Conference were limited to the most intransigent, and punishment of their allies to the most tactlessly outspoken. Other, more moderate Puritans actually helped in the great new translation of the Bible, commissioned under royal patronage, and published as the 'Authorised Version' in 1611. Nor was this surprising, for in theology James was at one with them. Something of an ecumenicist before his time, with over-ambitious not to say absurd hopes of re-unifying Christendom, he remained an orthodox Calvinist in belief, and his second Archbishop of Canterbury (George Abbott) was in this respect impeccably orthodox too. Only separatist Puritans and Baptists, and of course the diehard recusant Catholics, marred this harmony, as did the unsolved and indeed insoluble problem of the Papist majority in Ireland. In Scotland James advanced the cause of moderate episcopacy, reversing the trend towards Presbyterian clericalism of his middle years, but he prudently halted this process when the opposition stiffened.

Culturally the glories of the Elizabethan Age were not merely continued into the new reign but arguably surpassed. Of this, despite the early deaths of Marlowe, Kyd and Spenser (the latter a refugee from the Irish wars), ample record can be found in other chapters of this book. Why, then, has James I on the whole had such a bad press from posterity? Partly it is simply historical hindsight, the consequence of what was to happen in the next reign and after: but this is not the whole story.

In any system of personal monarchy the defects even more than the qualities of the ruler are magnified in their consequences. James was generous where Elizabeth had been stingy. But he carried this to excess, and within five years he had got so chronically into debt that the Crown was never able fully to recover solvency. Attempts were made to remedy the shortfall in several ways, some traditional, others innovatory. The King tried to restrain his own initially careless generosity, and appointed special advisers to stop his gifts—of offices, pensions, grants, titles and so on—from going through too easily. There were also campaigns to economise at court, of little effect until near the end of the reign. On the revenue side, the fundamental weakness of the Crown's position was due to the inflexibility of the tax system in relation to the falling value of money, the changing distribution of national wealth, and the absence of a long-term funded debt. The inadequacy of the tax system was partially remedied in the mid-century, the problem of public credit not really until the country was again subjected to the strains of a major European war, this time under King William III in the 1690s. In order to repay old loans and to provide security for new ones, Crown lands were sold as they had been under Henry VIII and Elizabeth I. Other sections of the royal revenues were either mortgaged in advance to creditors, or leased out to tax-farmers who were also often lenders to the Crown themselves. Efforts were made to increase the yield of existing revenues, notably of the remaining Crown lands, of the feudal and prerogative dues, and above all of the customs duties on exports and imports. There Tudor precedents could be invoked, and the common-law Judges upheld the King and his Ministers in a test case which vindicated the so-called Impositions and the new Book of Rates. But in these same years James's attempt to obtain a full legal, political and economic union between his southern and northern kingdoms was frustrated by a combination of prejudice and mutual suspicion, English commercial jealousy and resentment against Scottish courtiers and favourites. Grievances over the Impositions, which had no parliamentary sanction, the royal rights of wardship and purveyance (well named 'fiscal feudalism'), petty quarrels about the rival jurisdictions of different courts, fears that the English Parliament might decline into atrophy like many of its Continental counterparts if the Crown were not kept in financial straits, sheer lack of imagination and understanding—all contributed to prevent agreement being reached in the last sessions of James's first Parliament.

The failure of the Great Contract—as we shall see—had important immediate consequences. And it is more than an interesting coincidence that in several respects the terms of this abortive bargain in 1610 anticipated those of the Restoration financial settlement in 1660. The Crown was to surrender its feudal revenues (from wardship, purveyance, homage, etc.) and in return the Commons would make a once-for-all grant to pay off the King's debts and also find a new source of regular taxation. In 1660 the new revenue was available by legitimising and making permanent part of the excise, which the Parliamentarians had begun in 1643 and which had been continued under the succeeding regimes of both Commonwealth and Protectorate. In 1610, however, it was assumed that some kind of annual levy on landed income and/or property would be unavoidable. The administrative resources of the time were quite unequal to levying a regular tax on incomes, especially those of professional and business people. Even the Williamite or so-called 'Dutch finance' of the 1690s involved making permanent the land tax as the third great prop of the British revenue system, together with the customs and the excise. Only a century after that could the Younger William Pitt and his successors undertake to replace this by an income tax, whose permanent existence in peacetime dates from as recently as Sir Robert Peel's administration in the 1840s.

The foundering of the Contract, largely on the rocks of mutual suspicion between King and Commons, led to a rapid political and financial deterioration. Cecil, since 1608 Lord Treasurer and first Earl of Salisbury, lost the confidence of his royal master; his health gave way, and he died, although still in office, less than two years later. While the King then tried to govern the country without a chief Minister and by means of favourites, resort was had to a series of financial expedients, some more damaging than others, few of much avail. Titles of honour and royal offices were sold; monopoly patents again became wide-spread, the worst, economically speaking, being an attempted reorganisation of the main branch of England's export trade, in heavy woollen cloth to northern and central Europe, the failure of which did grave financial damage, and the most vexatious being that for the licensing of inns and alehouses, traditionally under the control of the local Justices of the Peace and hence the business of each individual county community. The Crown's dependence on the Justices of the Peace for law enforcement and local government, and on members of the same social class in each shire for the collection of parliamentary subsidies and other fiscal needs, made the loss of their active co-operation potentially very serious. Meanwhile scandals at court and divisions in the upper ranks of government accompanied the total failure of James's next and shortest, the so-called Addled Parliament of 1614. Not a single item reached the statute book, and by the time another Parliament was called (late in 1620 for early 1621) both the internal and external situations had changed dramatically. The leading political figures of the years 1611 to 1618 (the King's Scottish favourite Robert Carr Earl of Somerset and the Howards Earls of Northampton and Suffolk) had either died or been disgraced, and all rivals were now eclipsed by the King's new favourite, George Villiers, first created Earl, then Marquis and finally Duke of Buckingham. Successfully exploiting the talents of far abler men than himself, notably Francis Bacon on the legal side of government and Lionel Cranfield on the financial, Buckingham was soon dominating the King's Council as well as enjoying a near monopoly of royal favour and hence of Crown patronage.

Soon the influence of foreign affairs again became decisive. The outbreak of war in central Europe, involving the King's son-in-law Frederick of the Palatinate and thus his only daughter Elizabeth of Bohemia, the 'Winter Queen', inevitably drew Britain towards the conflict against the Austrian branch of the house of Habsburg and their other Catholic allies. This gave new urgency to James's schemes for a marriage alliance between his only surviving son Charles, now Prince of Wales, and the Infanta, Philip III of Spain's daughter. James sincerely believed that he could exercise greater influence on Spanish foreign policy, and hence render more service to the Protestant cause in Europe, as a neutral power allied to Spain in this way than as an enemy joined to her opponents. He may well have been right in this; or rather his critics may have been at least as wrong as he was. Spain's terms for a marriage treaty were always such that James could only have accepted them at the price of a major breach with the bulk of his Protestant subjects; likewise he overestimated not what England could do on the Continent—this was much more his critics' mistake—but what neutrality or non-intervention would be worth to Spain. So first the King partly abandoned his previous policy, agreeing to 'volunteers' (*alias* mercenaries) and financial aid being sent to Frederick, and then wholly reversed it in 1624 after the ignominious but widely welcomed failure of Charles's and Buckingham's visit to Madrid in pursuance of the Prince's marital hopes, after which a breach with Spain soon followed.

But the opposite policy was not embraced with sufficient vigour to make it effective. With few exceptions, neither James's advisors nor the members of his last two Parliaments (in 1621 and 1624) could envisage the necessary scale of naval and military intervention, still less the kind of financial support which would be required to underpin this. Here the King was more realistic, at the end more so even than his son and his favourite. Certainly the cost of waging effective war on the Habsburgs, even of maintaining credibly large armed forces without actually committing them, seems to have been quite beyond the imaginative grasp of most MPs throughout the 1620s. It has often been argued that, if they had not been—rightly—suspicious of James and then of Charles I on religious and constitutional grounds, then they would have voted more generous supplies; but even at their least suspicious and most generous the supplies granted were utterly inadequate for the purposes intended. Not until the outbreak of the Second Dutch War in 1664 did any Parliament freely vote supplies larger than the government of the day had dared to request and more than the King's advisers considered the minimum needed for the purpose in hand. During these years rational discussion of foreign affairs, and of the strategic options open to the country, was rendered increasingly difficult, and often impossible, by the other issues which frequently came boiling up to the surface of political debate.

In the first effective parliamentary sitting for eleven years (1621), discontents over monopolies and the Palatinate were exacerbated by renewed economic difficulties. Scarcely had the export of heavy woollens been restored to its previous basis under the Merchant Adventurers than currency depreciation in the consumer countries, together with the physical dislocation caused by the war, saw English cloth largely priced out of its traditional Continental markets. The resulting slump from 1620 on had consequences far beyond the export merchants. It affected the clothiers who bought the raw wool and employed the spinners and weavers, mostly through the domestic, or 'putting out', system, and not yet in factories. This in turn affected the wool producers and their families and workpeople. As with all major depressions, a serious fall in the prosperity and so in the purchasing power of one important group led to falling demand all round. Against the long-term inflationary trend, and perhaps contributing to its subsequent reversal, the result was falling prices and rents, deflation and unemployment. Except for a brief and limited boom in the 1630s, largely due to renewed English neutrality in the European war, and a similar export recovery in the early to mid-1650s, unsettled and generally difficult conditions in the country's economy lasted on into the 1660s if not the 1670s. The other grievances of the early 1620s—monopolies, governmental and judicial corruption, jurisdictional disputes, Puritan suspicions of excessive leniency towards Catholics—were endemic in most Parliaments of the period, and need not in themselves have led to a political breakdown. True, among the consequences was the impeachment and removal from office of Bacon, the Lord Chancellor. This, the punishment of monopolists, the calling in of patents, the drafting of a Bill for their abolition, and other measures against grievances, all have earlier parallels. Probably James made an error of judgement in losing patience with the 1621 Parliament, and dissolving it after a short, stormy and barren second session (a remarkable repetition of events at the end of his first Parliament in 1610). But the Commons were plainly not going to vote him enough money to sustain the foreign policy for which many Members were clamouring.

His fourth and last Parliament, managed largely by an unholy alliance of the Prince and the favourite with the Crown's erstwhile critics in the Commons, saw a superficial restoration of harmony, indeed of positive co-operation. The Commons voted supplies for the war, even though still an inadequate amount, and the Crown actually invited them to appoint their own nominees as commissioners for the auditing and supervision of these sums. Nor did the Crown oppose their renewed attack on monopolists and the Bill of 1621—duly amended to satisfy the great London export merchants and financiers and the syndicates of colonial investors—was soon passed into law. It is the first statutory limitation of the royal prerogative achieved by Parliament in this period and seems to show James conceding what Elizabeth had refused. But the loophole left to accommodate the interests of the overseas trading and colonising companies was to enable Charles I and his advisers to make a mockery of it in the 1630s. Likewise the successful impeachment and removal of James's last reforming finance Minister, Lionel Cranfield, the ex-merchant by then Earl of Middlesex and Lord Treasurer, once more for corruption, satisfied the self-righteous appetites of some in the Commons, pleased the victims of his economies at court and in the administration, and represented a victory for the war party in government and Parliament alike, but was also—as James pointed out—an unwise precedent for the Crown to have set.

CHARLES I

As in the case of his father in 1603, so Charles I began his reign in 1625 with a considerable fund of good will. His mistakes, or the circumstances that made for most difficulty with Parliament in his early years, were his retention of Buckingham as his principal adviser and as head of the navy, and his support for the Arminians or high-church party, the anti-Calvinist ritualists within the Church of England. Neither Charles himself nor the great majority of the Arminian clergy (so named after a revisionist Dutch theologian) were secret Papists, or even fellow-travellers with Rome. But they appeared so to an increasing number of their more militantly Protestant contemporaries. This became even truer as high-churchmen, having been promoted to bishoprics and other senior posts, began to use their authority and powers of ecclesiastical discipline against their Puritan critics in a way that had not happened since the death of Archbishop Bancroft in 1610 and which went further than anything attempted by Elizabeth's last primate, John Whitgift (Archbishop of Canterbury,

1583–1604). Here the crucial steps were the promotion of William Laud first to the see of London in 1628 and then to Canterbury in 1633. But relations had already deteriorated before that. By the end of his second Parliament in 1626 Charles was at odds with the majority in the Commons over money for the war, over religion, and over Buckingham; and this led to experiments which some believed to presage the end of parliaments and of traditional constitutional government. By then, owing to Buckingham's vanity and ineptitude, England was at war with France as well as with Spain. Fortunately, although not then at war with each other, the two great monarchies of Bourbon and Habsburg were very unlikely to join forces against Britain. Even so, this double commitment called for a war effort on a massive scale. The outcome was military fiasco and political embitterment. Having been repulsed from Cadiz in 1625, the English forces—this time under Buckingham in person—failed to raise the siege of La Rochelle to relieve the French Protestants there in 1627. Because Parliament's grants had been derisory in 1625 and non-existent in 1626 the King and his advisers raised a forced loan to finance the war, equivalent to a multiple grant of five subsidies. It was called a loan because a statute of Edward IV's reign had made the levying of 'benevolences', or involuntary gifts from the subject, illegal. But in practice the prospects of repayment were, quite correctly, seen as remote. The many refusals on the part of prominent country gentlemen to lend resulted in dismissals from local offices and even in arrests. The failure to charge those arrested with any specific criminal offence in turn led to the Habeas Corpus issue in the 'Five Knights' Case', wherein the common-law Judges refused to issue a writ ordering the release of the prisoners unless they were brought to trial.

In fact, neither Buckingham nor the King had yet turned finally against parliaments. Indeed, in constitutional as in religious matters, Villiers was more flexible and pragmatic, perhaps because less principled, than his royal master. Not for nothing had he made his way to the top in the dirty politics of James's middle years when Charles was still an adolescent. Once the King had decided to call a new Parliament, all those under arrest for having refused the loan were released. But the presence of considerable armed forces, stationed mainly in the southern seaboard counties, had by this time produced two further grievances, which also came to be seen as matters of principle: the Crown's right to billet troops in people's homes, except in the face of imminent foreign invasion, and its right to impose martial law in the districts where the soldiers were stationed. Together with wrongful arrest and detention without trial, these questions temporarily eclipsed even those of religion and Buckingham's influence in the first session of Charles's third Parliament (March–June 1628). By formulating their grievances as a Petition of Right, ostensibly to declare what the law already was and not to alter it, the Commons won the support of the Lords, and eventually the King's reluctant assent. Even so, before Charles ended the session they had renewed their attacks on Buckingham and the most unpopular of the Arminian churchmen.

While Charles was apparently ready to give this Parliament another chance by keeping it in being and recalling it early in 1629, other developments including some of his own actions were hardly conducive to a favourable outcome. Buckingham was assassinated by an unbalanced ex-officer whose sense of grievance amounted to mania, for which the King seems to have held the favourite's political enemies in Parliament partly to blame. His new advisers urged peace, and this meant that active parliamentary support was less necessary. But this was liable to cut both ways: it fed the anti-Catholic suspicions of those in Parliament who identified Arminians with Spain and with Rome. The elevation of Laud and others could only intensify this feeling. Likewise the King's personal involvement in the collection of customs duties which many regarded as illegal (Tonnage and Poundage too were without parliamentary sanction from 1626) meant that any clash between MPs and revenue officials was all too likely to become a confrontation with the monarch himself. Charles neither could nor would abandon his ecclesiastical and financial agents, as Bacon and Mompesson (the alehouse patentee) had been abandoned in 1621 by his father, and Cranfield in 1624 by both. Because one of the merchants arrested for non-payment of the controversial duties was an MP, this soon became an issue of parliamentary privilege—again one which had come up under the Tudors and James I, but never before with so explosively divisive an effect.

In their 1629 session the Commons largely concentrated on religion and finance, the latter including the issue of parliamentary privilege. The King's closest advisers were attacked, among them the new Lord Treasurer, a Buckingham appointee but one who had begun substantially to reverse his erstwhile patron's policy by helping to disengage Britain from the wars against both France and Spain. Tactically too the Commons overreached themselves. Hence when Charles ended the session in early March he was in a stronger position than his father or he had been after any previous Parliament of the decade. How long he would remain so was another matter. Opinion in the Commons had latterly been divided, and in the Lords had definitely been swinging back towards the Crown; the same may have been true outside Parliament too, though we have perilously little means of gauging 'public opinion' even among the upper and middle levels of society in Stuart England, except as measured by election results, and there were to be no more of these for eleven years.

When we talk of constitutional conflict between Crown and Parliament, or even King and Commons, there is a danger of making such political divisions seem more fixed and clear-cut than they were in reality. In all the Parliaments of the years from 1604 to 1629 there were always some royal officials and even courtiers and Crown pensioners who were critical of particular royal policies. The 'Court' did not act, speak and vote like a united modern pro-government political party. Likewise non-office-holding MPs and peers were by no means all equally critical of government on all issues; still less did they form a coherent opposition party. Men could be violently anti-Arminian and rabidly phobic about Popery, yet moderate, indeed positively responsible Crown supporters on financial matters. A few MPs and peers of the 'Country' were truly oppositionist by temperament; but many more were usually prepared to give the Crown the benefit of the doubt. Some were always hoping for office themselves and, with this object in view, modulated their criticisms, even their outright attacks on royal policies and Ministers. To mention only some of the most famous instances, Sir Edward Coke had first sat in the Commons in the late 1580s, already a rising lawyer; he had served as Attorney General (that is, as official prosecutor in treason and other major cases) under two successive monarchs from 1594 to 1606; then, as Chief Justice successively of the two great common-law courts, of Common Pleas and King's Bench, he began to develop dangerous notions of judicial discretion and even independence, and through rivalries with the Church courts and then with Chancery soon came into collision with the King; dismissed by James in 1616, he still aspired to recover high office when he played the part of a responsible critic in 1621 and 1624, but, ageing and frustrated, he became a more out-and-out Country spokesman by the time of the Parliaments of 1625 and 1628. Sir Thomas Wentworth, later Viscount Wentworth and finally Earl of Strafford, held only local offices until 1628, and even lost most of these at one stage, but he always aspired to a great position in the State, and seems to have felt (perhaps incorrectly) that Buckingham stood in the way. In the three Parliaments of 1621, 1625 and 1628 he was a moderate, if at times a severe critic of particular royal policies and of misdeeds by members of the government. Yet between the two sessions of Charles's third Parliament Wentworth accepted a peerage and the Lord Presidency of the North and soon became one of the great pillars of the King's regime. Sir John Eliot lost an important local office in the south-west for his violent attacks on Buckingham in 1625–26 and was imprisoned after the dissolution of 1629 for his leading part in the final disorderly scene when the Speaker was prevented from adjourning the House and Eliot's three resolutions, condemning Arminianism and Popery, and against the levying and paying of Tonnage and Poundage, were read and carried; but, although he died in the Tower (probably of tuberculosis) because he refused to apologise and recant, Eliot spent much of his time there either translating Continental writings or composing his own in which monarchy was extolled as the best if not the only legitimate form of government. Finally, John Pym, the great Parliamentarian leader of the early 1640s, was a minor revenue official from 1612 to 1638, and perhaps for this reason always took a more conciliatory, even constructive line on finance, in contrast to his militancy on religious issues. In 1629 he clearly thought that Eliot and others were making a grave error of judgement in fighting on the ground of parliamentary privilege.

So the 'Country', like the 'Court', was far from being a monolithic political force, or from resembling a modern party. Nonetheless the system that had worked, with whatever stresses and strains, under the Tudors and even under James I, of periodic Parliaments with a certain measure of give and take between the Crown and its critics, and an underlying mutual respect, did seem to have reached deadlock by 1629. This was emphatically not because Charles was a would-be absolutist; nor was it because the House of Commons wanted to take over the government of the country from the King and his Council. But the combined effects of inflation, war, economic difficulties, religious disagreements and plain incomprehension of each other's needs and motives had led to a mistrust so fundamental as to have brought about what may fairly be called a functional breakdown in government. It is tempting to suggest that after this things were bound to shift one way or the other: either towards greater effective royal power, or towards more effective parliamentary participation in running the country. At first the swing was to be in the Crown's favour.

One of the most authentically new features of the early seventeenth century is the creation of an English colonial empire in the Americas. This was a logical extension of what contemporaries called 'plantation' in Ireland, and it overlapped in date with the Anglo-Scottish settlement of Ulster after the 'flight of the Earls' (Tyrone and others) in 1607. Much argument has been focused on the motives and character of the early settlers in North America and to a lesser extent in the West Indies: separatist Puritans seeking to create a new kind of Christian commonwealth in New Plymouth; non-separating Congregationalists attempting to build a 'city upon a hill', to be an example to those at home, in Massachusetts and what became Connecticut; low-church Anglicans motivated by the desire for gain in Virginia and the Caribbean. There is an element of truth in these distinctions, but all tend to oversimplify. The early New England settlements did have a more uniform denominational complexion and a somewhat stronger religious commitment than those farther south. Yet many who went to New England did not do so out of Puritan idealism, or as religious refugees from Laud and the bishops. Likewise some who went to Maryland did so because it was a refuge for Catholics; and not everyone who headed for Virginia and the Barbados was simply a cynical, irreligious, materialistic adventurer. Begun as a primarily commercial venture with the founding of Virginia in 1607 (and one which came near to total failure and collapse until the first tobacco boom of the 1620s), by Charles I's reign emigration can be seen as a kind of safety valve for demographic pressures and social tensions at home, as well as for religious and political discontents.

Inside England the single most striking feature of the social scene was the rapid—to many contemporaries, the inordinate—growth of the capital city. Such disproportionate growth, out of relation to other towns or to the country as a whole, is of course a commonplace in developing countries of the twentieth century. Nor was the growth of London new in the time of James and Charles I; but the capital's preponderance in wealth and numbers excited much attention, mainly hostile. The rural–urban antithesis, country suspicion of the city, of what Lewis Mumford has called megalopolis,[3] is not to be confused with the political, social and even cultural dichotomy of country and court. Many Londoners were certainly critical of the royal court and of Crown policies in Church and State, especially by the 1630s; at the same time many non-office-holding country gentlemen without court connections, and many lesser inhabitants of rural and provincial England, were deeply suspicious of what they considered the over-sophistication and corruption of court and city alike, yet were entirely loyal to Church and King.

Characterised by some nineteenth-century Whig historians as the Eleven

Years Tyranny, Charles I's rule without Parliament (1629–40) has been radically reassessed in recent years. Firstly, by twentieth-century standards, it was no tyranny. Apart from Eliot's death in the Tower (and we cannot know that he would not have died of the same illness back in his native Cornwall), there was no single execution for religious or political offences against the State until the spring of 1640. At no time did the number of those in prison on what we should call grounds of conscience or ideology reach double figures. There was no standing army, no police force, no regular corps of government informers, no local bureaucracy. The censorship of printed books was severe but scarcely more so than under Henry VIII or Elizabeth I. Controls and restrictions on people's movements and on some of their economic activities were not peculiar to England in these years, nor were they appreciably stricter and more far-reaching than at other times or in Continental States of the same date.

Until 1637 the government's successes were considerable. Peace was made with France and then with Spain (in 1629 and 1630), and England undoubtedly profited commercially from her subsequent neutrality. After an ineffectual resistance campaign by some merchants had been overcome, the full range of customs duties, including Impositions and Tonnage and Poundage, were successfully collected, and latterly additional New Impositions and then new New Impositions were also levied. Existing feudal revenues like wardship were made to yield more than ever before; ancient rights of the Crown were exploited to establish and justify new or revived forms of taxation; for the time being the sale of Crown lands, of offices and titles was halted; some reforms were even achieved within government departments, and expenditure was reduced. Something approaching solvency was attained, Crown income and expenditure came into balance, debts were even reduced. According to the great royalist historian, Edward Hyde later Earl of Clarendon, the country as a whole was never more peaceful, prosperous and contented than in these years. How, then, did Charles and his government come to be so isolated by 1640 that the whole regime was to be swept away with such startling ease?

We may refer to the government, but it was in fact at all times a deeply divided one, on issues of personality and policy alike. Laud and Wentworth had a vision of what they called 'Thorough,' an ideal of tough, efficient but also just and honest rule. But it was only their own private name for what they wanted in Church and State; it was not the King's policy, still less that of the whole Privy Council. Except briefly when Laud was senior Treasury Commissioner in 1635–36, neither of them ever had charge of royal finance. And Wentworth was absent, in the north of England or in Ireland, for most of the time until 1640. Both men were disliked on grounds of personality as well as principle. And so both could all too easily become scapegoats for their colleagues, if and when things became difficult. Some feared that Wentworth's high-handed ruthless-ness, already evident in the north and in Ireland, was to be applied on a nationwide basis. Many regarded Laud as a fellow-traveller with Rome, if not as a crypto-Papist, who was attempting to subvert the Protestant Church as by law established. Increasing numbers of clergy as well as laymen were alienated from the establishment, and from the very institution of episcopacy, because of Laud and the Arminians. Ironically Laud was a strong opponent of the Queen's religious and political influence and of other Roman Catholics at court. And in the country at large the penal taxation of recusant Catholics was enforced more rigorously than ever before.

Such suspicions, extending even to the King himself, were inevitably also nurtured by Charles's foreign policy. This was partly due to the shame aroused at England's apparent impotence to aid the Protestant cause abroad, when it was first threatened by Habsburg victories and then saved by the brilliant intervention of Gustavus Adolphus and the Swedish army, together with the continued dogged resistance of the Dutch to Spanish power (the twelve years' truce having lapsed in 1621). The King's complete failure to recover even a part of the Palatinate for his brother-in-law Frederick, and then for his nephew the new claimant to the lost Electorate, was a constant irritant and highlighted the ineffectuality of English diplomacy; it also underlined the slight value set on English neutrality and intervention alike by the major Continental States. There were also suspicions, all too well founded in fact, that the King was at the least toying with a more positively pro-Spanish and anti-Dutch policy, harking back to some of his father's schemes before 1624. While the King and his Archbishop were what we should call sincere high-church Anglicans, or in contemporary terms Arminian episcopalians, there were indeed secret and even open Catholics in high places, while Charles's apparent reliance on the Queen's advice and the freedom which she enjoyed as a centre of Catholic worship and intrigue at court could only make the darkest suspicions all the more credible.

Moreover financial improvement was bought at a heavy cost. Some of the new and revived levies were merely tiresome or else affected only small minorities—such as some of the monopolies, fines for not being knighted at the coronation, reactivation of the forest laws. Others were felt more widely, and were believed to threaten the very existence of Parliament if they came to provide the Crown with the means of remaining permanently solvent without resort to parliamentary grants. Monopolies on near necessities, such as salt and soap, posed such a threat. But easily the most important quantitatively and so also politically were the additional customs duties, both those regarded as illegal since the 1600s and 1620s respectively and those innovated subsequently, and Ship Money, which was extended from the sea-coast areas to the whole country after a year (in 1635–36), and two years later looked like becoming a regular tax which would enable the entire cost of the navy to be met outside the normal royal budget. In retrospect we can see that the real objection can hardly have been to the absolute weight of these and the other tax burdens; even by seventeenth-century standards England was still a lightly taxed country and by twentieth-century standards ludicrously so. It was the very existence of such burdens and their political implications for the future which aroused such resentment and alarm.

It is also possible that the Crown's invisible or 'below the line' revenue was increasing faster in proportion to the value of money than its visible, 'official' income from taxes and other revenues. Royal officials from the most senior to junior, their employees and hangers on had become more and more dependent on fees and gratuities received from members of the public or in turn from other officials making use of their services, and on various perquisites in money and in kind, some at the expense of the Crown, some of the public. This development arose in part from the very nature of office, which was regarded as a species of property; but it was due more immediately to the growing inadequacy of stipendiary fees and salary or wage payments from the Crown, or from superiors in office, and to the utter failure of those to keep up with the inflation. The repeated outcry against 'exacted fees and innovated offices', which is almost constantly in evidence from Elizabeth's last years to the eve of the Civil War, and on which there was an active—if ultimately ineffectual—royal commission in being from 1627 to 1640, may suggest a swelling bureaucracy, battening upon the rest of society. Even if the administration remained, both comparatively and in absolute terms, very small, the total takings of office-holders and their subordinates may well have been increasing faster than the Crown's other income. The growing alienation of the country from the court was not simply along material, economic lines, between the 'have nots' and the 'haves'. Still, envy is often an irrational force, in politics as in individual human relations.

The legal system is an important part of any government. When the rest of government was on so small a scale and its activities so circumscribed, this was perhaps even more the case in the seventeenth century than it is today. Charles I and his Ministers were well aware of this, and incurred further disapproval for their more systematic use of the common-law Judges as political instruments. Even so, by 1640 it was the so-called prerogative courts—especially Star Chamber, the High Commission for Ecclesiastical Causes, and the Council in the North—which had become the main focus of popular fear and hatred. This resulted from a small minority of ideologically motivated cases, such as that against the Puritan pamphleteers and their helpers in 1637, where Laud and other bishops appeared both as parties and judges. Ironically, however, it was the King's successful use of the common-law machinery, and the compliance of most of the Judges there, which posed the greater long-term threat to what contemporaries would have regarded as the traditional rights and liberties of freeborn Englishmen. This of course meant mainly, if not exclusively, the rights of Protestant propertied males; only during the 1640s did a wider, more inclusive, even democratic concept of human rights begin to emerge.

Ship Money was collected with increasing difficulty. There were delays, evasions, and some outright refusals to pay. Of the latter, the most notorious were by the Puritan peer, Lord Saye and Sele, who could only have been tried by a jury of his peers, which the Crown decided not to risk, and by John Hampden, a Buckinghamshire gentleman, who had sat in all the Parliaments of the 1620s and took a prominent part in the last of them. Charles I had used his Chief Justice, the self-same Sir John Finch who had as Speaker to be prevented forcibly from adjourning the House on 2 March 1629, to sound out the other Judges in advance as to the legality of Ship Money. All apparently agreed that it fell within the King's emergency prerogative powers to levy it for immediate purposes of national defence. When 'Hampden's Case' was finally heard before all twelve common-law Judges in Exchequer Chamber (the nearest to an appeal court that then existed), his counsel admitted the King's legal powers, but denied—in effect—that an emergency could continue indefinitely without the country actually going to war, or being attacked. On this basis the Judges found for the King by the narrow majority of only seven to five. (There was no jury in Exchequer Chambers.) This is often described as a pyrrhic victory for the King, but the verdict by no means led to a sudden or general cessation of payments. Less Ship Money was demanded in 1638 (for payment in the following year), and it was only after the last writ to be issued (in 1639 for 1640) that refusal became general.

By then much else had happened also to undermine the Crown's authority. The immediate cause of Charles's downfall was his decision to back the high-church episcopalian party in Scotland, and to try to push the Scottish Church further away from Calvinist Presbyterianism, at the expense of the laity as well as the ministers. Widespread rejection of the new Prayer Book, modelled on that of England, and of the authority exercised there on the King's behalf, together with the opposition organised in the form of the National Covenant, led to the next fatal step: Charles's decision, abetted by Laud, Wentworth and a few other advisers but not backed by his full Council, to coerce the Scots, if necessary by an armed invasion. This led to the first of the so-called 'Bishops' Wars' in the summer of 1639, when the King was obliged to make a truce with the Covenanters as the two armies faced each other across the Tweed. But the concessions that he made to the Scottish Parliament and Church Assembly were intended by Charles to be no more than delaying tactics. Wentworth, now created Earl of Strafford, was recalled from Ireland, and his advice to call a Parliament once again was accepted.

At this stage the King's position was serious, potentially critical, but not desperate, still less hopeless. When the body known to history as the Short Parliament met in April 1640 the truce with the Covenanters was still operative, although Charles had effectively lost control of his northern kingdom. There was much passive, and some more active resistance to the renewed military preparations and to the intensified financial levies under way in England, but nothing as yet anywhere near armed revolt. Crown finances had deteriorated sharply as a result of the military expenditure of 1638–39; royal credit was once more dangerously extended, and lenders were showing increasing reluctance. But the Crown was not yet insolvent, nor totally unable to raise more in loans. At this stage Charles could have cut his losses, and yielded with as good grace as he could muster to the Kirk and the Covenanters; alternatively he would have had to make sufficient concessions—on religion, unparliamentary taxation, and other grievances—to win the support of the English Parliament for further military action and to obtain the vote of supplies essential for this. In the event he did neither. The Short Parliament was dissolved in May with not a measure passed, not a tax voted. Despite this, on the advice of Strafford and others,

Charles proceeded with further military preparations, leading to the fiasco of the Second Bishops' War. After one skirmish the English army fled without standing battle, and the Scots occupied the north-east of England. By the time of the ignominious settlement negotiated at Ripon in September the Crown had lost all financial credibility and was on the verge of bankruptcy.

The King called a Great Council of all the peers at York, but he had already decided that another Parliament was unavoidable. The membership of the new Parliament, elected in September and which met on 3 November, was largely the same as that of its predecessor in the spring; but the temper and mood of the Long Parliament, as it was understandably to become known, was from the outset very different. And the King's bargaining position was now catastrophically worse. Clarendon indeed did not disguise his opinion that the premature dissolution of the Short Parliament was one of Charles I's most egregious and costly political blunders. Above all, the presence of a Scottish army in the north of England, which had to be paid regularly in cash to prevent it living off the country, put the Crown and the court at an extreme tactical disadvantage in the new Parliament. Combined with the strength of feeling against the Laudian innovations in the Church, against Strafford and all that he stood for, against the Judges who had upheld the prerogative, and against monopolists and Papists, this made the session of 1640–41 disastrous for the Stuart monarchy.

By the following summer the whole structure of Charles's personal rule had disappeared, together with much vital apparatus of the Tudor State. Strafford was executed, Laud was in the Tower, lesser objects of Parliament's fury were either in prison or in exile. Besides the attainder of his great Minister, Charles had consented to an Act providing for a Parliament to meet every three years, and another (to help encourage creditors in the City) providing that the existing Parliament should not be dissolved, prorogued or even adjourned for any length of time without its own consent. Many of the Long Parliament's early measures of reform appear to have been carried without a division, such as those to abolish unparliamentary taxation and the prerogative courts. But attendance in the House was low by modern standards, and since abstention was not allowed, absence may often indicate disapproval—or indifference either way. The decisive vote on Strafford's attainder (by then the impeachment was clearly going to fail in the Lords) was carried by 204 to 59: overwhelming enough, yet the whole House of Commons numbered over 500. Only after the summer recess of 1641 did more even and deeper divisions begin to appear in the Commons and between the two Houses.

CIVIL WAR

Much unnecessary disagreement and confusion has been generated by historians failing to distinguish clearly enough between the reasons for the events of 1640–41 and those of 1641–42. In the former case the only real problem is how Charles I had come to be so weak and vulnerable; in the latter, how and why he regained enough support to fight a civil war, and for some time to contest it on remarkably even terms. It is of course possible that long-run developments and some common causes can be found to help explain the whole sequence of events of the 1640s; but the more immediate explanations of such very different happenings are hardly likely to be the same.[4] We need not commit ourselves to the depressing, and actually rather absurd, conclusion that 'history is just one damned thing after another', a mere mish-mash of episodes without cause or explanation, to suppose that contingent circumstances may sometimes be as important as economic, social, political or religious developments—for example, the premature death of James's elder son Henry, and the survival of his younger son Charles; and the unusual longevity of William Laud, who only became Archbishop at sixty and was still remarkably fit for his years when executed at the age of seventy-two. Looking further ahead, into the Interregnum, who can gauge how different the course of events would have been if Pym or Hampden had survived after 1643, or if Cromwell had been killed in battle early on, or indeed had died at any time before the mid-1650s? Looking outside the British Isles, events on the Continent had momentous consequences, especially those of 1618–29 in central Europe. The influence of Scottish on English affairs was decisive in 1637–40, while the effect of events in Ireland was to be equally important in 1641–42. Of course individuals, and coincidental or contingent circumstances, do not count for everything in history; but in a highly stratified society the personalities of those born at the top and of those who make their way there do certainly count for a good deal.

The rebellion of October 1641 in Ireland developed into the longest-drawn-out and largest-scale attempted war of liberation ever waged by the Irish against their English invaders and conquerors. The decisive question of who was to command and control the armed forces that would be needed to suppress the Irish was not the only new element in the English situation of 1641–42 which led to political polarisation and eventually to armed conflict. Just as the political actions of the Long Parliament involved far more than merely rectifying the abuses—real or alleged—of the 1630s, so too in religion many Puritans were not content with the overthrow of Laud and the Arminians. The campaign to destroy episcopacy 'root and branch'[5] depended on an alliance of groups and denominations who knew what they wanted to get rid of but were deeply divided on what they wanted in its place. The Presbyterians wanted a national Church, and all except a few of their clergy assumed it would be one under lay, that is, parliamentary, control; but it was to be modelled on the Churches of Geneva, the Dutch Republic, and (since 1638–39) of Scotland. The Independents, or as we should call them Congregationalists, and the other Puritan sects of whom the Baptists were much the most important, either wanted an extremely decentralised State Church with toleration for other Puritan Churches outside it, or no ecclesiastical establishment at all but equal freedom for themselves and other Puritans, though not for Episcopalians or Catholics. Most Presbyterians opposed any toleration of erroneous doctrines and practices; very few people of any persuasion yet envisaged extending toleration to all religions and to none.

Of all the denominations involved in the conflicts of the 1640s, the Presbyterians were the most intolerant and rigid. Some radical Puritans, or deviants from Puritanism, and some on the far right—Erastians and ecumenicists—were among the least rigid and intolerant. Members of sectarian congregations often met outside consecrated church buildings, and their preachers were often ordained laymen, sometimes uneducated and of humble origin, occasionally—horror of horrors to orthodox Puritans and Anglicans alike—even women. It seems to have been the social and thus the political implications of the radical sects which aroused as much alarm and opposition as the heterodox content of their theology, their views on Church government, or their religious observances, although all these are in practice hard to separate. In this maelstrom of opposing views and forms of worship, this great outburst of preaching and publishing when censorship and episcopalian discipline had broken down, Milton first appeared as a pamphleteer on religion and Church government. At first simply anti-episcopalian as an extension of his being naturally anti-Catholic and so anti-Laudian, he was soon to see, more clearly than most, the potential threat to freedom of worship, expression and conscience posed by a Presbyterian State Church. But by then he was himself regarded as highly suspect because of his views on divorce and his other heretical tendencies.[6]

In the resumed sitting of the Long Parliament the divisions among the once united reformers were swift to appear. The Grand Remonstrance, a long recital of past and present grievances against the King and his regime and of future radical aspirations, implied drastic further restrictions on the King's power and encroachment on his traditional authority as head of the executive arm of government. The shift of opinion, even inside the Commons, can be seen in the narrowness of the vote for its passage (158 to 147), and in the bitterness of the debates both on its contents and on the question of printing and publishing it as well as presenting the Remonstrance to the King. Above all, it seems to have been this appeal to a wider, extra-parliamentary audience and readership which shocked the more conservative MPs as much as what the Remonstrance actually contained.

The political atmosphere was already poisoned with suspicion. The King and the court, and most of all the Catholic Queen, Henrietta Maria, were suspected of planning an armed counter-coup, to be led by demobilised ex-officers from the Scottish campaigns of 1639–40. And the fact of the Scots having now withdrawn their army from English soil gave Charles greater freedom of action because he might now dispense with further parliamentary taxation. The radicals in the Commons and their very few allies in the Lords were increasingly suspected of using crowds of Londoners, organised in mass demonstrations and shows of physical force, to push their programme through, to impose it even on their one-time allies, now opponents in the two Houses. The political role of the bishops in the upper House was particularly obnoxious to both committed Puritans and political radicals. Control of the Tower of London, the great arsenal and fortress of the capital, became another issue serving to heighten the tension.

In the event it was Charles who lost his nerve and resorted to direct action first, apparently fearing that his wife was about to be impeached. It was much less the fact of his accusing five MPs and one peer of treason than of his coming into the chamber of the Commons for the five with a large posse of armed men waiting in the lobby outside that was the fatal step. The Five Members escaped just in time and took refuge in the City of London, where the political ascendancy had been gained by the radicals immediately before this. Like almost any unsuccessful use of force, this failure left Charles in a worse situation than before, and probably checked the swing of moderate, middle-of-the-road opinion in his favour. Parliament in turn crossed the Rubicon into revolutionary action over control of the armed forces, ostensibly to reconquer Ireland, less plausibly to defend the country from possible Irish or foreign attack, and actually to prevent the King having command and use of the militia, the home defence levies, in the cities and counties of England and Wales. Since Tudor times the monarch had appointed the Lords Lieutenant (normally one or two influential peers for each county), and they in turn chose Deputies (from the resident peers and greater gentry of the county—much the same kind of men who would be Sheriffs, MPs or JPs); once royal approval had been given for their nomination, the Deputy Lieutenants had charge of the respective county militias, of which the immediately active and useful part was known appropriately as the Trained Bands. Now the Commons majority, led by Pym, tried to get a Bill passed into law, naming Lords Lieutenant of their own choice (who would then, it was assumed, choose acceptable Deputies). The Lords eventually agreed to this, after being threatened with popular action against themselves and their House, as they already had been over the continued presence of the bishops. The King, who had left London in January, finally refused his assent; the remaining peers gave way to the Commons, and thus the Militia Ordinance of March 1642 was the first legislative measure passed without the King's consent, and which the Parliamentarians claimed had the same force as a statute.

A period of propaganda war and military preparations followed, with evidence of much unwillingness to fight for either side among many people in the provinces. Now helped by Edward Hyde and other ex-reforming peers and MPs, Charles was on the whole successful in representing his opponents as the constitutional innovators. In many counties widespread movements for neutrality were led by the gentry; meanwhile, as armed conflict seemed to draw inevitably nearer, the religious issue—Root and Branch Puritanism versus Episcopalians and Catholics—came increasingly to the fore and nerved the militant minorities on both sides against each other. As early as the summer of 1641, and irrevocably from the winter following, mutual mistrust between the opposing leaders, and most of all between John Pym and Charles I, was perhaps the single most obvious, immediate influence making for civil war. But it was a war which was slow to break out, unwillingly undertaken by almost everyone, and not a clean-cut division between two fundamentally opposing sides.

There are many histories of the English Civil War, some of them in the Bibliography of this volume (pp. 394 ff.); and for that reason no summary of the military events will be given here. With important exceptions there was a broad geographical division, with the King controlling more of the north and west, Parliament more of the east and south. The majority of the peerage, and probably of the upper or greater gentry, were for the King; proportionately more of those in the middle levels of society were for the Parliament. For some of those on both sides social values, political principles and religious beliefs were in full harmony. But the accident of where people lived, and who their neighbours, relatives, landlords and employers were, often mattered more than class or ideology. The King had greater initial advantages, Parliament greater potential long-term resources. As late as 1644 it seemed that, even if the royalists were no longer likely to win an outright military victory, they might well fight their opponents to a standstill, exploit the deep political and religious divisions within the ranks of the Parliamentarians and Puritans, and so come out on top from a position of stalemate. The war was not finally won by Parliament until 1645–46, and Charles I spent the next three years trying to snatch political victory out of military defeat, by taking advantage of the disagreements and even conflicts between the English Presbyterians and their Scottish allies, the Independents and the other sects, above all between Parliament and the very army which it had created and which had gained it eventual victory.

Perhaps Charles I was a 'late developer' as a politician. Certainly he showed greater skill in this last phase of his reign than ever before. In 1647 a further division arose within the army itself between the Grandees (or senior officers, in particular Oliver Cromwell and his son-in-law Henry Ireton) and the elected delegates of the soldiers called Agitators, and their civilian allies, the Levellers, together with a very few more senior officers. But the Grandees and their supporters among the other officers kept control of the army; the attempted royalist come-back in the Second Civil War of 1648 failed disastrously, and the Scottish change of sides and invasion of England was overwhelmingly defeated. Those in the army and elsewhere (some in Parliament, more among the radical Puritan preachers) who held Charles personally responsible for the bloodshed and sufferings of civil war now carried the day, and—against a background of continued negotiations between the King and the parliamentary majority, the so-called Presbyterians—demanded exemplary justice upon 'that man of blood'.

This precipitated the final stage of the revolution. In early December Pride's Purge removed at a stroke well over half the MPs still alive and eligible to sit; when the Lords refused to co-operate in proceeding to the trial of the King, the Commons assumed sole legislative power in the name of the people; the King's trial and execution were soon followed by the abolition of the monarchy and of the House of Lords (but significantly not of the hereditary peerage); and a unicameral republican Commonwealth was formally declared the following spring. It has been called a limited, moderate, even—if the term is not too contradictory—a conservative revolution. Certainly Cromwell and with few exceptions the other leaders can fairly be called reluctant and became republicans almost in spite of themselves.

But in other respects the country's new rulers were less moderate, and hardly conservative. The Church of England as it has existed since Elizabethan times had been completely overthrown; episcopacy and the Prayer Book had been replaced by a modified, State-controlled Presbyterian system with a Genevan or Scottish type 'Directory of Worship'. Heavy penal taxation had been imposed on royalists and neutrals; the landed and other property of the bishops, deans and chapters of cathedrals, of the Crown (the King and the rest of the royal family), and of Cavalier activists and many Papists, was confiscated outright and sold to meet the cost of war and Parliament's other debts. In some counties and towns power shifted to new men, often drawn from the middling and lesser gentry and from citizens below the level in wealth and status of the previous elite. This was particularly so in districts where Parliament and its armed forces gained control later rather than sooner, and where the previous local rulers (JPs etc.) had been mainly royalists. This was true of other institutions too. Thus the University of Oxford was only captured in 1646 and so was more radicalised than Cambridge, which was under Puritan-Parliamentarian control from August 1642. Counties like Worcestershire and Herefordshire, only won for Parliament in 1645, were more affected in this way than (say) Suffolk and Essex, which, except for brief royalist incursions, were Parliamentarian throughout. The various county committees, appointed by the Long Parliament, whose responsibilities included security and local defence, the implementation and enforcement of the religious changes, and penal taxation, were particularly unpopular; indeed, by the years 1646–50 they had come to be thoroughly detested even by many one-time Parliamentarian supporters, not only those who had parted company with the revolution on—to use the terminology of more modern times—both left- and right-wing grounds. The religious aspect of the Civil War also had what may be called a moral dimension, symbolised in the opprobrious nicknames 'Round-head' and 'Cavalier'. Maybe the losers deserve the best lines: a contemporary history tells of a royalist who wrote to an old friend on the other side, 'in our army, we have the sins of men, (drinking and wenching), but in yours, you have those of devils, spiritual pride and rebellion'.[7] And, more light-heartedly, this aspect is well summed up by the authors of that immortal parody of school textbooks, *1066 and All That*, who tell us that the Cavaliers were 'Wrong but Wromantic' and the Roundheads 'Right but Repulsive'.[8]

It is worth distinguishing what is meant by Parliament in these years. From 1642 to 1645 the Parliamentarians comprised about three-fifths of the Commons and rather under a quarter of the Lords. From 1646 to 1648 the lower House was 'recruited', that is to say batches of bye-elections were held to replace those MPs who had died, been killed in the war, or expelled as royalists. The decisive vote, to continue negotiations with the King, which precipitated Pride's Purge, was smaller (129 to 83) than that taken earlier the same day, to adjourn for a few hours (144 to 93); but even the larger total leaves a good many who must have been avoidably absent.[9] Already before this the upper House had dwindled, and were often down to below twenty, sometimes into single figures. They may have mustered as many as fourteen or even sixteen when they rejected the first ordinance for the King's trial which led to the Commons' decision to 'go it alone'. Certainly this demoralised disappearing trick makes their subsequent abolition easier to understand. From early 1649 Parliament means the so-called 'Rump' House of Commons, consisting of those who had survived Pride's Purge, or had later disavowed the vote which had precipitated it, plus a few more subsequent recruiters. Just over 200 MPs may have sat in the Rump at one time or other between December 1648 and April 1653, but 120 was the maximum turn-out[10] and eighty a good showing. Numerous constituencies were not represented at all, and many others by only one Member, a large proportion of whom had been elected as long ago as September 1640! Whatever else had been at stake in the Civil War, a better representative system had hardly come out of it.

For many contemporaries the events of December 1648 to early 1649 produced even sharper divisions of allegiance than those leading up to the outbreak of civil war in 1641–42. A majority of the MPs still eligible to sit were removed by imprisonment or 'seclusion' from the House. Sole legislative power was then assumed, in the name of the people, by this attenuated House of Commons. A special High Court of Justice, whose members were to act as both judges and jurors, was then appointed by the House, to try the King. The monarch was convicted, sentenced and executed for levying war against his people, and for other retrospective 'treasons' previously unknown in English law. In the wake of this, the monarchy and the House of Lords were abolished, and a little later England and its people declared to constitute a 'Free Commonwealth'. None of this can have seemed conservative, or moderate, or unrevolutionary to many contemporaries. For others, however—including Milton, who had become extremely disillusioned with the Long Parliament and its clerical allies in the preceding few years—the overthrow of the old order, of Presbyterianism as well as royalty, seemed to herald a brave new world. Millenarian Christians, vividly anticipating the rule of the saints which must precede the Second Coming of Christ, and more secular-minded but not necessarily irreligious radicals, alike saw the changes of that winter as a decisive step towards better times to come. Milton himself began his career as a political pamphleteer for the Commonwealth and as a republican official within weeks of the King's execution.[11]

The story of the next eleven years is partly one of progressive alienation from the Good Old Cause of many who had originally supported it. Correspondingly, successive regimes failed to win over enough more conservative elements or previously uncommitted groups to counterbalance this loss of radical support and the cumulative defection from the Puritan-republican cause of all but its most diehard adherents. Not that we should leap to the conclusion that the events of 1660 were all implicit, still less inevitable, from the beginning of 1649, let alone earlier than that. There were many ways in which things might well have worked out very differently.

INTERREGNUM AND RESTORATION

Historians remain divided about the character of the Commonwealth, the regime which survived until Oliver Cromwell dissolved both the Rump and its Council of State (almost all its members were also MPs) in April 1653. Just as it remains open to argument how lackadaisical and dishonest was the government of James I, and how much this contributed to its other failings, and how arbitrary the rule of Charles I, so there is continuing disagreement about the irresponsibility and self-seeking character of the Rump. Its achievements should not be underrated. Ireland was successfully reconquered, at the price of the Cromwellian 'atrocities' and the subsequent legacy of hatred which they engendered, and a vast new transplantation of the native landowners begun, to make way for new English settlers. The royalists and their new-found Scottish allies were decisively defeated, and Scotland was joined in a forced union with the English Commonwealth. A hard-fought war at sea with the premier naval power of the age led eventually to the English fleet gaining complete ascendancy over the Dutch, who were forced into harbour and faced with imminent commercial ruin in consequence. Unprecedented sums of money were raised by the sale of Church, Crown and royalist property, and through an onerous but effective system of taxation. Law and order were preserved and a measure of economic recovery was made possible. A few minor legal and other domestic reforms were carried out, and many more—some of real substance—were discussed or projected. But from 'the crowning mercy', as Cromwell called the battle of Worcester on 3 September 1651, more and more of the army officers and of the more radical Puritans, both clergy and laity, became increasingly dissatisfied with the Rump and its leading civilian members. Just as the Purge of December 1648 and the regicide had led to an irrevocable breach between their supporters and many of the original Parliamentarians, the religious and political Presbyterians, so the forced dissolution of 20 April 1653 alienated the parliamentary republicans.

The calling of the Nominated Assembly, known to history as the Barebone's Parliament (July–December 1653), was meant by Cromwell and his fellow officers to settle the country's constitutional future. They hoped that it would succeed where the Rump had failed: namely by producing an acceptable plan for future Parliaments, which might indeed be more representative—but only of the right people. The fundamental contradiction in every one of these schemes—Grandee, Leveller, Rump, Protectoral—from the King's defeat to the Restoration, was how to reconcile a wider, slightly more popular franchise, constituencies which corresponded better to the distribution of wealth and numbers, and what the seventeenth-century understood by 'free elections', with a guarantee of continued Puritan-Parliamentarian, and latterly republican, rule. Increasingly the role of the army as a vested interest, almost as an additional 'estate of the realm', came to be the greatest apparent obstacle to a constitutional settlement and a free Parliament: yet without the army would the Puritan republic survive at all? The failure of the Barebone's Parliament was perhaps inherent in the uncertainty of purpose in its being called: the majority of its members were sincere, inexperienced reformers, not particularly extreme, but radical enough in regard to Church and law reform, and evident enough in their preference for the naval war against the Dutch over the upkeep of the army, to alarm both the inner circle of Cromwellians and the senior officers in general. The more conservative Members voluntarily surrendered their authority back to the Lord General from whom they had received it; the radicals were in turn forcibly dissolved, and the Protectorate instituted within a matter of days, its constitutional basis, the Instrument of Government, having obviously been prepared by Major-General John Lambert, with this occasion in view.

The transition from Barebone's to Protectorate alienated many millenarian Puritans and army republicans who had accepted, and many welcomed, the removal of the Rump. Cromwell's attempts to govern, under the terms of the Instrument, with an elected Parliament (1654–55 and 1656–58) can hardly be called successful; they prove that he had no wish to be an absolutist ruler or a mere military dictator, but the story of both these Parliaments demonstrates the narrow basis of support for the regime. The adoption in 1657 of a revised protectoral constitution, the Humble Petition and Advice, gave more power to Parliament, re-created a second chamber of nominated life peers, and reduced the Council of State to an advisory role more like that of the royal Privy Council before 1640 and after 1660. This in turn alienated Lambert, the leading political figure in the army since Ireton's death in Ireland earlier in the 1650s, and it helped to disillusion other republican-minded officers. Yet at the very same time Cromwell's refusal of the crown undermined the very purpose of the Humble Petition in the eyes of its authors and supporters; this, together with the earlier interlude of the Major-Generals (1655–56) had damaged, perhaps fatally, the Cromwellian policy of reconciling more of the traditional ruling class without losing the support of the army and the Puritan sects. These were probably incompatible objectives. But with the passing of time more and more people might have come to terms with the Cromwellian regime while the exiled king Charles II and his emigré court increasingly lost credibility as an alternative.

The peaceful succession of Oliver's eldest son Richard at first seemed to point in this direction. Undoubtedly the English republic disintegrated between the winter of 1658–59 and the spring of 1660 through internal divisions, utterly inadequate leadership, and lack of positive popular support, eventually even from the rank and file of its own army, and emphatically not because of the strength of royalism either at home or overseas.

The burden of taxation remained heavier than under the monarchy, even during the brief intervals of both internal and external peace in the earlier 1650s, and again after reductions in the army, especially during the second Protectorate Parliament. Only in respect of the fees, gratuities and bribes paid by the public to officials and clerks in the government and the courts, that is by the country to the court, and in expenditure on the formal, ceremonial side of government, were there significant reductions; some of the reforms initiated or half begun indeed pointed forward towards a fully salaried civil service such as was not to be achieved until the nineteenth-century. Meanwhile the renewed naval war, this time with Spain, together with commitments in Flanders and the Caribbean, intensified the bad effects of a recession; trade contracted and the customs revenue fell in consequence; general economic difficulties in turn affected government credit, already dangerously vulnerable through political uncertainty. A major show of naval strength against the Dutch, arising from the Baltic conflict between Denmark and Sweden, further undermined finances already perilously stretched. Only during the military junta rule of October to December 1659 was there anything approaching a general cessation of tax payments, but the republic was by then spiralling downwards into insolvency. That General George Monck was able to pay his army when his rivals could not do so lent credibility to the Cavalier and Presbyterian refrain that only a restoration of the monarchy could save the whole country from trade collapse and national bankruptcy.

To the last, the number of royalists prepared to risk life and limb, freedom and property on the King's behalf was really very small. Ironically it was a Presbyterian ex-Parliamentarian, Sir George Booth, who raised the only actual royalist revolt in 1659. A Stuart restoration only became inevitable at a very late date. At least until the re-entry into the Commons under Monck's auspices of the 'Secluded Members', the survivors of those purged by Colonel Pride, in February 1660, and the voluntary dissolution of the Rump and its replacement by a Convention Parliament in April, the republicans might still have kept control of the situation, if they could only have acted together. They seemed, however, bent on hanging separately, as some all too literally were shortly to do. The astonishing thing about the Restoration is its virtually unconditional character, combined with the political compromise involved in the combination of those who brought it about. As Charles II wittily remarked, everyone seemed so happy to welcome him back that he could not think why he had had to stay away so long!

The Restoration Settlement was a compromise in more respects than one. It rested on an alliance between ex-Parliamentarians and ex-Cromwellians, who engineered the King's bloodless return, and Cavaliers, both those who had fought for Charles I and the younger generation, including exiles as well as those who had stayed at home. On the strict legalistic view, all laws passed by Charles I down to the summer of 1642 were still in force, and none of the ordinances or Acts passed without the royal assent; in practice some statutes of 1641–42 were modified or even reversed, while several parliamentary measures were re-enacted, especially in the revenue settlement of 1660–61. Ordinary, that is non-political, legal decisions of the whole period 1640–60 were given formal validity by statute, unless specifically annulled by Act or by subsequent legal decisions. Steps were taken against what the royalists and now many of the more conservative ex-Parliamentarians regarded as the worst abuses of the times: mass petitioning and lobbying of Crown or Parliament, and any restraints on the King's control of the established Church and of the armed forces, including the county militias. The settlement was less of a compromise and more partisan in Scotland than in England; and in some ways, because of the alignment of Protestant against Catholic, of English and Scots against Irish, more of a compromise in Ireland. Apart from the execution of the regicides and a few others (fourteen people in 1660–62, plus those who died in prison) and the banishment of others to escape execution, the settlement was more one-sided and severe in religion than in politics. The Uniformity Act of 1662 and the measures which accompanied it, unfairly fathered on Hyde and known as the Clarendon Code, marked a new and—as it turned out—permanent division within the body of English Protestantism, between Church and Dissent (or Nonconformity). For some of the one-time Laudians this was deliberate, a compromise with even the most moderate and anti-republican Puritans being no part of their scheme. But for others the failure to reach a compromise and to 'comprehend' the moderate Puritans within the restored Church of England was a great and unnecessary tragedy. As with the republican political collapse of 1659–60, the failure of ecclesiastical moderation in 1660–62 was due as much to inadequate leadership and unreadiness to compromise as to the implacable enmity of conflicting extremes. The failure of comprehension was, however, to mean that the issue of toleration for those outside the State Church—to whom it should be extended and on what conditions—was to be a continuing and often urgent priority under the later Stuarts.

CONTINUITY AND CHANGE

It should be possible to draw up a rough-and-ready balance sheet of old and new, of continuity and change, comparing the England of Charles II with that of his father and his grandfather.

To take first England in relation to the rest of the world outside, foreign relations were in a state of constant interaction with affairs at home, with cultural developments as well as with politics, but by no means always in the same way. From the mid-1580s to the early 1600s the war with Spain dominated all else. It involved alliance with the Dutch and, from 1589 to 1598, with Henri IV of France. The years 1601 to 1609 saw the west European scene transformed. Reunited and freed from internal strife, France rapidly regained her position as the leading power. England made peace with Spain in 1604, and the Dutch followed suit in 1609. The English conquest of Ireland was effectively completed in 1603, and large-scale British settlement of Ulster began in 1610. The Anglo-Scottish border ceased to be a frontier along which war might at any time erupt, although there were of course Anglo-Scottish wars of varying character from 1639 to 1651. In 1610 the French king was assassinated and his country plunged back into all the insecurity and at times factional conflict of a minority; from this it only fully emerged with the appointment of Cardinal Richelieu as the new king's chief Minister in the mid-1620s. Meanwhile the heir apparent to the British throne, Prince Henry, died in 1612; a martial-minded young man, he might well have involved his country in Continental wars alongside the militant Protestants, against the Habsburgs and the Counter-Reformation; in the same year his sister married the Elector Palatine, leader of the most intransigent of the German Calvinists.

It was Frederick's acceptance of the Bohemian crown in 1618 which led to war in Europe and helped to destroy James I's policies of neutrality and marriage alliance with Spain. The French marriage of 1624–25 in turn produced a further temporary realignment: detente with France and war with Spain. The subsequent breach with France also, partly over the fate of the Huguenots in La Rochelle, can only be called an aberration, when from 1627 to 1629 Britain was at war simultaneously with both the great Catholic powers of Europe, fortunately themselves bitter dynastic and political rivals. In the 1630s Charles I returned to his father's earlier policy of neutrality. The recovery of the Palatinate, conquered by the Spanish and Imperial armies after Frederick's defeat in Bohemia, was the main declared objective of Britain's Continental policy. Behind the façade of non-parliamentary, prerogative government there were divisions between pro-French and pro-Spanish factions, or rather perhaps between those who were more anti-Spanish and others more anti-French. This was complicated by a further division between those who saw foreign policy in primarily religious terms, and favoured a general Protestant alliance—with the German princes, the Dutch and the Scandinavians—against Rome and the Habsburgs, and those who put strategic and economic considerations first. On the latter view, if France was weak, then England's weight should be thrown into the balance against Spain, and vice versa. Yet English trading and colonial interests were most in conflict with those of the Dutch, who were potential allies against Spain (with whom they had resumed war in 1621).

The outbreak of the Civil War may seem to have effectively neutralised Britain in foreign affairs. But these conflicting interests and principles remained unresolved. The royalist cause received a little help from other European monarchies, but more from Protestant Denmark than from Catholic Spain or France. The Stuarts were more firmly backed by the house of Orange-Nassau (their new in-laws since 1641) than by the Queen's family and the two great Cardinals who ruled France under her brother and then her sister-in-law. The infant Louis XIV succeeded his father in 1643, initiating yet another period of regency and minority, culminating in the upheaval of the Fronde (1648—53). The end of the Thirty Years War in 1648 raised the spectre of possibly united intervention against the new heretic, regicidal republic. But the Dutch stadtholder died in 1650, leaving only an infant heir—the future King William III; France was again plunged into internal confusion, and Spain was in no condition to intervene and help either Charles II or the Irish against the Commonwealth. At first the republic's relations were worse with France than with Spain. But the English, having been spurned in their offer of an alliance so close as to be a union, then began to discriminate against Dutch shipping, and it was with the Dutch that the first foreign war was fought (1652–54). Having in turn made a compromise peace with the United Provinces, but if anything one in England's favour, Cromwell and his Council then launched 'the Western Design', a major amphibious expedition against the Spanish Indies, apparently on the mistaken postulate that it would be compatible with remaining at peace in Europe. Not surprisingly, however, the Spaniards retaliated against English commerce; and in 1655 war became general, with the Protector subsequently joining Cardinal Mazarin in a military alliance and Britain fighting alongside France against Spain in the Flanders theatre.

The exclusion of the exiled royal court, and denial of any aid or facilities to them, formed an important part of this French alliance. Indeed, security against a foreign-backed royalist invasion was perhaps the strongest single thread in both the Commonwealth's and the Protectorate's foreign policy. In so far as Denmark was a client ally of the Dutch, England's natural ally in the Baltic was the Danes' hereditary rival, Sweden. In Cromwell's case this was camouflaged by anti-Habsburg sentiment, and the alleged danger of the Austrians interfering in north Germany and the Baltic. The great Franco-Spanish war, which had finally broken out in 1635, long outlasted the general European conflict of which it was a by-product; indeed, it almost outlived the English republic. The Peace of the Pyrenees, concluded in April 1659, led some English royalists to hope—at last—for united Bourbon–Habsburg aid for their cause. But no such move came, and it was in fact from Calvinist-republican Holland that Charles II and his entourage re-embarked for England in May 1660. Not merely did the Restoration not come about through foreign intervention; any such attempt might well have rallied the divided republicans and so have delayed restoration rather than hastening it.

Charles II and his Ministers faced many of the same problems as previous governments had done. At first Charles II's Portuguese marriage alliance suggested a continuation of Cromwellian policy: anti-Spanish and thus by default pro-French. In the event it was again with the Dutch that war was first to be fought (1664–67). But this time the outcome was far less favourable to England than in the previous decade. And the domestic political repercussions of naval disgrace and squandered resources were correspondingly severe. A brief flirtation with a pro-Protestant, anti-French policy followed, embodied in the Triple Alliance of 1667–68; but soon after that Charles II's foreign policy was drastically reoriented in a pro-French, pro-Catholic direction, with the two Treaties of Dover (one secret, one open) in 1670, and intervention on the French side in the third Anglo-Dutch war of 1672–74. France under Louis XIV was by then incomparably the strongest power in Europe, the super-power to whose tune all others danced, much as had been the case with the Spain of Philip II in the previous century.

French influences in art, literature and social life grew increasingly dominant. Only in the 1680s, and above all after the second English revolution (of 1688–89) did Britain both begin to emancipate herself from French cultural hegemony and to redirect her foreign policy in a fundamentally different direction, one in which she was to persist until the nineteenth century: imperial, commercial, and anti-French. It would be simplistic to say that nothing had changed except that France and Spain had exchanged roles as England's main opponent. In spite of James II's policies and his consequent downfall, religion had become less important as a factor in foreign relations than it had been under Elizabeth I and the early Stuarts. Colonial and commercial considerations counted for much more. The army and navy now had a continuous existence in times of peace as well as when the country was at war. This in turn helped to hasten the 'financial revolution': heavier and more efficient taxes, a long-term system of government borrowing, and a note-issuing national bank, again a process only consummated in that decade of decisive changes, the 1690s.

At home some continuities seem more obvious than others. Anti-Catholicism, amounting at times to a national phobia or collective paranoia, remained a dominant theme at least until after the fall of James II in 1688. Except in times of the most acute political and social conflict (as in 1641–53, 1659–61 and 1678–83) the political antithesis of country versus court, while not a master key to explain all else, was the prevailing influence, especially within Parliament. Equally significant, however, was the dichotomy, and resultant tension, between centralism and localism. The strength of local, especially county feeling, had inspired much of the opposition to the policies of Charles I, and equally to those of the Long Parliament and of Cromwell. It remains very evident under Charles and James II. Fears of absolutism, yet at the same time fears of popular upheaval, both of which were related to standing armies and the interference of the military in politics, cut across the party and denominational allegiances of the propertied classes.

In politics, and most especially in the House of Commons, and in the restored Lords of the 1660s–70s, we should not think of two monolithic entities, government and opposition. This would be as misleading applied to Charles II's reign as to the period from the Armada to the Petition of Right. England remained a small country, measured in terms of population: with perhaps one inhabitant for every eleven today, and proportionately more of those being children. Above all it possessed a close-knit, homogeneous ruling class; yet there was some genuine scope for popular participation, in parliamentary elections, local government, and the administration of justice. In respect of numbers there probably was a change towards the end of the Age of Milton. Between about 1630 and 1670 population growth seems to have levelled off: war, emigration, plague and other epidemics, and hard times may all have contributed to this. And, except for short-term fluctuations due to harvest failures or wartime trade dislocations, the price rise also came to an end. Indeed, the value of money was not merely stabilised but even rose as some agricultural commodity prices and rents fell during the 1660s and 1670s. Real wages stopped falling, and may even have begun to rise during the second half of the seventeenth century.

In contrast to theoretical science and mathematics, practical developments in applied science and technology were much more limited. Improvements in agricultural methods were beginning to show results, but heavy and often lucrative investment in overseas trade and in finance contrasted with relative stagnation in most of the main industrial techniques and in communications. Milton's lifetime coincided with the establishment of England's overseas empire outside Europe, and with the growth of trade beyond the traditional areas of northern Europe. These same years marked a decisive stage in the hegemony of

England over the rest of the British Isles, the anglicisation of the Celtic realms.

Inside England it can be argued that the political effects of what happened from 1640 to 1660 were more negative than positive. There was not to be an absolute monarchy, ruling either without Parliament altogether or at most with a 'rubber stamp' assembly.[12] Nor was there to be a middle-class Puritan republic, still less anything nearer to a popular democracy. The failure of the republic may well have contributed to the upper-class, even aristocratic, reaction which is evident from 1660, and thus very likely helped to delay many much-needed social and legal, as well as political, reforms for a century or more. These questions are as controversial, and remain as open, as the debate about the causes of the mid-century upheaval. The extent to which this was a traumatic experience for many who lived through it, and retrospectively in memory for many who came after, seems beyond dispute. Only exclusive emphasis on social and economic transformation, as opposed to political and religious cataclysm, would make the word 'revolution' inappropriate to describe what happened in England during the 1640s. By those criteria there probably were no revolutions in history before 1917.

If we contrast the England of Charles II with that of late Elizabethan and Jacobean times, some of the differences are striking but perhaps superficial. Men's and women's clothing and hairstyles had changed dramatically—so they looked different, or they certainly do so to us in surviving pictures. The ruff had gone out and the wig was coming in. Clearly the historian must try to distinguish between possibly superficial changes of fashion and idiom or style, and genuinely new phenomena—changes of underlying substance. That many contemporaries thought that they had lived through a period of tumultuous upheaval and striking novelty—whether in their view for good or for ill—proves something but not everything. They may have been deceived as to what were the most important developments; they may have been over-influenced by subjective reactions to external circumstances. In cultural history, the return of the exiled court and of the Church hierarchy, the reappearance of aristocratic patronage and the official reopening of the theatres, together with the return of pre-publication censorship, civil and ecclesiastical, make it only reasonable to treat the Restoration as some kind of watershed. Dryden's first great political 'face-about', Milton's disappearance from the public scene, and Marvell's temporary silence provide, as it were, the poetic documentation for this generalisation. Yet the successful career of Samuel Cooper, among the greatest of portrait miniaturists and 'limner' successively to the Cromwellian circle and then to King Charles II, is as much a reminder of continuity from the 1650s to the 1660s as the public careers of Monck and Ashley Cooper, Pepys's Diary and his career as a naval administrator, the links between the scientific groups and meetings of the Interregnum and the newly instituted Royal Society. 'Continuity and change' is a fitting overall theme, provided it is not used mechaniclly or as any kind of talismanic explanation, and so long as it does not lead us to lose sight of the aspirations, achievements, failures, passions, sufferings, absurdities and sheer endurance of individual human beings living out their lives—whether these seem to us ordinary or exceptional—in an epoch of violence and revolution.

NOTES

The reader will find many topics discussed more fully elsewhere, especially in Chapters 2 and 3. I am particularly grateful to Professors Austin Woolrych and Theodore K. Rabb for having discussed the contents of their chapters with me by post and for having provided full synopses. Where there is a difference of emphasis or disagreement, it has seemed best to allow some overlap to remain: e.g. on the events of 1641–42 and on public finance and the effects of inflation.

1 The fullest and best account is now by D. B. Quinn (§S–117), especially Chapters XI and XVII.

2 In my own textbook (§S–6), if anything too severe a view is taken—I now think—of James as king and too little allowance made for his difficulties. Conrad Russell (§S–129) provides a juster, more balanced view.

3 In *The Culture of Cities* (1938).

4 See §§S–124, S–141 (Ch. III), and S–130.

5 So named after the London petition of December 1640, which spoke of abolishing episcopacy 'with all the roots, branches and dependencies thereof'; the phrase was later embodied in a parliamentary Bill of the following summer.

6 Christopher Hill's *Milton and the English Revolution* (§S–69), especially Parts II and V, is now in my view the most lucid and compelling, as well as the most recent, serious scholarly treatment. It relates the great Christian poet's intellectual development to the contemporary context with great skill and effect, but without committing the vulgar heresy of 'reductionism'.

7 Cited by Sir Philip Warwick (1609–83) in his *Memoires of the reigne of King Charles I . . .* (1701), pp. 253–4.

8 By W. C. Sellar and R. J. Yeatman (1930), Ch. XXXV, p. 63.

9 It is of course necessary to add on five, for the Tellers on each side and the Speaker; but this is still under seven-tenths of the possible attendance.

10 Sometimes reached in the annual voting for the Council of State, whose members were elected by ballot from 1651 on.

11 For a fuller discussion, especially of Milton's activities as a political writer, see below, Ch. 2.

12 Contrary to the views of some present-day historians, I do not think that the rule of Charles II and of James II from 1681 to 1688 invalidates this generalisation.

2

Political theory and political practice

THE COMMON-LAW MIND AND THE ANCIENT CONSTITUTION

In the early seventeenth century most political thinking in England was narrow, unsystematic and set in ancient modes. During more than a century before the Civil War, no Englishman published a political treatise that made any significant impact outside his own country, or is still read by any but specialists today. Those native writers who did substantially influence contemporary thought on the subject were primarily concerned with other matters: Richard Hooker, for example, with the relations between Church and State, and Sir Edward Coke with the common law. There was nothing to presage the outburst of original and creative political theory that began in 1642. The Great Rebellion was not the outcome of radical political ideologies; it generated them. Radical ideas were prompted at first by the need to justify revolutionary actions which the old channels of thought could not accommodate, but the momentum of the great debate became self-sustaining, and the result was the richest and most exciting period in the history of English political philosophy.

The lateness of this development needs some explaining, for there was plenty of friction in the previous forty years to stimulate fresh thinking on the subject, and in the course of James I's reign two intellectual currents began to flow which would powerfully encourage a new spirit of inquiry over a whole range of subjects. One had its main impetus from Bacon's vision of the vast improvement in man's lot which the new philosophy would achieve through the systematic and scientific pursuit of knowledge, and from the broad programme for this which he sketched in his *Instauratio Magna* (1620–23). The other sprang from the rapid intensification of interest, chiefly but not solely among Puritans, in millenarianism. It may be wondered why the conviction that the prophecies in Daniel and Revelation were to be strictly fulfilled in historical time, probably quite soon, and that the expected overthrow of Antichrist would open the way to the new Jerusalem, should be a strong stimulus to intellectual inquiry. Yet it was so, because the millennium was expected not only to restore man to a state of grace, but to recover for him the encyclopaedic knowledge and the power over nature which Adam had enjoyed at the Creation but lost through the Fall. Baconianism and millenarianism came consciously together, because they both conceived the quest for knowledge and mastery not as a Promethean challenge to divine providence but as the acting out of God's purpose (§S–577: Ch. I and *passim*).

Such ideas ran counter to the older assumption, which still persisted, that ancient wisdom was superior to modern because the world was in a state of progressive decay and approaching its end. The hopeful projects and the large achievements which they inspired came mainly after 1640; during the preceding quarter-century the prevailing intellectual climate was predominantly pessimistic, and official policies were repressive and discouraging (§S–68: pp. 7–13). Yet while there were many forerunners of the great mid-century flowering in natural philosophy there was virtually none to hint at the coming breakthrough in political thought, and neither the tightening of the licensing laws nor the activities of the Court of Star Chamber are sufficient to explain why this was so.

One reason was that Englishmen were on the whole highly contented with the political system they had inherited. When things went wrong they blamed their governors, not the 'fundamental laws' under which government was carried on. A certain smugness about the superiority of English institutions and English liberties went back at least as far as Sir John Fortescue, the Lord Chief Justice during the Wars of the Roses who had contrasted English kingship, which operated within a framework of law that enshrined the subject's rights as well as the king's prerogative, with the Continental monarchies which were bound by no such restraints. By a century later the idea had taken shape that England's was a mixed monarchy, embodying all the advantages of each of Aristotle's categories of government (monarchy, aristocracy, democracy) while avoiding the possible abuses of all three. As John Aylmer put it shortly after Elizabeth I's accession,

> The regiment of England is not a mere monarchy, as some for lack of consideration think, nor a mere oligarchy, nor democracy, but a rule mixed of all these . . . the image whereof, and not the image but the thing indeed, is to be seen in the Parliament House, wherein you shall find these three estates: the king or queen, which representeth the monarch; the noblemen which be the aristocracy; and the burgesses and knights the democracy.[1]

It is worth noting that this conception of mixed government was a Tudor growth with its roots in antiquity, because although it was not much voiced in the earlier seventeenth century it came very much to the fore again in the early 1640s. So did the meaning which Aylmer attached to the three estates. In mediaeval usage these had been the clergy, the nobility (with whom knights were then included) and the commonalty, but Aylmer identified them as King, Lords and Commons—political rather than social entities. This too passed into common currency, but those royalists who deplored that the King was being degraded from a position of unique transcendence to a mere estate of the realm, conceptually on a par with the two others, were doubtless unaware that the idea had gone apparently unchallenged in the days of Queen Elizabeth of blessed memory.

Yet despite such limitations on royal autocracy, belief in the divine right of kings remained as widespread in the early Stuart period as in the Tudor. It may have been strained by James I's more extravagant formulations of it, and it certainly was when the court divines inflated it more grossly under his son, but until the Civil War it still commanded general assent. It was not just the doctrine of a party, for it was affirmed by parliamentary politicians like Sir John Eliot, John Pym and Dudley Digges, and by Puritan preachers from William Perkins and Robert Bolton to John Downame and Stephen Marshall.[2]

There is no paradox here. It would have seemed quite wrong and unnatural to divorce political theory from religious precepts and sanctions; no Englishmen did it completely before Hobbes, and some authorities deny that even he did. Government, it was agreed, was decreed by God as a necessity to fallen man, and human societies were composed of souls that had an end beyond this world. Machiavelli, who had made the great separation, had fascinated, shocked and sometimes even, within limits, influenced English writers since Henry VIII's reign, but *The Prince* was not published in English until 1640, and his mode of thought remained alien (§ S–119). It would take the upheavals of the English revolution to change the primary political question from 'What kind of government do God and the law prescribe?' to 'What institutions will best satisfy the interests which induce men to submit to political authority?'

Prior to that change, several lines of thought converged to raise kings to the status of God's lieutenants on earth and the images of his own power. The Great Chain of Being was one, the world picture which displayed hierarchy as a principle pervading the entire cosmos, so that a king stood in the same relation to the ranks and orders of men in the microcosm of his realm as God did to the whole scale of creatures from angels to earthworms in the universe at large (§ S–388). Then there was that other pervading image of the commonwealth as a body politic, with the king as head and all his subjects as members, each performing his organic function according to his degree. Just as the head was unique as the seat of the divine faculty of reason, so kings were supposed to be endowed by God with a special capacity to judge aright in the weighty decisions that constantly faced them. The attribution to kings of faculties beyond those of ordinary mortals was very ancient; it was perpetuated in their solemn anointing at their coronation, and the popularity of the practice of touching for 'the king's evil' showed that it still met an emotional need. The specific doctrine of divine right went back also to the claims of mediaeval emperors, when in conflict with the Papacy, that the authority of the temporal sword was no less ordained by God than that of the spiritual. Kings of sovereign States claimed to be emperors in their own realms, and in England the sacred character of their office (if not of their conduct) had been enhanced by their assumption of royal supremacy over the Church. Even national pride entered into it; popular feeling craved for a more than human figure to personify the majesty of the State and the aspirations of the nation, and would have been offended if the King of England were held any less sacred in his person than his cousins of France and Spain. Moreover John Foxe had supplied a special reason for holding him so. Far more widely read than any other book except the Bible, his *Book of Martyrs* (§P–6) had taught generations of Englishmen to believe that they were an elect nation, predestined to play a very special part in the final overthrow of Antichrist. In this great enterprise the Godly Prince was cast for a heroic role, recalling that which a potent and persistent mediaeval tradition had accorded to the Emperor of the Last Days. Eventually the gap between Stuart policies and Protestant hopes would dim the vision of the Godly Prince, but the upsurge of millenarianism kept it alight surprisingly long.[3]

Yet what gave divine right its special character and prominence in this age, throughout western Europe, was the need that monarchs felt to counter the doctrines of resistance which developed during the various wars of religion. French and Dutch Calvinists, going far beyond Calvin himself, affirmed the right and duty of the faithful to take up arms against princes who persecuted the gospel; Catholics, particularly Jesuits, invoked the same against heretic kings. James I encountered such doctrines in Scotland, and it was these and the actual plots against him which inspired his higher flights on divine right. But in the whole period from Elizabeth I's accession to the very eve of the Civil War the English Puritans conspicuously refrained from justifying resistance; indeed, they frequently condemned it, and differed little from their Anglican brethren over the duty of passive obedience.[4] The divine right of kings troubled them far less than the Arminian divines' doctrine of the *jus divinum* of episcopacy.

Divine right was the easier to accept because it did not at all necessarily imply royal absolution. To the Arminians it did, but most Englishmen found it quite consistent to believe the king's person and office were sacred, and that his lawful commands could not be disobeyed without sin, and yet to hold that he was bound to exercise his divinely sanctioned authority within the bounds set by the law of the land. For the law itself was divinely ordained, and the immemorially ancient common law of England stood only one degree below the law of nature and the law of God in the hierarchy of authority through which God gave order to mankind. As far back as the thirteenth century, Bracton had written that though the king was superior to everyone else in his realm, he was subject to God and the law, since the law made him king. Hooker said much the same towards the end of Elizabeth's reign:

> Though no manner person or cause be unsubject to the king's power, yet so is the power of the king over all and in all limited that unto all his proceedings the law itself is a rule. The axioms of our regal government are these: 'Lex facit regem': the king's grant of any favour made contrary to the law is void: 'Rex nihil potest nisi quod iure potest'.[5]

The common law coloured the average educated Englishman's thinking on matters of politics to a remarkable degree—the more remarkable because in many respects the law was obscure, archaic and fearsomely technical. But it was the law which the greater gentry administered in their counties as Justices of the Peace, and in early seventeenth-century Parliaments between a half and three-fifths of the MPs were also JPs. It was the law which many of them had studied when they went to one of the Inns of Court to complete their education—about 330 out of the original 547 members of the Long Parliament, for instance, which was a shade more than had been to Oxford or Cambridge.[6] It has been doubted whether most of them penetrated far into the law's mysteries unless they were among the smallish minority who were training to practise it professionally (§S–320: Ch. VII), but their veneration for it was not limited by their comprehension and they absorbed the ethos of the Inns even if they absorbed little else. A high proportion of the leaders of parliamentary opposition possessed legal expertise.

The common law was of course basically case law, embodying age-old maxims but subject to modification by parliamentary statutes. This largely explains the Commons' devotion to precedent, for what had once been done, however long ago, could lawfully be done again. When they did manage to do something unprecedented, such as determining disputed elections to the House, it rapidly became enshrined as part of the ancient and undoubted birthright of Englishmen. When in the 1620s they were emboldened to force unpopular Ministers of the Crown from office, which they had never dared to attempt under the Tudors, they did not have to make their case from first principles; they revived the process of impeachment, which had lain disused since the Lancastrian era. From Elizabeth's reign onwards they scoured the statutes of the Middle Ages, quarried the musty records in the Tower and read strange unhistorical meanings into Magna Carta. They were in fact harnessing antiquarianism to radicalism, though they would never have admitted to being radicals, even if they could have understood the term. This tendency to argue from what had been rather than what should be goes far to explain why English political thought before 1640 was so limited and unphilosophical. The approach worked fairly satisfactorily while the main issues arose over specific clashes between the Commons and the Crown, or between the county communities and the central administration. It would break down completely, however, during the crisis which led directly to the Civil War.

Before that unforeseen catastrophe, a comfortable belief prevailed that the prerogative of the Crown, the privileges of Parliament, the jurisdiction of the various courts and the liberty and property of the subject were all sustained in perfect equipoise by the law of the land. It was quite understood that there was a large area of government, embracing decisions of policy rather than of right, which was not susceptible to regulation by law. In these 'matters of state', which included the whole sphere of foreign policy until the Commons first began to encroach on it in 1621, it was freely agreed that the power of decision lay with the king. It was equally acknowledged that there must in every State be a residuary power to act for the safety of the people, even if in a case of emergency it meant overriding the law. This too belonged indisputably to the king, but it did not make him absolute. James I himself accepted this, for though he sometimes spoke the rhetoric of absolutism he acknowledged to Parliament in 1610 that 'though he did derive his tytle from the loynes of his ancestors, yet the lawe did set the Crowne upon his head, and he is a Kinge by the comon lawe of the land'. In particular he owned that he could neither make laws nor levy subsidies without the consent of the estates in Parliament.[7]

This general belief in a 'balanced polity', in which the king presided over a plurality of authorities, each of which, including the royal prerogative itself, had its functions defined by an unwritten fundamental law, made Englishmen resistant to the more modern concept of sovereignty, which the Frenchman Jean Bodin had formulated in 1576, though many of them read him. According to Bodin, there must be in every well-ordered State a single sovereign authority from which all others derive, and which is unrestrained by law because the law is simply what the sovereign commands. In practice, sovereignty in England effectively resided in the King-in-Parliament, since King, Lords and Commons acting jointly could make and unmake laws, levy taxes and do whatever else Bodin's sovereign was supposed to do. James Whitelocke almost grasped this when, in a remarkable speech in the Commons in 1610, he said that the King's power in Parliament was supreme, but out of Parliament subordinate (§S–84: pp. 70–1); yet the concept of sovereignty played little part in political debate before 1642 and few Englishmen seem to have fully understood it. Some were positively hostile to it, especially the common lawyers. 'Magna Charta is such a fellow that he will have no sovereign,' said Sir Edward Coke.[8]

Not only did those who engaged in the major political conflicts prior to 1640 fail to conceive them in terms of a struggle for sovereignty, but it is misleading to view them thus even with hindsight until a fairly late stage.[9] All parties concerned had a high regard for the constitution that they had inherited, and until at least the 1630s they tried to resolve their differences within its framework. It is significant that three of the major constitutional disputes were brought before the courts to be determined, and that in each one the royal power that was challenged was such as the kings of France and Spain and many a lesser prince were accustomed to exercise without question. They were the imposition of additional import duties by royal prerogative (1606), the King's right to imprison men for reasons of state without declaring any further cause (1627), and Charles I's annual levy of Ship Money (1637–38). In each case the Judges accepted a distinction between the King's ordinary power (*potestas*) and his absolute power. The former embraced all the civil and criminal justice that was executed in the King's name, and all the ordinary dealings between government and subjects; it was of course bounded by the laws of the land, mediated through the courts, and not subject to his personal interference. His absolute power (or prerogative), by contrast, was that which he exercised in all those matters of state—decisions of policy, conduct of foreign relations, emergency measures for the safety of the people, and so on—for which the law could not possibly prescribe.[10] So much was agreed; the Judges were careful to explain that it was not a power to do as he pleased. But was it a power which the king exercised by virtue of the law of the land, and within limits which the law set, or was it a power *above* the law? Coke thought the former: 'The King,' he once affirmed, 'has no prerogative but that which the law of the land allows him.'[11] But when it was argued before Sir Robert Berkeley in the Ship Money Case that the King was restrained by a 'fundamental policy' in the constitution from levying any money without the consent of Parliament, that Judge retorted:

> The law knows no such king-yoking policy. The law is of itself an old and trusty servant of the king's; it is his instrument or means which he useth to govern his people by. I never read or heard that *lex* was *rex*; but it is common and most true that *rex* is *lex*, for he is *lex loquens*, a living, a speaking, an acting law.
>
> (§S–84: p. 113).

But the Judges in this case were deeply divided, and Berkeley himself conceded much concerning fundamental law and the Englishman's birthright which muted the absolutist ring in the words quoted above.[12] (This did not save him from being impeached by the Long Parliament in 1641.)

The fundamental law, or laws, became a favourite stick with which to beat those who were believed to be encroaching on the subject's liberties or innovating upon time-honoured constitutional practice. They were much invoked in the busy Parliaments of the 1620s, and still more by the Long Parliament. Strafford, Laud and Berkeley were impeached for endeavouring to subvert them. Charles I retorted the charge on the Five Members, but it was for allegedly overthrowing the fundamental laws that he was eventually sentenced to death. The trouble was that nobody could state exactly what they were, and that until they were established with more precision they were a two-edged weapon. James I perceived that in his time, and the royalists made much play with them from 1641 onwards (§S–57: Ch. IV–V). Coke became so dissatisfied with the vagueness of the concept that in 1628 he rejected 'fundamental' as 'a word I understand not', but he was not wholly consistent, for there are many statements of his which assume the existence of fundamental laws.[13]

Coke was certainly not consistently a figure of opposition, and it was only after he was finally disappointed of high political office in 1621 that he became the intellectual leader of the more responsible country politicians in the Commons. But the influence of his legal opinions went back further, and that of his writings went on increasing after his death in 1634. In so far as a parliamentarian ideology developed in the course of Charles I's reign, Coke did more than any other individual to shape it. He was the main deviser of the Petition of Right, which for all its lack of immediate effect was important for its vindication of Parliament's power to declare what the law of the land was, in matters which deeply concerned the liberty of the subject.

But his writings wrought more than his actions, and despite the limitations of his vision he must be reckoned, as he was reckoned at the time, one of the intellectual giants of his age. His great enterprise was to systematise and synthesise the bewildering tangle of custom, case law and statutes which the judges and lawyers of his time had to interpret. In doing this he gave the law a distinct bent, favourable to the rights of the subject and restrictive of the royal prerogative. He dealt with case law in the thirteen volumes of his *Reports*, eleven of which were published between 1600 and 1615 with prefaces in English that carried his message far beyond his fellow professionals. He portrayed the common law as immemorially ancient, immutable in its basic principles, yet in continuous process of refinement and renewal through interpretation by genera-tion after generation of judges, so that it both distilled the accumulated wisdom of the nation and adapted itself perfectly to change. How, he implied, could a particular man's judgement, even a king's, stand against this massive 'artificial reason' of the law? James I tried vainly to make Coke expurgate his *Reports*, but they were not as directly threatening to the prerogative as his later *Institutes*, which attempted to educe the fundamental principles of the law and the constitution. Only the first part was published in his lifetime, in 1628. When he lay dying all his manuscripts were seized, not for the first time, and the other three parts remained suppressed until the Long Parliament ordered their publication in 1641.[14]

In these works Coke developed an extraordinary myth. He assumed that not only the basic principles of English common law but the whole structure of the English constitution had descended without essential change from the mists of antiquity. The present courts of common law and equity, the writs they employed and the sheriffs who executed them, all dated from untold centuries before the Norman Conquest; so did Parliament, and the presence in it of elected knights and burgesses. Coke not only cited the apocryphal laws of pre-Conquest kings from Alfred onwards, calling them statutes, but he invoked such wholly mythical British monarchs as Brutus the Trojan and Dunwallo Molmutius, though in their case it was to illustrate rather than to establish the antiquity of the constitution. This appeal to a legendary past was not novel or bizarre in itself. Henry VIII and his Ministers had seriously examined the stories of Brutus, Brennus and Arthur for evidence of the earliest English kings' independence of Rome, and Milton in his *History of Britain* was only half sceptical about their descent through Brutus from Aeneas.[15] But it is surprising how easily Coke persuaded his readers that the Norman Conquest had wrought little change in England's laws and institutions, for the popular historians of the day whom the gentry were likely to read, such as Sir Richard Baker, William Martyn and John Hayward, depicted it as causing a drastic break in both laws and customs, and none of them set an earlier date to Parliament than the twelfth century. Sir Henry Spelman and other legal antiquarians had been busy discovering the profound differences between pre-feudal and feudal institutions, and correctly tracing the origins of Parliament in the latter.[16]

But Spelman's key works were not published until after his death in 1641, and the common-law mind was profoundly resistant to the kind of true historical sense that they exemplified. Whether Coke was consciously myth-making we cannot know, but it was highly satisfying to him and his readers to think that no legislator, however remote, had devised the ancient constitution of England, which was as perfect and as sacrosanct as it was immemorially old. The full doctrine caught on slowly; in the Parliament of 1628 only John Pym and Sir Dudley Digges are recorded as expounding it.[17] But by the time of the Long Parliament it was widely current, and it became more so after the full publication of the *Institutes*. Ironically it put out its strongest appeal just when the quarrel between King and Parliament was carrying the latter into waters where the ancient constitution offered no landmarks, but that did not extinguish its potency. Even in 1647, when the chief officers of the New Model Army were contending in Putney Church with the Agitators' claim that every free man should have an equal voice in parliamentary elections, Commissary-General Ireton argued that the franchise was restricted to those who then possessed it 'by the civil constitution of this kingdom, which is original and fundamental, and beyond which I am sure no memory of record does go'. 'Not before the Conquest,' interjected one of his opponents, appealing to an imagined Anglo-Saxon democracy, and so countering myth with myth. 'But before the Conquest it was so,' retorted Ireton with sublime certainty (§S–8: p. 99).

PARLIAMENTARIANS AND ROYALISTS

By that time the ancient constitution was shortly to be torn to shreds, but for the first year or two of the Long Parliament it dominated most Members' thinking. The acts of 1641, which in fact changed the balance of the constitution quite drastically—the Triennial Act and those which abolished the prerogative courts and all forms of non-parliamentary taxation—made out that they were merely restoring it to its pristine excellence by removing recent abuses and excrescences. The King's sacred image was saved from too much tarnishing by blaming all the misrule of his reign on his 'evil counsellors'. Most members would have been content to go no further than these measures of 1641, if only the King could have been trusted to abide by them, and if the appalling rebellion in Ireland had not created a new crisis in the autumn. In those circumstances, Pym and his allies persuaded the two Houses to advance two demands far more radical than any previous ones, namely that the King should employ only such councillors and Ministers as Parliament should approve, and that Parliament should control the militia—in other words the State's ultimate sanction, its armed forces. The situation caused a major political realignment, and the gradual emergence of parties which for the first time can legitimately be called royalist and Parliamentarian, although a substantial proportion of the political nation maintained a neutral position for as long as possible.

The new demands had no respectable precedents and could claim no convincing justification from the fundamental laws, which the royalists could now claim to be defending. This probably played as great a part in rallying a party to the King as the rising Puritan threat to the Anglican Church and the support which the opposition was receiving from mass petitions and riotous popular demonstrations. The King could and did now take his stand as the defender of the ancient constitution, of the true Protestant religion embodied in the Church of England, and of the traditional social order that was being threatened from below.

There is no doubt that popular demonstrations and riots played a significant part in the events of 1640–42, and that the general political dislocation took the lid off a great deal of simmering discontent among craftsmen, small traders, artisans and peasants. Nor can it be doubted that the parliamentary leaders welcomed their support, though there is little evidence to show whether or not they organised its rowdier manifestations. It has recently been argued that these popular movements took over the political initiative and swung the course of events towards civil war, thereby transforming a conflict within the governing class into a primarily social struggle.[18] This is to exaggerate their significance at this stage. It is true that since at least the 1620s the country faction in the Commons had favoured a widening of the electorate, particularly in those 'close' boroughs where the ruling oligarchies were disposed to return candidates supported by the court. Indeed, in the Long Parliament the Commons generally decided disputed elections on the assumption that in borough constituencies, which accounted for more than four-fifths of the membership, all adult male residents were entitled to vote unless there was a specific statute to the contrary (§S–72). But though the Commons made much of their claim to speak as representatives of the people, this electoral policy was not so much an expression of democratic principles as a means to an end, namely the defeat of as many court candidates as possible. There was nothing notably democratic in the aims for which the Long Parliament embarked on the Civil War, and few Members had any desire to admit the lower orders to any real share in political power. The conflict remained essentially one between sections of the governing class until well after the war had begun, and in very many cases their differences were not ideological or social at all, but only as to whether King Charles or King Pym presented the greater menace to the interests that they nearly all wanted to preserve.

Nevertheless those who followed Pym were hard put to it to find respectable arguments for their actions within the terms of conventional wisdom, especially after the two Houses usurped the legislative power by passing the Militia Ordinance in March 1642. The King naturally forbade his subjects to obey it, for nothing was more central to his prerogative than his exclusive right to call them to arms. Parliament in reply was driven to such sophistry as this:

> The High Court of Parliament is not only a court of judicature, . . . but it is likewise a council, to provide for the necessities, prevent the imminent dangers, and preserve the public peace and safety of the kingdom, and to declare the king's pleasure in those things that are requisite thereunto; and what they do herein hath the stamp of the royal authority, although His Majesty, seduced by evil counsel, do in his own person oppose or interrupt the same; for the king's supreme and royal pleasure is exercised and declared in this High Court of law and council, after a more eminent and obligatory manner than it can be by personal act or resolution of his own.[19]

Parliament was arguing tendentiously from the judicial power, which was exercised in the King's name by the courts, to the political function of deciding matters of state, which historically belonged to the King and in which Parliament's role was at the most advisory. In contemporary terms, it utterly confused his 'ordinary' and 'absolute' powers, and bound both equally in chains.

A long paper war preceded the actual fighting, but despite the skill and persuasiveness with which Sir Edward Hyde, the future Earl of Clarendon, put the King's case to the public, it contributed little new to political theory. Both sides dwelt on their legal rights; but, while the penners of official declarations were battling it out in terms which the tide of events was rendering increasingly unreal, some other writers were prepared to acknowledge that the struggle really was now over sovereignty. Outstanding on the Parliamentarian side was Henry Parker, a lawyer sprung from a solid Sussex family which sent Members to most Parliaments during the century. Of his score or so of tracts the most influential was *Observations upon Some of His Majesty's Late Answers and Expresses* (July 1642).[20] 'Power is originally inherent in the people,' its first page boldly proclaimed. God is no more the author of royal authority than of any other, whether supreme or subordinate, since all just authority is conferred in accordance with laws based on common consent and agreement. When the people thus bestow it, 'man is the free and voluntary Author, the Law is the Instrument, and God is the establisher of both'. Parker acknowledged that by the laws of England the supreme authority in England was normally exercised by King, Lords and Commons conjointly; but who should be obeyed if the King deserted his Parliament—Parker's way of describing Charles I's withdrawal to York—and if he and they issued directly contrary commands? His answer was unequivocal. King and Parliament both derived their power from the people, but whereas the King's was 'conditionate and fiduciary', Parliament did not merely represent the people; it *was* the people, for 'the whole Kingdome is not so properly the Author as the essence it selfe of Parliaments'. The King had asserted, all too plausibly, that the Parliamentarian leaders no longer expressed the desires of most of the people. Parker indignantly denounced this attempt to impugn 'that great Priviledge of all Priviledges, that unmoveable Basis of all honour and power, whereby the House of Commons claimes the entire rite [*sic*] of all the Gentry and Commonalty of *England*'. Since it was inconceivable that the people, so perfectly embodied, could command anything injurious to themselves, Parliament must have the ultimate authority to declare what the law of the land was, and to do whatever was necessary to preserve the safety of the people (pp. 1, 4, 5, 9, 15, 21 ff., 34–9).

Although Parker is justly famous as England's first unequivocal exponent of the sovereignty of the people, he was hardly a democrat. He thought it quite proper that 'the multitude hath onely a representative influence, so that they are not likely to sway'. He saw the Lords and Commons as together forming 'an excellent Skreene and banke . . . to assist both King and people against the encroachment of each other', for they 'peaceably and sweetly arbitrate betwixt the Prince and his poorest Vassals, . . . declining Tyranny on the one side, and

Ochlocracy [mob rule] on the other' (p. 23). The weakness of his case was that he never adequately demonstrated *why* a body so dubiously representative and so dominated by landowners as the unreformed Parliament should be held to incarnate the interests of the whole people so perfectly that everything it voted must infallibly be for their good. Within five years the Levellers were to attack this whole assumption, and Parker was to denounce them virulently for it. Yet his ideas seemed shockingly radical in their day.

A more moderate Parliamentarian theorist than Parker, but more in the mainstream of English political thinking, was Philip Hunton, who published his *Treatise of Monarchy* in 1643. In it he expounded at length the theory of mixed monarchy, but he also showed a clear grasp of the concept of sovereignty, which he identified as essentially the law-making power and located in the King-in-Parliament. Unlike Parker, he did not think there was any Judge who could legally pronounce when the partners in the sovereign power fell out with each other; he saw the Civil War as a tragic outcome of the breakdown of government rather than as a means of attaining any desired change. Yet he supported Parliament, and as a clergyman he urged others to do so, on the ground that the judgement of the best men was the safest guide for individual consciences to follow if the King appeared to be transgressing the fundamental constitution.[21]

A notable feature of Hunton's treatise was its emphasis on 'the consent and fundamental contract of a nation' as 'the root of all sovereignty'. The notion that government depends on a contract, implied if not actually historical, has sometimes been given an older ancestry than it can truly claim. The principle that government should rest on agreement was familiar to mediaeval schoolmen, and for that matter to Hooker and James I; but a covenant that bound both ruler and ruled was a more recent concept, evolved mainly by the Huguenots and the Netherlanders, and it was one of several points on which two notable royalist polemicists took up Hunton.

The first was Dr Henry Ferne, who became a chaplain to Charles I and attracted considerable attention with three well argued tracts in 1642–43.[22] His views were remarkably moderate compared with the near-absolutism preached by Mainwaring, Sibthorpe, Laud and the Arminians earlier in the reign. This was politic as well as sincere, for to most royalists—and still more to the thousands of as yet uncommitted neutrals—the Arminians were almost as obnoxious as they were to the Parliamentarians. Ferne accepted that the King's prerogative was limited by the law of the land. He agreed that the supreme power in the State was the legislative power, and that in this the two Houses were 'in a sort coordinate with His Majesty . . . by a fundamental constitution'.[23] But against Parker he denied that they had any right to frame laws without the King's consent, or to usurp his supreme authority in matters of state; against Hunton he denied that subjects might in any circumstances take up arms against their king; and against both he denied that power was derived from the people.

Hunton's other adversary, however, was eventually to achieve much greater fame and influence, though mainly long after his death. Sir Robert Filmer was a

Kentish gentleman who had been an intimate friend of George Herbert and the antiquary William Camden, and had known Cotton, Selden and Spelman among the great legal and historical scholars of his age. He won some reputation with three tracts which he published in 1648, notably *The Freeholder's Grand Inquest*, which brought much antiquarian learning and devastating force of argument to bear against the prevalent belief in the immemorial antiquity of the House of Commons. His now much more famous *Patriarcha*, however, was not printed until 1680. Nevertheless it circulated in manuscript, and it is the most important exposition of high royalism written in the Age of Milton. Just when he wrote it is doubtful: probably in 1648 in its final form, though some elements in it may date from 1642–43.[24]

To appreciate the force which Filmer's argument had for his century, it is necessary to suspend the disbelief or repugnance that we feel today towards a number of assumptions which were then generally current. These include the literal historical truth of the entire Old Testament, the divinely ordained superiority of the male sex, the absolute authority of a father over his children, and the justice and necessity of both social and political subordination. From such premises Filmer made out a formidable case that political authority is not in its nature contractual at all, nor derived either directly from the people nor from fundamental laws. It is natural, for it springs from the father's authority over his family, in which it originated, and whose divine sanction it shares. This was not a novel doctrine—James I among others had appealed to it[25]—but Filmer built upon it more systematically than any earlier writer. Locke and others were to make fun of his derivation of all kings' authority from God's grant to Adam of the sovereignty over all created things and his reliance on Noah's division of the world among his sons to explain why Adam had many royal heirs rather than one. But this biblical underpinning did not make him nearly so implausible to his own age as has generally been thought,[26] and his central thesis could have stood quite strongly without it. This was that political authority was a natural growth, expanding organically as families had broadened into clans and clans into nations, and not a legal artifact based on an imagined contract. He caustically dismissed the whole implausible concept of a pre-political state of nature. He knew perfectly well that most dynasties derived their right ultimately from conquest, but it did not detract from the essentially paternal nature of royal authority. 'Every man is born subject to the power of a father,' he wrote:

> In all kingdoms or commonwealths in the world, whether the Prince be the supreme Father of the people or but the true heir of such a Father, or whether he came to the Crown by usurpation, or by election of the nobles or of the people, . . . yet still the authority . . . is the only right and natural authority of a supreme Father.[27]

But he strongly disapproved of elective monarchy, and he dismissed mixed monarchy or mixed government of any kind as 'a mere impossibility or contradiction'. He would allow no right of resistance against tyrannical kings, and no right in the people either to choose what government they pleased or to reserve any powers from the sovereign. Kings are morally obliged by the law of God and the law of nature, but are not to be limited by their subjects:

> For as kingly power is by the law of God, so it hath no inferior laws to limit it. The father of a family governs by no other law than by his own will, not by the laws or wills of his sons or servants.[28]

Filmer arrived at his doctrine of indivisible sovereignty by a very different route from Hobbes's, and he quite lacked the philosophical sweep with which Hobbes framed a political theory capable of standing without biblical and providential props. But it was precisely his revivification of divine right and his vindication of monarchy *per se* that commended him to thoroughgoing royalists in his own age and to high Tories in the next.

RADICALS AND REVOLUTIONARIES

All writers whom we have considered so far took it for granted that active involvement in politics, with limited exceptions at election-time, was confined to about five per cent of the families in the land at the most. But it is impossible to wage civil war without putting arms into the hands of many of the other ninety-five per cent, and the results were distinctly bad for traditional social deference, especially in the case of men who (as Cromwell put it) knew what they fought for and loved what they knew. Richard Baxter, when he was a chaplain in the New Model Army, heard the soldiers asking 'What were the Lords of England but William the Conqueror's colonels, or the Barons but his majors, or the knights but his captains?'[29] Men who constantly risked their lives in what they were told was a war of ideals were bound sooner or later to start thinking about those ideals for themselves. The political awakening was especially strong in the cavalry of the New Model, who were recruited largely from the 'middling sort' in the towns and countryside of Puritan East Anglia. But it was by no means confined to the soldiery, and its leaven worked powerfully among the lesser citizens of London—not least the apprentices, who like twentieth-century students were idealistic, impressionable, combustible, and as yet free of the cares of family and property which enjoined caution on their elders. Not all the manifestations of popular political consciousness, however, were radical. The Clubmen who rose in several regions to resist the pillaging forces of both sides demanded the restoration of the ancient laws, the old gentry-dominated local government, and quite often the Book of Common Prayer too (§S–97: pp. 98–111); and it was a crowd of miscellaneous London citizens who invaded the Palace of Westminster in July 1647, forcing the Commons to invite the King to London with a view to his immediate reinstatement.

Nevertheless the most striking development from the mid-'40s onwards was a body of political theory which questioned every traditional assumption about political and social hierarchy, and based itself on the natural rights of men as men. Partly it arose from typical class feeling, sharpened by all that tenants had suffered from their landlords and craftsmen-producers from capitalist merchants in two decades or more of chronic depression. Partly it grew from the very rhetoric of the parliamentary cause, since if the war were really fought for the people's liberties it was natural for articulate yeomen, shopkeepers and artisans, who suffered loss, hardship and heavy taxation even if they did not face death in the army or the trained bands, to expect victory to bring tangible benefits to themselves as well as to their gentry betters.

Political radicalism was also powerfully fuelled by religion. The preachers of the sectarian and lower-class Independent congregations were far readier than the orthodox Presbyterians to cry down all worldly hierarchies, and many of the leading Levellers had imbibed their doctrine. The intensity of radical religious convictions in the New Model Army was notorious, and Baxter heard the soldiers arguing 'sometimes for state-democracy, and sometimes for church-democracy' (§S–164: p. 388). It has often been said that the self-governing congregations, each one bonded by a voluntary mutual covenant among its members and electing its own pastor, furnished a paradigm for the democratic political theories of the mid-century. This is convincing only up to a point, for the purpose of the covenant was not so much to give expression to the wills of the individual church members as to submit them all to the will of God and to a rigorous communal discipline. But the very existence of alternative religions was a powerful solvent to traditional political assumptions, and the Long Parliament's persistent refusal to tolerate them—at any rate before 1650—spurred the more militant Independents and sectaries towards political action. Popular millenarianism was another strong current running the same way, for although its aims would eventually clash with the Levellers', its preachers often predicted that the saints who were to rule the thousand-year kingdom would be found among the humbly born.

The previous chapter has mentioned how the army made its dramatic incursion into politics in 1647, just when the Leveller movement was building up its organisation in London and assembling the planks in its political platform. Here we are concerned with the Levellers' ideas rather than their actual political involvement or the contrasted personalities of their leaders.[30] The separation is slightly false, because they did not all think alike and they modified their policy on some important matters under the impact of current events. But some over-generalisation must be risked, for the Leveller literature is one of the most astonishing phenomena in the whole history of ideas, and all the more rewarding if it is studied in relation to the modes of thought that had hitherto prevailed rather than as a primitive precursor of Chartism or modern democracy.

We must pass over the formative stages, which were much influenced by the particular issues over which John Lilburne and other leaders suffered at the hands of their parliamentary persecutors. But during 1646 Lilburne formulated what was to be the central doctrine of the whole movement, namely that all men—the Levellers were not consistent about women—were born alike with certain indefeasible natural rights, among which was freedom from obligation to any authority to which they had not given their assent. He derived it from God's grant to Adam of sovereignty over all the rest of his creatures—the very ground on which Filmer had built his edifice of absolute monarchy. Lilburne drew the opposite conclusion:

> But [God] made him not Lord, or gave him dominion over the individuals of Mankind, no further then by free consent, or agreement, by giving up their power, each to other, for their better being.[31]

By their common descent from Adam and Eve, all men and women in the world 'are, and were, by nature all equal and alike in power, dignity, authority and majesty, none of them having by nature any authority, dominion, or magisterial power one over or above another'.[32] Richard Overton argued for equal natural rights with rather more emphasis on every individual's 'selfe-propriety', or property in his own person and capacities. This is invaded whenever another seeks to impose authority on him without his consent:

> For by naturall birth, all men are equally and alike borne to like propriety, liberty and freedome, and . . . we are delivered of God by the hand of nature into this world, every one with a naturall, innate, freedome and propriety.[33]

Overton utterly rejected Henry Parker's assumption that Parliament perfectly embodied and promoted the interest of the people. On the contrary, he accused the Long Parliament in 1647 of failing to redress the people's most fundamental grievances and of imposing new oppressions on them. He therefore appealed against it to the authors of its authority:

> Therefore, if I prove a forfeiture of the *peoples trust* in the prevalent party at *Westminster* in Parliament assembled then an *Appeal* from them to people is not *Anti-parliamentary*, Anti-magesteriall, not *from* that *Soveraign power*, but *to* that *Soveraign power*.[34]

In place of Parliament the Levellers aimed to establish a single-chamber Representative of the People which should live up to its name and exercise no further authority than the sovereign people entrusted to it. Its foundation, and that of every other power in the State, was to be an Agreement of the People, a written statement of the fundamental laws which was to be subscribed by literally all free citizens of the commonwealth. Thereby they would register their consent, and the social contract imagined by the theorists would become a reality. The Agreement was elaborated and modified in successive versions between October 1647 and May 1649, but the principles remained the same. The power to make laws, to lead the people into war or peace, and to control every officer of the State was to be vested in the Representative of the People, which was to be democratically elected on the basis of equal constituencies every two years (reduced to one in the final Agreement). But each biennial Representative was to sit no longer than about six months,[35] and certain fundamental rights were to be reserved from it altogether. They included liberty of conscience and worship, the full equality of every subject before the law, freedom from compulsory military or naval service, and (from 1648 onwards) the right to private property, for no Representative was to be permitted to 'level mens Estates, destroy Propriety, or make all things Common'.[36]

There has been much controversy as to just how democratic the Levellers were. Their earlier manifestoes called simply for manhood suffrage, but from the time that their spokesmen debated the first Agreement with the General Council of Officers in Putney Church in the autumn of 1647 most of them (though not all) would have excluded servants and recipients of alms. Professor Macpherson has contended that thereby they meant everyone who earned his living by wages or who ever needed help under the Poor Law, which would have denied the vote to well over half the adult males in the country. But it has been more plausibly argued that in contemporary usage 'servants' generally signified not all wage-earners but only 'in-servants' who lived in their masters' households, and that alms-takers referred to those who lived permanently on charity or public relief.[37] Such men could be reckoned, in those days of open voting, to have forfeited the independence of choice on which a genuinely popular commonwealth depended, and also some part of that 'selfe-propriety' from which Overton derived the right of consent. Neither their exclusion nor that of men who had fought for the King detracts seriously from the Levellers' reputation as pioneer democrats. But did they intend to restrict voting rights to those who signed the Agreement? One version of it said so, though it was one which others besides Levellers helped to draft (§S–164: p. 357). That could have excluded very many who would have objected on religious grounds (upon which the Agreements were highly contentious) as well as political. But there is not enough evidence to say whether this was firm policy, or fully thought through, and it would be an anachronistic distortion to suggest that the Levellers were aiming at anything like a one-party State.

Historians have been more obsessed with the franchise than most of the Levellers themselves probably were. This is not only because of recent controversy, or because of the fascinating parallels with nineteenth-century polemics over manhood suffrage, but also partly because Ireton made such an issue of it on one day of the Putney Debates which by marvellous fortune was recorded almost verbatim. The Leveller programme needs to be viewed as a whole. Until a late stage it envisaged the Representative of the People as sitting for only a quarter of the time at most, and primarily to pass laws, though the hope was that the laws would be few and simple. To those men of the middling sort from whom the movement drew its strength, authority was represented not so much by intermittent Parliaments as by the law of the land and the magistrates and courts that administered it. Perhaps the most revolutionary Leveller demands were that all justices, sheriffs, mayors and other magistrates should be elected annually by the people, and that the law of the land should be so drastically simplified that it could be executed without the need for professional lawyers to interpret it. When one considers how long the greater landed families had dominated the commission of the peace, almost by prescriptive right, and how much the arcane law of property pertaining to their class kept the higher courts busy and the lawyers fat, one appreciates that franchise reform was only part of a larger programme.

Other parts were no less alarming. The Levellers' demand for the abolition of tithes, and even of an established Church as previously understood, would have greatly altered the status of the clergy and the governing class's indirect power over the pulpit, and had disturbing implications for property itself. Their desire to abolish the monopoly of the Merchant Adventurers and their attempts to democratise some London livery companies expressed their bid for equality of economic opportunity. They wanted an end to the excise and to imprisonment for debt; a sharp check on the extortions of gaolers; nation-wide provision of free schools and hospitals, and much more effective relief of poverty and unemployment. Occasionally they called for the abolition of copyhold tenures and the throwing open of all common land that had been enclosed, but on the whole they tended rather to neglect rural grievances and to concentrate on those of the smaller townsmen who were their backbone.

The political theory of the Levellers marked as clear a break with the past as their practical objectives. It rejected the ideal of mixed government, for it allowed no place for a privileged aristocracy or a House of Lords, and if the Levellers were not always as explicit in ruling out monarchy as their principles logically required, the reasons were merely tactical. They had no patience with fundamental laws or the ancient constitution; in their view the people's victory had freed them from bondage and created a *tabula rasa*. As John Wildman put it at Putney:

> Our very laws were made by our conquerors; and whereas it's spoken much of chronicles, I conceive there is no credit to be given to any of them; and the reason is because those that were our lords, and made us their vassals, would suffer nothing else to be chronicled. We are now engaged for our freedom; that's the end of parliaments, not to constitute what is already. (§S–8: p. 109)

Richard Overton called Magna Carta itself 'but a beggarly thing, containing many markes of intollerable bondage'. Lilburne and Wildman concurred.[38] Most of them imagined a Golden Age of popular rights and liberties in the remote past; it was the Norman Conquest that had subjected a free people to wholesale dispossession, to alien laws and to hereditary social subordination. The Levellers did not invent the potent myth of the Norman yoke or possess exclusive rights in it, but they worked it for all it was worth.[39]

There is so much in the courage and humanity of the Leveller movement that warms the heart that it is sad to record how swiftly it declined after Fairfax and Cromwell crushed the last Leveller mutinies in May 1649. It never stood a chance of gaining its ends by constitutional means, since its whole programme was anathema to the entrenched governing class. When it failed to forge the army into an instrument of revolutionary action it was left without any strategy for attaining power. The Levellers indeed thought little about how they would actually exercise power if they got it, for it was not until a few working politicians joined them in drafting the second Agreement towards the end of 1648 that they made any proposals as to how government should be carried on in the long intervals between biennial Representatives. As a pressure group they were tremendous, with their stream of pamphlets, their own newspaper, their mass petitions and their occasional well organised demonstrations. As practical revolutionaries they were non-starters. To be fair, their leaders did not think in terms of violent revolution; in their own way they were constitutionalists, believing in persuasion and law, and they were singularly free of that ruthless lust for personal power which has stamped so many later revolutionaries.

They probably did not realise how revolutionary they were, or what large effects their proposed power structure could have had on the distribution of wealth. When challenged on the possible implications at Putney, they simply denied them. They were probably naïve to hope that the democracy at which they aimed was attainable while wealth was as unequally shared as it then was. But there was another reason peculiar to their own time why their appeal was limited even among their own kind, and especially among the more literate ranks of the army. There were many radical Puritans, both soldiers and civilians, who saw the Civil War as a crucial phase in the final battle with Antichrist, and who were not persuaded that the Lord had given victory to his people for them to set up a secular commonwealth which would renounce almost all power over religion and allow equal political rights to saints and sinners alike. Soon after the Putney Debates a group of London's more radical Independent congregations published a firm condemnation of political and social egalitarianism,[40] and by 1649 some Independents and Baptists were attacking the Leveller leaders as atheists and libertines. By that time, too, the Fifth Monarchists were campaigning for a course of action quite irreconcilable with theirs; but before turning to that particular extreme there is another band in the radical spectrum to consider.

The Levellers, as we have seen, not only believed in private property but would have made it a fundamental native right which no government might take away. There were two or three small groups on their fringe which thought differently about it, but their existence hardly seems to justify a recent thesis[41] that the movement was fundamentally split between reforming 'possessive individualists' and communistic revolutionaries. They do, however, suggest a link between the left wing of the Levellers and the more unequivocally communistic Diggers, who sometimes called themselves the True Levellers, and who have an interest out of all proportion to their small numbers because in Gerrard Winstanley they had a leader and pamphleteer of genius. The pathetic story of their attempt—inevitably crushed—to live as a commune by cultivating some common land in Surrey cannot be told here. There were at least nine similar enterprises, in almost as many counties.[42] But though he made the merest ripple on the surface of political history in his own time, Winstanley claims our attention not only because he wrote memorably well but because his ideas still challenge and move us today while those of many of his more immediately influential contemporaries lie dead on the page.

Winstanley was a Lancashireman who came to London to try his fortune in the cloth trade, failed during the Civil War, and subsequently earned his bread as a cowherd. He was nearly forty when he first appeared in print in 1648 with three lengthy tracts which, like many another self-schooled millenarian's outpourings, searched the visions of Daniel and Revelation for assurances that Christ was about to raise up his despised saints in England. But his doctrine of a God immanent in the whole creation became more and more unorthodox, and his teaching that Christ was a spirit to be sought and found by every believer in his own heart linked him closely with the founders of the Quakers. His tracts were certainly among the early Quakers' devotional reading.

Early in 1649, however, his mysticism suddenly took an active and practical turn. He was moved to launch the Digging enterprise by a revelation which came to him in a state of trance.[43] He was now rationalising the scriptural myths and archetypes in the boldest way; 'the Spirit Reason and Righteousness' became his highest name for God. The garden of Eden signified the world's first age, when men in innocence had shared the earth and its fruits freely. Adam's fall allegorised the first and cardinal sin against the Spirit Reason whereby the strong had enslaved the weak and carved up the earth into parcels of private property. But now Christ, the second Adam, was to rise within the breast of every man and woman and inspire them to redeem the sin of the first by renouncing lordship and property. It was to be an act of spiritual, indeed millennial significance, for Winstanley's God remained transcendent as well as immanent:

> For talking of love is no love, it is acting of love in righteousness, which the Spirit Reason, our Father delights in. And this is to relieve the oppressed, to let goe the prisoner, to open bags and barns that the earth may be a common treasury to preserve all without complainings.[44]

Property was the curse that had imposed bondage on all mankind, and all landlords had acquired it originally by oppression or murder or theft. Israel's bondage was a 'type' prefiguring England's and all others; their fortunes intertwine in Winstanley's vision of history:

> And the last enslaving Conquest which the Enemy got over Israel, was the *Norman* over *England*; and from that time, Kings, Lords, Judges, Justices, Bayliffs, and the violent bitter people that are Free-holders, are and have been Successively: The *Norman* Bastard *William* himself, his Colonels, Captains, inferiour Officers, and Common Souldiers, who are still from that time to this day in pursuite of that victory, imprisoning, Robbing and killing the poor enslaved *English* Israelites.[45]

Redemption and the millennium were to be achieved together, for 'The word of life, Christ the restoring spirit, is to be found within you, even in your mouth, and in your heart'.[46] This is how Winstanley proclaimed the significance of the Diggers' action:

> In that we begin to Digge upon *George-Hill*, to eate our Bread together by
> righteous labour, and sweat of our browes; it was shewed us by Vision in
> Dreams, and out of Dreams, That that should be the Place we should begin upon
> . . . It is shewed us, That all the Prophecies, Visions and Revelations of
> Scriptures, of Prophets, and Apostles, concerning the calling of the Jews, the
> Restauration of Israel; and making of that People, the Inheritors of the whole
> Earth; doth all seat themselves in this work of making the Earth a Common
> Treasury.[47]

For a year or two the strands of mysticism and socialism were fused in
Winstanley's thought at white heat. The tone, however, of his last and most
detailed work, *The Law of Freedom in a Platform*, is markedly more practical and
sceptical, so much so that many commentators have seen in it his final arrival at
a wholly secular socialist commonwealth, free of doctrinal trappings.[48] This is to
ignore its many invocations of the scriptural prophecies and its continuing
emphasis on the spiritual regeneration that will accompany the sharing of the
earth and its fruits.[49] The flame burns lower in it, certainly, but its purpose is
different from that of the earlier manifestoes. He wrote it in 1651, and addressed
it to Cromwell, in an attempt to demonstrate that a polity based on common
ownership was a practical proposition. He did not demand that all existing
landowners should be dispossessed; his proposed laws and institutions were to
extend initially only to the inhabitants of 'commonwealth's land', by which he
meant the ancient commons, the former monastic estates, and all the lands of
the Crown, the Church and the beaten royalists which Parliament's victory had
won back for the people.[50] Other landlords would be left undisturbed, but he
hoped they would gradually be persuaded of the uselessness of owning land
beyond their needs, especially as they would soon be short of hands to work it
for them. Within his commonwealth, the giving or taking of hire for labour for
the community was to be compulsory up to the age of forty. On reaching it men
would become eligible for the various public offices, including judge and
minister, which were to be held for a year only. All the yield of the earth and the
products of the handicrafts were to be delivered to common storehouses, from
which each family would draw what it needed. Community of property was not
to extend to houses, household goods, wives or children, but in all else it was to
be most rigorously maintained. *The Law of Freedom* decreed the death penalty not
only for murder and rape but among other things for buying or selling land or its
produce, administering the law for gain, or making a trade of preaching and
praying. The annually elected ministers were forbidden to preach of a heaven
and hell after death, 'which neither they nor we know what will be', but to
devote their Sunday lectures to current affairs, the laws of the commonwealth,
improving episodes from history, the practical arts and sciences, and for good
measure the whole nature of man. 'There must be suitable laws for every
occasion, and almost for every action that men do,' wrote Winstanley, and their
principle was to be the harsh Mosaic one of life for life, eye for eye, and tooth for
tooth.[51] He would not be the last apostle of a communist paradise to realise that
it could only be kept going by draconian laws, but many pages in *The Law of*

Freedom make sad reading after the earlier tracts, with their intense compassion and their faith that man's humanity to man would break forth freely when the fetters of property and exploitation were struck away.

Winstanley's vision of the millennium as a transformation of society by regenerate men, vibrant with religious resonances though it was, stood a world away from that of the Fifth Monarchists. They were the most extreme biblical fundamentalists of their time. They were of course by no means alone in expecting the early fulfilment of Daniel's and St John the Divine's intoxicating prophecies, and in reading into the events of their own time the portents of the imminent overthrow of Antichrist. What distinguished them from the more sober millenarians was the dogmatic literalness with which they related each detail in those ancient visions to events and persons in the England of their time, and their belief that God was now calling his English saints to drastic political action. Assuming the four beasts in the Book of Daniel to signify the four great monarchies or empires of world history, they confidently identified the tenth horn on the fourth beast as Charles I—at least until after 1653, when some of them came to think it meant Cromwell. The victory of the saints in the Civil War and the execution of the King marked for them the crucial defeat of the fourth monarchy, whose chief throne was still in Rome, and they saw it as England's role in the cosmic struggle to set about establishing the fifth monarchy, that of Christ as King.

Most Fifth Monarchists believed, however, that Christ would not appear in person until Judgement Day, and that his thousand-year kingdom was to be ruled in his name by the saints. It was to be no merely internal and spiritual kingdom but an outward and highly authoritarian one, and they felt a divine call to erect it by militant means. 'Overturn, overturn, overturn' was a favourite text of theirs; all wordly institutions must be pulled down, parliaments in their present form no less than kings. They rejected as impious the Leveller argument that sanctity was irrelevant to political rights because the commonwealth's authority should be restricted to men's temporal concerns. This was not the purpose for which the Lord had led his people to victory. 'How can the kingdom be the Saints,' they asked, 'when the ungodly are electors, and elected to govern?'[52] To those who argued that power should derive from the people, William Aspinwall retorted by asking, 'when did Christ betrust the people with power to make Lawes; otherwise they can have no such power to confer'. 'Under the fifth monarchy, Christ alone shalbe Law-giver,' he proclaimed, and 'he will own no other Laws but what himself hath given.'[53] The Fifth Monarchists were not a single homogeneous sect, and they did not all think alike about what sort of government Christ's kingdom should have, but one of their favourite ideas was that its officers and magistrates should be chosen solely by the Independent and separatist congregations like their own. Their hopes rose highest after Cromwell dissolved the Rump in 1653, and when he and his Council of Officers were selecting the assembly soon to be known as Barebone's Parliament some of these congregations sent in the names of candidates whom they wished to see chosen. But only a dozen confessed Fifth Monarchists were actually nominated, though there was a rather larger number of millenarian fellow-travellers in the House. The extreme measures that they sought to promote, and their pretensions to a special call from Christ, finally drove the moderate majority to resign their power back into the hands of Cromwell. One of these firebrands later told him to his face that when he became Protector he 'tooke the Crowne off from the heade of Christ, and put it upon his owne'.[54]

By that time the movement was past its peak, though it did not decline as rapidly as the Levellers and Diggers had done—partly because Cromwell was more reluctant to trample on it. It had waxed as the Levellers waned, though there is little evidence to support the tempting assumption that this represented a massive transfer of popular hopes from rational secular remedies to an apocalyptic deliverance.[55] The Fifth Monarchists' aspirations may seem almost too bizarre to include in an account of political theory, but their strength in the early '50s is a reminder that popular radicalism took many forms, and that some of them were inimical to both democracy and republicanism. Others were simply apolitical; the Ranters and the early Quakers, so unlike in many respects, were akin in this. But it is time to return to the ideas that were preoccupying the established political nation, and particularly to the questions of principle and of duty that were posed by the execution of the King.

POLITICAL THEORY UNDER THE COMMONWEALTH AND PROTECTORATE

When the Rump of the Long Parliament set up the High Court of Justice to try Charles I in January 1649, it staked its claim to sole sovereignty with resounding votes 'That the people are, under God, the original of all just power', and 'That the Commons of England, in Parliament assembled, being chosen by, and representing the people, have the supreme power in this nation'.[56] But only a small minority of the people would have agreed that power belonged by law or right to what Pride's Purge had left of just one House of Parliament, first elected over eight years earlier. The Rump dared not appeal to the people through a general election, and it badly needed arguments to persuade the majority of its reluctant subjects that they morally owed it obedience. After a year of rather shaky power it required every adult male to take an Engagement to be 'true and faithful to the Commonwealth of England, as it is now established, without a King or House of Lords'.[57] Refusal could carry serious penalties, and the great question of conscience was whether those who regarded the regicide as a crime and the present rulers as usurpers might secure themselves a quiet life by subscribing—or whether it was even their duty to subscribe.

The most obvious appeal was to St Paul's injunction to obey the powers that be because they are ordained of God, which as Francis Rous recalled in *The Lawfullness of Obeying the Present Government* (1649) was written under an emperor who had come to power irregularly, through the soldiery. 'For the power is one thing which is of God,' wrote Rous, 'and the getting and the use of the power is another.' It is not for the people at large to judge who has the title to it, for the result would be a confusion worse than tyranny. Where power actually lies, there obedience is due (§P–70: pp. 7–9). John Dury invoked the authority of Calvin for very similar arguments.[58] But Rous's critics objected that his doctrine was both a blanket justification of successful rebellion and a total prohibition of resistance to tyranny. It is true that in this simple form the argument for submitting to *de facto* government took no account of whether a regime was lawful or not, and that Rous could make no case that the present one had any basis in law or right.

Milton, to whom I shall shortly turn, argued vehemently in *The Tenure of Kings and Magistrates* that right was on the Commonwealth's side, but he did so from premises so outrageous to Presbyterians and royalists that he can have preached only to the converted. Anthony Ascham in three tracts that he published during 1649 appealed more persuasively to the moderates whose allegiance the Rump so badly needed. His main case was that a government's claim to obedience does not rest primarily on the legitimacy with which it has come to power but on its capacity to maintain internal peace and protect its subjects' persons and property. Its sanction, in fact, lies in its ability to perform the functions without which civil society cannot subsist. To the objection that the Commonwealth had destroyed the mixed government in which both sides in the Civil War had believed, he replied that King, Lords and Commons had been 'a mixture of things very heterogeneous', and inherently unstable. Better, he urged, to have a unified authority based on the people's suffrages. Wars over monarchs' claims to titles or territories could not be justified:

> The Houses which are burnt, and the millions of bodies left dead in the field, are the peoples; and Princes scorning to derive from them, still trample them to dung . . . Who is it then that can right wronged Titles but he alone who makes all Titles right?[59]

For Ascham, in contrast with the royalists and most of the Presbyterians, God had given judgement and the war was over; the subject's duty was to help heal its scars, not work for its renewal. He came close to arguing that if a government provided peace, protection and reasonable equity it could not be unlawful, and in this he was no more than the first of a small school of writers which included such considerable talents as Marchamont Nedham and Francis Osborne.

If this seems rather a low key in which to be vindicating so revolutionary-seeming a regime as the Commonwealth, much of the explanation lies in the fact that most of the Commonwealth's actual governors were men whose temper was far from revolutionary.[60] Only a small minority of the Rumpers had actively associated themselves with the trial of the King, or were republicans by conviction when the republic was first established. Many clung to their seats mainly to prevent the government from being taken over by the army, or by any of those real revolutionaries whose objectives we have just examined. They were averse to radical reform not only by personal inclination but from a fear of alienating any further the predominantly conservative country gentry, the cautious merchants who governed the major towns, the legal profession, the orthodox ministers—indeed, all those on whose co-operation any regime had to depend, in default of that drastic enlargement of political participation which was the last thing that most Rumpers wanted. Those initial votes of theirs about power originating in the people and devolving by right on their representatives drew a cheque on democracy that they were not prepared to honour, especially after they had followed up their fierce suppression of the Levellers by sentencing Lilburne to exile, not by due process of law but by Act of Parliament.

So they were driven back upon the argument that *de facto* government must be obeyed because it discharges the functions without which civil society would disintegrate, and because every questioning of it risks that disintegration. Logically this is an argument for absolute authority; it leaves no room for that balance between the sovereign's prerogative and the subject's rights that the concept of mixed government enshrined. Theory here matched practice, for although the Rumpers were not absolutists by intent and their officials were on the whole honest and competent, their government was more arbitrary, more apt to encroach on the judicial sphere, and far heavier in its demands on its subjects' purses than the monarchy had ever been.

It is in the context of the Engagement controversy and of the *de facto* school of State apologetics that we should consider the most famous political treatise in the English language, Thomas Hobbes's *Leviathan*. Recent research has demonstrated that the political ideas in *Leviathan* were much less isolated, and in themselves less original, than had been generally thought.[61] This is not to say that Hobbes derived them from the *de facto* theorists or to deny *Leviathan* the status of a masterpiece. Hobbes had been working out his ideas for many years; he had published *De Cive* in 1642 and again in 1647, but only abroad, only in Latin, and in very small editions. He had had strongly royalist connections before and during the Civil War, which he had spent in France, and since 1645 he had been tutor in mathematics to the future Charles II. But he had probably viewed the war with more abhorrence than commitment, and more as a neutralist than as a royalist. *De Cive* was his first attempt to delineate a system of politics that would be proof against the convulsions that drove him abroad in 1642. *Leviathan*, for all its uncompromising argument in favour of absolute monarchy, should no more be read as an expression of his royalism than as an attempt to flatter Cromwell, which is what Clarendon accused it of being. But Hobbes's publication of it in 1651, close in time to the first English translation of *De Cive*, was not unconnected with his desire to return to England, which he did soon afterwards. As soon as these and his other political works began to circulate in England they were cited with approval by the Commonwealth's defenders of the *de facto* school, whereas nearly all royalists were hostile to *Leviathan* from the start. No wonder, since it eliminated divine right, offered no reason for preferring the Stuart monarchy to any other, and did not even maintain monarchy to be the only rightful form of government.

Leviathan is the ultimate statement of the argument that would justify political authority entirely by its capacity to curb men's mutually destructive impulses and to provide the order and protection without which civil society can have no being. It argues its case with a force, a philosophic sweep and a massive consistency which were beyond the range of Ascham, Nedham and their fellows. Superficially it is not a very different case; yet it is vastly more than a political tract for the times. It is the first comprehensive attempt to construct a system of politics according to the principles of the new philosophy which took for its subject-matter only what could be apprehended and calculated by unaided human reason. Its whole edifice is built stage by stage upon a startlingly original and secular theory of the nature of man and his motivation. To summarise its political doctrines without more than a glance at its psychology and epistemology is an injustice to Hobbes's genius, but this is partly repaired later in this book (see below, pp. 162 ff.).

Leviathan begins by presenting man as a creature who apprehends external reality wholly through his senses, and responds to it with either desire ('appetite') or aversion. Men, and on a lower level the beasts, have a rational faculty of deliberating, whereby they weigh short-term satisfactions against longer-term ones. 'In *Deliberation*, the last Appetite, or Aversion, immediately adhering to the action, or to the omission thereof, is that we call the WILL . . . *Will* therefore *is the last Appetite in Deliberating*.'[62] On this basis Hobbes identifies and defines the entire range of human passions, rigorously (and to his contemporaries shockingly) excluding any source of motivation but enlightened self-interest. Of all passions he holds the fear of death to be supreme, and the one indefeasible right of nature that he allows is that of every individual to use whatever power he has to preserve his own life. The venerable concept of the law of nature is disturbingly transformed in *Leviathan*. From St Thomas Aquinas to Hooker it had embraced all those universally accepted precepts of equity and justice that man derives from his rational perception of the world rather than from God's direct command, but it was morally imperative because it was all part of God's law, though communicated through his creation rather than expressly through his Word. For Hobbes, by contrast, 'A LAW OF NATURE . . . is a Precept, or generall Rule, found out by Reason, by which a man is forbidden to do, that, which is destructive of his life, or taketh away the means of preserving the same'. His laws of nature, as he admits, are strictly not laws at all but maxims which men deduce from their calculation of long-term advantage, or 'Theoremes concerning what conduceth to the conservation and defence of themselves' (pp. 99, 122–3).

Law and right are quite distinct in his conception, and largely opposed. Laws proper are backed by the power to command, and since that power is vested solely in the sovereign, law lies simply in the sovereign's will. But why should people submit to a sovereign whose will, so long as he can enforce it, is not subject to their questioning or consent? Hobbes's answer is that the alternative would be more wretched than subjection to even the most arbitrary of settled government. *Leviathan* paints a stark picture of men in an imagined state of nature, utterly unrestrained in their desperate efforts to preserve their own lives and the means of maintaining life, and therefore engaged in a continual war of all against all. In such a state there are no divinely implanted notions of right and wrong, for such ideas can have no meaning where civil society does not exist. There can be no rights of property, no settled agriculture or navigation, no arts and letters; only 'continuall feare, and danger of violent death; And the life of men, solitary, poore, nasty, brutish, and short' (p. 97). It is a wry thought that this assessment of human nature in the raw, which offended Hobbes's critics from his own until recent times, has become a commonplace in modern science fiction. He himself conceived the state of nature as a hypothetical rather than a historical or actual condition of mankind, though he thought that something near to it existed among the American Indians and he feared lest chronic strife and instability should plunge England back into it.

The only sure escape from it, according to his inexorable argument, lies in all the individual human bodies in the community incorporating themselves in the great artificial body of Leviathan, the State, and surrendering their puny personal powers of self-preservation to its sovereign. In contrast with Filmer, but in common with Harrington, Hobbes sees the State not as part of the natural order of things or as a dispensation of divine providence but as an artifact, created and sustained by the will of man. Its foundation lies, implicitly even if not historically, in a mutual contract or covenant by all its citizens, one with another, to accept the absolute authority of the sovereign. The sovereign is not a party to the contract, nor bound by it, so subjects have no right to call him to account. 'He' may be a single person or an assembly—Hobbes in the context of 1651 carefully preserves the alternatives—but either way sovereignty is indivisible. Subjects must not have any share in its essential functions or any right to question its decisions, for that would negate the purpose of the contract and expose the commonwealth to dissolution. Consequently there must be no limitations upon the sovereign's power to make laws, levy taxes, appoint officers of state, confer rewards, impose punishments, take decisions of peace and war, or do whatever else is required for the safety of the people.

Hobbes knew very well, of course, that few States in his time were founded upon an explicit contract. He distinguished those that were ('commonwealths by institution') from the majority whose authority had come by succession or conquest, but he insisted that the basis of both types is in essence contractual. The contract may be a historical event or just a postulate of reason, but the submission of the vanquished to a conqueror is as valid a covenant as any other. The limits to the obligation of absolute obedience are very few: the subject may, if condemned to death, resist his executioner or seek to escape; he cannot, if conscripted for military service, be expected to expose himself to death against his will; and he is released from his allegiance if the sovereign loses the power to protect him.

Hobbes was in agreement (for once) with Cromwell and Milton, and at odds with most contemporary theorists, in holding the actual form of government to be of secondary importance. He was frank in his preference for monarchy over aristocracy or democracy, but condemned any attempt to seek a change:

And of the three sorts, which is the best, is not be disputed, where any one of them is already established; but the present ought alwaies to be preferred, maintained, and accounted best (p. 429).

Leviathan's is a bleak doctrine, and the crucial practical questions for its readers then and ever since have been whether total submission does inevitably entail results less unbearable than the miseries of anarchy, and whether anarchy cannot be obviated by means less oppressive than absolutism. To most of us today the answers seem less obvious than they did to our liberal grandfathers, and they did not seem obvious to Hobbes's contemporaries either. It used to be thought that early reactions to *Leviathan* were almost uniformly hostile and that its influence on political practice was negligible. In fact it was welcomed, and its ideas cited and borrowed, by defenders of both the Commonwealth and the Protectorate. Although most royalists disliked it, Filmer praised it and Matthew Wren drew heavily upon its arguments.[63] Those who attacked Hobbes did so much more for his alleged atheism and materialism than for his absolutist doctrines, and his critics were as varied in their political and religious allegiances as his approvers (§S–392). In our own time some attempts have been made to portray him as essentially a natural-law philosopher, holding forth the laws of nature as eternal and immutable and attributing a moral imperative to them because they are God's commands. But this is not only very hard to square with some of his own statements; it also asks us to suppose both that all his contemporaries misunderstood him and that he made no attempt to put them right.[64]

One other Englishman endeavoured to construct a system of politics as demonstrable and irrefutable as the discoveries of the new natural philosophy. Except in this common aim, however, James Harrington, who published *Oceana* in 1656, differed from Hobbes profoundly. Whereas Hobbes was not concerned with specific forms and institutions of government, and considered them of secondary importance, to Harrington they were of the essence. *Leviathan* was not written to prescribe precise remedies for England's current political ills; *Oceana* was, and it set out the manner of establishing the 'equal commonwealth' in extravagant detail. Harrington followed it up with two plainer expositions, aimed largely at convincing the working politicians of his time, and after the fall of the Cromwellian Protectorate in 1659 he launched a whole campaign of pamphlets, petitions and public debates in an effort to get the restored republic remodelled according to his design. Whereas Hobbes based his system on his analysis of universal human nature, Harrington argued that the form of every State should be, and in the end must be, determined primarily by the distribution of property within it. Hobbes, holding human nature to be everywhere the same, logically took no account of time or place; Harrington, to an extent unique in his age, turned to history to account for the political and social structures of particular nations, and believed that their political needs must be diagnosed in the light of their whole economic, social and geographical circumstances. Whereas Hobbes's argument led inexorably to undivided and absolute sovereignty, Harrington's equal commonwealth was based on a separation of powers and a constant rotation of the men who exercised them. And though Hobbes was never so isolated or unacceptable as used to be thought, Harrington was far more widely discussed in print in the later 1650s, and his ideas had their advocates in more than one Parliament.[65]

At the heart of his theory lies the 'balance of property', by which he meant landed property in all but those few commonwealths which, like the Dutch Republic, subsisted mainly by trade. Where one man owns all the land, as in the Ottoman Empire, the result is absolute monarchy. Where the balance is in the hands of a landed aristocracy, mixed monarchy is the natural form, but where land ownership is more widely distributed only a republic will fit the economic facts. Where the form or 'superstructures' fail to match the foundations, the result is inevitable conflict and instability until the more appropriate form is established. In mediaeval England, according to Harrington, the nobility had held enough of the land to sustain a mixed or feudal monarchy, but through various Tudor measures, together with the huge sales of monastic land, the balance had shifted decisively from aristocratic to popular. Elizabeth's skill in statecraft had concealed the fatal fact for a time, but the Stuarts' ineptitude had exposed the monarchy to its ultimately inevitable doom: *'Wherefore the dissolution of this Government caused the Civil War, not the war the dissolution of this Government'*.[66] Land was vital not simply as wealth but as the foundation of armed power. Feudal monarchy had fallen when nobles lost the power to command the military services of their vassals; the means of preserving the commonwealth must be a citizen militia in which every landowner of military age had the duty and privilege of bearing arms.

Harrington thought that the devising of superstructures or specific institutions to fit the social and economic foundations of the national community should be the task of a sole Legislator. While councils may excel in judgement, he argued, invention is the achievement of individuals: 'A parliament of physicians would never have found out the circulation of the blood, nor could a parliament of poets have written Virgil's *Aeneis'*.[67] The task was to be both a scientific one and a work of art, and it was to have a religious, even a millennial, dimension as well (§S–114: pp. 72 ff.).

Since the commonwealth's stability depended on maintaining the distribution of land ownership, one of the Legislator's first priorities must be an 'agrarian law' to set a maximum to individual holdings. The limit that Harrington proposed for England was an annual value as high as £2,000. He calculated that it would ensure at least 5,000 landowners, even if each one held the full £2,000-worth, and since most would in fact hold far less he thought that this would suffice to keep the balance popular. Those who already held more than the maximum—at the most 300 men, he reckoned, and the estimate was generous—would not be dispossessed; they would simply be required to bequeath the surplus among their younger children. Harrington was a democrat of a kind, but he was certainly no egalitarian; in fact one of the few things he had in common with Hobbes and Milton, besides anti-clericalism, was an assumption that government is essentially a business for gentlemen:

There is something first in the making of a *Common-wealth*, then in the governing of her, and last of all in the leading of her Armies; which, though there be great *Divines*, great *Lawyers*, great men in all professions, seems to be peculiar unto the Genius of a Gentleman.[68]

In Harrington's commonwealth there was to be a basic distinction between men worth £100 a year or more in land or goods, styled the horse because they would serve in the mounted militia, and the foot, who were worth less and would serve as infantrymen. Horse and foot were to enjoy very different levels of political participation, and servants, who lacked the minimal independence required even of the foot, were not to participate at all.

Totally rejecting Hobbes's contention that law is merely what the sovereign wills, Harrington upheld Aristotle's maxim that a just commonwealth is ruled by known laws rather than by the arbitrary will of men. Against Hobbes, too, he argued for the intrinsic superiority of a well constituted republic over even the best of monarchies. But he acknowledged Hobbes to be 'the best writer at this day in the world',[69] and accepted, if only for argument's sake, his contention that men's actions are wholly determined by their passions or interests. That being so, he set himself to devise institutions which would neutralise selfish and sectional ambitions and advance the interest of the people as a whole. The essential means he proposed for achieving this were five, in addition to the agrarian law and the citizen militia already mentioned.

The first was a legislature consisting of two elected assemblies, radically different from the traditional houses of Parliament. A senate of three hundred, intended to embody the wisdom of the commonwealth and drawn exclusively from the horse, was to have the sole right to initiate and debate laws, but none to enact them; while a body of more than a thousand, representing the 'interest' of the people and composed of horse and foot in the ratio of three to four, was to meet solely to accept or reject them, without either debate or amendment. One may smile at the thought that a thousand Englishmen would travel by vile roads to Westminster merely to ballot in silence for measures that they could have no share in shaping, and at the assumption that wisdom went with wealth. Nevertheless a scheme which sought to harness the talents of the leisured and educated while checking their self-interest, and which gave the last voice in law-making to a body with a built-in majority of the middling sort, was liberal for its time. Few men worth less than £100 a year can have played *any* direct part in legislation in Harrington's lifetime, or for long before and after it.

His second fundamental device was rotation, for he distrusted professional politicians as much as professional soldiers. Members of both assemblies were to be elected for three years, without the possibility of immediate re-election, and one third of each body was to retire and be replaced annually, so that both remained perennially in being. The highest officers of state were to be elected from and by the senate, some for annual and some for triennial terms. Thirdly, Harrington insisted that the 'magistracy' which executed the laws, from the highest judges to the local JPs, must be separate from the legislature, though equally subject to election and rotation. His fourth basic institution was the secret ballot, which was to be used in elections at all levels as well as at the popular assembly's votes upon the senate's Bills. Finally—though there were many refinements which a brief summary must pass over—no men, not even avowed royalists, should be debarred from full citizenship by their political or religious convictions:

> To the *Common-wealths-man* I have no more to say, but that if he exclude any party, he is not truly such; . . . a *Common-wealth* consisting of a party will be in perpetuall labour of her own destruction.[70]

Harrington had a rather touching faith that if a commonwealth had its basic institutions or 'orders' rightly framed it would not only be invulnerable to internal enemies but would actually convert them, and make them better men as well as better citizens. This was his retort to the common Puritan argument that constitutions matter little so long as power is entrusted to godly men:

> *Give us good men and they will makes us good Lawes*, is the *Maxime of a Demagogue*, and . . . exceeding *fallible*. But *give us good orders, and they will make us good men*, is the *Maxime of a Legislator*, and the most infallible in the *Politickes*.[71]

Some of his notions betray the fact that he had no practical experience of the rough world of politics, despite his close personal attendance upon Charles I during the latter's captivity. The baroque extravagances in *Oceana* certainly invited the philistine to blaspheme, and though he toned them down in several later tracts they came in for much ridicule at the Restoration. But his ideas were by no means forgotten thereafter, and they deserved the intense interest and discussion that they aroused in their time. No other republican theorist approached him in stature. His bold but crude attempts at quantification would in themselves give him a place among those who first strove to elevate politics into a science, but his claim to stand high among these pioneers rests more on his perception of the dependence of the structure of politics on the structure of society, and of the shaping of both as a historical process varying according to time, place and custom.

Between the publication of *Leviathan* and *Oceana* the Commonwealth gave way to the Protectorate of Oliver Cromwell, after the brief experiment of Barebone's Parliament. The written constitution of the Protectorate, the Instrument of Government, marked a conscious return to the ideal of a balanced polity; its authors sought to read the successive lessons of a would-be absolute monarchy, an unrestrained oligarchy (the Rump), and the still more arbitrary pretensions of those who had lately aimed at a rule of the saints. Cromwell himself commended it as 'most likely to avoid the extremes of monarchy on the one hand, and democracy on the other, and yet not to found *dominium in gratia*'.[72] It is understandable therefore that the Protectorate did not in itself generate much original political thought. Ironically, the most skilful apologist for its system of checks and balances was that political chameleon Marchamont Nedham, who had lent his expert journalistic talents first to the radical Parliamentarians, then in 1648 to the royalists, and next to defending the Engagement and extolling a pure republic. Now he found the acme of politics to consist in separating the legislative and executive powers.[73]

But the Protectorate had a more illustrious defender than Nedham. He was John Milton, though this is not the role in which the poet in his later years would have cared to be remembered by posterity. In a volume devoted to the Age of Milton it may seem perverse to accord him no greater prominence here. His commitment to the English revolution was certainly wholehearted. At its very outset he deferred indefinitely the fulfilment of his vocation to write a great Christian epic so that he could serve the cause with his pen, and with a still greater sacrifice he spent the last of his failing sight on vindicating the Commonwealth against its enemies. He was its salaried official for more than a decade, and when it was finally on the point of collapse he risked not only his liberty but his life and his still unwritten masterpieces to pour out his eloquence against the inevitable restoration of monarchy.

But this chapter is concerned with political theory and political practice, and his contribution to both was slight. It is no derogation to say that he was a rhetorician rather than a political philosopher, for rhetoric can be a worthy servant of great causes, and Milton's at its best is supremely noble. His prose works were not even primarily concerned with politics except in the years 1649–54 and 1660. He made the conventional distinction between religious and civil liberty, and he clearly cared more about the former. Such political ideas as he handled were for the most part unoriginal and unsystematic, and they changed considerably over the years. In 1644 he still believed in mixed monarchy, with the balance tilted towards Parliament:

> There is no Civill *Goverment* that hath been known, . . . more divinely and harmoniously tun'd, more equally ballanc'd as it were by the hand and scale of justice, then is the Common-wealth of *England*: where under a free, and untutor'd *Monarch*, the noblest, worthiest, and most prudent men, with full approbation, and suffrage of the People have in their power the supreame, and finall determination of highest Affaires.[74]

At what point he became a republican is unknown, but he wrote *The Tenure of Kings and Magistrates* early in 1649 to justify the trial of Charles I. Yet he was motivated more by indignation against the Presbyterians, and by concern for the fate of Christian liberty if they had their way and reinstated the King, than by any positive convictions about the superiority of one mode of government over another. *The Tenure* argues an age-old case for resisting tyrants, and its method is to pile authority on authority: the Scriptures, the classics, the Protestant reformers, the example of the Dutch, and so on. Nor is there much more of sustained republican theory in the larger vindications of the Commonwealth which were his chief tasks as Secretary for Foreign Tongues to the Council of State. Both the *Eikonoklastes* of 1649 and the Latin *Defence of the People of England* which made his European reputation in 1651 affirm the superiority of republics over monarchies, though more by way of assertion than argument.

When he came to write his *Second Defence of the People of England* the Commonwealth had just given way to the Protectorate, and he celebrated its arrival not only with a full-throated panegyric to Cromwell but with a strong profession that the man most fit to rule has a positive right to rule, in the eyes of God and man. He accompanied this, however, with some rather large advice to the Protector on the manner in which he should execute his trust, and Cromwell's understandable disinclination to follow most of it accounts for Milton's growing disillusionment with the regime. In particular Milton believed, as Cromwell did not, that the State should renounce all authority over matters of religion and should cease to maintain an established clergy by tithes or any other form of compulsory contribution. As he focused his mind increasingly on formulating the highly unorthodox beliefs which he expounded in *De Doctrina Christiana*, the aim to remove religion entirely from the civil power preoccupied him more and more. Although he never published a word in direct criticism of Cromwell, this objective largely explains the enthusiasm—sadly misplaced, as it turned out—with which he greeted the restoration of the Rump and of the republic after the downfall of the Protectorate in 1659. When the revived Commonwealth began in turn to collapse, he proposed that all who served it should be required to make two pledges: to abjure one-man rule in any form, and to renounce all civil authority over matters ecclesiastical.

Milton soon ceased to be a democrat, if he ever was one. His optimism in *Areopagitica* about the capacity of the people of England to order their own destinies declined by degrees into the contempt for the judgement of the public at large that crackles from the pages of *The Readie and Easie Way* (early 1660). Even in 1649, when contending for the people's right not only to choose but to depose their kings, he was driven to argue that the upright minority, 'though in number less by many', could and should 'judge as they find cause' in such grave cases. Eleven years later, when the Commonwealth was finally tottering, he was still asserting, even more nakedly, the right of a freedom-loving minority to override a base majority.[75] But he never specified the political means whereby the righteous few could be identified and invested with authority, nor did he satisfactorily explain by what right they might command the obedience of the unregenerate many. His ideal was an aristocracy of grace, but he could not base that right on godliness or spiritual election because it was his purpose to segregate the spiritual sphere from the temporal and to confine the civil magistrate's authority to the outward man. He never thought it his business to prescribe ways and means of government until the last winter and spring before the Restoration, by which time the options were narrowing month by month. The expedients that he finally proposed in the two editions of *The Readie and the Easie Way* were so desperate, and probably so far from any ideal commonwealth that he might have delineated in happier times, that it is kinder to draw a veil over them (cf. §S–89).

Yet although Milton's impact on the English revolution was slighter than that of many a lesser writer, the impact of the revolution on Milton was tremendous.

Christopher Hill has recently shown, with unique insight, how the poet's experience of it is reflected in the three great epics, and what messages he meant them to convey to those who had grieved with him to see the Good Old Cause go down to defeat (§S–69: esp. Part VI). Dr Hill has also taken a new reading of Milton's intellectual bearings, orientating him somewhere between the traditional Puritan culture of the 'Country' (as opposed to the court) and a plebeian, heretical 'third culture' which was variously embodied in the Levellers, the Diggers and the extremer sects. This popular culture, he argues, exerted the stronger pull. But although Milton's political stance was certainly more radical than that of every government under which he lived, and although his religious unorthodoxy had features in common with several of the sects, his radicalism was qualitatively different from that of most lower-class revolutionaries and derived mainly from other sources. He was a thoroughgoing elitist, as unsympathetic towards Leveller democracy as he was towards Digger communism or the crude theocracy of the Fifth Monarchists.

Nevertheless he was a true revolutionary, and the best of his political works have enduring value not only for their frequent splendour of utterance but for their expression of the moral and spiritual values which the revolutionary cause had for a very great mind that was deeply committed to it. Little though they had to offer about the means whereby a commonwealth fit for an elect nation might be established and maintained, they were uniquely eloquent about the virtues that it should promote—probity, public spirit, self-respect, temperance, above all spiritual and intellectual liberty—in contrast with the servility, the corruption of manners, the graft, the extravagance, the persecution and mental straitjacketing that he associated with monarchy.

Any short survey of this subject must involve some distortion, because it is obliged to pass over so much. The explosion of political theory that began in 1642 was enormous; of the 22,000 tracts and newspapers which the bookseller George Thomason collected in just over twenty years, a striking proportion debated questions of principle or proposed radical innovations in political practice. The tighter licensing laws of 1655 only slightly restricted the output; the Restoration naturally cut it off much more sharply, especially after the Act of Uniformity and the Licensing Act were passed in 1662. The King's promise of a liberty to tender consciences was broken by the Cavalier Parliament, which made it a treasonable offence to propose any alterations in the government of Church or State. Anglican pulpits trumpeted the doctrine of divine right louder than ever. The ancient constitution and the fundamental laws made a come-back too, for the Act which restored the bishops to the House of Lords condemned the one which had excluded them in 1642 as 'contrary to the laws of the land', even though it had received the royal assent.[76]

But the constitution had suffered a sea change, and English political thought would never be the same again. When the honeymoon period of the Restoration was over, the first Whigs would find a whole armoury of refurbishable arguments in the contractualist literature of their fathers' time, Harrington's ideas would get a fresh airing, and the Tories would reply with Filmer's *Patriarcha*, which they published for the first time in 1680. Locke's synthesis in his second treatise *Of Civil Government* was his own, but there were few ideas in it that had not appeared in print during the Interregnum. The Leveller literature had to wait longer for its resuscitation, but it would be remembered when the time was ripe, on both sides of the Atlantic. How deep and lasting an effect the revolutionary decades had on the structure of society and on the political system is still a matter of controversy, but the enduring influence of their legacy of political theory is beyond all doubt.

NOTES

I am indebted to Mr Harro Höpfl of the University of Lancaster for reading this chapter in draft and offering many helpful comments and criticism.

1 *An Harborowe for Faithfull and Trewe Subjects* (Strasbourg, 1559); extract in §S–105: p. 16. For the whole subject, see Corinne C. Weston, 'The Theory of Mixed Monarchy under Charles I and After', *English Historical Review*, LXXV (1960), 426–43.

2 For evidence and quotations, see §S–81: pp. 17–19; §S–205: pp. 216–20; and Harold Hulme, *The Life of Sir John Eliot* (1957), pp. 374–9. On divine right generally, see G. R. Elton's Introduction to §S–43, and W. H. Greenleaf, *Order, Empiricism and Politics: Two Traditions of English Political Thought 1500—1700* (Oxford, 1964), Ch. I–IV.

3 §S–466: Ch. I–II; §S–60; §S–438A; Ch. VI and *passim*.

4 Michael Walzer (§S–152) portrays Calvinism as inherently a revolutionary ideology, but he notably fails to offer convincing evidence that his thesis is valid for England before c. 1640.

5 Hooker (§P–261), VIII, ii, 13; extract in §S–40: p. 17.

6 Mary F. Keeler, *The Long Parliament, 1640—1641* (Philadelphia, 1954), p. 27. The number of seats in the Commons was 507; 547 includes members returned in bye-elections to the end of 1641.

7 *Parliamentary Debates in 1610*, ed. S. R. Gardiner, Camden Society (1862), p. 24.

8 Quoted in full context in §S–57: p. 64.

9 For a contrary interpretation, see George L. Mosse, *The Struggle for Sovereignty in England* (East Lansing, 1950).

10 §S–84: pp. 62–4, 106–16; S. R. Gardiner, *Constitutional Documents of the Puritan Revolution*, 3rd ed. (Oxford, 1906), pp. 57–64, 108–24.

11 12 Reports 74 (1610), quoted in F. D. Wormuth, *The Royal Prerogative 1603—1649* (Ithaca, N.Y., 1939), p. 54.

12 §S–57: pp. 71–2. *Res est lex loquens* was a maxim familiar from the Roman law; James I had quoted it in a speech in 1607: Mosse (as above, note 9), p. 70, n. 72.

13 §S–81: pp. 247–8; §S–68: pp. 253–7. Gough goes far to reconcile Coke's inconsistencies (§S–57: especially Ch. III).

14 For Coke's ideas and influence, see §S–112: Ch. II–III, and §S–68: Ch. V.

15 J. J. Scarisbrick, *Henry VIII* (1968), pp. 270–3; Milton, *CE*, X, 6 ff.

16 §S–137a: pp. 157–60; §S–112: Ch. V.

17 I owe this point to Mr Conrad Russell.

18 Brian S. Manning, *The English People and the English Revolution 1640—1649* (1976).

19 Declaration of the Houses, 6 June 1642, in Gardiner (as above, note 10), pp. 256–7.

20 Reproduced in facsimile in §S–62: Vol. II. There are good commentaries on Parker in W. K. Jordan, *Men of Substance* (Chicago, 1942), especially Ch. V, and in §S–81: pp. 416–32.

21 *A Treatise of Monarchy* has not been reprinted, but it is discussed in C. H. McIlwain, *Constitutionalism and the Changing World* (Cambridge, 1939); §S–81: pp. 396–407; §S–2: pp. 449–55.

22 *The Resolving of Conscience* (Cambridge and London, 1642); *Conscience Satisfied* (Oxford, 1643); *A Reply unto Several Treatises* (Oxford, 1643).

23 *Conscience Satisfied*, p. 6; quoted in §S–81: p. 389. On the extent of the disaster of Charles I's championship of the Arminians, see Nicholas Tyacke, 'Puritanism, Arminianism and Counter-Revolution', in §S–130: pp. 119–43.

24 Peter Laslett in his edition of *Patriarcha and other Political Works of Sir Robert Filmer* (Oxford, 1949), p. 3, dates it somewhere between 1635 and 1642. John M. Wallace argues persuasively for 1648 in 'The Date of Sir Robert Filmer's *Patriarcha*', *Historical Journal*, XXII (1979). He shows, however, that Filmer borrowed from earlier writings in it, and passages on pp. 55 and 95 in Laslett's edition suggest to me that important parts of it were first written not long before or after the outbreak of the Civil War.

25 Mosse (as above, note 9), pp. 61–2; Gordon S. Schochet, *Patriarchalism in Political Thought* (Oxford, 1975), especially pp. 86 ff.

26 Greenleaf (as above, note 2), Ch. V, and 'Filmer's Patriarchal History', *Historical Journal*, IX (1966), 157–71.

27 *Patriarcha*, ed. Laslett (as above, note 25), pp. 62, 74.

28 *Ibid.*, pp. 93, 96; also pp. 66 ff.

29 *Reliquiae Baxteriana* (1696), Part I, Sect. 71; extract in §S–164: p. 388.

30 For the best short account of all these aspects, see G. E. Aylmer's introduction in §S–8.

31 Postscript to *Londons Liberty* (1646); extract in §S–8: p. 71.

32 *The Free-man's Freedom Vindicated* (1646); extract in §S–164: p. 317.

33 Overton, *An Arrow against all Tyrants* (1646, reprinted by The Rota, Exeter, 1976); extract in §S–8: pp. 68–9.

34 Overton, *An Appeale from the Degenerate Representative Body the Commons . . . To the Body Represented* (1647), reprinted in §S–163: p. 163.

35 The Levellers carefully stipulated a *maximum* duration until 1649, when they came to fear the army more than a self-perpetuating Parliament. In May 1649 the third Agreement proposed a *minimum* duration of four months.

36 §S–164: p. 363; §S–8: p. 167.

37 §S–93: Part III; and for the fullest critiques: Keith Thomas, 'The Levellers and the Franchise', in §S–7: pp. 57–78, and Iain Hampsher-Monck, 'The Political Theory of the Levellers: Putney, Property and Professor Macpherson', *Political Studies*, XXIV (1976), 397–422.

38 *A Remonstrance of Many Thousand Citizens* (1646), p. 15, reproduced in facsimile in §S–62: Vol. II. For Lilburne on the limitations of Magna Carta, see §S–8: pp. 65–7; and for Wildman, §S–164: pp. 370–1.

39 Christopher Hill's classic essay 'The Norman Yoke' is reprinted in §S–70.

40 *A Declaration by Congregationall Societies in and about London . . . touching Liberty, Magistracy, Propriety, Polygamie* (1647), p. 7.

41 By the Soviet historian M. A. Barg; expounded by Christopher Hill in §S–71: Ch. VII, and briefly criticised by G. E. Aylmer in §S–8: pp. 48–9.

42 Keith Thomas, 'Another Digger Broadside', *Past and Present*, XL (1969), 57–69. The fullest and profoundest study of Winstanley and the Diggers is by Olivier Lutaud, *Winstanley: Socialisme et Christianisme sous Cromwell* (Paris, 1976).

43 *The New Law of Righteousness* (1649), reprinted in *The Works of Gerrard Winstanley*, ed. G. H. Sabine (1941), p. 190.

44 *Ibid.*, p. 193.

45 *The True Levellers Standard Advanced* (1649), in Sabine (as above, note 44), p. 259.

46 *The New Law of Righteousness*, in Sabine, p. 213.

47 *The True Levellers Standard Advanced*, in Sabine, p. 260.

48 E.g., recently by Christopher Hill in §S–71 and in his introduction to his edition of *Winstanley: The Law of Freedom and Other Writings* (1973), and by G. M. Juretic, 'The Revolutionising of Gerrard Winstanley', *Journal of the History of Ideas*, XXXVI (1975), 263–80. But this interpretation has been generally current since D. W. Petegorsky expounded it in *Left-Wing Democracy in the English Civil War* (1940).

49 L. Mulligan, J. K. Graham and J. Richards, 'Winstanley: A Case for the Man as He Said He Was', *Journal of Ecclesiastical History*, XXVIII (1975), 57–75.

50 See J. C. Davis, 'Gerrard Winstanley and the Restoration of True Magistracy', *Past and Present*, LXX (1976), 76–93.

51 *Works* (as above, note 44), pp. 523, 562 ff., 528, 591–2.

52 *Certain Queries Presented by Many Christian People* (1649); extract in §S–164: p. 246.

53 *A Brief Description of the Fifth Monarchy* (1653), pp. 9–10.

54 *The Clarke Papers*, ed. C. H. Firth (1891–1901), II, 244.

55 On this see the excellent general account of the movement by B. S. Capp (§S–25), especially pp. 89–92.

56 *Journals of the House of Commons*, VI, 111.

57 Gardiner (as above, note 10), p. 391. The following paragraphs are heavily indebted to John M. Wallace (§S–151), Ch. I; to Quentin Skinner's article (§S–137a); and to Skinner's chapter on 'Conquest and Consent' (§S–7: pp. 79–98).

58 *A Case of Conscience Resolved* (1649), summarised by Skinner in §S–7: p. 81.

59 *The Bounds & Bonds of Publique Obedience* (1649), pp. 16, 34, 36–7; formerly attributed to Francis Rous but identified as Ascham's work by John M. Wallace, 'The Engagement Controversy, 1649–1652: An Annotated List of Pamphlets', *Bulletin of the New York Public Library*, LXVIII (1964), 384–405.

60 Three fine studies have transformed our knowledge of the Rump and its agencies in government: see David Underdown (§S–150), Ch. VI–XI; Blair Worden (§S–165); and G. E. Aylmer, *The State's Servants* (§S–5).

61 To the works by Wallace and Skinner cited above (notes 16 and 58), add Skinner's article (§S–137b).

62 *Leviathan*, reprinted from the 1651 edition (Oxford, 1909), pp. 56–7.

63 Quentin Skinner (§S–137b). This is a valuable corrective to John Bowle, *Hobbes and his Critics*, 2nd ed. (1969). Wren's main work was *Monarchy Asserted* (1659); its debt to Hobbes, though large, is unacknowledged.

64 See Skinner (§S–137b), pp. 313–17, and the essays by A. E. Taylor, Stuart M. Brown, John Plamenatz and Howard Warrender in *Hobbes Studies*, ed. K. C. Brown (Oxford, 1965).

65 The best commentary on Harrington is J. G. A. Pocock's introduction to §S–114. Excellent too is Felix Raab (§S–119), Ch. VI.

66 *Oceana* (1656), p. 41; in §S–114: p. 198. I cite the page numbers of the edition—one of two in 1656—printed for D. Pakeman, which is the text used by S. B. Liljegren in his edition (Lund and Heidelberg, 1924), and the corresponding page numbers of Pocock's edition (§S–114), which modernises the spelling and punctuation. On the texts see Pocock (§S–114), pp. xiv–xv, 6–14.

67 *A System of Politics* (written *c.* 1660, unpublished until 1700), in §S–114: p. 842; cf. p. 779.

68 *Oceana*, p. 25; §S–114: p. 183. For an attempt to portray Hobbes and Harrington as theorists of a 'bourgeois' society, see §S–93: Part II and IV; and for critiques thereof: Keith Thomas, 'The Social Origins of Hobbes's Political Thought', in Brown (as above, note 64), pp. 185–236, and §S–114: pp. 56–64, 88–9.

69 *The Prerogative of Popular Government* (1658), in §S–114: p. 423.

70 *Oceana*, p. 46; §S–114: p. 203.

71 *Oceana*, p. 48; §S–114: p. 205.

72 *Writings and Speeches of Oliver Cromwell*, ed. W. C. Abbott (Cambridge, Mass., 1937–47), III, 587.

73 [M. Nedham], *A True State of the Case of the Commonwealth* (1654). This has been republished in facsimile by The Rota (Exeter, 1978). Nedham's earlier *The Case of the Commonwealth of England States* (1650) has been edited by Philip A. Knachel (Charlottesville, Va., 1969).

74 *Of Reformation in England* (1641), in CE, III, 63.

75 CE, V, 6–7; VI, 114, 140–41; and my introduction to the seventh volume of Milton's *Complete Prose Works* (New Haven, 1974), especially pp. 207–9.

76 *English Historical Documents*, VIII: *1660—1714*, ed. Andrew Browning (1973), p. 208. In 1689 the Commons charged James II with having 'violated the fundamental law'.

THEODORE K. RABB

3

Population, economy and society in Milton's England

The England in which Milton was born was at an early stage of remarkable economic change. For centuries she had been of secondary significance in European commerce, often reliant on the merchants of other countries for her place in international trade. During the reign of Elizabeth I, however, signs of transformation appeared. New direct links were developed with the Baltic, with Muscovy, and with the Levant. The traditional reliance on two major export commodities, cloth and wool, began to give way to more diverse interests; and investments in industry, notably coal mining, shipbuilding, glassmaking, and metallurgy, gathered momentum. Two events in the last years of the reign symbolised this growing independence and expertise: in 1598 the Hanseatic League, which had controlled much of England's trade, particularly with the Baltic and the Netherlands, was forced to close its enormous London headquarters, the Steelyard; three years later a new organisation, the East India Company, dispatched a fleet of four ships on the first English spice-trading voyage across the immense distance to the Far East. These advances accelerated under the Stuarts until, by the end of the seventeenth century, London had become the principal financial centre and entrepôt for colonial goods in Europe, and England's commitments extended throughout the world.

Economic change is frequently both a result and a cause of social change, and this case was no exception. To give but two instances: the inflation of prices that helped stimulate economic growth in the sixteenth century was largely the result of a rise in population; and the increase in the value of farm goods encouraged landlords to exploit the labours of their tenants more effectively. On the whole, the seventeenth century was a time of slackening economic advance and of increasing strain in social relationships, brought to a rupture during the Civil War, and thereafter gradually relieved as new patterns took shape. But the picture in social history is far less sharp than it is in commerce or agriculture.

There are no representative statistics, no easily recognisable differences between one period and the next. If on some subjects, including population and urban–rural divisions, reasonably precise information is available, on others, such as attitudes or tensions, the evidence is less clear-cut, and the historian must rely on depiction rather than definition to suggest the nature of English society.

For all the uncertain or unresearched areas, though, certain features will stand out in the survey that follows. Between the late sixteenth and late seventeenth centuries England was transformed. Put in terms that may exaggerate but which do convey the flavour of what happened, a traditional society—essentially static, rural, and with limited types of occupation—reached the brink of modernity. Many changes still lay ahead in 1700, but by that date a great metropolis had arisen, a national economy was formed, personal mobility and the experience of urban life were commonplace, polarisation between the secure and the insecure was widening, agriculture was becoming rationalised, and an increasingly sophisticated consumer and service economy was developing. Moreover, manufacturing and industry, as well as overseas empire and shipping, were coming to be England's hallmarks—although in Elizabeth's reign they had been of secondary significance at most.

Milton lived through the central period of this transformation; and, as a Londoner, he was at the very heart of the most remarkable advances of the day. He experienced at first hand the growth of the capital, the appearance of new goods, wealth and trade, and the sharpening distinction between fine society and the labouring classes. His lifetime is a fitting epitome of an age that witnessed the most rapid and far-reaching changes in English society since the Norman Conquest.

DEMOGRAPHIC PATTERNS

At some point during Milton's lifetime, probably around 1630, the striking growth of England's population that had started around 1500 came to an end, to be succeeded by about a century of stagnation or at most modest increase. The estimates presented in Table I should be taken as very rough figures—there were no nationwide censuses until the nineteenth century—but they can be regarded as reasonably accurate indications of orders of magnitude. As the table shows, the number of people living within the country's 150,000 square kilometres more than doubled between 1500 and 1650, but increased by little more than twenty per cent during the following century. In other words, the rate of increase was three times as fast before 1650 as after.

Historians are still uncertain about the reasons, either for the rise or for the levelling off. There has been some speculation about climate, for there are hints that temperatures were slightly higher during the period of expansion, and that a 'little ice age' caused a drop in the seventeenth century, but it has been difficult to link these estimates with specific demographic developments. Nor can one

Table I
Estimates of the population of England and Wales, 1500–1750[1]

Date	Population
1500	Slightly over 2 million
1550	Almost 3 million
1600	About 3·75 million
1650	Between 4·5 and 5 million
1700	Slightly over 5 million
1750	Close to 6 million

always identify the causes of significant shifts in the birth rate or the death rate. Plagues and harvest failures were traditional decimators of the population, though they seem to have become somewhat more frequent (especially small-pox) in the seventeenth century than they had been in the sixteenth. A noticeable break in the patterns of baptism, marriage and burial came in the 1640s, and was undoubtedly associated with the turmoil of the Civil War. There is even evidence of family limitation in this period—couples married later in life, and the interval between births became longer, indicating that parents were delaying the appearance of new children and thus reducing the total size of the family. The most careful detailed study of a single village, Colyton in Devon, has produced the figures in Table II, which demonstrate the importance of the 1640s, and the distinctiveness of the seventeenth century in general.[2]

Table II
The demography of Colyton, sixteenth to eighteenth centuries

	Age at first marriage		No. of children born to women marrying before age 30 who were still married at 45	Life expectancy at birth	
	Male	Female			
1560–1646	27	27	6·4	1538–1624	43
1647–1719	28	30	4·2	1625–1699	37
1720–1769	26	27	4·4	1700–1774	42

While the 1640s were clearly very important—overall figures for baptisms, marriages and burials throughout England reinforce the conclusions that can be derived from the Colyton materials—once cannot make a simple connection between the Civil War and population trends, especially since wartime records were poorly kept. But longer-term trends are significant. Signs of decline had begun before the Civil War; baptisms did not return to their 1630s level until long after the fighting ended—indeed, not until after 1720; and the turbulence of the sixteenth century, including the Reformation and repeated uprisings, had not slowed the growth of the population. What is unmistakeable is that even small shifts, such as an additional six months between births, postponement of marriage by a few months, can make a major cumulative difference to population trends when multiplied by the hundreds of thousands of such events that took place each year. In the end, the historian can record only that the changes happened; more precise explanations will have to await further research.[3]

Regardless of the larger movements of growth and decline, certain characteristics of life remained fairly constant throughout this period. The prevailing household arrangement for most Englishmen was the so-called nuclear family—parents and their children living together by themselves, or perhaps with a servant. There are examples of other people beyond a servant joining this group. In the stem family, one or more grandparents would come under the same roof; in the extended family, various relatives (an unmarried aunt, or perhaps the mother's brother and his wife) would live with the nuclear family. But these were usually brief stages in the life history of a family—for instance, a married couple and their child might live with the grandparents for a short while after the wedding until they could strike out on their own. The common expectation was the establishment of a nuclear family.[4]

The one significant change that was taking place during this period was in the relationship between the various members of the family. At least in the comfortable, articulate classes, there is evidence of a gradual rejection of the cold, formal, patriarch-dominated family, and its replacement by an atmosphere of kindness rather than severity towards children, affection, warmth, greater equality, and marriages based on love. A transformation as subtle, as inward and as pervasive as this defies explanation, but one can suggest some influences: Protestantism, with its emphasis on the individual and its attention to the spiritual well-being of the young; technological change, which made the glass-insulated house, containing separate rooms, and hence the possibility of privacy, more common; and larger social and intellectual developments, such as the interest in education, which benefited women and children as well as men. Whatever the explanation, the manifestations were unmistakable. By the time John Locke published his *Some Thoughts Concerning Education* (1693)—a powerful assertion of the need to rear children with love and encouragement—the behaviour of families was already moving in the direction to which he was pointing.

One sign, visible first among the wealthier Londoners and more generally among the upper classes, was a rising belief in marriage as companionship. The vanguard were Puritan preachers, but they were followed by the likes of Milton and Defoe, who insisted that love was essential for all couples. Equally significant was the growing inclination of nuclear families to look inward, loosening their ties with an extended kin, and depending on mutual friendship and support. Mistreatment of wives was increasingly condemned, as was the beating of children. And harsh traditional practices, such as the swaddling of infants, slowly fell out of fashion as a nurturant, rather than authoritative, atmosphere began to pervade. Courtship became more important, wives gained status and authority, and children's development became a matter of fond, personal concern instead of formal arrangement.

These were very slow processes, which took centuries to spread throughout society; but their beginnings can be detected in the few generations around Milton's lifetime, and the poet himself made a notable contribution to their advance. In his own day he was probably more famous for his tracts on divorce than for any other work, especially as he asserted in the very title of *The Doctrine and Discipline of Divorce*, his principal tract, that divorce should work 'to the good of both sexes'. He insisted on the equality inherent in marriage, which had to be sustained 'by that sociable and helpfull aptitude which God implanted between man and woman toward each other'. It was precisely when the *mutual* love and support faded that, in his opinion, divorce became the best remedy. Milton's views were shocking to many of his countrymen, but the new attitude he epitomised was gradually bringing about a revolution in the nature of England's most fundamental institution, the family.

Yet one must remember that the late age at marriage and the likelihood of early death prevented long-lasting arrangements. Between the wedding of a couple who were, say, twenty-seven years old, and the predictable death of one of the partners around forty, there was not enough time for even their first-born to reach adulthood. It was a rare child that knew two of its grandparents, and even rarer if it did not have to begin working to help earn its keep well before it reached its tenth year. That is, if it lived that long: up to a quarter of babies did not survive beyond twelve months. The omnipresence of death in an age without effective medicine or a secure supply of food put a curb on any notions of permanence or stability.

One consequence of these inescapable constraints was that England was dominated by its young. Over a third of the people were under fifteen (the figure for the United Kingdom today is less than a quarter), which put a tremendous burden on their elders, because the young could not work as productively as the adults who had to maintain them. That is why even poor families often had a servant: it was a way of sending an extra child to a household that was short-handed. Moreover, a talented person could make a mark in his twenties, since there were proportionately fewer old people holding on to their positions and bottling up opportunities for advancement. A signifi-cant number of the members of the House of Commons, to give one example, were in their early twenties, and many of their leaders were first elected before they were thirty.[5]

In addition to the high incidence of death, the chief reason for instability in family life was the rate of geographic mobility. For the population in some cities was growing much faster than in the country at large, almost entirely because of internal migration. It has been estimated that, taking into account deaths and emigration, there were 8,000 additional inhabitants settled in London each year by the late Stuart period. The capital was the main beneficiary of the migration, but other towns and cities also grew at this time, as is apparent from Table III. This sampling indicates that there was growth at all levels of England's urban centres. Salisbury and Coventry were losing their importance in the economies of their regions, but were still maintaining their size. In addition, many small towns, such as Bury St Edmunds, were growing; Newcastle, Yarmouth and Colchester also had over 10,000 inhabitants in the late seventeenth century; and

Table III
Population of English towns and cities

	c. 1520	c. 1603	c. 1670	c. 1695
London and suburbs	60,000	200,000	—	575,000
Norwich	12,000	15,000	—	29,300
Bristol	10,000	12,000	—	19,400
York	8,000	11,000	12,000	—
Exeter	8,000	9,000	12,500	—
Salisbury	8,000	7,000	—	7,000
Coventry	6,600	6,500	—	6,700
Bury St Edmunds	3,600	4,500	6,200	—
Leicester	3,000	3,500	5,000	—
Warwick	2,000	3,000	3,300	—

a number of places, including Hull and Plymouth, were approaching the 10,000 figure in 1700.[6] It should be noted that only London and Norwich, of the cities in Table III, were growing faster than the national population (Table I). London was of crucial importance, but elsewhere the increase was primarily the result of general population pressure. Yet that is not to deny the importance of urbanisation. The very fact that substantial towns were becoming a familiar part of the landscape, and that the expansion was not contained within rural areas, helped change the nature of English society.

By European standards, a town with 10,000 inhabitants was not of unusual size; but one might recall that England's total population in 1700 was only five million, over ten per cent of whom lived in London. As recently as 1520 the country had had only seven towns (including London) with 7,000 people or more. In the interim, not only had there been growth in existing locations, but nearly thirty new towns of over 1,000 inhabitants had appeared. Some, like Bath (with 3,000 inhabitants by 1700) and Tunbridge Wells, were spas. Others, including Chatham (more than 5,000 strong by 1700), served military purposes. The most important, however, were the new industrial centres, led by Birmingham and Leeds, which had around 8,000 inhabitants apiece in the early eighteenth century. About a dozen of these industrial centres had sprung up in the Midlands and the north, the beginning of a movement that was to turn this first stage of the urbanisation of England into a total transformation of the country's traditional agricultural existence.

The process still had a long way to go in 1700. At most, somewhere between fifteen and twenty per cent of Englishmen lived in a town with more than 7,000 inhabitants at that date. But the number who had had experience of life in such towns was much larger. Leaving aside those who came to a town briefly to sell or buy goods, to find medical or legal help, or for any specific reason, there were thousands who migrated from the countryside and then either returned or died. To maintain urban growth, a far greater influx was needed than appears in the aggregate figures. To say that London experienced a net annual increase of 8,000 people does not mean that a mere 8,000 moved to the capital. The new settlers would have had to amount to 8,000 after deducting, first, the total of those who left the city, and, second, the excess of deaths over births during that year. Mortality was consistently higher in urban areas, and in a plague year anywhere from a sixth to a quarter of the population could be destroyed, a proportion that was very rare in a village. It has been estimated that in the plague years of 1603, 1625 and 1665 London experienced 43,000, 63,000 and 97,000 deaths, respectively, and that to replace such losses and maintain a yearly aggregate growth of 8,000 in the late seventeenth century the capital had to absorb the entire natural increase of a population of two million—that is, of about forty per cent of the country as a whole. The city could scarcely maintain itself, let alone grow. The following were the annual deficits and surpluses (births minus deaths) in London during seven years in the 1620s, including the plague year of 1625:

1622	−1,100
1623	−3,200
1624	−3,900
1625	−47,300
1626	+800
1627	+700
1628	+800

To grow a mere 10,000 during this period (and it is likely to have grown more), even ignoring emigration (probably a few thousand), London would have needed over 60,000 new inhabitants in the course of seven years. Close to two per cent of all Englishmen outside London would, in other words, have had to move to the capital.[7]

Assuming that provincial towns accounted for about half as many people again as London, one can readily appreciate the extent to which urbanisation was affecting English life during the sixteenth and seventeenth centuries. Increasingly mobile geographically, more and more people were becoming familiar with the experience of living in a town, whose society, as we shall see, was markedly different from its rural counterpart. The movement to new locations was another reason, as important as early death, why long-lived, stable family patterns were the exception rather than the norm. Mortality can be explained by deprivation and disease; but to understand the causes of the mobility one must look to the changes taking place in England's economy, where, in addition, the differences between various social groups emerge more clearly than they do from demographic patterns.

COUNTRY LIFE

The principal occupation of Englishmen during the seventeenth century, as in all previous centuries, was agriculture. Consequently, the chief determinant of how people spent their lives was the nature of their physical environment and the kind of farming it could sustain. England may be divided into two basic types of land, highlands and lowlands. The former prevail in most areas of the north and west, where grassland, grazing and thus animal husbandry dominated the countryside; the latter extend throughout much of the south and east, where the richer soil and drier climate permitted a mixture of pasture and arable: cattle- or sheep-raising alongside the cultivation of crops such as corn. In the highland areas the enclosure of fields was a familiar means of improving animal farming, and had been taking place for centuries. In the lowlands common areas—owned by a village as a whole—might contain arable plots as well as the pasture to which villagers had grazing rights; here the efforts to enclose fields for the exclusive use of animals caused tension and resentment.[8] Physical setting was therefore an important determinant of both economic activity and social relations.

Among the inhabitants of rural villages and farms, distinctions of status and prosperity were often blurred, but different groups are nevertheless visible. At the bottom of the scale was the propertyless day labourer who relied completely on the needs of local farmers for whatever employment and livelihood he could find. At best his jobs were seasonal; they were nearly always sporadic and uncertain. He was constantly on the verge of starvation, barely able to maintain himself in a flimsy, shabby hut, probably made of mud and sticks. Considerably better off was the labourer who lived with his employer in a farmhouse, or had quarters somewhere on a farm. His independence was limited, and he had no property, but at least his wages and his future were reasonably secure. If things went well he might even be able to move to a cottage in the village and establish a family. At that point the border between the propertied and the propertyless was crossed, though security was by no means assured. Even among the more independent of the labourers, those who owned some land and perhaps some animals, there was a significant divide between those who were essentially self-supporting but took additional wage work to make ends meet, and those who still relied on outside jobs for their basic livelihood, supplementing that income with the product of their own holdings. In other words, the ownership of land did not assure security, although it did strengthen a family's economic position. An Act of 1589 decreed (so as to protect established property) that no cottage could be erected unless it was attached to four acres of land, and it has been assumed that about five good acres were needed for real self-sufficiency.[9]

The best estimates of the number of Englishmen who were either below, or just at, the self-sufficiency level—that is, who at some time had to labour for wages—suggest that about one third of the population fell in this category in 1600. However, the number was rising steadily, especially in the less prosperous times of the seventeenth century; by 1700 the figure had probably risen to over forty per cent. They were more numerous, proportionately, in the south and east, where mixed farming required considerable labour. And there were real differences, too, between the lives of shepherds, who were needed the year round and whose fortunes depended on the well-being of their flocks, and, say, the seasonal hop pickers of East Anglia or Kent. Equally important were variations in landholding. In a few areas, especially near Wales, outright ownership of four or five acres was not exceptional; in most areas, by contrast, farmers had to rent the additional acres they needed to support themselves—it was unusual to find as many as ten per cent of the labourers possessing the minimal acreage for survival. Obviously, the renter was less secure than the owner.[10]

There were considerable efforts during the seventeenth century to improve the yield of agricultural land by new techniques. For instance, once sufficiently extensive lands had been enclosed by a landowner, and were thus under his control, he could begin to practise 'up-and-down' husbandry, which increased productivity by alternating fields every few years between pasture and tillage. Other ways of evading the traditional fallow year, which removed acreage from productivity so that the soil could recover its nutrients, were also devised: water meadows, which enriched low-lying land by flooding and draining, or the sowing of fertilising crops such as clover and, later, turnips. There were experiments with new kinds of ploughs, and in general a major interest—exemplified by dozens of books on husbandry—in getting more out of the land. The extent of the increase in yields is not clear, but the attention to the issue was symptomatic of landowners' growing interest in the full exploitation of their assets. It was part of the same drive that saw rents increase sharply in most areas of England during the half-century before 1640, following a long period when they had lagged behind prices. The more intensive use of the land was thus eventually of benefit to the great landowners, not to the small farmers or the peasants, more and more of whom were forced to struggle for subsistence.[11]

For the lower orders, the only way to supplement their meagre income from the land was to turn to other forms of employment. The most common was the cloth industry, England's principal contribution to Europe's economy. This was the country's largest economic commitment, after farming, and it employed thousands of spinners, weavers, dyers, knitters, and similar workers of wool. There was scarcely a region of England that did not raise sheep, and few that did not offer employment in the cloth industry. That is not to say that it was a localised undertaking. Wool was cheap to transport; consequently, entrepreneurs developed elaborate connections between sheep-raising, cloth-producing and marketing centres. Gradually there developed what has come to be known as domestic or cottage industry, or the putting-out system, in which spinners and weavers became entirely dependent on merchants who brought them wool and then took the finished goods they had produced to market. The advantage for the labourer or his wife was the opportunity to join an industrial enterprise without leaving home; but they were also more vulnerable because they now relied on the merchant for materials and payments. For the entrepreneur, although the system created logistical problems, it provided a new source of labour which was free from restrictions imposed by guilds in towns. Cottage industry held immense importance for England's future, because the entrepreneurial organisation that it required was an essential stepping-stone towards the factory system of the industrial revolution. Even in the seventeenth century, though, it played an important part in improving the livelihood of the tens of thousands of English men and women who wove or spun as part of a complex national undertaking.

Since the cloth industry was not restricted to specific regions by the unavailability of natural resources, it thrived throughout the country, though it was particularly associated with areas whose occupations permitted spare time from agriculture. Dairy farming, for example, provided an appropriate labour force, and was closely linked with domestic industry in the West Country; similarly, an unusual concentration of population, as in the fell valleys in Westmorland, forced the inhabitants to look beyond farming for a livelihood.[12] But they did not always have to look to wool and its products. Other industries flourished, and although they were often tied to local natural resources and could not match the scale of cloth production, they did offer significant opportunities for employment.

The fastest-growing of these new industries was coal mining. Especially in the north-east, there was a spectacular boom in production from the mid-sixteenth century onward. In the 1680s, according to the best estimates, the output of England's coalfields was *sixteen* times as high as it had been in the 1550s.[13] The increased activity had multiplying effects, for it created a large new labour force that had to be housed, clothed and fed, and more ships were needed to bring the coal from Newcastle and other mining centres to the hearths where it was burned. Without the rise in production it would have been impossible to keep the soaring population of London warm; the trade between Newcastle and London alone employed thousands of sailors and shipbuilders by the early eighteenth century. Moreover, a number of other industries, such as glass-making and salt production, which required heat in their manufacturing processes, became capable of expansion only because coal was available to replace the shrinking supplies of wood and charcoal from England's dwindling woodlands.

The industrial growth of the late sixteenth and seventeenth centuries, spearheaded by the boom in coal mining, has led one historian to call this the age of the first industrial revolution. The idea encourages an exaggerated notion of the advances that took place, for the scale of change a hundred years later was immensely greater, and nothing like the factory system appeared until the late eighteenth century. Nevertheless, there can be no doubt that the expertise, labour force and capital that accumulated during the earlier period provided a

significant basis for the subsequent take-off. The diversity of the growth was
certainly remarkable. In shipbuilding, for example, between 1660 and 1688 alone
the tonnage of English shipping nearly doubled, to about 340,000 tons. By 1700
this industry employed more than ten per cent of those Englishmen who were
not engaged in agricultural work. In the iron industry notable growth took place
before Milton was born. Between the 1570s and 1600 the number of blast
furnaces rose from around fifty to around eighty. Then, because of technological
obstacles, expansion slowed: by the 1650s there had been no more than a slight
increase, and output had risen only from around 18,000 tons per year in 1600 to
around 23,000 tons in 1650. Thereafter the number of furnaces declined, yet total
production still continued to mount slowly; in the course of the seventeenth
century the location of the industry spread from its previous concentration in the
south-east to the Midlands, Yorkshire and Wales.

There were similar indications of health and vigour in the many other
industries that had become a part of the English countryside by 1700. It has been
estimated that in the early eighteenth century some 150,000 people were
involved in the leather industry, primarily in small towns such as Leicester and
Northampton. Glassmaking, the mining of lead, tin, copper, chalk and alum
were all rural industries, as at first was the metalwork, such as nail making, that
was helping to create new towns in the Midlands by 1700. Long before that date
the small town of Sheffield had become well known for its cutlery, and similar
specialities—such as the knitting of stockings in the West Yorkshire dales and
East Midlands—had sprung up in localities throughout the country. Moreover,
in almost every region of England there was a remarkable boom in the building
of houses between the late sixteenth and early eighteenth centuries. From the
grand country houses to the lowly cottages, the face of the land was transformed—a massive undertaking that again provided work for tens of
thousands.[14]

In other words, a wide variety of alternatives to agriculture offered means of
livelihood to the ordinary seventeenth-century Englishman. A substantial
majority still depended on farming. But many of those on the land were also
involved in some form of industry like mining or cloth production. And a
substantial proportion of the Englishmen who lived in cities or towns were
engaged in artisanal activities such as leather finishing that were closely related
to the growth of rural industrial activity. The switch away from an essentially
agricultural economy still lay in the future, but already in 1700 the traditional
distinctions among the agricultural population that were outlined above—rising
from the propertyless day labourer to the independent small landowner—were
being transformed by the broadening opportunities for earning a living away
from the fields.

PROVINCIAL TOWNS

The blurring of the distinctiveness of the farming life was accomplished not only
by the increasing importance of industry, by the putting-out system, and by the

growing demands of cities, but also by the mobility of people who once had remained tied to the area of their birth. The motives for leaving one's village varied enormously—overpopulation, enclosure, the quest for a different kind of life—but the dominant stimulus was undoubtedly economic hardship. We have seen that in the course of the seventeenth century the proportion of Englishmen living at or below the subsistence level was rising, and this at a time when the population was becoming steadily larger; by 1700 well over one million persons had been added to this category since 1600. The rough figures that can be calculated for the prices of agricultural produce, average farm wages and the cost of living show the dimensions of the problem. Between the 1570s and the 1640s prices more than doubled, but in the same period average wages rose only fifty per cent. In other words, purchasing power dropped, and the ordinary person's standard of living declined by about twenty-five per cent.[15] The result was a flight from the land that—in the eyes of contemporaries—was manifested almost as much by roving armies of vagabonds as by the influx into the cities.

The awareness of vagrant bands gave rise to the conviction that the country was overpopulated. According to Sir John Hawkins, Englishmen were so crowded that 'for the want of place they crawl one o'er another's back'.[16] Since the traditional sources of charity, the monasteries, had been dissolved in the 1530s, the government was forced to devise means of controlling the mounting problems of poverty and vagabondage. The result was a series of statutes, starting with the Statute of Artificers in 1563, and culminating with the promulgation of the Elizabethan poor relief law in two Acts in 1597 and 1601. One purpose of the legislation was to impose stability—people were supposed to stay where they had been raised, and to remain in the work for which they had been prepared—but the other was to create a system of poor relief, with the prime responsibility for welfare vested in each parish. Although neither objective was fully realised, the system was working quite well by the 1630s, and the very effort was an indication of the severity of the disruptions caused by economic change.[17]

Once the rural labourers set out on their travels, their destinations varied widely. Some did not settle down again, remaining for years in vagrant bands that were a feature of the seventeenth-century English countryside. Others stayed in the half-way house between rural and urban life, the market town. There were over 750 market towns in England during this period, located every few miles, and in some cases performing functions they had pursued for six hundred years or more. The smallest, such as Billesdon in Leicestershire, had only three or four hundred inhabitants, and served a few thousand rural workers within a limited area. More common were market towns with at least six hundred and sometimes as many as two thousand inhabitants, a few of which—like Tonbridge or Reading—were to be found in every county. The largest were indistinguishable from county towns like Winchester or from the smaller cities such as Bury St Edmunds (also a county town), whose growth has already been discussed.[18] Certainly men and women on the move would have passed through these regional centres, which offered some opportunities for a new start in life.

The prime function of the market towns was the sale and distribution of agricultural products. Here local farmers sold their surplus crops and purchased the food or supplies they needed. One day each week was officially designated market day—at some of the larger centres, more than one day a week—and a few times a year there would be major fairs. Artisans and craftsmen could also sell their goods at markets and fairs; they therefore often became inhabitants of the towns, giving the population a diversity not to be found in the villages. The more successful of these communities also took on a role as local social centres when they reached sufficient size. Daniel Defoe referred to Maidstone as 'a very agreeable place to live in, where a man of letters, and of manners, will always find suitable society . . . ful of gentry, of mirth, and of good company' (§S–192: p. 479). Most of them had their own schools, a number hosted sessions of courts, and a few even boasted such insignia of culture as stationers and booksellers.

The country towns retained their links with agriculture—in many cases, a quarter or more of the inhabitants were engaged in pursuits no different from those of their village counterparts. A good proportion of the traders and craftsmen supplemented their income with a stake in husbandry. But the markets, the social and intellectual life, and the possibility of specialisation did mark them apart. Even the little town of Bewdley in Worcestershire, for example, could become known widely for the caps it made. There was no question that in these centres opportunities for employment (as day labourers, apprentices or servants) must have seemed better for those who had been forced off the land—though in hard times the market towns were no less depressed than the surrounding country, and many had large pauper populations.

If they moved on to the major county towns, especially to places such as York or Exeter which were important enough to be considered provincial capitals rather than mere county towns, the change would have been even more pronounced. In addition to larger concentrations of people, these cities were distinguished by complex organisations: elaborate structures of self-government, powerful oligarchies, and in some strong guild systems. Moreover, they often had international contacts: Exeter, for example, maintained a substantial trade with France, while Bristol and Plymouth had links with the New World and fishing fleets exceeded only by London's. Opportunities for employment in centres such as these were excellent, and they became natural magnets for those leaving the land (§S–192: Ch. IV).

In most of the provincial capitals there were large concentrations of merchants, notably companies of Merchant Adventurers, who specialised in long-distance trades, particularly in cloth. To gain admission to such a company required a seven-year unmarried apprenticeship, as did admission to a craft guild. For many migrants this was not a serious option because masters tended to take apprentices only from families they knew or in return for payment or other inducements. More feasible were the jobs in the industrial enterprises that were also a feature of the provincial capitals. Cloth-finishing, soap making and sugar refining were only a few of the many possibilities that were available. In addition, there were hundreds of shops and services that flourished as the cities became centres of consumption, attracting the gentry to social 'seasons', entertainments, and contacts with a wider world. Here the dispossessed labourer might find new ways of earning a livelihood, whether in the most menial positions in the docks of a port or at a hostelry, or in more promising situations attached to a gentry household. Dick Whittington stories of spectacular rises to fortune were virtually non-existent in real life, but the fact that this story became a popular tale throughout England at the time was an indication of the hopes that continued to lure people to the cities. And for most of them the ultimate objective was the greatest lure of all, the sprawling capital itself. If the local centres had hundreds of opportunities, London had tens of thousands. For all the disappointments and poverty that the metropolis in fact promoted, its magnetism only increased as the seventeenth century went by.

LONDON

Milton in *Areopagitica* described London as 'this vast City; a City of refuge, the mansion house of liberty, encompast and surrounded with [God's] protection; the shop of warre hath not there more anvils and hammers waking, to fashion out the plates and instruments of armed Justice in defence of beleaguer'd Truth, then there be pens and heads there, sitting by their studious lamps, musing, searching, revolving new notions and ideas wherewith to present . . . the approaching Reformation: others as fast reading, trying all things, assenting to the force of reason and convincement'.[19] It was an extraordinary homage to the capital's intellectual vitality and its leadership in the new ideas sweeping England during the revolution. Significantly, he emphasised its quality as 'a City of refuge', for here was taken many stages further the mingling of diverse peoples and occupations that was characteristic even of provincial cities. Milton had experienced at first hand what he was describing, for he had taken part in the flow of people, and he knew well the life of London's artisans (like his father) and intellectuals. His enthusiasm for the capital and its ways typified the excitement and sense of opportunity that brought men and women in such numbers to its teeming wards. The very masses seemed appealing, for he wrote in his seventh elegy of the 'crowds close compacted, crowds like in faces to goddesses, [who] moved in brilliance to and fro through the midst of the streets and roads'. Both the quantity of humanity and the way it was organised were unique in England, because the metropolis drew on the entire nation for its inhabitants and commerce, and to absorb them it developed social and economic patterns that were far more elaborate and complex than any that its immigrants could have experienced before.

The central institution of the city was the livery company, the descendant of the mediaeval guild. There were dozens of these organisations, formed to regulate and maintain standards in every trade, whether the members were as familiar as the apothecary or as specialised as the loriner (who made harnesses for horses). But the dominant groups were the so-called twelve greater companies—in order of civic precedence, the Mercers, Grocers, Drapers, Fishmongers, Goldsmiths, Skinners, Merchant Taylors, Haberdashers, Salters, Ironmongers, Vintners, and Clothworkers. It was primarily from their leaders that the aldermen who ruled London were chosen; they could count the richest and most powerful merchants of the day among their members; and their freemen and masters were the chief beneficiaries of the profits to be made from an ever growing population of consumers. To become a citizen of London one had to gain the 'freedom' of one of the livery companies, which meant either serving a seven-year apprenticeship or acting as a benefactor to the company.

It has been estimated that there were approximately 20,000 apprentices at any one time in mid-seventeenth century London.[20] If, as an estimate, one multiplies that cohort by four (on the assumption that most people lived to enjoy some twenty-eight years as fully fledged skinners, vintners, and so forth), one can guess that about 100,000 of the city's inhabitants—approximately a third—were apprenticed to or members of a livery company. These were essentially the middle ranks of the population, whose most fortunate or skilful representatives could reach the very highest levels of wealth, status and influence. A great merchant like Sir Thomas Smythe or Sir Baptist Hicks (later Viscount Campden) was a national figure, of importance in politics as well as commerce. Such a position did not seem anomalous, because the links between the country gentry and the livery companies of London were always close: the two groups intermingled constantly, and formed as homogeneous a landed/trading class as any in Europe.

Even more so than in provincial cities, apprenticeships in London were the reward of the well-connected. Younger sons of gentry, who in a country of primogeniture could expect to inherit little of the family wealth, frequently turned to trade for a livelihood. The sons of established London or provincial merchants or of other masters were also a source of apprentices, who thus constituted a fairly uniform, well defined and privileged (though rowdy) group. It was possible, but not too common, for someone from outside the traditional sources of recruitment to get a foot on this first step towards the relatively secure and respected occupation that awaited any freeman of a livery company. The most successful, like Smythe, could establish themselves as landed gentry quite easily once their fortunes had been made. The mingling of the two classes, which was formalised in the House of Commons—where, unlike Continental assemblies, townsmen and the landed sat together, rather than in separate Houses—was constantly renewed by marriage, and by the move from country to town and back again.

A good example of the constant interchange was the Wolstenholme family. John Wolstenholme was a solid and reputable minor gentlemen with ancient roots in Derbyshire. When his second son, also John, was born in 1562 it was clear that the boy would have to leave the ancestral estate, which his older brother would inherit. Young John came to London, where his father had obtained a foothold by obtaining a post in the customs. The son prospered, and by the early seventeenth century was one of the capital's richest merchants, a major supporter of new overseas ventures. In 1617 he received a knighthood, but long before then his ties to his origins had been strengthened by a marriage to the daughter of one of his father's notable Derbyshire neighbours, Thomas Fanshawe, an official of the Exchequer under Queen Elizabeth, the father of a number of courtiers, and the grandfather of the first Viscount Fanshawe. One of Wolstenholme's daughters married another Fanshawe, through whom both families were also related to Sir Thomas Smythe. Sir John's eldest son, also to be Sir John Wolstenholme, increased the family fortunes further until his son could return to the land as a prominent member of the Derbyshire gentry.

On a lesser scale, this story was repeated throughout London's elite and at most of the higher levels of the livery companies. There were many stories of failure, of course, but sufficient success for both gentry and merchant classes to renew themselves in each generation. And during Elizabeth's reign and the seventeenth century the merchants of London were passing through the most remarkable expansion of their history. Not only were they driving out the foreigners who had played a large role in England's export and import trade until the late sixteenth century, but they were opening links with an extraordinary variety of new markets.

Until 1600 the dominant force in overseas trade was the Company of Merchant Adventurers, which dealt in England's one great export commodity, woollen goods (usually unfinished cloth). A mere twenty years later it had been joined by more than twenty companies either trading with new markets—in the Baltic, the Levant or the East Indies (the first two enterprises founded in the sixteenth century, the last in 1600)—or trying to settle new areas which would in turn become new trading partners, for example, Virginia, Newfoundland and New England. Many of these companies were organised not under the regulated system of the Merchant Adventurers, who required an apprenticeship before a merchant was admitted to the trade, but under the joint-stock system, which enabled anyone (including many gentry) with sufficient funds to buy a share in a venture. The joint-stock system permitted companies to draw on non-mercantile wealth for their capital, and was a major reason both for the success of the overseas efforts that eventually created an empire and for the continued closeness between merchants and gentry.[21]

Foreign trade, especially beyond Europe, may have been the glamourous enterprise within commerce as a whole; but it still followed traditional paths and was not yet the dominant sector of London's economy. It is true that the fastest-growing source of wealth during the seventeenth century was the re-export business—the re-shipping to foreign ports, primarily on the Continent, of goods brought to London from abroad. By the end of the century, re-exports may have accounted for one third of the city's foreign ventures; but even then cloth remained the principal trade. This was so despite the reorientation of the cloth industry that had started in the 1610s with the so-called Cokayne project. The brainchild of Sir William Cokayne, a London alderman, the project had been an attempt to centre all English cloth production on the 'new' draperies—that is, to complete the finishing of the wool that until then was carried out primarily on the Continent. Since the greatest profits were made after the cloth had been dyed, Cokayne particularly wanted Englishmen to take over that function, helped by the influx from the intolerant Spanish Netherlands of Protestant clothworkers skilled in finishing processes. By prohibiting the export of undyed wool, Cokayne expected to concentrate all stages of production in English hands; and, in the long run, this was the direction the country's cloth trade was to take. In the short run, however, the project was disastrous, because the Dutch refused to import the finished goods, unemployment rose, and the English had to face the terrible trade depression that struck Europe in the early 1620s, following a series of coinage debasements and wild inflation in the Baltic areas. Nevertheless, the cloth trade survived and continued to dominate London's exports in 1640, as is indicated in Table IV.

Table IV
English merchants' exports from London, 1640

	£	%
'Old' draperies	580,000	48·7
'New' draperies and hosiery	455,000	38·2
Other manufactured goods	27,000	2·3
Re-exports	76,000	6·4
Minerals	35,000	3·0
Agricultural produce	17,000	1·4
Total	1,190,000	100·0

As for markets, even in 1700, when the West Indies were booming, England's trade with Europe and the Mediterranean was still over three times as valuable as the overseas trade.[22]

   Equally striking was the continued significance of domestic trade. No sample of London's leading merchants in the seventeenth century reveals less than half engaged primarily in business at home rather than abroad. Supplying the capital with food was alone an enormous business—imports of grain to the city, for example, almost tripled between 1615 and 1681. London was the chief market for Newcastle coal, for timber from the whole kingdom, and for the food grown in the home counties. The sale of wholesale goods was concentrated there, too; when, in 1688, an enterprising young man named William Stout decided to open up a general store in his home of Lancaster, in the north-west corner of England, it was clear across the nation, to London, that he travelled to buy the stock that he needed. He may have stopped off in Sheffield and Birmingham to pick up some of the goods for which those towns were becoming known, and from his own region he may have obtained some of his inventory, notably the nails produced by the Lancashire lead industry, but the bulk of his purchases had to be made in London. Thanks to its easy access to the main routes of transport, the sea and rivers, the capital was the natural entrepôt for the whole country, the centre of its financial institutions and trade no less than of its law and politics, the heart of an emerging national economy. Here were more than enough good prospects to keep the merchant community committed to domestic enterprises.[23]

London was also the most important industrial centre in England. It had always been the headquarters of luxury goods, and such craftsmen as the goldsmiths continued to flourish, as did more recent arrivals like sugar refiners or the silkmakers of Spitalfields—primarily Huguenot exiles from France. With the constant need for more housing, building was also a lucrative profession. The most remarkable expansion, however, was in shipbuilding. Shipyards opened on the Thames from Chatham up river; and it has been estimated that by the 1690s about a quarter of London's population was employed in some kind of port work or shipbuilding. Specific figures for London are not available, but it has been calculated that the total tonnage owned by Englishmen rose from 50,000 in the 1560s to 115,000 in 1629, and reached over 350,000 by the end of the century. Many times that tonnage had to be produced, of course, because of the high rate of loss and wear, and the majority of it was built along the Thames.[24]

The spectacular growth of the capital was not, however, without its critics. In addition to local worries about housing, food supply, overcrowding and disease, there were bitter resentments elsewhere in the kingdom at the dominance of this one city in so many sectors of the economy. More than sixty per cent of the shipping tonnage in England was owned by Londoners in 1700. As the export of new draperies rose from about £350,000 in value in 1610 to over £600,000 in value in the 1640s, London's share, already overwhelming in 1610, increased from 77 to 85 per cent.[25] The hostility of provincial merchants towards the capital was a constant theme of seventeenth-century politics, though the protests were unavailing.

It is not difficult to see why government leaders took little notice of the complaints about London's avaricious behaviour. For the city's great merchants were far too useful to the Crown to be restrained. One financier alone, Paul Bayning, lent Charles I £40,000 between 1625 and 1628, and was rewarded with a viscountcy in the latter year. A decade later Sir Paul Pindar, who had profited enormously from the Levant trade and from customs farming, apparently lent Charles almost £100,000 in little more than a year. Groups of merchants were even more fruitful sources of money. In 1607, for example, the customs farmers formed a special syndicate to lend the Crown £120,000, quite apart from the regular advance rental they paid for the privilege of raising customs duties. The most bountiful loans of all were those raised through the corporation of London, that is, from the livery companies and whichever private citizens would contribute. This practice had begun before the Stuart period—one of the debts James I inherited was £60,000 that Elizabeth had raised in this way in 1590—but it rapidly took on new dimensions. By 1626 the Crown had borrowed almost £500,000 in additional loans from the city, and a further £200,000 was obtained in the 1630s. The repayments forced extensive sales of Crown lands, and the exactions themselves caused ill feeling between city and monarch, but the government was never able to find an equally munificent source. Support of London's economic needs was therefore almost unavoidable (§S–176).

The support took various forms. In the early seventeenth century, it was mainly a matter of charters for new corporations and monopolies in various branches of the new overseas trades. The full title of what was to become one of England's most powerful organisations was 'The Governor and Company of Merchants *of London* Trading into the East Indies', and it was not too surprising that James I later demanded a £10,000 loan from the company. Nor was it unusual for the government to look to the London community for its main advice in financial affairs—the most notable example being Lionel Cranfield, who eventually became Lord Treasurer. Increasingly, governments became inclined to intervene in economic matters through legislation. The first such effort was the Navigation Act of 1651, which proved to be a futile attempt to restrict all foreign trade in English ports to English ships. A more sophisticated series of Acts, passed between 1660 and 1696, established enormous advantages for English merchants and ship owners, especially in trade with the colonies, and helped confirm London's position as the commercial capital of the world.[26]

By 1700 much of England's foreign policy was determined by economic concerns; certainly her recent wars with the Dutch had been largely motivated by the struggle for trade, markets and resources, and these considerations remained important thereafter. The close ties between the government and London's merchants had been epitomised by the creation of the Bank of England in 1694. In just twelve days a group of city financiers raised £1,200,000 to capitalise the Bank, which then lent the entire sum to the Crown at eight per cent interest. It was thus entirely in the government's own interest to support in any way it could the merchant and financial leaders who had underwritten the founding of an empire, the creation of an unmatched commercial centre, the building of the world's largest trading fleet, and the building of the richest and most populous city on earth.[27]

For the very large majority of London's inhabitants these splendid achievements must have been incomprehensible. The area east of the original city walls was rapidly becoming an enormous slum in the seventeenth century. Here the day labourers, often little better off than they had been in their villages, and certainly living in far less hygienic conditions, made their homes. There were stories of seven or more people crowded into a single room. The main organisation for looking after homeless vagrants, Bridewell, faced a twelvefold increase in annual cases between 1560 and 1625, and its rolls were filled with repeated offenders. Crime was common, and except for the rich, whose carriages were a common sight by the end of the century, movement within the city was punctuated by encounters with beggars and thieves.[28]

For those unable to gain admission to the livery companies or find work in the ports the one major source of employment was what today would be called the service sector. Thanks to the presence of the Inns of Court, Parliament, and the royal court, London was developing a social 'season'—a round of parties and gatherings among the country gentry, who were finding it increasingly attractive to set themselves up in a house in or near the capital for a few months each winter. As the poor moved eastward from the city walls, so the rich moved westward, creating what is still known as the West End. Beautiful squares were laid out in the area of Covent Garden and Bloomsbury, and elegant homes were established. They needed provisioning, cleaning, painting, and the hundreds of services that menial labour could provide. London became a centre of fashion and conspicuous expenditures, all of which were potential sources of livelihood for both men and women.[29]

The city was thus a packed microcosm of the kingdom. Within its compact space—even with its crowds and spread into suburbs, it could have been traversed in 1700 in about an hour—lived extremes of wealth and poverty and toilers in every occupation of the day. The tensions of the time were also concentrated here, because London was the quickest disseminator of the latest rumours and beliefs. The first regular newspapers were begun in Milton's lifetime; indeed, he himself was licensor for the official weekly of the Commonwealth, the *Mercurius Politicus*, an early example of a regular organ of government propaganda. With free-flowing presses, many viewpoints found a hearing, and it was only natural for London to become the chief centre of Puritan preaching and radical ideas. More sharply than most other Englishmen, its citizens divided their loyalties: the great merchants who were doing so well out of their close links with the government supported the Crown in the Civil War, but lesser merchants, apprentices, and artisans, resentful of the control over the most lucrative trades exercised by the city's elite, were overwhelmingly Parliamentarian.[30] As governments knew only too well, the capital was a breeder of antagonisms as well as opportunities.

SOCIAL STRUCTURE

In 1695 one of England's first statisticians, Gregory King, produced a series of estimates of the nation's wealth, demography and physical features. He described the country's characteristics according to a number of different measures: population, with special attention to London, mortality, births, marriages, age, income distribution, types of land, number of houses, livestock, consumption of meat and drink, and taxes. His most famous table depicted the annual income of the different classes into which he divided Englishmen. Although its details cannot be verified, its broad outlines remain plausible, and give an excellent indication of the nation's social and economic structure in the late seventeenth century. Table V is adapted from King's figures.[31]

In King's view, about half the country (above the £20 mark) consisted of the comfortable and secure—or, in his words, those who 'increased' England's wealth—while the other half hovered on the brink of destitution and 'decreased' the kingdom's wealth. Leaving aside the mercantile rich, the landed elite

Table V
Annual income of different ranks and occupations, 1688

Family income	Rank/Occupation	No. of persons	% of total
£400 and up	Aristocrats/higher gentry/bishops	57,520	1·0
£400 and up	Great merchants	16,000	0·3
£100–£399	Gentry, office-holders, and great lawyers	236,000	4·3
£100–£399	Merchants and prosperous tradesmen	48,000	0·9
£50–£99	Clergy, small landowners, professionals, navy and army officers, and prosperous shopkeepers and artisans	1,103,000	20·0
£21–£49	Farmers and lesser shopkeepers and artisans	1,215,000	22·1
£10–£20	Labourers, soldiers and sailors	1,495,000	27·2
Under £10	Paupers and vagrants	1,330,000	24·2
Total		5,500,520	100·0

consisting of aristocrats, gentry, bishops and courtiers constituted slightly over five per cent of the population, yet accounted for about twenty-five per cent of the national income. This was the dominant class both in the counties and in the capital, yet it was not without its own problems and tensions.

The major social and economic change of the sixteenth and seventeenth centuries within the elite was the redefinition of the role of the peerage, the highest echelon in society. The titled families—the dukes, marquesses, viscounts, earls and lords—whose heads sat in the House of Lords were the traditional rulers of England. Their greatest clans, such as the Howards, embodied almost as much of the country's history as did the various ruling houses. Unlike their Continental counterparts, who would have considered as nobles all those who in England were *untitled* gentry, the peers were a small group. During Elizabeth's reign they had amounted to approximately sixty families. That figure had doubled by 1640, and had reached 160 by the time of Gregory King's estimates, but it was still a minuscule proportion of the landed class.[32]

By the late seventeenth century the holders of knighthoods and baronetcies (hereditary knighthoods instituted by James I), both of which were titles that did not carry membership of the House of Lords, totalled about 1,400, and King guessed that there were, in addition, perhaps 12,000 gentry families and 5,000 holders of major royal offices. In other words, something like 18,000 or 19,000 families constituted the landed and official elites. The relationship that was changing was the one between the vast majority of this class and the less than one per cent who made up the peerage.

For by 1640 it was completely clear—as it had not been as recently as 1560—that the peers were no longer a distinct ruling group. Various influences had helped bring the change about, among them the end of the nobility's traditional military function, the growing power of the House of Commons, Elizabeth's execution of the greatest aristocrat in the realm, Thomas Howard Duke of Norfolk, and the increasing use of non-nobles at the highest levels of government. But none was more important than the shifting economic situation of the different elements of the landed class. For the peers there was a drastic decline in average income during Elizabeth's reign which, though redressed by 1641, was both a severe shock and a blow to one of the main props of their social superiority. Largely because their numbers were reduced and their rents did not keep pace with inflation, they suffered a serious decline under Elizabeth, which was only just overcome during the next forty years by the recruitment of new nobles and sharply improved rents.[33]

By comparison with the upper levels of the gentry, often indistinguishable from the peers in terms of position at court or prominence within a county, the nobles barely held their own during the seventeenth century. In 1601 the sixty-one peer families earned about three per cent of the total income of England's peers and gentry; by 1688, though their numbers had risen to 160 (a 2·7-fold increase), the proportion had grown only to seven per cent (a 2·3-fold increase).[34] It should be noted, too, that the first date happened to be the low ebb of the peerage's fortunes. Although the aristocrats hung on thereafter, it is by comparison with this low point, and the absolute size of their percentage remains striking. They were the richest group in the country, but they did not overwhelm the gentry by any means. One nobleman in the House of Lords was heard to say in 1628 that the members of the House of Commons 'were able to buy the Upper House (His Majesty excepted) thrice over'. Unable to retain their distinctiveness in the realms of national or local politics, military prowess or economic advantage, the peers inevitably found themselves being equalled as possessors of power and status by the gentry.

The fortunes of the gentry in the seventeenth century have been the subject of the most intense debate among English historians during the past few decades. Some have argued that the gentry's wealth was increasing and that their political aggressiveness, culminating in the triumph of their institution, the House of Commons, following the Civil War, was the result of their demand for a say in national affairs commensurate with their economic position. Others claim that they were losing ground and that the revolution was a desperate attempt by a declining class to redeem its position by turning on the Crown. Although the economic questions have not been answered to general satisfaction—and probably never can be, given the lack of documentation and the

difficulty of interpreting what does exist—on the larger issue the first interpretation (positing a 'rising' gentry class) seems the more plausible.[35]

Amidst a class consisting of thousands of families there were bound to be
losers as well as winners. Some gentry were profligate, incompetent or unlucky,
but many were leaders of agricultural improvement, intensified exploitation of
the land, industrial development and investment in new trade ventures. It was
the gentry who promoted enclosure and who started the experiments with new
crops, with new rotation systems that obviated the need for fallow years, and
with the other new cultivation techniques that laid the basis for the agricultural
revolution of the late seventeenth and eighteenth centuries. As for industry,
they were quick to take advantage of the non-agricultural resources of their
lands, such as coal, and to encourage new manufactures. Sir Robert Mansell,
best known as a naval commander in the reign of James I, was also one of the
chief promoters of glass production in England. Over thirty per cent of the
investors in the companies formed under Elizabeth to invest in mining and wire
manufacture were gentry. And in new trading and colonising companies their
eagerness to participate was highly visible. Table VI indicates the role they
played in this arena.[36]

Table VI
Number and proportion of gentry among investors in companies

Company and dates of investments	No. of gentry investors	Proportion of membership (%)
Africa, 1618	27	71
Bermuda, 1612–20	41	27
East India Company, 1600–30	111	10
Gilbert Venturers, 1578–83	66	49
Guiana, 1594–1629	45	49
Irish Plantations, 1586–1618	157	23
Massachusetts Bay, 1628–29	25	31
New England, 1606–23	42	62
Newfoundland, 1610	11	22
North West Passage, 1584 and 1612	48	16
Virginia Company, 1606–24	472	38

In addition, about fourteen per cent of the investors in privateering in
Elizabeth's and Charles I's reigns were gentry.

The peers were certainly involved in all these activities. Simply because of
numbers, however, the gentry were far more conspicuous in this drive for
economic advantage. Moreover, they were certainly no less engaged than the
peers and could not be regarded as inferior in importance. In absolute numbers
they were capturing the largest share of the two most lucrative sources of quick
profit at the time: purchases of Crown land and incomes from Crown offices.

Indeed, all the signs point to extraordinary vigour—not least the unprecedented commitment to education that the gentry began to exhibit from the mid-sixteenth century onward. Just as they took over representation of boroughs in the Commons in order to make the House their own, so they took over the Inns of Court, the universities, and the means of education.

It has been estimated that more Englishmen, proportionately, were receiving higher education in the mid-seventeenth century than at any time until the late nineteenth century. Almost all the influx consisted of gentry in search of the new culture that Renaissance Italian humanists and their English followers had decreed to be the mark of the true gentleman. It is true that some did not take the education seriously, and that many (especially younger sons) received more education than they could use in later life—a phenomenon that both Bacon and Hobbes considered a cause of the restlessness that led to the Civil War, and that modern interpreters have described as the creation of a class of 'alienated intellectuals'. In the main, however, education was seen as a means of more effective participation in the life of the State (parliamentary debates were sprinkled with quotations from the classics) and of more intelligent management of the family's fortunes (in an age when investments had to be calculated and when new ideas about agriculture came from books that the gentry both read and wrote). The commitment to advanced schooling, enthusiastically shared by Milton himself, has to be taken as a confirmation of the new ambitions and expansiveness of the landed class.[37]

THE EMERGENCE OF A NEW SOCIETY

The consequences of the social and economic changes England was passing through in the sixteenth and seventeenth centuries were visible in the Civil War and revolution that rent the nation apart in Milton's middle years. The tensions in the elite drove what was a remarkably homogeneous 'establishment' into two camps, although it retained its unity until very late in the day. In 1640 very few members of the landed class sided with the King; their power and wealth had been growing, and they were united in their resistance to royal exactions. For his part, Charles I was finding it impossible to rule in an age of inflation and the mounting expenses of government without the additional income that he could obtain only by extraordinary means when requests for regular taxation were met by threats to his prerogatives in the Commons. Yet as parliamentary demands multiplied in 1641, a party of gentry and peers detached itself from opposition and joined the King, thus creating the second side in the Civil War. The royalists were disproportionately from the north and west of England, from areas least affected by economic change; it might also be suggested that the south and east, the chief beneficiaries of the boom of the sixteenth century, were particularly distressed by the depression that started in the 1620s—their expectations were thus higher and their discontent greater.

Nevertheless, economic and social stresses must not be given undue weight among the causes of the Civil War. The basic issues were political and religious, and, while these had other dimensions and contributory causes, they were also the only arenas in which the situation was significantly altered after 1660.[38] The directions of economic and social change continued undisturbed: growing urbanisation, rural industry and commercial advance, and the dominance of the gentry and London's merchants. It could be argued, therefore, that the most dramatic results of the developments of the sixteenth and seventeenth centuries in trade, agriculture and population are to be found not in the great upheaval of the Civil War but abroad, in the creation of an empire; and at home, not in the cities but in the villages, the last bastions of a dying way of life.

England's imperial status in 1700 was unmistakable, and to an observer would have seemed the most striking difference in the country's position from 1600. By the end of the seventeenth century about 300,000 Englishmen—more than one in twenty of the population at home—had settled along the east coast of the North American continent alone. Others were in Ireland, in the Caribbean, in India and in the Far East. The movement had started in Ireland, which had been conquered and subdued with considerable brutality by the Elizabethans and ultimately by Cromwell. It had spread throughout the world as London became the leader of international finance and commerce, and by the late seventeenth century it was transforming the mother country. New products, such as tobacco, the potato and coffee, had become a part of daily life. Former luxuries, such as sugar and pepper, had come within popular reach. The origins of the stock exchange lay in the dealings in the shares of companies venturing overseas, and insurance first became a large-scale enterprise to protect long-distance shipping. Indeed, the transaction of both stock and insurance business was in its early days associated with another institution made possible by the new products of empire: the coffee house, a ubiquitous feature of eighteenth-century London, where deals were made, the newly familiar newspapers read, and the class that was shaping England's world-wide power and prosperity cemented its connections.[39]

No less fundamental was the alteration of the conditions of village life. Both economic and political forces had contrived to end the traditional isolation and homogeneity of the ordinary village. The inflation, the rise of rural industry and the increasing migration to cities had accentuated the distinctions of wealth among the rural population and had undercut the sense that age-old customs and relationships would continue for ever. The gentry were turning their attention to national affairs and spending time in London, at the expense of their local commitments. Moreover, agents of the royal government, entrepreneurs in search of cheap labour, and in some areas dedicated Puritan preachers, were subjecting the village to powerful outside influences at the very time that its sense of community was breaking down.

The chief evidence of the disruptions taking place in country society was the epidemic of witchcraft accusations and persecution that reached its peak in the mid-seventeenth century and then slowly died away. Rural folk had always had elaborate systems of belief by which they explained the events of nature—light-ning, crop failure, the death of a cow, a cottage catching fire—that controlled their existence. Generally, they assumed that magical forces dominated the world. Nothing happened without purpose, by accident. If a jug of milk fell and broke, it had been willed to fall by some ill-intentioned force. The rituals they practised to ward off misfortune were a blend of paganism and Christianity, and from both roots they derived the assumption that there were certain people—usually old women—who had special powers that they obtained by some sort of arrangement with a demon.

Villages had their 'good' or 'white' witches as well as the evil kind. Good witches or cunning men were traditional repositories of wisdom. One went to them for advice when problems arose: a new bride who could not become pregnant, perhaps, or a family treasure that had been lost. They suggested the spell, or the ointment, or the procedures to set matters right again, and they were normally respected members of the community. But gratitude could easily turn to fear. As the closeness between the villagers weakened, as the distinctions among them widened and they felt less inclination to help one another, other instincts came into play. The records of witchcraft trials reveal that one common starting-point for an accusation might be the appearance at a relatively well-to-do home of an old widow (the most vulnerable member of this society as a result of age, sex and isolation) who begs for food. The housewife, less charitable than she might once have been, sends the old woman away, and hears her muttering to herself as she leaves. The next day there is some accident in the house, and the housewife, perhaps feeling guilty about her hardheartedness, absolves herself by spreading the tale that the old woman is a witch who put a spell on the house when refused food.[40]

The rash of trials in all parts of England continued from the mid-sixteenth until the mid-seventeenth century, aided and often stimulated by governmental or religious officials who were intent on extending their authority and the rule of law and Church to all localities. It may be that what we see as an epidemic was merely the appearance in official records of quarrels and tensions that villagers would have taken care of themselves until encouraged by prosecutors and churchmen to bring accusations before proper judges for resolution. Exactly the same thing was happening on the Continent at the same time, and for many of the same reasons. Eventually, however, as lawyers and governments began to realise how tenuous the evidence in witchcraft cases really was, as the uncontrollable hysteria and mass denunciations that a single accusation could unleash became serious threats to social order, and as villages began to adapt to their new social and economic situation, the great wave of persecution died away. By the 1690s the terrible outburst in Salem, Massachusetts, looked almost like an anachronism. (See also below, pp. 171 ff.)

Yet the conditions which the obsession with witches revealed had been no passing flurry. The better-educated clergy produced by the Reformation, and representatives of central government who were taking on new local functions like poor relief, were in the village to stay. So was the aggressive businessman organising rural industry. Equally permanent henceforth were the more withdrawn gentry and the better-off local farmers, both of whom felt fewer ties with their neighbours. And the day labourer remained likely to seek an easier life beyond the village—on the road, in a town or city, or at sea. This was the new situation, and eventually it was accepted, but not without a long period of tense and sometimes violent adjustment.

CONCLUSION

By the time of Milton's death England was well on her way to becoming the dominant economic power in the world, a position she was to hold for two centuries. Innovation, adventure and the ability to stimulate and absorb rapid change had been the hallmarks of the country's extraordinary advance between the reigns of Elizabeth and Anne. Contemporaries had a sense of what was happening, but nobody was more gifted than Milton at capturing his country-men's qualities, especially when, in full patriotic fervour, he described them as 'a Nation not slow and dull, but of a quick, ingenious, and piercing spirit, acute to invent, suttle and sinewy to discours, not beneath the reach of any point the highest that human capacity can soar to' (*CE, IV,* 339).

The rhetoric might seem excessively glowing, but Milton knew whereof he wrote. His father had been a scrivener, a member of a profession that had expanded its document-writing vocation to include the role of middleman or broker for loans and other financial transations. Milton thus had direct experi-ence of the business world, and did not hesitate to reject the traditional Christian opposition to the charging of interest. If he was an advocate of new economic attitudes, he was even more attuned to the other fundamental changes of his time: in the family, in education, and in the larger concerns of political and intellectual life. As a quintessential Londoner in a period of extraordinary fertility, he was both shaper and mirror of rapid social change, from the rise of the newspaper to the development of fresh attitudes towards authority. Above all, his 'quick, ingenious, and piercing spirit, acute to invent' epitomised the openness and unprecedented transformations which, during his lifetime, cre-ated a society in England that was a harbinger of future modernity for all of Europe.

NOTES

I wish to thank David Levine, Lawrence Stone, and the editors of this volume, for their very helpful comments on an earlier version of this chapter.

1 The basic sources for these estimates, which have been kept deliberately rough, are: Julian Cornwall, 'English Population in the Early Sixteenth Century', *Economic History Review* [henceforth abbreviated as *Ec.H.R.*], 2nd series, XXIII (1970), 32–44; G. S. L. Tucker, 'English Pre-industrial Population Trends', *ibid.,* XVI (1963), 205–8; D. V. Glass, 'Gregory King's Estimate of the Population of England and Wales, 1695',

Population Studies, II (1950), 338–74; and G. T. Griffith, *Population Problems in the Age of Malthus* (Cambridge, 1926).

2 Climate and its effects on population are discussed in G. Utterström, 'Climatic Fluctuations and Population Problems in Early Modern History', *Scandinavian Economic History Review*, II (1955), 3–47; Emmanuel Le Roy Ladurie, *Times of Feast, Times of Famine: A History of Climate since the Year 1000* (Garden City, N.Y., 1971); and John D. Post, 'Meteorological Historiography', *Journal of Interdisciplinary History*, III (1973), 721–32. The sources for Table II are: E. A. Wrigley, 'Family Limitation in Pre-industrial England', *Ec.H.R.*, 2nd series, XIX (1966), 82–109, and his *Population and History* (1969), table on p. 87.

3 For a general discussion of these issues, see Wrigley, *Population, passim.*

4 See L. Stone (§S–265), from which the next three paragraphs are also derived. Although noble families had much larger households, their demographic patterns were not essentially different from those of the rest of society. See T. H. Hollingsworth, 'The Demography of the British Peerage', Supplement to *Population Studies*, XVIII (1964).

5 Francis Bacon, Edwin Sandys, John Eliot, John Hampden and Oliver Cromwell all first sat in the House while in their twenties. For the data on age distribution, see §S–197: p. 19.

6 The source for Table III is §S–192: table on p. 83. The other figures in this and the next paragraph are drawn from Chapters II–IV of the same book.

7 Wrigley, *Population* (as above, note 2), ppp. 96 and 114, gives the birth and death figures for London.

8 The best survey of regional differences in agriculture and patterns of enclosure is §S–274: Ch. I, III and IV.

9 *Ibid.*, Ch. VII, especially pp. 398 ff.

10 *Ibid.*, and D. C. Coleman, 'Labour in the English Economy of the Seventeenth Century', *Ec.H.R.*, 2nd series, VIII (1956), 280–95.

11 §S–274: Ch. III; §S–197: pp. 31–41; and §S–225. The last somewhat overstates the case for the revolutionary consequences of the new husbandry, but certainly makes the clearest and strongest argument for its importance.

12 Joan Thirsk, 'Industries in the Countryside', in §S–202: pp. 70–88; E. L. Jones, 'Agricultural Origins of Industry', *Past and Present*, XL (1968), 58–71.

13 The estimates are given in J. U. Nef, *The Rise of the British Coal Industry* (1932), I, 19. It was Nef who referred to this period as the age of the 'first' industrial revolution: see below.

14 The best general survey of English industry is §S–198. See also §S–285: Ch. IV and IX; Rosemary O'Day, *Economy and Community: Economic and Social History of Pre-industrial England 1500—1700* (1975), Ch. IV; Ralph Davis, *The Rise of the English Shipping Industry in the Seventeenth and Eighteenth Centuries* (1962); and R. Machin, 'The Great Rebuilding: A Reassessment', *Past and Present*, LXXVII (1977), 33–56.

15 See §S–274: tables XIII, XV and XVI, pp. 862, 864 and 865. The basic sources on prices, wages and inflation are two articles by E. H. Phelps Brown and Sheila V. Hopkins, 'Seven Centuries of Building Wages', *Economica*, new series, XXII (1955),

195–206, and 'Seven Centuries of the Prices of Consumables, compared with Builders' Wage-rates', *ibid.*, XXIII (1956), 296–314; Y. S. Brenner, 'The Inflation of Prices in England, 1551–1650', *Ec.H.R.*, 2nd series, XV (1962), 266–84; and §S–242. For a general discussion of social mobility, see the articles by Lawrence Stone and Alan Everitt in *Past and Present*, XXXIII (1966), 16–73, and Carl Bridenbaugh, *Vexed and Troubled Englishmen 1590—1642* (1968).

16 Cited in K. E. Knorr, *British Colonial Theories, 1570—1850* (Toronto, 1944), p. 27. See also J. F. Pound, *Poverty and Vagrancy in Tudor England* (1971), and Paul Slack, 'Vagrants and Vagrancy in England 1598–1664', *Ec.H.R.*, 2nd series, XXVII (1974), 360–78.

17 The only substantial study of official policies towards the poor remains E. M. Leonard, *The Early History of English Poor Relief* (Cambridge, 1900).

18 On the subject of this and the next two paragraphs, see §S–192: Ch. II, and §S–274: Ch. VIII.

19 *Areopagitica*, in *CE*, IV, 340. The remark about crowds (below) is from Elegy VII (1628), in *CE*, I, 219.

20 S. R. Smith, 'Social and Geographical Origins of the London Apprentices 1630–60', *Guildhall Miscellany*, IV (1971–73), 195–206.

21 For general accounts, see §S–252, and W. R. Scott, *The Constitution and Finance of English, Scottish and Irish Joint-Stock Companies to 1720* (Cambridge, 1910–12), 3 vols.

22 Table IV is based on §S–197: table on p. 65. See also F. J. Fisher, 'London's Export Trade in the Early Seventeenth Century', *Ec.H.R.*, 2nd series, III (1950), 151–61; J. D. Gould, 'Cloth Exports, 1600–40', *ibid.*, XXIV (1971), 249–57; Astrid Friis, *Alderman Cockayne's Project and the Cloth Trade* (1927); and §S–269.

23 The best account of the emergence of a consumer economy is §S–272. See also F. J. Fisher, 'The Development of the London Food Market 1540–1640', *Ec.H.R.*, 1st series, V (1935), 46–64; §S–192: Ch. V; and *The Autobiography of William Stout of Lancaster, 1665—1752*, ed. J. D. Marshall, Chetham Society, 3rd series, XIV (1967), especially pp. 89–90.

24 Davis (as above, note 14), Ch. II; Fisher (previous note); D. C. Coleman, 'Naval Dockyards under the Later Stuarts', *Ec.H.R.*, 2nd series, VI (1953), 134–55; and §S–285: p. 171.

25 §S–197: p. 64, based on Gould (as above, note 22).

26 L. A. Harper, *The English Navigation Laws* (1929); and §S–286.

27 *Ibid.*; J. H. Clapham, *The Bank of England* (Cambridge, 1944), Vol. I: *1694—1797*.

28 §S–192: Ch. V; Lee Beier, 'Social Problems in Elizabethan London', *Journal of Interdisciplinary History*, IX (1978), 203–21.

29 F. J. Fisher, 'The Development of London as a Centre of Conspicuous Consumption in the Sixteenth and Seventeenth Centuries', *Transactions of the Royal Historical Society*, 4th series, XXX (1948), 37–50; D. V. Glass, 'Socio-economic Status and Occupations in the City of London at the end of the Seventeenth Century', in *Studies in London History presented to P. E. Jones*, ed. A. E. J. Hollaender and W. Kellaway (1969), pp. 373–89. Beier (previous note), p. 215, suggests that there were perhaps 100,000 domestic servants in late seventeenth-century London.

30 §S–110; Robert Brenner, 'The Civil War Politics of London's Merchant Community', *Past and Present*, LVIII (1973), 53–107.

31 King's original assessments, from which Table V is derived, have been reprinted in §S–275: pp. 780–1. On King and his estimates, see D. V. Glass, 'Two Papers on Gregory King', *Population in History: Essays in Historical Demography*, ed. D. V. Glass and D. E. C. Eversley (1965), pp. 159–220—the second paper is a slightly revised version of the article cited in note 1, above.

32 Lawrence Stone's *Crisis of the Aristocracy* (§S–264) is the standard work on the issues discussed in this and the next paragraphs.

33 The precise figures can be found in Stone (§S–264): App. IX (B), p. 762.

34 Detailed figures are given in Stone (§S–264): App. XII (1) and (2), p. 767. For the nobleman's remark, cited below, see British Library Harleian MS. 390, f. 365.

35 The best sampling of the literature, and guide to further bibliography, is §S–266: Part I.

36 Table VI is derived from §S–252: table 11, p. 104.

37 J. E. Neale, *The Elizabethan House of Commons* (§S–101), Ch. VII; G. E. Aylmer, *The King's Servants* (§S–5), Ch. IV–V; Mark H. Curtis, 'The Alienated Intellectual of Early Stuart England', *Past and Present*, XXIII (1962), 25–43; and §S–328.

38 The most succinct treatment of the origins of the Civil War, which, however, places more stress on social and economic factors than I have given here, is by Lawrence Stone (§S–141).

39 Williamson (§S–284) remains the best introduction. For the importance of Ireland, see §S–118. For the effects at home, see §S–192: Ch. V and X, and Scott (as above, note 21), Vol. I, Ch. XVII, and Vol. III, Division XI.

40 The standard works on popular customs and beliefs and the witchcraft persecution are Keith Thomas (§S–147) and Alan Macfarlane, *Witchcraft in Tudor and Stuart England: A Regional and Comparative Study* (1970). See also Christopher Hill (§S–217), Ch. XII: 'The Secularization of the Parish'.

KENNETH CHARLTON

4

The educational background

If we wish to understand that aspect of seventeenth-century English society which we label 'educational' we need to start by recognising that the term covers much more than what went on in schools and universities. These catered for a very small proportion of the population indeed, yet the non-fictional literature of the period reveals an increasing and sustained insistence on the religious and political education of the majority, the vast mass of illiterates who nevertheless had to be orally 'schooled' in appropriate religious and political attitudes and behaviour.

Primarily this means considering those explicit and overtly didactic attempts on the part of the few to influence the attitudes and behaviour of the many, since there is very little evidence of the latter undertaking their own education, save in the time-honoured vocational sense of parents initiating their children into ways of rearing a family and earning a livelihood. Of the importance of the task the few had no doubts, since, as Milton himself reminded his readers in *Areopagitica*, 'albeit whatever thing we hear or see, sitting, walking, travelling or conversing may be fitly called our book and is of the same effect as writings are'.

Two countervailing aspects of communal belief have at the same time to be noted. The first was the view that to be a good Christian one needed only to be imbued with spiritual grace, thus denying the need for mass education and asserting the dangers implicit in the education of the few. Book learning, it was claimed, inevitably led to spiritual pride and at the same time reinforced the hierarchical divisions of society. The simple democracy of a 'truly' Christian commonwealth was thus endangered rather than enhanced by education. The second view reflected the well recognised notion of the mutability of human society, to be found in the 'melancholic' characters of the fictional literature of the period, and thus denying the educational optimism implicit alike in Renaissance humanism and Protestant belief.[1]

One further variable in the complicated pattern of educational background has to be taken into account. We are, of course, concerned with 'what actually happened'. But the prescriptive literature also tells us something about the educational aspirations of the period. It would be too easy to dismiss this kind of evidence as 'utopian', impossible of achievement. But an awareness of it will complete our understanding of both the pessimistic and the optimistic aspects of the Age of Milton.

THE EDUCATION OF THE FEW

(i) At grammar school. For the majority of those who received institutional 'schooling' in any regular way this meant attendance at one of many endowed grammar schools, which by the seventeenth century were to be found fairly comprehensively distributed in both urban and rural areas of England.

In most cases the existence of an endowed grammar school meant the teaching of Latin grammar, first through the painfully repetitious study of the accidence and syntax of the language, and later by rhetorical and logical exercises—the composition of themes, orations, letters and so on—with finally (if the boy stayed on long enough at school) an acquaintance with the texts of Latin authors. The choice of authors would be decided by the foundation statutes of the school, or, in the absence of such prescription, by the master himself, and depended especially on attitudes to the inclusion of 'pagan' authors. Some followed Dean Colet's provision for St Paul's school in prescribing that none other than 'chaste' Christian authors be studied.[2] John Brinsley, in his *Ludus Literarius* (1612), made a similar stipulation,[3] and his view was echoed in mid-century by William Dell, though in characteristically more forceful terms, when he insisted

> that they learn the Greek and Latin tongues especially from Christians, and so without the lyes, fables, follies, vanities, whoredoms, lust, pride, revenge etc of the heathens . . . and most necessary it is that Christians should forget the names of their gods and muses, which were but devils and damned creatures, and all their mythology and fabulous inventions and let them all go to Satan from whence they came.[4]

The matter was still a live issue at the end of the century when, for example, the Anglican parson Thomas Brockbank recorded in his diary his regret that 'so much wanton and not to say obscene and profane poetry' was taught in school, advocating instead the use of 'bookes of morality and humane prudence . . . such as laye down ye principles of Christianity and teach language and religion at the same time',[5] and thus echoing the perennial ambition, in matters educational, to kill (at least) two birds with one stone.

Others, however, were willing to allow the study of pagan authors, though even here it was felt there was need for censorship to avoid exposure to the more libidinous writings of the pre-Christian era. Lucian, Ovid, Horace, Juvenal and

Martial had long been the subject of such strictures, notwithstanding occasional resort to the scriptural authority of St Paul: 'For whatsoever things were written aforetime were written for our learning'. That there was so much debate about the matter throughout the century (it was indeed perennial, and had been a matter of discussion ever since the early Christian Church faced the problem of education at this level) is indicative of the importance attached to the upbringing of boys in the context of a Christian morality. Far too often, critics noted, the medium of such upbringing—Latin language and literature—became an end in itself. But of what the purpose should be there was no doubt whatsoever.

Most endowed schools provided a master (and sometimes an usher) to teach a limited number of boys 'on the foundation' without charge and for a fixed salary derived from the revenues of the foundation. Inflation notwithstanding, the salary originally stipulated was rarely altered, so that (with or without the permission of the trustees) the master often admitted additional boys and charged them a variety of feés to supplement his stipend—admission fees, 'quarterage' fees for tuition, and a variety of *ad hoc* fees for paper and writing materials, for candles, even for the provision of 'birch for rods'. William Dugard, master of Colchester Grammar School, for example, charged 10s per quarter for tuition, together with 2d per pupil for sweeping the school at the end of each quarter, and 12d per quarter for 'fireing'. In addition, every Christmas, his pupils contributed 12d apiece 'to entertain ye company that repair to the schoole at that time to hear the schollers exercise'. Moreover, if any boy wished instruction in writing Dugard charged 20s (§S–300: pp. 310–11). When Abraham Colfe founded his grammar school at Lewisham in 1652 he provided free tuition for thirty-one boys being 'destitute orphans, the children of parish pensioners, and of Day-labourers, Handycrafts-men, mean Tradesmen, painful Husbandmen or of any other honest and godly poor persons'. The master was, however, allowed to take fee-paying pupils as well, and to charge the sons of yeomen 8s per quarter and of gentlemen 10s per quarter.[6] Shrewsbury School continued its sixteenth-century practice of charging differential fees: a lord's son paid 10s, a knight's son 6s 8d, the eldest son of a gentleman 3s 4d and his younger sons 2s 6d. For those of lower degree the fee was 2s if born outside Shropshire and 12d if born in the county. The sons of inhabitants of Shrewsbury itself paid 18d, whilst burgesses' sons paid only 4d.[7]

In these various ways masters of grammar schools were able to supplement the salary laid down in the statutes of their school, and since the numbers of scholars 'on the foundation' were limited by the statutes there were usually far more fee-payers on the school roll (§S–300: p. 310). Opportunities for a 'free' grammar school education leading on to a professional career were very limited indeed, and, in the same way, what was taught in the endowed grammar schools of the seventeenth century was determined as much by the recruitment possibilities of the area and the predisposition of the master and his trustees to satisfy the demands of parents as by the original statutes of the school.

Whatever the immediate cause, however, there is no doubt that the scope of the grammar school curriculum widened in the seventeenth century to meet particular needs. The revised statutes of Enfield Grammar School of 1621 provided for the teaching of 'crossrow or alphabetical letters, writing, and arithmetic' as well as of Latin grammar.[8] Colfe's grammar school at Lewisham had a writing master on the staff, as did the Royal Grammar School at Newcastle upon Tyne.[9] More important, however, the momentum for the teaching of the English language, originally discernible in the latter part of the sixteenth century with John Hart's *Orthographie* (1569) and his *Methode . . . to Reade English* (1570), William Bullokar's *Amendment of Orthographie of English Speech* (1580) and Richard Mulcaster's *Elementarie* (1582), was maintained and increased. Edmund Coote, master of Bury St Edmunds Grammar School, produced his *English Schoolmaster* in 1596. It reached a twenty-fifth edition in 1635 and a fifty-fourth in 1737. It made use of a full range of pedagogical techniques, from the use of dialogue and recapitulation to graded reading exercises at the end of each chapter. More advanced reading matter was provided in the form of a short catechism, extracts from the Bible and an alphabetically arranged vocabulary with instructions how to find words in it. When William Walker, master of Grantham Grammar School, produced *Some Improvements in the Art of Teaching* (3rd edn 1683) it was the teaching of English that he was concerned with, and his *Treatise of English Participles* (1655) reached a tenth edition in 1691. John Wharton's *New English Grammar* (1655) claimed in justification that after he left school only one boy in a hundred had any need at all for Latin, in the studying of which he had spent virtually all his school life. Books such as these were obviously not meant for the lowest levels of literacy, but Wharton's claim should remind us that, their availability notwithstanding, the prime purpose of a grammar school was the teaching of Latin grammar, and that the study of English grammar therein was but a means to that end. As Joshua Poole put it in his *English Accidence* (1655),

> my drift and scope therefore is to have a child so well-verst in his mother's tounge before he meddle into Latin that when he come to construing a Latine author he shall from the signification of his words in construing be in some good measure able to tell distinctly what part of speech every word is.
>
> ('Episte to the Reader', sig. A2^v)

In the same way Poole's *English Parnassus* (1657) was designed as an aid to composing verse in English preparatory to composing verse in Latin.

The early signs of the teaching of 'English' as a school subject are, therefore, to be found in the endowed grammar schools of Milton's day. The master of the endowed school was not, however, the sole representative of his profession, since some preferred to set up their own school free from the inhibitions of statutes and trustees. Many of these were clerics who welcomed the additional income from both day boys and boarders in their own house. Before going on to Eton, Sir Robert Walpole was taught by Richard Ransome, the rector of Great Dunham.[10] John Bowtell, master of the grammar school at Thaxted, preferred to send his son John to the adjoining parish of Tilney, where the vicar, Mr Houlden, kept a private school.[11] Many ejected ministers, both during the Civil

War and after the Restoration, set up their own schools. The royalist master of
Shrewsbury School, Thomas Chaloner, was deprived in 1645 and spent the next
eleven years teaching in a variety of private schools in Shropshire, Staffordshire
and North Wales, before returning to Shrewsbury at the Restoration.[12] Samuel
Ogden, on being deprived, set up school in Derby, competing with the already
existing endowed school there.[13]

Even so, not all private schoolteachers were either clerics or deprived
teachers. Some made a career of it, as did Robert Latimer, who taught for forty
years opposite the Three Cows in Malmesbury, where Thomas Hobbes was once
his pupil. The most famous private schoolmaster of his day, however, was
Thomas Farnaby (c. 1575–1647), 'that Atlas of grammar learning', as a fellow
schoolmaster called him.[14] Having started his career as an 'abcedarian' in the
Somerset village of Martock, he set up his own school in London, in 'a garden
house' in Goldsmith's Alley near Cricklegate. Farnaby was a prolific writer,
producing for use in schools editions of Juvenal's *Satires*, Martial's *Epigrams*,
Ovid's *Metamorphoses*, Seneca's *Tragedies* and Terence's *Comedies*, as well as
anthologies of prose and poetry and a Latin grammar, *Systema Grammatica*.[15]
Private schoolmasters were, then, not inconsiderable figures in the educational
scene. Though outnumbered by the masters of endowed schools, they nevertheless sent boys on to the universities, whose admissions registers are often the
only evidence we have of their existence.[16]

Motives for sending a boy to a private school (whether as a day boy or as a
boarder) rather than to a 'public' endowed grammar school were doubtless
mixed. The relative expense of the former would obviously be taken into
consideration, but among the upper classes at least there was little compunction
about sending a boy away to school at an early age. Certainly the availability of
private schooling was greater in the seventeenth century than hitherto. The
older method was to have the boy tutored at home (or in another's house), and
the debate as to which method was the better was continuous. Just as Roger
Ascham's *The Scholemaster* (1570) was concerned with the duties of a private
tutor, so too John Locke's *Some Thoughts Concerning Education* (1692) discussed
the education of a gentleman's son at home, Locke himself having been a tutor
in the household of the Earl of Shaftesbury. Robert Boyle was tutored at home in
both Latin and French before going off to Eton for a couple of years with his
brother Francis.[17] Gilbert Burnet, privately educated at home by his father,
before studying at Marischal (i.e. New) College, Aberdeen, weighed the
advantages of public and private education in his *Thoughts on Education* (c. 1668),
and concluded that a private education, not at home but in the house of another,
was the more advantageous.[18] John Clarke, the scholarly master of Hull
Grammar School, on the other hand, claimed the advantage lay with private
boarding schools of not more than twenty or thirty pupils.[19] The issue remained
an open one. The upper classes were just as likely to send their sons away to
school as to have them tutored at home; the middle classes tended to choose
between the local endowed grammar school or, if their finances could run to it, a
boarding school, whether endowed or private (cf. §S–300: p. 309). For those who

could pay—and despite 'free places' on the foundation this remained a crucial factor—provision of what we would now call secondary education, whether public or private, was relatively easy to come by. Indeed, it was argued, both at the beginning of the century and in retrospect after the Civil War, that there was not only over-provision of grammar school places but also cause for complaint in that grammar schools contributed, through the reading of 'republican' Latin authors, to the subversion which itself had led to the Civil War.

The argument was not a new one. It had been used by Mulcaster in the 1580s, and was repeated by Bacon, and by Hobbes and Newcastle after the Restoration.[20] 'When more are bred scholars than preferments can take off' (as Bacon put it) sedition is bound to follow from the ranks of the 'alienated intellectuals'. Yet the evidence is more complicated. For every Oliver Cromwell educated at Stamford Grammar School one can find a William Laud emerging from Reading Grammar School. Moreover, the schools (and universities) of the day were regularly castigated for concerning themselves only with 'the cobwebs of learning, admirable for their fineness of thread and work but of no substance and profit'[21]—and the criticism was applied to schoolmasters and tutors of Puritan and orthodox allegiance alike.

Nevertheless, through the increasing provision of grammar school education for the upper and middle classes during the first thirty years of the seventeenth century, more and more of the few were put in a position to make use of the histories and political works to which they had been introduced (in however tedious a fashion) at school. Even more important, most of these works were now available in translation through the work of George Chapman, Philemon Holland and others (cf. §§S–909 and S–941). An 'educated' man would draw what conclusions he wished from such reading, whether of approval or disapproval, but they were at least likely to be relatively better-informed conclusions, if only because the reader would be aware that he was forging allegiances within a tradition of political thought and action (of whatever variety). To argue 'over-supply', as Bacon and others did, in order either to inhibit expansion or to explain political movements of which one disapproved was, of course, to argue that all education is potentially subversive, as Socrates had come to know to his cost.

Yet none of the critics objected to the study of Latin grammar and literature as such, only to the painfully inefficient ways of studying them. Hartlib was entirely typical in publishing his *True and Readie Way to Learne the Latine Tongue* . . . (1654) in order, as he said, 'to abridge the time which is spent and to cease the toil which is taken therein', thereby avoiding 'the grammatical tyranny of teaching tongues' (sig. A3). Such writers acknowledged that the traditional grammar school curriculum was essential to the initial preparation of boys for the universities and the professions, though they argued, too, that, in addition to improving the methods of teaching, attention should be paid to the extension of the curriculum by the inclusion of studies which would not only be useful to the reformed commonwealth in a material sense, but would at the same time reduce social divisions. Milton's *Of Education*, Dury's *Reformed School*, Petty's

Advice and a host of less well known pamphlets all made the same point, which was classically stated in Comenius' *Great Didactic* (1657):

> not the children of the rich or of the powerful only, but of all alike, boys and girls, both noble and ignoble, rich and poor, in all cities and towns, villages and hamlets should be sent to school . . . All . . . must be brought on to the point at which, being properly imbued with wisdom and virtue and piety, they may usefully employ the present life and be worthily prepared for that to come. (ed. M. W. Keatinge [1896], p. 218)]

Yet they were not recommending a grammar school education for all. When they did turn their minds to the education of the many, it was to be in separate schools. For the sectaries on the extreme wing of the Puritan movement, however, this was the crucial problem, to be given first priority and requiring a more radical remedy, which either denied the necessity for a literary or scientific education at all or called for a switch of curricular emphasis away from classical language and literature to universal literacy, religious instruction and vocationally useful studies. Their educational prescriptions were concerned more with the abolition of social hierarchy than with the facilitation of social mobility. Even Milton, conservative humanist that he was in his *Of Education*, would go not further, in his *Considerations Touching the Likeliest Means to Remove Hirelings* (1659), than recommending the founding of schools in which youth

> may be at once brought up to a competence of learning and to an honest trade; and the hours of teaching so orderd, as thir studie may be no hindrance to thir labor or other calling.   (CE, VI, 80)

The printing presses of the middle decades of the century poured forth a stream of educational pamphlets and books, but in the event they had little effect either on the curriculum of secondary education (whether in endowed or private schools), or even on that of the increasing number of elementary schools, in which a curriculum consisting of the three Rs and the elements of vocational training predominated. Change did come, in an effective way, with the Restoration, which achieved by the enactment of the 'Clarendon Code' what the Commonwealth had been unable to achieve, the teaching of precisely that 'modern' curriculum for the few which Hartlib and his fellow writers had so urgently advocated.

The statutory prohibition of dissenters from teaching in grammar schools resulted in the setting up of the Dissenting Academies, at first clandestine and even nomadic, but later achieving a degree of permanence and acceptance, and a clientele which included the sons of Anglican parents.[22] In the curriculum of these schools we come nearest Milton's 'academies' which would serve as both school and university, and which would add to a sound foundation in classical languages and literature the study of theology, literature, history, mathematics and science, as well as occasionally commercial subjects. Since dissenting teachers could no longer continue to serve in endowed grammar schools, and since the sons of dissenters could not matriculate at university, the Dissenting

Academies served a dual function, but it has to be stressed that they taught a very small proportion of those who sought a secondary education. The majority of those who did seek it continued to receive it in one (or a combination) of the three traditional forms, in an endowed grammar school, in a private school, or at home under the supervision of a private tutor.

The success of the Dissenting Academies in achieving a modern curriculum and the influence of John Locke's arguments for education by a private tutor have led some historians to argue for a consequent 'decline' in grammar school education in the latter part of the century.[23] Certainly the earlier flow of new endowments slowed down considerably in that period, and an increasing number of grammar schools were adding the teaching of English (and other subjects) to their curriculum. Some even ceased to teach Latin altogether in the absence of a sufficiency of suitable candidates to maintain the master and his usher, a trend reinforced by the production of 'grammars of the English tongue' in profusion when hitherto they had been exceptional.

W. K. Jordan was surely right in remarking that previous estimates of grammar school foundations have been 'much too low'. He himself counted 437 in his sample of ten counties and suggested 'at least an equal number' for the rest of England (§S–223: p. 291). Christopher Wase's survey carried out in the 1670s produced a total of 704 schools. But, as P. J. Wallis has noted, counting schools is a hazardous business. Not all schools labelled grammar schools taught the same combination of subjects. Wase himself was interested only in free grammar schools, and he therefore excluded those which were not endowed. Wallis concluded, therefore, that 'it does not seem unreasonable to suggest at least 2,000 grammar schools for the seventeenth century'.[24] Even then, the frequent evidence of supplementation of existing foundations has also to be taken into account in any estimate of development.

It is, therefore, too simple a question to ask whether the grammar schools were in decline or not at the end of the century. They were a heterogeneous set of institutions, whether by foundation or continuance. Some flourished because their locality and its hinterland flourished; others because of the influence of an active patron or master. Some were in decline due to an unsatisfactory schoolmaster, declining locality, corrupt trustees, incompetent trustees, leaseholders of school lands who refused to pay the rent out of which the master's stipend came, and so on. Some declined in apparently prosperous times, others managed to survive in a declining town, whilst over all hung the varying contribution of the private grammar school, often prospering under a lively master but lacking the continuity which a completely run endowment could provide.

(ii) The 'daughters of gentlemen'. The *daughters* of the upper and middle classes did not, of course, attend the grammar schools. If they received an education it was either at the hands of a tutor at home or by attendance at establishments for the education of 'daughters of gentlemen'. If in the education of boys at grammar school we are talking about a relative minority, here we are talking about a much

smaller number. There were in the first place nothing like the same number of schools, and when they existed they had fewer pupils. Moreover, even by the end of the century there were still some (men, of course, and not a few women) who, echoing Ben Jonson's 'Lady Would-be' in *Volpone*, continued to argue that the education of girls in anything other than housewifery and the duties of motherhood was not only an unnecessary expenditure of money, but was also unseemly and in the end likely to endanger the chances of marriage itself. Robert Herrick was not unusual in praying for an 'unlearned' wife.[25]

For the girls of this class who did receive some kind of formal education, however, a change of emphasis may be noticed. At the beginning of the century opportunities for education other than at home at the hands of a tutor or in the household of another family were extremely limited. By the middle of the century, and certainly by its end, there is increasing evidence of girls being sent away to boarding school. As to the curriculum of such education, two strands have to be distinguished. Each would be present, but with a differential emphasis depending on parental preference. The first strand consisted of traditional classical studies, such, for example, as Thomas More gave his daughters and as Lady Jane Grey and Elizabeth Tudor received from Roger Ascham. Milton's daughters received a similar education, as did Lady Anne Clifford at the hands of Samuel Davies, the poet, though Lucy Apsley, who married the regicide Colonel John Hutchinson, recounts how 'when I was about seven years of age I remember I had at one time eight tutors in several qualities—language, music, dancing, writing, needlework—but my genius was quite averse from all but my book'.[26] She learned French from her nurse, and Latin from her father's chaplain, and her writings reveal her knowledge of Latin, Greek and Hebrew.

Yet in this she was unusual, since it was the second strand of Renaissance views about the education of girls and women, the acquisition of feminine 'accomplishments', that came to predominate in the education of upper and middle class girls in the seventeenth century, though even in the earlier period classical studies for girls were justified more in terms of social accomplishment than in the functional sense applied to boys. In addition, of course, moral education loomed large. Lady Anne Halkett's autobiographical description may stand exemplar for many of her class who received their education at home:

> My mother . . . paid masters for teaching my sister and mee to write, speake French, play on the lute and virginalls and dance, and kept a gentlewoman to teach us all kinds of needleworke . . . But my mother's greatest care . . . [was to ensure that we were] instructed never to neglect to begin and end the day with prayer, and orderly each morning to read the Bible, and ever to keepe the church as offten as there was occasion to meet there, either for prayers or preaching.

Notwithstanding this rather austere regime Anne recorded that she

> loved well to see plays and to walke in the Spring Garden sometimes (before itt grew somewhat scandalous by the abuse of some) . . . and I was the first that

proposed and practised itt for three or four of us going together withoutt any man, and everyone paying for themselves by giving money to a footman who waited on us, and he gave itt to the play-howse.[27]

It was the emphasis on the acquisition of 'accomplishments' that John Dury criticised in his *Advancement of Learning* (1653), when he complained of

the education of young gentlewomen which in most places tends onely to teach them how they may become objects of lusts and snares unto young gentlemen . . . [when instead] they should become modest, discreet, and industrious housewives.

Not surprisingly, he recommended that such schools should be 'lookt into and reformed by the Counsell of some grave and vertuous Matrons' (§S–338: p. 190). The middle-class parent, however, seeking an education for his daughter, increasingly turned to the school as an alternative to the tutor. John Evelyn noted in his diary for 17 May 1649 that he went 'to Putney . . . to see the Schools or Colledges of the Young Gentlewomen', and it was at Mrs Salmon's school at Hackney that, as Katherine Fowler, 'the matchless Orinda' went, aged eight to begin her formal education.[28] Mrs Playford's school opposite the church in Islington offered in the 1670s tuition 'in all manner of curious [needle] works . . . reading, writing, dancing and the French language', and it was for the pupils of Josias Priest's 'school for young gentlewomen' in Chelsea that Henry Purcell wrote his *Dido and Aeneas* (c. 1688–90).[29]

Nor were such schools confined to the metropolis and its rural surroundings. In mid-century the cleric-farmer Ralph Josselin sent his daughter Jane, aged ten, to Mrs Piggott's school in Colchester. His other daughters, Mary and Elizabeth, were sent to similar establishments at White Colne and Bury St Edmunds respectively.[30] Margaret and Elizabeth Oxinden, daughters of Henry Oxinden, were sent to a school at Mersham run by Mr Beavan, who assured their father that

besides the quallietyes of musicke, both for the virginalls and singing (if they have voices), and writing (and to cast account which will be usefull to them hereafter), he will be carefull also that theyr behaviour be modest and such as becomes theyr qualliety, and that they grow in knowledg and understanding of God, and theyr duty to Him, which is above all . . . I presume [he concluded] you will think £30 a year for both reasonable, when you consider the hardnes of the times [1647] and that there is more troble with girles then boys.[31]

It was, in fact, the proliferation of such schools that led Mary Astell, in her *Serious Proposal for Ladies* . . . (1694), to call for the setting up of a college 'rather acedemical than monastic' to 'stock the kingdom with pious and prudent ladies . . . able to teach in schools of a better sort' (pp. 73–4), a proposal which anticipated Charles Kingsley's Queen's College by 150 years.

The acceptance of such a proposal, however, would have required a far greater degree of general support for the education of girls than was forthcoming. Such education was not only satirised from Ben Jonson to Molière but discouraged in many of the treatises on women's status and education, as well as in individual cases. Sir Miles Sandys was merely repeating a well known standpoint when, in his conduct book *Prima Pars Parvi Opusculi* (1634), he insisted that 'to make them schollers were frivolous . . . learning in a woman is like a Sunnediall in a grave' (p. 128)—a view shared, not untypically, by Elizabeth Joceline, who urged her husband that, if her child were a girl, 'I desire that her bringing up may be learning the Bible, as my sisters doe, good housewifery, writing and good works; other learning a woman needs not'.[32]

With such viewpoints as commonplace as those which expressed the 'gallant' attitude to 'the fair sex', and which in their turn often degenerated into the stock question 'Pray, what need of metaphysics to make a pudding?', it is not surprising that at the end of the century Defoe still felt it necessary to proclaim that he 'wou'd have men take women for companions and educate them to be fit for it'.[33] Almost always the appeal was to man's sense of duty; only rarely did women's sense of injustice form the basis of an argument for the education of girls and women. It was not until the nineteenth century, in fact, that a kind of political arithmetic—Dicey's notion of women being 'half the nation'—brought the discussion into the arena of equality between the sexes.

(iii) At university. Following on from the grammar schools the main agencies for the education of the few were the two universities, and for these the basic questions remain the same: who attended and in what numbers? what did they study and with what end in view? what changes (if any) were discernible as the century progressed?

Starting with provision, the first thing to notice is that between the foundation of Sidney Sussex College in 1596 and Downing College in 1800 no new colleges were founded at Cambridge in our period, with only two foundations at Oxford, Wadham in 1609 and Pembroke (and that by enlarging Broadgates Hall) in 1624. This does not mean, of course, that the situation was static, since, in the early part of the century at least, the number of undergraduates admitted (as well as the number of those graduating, though the two were by no means the same) rose considerably, carrying forward a trend already noticeable at the end of the sixteenth century. Cambridge, for example, had about 3,000 students in the 1620s with admissions round the 300 mark, and at Oxford the numbers were only slightly lower. But these were peak years, Cambridge in the 1610s and 1620s, Oxford in the 1620s and 1630s. The Civil War inevitably played havoc with admissions and graduations, but numbers did not fully recover even after the Restoration, with a decline more marked in Cambridge, where numbers were less than half those of the earlier years of the century.[34]

One important change did take place, and this was the marked increase in the number of sons of wealthier parents who were arriving at university in Elizabeth's reign and just after. It has been claimed that not only did they become 'the dominant element in the student body' but that they did so at the expense of the traditional 'poor scholars'.[35] The debate about the social class distribution of these students has in a sense gone the way of the debate about the rise of the gentry, which in its early stages was so obsessed with establishing a rise and indicating its causes and effects that little attention was paid to defining 'the gentry', who turned out to be a much less homogeneous group than earlier protagonists had cared to admit.

The same has been true of the debate about the influx of the sons of the gentry into the universities. Sir John Neale[36] and Mark Curtis were so busy counting heads that other variables tended to be ignored. Joan Simon, for example, has shown that the percentage of gentlemen's sons entering university in fact remained stable during the period of expansion and that it was the sons of the urban mercantile professional middle class who increased their numbers at the expense of that mixed bag of students labelled in the admissions registers as *mediocris fortunae* or *filii plebei*. David Cressy has further shown that whilst the proportion of gentlemen's sons entering in the late sixteenth and early seventeenth centuries was relatively stable—about one third—in the period of greatest student expansion it was actually declining.[37] Much care has to be taken in using the sources available—the registers (matriculation and college) are imperfect on several counts and the literary evidence derives too often from those with axes to grind. In addition the vagueness of the social categories is compounded by the willingness of some parents to claim a status higher than would otherwise have been accorded them, and at the same time to pay the higher fees required from the higher social level.

A further aspect of the debate arising from the general increase in student numbers is the claim that, since the increase outpaced the number of occupational positions available to graduates, it produced a group of 'alienated intellectuals' who were not only superfluous to requirements but, being educated as they were for office, saw more clearly than most the venality of the early Stuart court, administration and Church, and were thus a prime cause of the Civil War.[38] These students were, of course, the products of the grammar schools, whose allegedly subversive influence we have already referred to. The major difficulty arises from the fact that we cannot support or deny the critical comments to be found in the literary evidence by reference to a satisfactory quantitative analysis of university graduates. We simply do not know the religious and political affiliation of those emerging from the universities (with or without degrees) in any particular decade during the period prior to the Civil War. More important, it would be extremely difficult to determine how far the universities were responsible for such affiliations. For example, how many disaffected graduates were sons of disaffected non-graduate fathers? There were of course 'Puritan' colleges, and Hobbes's membership of Magdalen Hall, that 'nest of Puritans', may perhaps have contributed to the formation of his views. But such colleges were in a minority, and in the half-century prior to the outbreak of war it could well be argued that royal and archiepiscopal control, through the revision of statutes and the appointment of masters and fellows, increased rather than decreased. The role of the universities in producing supporters or opponents of the King has, therefore, to remain an open question.

Though the steady increase in the founding of colleges in the sixteenth century was halted in the seventeenth, there is nevertheless plenty of evidence to show an expansion by the supplementation of existing provision. The most obviously apparent form of this supplementation is to be seen in the new building undertaken at both college and university level, and this was particularly so after the Restoration with the work of Christopher Wren at Cambridge—his chapels at Pembroke and Emmanuel, his library on the south side of Trinity's Nevile's Court (with woodwork by Grinling Gibbons)—as well as his work at Oxford, where the Sheldonian Theatre was built to house the public ceremonies of the university, hitherto held in St Mary's Church. The Old Ashmolean Museum, no longer attributed to Wren, was also a product of this period, with the Clarendon Building and the Randolph Camera being completed early in the new century, the former the work of Nicholas Hawksmoor.[39]

Not all new building, however, was on this impressive scale. More modest were the buildings initiated by William Laud, former President of St John's, in the college's Canterbury Quadrangle, and the extension of the west end of Bodley's Library in 1638–40, in which Laud was also involved. Some was even the result of initiative by college servants, as when in 1597 Thomas Bentley, the butler of Exeter College, Oxford, built a two-storey wooden structure over the fourteenth-century library to provide extra rooms for students, whose rents he was allowed to retain; and when Thomas Clarke, senior cook of St John's, Oxford, built a new kitchen with chambers above for four students in return for their rents for twenty years. Even so, with the peak of expansion of student numbers in the early part of the century overcrowding in the students' accommodation was the order of the day. At Sidney Sussex, Oxford, for example, in 1623, 130 students shared thirty-five rooms, and the effects of the recurring outbreaks of plague was the more noticeable as a result.[40]

In a less dramatic way than through fine new buildings in the wealthier colleges, individual benefactors continued to improve provision, by supplementing fellows' income and by endowing scholarships for boys from their own region or even their own school. Robert Lewis, for example, Puritan master of Colchester Grammar School and formerly fellow of St John's, left money in 1620 to found scholarships at his old college for boys from his own school. The same college benefited from one of its former students, Sir William Paddy, physician, of London, whose will of 1635 provided for the salary of the college organist and endowed the choral service. Samuel Ratcliffe, vicar of Steeple Aston in Oxfordshire and late Principal of Brasenose, having endowed a school in his parish in 1640, added land to provide scholarships for two boys at his old college. In 1654 John Goodridge, one of Wadham's original fellows, bequeathed his land in Walthamstow to provide seven exhibitions of £9 per annum each.[41]

Individual students were also maintained at university through personal patronage, as was the case with Timothy Rogers, who recorded his indebtedness to Lady Anne Bromley of Holt in Worcestershire, 'a bountiful friend unto me in the time of my minority and all the while I was at university many years together'.[42] Nor was this kind of provision simply a matter of private benefaction. At the beginning of the century the Common Council of Newcastle upon Tyne started to provide scholarships of £5 apiece for five freeman's sons on leaving the Royal Grammar School of the town, for periods of five to seven years each. Later in the century, in 1676, the governors of the King Edward VI Grammar School in Birmingham set aside £70 for two scholarships and two fellowships at St Catharine's Hall, Cambridge.[43] In these various ways, then (and the examples could be multiplied many times over), both the university and the colleges were able to supplement their existing provision.

The Civil War, of course, profoundly affected both universities, and neither was able to retreat into isolation in the face of it. After Edgehill the city of Oxford was occupied by the King and became his headquarters, until it was beseiged and taken by the Parliamentarians in 1646. Guns were lodged at Magdalen, powder and muskets at New College, food supplies at Brasenose. Cambridge, in the centre of radical Puritan country, became an important base for the Parliamentary army, contributing its plate to the Cromwellian cause and its students to the army. When Matthew Robinson entered St John's College 'in the very heat of the wars on May 10th 1644 . . . There was but nine admitted of that great college that year. And when I commenced Master of Arts (1652) of that year there was but three commencers in our college'. Not surprisingly the University petitioned Parliament for help—'our schools daily grow desolate . . . our members grow thin and our revenue short'—though with little tangible result.[44]

It was during the Civil War and Interregnum, too, that the universities were subjected to the most sustained criticism they had ever faced. Most Puritans were critical of the two universities, seeing them not only as centres of privilege which perpetuated unacceptable social divisions, both through their traditional ritual and (it was claimed) their outmoded scholastic curriculum,[45] but also as monopolistic producers of the nation's clergy. Some acknowledged the importance of the universities if only they could be reformed. Milton argued in *Of Education* that they had 'not yet well recovered from the scholastick grossness of barbarous ages'. He criticised them for introducing 'their young unmatriculated novices at first coming with the most intellective abstractions of logic and metaphysic' and was convinced that university theology served only to 'perplex and leaven pure doctrine with scholastical trash than enable any minister to the better preaching of a ministry'. John Hall in his *Advancement and Learning and Reformation of the Universities* (1649), John Webster in *Academarium Examen* (1642), William Dell in *Right Reformation of Learning, Schools and Universities* (1646), and many others, called not only for the abandonment of the 'peripatetick philosophy', but for its replacement by a curriculum which was (in Dell's words) 'politick, useful and profitable, enabling all kinds of undertakings both civil and military', and available 'in every great town in the nation'. In this way the old traditional forms and privileges would be abolished, more students would be able to attend and receive a more 'useful' education.[46] Some might even be able (as in one proposal) to split their time between studying and working 'at some lawful calling', and the new institutions would be able to produce a 'reformed' clergy drawn from a wider range of social class. Milton himself proposed, in *Of Education*, the founding of academies which would be 'at once both school and university . . . in every city throughout this land', thus anticipating the Dissenting Academies of the Restoration period. Petitions were received by the Long Parliament for the setting up of universities at Manchester and at York, and many other cities, including London, were nominated. Only one such rival to Oxford and Cambridge, however, came to fruition, at Durham, though despite the support of Cromwell himself it came too late to survive the Restoration when, opposed by Oxford and Cambridge from the start, it finally failed.[47]

Criticism of the monopoly of Oxford and Cambridge and of their curricula did, however, have one positive outcome of rather longer standing than the attempt at Durham. This was the founding in 1598 of Gresham College in London, with provision (by the will of Sir Thomas Gresham) for chairs in law, rhetoric, divinity, music, medicine, geometry and astronomy. Its early professors in the sciences and their applications (an innovatory emphasis) were a distinguished group. Henry Briggs, Professor of Geometry, popularised Napier's logarithms, recalculating them to the more convenient base 10 to produce our common logarithms. Henry Gellibrand, his successor, successfully solved the problem of the secular variation of the compass, which had been puzzling scientifically-minded mariners for a generation, in his *Discourse Mathematicall on the Variation of the Magneticall Needle* (1635). Edmund Gunter, Professor of Astronomy, also worked to provide a sound mathematical base to the problems of navigation, whilst John Mapletoft, the Professor of Medicine, popularised the work of William Harvey. However, though the college continued in existence it lost its momentum as the group centring on John Wilkins of Wadham College, Oxford, during the Commonwealth formed their 'experimentall philosophicall clubbe', before themselves being overtaken by the Restoration when scientific interest shifted back to London with the foundation of the Royal Society.[48]

(iv) The professions. Whatever debates took place about the curriculum of the universities, there was, nevertheless, no doubt in the minds of contemporaries about their main purpose—the influx of the sons of the gentry and the reservations of the sectaries notwithstanding—and that was the production of the future clergy of the country. All save the sectaries were agreed about the need for both scholar theologians and educated parish priests. Whitgift had needed no urging in the matter, though the criticisms of the 'puritans' of his day had contributed to the transformation of the clerical profession from one in which, at the beginning of the sixteenth century, only a minority were university graduates to one in which, at its end, a majority (and in certain favoured dioceses an overwhelming majority) were so qualified. Elizabeth I had seen dangers in such a trend; she perceived an overriding need for uniformity and conformity, as her opposition to and later prohibition of 'prophesyings' (clerical 'workshops' at which small groups of clerics were instructed in the Scriptures and their interpretation) was to show. But even in

Elizabeth's day Henry Barrow, Robert Browne and their radical followers were pressing the point which became a major feature of the Leveller critique. 'Human learning', it was claimed, was unnecessary in a priest, who needed only divine grace and the Inner Light to validate his ministry. The ritual and privileges of university education irreparably separated him from his flock and perpetuated social divisions which the sectaries were striving to remove.[49] Nevertheless, important as the learned ministry debate was for the larger issue of the role and function of the universities, Brownists and Levellers alike were a minority even amongst Puritans, the majority of whom, from Cromwell and Milton (in their respective spheres) downwards, saw the problem as one which needed reformed universities rather than (to use the pejorative term of the day) 'mechanick' preachers.

In the matter of their education and how it was to be achieved the clergy were a relatively homogeneous profession. The same could hardly be said of the other professions—and certainly not of the two other 'traditional' professions, the lawyers and doctors. Among the lawyers, the practice of the canon law of the Church Universal had ceased with the Henrician Reformation, along with its study at university. The ecclesiastical law as practised in the metropolitan and diocesan courts of the reformed Church continued to be part of divinity studies in the universities. A few 'Civilians', those who practised civil (or Roman) law at the Courts of Admiralty, Requests, Star Chamber, etc., also continued to study in and graduate from the universities.[50] But those who practised the common law in the royal courts of justice received their professional training not at university but in the Inns of Court. There, since the fifteenth century, a professional preparation was provided for barristers and attornies (though the latter had gradually been confined to the Inns of Chancery). But as a system of professional education both institutions had progressively declined until in the seventeenth century they were little more than centres of social education for the wealthy, despite a nearly fivefold increase in membership between 1540 and 1610. Much more socially exclusive even than the universities, they were, not surprisingly, subjected to severe criticism from the sectaries.[51]

The same kind of distinctions have to be made about the medical profession. For long a closely restricted group of physicians had received a bookish and outmoded education at the universities, some few going for further study at Continental universities such as Leiden and Padua. Their more lowly brethren, the barber-surgeons, had formed their own Company in 1540, and through apprenticeship, supplemented for those in London by regular Tuesday lectures in Barber-Surgeons Hall, had sought to marry theory and practice by reference to the most modern and up-to-date practice as laid down by such as John Bannister. In this way, they claimed with some justification, an increasingly sophisticated knowledge of the treatment of gunshot wounds could be utilised in the cause of general surgery. But the man who practised medicine in the way a modern general practitioner does was the apothecary, who sought profes- sional status by separating from his erstwhile colleagues the Grocers to form the Society of Apothecaries in 1607. Despite a constant battle with the College of

Physicians, the apothecaries gradually improved their efficiency (and status) by an increasing knowledge of both organic and inorganic compounds, and like the surgeons used apprenticeship and the oversight of their Society to maintain standards.[52] Their chief spokesman was Nicholas Culpepper, who translated the *Pharmacopoeia Londiniensis* into English in 1649 in an attempt to make medicine more widely available. 'To my knowledge', he said in his *Physicall Directory* (1650), 'many people have perished either for want of money to fee a physician or want of knowledge of a remedy happily growing in their own garden' (p. 242). It was, however, precisely the unqualified physicians whom Christopher Goodall attacked in his history of the Royal College of Physicians (1684), in much the same way as clerics attacked 'mechanick' preachers, or lawyers attacked radicals such as George Fox, who had urged that the law should be 'drawn up in a little short volumn, and all the rest burnt'.[53]

Those who saw the professions and their learning as socially divisive offered an unrealistic alternative—the 'empirick'. Those who reasonably resisted such arguments could hardly defend the monopolistic nature of the arrangements they were defending. The Presbyterian who advocated his particular brand of a 'learned ministry', and the apothecary who systematised the more traditional organic remedies and embraced the new chemo-therapy of the Paracelsans (§ S–561), could well stand exemplar for the new set of 'professional' attitudes—skill based on learning and an awareness of social need—which can be seen developing, though not without opposition (or apathy), in the seventeenth century. As Culpepper put it, 'My intent . . . is not to make fooles physitians, but to help those that are ingenious, rational and industrious.' But the 'barefoot doctors' and 'worker priests' of the late twentieth century (to say nothing of that latter-day sectary, Ivan Illich) remind us that the debate about the learned professions is by no means concluded.[54]

(v) The gentry. The criticism of the universities, then, not only came from a particular section of the community but was vehemently denied by others whose advocacy cannot be dismissed as wholly a matter of vested self-interest. Whatever judgements are made about the education of the professions, we are still left with the problem of assessing the general educational level of the gentry. Gilbert Burnet, towards the end of the century, was unequivocal in his judgement that they were 'for the most part the worst instructed and the least knowing of their rank I ever went amongst'.[55] The accuracy of the judgement, however, may be doubted. William Lambarde's estimate for the gentry of Kent in the 1570s that 'these gentlemen be also (for the most part) acquainted with good letters'[56] may be generalised to apply to at least some other counties of seventeenth-century England. Sir Thomas Knyvett of Ashwellthorpe, Norfolk, for example, having received a 'schooling' at the hands of his grandmother and a neighbouring clergyman and then gone on to Cambridge, left a library of books and manuscripts valued at £700, which included works on theology, philosophy, medicine, history, mathematics, Greek and Arabic science, Greek and Latin classical literature and law, as well as books by Chaucer, Spenser,

Heywood and Lydgate. Justinian Isham and his son Thomas, of Lamport Hall in Northamptonshire, left similar evidence, as did the Surrey royalist MP, Sir Thomas Bludder.[57]

Moreover, the by now traditional practice of some upper-class fathers of sending their sons for a period of travel on the Continent further contributed to the educational level of the gentry. At the beginning of the century the main motive and objective was that expressed by Sir Thomas Bodley, later benefactor of the university library at Oxford:

> to travell beyond the seas for attaining to the knowledge of some speciall moderne tongues, and for the encrease of any experience in the managing of affaires, being wholly then addicted to employing my selfe and all my cares in the publique service of the State.[58]

Bodley was then aged thirty-two, though others were sent much earlier than this. Sir Thomas Browne's son, Thomas, was fourteen when he went to France, and Robert Boyle was the same age when he went with his tutor to Rome in 1641. Many considered this to be far too young, Milton, for example, objecting in *Of Education* that it merely transformed youth 'into mimics, apes and kickshaws', a view shared by Gilbert Burnet, who thought that such a traveller should be 'a person of mature spirit and ripe judgment, who is well-confirmed in his religion and hath a true sense of piety and virtue and is not of a light or gadding mind.'[59] For some, of course, this was the overriding objection which invalidated all notion of travel abroad as a part of a young man's education.

The evidence for this informal aspect of a gentleman's education is fortunately varied, ranging from the *Advice to a Son* to the prescriptive manuals written by travelling tutors such as James Howell, Richard Lassels, John Gailhard and many others, and the autobiographical letters and reports of the young men themselves. The particular and varied interests of individual parents and sons, of course, preclude too firm a generalisation, but nevertheless a shift of emphasis in the purpose for which such travels were undertaken may be detected, away from the mainly political at the beginning of the century towards the scientific and aesthetic at the end. For the fully fledged and highly organised Grand Tour we have, of course, to wait until the eighteenth century, when the historical and aesthetic predominated.

THE EDUCATION OF THE MANY

When we come to consider the education of 'the many' we enter a quite different arena which, though sharing a common end—'to repair the ruins of our first parents by regaining to know God aright'[60]—utilised quite different methods, since it was subject to a different set of constraints.

It was generally recognised as desirable that each person should be able to read the Bible and, as part of his 'Godly calling', to contribute to the economy through work. Most of those who contributed to the educational debate were realistic enough to see, however, that sufficient resources were not available to meet the requirement. Emphasis was therefore laid on the need for a more efficient (by which was meant a more closely controlled) use of oral methods of education within both the family and the congregation. Again the aim was identical, a religious education which was at the same time political. However, social mobility through education of a traditional kind and in traditional institutions, though considered an acceptable consequence for a few, rarely figured as an explicit aim for the many. Those who put their minds and their pens to the education of the many faced a real dilemma: how, whilst expanding 'the political nation' and particularly a 'priesthood of all believers', could they avoid the obviously consequent dangers of independence of mind on the part, say, of craftsmen, artisans and yeoman farmers for whom political and religious issues were no longer expressly a matter for their 'betters'.[61] With an increasing number of contested elections, for example, and with continued debate about the nature of the electorate, candidates recognised that perhaps they would do better to rely rather more on persuasion (even if this meant cajoling) than on browbeating with threats of economic sanctions.

The publication of political pamphlets (to say nothing of news-sheets and ballads), ostensibly for sale but often distributed free of charge, increased markedly during the century, as did the means of distributing them over large areas by the development of the cross-posts and stage-coaches. They were directed, too, towards a county electorate increased in number through inflation, and to a borough electorate increased through the creation of new boroughs and the revival of hitherto obsolete categories of voters. By the end of the century general elections occurred much more frequently and contested elections were commonplace, but even so we are still talking about a small minority, not much more (it has been estimated) than fifteen per cent of the adult male population. When the suffrage was considered during the Putney Debates, not even the Levellers argued for universal suffrage, even for men, excluding servants, labourers and beggars (about one third of the total population) on the grounds that their economic dependence precluded political independence.[62]

Nevertheless, the notion of 'authority freely consented to' had serious implications for the education of the masses and could not be ignored. Milton himself shared in the dilemma which faced all concerned with the matter. In *Areopagitica* (1644) he urged Parliament to

> consider what Nation it is whereof ye are, and whereof ye are governors: a Nation not slow and dull, but of a quick, ingenious, and piercing spirit, acute to invent, suttle and sinewy in discours, not beneath the reach of any point the highest that human capacity can soar to.　　　　　(CE, IV, 339)

He insisted that licensing the press was as much a 'reproach' to the common people as it was to the clergy and universities,

> for if we be so jealous over them, as that we dare not trust them with an English

pamphlet, what doe we but censure them for a giddy, vitious, and ungrounded people; in such a sick and weak estate of faith and discretion, as to be able to take nothing down but through the pipe of a licencer. (CE, IV, 328)

In a nice pedagogical metaphor, he asked

What advantage is it to be a man over it is to be a boy at school, if we have only scapt the ferular [cane], to come under the fescu [twig = pointer in classroom] of an *Imprimatur*? if serious and elaborat writings, as if they were no more than the theam of a Grammar lad under his Pedagogue must not be utter'd without the cursory eye of a temporizing and extemporizing licencer. (CE, IV, 324)

In *Areopagitica*—itself unlicensed, but boldly carrying Milton's name, though not those of printer or bookseller—he is willing to accept that 'books are not absolute dead things, but do contain a potencie of life in them to be as active as that soule was whose progeny they are'. Yet what he says there about 'the capacity of the plain artisan' and 'the common people' is not echoed in his other works. In *Of Education* (written in the same year) he was, of course, concerned only with the education on traditional humanist lines of the very few, but he had little respect for majority decisions, 'there being in numbers but little virtue', and he was not alone in being apprehensive of 'the inconstant, irrational and image-doting rabble' (§S–162: pp. 268 ff.)

All this, however, was debate and prescription. The question has also to be asked, how far were the prescriptions implemented? By what methods? And with what success? In the first place we must note an expansion of what was later to be called an elementary education in the three Rs, and especially of reading and writing. This expanded in two ways. First of all the masters of endowed grammar schools, increasingly required by their trustees to provide the 'elements' of English as well as of Latin, often responded to parental demand by offering (for a lower fee) the teaching of English at an elementary level. In addition, however, a relatively new type of institution was appearing in the seventeenth century, the endowed elementary school for the children of the poor. Occasionally such schools were generously endowed. In 1646, for example, Richard Aldworth left £4,000 to purchase lands whose revenues were to provide a boarding education of this kind for twenty boys, with a further thirty non-boarders also provided for. The Civil War delayed the purchase of the land until 1660, but eventually the Reading Bluecoat School came into existence.[63] More often, however, the endowment of these elementary schools was much less generous, on the grounds that the teacher required a smaller stipend and the pupils less lavish surroundings. Of the £500 left by Simon, Lord Digby, in 1694, for 'good pious and charitable uses', the princely sum of £4 was allocated for the teaching of the daughters of the poor in Coleshill, Warwickshire, to read, spin, knit and sew, a similar sum being allocated to teach boys to 'write and cast accounts' so as to qualify them to become bailiffs, or gentlemen's servants, or 'some honest trade'.[64]

The difficulties of quantifying the education of the few in grammar schools seem paltry compared with those relating to elementary education. None of the latter kept admission registers, and, lacking the status attached to grammar schools and less securely endowed, their survival was more hazardous. But we have the evidence of their endowment, and many of them survived to be recorded in the surveys initiated by Lord Brougham in the early nineteenth century. As always, the main emphasis was on the religious and moral education of the children through the Bible and the catechism. Much less attention was paid to arithmetic—'the casting of accounts' by the use of bone or metal counters on a counting board. 'Cyphering', or 'arithmetic by the pen', was, with writing, considered to be a skilled matter, best left to specialists in their private schools preparing boys for apprenticeship in merchants' counting houses, and using the texts of James Hodder, Noah Bridges and others.[65] George Robertson's *Learning's Foundation firmly laide in a short method of treating to read English more exact and easie than ever was yet published by anie* (1651) had a wider use in mind, and was but one of many following in the footsteps of Edmund Coote's *English Schoolemaster* (1596), which was continually reprinted throughout the seventeenth century, and was considered to be the English teacher's equivalent of Lily's Latin grammar.

Right at the end of the century a new dimension was added to the elementary school scene with the founding in 1698 of the Society for the Propagation of Christian Knowledge, an expressly Anglican body designed to promote the founding of elementary schools which would act as 'little garrisons against Popery', and would be supported not by the endowment of an individual but by the subscriptions and donations of groups of individuals in particular localities. Thus a new method of funding elementary education in what came to be known as charity schools, 'in correspondence' with the parent body in London, came into being. Whether there was a 'Charity School Movement' is very much a matter of definition, both of 'movement' and of 'charity school', for though the latter term has been identified with the so-called SPCK schools, there were plenty of others which had their origins in the charitable wishes of pious philanthropists who had no connection with the Society.[66] More important, however, the schools associated with the SPCK abandoned the relative optimism about the education of the masses which was to be found in much of the writing of the 'Puritan reformers' for a relative pessimism which saw a prime need to control the masses, who were, by the end of the century, increasingly regarded as a potential 'mob' whose passions could be swayed by those intent on sedition.

The terms 'literate' and 'literacy' have so far been studiously avoided, but the question has obviously to be posed: how far did this provision of elementary schooling improve the levels of literacy in seventeenth-century England?[67] A good deal of energy has been devoted to the calculation of the levels of literacy or illiteracy in different social classes and in different parts of the country. Much of it has been based on the evidence of signatures in a variety of official records, where the ability to sign one's name has been taken as an index of literacy. Whether such a criterion can be used as an adequate index of functional literacy, the ability to write a document or a letter, is doubtful. More important, it relates only to one aspect of literacy, the ability to write (at least one's name), and ignores the other and infinitely more important aspect, especially to the people of the seventeenth century, the ability to read (at least one's Bible). In the seventeenth century the ability of applicants for marriage licences to sign their allegation bonds provides a continuously uniform record over a period of years, as do signed depositions to ecclesiastical courts, and may be supplemented by the occasional evidence of documents such as the Protestation Returns and Hearth Tax lists. Yet they tell us only that, on one particular occasion in their lives, the individuals concerned signed their names. Whether they could 'write' in the modern usage of that term, or even 'write with a good fist' we do not know. It may be reasonable to claim, on the other hand, that there was no incentive to learn to write one's name without also being able to write other things. It may also be claimed that, since reading was usually taught before writing, estimates of literacy based on writing will be underestimates of ability to read. By the same token this estimate would also be reinforced by arguing that some who could not write might nevertheless be able to read.

Queen Elizabeth had already assumed a reasonable level of reading ability when she enjoined each parish priest to provide an English Bible and the *Paraphrases* of Erasmus in English in a place where 'their parishioners may most commodiously resort unto the same'. Moreover, she had ordered that they should 'discourage no man from reading any part of the Bible either in Latin or English, but rather shall exhort every person to read the same with great humility and reverence, as the very lively word of God and the special food of man's soul'.[68] Even so, a hundred years later it was still part of John Dury's *plan*, in *The Advancement of Learning* (1653), that 'every one should be able to read distinctly and write truly and legibly in his mother tongue', and that this would not be achieved until and unless 'there should be common schools throughout all the parts of the nation' (pp. 10, 13). For all the enjoinders and prescriptions, and despite the relative increase in provision of elementary schooling, we have always to bear in mind their relative inefficiency in achieving even the limited end looked for by Dury.

Any discussion of the education of the many must, of course, include the education of women and girls, and in debates and controversies about this in the seventeenth century, though essentially about the same problem—the place of women in society and their preparation for such a place—we have to distinguish a quite different line of thought from that which provided the main thrust of calls for the education of girls and women of the upper and middle class. Whereas ideas for the education of the latter came from Renaissance humanism, justifications for the education of the mass of females came from the Protestant Reformation, which took the idea of a participatory flock to its logical conclusion to include girls and women of all classes. Not all Protestant denominations took the prescription that far, of course, since—if it suited their purposes—some members could take the (allegedly) 'Pauline' view of women and their place in society to prescribe a relatively restricted role and therefore a relatively restricted education.

As always, by far the largest proportion of literature about the role, status and education of girls and women was written by men, and it is their claims or strictures which provide the bulk of the evidence. Because it was infinitely smaller in quantity the evidence from women's writing has to be used with even greater caution, since it was less likely to be representative even of female aspirations. An additional aspect of the matter derives from the emphasis on a 'godly household', and the role of the wife and mother therein. Contemporary views about the nature of marriage and its purposes, and the relative importance and standing of the wife in the marriage relationship, are clearly crucial in determining to what degree a wife and mother should be educated, and what kind of education would best prepare her for whatever duties and responsibilities were assigned to her. In the end, however, and despite the views of the radical wing of the Puritan movement (who echoed those of the fifteenth century in these matters), it was a wife's duties rather than her responsibilities that were emphasised, and particularly her duty to accept a position subservient to that of her husband.

But in this, as always in matters relating to the education of a hitherto uneducated group, the husband faced a real dilemma. Francis Cheynell was not unusual in reminding a husband, 'Do not forget your beloved wife . . . she will never be at your command unlesse you teach her to be at Christ's command.'[69] The difficulty arose when a wife decided that what appeared to her to be Christ's command did not coincide with that of her husband. Then, as Thomas Edwards feared—and again he was not alone—'If toleration be granted they should never have peace in their families more, or ever have command of their wives, children and servants'.[70] Ralph Verney may have been a Cavalier, but many Puritan fathers would have agreed with him when he advised his god-daughter, 'beleeve me, a Bible . . . and a good plaine cattichisme in your Mother Tongue, being well read and practised, is well worth all the rest and much more sutable to your sex';[71] and in the end a majority of husbands, Diggers, Ranters and their kind apart, would have subscribed to the view of the Elizabethan Homily 'Of the State of Matrimony' that, though the husband should 'give honour to the wife', it should be 'as to the weaker vessel . . . for the woman is a weak creature not endued with like strength and constancy of mind; therefore they be the more prone to all weak affections and dispositions of the mind, more than men be; and lighter they be and more vain in their phantasies and opinions' (§P–342).

Milton himself shared the dilemma. Though his daughters were able to read to him during his blindness in both classical and modern languages, *Of Education* makes no mention whatsoever of the education of girls. His divorce tracts, however, make plain his views about the status and rights of all women, and it would be unthinkable that he was attributing such a position to an uneducated woman.[72] The precise degree of mutuality and assent attributed to the marriage bond—whether in Milton or in most other writers on the topic—is debatable. What is inescapable is the need (acknowledged by Anglican and Puritan alike) for a wife sufficiently educated to be both a companion to her husband and an active partner in the religious and social education of their children.

That a few such women achieved not only the education but also the status claimed for them or by them is clearly evident. Some women not only took it upon themselves to preach (the ultimate claim in many eyes), but were permitted to do so among many Independent congregations both in London and in the country at large.[73] For the Quakers the Inner Light knew no sex barriers, and the setting up of the Women's Fortnightly Meetings gave them a formal share in church government.[74] Women writers on religious matters such as Catherine Chidley, Mary Cary and Lady Eleanor Davies were obviously 'educated' in the traditional sense of the term. But we do well to remember that it was the sound of 'three or four women sitting at a door in the sun and talking about the things of God' which set John Bunyan on the path to piety, and it is hardly likely that the scene he described in *Grace Abounding* was unusual. Right at the end of the century Thomas Tryon commented on the importance of the mother's role in the first seven years of a child's upbringing, and claimed therefore 'that the females ought to have the principal and best education, they being the first planters or tutors, having the children always with them when they will imitate and observe'.[75] However, such a view of women as self-directing individuals, who were not only aware of their responsibilities but educated to carry them out, exemplifies aspiration rather than practice.

Local studies for both the beginning and the end of the century nevertheless show that an increasing number of elementary schools were being founded to teach the poor to read and write, and it would not be unreasonable to assume that girls as well as boys attended such schools, since some provided for both sexes and others were explicitly endowed for 'teaching and instructing the daughters of the poor inhabitants to read, spin, sew, knit and acquire any other skills useful for getting an honest living'.[76] Thomas Offley, merchant, of London, provided in his will of 1645 for both a boys' and a girls' school in his native village of Madeley in Staffordshire, though delays in proving the will, as a result of the war, meant that they were not built until after the Restoration. Sir Francis Nethersole's foundation of 1655 at Polesworth, Warwickshire, provided for one school but separate classes for boys and girls, with a master and a mistress for each, the latter to teach the girls to 'read, write, work the needle, and principles of Christian religion'.[77] Such schools were by no means widespread, though there is increasing evidence of their existence. Again, they catered for a relatively small number of girls, and it was not until the Charity Schools of the eighteenth century, and the later Sunday schools and schools of the voluntary societies (Anglican and Nonconformist) that girls in any number began to receive an elementary education.

When we consider, then, either a notion or an index of reading literacy, or indeed writing literacy, and the part played by both grammar and elementary schools in contributing to this, we are still referring to a relative minority of the population. If such schooling had been a necessary prerequisite for achieving a 'priesthood of all believers', for achieving the kind of religious education implicit in that aspiration, then failure would have been inevitable, for the majority of the population and the majority of any congregation would have been unable to read.

Fortunately those concerned with the religious education of the masses clearly recognised the constraints within which they were working. They were only too well aware, for example, that even the purchase of books did not inevitably result in their being read. As Daniel Rogers put it, 'it may be once a quarter if they hit upon a new booke, read a few pages and cast it away, and so it lies upon the cupbord ouergrowne with cobwebs'.[78] Nor, indeed, is this surprising, for there was little in the didactic literature that, at one and the same time, was written expressly for the lower levels of reading literacy, whether in children or in adults, and would in content, style and brevity appeal to its ostensible readership. The two books which John Bunyan's wife brought with her on marriage, Arthur Dent's *Plain Man's Pathway to Heaven* (1601) and Lewis Bayly's *Practice of Pietie* (1612), each many times reprinted, were nevertheless over 400 and 500 pages in length respectively, and when Dent came to write his *Pastime for Parents* (1606), intended, as he said, to be 'a recreation to pass away the time' with children, he included passages such as this:

> Father: How then doe you conceiue the Essence and Being of the Godhead?
> Child: That the Substance or Essence of the Deitie is of all things most simple and single, and is neither divided, multiplyed nor compact of any elementarie qualitie
> Father: Expresse your minde more fully
> Child: This I meane, that the divine nature is one, simple, uniforme, immateriall, impassible, immutable, illocall, eternall, omnipotent, omniscient, infinite, void of al mixture . . .   (sig. A2v)

Thomas Hooker was perhaps more realistic when he acknowledged in his *The Unbeliever's Preparing for Christ* (1638) that 'for a child to consider of the mysteries of life and salvation is almost impossible; he is not yet come to that ripenesse of judgement' (p. 199). The Presbyterian minister Henry Newcome was unusual in voicing his thoughts in his diary, but most parents would have echoed the note of exasperation and resignation in the entry, 'What a deale of patience is requisite to beare any converse with our little children. How foolish and peevish are they.'[79] There was, in fact, very little to match, say, the Cheap Repository Tracts, produced by Hannah More at the end of the eighteenth century for just such a readership and showing a clear awareness that she was competing for the attention of her readers with the chapbooks of the day. In the seventeenth century almanacs, ballads and news-sheets competed on very favourable terms for the attention of readers at this level. Criticism and exhortation seemed to have little effect if the continual need for such is anything to go by, and John Bunyan vividly recounts how such reading diverted him from the Bible in his youth.[80] His own *Book for Boys and Girls* was an honest attempt, but lacked the immediacy of the books of Thomas Newbery, which appeared fifty years later.

There is, however, another aspect to be considered, namely the recognition by many who were concerned with the religious education of the masses that oral education could be realistically effective in achieving their limited purposes. In his *Practice of Christianitie* (1603) Richard Rogers, Puritan lecturer and school-master at Wethersfield in Essex, asked the rhetorical question 'who shall read?' and had the remedy for those who could not: 'let them use the more diligence in praying, hearing the word preached and godly books read by others' (p. 598). Comenius was merely repeating what was regarded as a truism when he claimed that 'the learned seldome excell those who are illiterate in the study of Vertue' (p. 8). As the Puritan reformers never ceased to remind their hearers, there was no shortage of oral means which might aid the achieving of universal grace and which could be used both in the home and in the chapel: the use of the catechism, the reading aloud of godly books, the psalter and the Bible, and the sermon.

It was the sermon, however, which was to provide the chief means. For the Puritans an 'unlearned' priest was above all one who could not *preach*, and the pulpit was *par excellence* the place from which to propound the word of the Lord to literate and illiterate alike. It was not for nothing that Elizabeth, on her accession, had thought it wise to issue a proclamation forbidding all preaching 'until consultation may be had by parliament', and that subsequently she attempted to control her clergy by the issue of licences to preach and by insisting on the reading of the Homilies by those not licensed. It was from the pulpit rather than the university divinity schools that authoritative statements should come. The highest praise was reserved for preachers such as William Perkins, who 'brought the schools to the pulpit and, marshalling their controversies out of their hard school-terms, made thereof plain and wholesome meat for his people'. The cultivation of 'the plain style' was thus entirely functional for the Puritan who disdained the academic and rhetorical style of the typical Anglican sermon (§S–217: Ch. II).

For the more orthodox Anglican, however, the dangers of such use of the pulpit loomed larger than the benefits. 'Gadding to sermons' was seen as an offence. James I complained of 'itching tongues' and banned the afternoon service and its sermon, which were becoming increasingly popular with Puritan congregations. Charles I was merely acknowledging what was usual when he remarked that 'people are governed by pulpits more than the sword in times of peace'.[81] No homilies were more popular with the hierarchy than those 'On Obedience' and 'Against Disobedience and Wilful Rebellion', and Winstanley was not alone in noticing how Anglican parsons 'most commonly in their sermons meddled with little but state matters'.[82]

An equally dangerous influence in the eyes of the establishment were the 'lecturers', nominees of laymen and corporations and therefore less subject to Church control than beneficed clergy (§S–324). Though relatively few in number, and lacking permanent tenure, they were nevertheless recognised (by Charles I) as 'the most furious promoters of the most dangerous innovations', and Laud quickly stifled a plan by a group of London merchants to establish such lectureships in their home counties.[83] Their weekday sermons tended to attract the better-educated Puritan, but through that audience their ideas, religious and political, filtered down to that other crucial educational agency, the household. The responsibility placed on heads of households had long been part of Protestant doctrine—from Luther's *Shorter Catechism* (1529) and the Genevan Bible's marginal gloss on Genesis 17:23, which insisted that 'Masters in their families ought to be as preachers to their families, that from the highest to the lowest they may obey the will of God'. The responsibility was recognised to be heavy and not without its difficulties:

> parents will doo them more harme at home then both pastor and schoolemaister can doo abroad . . . it is not inough to bring thy children to bee catechised at the church, but thou must labor with them at home after a more plaine and easie maner of instruction that so they may the better profit by the publike teaching.
> (§P–84: pp. 305 and 38)

Occasionally we get direct insights into this kind of familial education. Oliver Heywood, for example, recorded in his diary that 'my sons have been very towardly, plyed their books, read chapters, learned chatichismes, got some chapters and psalmes without book; John repeated the 12th, Eliezer the 10th of Revelation last night in bed, blessed be God'; and he recalled his own childhood, when his father

> associated himself with God's people, promoted days of fasting and of prayer, conference and other Christian exercises. In my childhood I am remembering many days of that nature and the Apparitor searching them out; and one appointed in the entry to deafen the noyse of such as were praying in the parlour.[84]

At another social level Samuel Fairclough, domestic chaplain to the Barnardiston family of Kedington in Suffolk, recollected the piety of Sir Nathaniel Barnardiston, who had

> at one time ten or more servants of that eminency for piety and sincerity that I never yet saw their like at one time . . . truely they made his house a spirituall church and temple wherein were dayly offered up the spirituall sacrifices of reading the Word, and prayer morning and evening, of singing psalmes constantly after evening meal, before any servant did rise from the table.[85]

Not all households reached that level of piety and practice, of course. Indeed, it was a perennial complaint of many schoolmasters that 'Now the parent doth just nothing, the master must do all, look to the child's book and manners both'.[86] Moreover, the emphasis was essentially a Puritan one. The established Church saw the enlargement of family groups for religious worship and mutual education as the setting up of 'conventicles', to be suppressed at the earliest opportunity. The clergy themselves saw heads of households as rivals, likely to swell the member of 'mechanick preachers', who would preach not only a variant 'Word of God' but an egalitarian approach to politics as well. Even so, though the limited 'priesthood of all believers' of the sixteenth century had been widened to allow for 'universal grace' in the seventeenth, the households referred to were substantial rather than poor, despite the aspirations of Richard Baxter and his like. Important as the 'spiritualisation of the household' was to become as an article of belief, it by no means affected every household in the country, and there was a mixed note of resignation and hope in Baxter's warning to ministers, 'you are like to see no general reformation till you procure family reformation'.[87]

Catechising, in both household and church, was of course one of the oldest forms of religious education for young and old alike—John Donne called it 'that primitive form of preaching'—and though Elizabeth had tried to control its use by prescribing an 'official' catechism (that of Alexander Nowell) in 1580, over one hundred unauthorised catechisms were printed during her reign alone.[88] Despite the requirement that Nowell's catechism be used for half an hour before evening prayer each Sunday, many parish priests and their curates used the alternative versions and were regularly hauled before the Consistory Court accused of 'teaching or suffering to be taught another catechism than that which is set down in the Book of Common Prayer'. Among the unauthorised catechisms were those written especially for the use of householders with their families, one of the earliest, Edward Dering's *Briefe and Necessarie Catechisme for all Householders* (1572), appearing regularly in reprints during the seventeenth century. But the need for uniformity was reaffirmed by the Westminster Assembly, which produced both a larger (forty-three pages) and a shorter (eighteen pages) catechism, the latter appearing subsequently in a variety of editions by John Walters (1662), John Alleine (1672), Thomas Lye (1674), John Flavell (1692) and finally by Isaac Watts (1731), all explicitly prepared for the use and help of 'masters of households'.

The importance attached to catechising as an essential part of the religious education of the masses is thus indicated both by the proliferation of different versions and by the attempt the authorities (of whatever religious persuasion) made to control the situation by prescribing an authorised version. It would be too simple a distinction to say that Puritans aimed through their religious education to help their members to a reasoned awareness of their faith, whilst Anglicans were happy to achieve a rote-learned word-perfect repetition of parts of the Book of Common Prayer. But the differences of emphasis were there, even though Presbyterians and Independents shared with the Anglicans an apprehension of the dangers implicit in heterogeneity of view. George Abbott, speaking in the Court of High Commission, was voicing a view which most Anglican clergy would have echoed when he insisted that 'when you have readinge, preaching, singinge, teaching you are your owne ministers; the blinde lead the blinde'.[89] The Puritans would have accepted the first but denied the second of these assertions, claiming that such activities would, on the contrary, lead to *clarity* of vision. But it was only the radical wing of the movement which would have denied the need for an authoritative statement of what was to be viewed.

With the Restoration uniformity and conformity in religious education became the norm, and this was as true of the education of the many as of the few. The

Book of Common Prayer and its catechism were firmly reinstated, as the notion of a thinking (even participating) congregation flew out of the window. If the flock needed reading matter it would be *The Whole Duty of Man*, advocating a quiescent acceptance of the worldly state in anticipation of the 'joys laid up for those in heaven'. The Licensing Act (1662–95) controlled both books and press, and the founding of the Society for the Propagation of Christian Knowledge, with its proposals to set up charity schools throughout the country, sowed the seeds of that authoritarian kind of elementary education in which patient acceptance of one's station in life became the all-pervasive aim in the education of the children of the 'labouring poor'. Despite the flood of didactic literature for the education of the many, much of it Puritan in its emphasis and aspiration, the century ended with a relatively pessimistic response to the major educational problem, the problem of knowing and especially of knowing God. The oft-quoted 'He that refuseth instruction despiseth his own soul' (Proverbs 15:32) begged the main questions—what kinds of instruction and with what ends in view? Locke was expressing a general view when he wrote, 'Reason must be our last judge and guide . . . [but] . . . the greatest part cannot know and therefore must believe'[90]—what they were told, presumably! It was a far cry from the aspirations of the beginning of the century, when John Rogers spurred on his congregation and readers with the question 'But doe you beleeve, and cannot prove it?'[91]

CONCLUSION: EDUCATION AND REVOLUTION

The century as a whole has been described by one historian as 'The Century of Revolution'. Others have discerned an 'intellectual revolution' and a 'cultural revolution'; and still others have seen these as part of a wider European phenomenon, 'the general crisis of the seventeenth century'.[92]

Any consideration of the educational background to the Age of Milton has, then, to include the question: how far did this diagnosis apply to education? For the period 1560–1640 at least, it has been claimed that changes took place which were 'astonishing', 'extraordinary' and 'unprecedented', and, more crucially, that these changes were 'a necessary, though not of course a sufficient, cause of the peculiar and ultimately radical course the revolution took . . . Few revolutions of a revolutionary age were of greater importance' (§S–328). Two claims are being made here, and they should be kept separate. The first depends on how the words 'revolution' and 'revolutionary' are to be used—in this case, in what sense are the changes that took place in education of sufficient originality and proportion to merit the adjective 'revolutionary' (even if they did not result in a revolution in the usual sense of the term, as in Puritan Revolution, Glorious Revolution, French Revolution, etc.); the second claim requires an answer to the question whether these changes made a causal contribution to the Puritan Revolution.

Changes undoubtedly took place, as we have seen, and in very general terms they included, at one level, a confirmation of the late sixteenth-century trend towards a proportion (about one third of the total) of upper-class undergraduates, at universities in which collegiate teaching had become vastly more important than the teaching in the university 'schools', and at another level an increase in the provision of elementary education, even if not on a national scale and certainly not conceived of as part of a national *system*, which resulted in a modest narrowing of the traditional gap between the educated clerk and the illiterate layman. But the content of education, whether at the upper or the lower level, hardly changed at all, the forceful advocacy of Comenius and his followers notwithstanding. Neither the new philosophy nor the new science found its way into undergraduate teaching, save when individual tutors or small groups, such as the Cambridge Platonists, made their limited and inevitably impermanent attempts.[93] Scholars there were, but (especially after the Restoration) they were more likely to be found among the Anglican bishops than the university professors and college fellows, the latter proving singularly unable or unwilling to alter what has accurately been called 'the circumscribed limits of an outworn curriculum'.[94] Even the remarkable transformation of classical studies initiated by Richard Bentley had little general impact. Gresham College, for all its distinguished professors at the beginning of the century, remained a minority force and by the end of the century, had failed to maintain its early promise. The same may be said of the Royal Society, which failed to diffuse its contribution beyond its restricted circle of members, coming to accept with John Locke that 'in a learned age a gentleman must look into natural philosophy to fit himself for conversation'.[95] The chemistry of Boyle, the botany of Ray, the medicine of Sydenham and the astronomy of Flamsteed had not by the end of the century been incorporated in any systematic way into the undergraduate curriculum, which took remarkably little account of science, whether Baconian, Cartesian or Newtonian.

The same conclusion, though for different reasons, must be reached after a consideration of the field of elementary education. When we read that 'the Puritans advocated educational revolution as part of the general revolution'[96] we have to remind ourselves that only *some* Puritans held this view over the whole range of educational provision, and that if there was an 'educational Renascence'[97] during the Commonwealth period it was a 'renascence' of advocacy which was not *achieved* even during that ostensibly favourable period. The relative optimism of Puritan calls for an educated flock has to be set against a conflicting insistence on uniformity, saddling such provision with an authoritarian motive, which was as evident after the Restoration, with the efforts of the SPCK to produce a God-fearing and obedient populace, as before. The seventeenth century, like other centuries, recognised that the setting of education to solve social problems by producing a social and spiritual regeneration itself produced other problems, not least the problem of where the seat of authority lay, or more specifically in whom lay the seat of authority, whether political or religious. It was one thing for Samuel Hartlib to claim that 'the readiest way to reform church and commonwealth is to reform the schools of education therein, and that the way to reform these is to send forth reformed schoolmasters amongst them'.[98] But this depended on the reformed school-master accepting that the seat of authority lay elsewhere than in himself. When he did not, then the not inconsiderable powers of those in authority saw to it that he changed his view, or he lost his office. In the same way the Age of Milton was not alone in recognising that those in receipt of an education designed to lead them to a predetermined answer to the question very often arrived at an alternative answer. Just as in the sixteenth century the distinction between sedition and heresy dissolved into synonymity, so too in the seventeenth century an educative godly household became, in the eyes of authority, a conventicle, and was searched out and punished as such by the Court of High Commission, whose officers applied their criteria to Puritan and Catholic alike.[99]

Nor should we be surprised too much by all this, since perennially the essence of education has been a conservative activity, consciously planned to hand on to younger generations a society's heritage, that parcel of values, ethos, culture, behavioural patterns and so on, which are approved of and valued by the handing-on generation. Moreover, the young grow older; increasing experience and the exigencies of practical decision-making alike make relative conservatives of us all, and 'of all institutions of civilized society none is more resistant to change than education. Even constitutions are altered more frequently and with less fuss.'[100] In the Age of Milton the English constitution was changed in quite a revolutionary way more than once. Yet despite radical criticism and radical prescription English education changed relatively little. Whether for good or ill will depend on prior premises which remain all too often undeclared when the questions 'Who shall be educated?' 'By whom?' and 'For what purposes?' are perennially asked.

NOTES

1   See §S–426, S–549 (Ch. II), S–369; and J. A. Bryant, Jr., 'Milton's View on Universal and Civil Decay', in *SAMLA Studies in Milton*, ed. J. Max Patrick (Gainesville, Fla., 1953), pp. 1–19.

2   St Paul's School statutes, in J. H. Lupton, *A Life of John Colet* (1909), p. 279.

3   *Ludus Literarius*, ed. E. T. Campagnac (Liverpool, 1917), p. 45.

4   *The Right Reformation of Learning, Schools and Universities*, appended to *The Tryall of Spirits* (1653), p. 27.

5   *Diary and Letter-Book of the Rev. Thomas Brockbank 1671—1709*, ed. R. Trappes-Lomax, Chetham Society, n.s., LXXXIX (1930), 200.

6   N. Carlisle, *A Concise Description of the Endowed Grammar Schools of England and Wales* (1818), I, 581.

7   J. B. Oldham, *A History of Shrewsbury School 1552—1952* (Oxford, 1952), pp. 17–18.

8   L. B. Marshall, *A Brief History of Enfield Grammar School 1558—1958* (1958), p. 23.

9 Carlisle (as above, note 6), I, 581; R. Howell, Jr., *Newcastle-upon-Tyne and the Puritan Revolution* (Oxford, 1967), p. 329.

10 J. H. Plumb, *Sir Robert Walpole: The Making of a Statesman* (1956), pp. 87–8.

11 Victoria County History, *Essex*, II, 554.

12 Oldham (as above, note 7), pp. 49–52.

13 Victoria County History, *Derbyshire*, II, 219–20.

14 Edward Burles, *Grammatica Burlesa* (1652), 'To the Reader', sig. A7.

15 Victoria County History, *Somerset*, II, 458, and R. Nadeau, 'Thomas Farnaby: Schoolmaster and Rhetorician of the English Renaissance', *Quarterly Journal of Speech*, XXXVI (1950), 340–4.

16 A. Smith, 'Private Schools and Schoolmasters in the Diocese of Lichfield and Coventry in the Seventeenth Century', *History of Education*, V (1976), 117–26; and §S–262.

17 R. Birley, 'Robert Boyle at Eton', *Notes and Records of the Royal Society of London*, XIV (1959), 191.

18 Burnet, *Thoughts on Education*, ed. J. M. Clarke (Aberdeen, 1914).

19 Clarke, *Essay upon the Education of Youth in Grammar Schools* (1720), p. 240.

20 Mulcaster (§P–167), pp. 133 ff.; Bacon, *Essays*: 'Of Seditions and Troubles'; Hobbes, *Behemoth*, ed. T. Tonnies (1969), pp. 147–8; C. H. Firth (ed.), *Memoirs of William Cavendish, Duke of Newcastle* (n.d.), p. 188; see also Edward Chamberlayne, *Angliae Notitia: the Second Parte of the State of England* (1682), pp. 320–2.

21 *The Works of Francis Bacon*, ed. J. Spedding *et al.* (1887), III, 286.

22 Cf. J. W. Ashley Smith, *The Birth of Modern Education: The Contribution of the Dissenting Academies 1660—1800* (1954).

23 Cf. §S–333, and J. A. G. Montmorency, *State Intervention in English Education* (1902).

24 'The Wase School Collection: A Neglected Source in Educational History', *Bodleian Library Record*, IV (1952), 78–104. Cf. A. M. d'I. Oakeshott, 'The Education Enquiry Papers of Christopher Wase', *British Journal of Educational Studies*, XIX (1971), 301–32.

25 'His Wish', in *Poems*, ed. L. C. Martin (1965), p. 294.

26 *Memoirs of the Life of Colonel Hutchinson*, ed. J. Sutherland (Oxford, 1973), p. 288.

27 *Autobiography of Anne, Lady Halkett*, ed. J. G. Nichols, Camden Society, n.s., XIII (1875), 2–3. Cf. the cases of Margaret Duchess of Newcastle, 'A True Relation of my Birth, Breeding and Life', appended to *The Life of William Cavendish, Duke of Newcastle*, ed. C. H. Firth (1886), pp. 280 ff., and of Anne Lady Fanshawe, in her *Memoir* (1907), p. 13.

28 *The Diary of John Evelyn*, ed. E. S. de Beer (Oxford, 1955), II, 555; P. W. Somers, *The Matchless Orinda* (Cambridge, Mass., 1931).

29 Victoria County History, *Middlesex*, I, 252; *Sammelbande der Internationalen Musik Gesellschaft*, V (1903–04), 506 ff.

30 A. Macfarlane, *Family Life of Ralph Josselin* (Cambridge, 1970), pp. 49 and 93.

31 D. M. Gardiner (ed.). *The Oxinden Letters: II* (1937), p. 128; and G. R. Parkinson (ed.), *Life*

of Adam Martindale, Chetham Society, IV (1845), 206–9, and C. Morris (ed.), *The Journeys of Celia Fiennes*, rev. ed. (1949), p. 227.

32   *The Mothers Legacie to her Unborne Childe* (1624), The Epistle Dedicatorie, sig. B5v.

33   Essay Upon Projects (1697), pp. 302–3.

34   J. A. Venn, *Oxford and Cambridge Matriculations 1594—1906* (Cambridge, 1908); L. Stone, 'The Size and Composition of the Oxford Student Body', in *The University and Society*, ed. L. Stone (Oxford, 1974), I, 3–110.

35   M. H. Curtis (§S–301). For literary examples of 'first generation' undergraduates, cf. §S–226: p. 222.

36   In *The Elizabethan House of Commons* (§S–101), pp. 302 ff.; cf. §S–294: pp. 137 ff.

37   Simon, 'The Social Origins of Cambridge Students 1603–40', *Past and Present*; XXVI (1963), 58–67, and Cressy, 'The Social Composition of Caius College, Cambridge, 1558–1640', *ibid.*, XLVII (1970), 113–15.

38   M. H. Curtis, 'The Alienated Intellectuals of Early Stuart England', *Past and Present*, XXIII (1962), 25–43; cf. J. H. Hexter's use of the term to describe the early sixteenth-century Christian humanists in his *More's Utopia: The Biography of an Idea* (Princeton, 1952), p. 115.

39   Victoria County History, *Cambridge*, III, 349, 477, 465; *Oxford*, III, 47 ff.

40   V.C.H., *Oxford*, III, 261–2, 116–17; *Cambridge*, III, 484.

41   V.C.H., *Oxford*, III, 256, 279, 255; Carlisle (as above, note 6), p. 426.

42   In his *Good Newes from Heaven* (1626), Preface.

43   Howell (as above, note 9), pp. 323 and 328; Carlisle (note 6), p. 625. Jordan (§S–223: p. 294) estimates that 500 new scholarships to Oxford and Cambridge were endowed in the period 1560–1640.

44   J. E. B. Mayor (ed.), *Cambridge in the Seventeenth Century*, II: *The Autobiography of Matthew Robinson* (Cambridge, 1856), p. 16, n. 2; W. Scott (ed.), *Somers Tracts* (1809), I, 443.

45   Curtis (§S–301) claims that the curriculum had been modernised by the teaching of college tutors; but cf. §§S–299 and S–68 (pp. 301–14).

46   Dell, *Several Sermons and Discourses* (1709), pp. 642 ff.; cf. §§S–337 and S–309.

47   For the Manchester and York petitions: G. W. Johnson (ed.), *The Fairfax Correspondence* (1848), II, 271–80; for Durham: G. H. Turnbull, 'Oliver Cromwell's College at Durham', *Durham Research Review*, III (September 1952), 1–7, and Victoria County History, *Durham*, I, 380–1; §S–68: pp. 108–9, 124; for the London proposal: *Motives Grounded upon the Word of God and upon Honour, Profit and Pleasure for the Present Founding of a University* (1647).

48   J. Ward, *Lives of the Professors of Gresham College* (1740). There is no modern work on Gresham College but cf. I. R. Adamson, 'The Foundation and Early History of Gresham College, London, 1596–1704', Cambridge Ph.D. thesis, 1976; F. R. Johnson, 'Gresham College, the Precursor of the Royal Society', *Journal of the History of Ideas*, I (1940), 413–38; C. Webster, 'The Origins of the Royal Society', *History of Science*, VI (1967), 106–29; M. d'Espinasse, 'The Decline and Fall of Restoration Science', *Past and Present*, XIV (1958), 71–89; R. P. Ross, 'Social and Economic Causes of the Revolution in Mathematical Sciences in Mid-Seventeenth Century England', *Journal of British Studies*, XV (1975), 46–66.

49 Cf. Dell (as above, note 46), p. 398, cited in §S–71: p. 303. Cf. §S–311 and §S–323.

50 Cf. B. F. Levack, *The Civil Lawyers in England 1603—41* (Oxford, 1973).

51 W. R. Prest, §S–320; §S–294: Ch. VI.

52 Cf. §§S–215, S–513, S–577; R. G. Frank, Jr., 'Science, Medicine and the Universities in Early Modern England: Background and Sources', *History of Science*, XI (1973), 239–69; A. Rook, 'Medicine at Cambridge 1660–1700', *Medical History*, XIII (1969), 107–22; Sir George Clark, *A History of the Royal College of Physicians*, I (Oxford, 1964); C. Wall, *A History of the Worshipful Company of Apothecaries: I*, rev. by E. A. Underwood (1963).

53 *Several Papers given forth* (1660), pp. 32–3.

54 Culpepper, *Medicaments for the Poor* (1656), sig. B4. For the education of the 'new' professions of merchant, navigator and surveyor, see §S–294: Ch. IX.

55 *A History of My Own Time* (1724), II, 648: 'The Scotch though less able to bear the expence of a learned education are much more knowing'.

56 *Perambulation of Kent* (1576), cited by P. Laslett, 'The Gentry of Kent in 1640', *Cambridge Historical Journal*, IX (1948), 148–64.

57 B. Schofield (ed.), *The Knyvett Letters 1620—44*, Norfolk Record Society, XX (1949), 17; Sir Gyles Isham (ed.), *The Diary of Thomas Isham of Lamport 1658–81* (1971), Introduction; J. Lievsay and R. B. Davis, 'A Cavalier Library, 1643', *Studies in Bibliography*, VI (1954), 141–60. For urban examples, cf. H. M. Colvin and L. M. Wodehouse, 'Henry Bell of King's Lynn', *Architectural History*, IV (1961), 41–62, cited by L. Stone, 'Social Mobility in England 1500–1700', *Past and Present*, XXXIII (1966), p. 54, and P. Clarke, 'The Ownership of Books in England 1560–1640: The Examples of some Kentish Townsfolk', in *Schooling and Society*, ed. L. Stone (1976), pp. 75–114.

58 *Life . . . written by himself* (Oxford, 1647), p. 4.

59 Burnet (as above, note 18), p. 80. For similar views cf. Hezekiah Woodward, *The Childes Patrimony* (1640), p. 164, and Edward Hyde, Lord Clarendon, *A Dialogue . . . concerning Education*, in *Miscellaneous Tracts* (1751), pp. 322–3; G. B. Parks, 'John Evelyn and the Art of Travel', *Huntington Library Quarterly*, X (1946–47), 251–73, and 'Travel as Education', in §S–931. pp. 264–81.

60 Milton, *Of Education*. Cf. the concise but comprehensive statement in J. Bury, *The Reformed School* (1650), in §S–338: p. 148.

61 Cf. Milton's *Areopagitica*: 'where there is much desire to learn there of necessity will be much arguing, much writing, many opinions'.

62 J. H. Plumb, 'The Growth of the Electorate in England 1600–1715', *Past and Present*, XLV (1969), 90–116; R. L. Bushman, 'English Franchise Reform in the Seventeenth Century', *Journal of British Studies*, III (1963), 36–56; K. Thomas, 'The Levellers and the Franchise', in §S–7: pp. 57–78.

63 V.C.H., *Berkshire*, II, 282; cf. *Essex*, II, 562, and *Derbyshire*, II, 273.

64 V.C.H., *Warwickshire*, II, 370; cf. G. Griffiths, *Free Schools of Staffordshire* (1860), pp. 96, 205–6.

65 Cf. H. C. Schultz, 'The Teaching of Handwriting in Tudor and Stuart Times', *Huntington Library Quarterly*, III (1943), 381–425; A. Heal, *English Writing School*

Masters and their Copy Books 1570—1800 (Cambridge, 1931); F. P. Barnard, *The Casting Côunter and the Counting Board* (Oxford, 1916); F. Yeldman, *The Teaching of Arithmetic through Five Centuries* (1936).

66 M. G. James, *The Charity School Movement* (1964); Joan Simon, 'Was there a Charity School Movement?' in *Education in Leicestershire*, ed. B. Simon (Leicester, 1968), pp. 55–100.

67 L. Stone, 'Literacy and Education 1640–1900', *Past and Present*, XLIII (1968), 67–139; D. Cressy, 'Levels of Literacy in England 1550–1730', *Historical Journal*, XX (1977), 1–24; T. W. Laqueur, 'The Cultural Origins of Popular Literacy in England 1500–1850', *Oxford Review of Education*, II (1976), 255–75; R. T. Vann, 'Literacy in the Seventeenth Century: Some Hearth Tax Evidence', *Journal of Interdisciplinary History*, V (1974), 287–93.

68 W. H. Frere, *Visitation Articles and Injunctions of the Period of the Reformation* (Alcuin Club Collections, XIV–VI, 1910), III, 10.

69 *A Plot for the Good of Posterity* (1646), p. 28.

70 *Gangraena* (1646), I, 116–19, 187.

71 V. M. Verney, *Memoirs of the Verney Family* (1894), III, 73.

72 Cf. §S–204, S–207, S–260; K. M. Davies, 'The Sacred Condition of Equality: How Original were Puritan Marriage Doctrines?' *Social History*, V (1977), 563–80.

73 K. V. Thomas, 'Women and the Civil War Sects', *Past and Present*, XIII (1958), 42–62; E. M. Williams, 'Women Preachers in the Civil War', *Journal of Modern History*, I (1929), 561–9.

74 Cf. G. Fox, *Gospel Truth* (1656), pp. 81, 331 and 724.

75 *A New Method of Educating Children* (1695), pp. 14 ff. and 30.

76 V.C.H., *Warwickshire*, II, 370.

77 *Ibid.*, p. 369.

78 *David's Cost* (1619), p. 304. Cf. Richard Rogers, *The Practice of Christianitie* (1603), sig. A3, on 'your well-bound volumes motheaten or mouseaten'.

79 *Diary of the Rev. Henry Newcome 1661—63*, ed. T. Heywood, Chetham Society, XVIII (1849), 16.

80 *A Few Signs from Hell* (1658), in *Works*, ed. G. Offor (1860–62), III, 711. For a typical and early criticism, cf. Henry Crosse, *Vertues Commonwealth* (1603). See also C. Blagden, 'Notes on the Ballad Market in the Second Half of the Seventeenth Century', *Studies in Bibliography*, VI (1954), 161–80.

81 S. R. Gardiner, *History of the Great Civil War* (1898), III, 135.

82 *A New Year's Gift for Parliament and the Army* (1650), in *Winstanley: The Law of Freedom and Other Writings*, ed. Christopher Hill (1973), p. 200.

83 C. Jackson (ed.), *Yorkshire Diaries and Autobiographies of the Seventeenth and Eighteenth Centuries*, Surtees Society, LXV (1877), 127–8.

84 J. Horsfall Turner (ed.), *The Reverend Oliver Heywood BA 1630—72: His Autobiography, Diaries etc.* (1882–85), I, 234 and 77.

85 *The Saint's Worthiness* (1653), p. 17.

86 Woodward (as above, note 59), p. 14.

87 Cf. §S–217: Ch. XIII; Baxter, *Reformed Pastor* (1655), p. 59.

88 H. S. Bennett, *Books and Readers 1558—1603* (Cambridge, 1965), p. 147.

89 S. R. Gardiner (ed.), *Reports of Cases in the Courts of Star Chamber and High Commission*, Camden Society, n.s., XXXIX (1886), 309.

90 *An Essay concerning Human Understanding* (1690), IV, xix, 14.

91 *Doctrine of Faith* (1629), p. 32.

92 See §S–66 and S–155; also S. L. Bethel, *The Intellectual Revolution of the Seventeenth Century* (1951); E. J. Hobsbawm, 'The General Crisis of the European Economy in the Seventeenth Century', *Past and Present*, V (May 1954), 33–53, and VI (November 1954), 44–65; though cf. V. F. Snow, 'The Concept of Revolution and Seventeenth Century England', *Historical Journal*, V (1962), 67–74, and J. H. Elliott, 'Revolution and Continuity in Early Modern England', *Past and Present*, XLII (1969), 35–56.

93 See §S–387, S–393, S–397.

94 D. C. Douglas, *English Scholars 1660—1730*, rev. ed. (1951), p. 250.

95 *Some Thoughts . . . concerning Education* (1693), Section 193.

96 R. Schlatter, in his introduction to §S–305.

97 Foster Watson, 'The English Educational Renascence', *English Review*, III (November 1909), 730–41.

98 Preface to John Dury's *The Reformed Schoolmaster* (c. 1649), ed. H. M. Knox (Liverpool, 1958), p. 20.

99 Gardiner (as above, note 89), *passim*.

100 Lawrence Stone, in his introduction (p. ix) to the 1967 reprint of §S–339.

SAMUEL I. MINTZ

5

The motion of thought: intellectual and philosophical backgrounds

'In 1600,' said Douglas Bush, 'the educated Englishman's mind and world were more than half medieval; by 1660 they were more than half modern' (§S–900: p. 1). To the reader who comes to seventeenth-century thought for the first time, the changes wrought in the intellectual landscape must seem confusing; new ideas and old ones sometimes coexist in the same minds; and the process of change itself is not regular, having both forward and backward motions, cross-currents, interactions, moving in a manner similar to the way Robert Burton described the course of his own prose, which like a river 'runs sometimes precipitate and swift, then dull and slow, now direct, then *per ambages*, now deep, then shallow, now muddy, then clear, now broad, then narrow'.[1]

Nevertheless it is possible to observe a pattern of change. At the beginning of the century, the human world and the natural sublunary world were seen as in decline, unstable, transient, while above and behind that world, it was felt, lay a structured universe of order, an eternal coherence, a world of spirit and spiritual creatures, of right reason and the moral law, the law of nature, that God had planted in the hearts of men. Gradually that belief in a structure of order began to crumble when it felt what Basil Willey (quoting Keats) has called 'the touch of cold philosophy' (§S–378)—the impact, that is, of the modern scientific outlook. This new outlook did not spring into being *ex nihilo*. Like every intellectual revolution, its roots were in the past. But it selected its antecedents; it emphasised those aspects of the past that were most congenial to its style of thought. In particular it related to those philosophies or parts of philosophies that sorted best with its own emphasis upon experience, its distrust of arguments based on authority, its seeking out of second causes and its refusal to interpret natural events in all their intimate details as the working out of a divine plan, its bias for mechanical explanations, its rejection of the occult, its suspicion of metaphor and analogical thinking.

Even where the modern outlook preserved aspects of the old, the older ideas were given new meaning. Consider for example two expressions of the familiar idea of a scale or chain of being. The first is from *Paradise Lost*:

> O Adam, [said Raphael] one Almighty is, from whom
> All things proceed, and up to him return,
> If not depraved from good, created all
> Such to perfection, one first matter all,
> Endued with various forms, various degrees
> Of substance, and in things that live, of life;
> But more refined, more spiritous, and pure,
> As nearer to him placed or nearer tending,
> Each in their several active spheres assigned,
> Till body up to spirit work, in bounds
> Proportioned to each kind. So from the root
> Springs lighter the green stalk, from thence the leaves
> More airy, last the bright consummate flow'r
> Spirits odorous breathes: flow'rs and their fruit,
> Man's nourishment, by gradual scale sublimed,
> To vital spirits aspire, to animal,
> To intellectual; give both life and sense,
> Fancy and understanding, whence the soul
> Reason receives, and reason is her being . . .
>
> (V, 469–87)

Milton's picture of nature proceeding from God and returning up to him, of spirit descending into matter and matter returning to spirit in a series of continuous gradations, is mainly traditional (§S–388). Compare it with the exposition of the idea by Thomas Sprat in *The History of the Royal Society*, a very manifesto of the new philosophy, published in 1667, the same year as *Paradise Lost*, but breathing a different atmosphere:

> Such is the dependence amongst all the orders of creatures; the inanimate, the sensitive, the rational, the natural, the artificial: that the apprehension of one of them, is a good step towards the understanding of the rest: And this is the highest pitch of *humane reason*; to follow all the links of this chain, till all their secrets are open to our minds; and their works advanc'd, or imitated by our hands. This is truly to command the world; to rank all the *varieties*, and degrees of things, so orderly one upon another; that standing on the top of them, we may perfectly behold all that are below, and make them all serviceable to the quiet, and peace, and plenty of Man's life.
>
> (ed. J. I. Cope and H. W. Jones [1959], pp. 110–11)

For Bishop Sprat the chain of being serves a utilitarian purpose: it makes nature 'shew it self the clearer'. It is a system of taxonomy for the promotion of scientific knowledge. Its sense of order is derived from a fundamentally mechanical conception of nature. And it is man-oriented, where Milton's view is God-oriented. Nature in Milton's view is organic, anti-mechanical; matter and spirit are both endowed with ethical properties; and the whole structure is designed to reveal a divine purpose rather than to serve strictly human ends. 'There can be no doubt,' wrote Milton in *De Doctrina Christiana*, 'that every thing in the world, by the beauty of its order, and evidence of a determinate and beneficial purpose which pervades it, testifies that some supreme efficient Power must have pre-existed, by which the whole was ordained for a special end.'[2]

Supporting the older outlook, serving as its intellectual and philosophical understructure, are the great traditions of Platonism and Aristotelianism. Of the two, Platonism may be said to be more important, because while Aristotelianism contributed many individual ideas to the set of assumptions that has come to be called the philosophy of order, Platonism gave it its general philosophical character. Aristotelianism survived into the seventeenth century and retained a good part of its energy in spite of the revolt against the mediaeval scholastic tradition; but whereas Aristotelianism survived, Platonism flourished. This does not mean that every writer tried to 'unsphere the spirit of Plato', or that every or even most writers agreed with Henry More that Plato's philosophy is 'the most consistent and coherent Metaphysicall *Hypothesis*, that has yet been found out by the wit of man';[3] it means rather that Platonism defined a characteristic philosophical attitude of the seventeenth century. This attitude may be stated in the following way: behind the phenomenal world lies a world of spiritual and intellectual entities, an invisible world that is real and that nourishes our life in the visible world. This habit of thought, this attitude that accepted the reality as well as the primacy of the supersensory world, persisted until it began to be eroded by the philosophies of Bacon and of Hobbes.

The purpose of this chapter will be to examine some of the more important ideas belonging to the Platonic tradition (and some few that are Aristotelian) that flowed into the seventeenth century and gave it its philosophical shape, to set these ideas briefly in the perspective of the history of thought, and to see what happened to them when they collided with the new outlook. By doing these things in a short space I will doubtless inflict an injury on the complexity of intellectual history, for which I apologise; at least I will not consciously distort anyone's thoughts and I will try not to commit the fault which John Locke charged against Sir Robert Filmer of doing 'with the Words and Sense of Authors' what '*Procrustes* did with his guests, lop or stretch them, as may best fit them to the size of their Notions'.[4]

PLATO: THE THEORY OF FORMS

Plato's theory of forms (sometimes called the theory of ideas) was first expressed in the *Symposium*, expounded in the *Phaedo* and in the *Republic*, and defended briefly in the *Timaeus* and in other dialogues. Although by no means the whole of Plato's thought, it is the most characteristic of his conceptions, the one that comes to mind when the term 'Platonism' is used. Certainly it is that aspect of Plato's thought which exerted the greatest influence on subsequent times.

Plato developed his theory by means of dialectical arguments, and he expressed it also through parable and myth. Let us consider the celebrated parable of the cave, given in the seventh book of the *Republic*. Socrates asks the other members of the dialogue to imagine an underground cave with a long passage leading to an entrance open to the light. In the cave are prisoners kept from childhood, chained in such a way that they can see only the rear wall of the cave. A certain distance behind them is a fire, and between them and the fire is a parapet on which men are carrying carved wooden or stone figures. The prisoners see only the shadows of these carved objects projected on the wall of the cave, and, knowing nothing else, they imagine that these shadows, these insubstantial things, are real, are the whole of reality. Even the occasional words exchanged by the men carrying the carved objects are thought by the prisoners to be speech made by the shadows on the wall. When a prisoner is released from his chains and allowed to turn round, his eyes are dazzled by the light of the fire, so that, at least momentarily, he retains his faith in the reality of the shadows; but when he goes up the passage and out into the light of day, and when he adjusts his sight to the new world before him, and especially to the sun in whose light that world is bathed, he comes to realise that he is now in the presence of what is real and that the world of shadows he has left below is but an illusion. Socrates drives home the meaning of the allegory in these words: 'the prison-house is the world of sight, the light of the fire is the sun, and you will not misapprehend me if you interpret the journey upwards to be the ascent of the soul into the intellectual world'. The meaning of the sun in the allegory is further explained to be the idea of good, the supreme Form or Idea in a hierarchy of forms:

> In the world of knowledge the idea of good appears last of all, and is seen only with an effort; and, when seen, is also inferred to be the universal author of all things beautiful and right, parent of light and of the lord of light in this visible world, and the immediate source of reason and truth in the intellectual; and . . . this is the power upon which he who would act rationally either in public or private life must have his eyes fixed.[5]

The theory of forms is elaborated at greater length in the *elenchus*—that is, the dialectical method of eliciting the truth through a process of questions and answers. When he was not resorting to parable or myth, Socrates cross-examined his auditors relentlessly.[6] Plato was convinced that the Socratic questions were instruments of precise thinking; they were designed to uncover the truth about the nature of Truth, and in that great enterprise, Plato said, they succeeded. The theory of forms expressed through them is a theory of transcendental truth. The forms are patterns or ideals of things. But they exist independently of things and they are both prior to and antecedent to the things that bear their names. They are absolute, eternal, and immutable, whereas things are subject to alteration and decay. The form of Beauty can never be anything but itself, whereas a beautiful object may have an admixture of ugliness in it, or may be regarded by some as beautiful and by others as ugly. Plato defines knowledge as the apprehension of the forms; what we discover through our senses Plato calls mere opinion. Our whole object should be to ascend from the sensory world of opinion to the intellectual realm of pure forms.

'Poore soule', said John Donne,

> 'what wilt thou doe?
> When wilt thou shake off this Pedantery,
> Of being taught by sense, and Fantasie?
> Thou lookst through spectacles; small things seem great
> Below; But up into the watch-towre get,
> And see all things despoyld of fallacies:
> Thou shalt not peepe through lattices of eyes,
> Nor heare through Labyrinths of eares . . .
>
> ('The Second Anniversarie', ll. 290–7)

The devaluation of sense-experience and the corresponding exaltation of the forms are an aspect of the dualism that colours Plato's thought. His mind perceived bifurcations; habitually he thought of pairs like Soul and Body, knowledge and opinion, reality and appearance, the intelligible and the visible or the rational and the sensible. In each of these pairs the first member is superior to the second, and, in respect of the division between the supersensory forms and their appearances in the world of things, the first is also anterior to the second, having an independent existence outside time and space, permanent, not transient.

This devaluation of sense-experience is further accompanied by an appreciation of mathematics; for mathematics is an excellent paradigm of the superiority of the intellectual over the visible. A perfect triangle does not exist in the natural world, but the concept of it does exist and can be understood. Mathematical principles are not themselves forms, but, being independent of the sensory world and (or so Plato thought) absolute and immutable, they are closer to the forms than is the world of appearances.

Plato's attitude towards body and matter was not exactly contemptuous—for instance, he advocated moderation rather than absolute self-denial in those activities that give bodily pleasure—but there is no denying the ascetic implications of his theory of forms. To withdraw from the life of the body into the life of the mind is at least in part a Platonic impulse.

The problem of what a form is when considered separate from things, or indeed of how such a form can be conceived at all—a question that troubled Aristotle and continues to be raised by Plato's critics—is left unresolved in the dialogues. The question is taken up in the *Sophist* and the *Parmenides*, where the argument against the separate existence of forms is pursued with so much force and pertinacity that at least one modern commentator, Gilbert Ryle, has concluded that Plato was no longer a Platonist in the sense already described and that he had now rejected the separate existence of concepts.[7] Ryle's view is a minority opinion among modern scholars and certainly at variance with the Platonist tradition of the Middle Ages and the Renaissance, which held that Plato believed consistently in the independent ontological status of the forms.

IMMORTALITY AND MEMORY

The Platonic theory of immortality was developed in the *Phaedo* and in the *Meno*. It is a doctrine not only of the persistence of the soul after the death of the body but also of the soul's pre-existence. In defence of the theory Socrates offered a number of logical proofs not remarkable for their acuity; his argument finally came to rest on the doctrine of latent knowledge or knowledge as recollection. Education is the uncovering of what was once known and has since been forgotten. To demonstrate this Socrates elicits the Pythagorean theorem from a slave-boy who had never studied geometry. How could the boy have known the truth of what he was saying? Having never learnt geometry in this life, he must have acquired it in a previous incorporeal existence. This is the life of the pre-natal soul, whose 'Bright shootes of everlastingnesse' Henry Vaughan still felt in his childhood:

> Some men a forward motion love,
> But I by backward steps would move,
> And when this dust falls to the urn
> In that state I came return.
>
> ('The Retreate', ll. 29–32)

In the psychology of Plato the soul has three parts or elements—the rational, the courageous, and the appetitive (depicted as a charioteer and his two horses in the famous myth of the *Phaedrus*). Plato evidently believed that only the rational part of the soul survives the death of the body, although the soul may retain a memory of some of its residence in the body. He also suggested but did not elaborate a theory of metempsychosis: after the death of the body the soul migrates to another body and thence to another in a continuous cycle of reincarnations. This idea of the transmigration of souls is conveyed only through myths, so that it is not clear how strongly Plato believed in it. What is certain is that Plato believed that the soul is a non-material entity, that it is immortal, that it exists before the individual human body to which it is attached comes into being and that it survives the death of that body. One hardly needs to underline the parallel between these ideas and Christian belief.

PLOTINUS AND NEOPLATONISM

The profound influence exerted by Plato on Christian philosophers, especially on St Augustine, will not be treated here. Nor will I speak of Middle Platonism, the long period of Platonic influence between the time of Plato (d. 348 B.C.) and Plotinus (c. A.D. 203–269). One writer of that period must, however, be mentioned. This is the Jewish thinker Philo of Alexandria (25 B.C.–A.D. 40).[8] Philo tried to reconcile Plato with Jewish tradition. (There are Stoic and neo-Pythagorean elements in Philo's thought, but these do not disguise his essential Platonism.) God is conceived of by Philo as absolutely transcendent, ineffable, not located in space, a kind of meta-form or form of forms, except that whereas Plato thought the forms could be known through a rational process, Philo believed in an unknowable God who can be attained only through intuition or ecstasy. The problem for Philo was how to harmonise this conception of an absolutely transcendent, self-sufficient God with the anthropomorphic Yahveh of the Book of Genesis or indeed with the immanent God of the later books of Scripture. The solution was allegory. The God of Genesis who appears to occupy space and have social intercourse is a metaphor, a shadow or type of a higher non-sensory meaning. He is rendered in human terms as an accommodation to the inferior sensory understanding of human beings. Milton adopted a similar theory of accommodation in *Paradise Lost* (§ S–461: pp. 159–63; § S–486: pp. 9–15). How, Raphael asks, is he to 'relate / To human sense th' invisible exploits / Of warring Spirits'?

> What surmounts the reach
> Of human sense I shall delineate so,
> By lik'ning spiritual to corporal forms,
> As may express them best.
>
> (V, 571–74)

Analogy and allegory are typically Philonic. Although he did not invent this way of thinking—it was present in Plato's treatment of things as shadows of the forms—Philo perfected it and transmitted it to later times. It was Philo who generalised into a philosophical principle the scattered references in the pre-Socratics, Plato and Aristotle to the image of man as a microcosm, Donne's 'little world made cunningly'.

The primary source of Renaissance Neoplatonism was, however, not Philo but Plotinus (A.D. 204–270). His six treatises, collected by their editor Porphyry into nine parts each (hence their name *Enneads*), form a metaphysical system of great rigour and no inconsiderable beauty.[9] The mysticism that is latent in Plato is brought to the surface in Plotinus. The otherworldliness of Plato, the immersion in a supersensory realm, is given its most finished expression in Plotinus. There are elements of Pythagoreanism, Stoicism and Philonism in his thought, but it was Plato whom he revered as his master, and it is the Platonic letters and dialogues, especially Plato's cosmological *Timaeus*, to which he returns again and again for reference. Nevertheless Plotinus is *sui generis*; his thought is rather a transformation than an extension of Plato. We might, in the manner of Harold Bloom, think of his approach to his great predecessor as a 'misreading' or misprision, although evidently accomplished without anxiety.

Essential to Neoplatonism is a belief in the supra-rational, in a Being that lies beyond reason and beyond reality. Plotinus calls this being by various names—the Absolute, the Supreme, the First, the Unity, or, most frequently, the One. It is not a Platonic form, although it is the source of all forms. It is not number, although all numbers are derived from it. It has no moral attributes, although, since all things strive to return to it, it would not be inappropriate to nominate it the Good. In fact it has no attributes whatsoever—neither shape nor magnitude nor place nor essence nor spirit—since attributes imply limitations, and the One cannot be bounded. 'Its nature is that nothing can be affirmed of it—not existence, not essence, not life—since it is that which transcends all these' (III, viii, 10). How, then, can it be known? Certainly not through the senses; but not by reason either. It is known mystically by intuition and by ecstasy in a contemplative process, and a sign that it is known is an irradiation of the soul, a burst of radiance not remote from the experience of Henry Vaughan when he said

> I saw Eternity the other night
> Like a great *Ring* of pure and endless light . . .
>
> ('The World', ll. 1–2)

According to Porphyry, Plotinus had four such illuminations of the One in a period of six years.

In the Plotinian world the One is supreme; ranged below it in a descending hierarchy are, first, the Intelligence of *Nous* and, second, the Soul. These belong to the invisible Platonic realm of supersensory beings; below them, inferior in every way, are the visible world of Body and of Matter. Each of these both in the invisible and in the visible world is derived from what is immediately above it in the hierarchy so that each is derived ultimately from the One and the presence of the One is felt in each, although that presence becomes more remote in every lower stage of the system. In the lowest stage, dull, inert Matter, that is to say matter utterly uninformed by Soul, the presence of the One is extinguished altogether. Plotinus therefore equates this stage of matter with evil, or total privation of the Absolute. We will note that Plotinus has a slightly better opinion of Body, which, though low on the scale, still bears some imprint of the Divine or One. Thinking this way did not, however, prevent Plotinus from feeling uncomfortable about having a body.[10]

To the question how can a perfect One or Unity that transcends existence create the multiplicity of things that exist in the world, Plotinus answered with a theory of emanation that he took from Philo and the Middle Platonists. The One did not create the world freely; that would imply activity, and the One is beyond activity. Rather it emitted or emanated a force out of which the world was created. This is described as a necessary result and is explained according to the principle that the less perfect must always be generated out of the more perfect.

The first emanation is the Intelligence of Mind (*Nous*). It is an existent thing but beyond time and space. It is the perfect image of the One but inferior to it. It is the abode of all the individual forms and at the same time the archetypical Form or Idea. Beauty is comprehended by it. Plotinus thought of it as analogous to the Demiurge of Plato's *Timaeus*. It is motionless, having only contemplative activity, which is the contemplation of the One and of itself.

Emanating from *Nous* is the Soul. Like the *Nous*, which is all the separate forms and one overarching meta-Form, so the Soul is all the individual souls and also the Soul of the whole world, the *anima mundi*, a conception borrowed from the *Timaeus*. The Soul looks upward towards *Nous* and downward towards

Body, which emanates from it and with which it joins; thus the Soul is the mediating agency between the intelligible and the phenomenal world. In that lower world of things it may be weighed down by lust and sensuality; this happens when Soul is dominated by Body, a condition from which it can escape only when it is instructed by virtue. Virtue enables it to reassert its intelligible nature and to satisfy its deep, passionate yearning to return to its origins, to *Nous*, and ultimately to the One. The dialectic of the descent and ascent of the Soul is the most dramatic part of Plotinus's system; it expresses the meaning of the assertion that in our end is our beginning. 'The starting-point is, universally, the goal' (III, viii, 7). And when the goal is reached, when the Soul has discarded all self-consciousness, all distinction between its object and itself, when it has ascended into or been illuminated by the One, when 'the flight of the alone to the alone' is complete, then Plotinus is at his most moving and his prose is incandescent. 'This is the life of the gods and of the godlike and blessed among men, liberation from the alien that besets us here, a life taking no pleasure in the things of the earth . . .'[11]

The Neoplatonism of Plotinus has qualities of religion in it, but it never became a religion, most probably because of its intellectual complexity. Its relations with early Christian thought lie outside the scope of this chapter. In the Middle Ages the *Enneads* was unknown. It was rediscovered in the Renaissance, when it became a powerful current of Platonist thought and a fructifying source in the history of mysticism. Although it can claim few adherents in our own time,[12] it continues to exercise an imaginative appeal. Bertrand Russell, who did not believe that the philosophy of Plotinus was true, and who charged it with 'the defect of encouraging men to look within rather than to look without', was nevertheless moved to praise its beauty and to compare it with Dante and with Milton.[13]

In the early Middle Ages Platonism and Neoplatonism retained some of their force; by their scholarship and through their translations the late Roman writers Chalcidius, Marius Victorinus, Macrobius and Boethius helped to transmit the Platonic tradition to later times; the presence of Plato and Plotinus is felt strongly in St Augustine; and Plotinus and his important successors Porphyry, Iamblichus and Proclus were known to Byzantine and Arab philosophers. Nor was Platonism completely extinguished in the later Middle Ages; the *Timaeus* was known in a Latin translation, and Platonic doctrines drifted in through secondary sources.[14] Nevertheless it is correct to say that the later Middle Ages mark the triumph of Aristotelianism. Chaucer's Clerk of Oxenford preferred to have twenty volumes of Aristotle and not of Plato at the head of his bed. Platonism during this period was not dead, but it slumbered, to be reawakened in the Italian Renaissance of the fifteenth century.

RENAISSANCE PLATONISM

We shall now speak briefly of Marsilio Ficino (1433–99), founder of the Florentine Academy, and of his younger contemporary Giovanni Pico della

Mirandola (1463–94).[15] These two philosophers reinvigorated Platonism; they nourished it with their enthusiasm; in their hands it became an instrument of reconciliation between pagan philosophy and Christianity; and they reshaped it and enlarged it with liberal infusions of Pythagorean, Orphic, Hermetic and (in the case of Pico) Cabalist ideas. One is tempted to think of these latter accretions as the moraine and detritus of Platonism, but it must be remembered that occult ideas were treated seriously in the Renaissance and cannot be dismissed lightly by anyone who wants to understand the Renaissance mind.

Ficino never repudiated Aristotle. Ficino's logic, his use of categories, his method of demonstration, his doctrine of essence and being, his concept of natural appetite—all these belong to scholasticism. But the centre of his interest was Plato. Responding to the stimulus of humanism, that vast enterprise of teaching and scholarship whose aim was to recover and interpret the ancient texts, Ficino made a complete translation into Latin of Plato and of Plotinus; and with the support of his learned, delightful patron Cosimo de' Medici he founded an academy in Florence where men of like mind discoursed together on Platonic questions.

In the philosophy of Ficino, Platonic and Plotinist doctrines are blended and fused with Christian ideas. Ficino accepted the traditional cosmology—that is to say, the conception of a chain of being descending from God at the top to inert matter at the bottom. But he modified the picture, making it dynamic rather than static, with its various parts capable of influencing one another through affinities or active forces (§S–382: p. 43). This is how he brought astrology and the occult into his system, and why he laid so much emphasis upon the idea (drawn first from the *Timaeus* and then from the *Enneads*) of a world-soul. Moreover the peculiar position of the soul in the hierarchy as a meeting-place of spirit and matter was for him a doctrine of central importance. It accorded with his humanist belief in the dignity of man; and it was at the heart of his belief in the value of the contemplative life. Repelled by the ugliness of the phenomenal world, the mind turns in on itself, contemplates itself, and thus releases the soul to make a Plotinian ascent which carries it into the intelligible world, a journey that culminates in a direct, intuitive, mystical apprehension of God. According to Kristeller, it was Ficino's refusal to accept the idea that this contemplative process ends in death which persuaded him, more than any other reason, of the immortality of the soul.[16]

Ficino's most important bequest to European literature was his doctrine of Platonic love. (The very phrase was his coinage.) He developed the concept in his *Commentary on Plato's 'Symposium'* (composed 1475), an attractively written dialogue that established the vogue in sixteenth-century Italy of the *trattato d'amore*. Ficino equated the idea of love in Plato with divine love, and he further asserted that when two persons love one another, what they truly love is the reflection of divine beauty and goodness that is in each of them. Hence it was that Ficino depreciated sexual and celebrated spiritual love: 'the passion of a lover is not quenched by the mere touch or sight of a body, for it does not desire this or that body, but desires the splendour of the divine light shining through bodies, and is amazed and awed by it.'[17] This conflation of human and divine love, of the love of soul for soul, established the tradition that lay behind Donne's 'The Extasie' and behind the whole sub-genre of 'Platonicks' in English poetry.[18] Milton's interest in angelical love (the subject broached by Adam which brought a blush to the angel Raphael's cheek) owes something to this tradition.

HERMETIC PHILOSOPHY, CABALISM AND THE OCCULT

Whereas Ficino aimed at a synthesis of Platonism and Christianity, Pico della Mirandola cast a wider net. His goal was the reconciliation of Plato with Aristotle, and of both with Christianity. Whether he could have succeeded in this large purpose even if he had lived longer (he died at the age of thirty-one) is a moot question. What is interesting to the student of the seventeenth century is the impulse Pico gave to occult studies. Pico was attracted to occult doctrines as a result of his syncretism; that is to say, he believed that a common core of truth could be extracted from all philosophies and all theologies. Consequently he opened his mind not only to Platonism (in which he followed his teacher and friend Ficino), and not only to mediaeval Aristotelianism (in which he went beyond Ficino), but also to systems of occult thought such as Cabalism, Hermeticism, Orphism, Zoroastrianism and magic. It may seem surprising, given these beliefs, that Pico made a powerful attack on astrology; but astrology is a form of determinism which undermines the theory of magic; as C. S. Lewis has pointed out, 'magic and astrology . . . are in tendency opposed. The magician asserts human omnipotence; the astrologer, human impotence.'[19] So Pico, persuaded of man's dignity and of his free-will, rejected astrology. Instead, he embraced Jewish Cabalism and pagan Hermeticism, both of which he viewed as reaching conclusions which anticipate and also confirm Christian doctrine.

Jewish Cabalism rose approximately in the third century in pre-Muslim Spain. At that time, and for seven centuries thereafter, it devoted itself to mystical contemplation and elaboration of Ezekiel's vision of God's throne and chariot (the 'Merkabah'). Both Merkabah mysticism and the later mediaeval Cabala which followed it have their roots in earlier Jewish speculation and in Gnosticism, but the mediaeval Cabala has a distinctive character. It is exegetical and allegorical. Its affinities are with Philo and with Plotinus. Particularly is this so in its emphasis upon the transcendence of God, the *En-Soph*, the Infinite, who lies beyond definition and beyond existence. Similarly, the theory of emanations in Philo and Plotinus is represented in mediaeval Cabalism by the doctrine of the *Sephiroth*, a complex hierarchy of intermediaries who created and govern the world, but whose power emanates ultimately from the *En-Soph*.

Pico's knowledge of the Cabala was not profound. He could read Hebrew, having sought out Jewish teachers of the language, and while it is doubtful whether he read the *Zohar*, the major text of mediaeval Cabalism, he did read a commentary on that work by Menachem Recanati, and he had in his library a

Latin translation of a manuscript by Joseph Gikatilia, who was the most systematic thinker among the mediaeval Cabalists (§S–345: p. 19). What appealed to him were the hermeneutic techniques of the Cabalists. They strove always to uncover hidden meanings through the use of analogy, allegory and numerology—all these methods obviously presupposing that they had a theory of the unity of knowledge. They believed that all things are connected to all other things in a network of symbolic relationships and actual correspondences. Pico thought that the Cabalists learned these techniques from Plato, who 'himself concealed his doctrines beneath coverings of allegory, veils of myth, mathematical images, and unintelligible signs of fugitive meaning',[20] and who derived this special knowledge from Moses and ultimately from the Egyptians.

Pico was not an adept at numerology, but his praise gave it currency in the later Renaissance and seventeenth century. In the Cabala it is based on the fact that the letters of the Hebrew alphabet are used also as numbers. Accordingly, in the technique called *Gematria*, the Cabalists would look for words having the same numerical value and they would feel at liberty to use these words interchangeably for meaning.[21] Christian Cabalists applied the method to Greek and Latin texts; and they broadened the Cabalist interest in number to include Pythagorean and Platonic ideas as well as the ideas of that extremely interesting Platonist nearer to their own time, namely Nicholas of Cusa (1401–64), who viewed mathematics as a key to the understanding of the universe and, beyond that, to the knowledge of God.[22] Among the philosophers of the occult who were attracted to the metaphysical status of number were Cornelius Agrippa, John Dee and Robert Fludd. Because the minds of these thinkers were saturated in cosmic analogies, they sought out various permutations of number—five and three were favourites, the latter from its association with the Trinity—and linked them with other aspects of the cosmos, after which they read them as principles of the structure of Creation. John Dee said that God's 'Numbryng was his Creatyng of all thinges', and that if God were to take away the 'Unit' of a thing then that thing would be '*discreated*'.[23]

This 'mathematicism' was known in the seventeenth century, but it must be said that it played only a minor part in the literature of that time. Cleveland was amused by it when he said that 'Numbring of kisses Arithmeticke proves',[24] although by saying so he acknowledged the presence of the idea. On the other hand Sir Thomas Browne entertained the idea seriously (with a mixture of playfulness that kept the work from becoming ridiculous) in the *The Garden of Cyrus*, an amazing evocation of the number five in the shape of a quincunx. Browne saw this figure almost everywhere and he read it as the signature of God. It is the structural principle of order 'according to the ordainer of order and mystical Mathematicks of the City of Heaven'.[25]

Browne's eclectic mind was hospitable to the Cabala, not only for its numerological interests but for its general concern with hidden meanings. It was one further confirmation of his belief that 'this visible world is but a picture of the invisible'.[26] The question is, Browne aside, how far did Cabalism penetrate the literature of the seventeenth century? It was widely known but, except by a few, it was not deeply held. Robert Fludd and Thomas Vaughan, brother of the poet Henry, were its theorists. Fludd believed he had completed the work begun by Pico of reconciling Plato and Aristotle. He identified the ten spheres of Aristotle with the ten Sephiroth—and this on the basis of a false etymology of the Greek *Sphera* from the Hebrew *Sephira*.[27] Vaughan was a follower of Agrippa, for whom the Cabala was a branch of alchemy. In Vaughan's fantastic system the ten principles of alchemy are the ten Sephiroth of the Cabala. Other writers who were versed in the Cabala but who did not make it a central feature of their doctrine were Henry Reynolds and the Cambridge Platonists Henry More and Ralph Cudworth.[28] Still other writers made only casual references to it, as did Burton in *The Anatomy of Melancholy*. What was Milton's attitude? He had read More's *Conjectures on the Cabala* and probably also Pico's *Heptaplus*; but there is no Cabala in the *De Doctrina Christiana* and there are only a few mild suggestions of it in *Paradise Lost*. One of these resemblances is to the Cabalist doctrine known as *Zimzum*, which appears to have been in Milton's mind when he described the creation of the cosmos as the result of God's voluntary self-limitation or retirement from a portion of space (*Paradise Lost*, VII, 166–73). But this idea is hardly sufficient evidence to support the claim that Milton was immersed in the Cabala and that his most essential ideas are reducible to a Cabalistic mysticism of light. Milton's Cabalism is slight, and metaphysical conceptions of light play only a minor role in the Cabala.[29]

Probably the best answer to the question of Cabalist influence was given by Marjorie H. Nicolson, who wrote that although Cabalism 'permeates much seventeenth century literature, it is as impossible to separate it sharply from other ideas of a particular author as it is to define exactly the particular brand of Platonism he held. By the seventeenth century, Cabalism had become so fused and intermingled with other ways of thinking that we look for it less in defined doctrine and creed than in an attitude toward a question.'[30] That attitude has been described as 'the emphasis on ethical conduct as a guide along the paths toward a transcendent God'.[31] Possibly a subtler understanding of the question, one that is closer to literature, is expressed by Gershom Scholem: 'Kabbalism is distinguished by an attitude towards language . . . Kabbalists who differ in almost everything else are at one in regarding language as something more precious than an inadequate instrument for contact between human beings . . . Language in its purest form has a mystical value. Speech reaches God because it comes from God' (§ S–406: p. 17). The search for 'language in its purest form', for a plainness of utterance that reaches directly to God, is an attribute of the poetry of George Herbert. Other writers wanted to expunge the false colours of rhetoric; some, like Bacon and Hobbes, and, later, Sprat, wrote from the standpoint of a scientific theory of truth. But Herbert thought of language, that is, of the language of poetry, as a spiritual instrument, as speech that reaches God because it comes from God. According to his 'Prayer' (I), it is 'Gods breath in man returning to his birth', it is 'The soul in paraphrase'. In this sense of language transcending the normal functions of language we may see a tincture of Cabalism in Herbert, acquired indirectly from a variety of Christian sources.

Much that has been said concerning Renaissance Cabalism can be said also of Hermeticism. Whereas Pico set Christian Cabalism in motion, Ficino was the progenitor of the Renaissance interest in Hermeticism. When Ficino was ready to begin his translation of Plato, in 1463, his patron Cosimo brought him a new set of manuscripts in Greek, fourteen treatises by an author whom Ficino believed to be an Egyptian priest called Hermes Trismegistus. Cosimo ordered Ficino to put aside Plato and begin work immediately on Hermes. This notion of priority reflects both Cosimo and Ficino's belief in the greater antiquity of the Hermetic texts and their feeling, characteristic of Renaissance attitudes towards the past, that what is older must also be wiser. Ficino translated the manuscripts into Latin and called them by the name of the first treatise in the group, *Pimander*; they are now referred to as the *Corpus Hermeticum*. The other surviving Hermetic texts also known to Ficino and used by him were the *Asclepius* in a Latin translation wrongly ascribed to Apuleius and fragments preserved in an anthology of Stobaeus.

Of the single authorship of these texts, of their great antiquity, and of the historicity of their author Hermes Trismegistus, Ficino entertained no doubts whatsoever. He believed that Hermes lives in the time of Moses, that he wrote in ancient Egyptian which was later translated into Greek, and that he founded an ancient theology, *prisca theologia*, which proceeded from him to Orpheus, thence to Pythagoras, to Plato's teacher Philolaus, and finally to 'our Divine Plato' himself.[32] On all these points Ficino was wrong. The Hermetic texts were written not in Egyptian but in Greek, and Egyptian influence on their content is barely perceptible, if it exists at all; they were not by a single author but by many; they did not antedate Plato but were produced approximately between A.D. 100 and 300. Thus they could not have influenced Plato; but they were certainly influenced by him. Their sources were Platonic and Neoplatonic, Persian and Jewish (the latter for affinities between *Pimander* and the account of creation in the Book of Genesis).

Ficino's defective scholarship—his peculiar view of the history of the Hermetic texts—was supported by a Christian tradition. Both Lactantius and Augustine were acquainted with portions of the texts and both believed that Hermes Trismegistus was the real author and that they were very old, older than Plato. Lactantius in particular was impressed by passages in the *Asclepius* and the *Pimander* which referred to the Son of God; he read those passages as gentile prophecies of Christianity. Augustine was less enthusiastic; he conceded that Hermes had intimations of the truth concerning God; but he was repelled by a long, idolatrous passage in *Asclepius* in which are described the magical techniques used by the Egyptians to animate their statues by drawing down into them the spirits of their gods. Ficino, who believed in the power of magic to effect good ends, conveniently omitted Augustine's criticism, preferring to concentrate on Lactantius's interpretation of Christian prophecy. Ficino's translation, and his *Argumentum* prefaced to it, launched Hermetic philosophy on its career in the Renaissance.

It was a philosophy that breathed an atmosphere of piety and asceticism.

Fantastic, magical and theurgical elements were mixed in plentifully. The cosmological frame of reference was astrological. Most pervasive in the texts is the outlook of gnosis, of the possession of spiritual insights into which a young disciple is initiated by an older master. Having been produced by different authors over a period of two centuries, the texts naturally express a variety of doctrines, some of which are mutually contradictory. Frances Yates says that 'it is their religious approach, their character as documents of religious experience, which give the *Hermetica* a unity which they entirely lack as a thought system' (§S–427: p. 22). Another student of these texts, A.-J. Festugière, finds two predominant, opposing strains: pessimist gnosis and optimist gnosis. Pessimist gnosis sees the material world as evil, guided by the baneful influence of the stars. The whole object of the Hermetic philosopher in this view is to lead an ascetic life which will enable him to transcend contaminated matter and rise into the spiritual world of the divine mind. Optimist gnosis, on the other hand, is pantheistic. The universe is impregnated with God. The earth, the sun, the stars and planets are alive, moved by God's power, animated by his spirit, made beneficent by his presence.[33] To contemplate this living universe, to possess it, as it were, in the mind, is to enter the *mens*, the Divine Intellect.

Hermetic philosophy had a wide circulation in the sixteenth century; Kristeller has counted sixteen separate printed editions of Ficino's translations besides numerous manuscript copies (§S–385: pp. 223 ff.). Not all who knew it were its adherents; but it doubtless exerted an influence. In seventeenth-century England it had a smaller diffusion. It was mentioned favourably by Henry Reynolds in *Mythomystes* (1632), and the *Corpus Hermeticum* was translated into English by J. Everard in 1650. Burton refers to it frequently, although rather as a student of curiosities than as a believer.[34] Milton makes only three direct allusions, of which the most famous is to 'thrice great Hermes' in *Il Penseroso* (l. 88); but I do not believe he was deeply affected by Hermetic thought. Whether or not the poetry of Henry Vaughan expresses Hermetic doctrines is a disputed question into which I shall not enter; his twin brother Thomas was certainly an enthusiastic believer.

What we can say about seventeenth-century Hermeticism generally is that, like Cabalism, it was less a matter of doctrine than of habits of thought, of mental coloration. Two attitudes in particular flowed into the seventeenth century from their Hermetic source. The first is vitalism, the belief (sometimes no more than a submerged feeling) that the natural world is animate; and the second is 'correspondency' or what may be called 'reflectionism', according to which the visible world is a mirror or reflection of the invisible. This latter outlook had an important corollary, namely the belief that the human mind is, like the mind of God, creative, and can generate within itself the invisible out of the visible. At the close of the sixteenth century, and in the early decades of the seventeenth, these attitudes were consciously held by conservative thinkers, by those for whom the intellectual past was a primary source of truth. But vitalism can be detected in such an unlikely place as the mind of Francis Bacon, and correspondence is present in Lord Herbert of Cherbury and is writ large in Sir

Thomas Browne, both of whom responded to the newer, 'modern' outlook while they preserved important features of the old.

BACON, LORD HERBERT, AND BROWNE

Bacon, Herbert and Browne are figures of transition in the intellectual history of the seventeenth century. They are Janus-faced. They look backward and forward, although Bacon looked forward more than he looked backward and more than the other two looked forward. He regarded himself as the founder of the scientific outlook, as *buccinator novi temporis*, the trumpeter of the new age, and in the later seventeenth century this was how he was perceived and how his influence was felt. Nor can it be denied that *The Advancement of Learning* and *Novum Organum* are revolutionary works. They try to revise traditional attitudes towards nature, to free matter from the contempt in which it was held in the Platonic tradition, to remove the stigma conveyed by the phrase 'forbidden knowledge'. Bacon wanted to open the mind to the truth of nature; he asked men to confront nature with humility, 'to dwell among things soberly'. He understood that error is built into the very structure of thought. There are, he said, 'Idols of the Mind', characteristic postures of thought—some are common to all men, some are peculiar to individuals, some arise from the confusion of words for things, and some derive from the vain speculations of the various philosophical schools—which predispose us to see in nature what we want to see and not what is truly there. Bacon would sweep these cobwebs away and replace them with a scientific method of observation and experiment. Because he lacked a mathematical sense he did not sufficiently appreciate the role played by reason itself in the scientific process; but he did try to penetrate to the essence, or, as he called them, the 'Formes' of things, and he constructed a theory of forms based (paradoxically) on the scholastic principle that the nature of objects can be understood by naming their *differentiae* until their own essential character, their 'whatness' or 'quidditas', is reached. But although Bacon's theory of Forms has a mediaeval ring, it is put in the service of a distinctly modern idea of science. Bacon thought always of the social implications of science, of science for the 'relief of man's estate'. His advocacy of this idea is remote from the contemplative atmosphere of the Platonic tradition.

Nor did Bacon compromise his modernity by his belief in the truth of revelation. Bacon conceived of truth as a bifurcation: there is the truth of God's word and the truth of God's works, of revelation and of natural science. These truths must be kept apart, for if religion is applied to science or science to religion, then what results is not the truth but only false religion and false science. Bacon would have agreed that all truth is ultimately religious in the sense that the truth of Nature is the truth of *God's* works; but he insisted that we can understand Nature, God's works, only through our knowledge of second causes, that is to say, of the natural causes of things. These causes are not to be found in revelation but in the observation of Nature itself, whereas the search for final causes, for purpose in Nature, is barren, 'and like a virgin consecrated to God, produces nothing'.[35] Although Bacon accepted religious truth, and there is no reason to doubt his sincerity on this point, his bias is to scientific truth. As Basil Willey has written, 'In *theory* [Bacon] seeks the Kingdom of Heaven first . . . But the effect of his teaching is to put the Kingdom of Man first'.[36]

Having said these things about the great propagandist of modern science, I return to my original point, which is that notwithstanding Bacon's unquestioned modernity, his thought was yet tinctured with the vitalism of Hermetic philosophy. His vitalism was not explicit, as it was in his contemporary William Gilbert, who reproved Aristotle for believing that the earth is 'imperfect, dead, inanimate, and subject to decay', whereas 'Hermes, Zoroaster, Orpheus, recognise a universal soul. As for us, we deem the whole world animate.'[37] Bacon, on the other hand, did not speak of matter impregnated by soul, but he did believe in 'vital spirits', a kind of rarified or refined matter, residing in all things, whether animal, vegetable or mineral, actuating all things, endowing them with appetite and life; 'for tangible parts in bodies are stupid things; and the spirits do (in effect) all'.[38] Bacon derived this doctrine from the Hermetical alchemists, and like one of them, Paracelsus, he thought that the spirits originate in the stars.[39] Thus do we have a paradox: the advocate of new ideas is caught in the grip of old ones; but the paradox evaporates when we realise that the history of thought, particularly in the seventeenth century, is not a series of discrete forward motions but something closer to a continuum that moves by accretion.

This quality of rejecting the past while embracing it is also characteristic of Lord Herbert of Cherbury (1583–1648). He was the brother of George Herbert and himself a poet, as well as a diplomatist, a soldier and, as we gather from his *Autobiography*, a vain, mercurial personality, much given to taking offence and to fighting duels. He was also a philosopher. In France, where he served as ambassador, he became acquainted with the new currents of sceptical thought in reaction to which he produced his philosophical treatise *De Veritate*, which he published in Paris in 1624. Herbert tells us in a well known passage in the *Autobiography* that he had doubts about publishing the work, fearing a critical reception, but that his doubts were resolved when he received a sign from heaven in the form of a 'loud though gentle noise'.[40]

The object of *De Veritate* is to find a principle of absolute truth. That such truth exists, that things exist independently of our perception of them, is Herbert's first premise, which he asserts 'against imbeciles and sceptics'. In addition to absolute truth (*veritas rei*), there are, according to Herbert, three types of conditional truth. These are phenomenal truth or the truth of things as they appear to us (*veritas apparentiae*); conceptual truth or the truth of conceptions of things formed in the mind; and intellectual truth, the truth of innate ideas. The problem is how to make our perceptions and conceptions of things conform to the things in themselves. Clearly it will not suffice simply to say that appearance and reality are in agreement, since appearances can be vitiated 'if the sense organ is imperfect, or if it is of poor quality, [or] if the mind is filled with deceitful prejudices'.[41] What is needed is an arbiter between the thing perceived and the percept, a criterion for judging the truth of the conformity between appearance and reality. The solution lies in the power of the intellect to form Common Notions—conceptions of things which are universally admitted to be true by all those whose intellect is unimpaired. The Common Notions arise out of a natural instinct. They are innate ideas and they were planted in us by God, and 'We must listen to these Notions unless we prefer uncertainty'. So the question of whether our perceptions and conceptions of things conform to reality is settled for Herbert by an appeal to the Common Notions, ideas that have universal consent and that are summoned by the instinctive power of the intellect to comprehend the truth. Obviously this theory has its difficulties. How can we know that an idea is universally assented to? And even if it is, can it not be universally wrong? Herbert tried to meet these objections by that part of his treatise which is most indebted to the past. He argued that Natural Instinct, the immediate source of the Common Notions, is not confined to human beings alone, but is present in all animal species, where it is expressed as an urge to self-preservation; in fact, he said, following the Hermetic philosophers, the instinct is diffused through the whole universe, and that universe is a living organism. Natural instinct 'promotes self-preservation in the elements, the zoophytes, and even the embryo', and 'if, throughout the elements, minerals, plants and animals it promotes precisely similar functions, why should it not manifest itself in ourselves?' While this argument is not a satisfactory reply to the objections raised against Herbert's theory of truth, it does show us Herbert's mind moving among Renaissance presuppositions. He believed that human beings can instinctively know the truth of the world outside themselves because they are a part of that world, linked to it in a series of gradations on a chain or scale of being. He spoke frequently of the correspondence between microcosm and macrocosm, of 'the common character of things, or that law of correspondence between man and the world as a whole'. So he believed that 'the principles of all the differences in the world are inscribed in man'.

But if Herbert took much from the past, he pointed in the direction of modern philosophy. His rationalism, his belief in the possibility of knowledge through introspection, anticipates Descartes. His doctrine of innate ideas appealed to Leibniz and it contains more than a hint of Kant. Moreover, his rational theology, his insistence that religious ideas be subjected to the judgement of reason, and especially his exposition of the five Common Notions of Religion,[42] mark him as a precursor of Deism.

In Lord Herbert a modern and a Renaissance outlook sit uneasily together. Both outlooks are present in Sir Thomas Browne, but in him they appear to be more compatible with one another. This is due partly to Browne's temperament, which is more serene than Herbert's, but also to the fact that Browne positively welcomed paradox. He loved to lose himself in a mystery. In the tension between faith and reason, to both of which he gave his allegiance, he thought he could perceive a higher knowledge, a knowledge of the harmony, the cohesiveness of things, which for him meant a knowledge of God. Nature is a diversity;

behind it lies a unity imposed by God, so that God stands in relation to nature as an artist does to a work of art. As a man of science Browne studied nature in its diversity; as a thinker (although not a technical philosopher) he looked for the divine artistry, the principle of unity. He thought he could detect this unity in various ways—through a mystical faith in its presence; through the discovery of God's signatures or 'hieroglyphics' in nature; through the apprehension of Platonic forms, which he interpreted as ideas in the mind of God; through his belief (which he shared with Lord Herbert) in the great ladder or scale of being and the links, gradations and correspondences among its various parts. This latter idea fascinated Browne. He felt the links between himself and nature and was encouraged by that feeling to pursue his study of nature; it also nourished his tolerance of other human cultures; and it made him look inward as much as he looked outward. The old Stoic belief in the virtue of self-knowledge was raised by Browne to the assertion that inner knowledge is also knowledge of the world. 'We carry within us the wonders we seek without us; there is all Africa and her prodigies within us . . .' In *Christian Morals* he urges us to 'Astronomize in Caves', to 'delight to be alone and single with Omnipresency'. He who is thus prepared may lie in bed and be in all quarters of the Earth, 'may speculate the Universe, and enjoy the whole World in the Hermitage of himself'. These remarks do not contradict the scientific outlook of Browne's *Pseudodoxia Epidemica*; they complement it. Browne the naturalist and Browne the mystic and moralist sit well together. He was not affected by the Cartesian separation of body and mind. His impulse was to 'Joyn Sense unto Reason, and Experiment unto Speculation'.[43] He believed that the knowledge of 'sense and ocular Observation' and the knowledge of inner vision are two sides of an equation whose meaning is truth.

THE CAMBRIDGE PLATONISTS

The conviction held by Browne that the world is a unity was shared by the Cambridge Platonists. This group of theologians, philosophers and teachers flourished in the middle years of the century. Its members included Benjamin Whichcote, their spiritual founder and most revered by the others; John Smith, who died prematurely at the age of thirty-four and who was the finest writer in the group; Henry More, a prolific writer and controversialist, an erratic but always interesting mind; and Ralph Cudworth, the most penetrating thinker in the group and an important figure in the history of English idealism, who, however, wrote at interminable length, so that even sympathetic readers have been moved to call his *True Intellectual System of the Universe* 'vast and unwieldy' and 'monstrously obese'.[44]

Again and again these thinkers went back to Plato and Plotinus, to the whole Platonic tradition including Ficino and Pico, for some including also the Cabala and the *Hermetica*. Plato's belief in a world of supersensory forms was *their* belief. It is true that they quoted Plotinus more often than they quoted

Plato—Coleridge thought they should have been called the Cambridge 'Plotinists'—but Plato's theory of forms is the ground of their whole philosophical creed. As Christian Platonists they believed that Platonic idealism provided the philosophical confirmation of their faith.

That faith was tolerant and non-dogmatic. Having assimilated the syncretic tendencies in the thought of Pico and Ficino, the Cambridge Platonists believed with Herbert that Christianity was not a narrow creed, that, at least within the Protestant spectrum, it was broad enough to embrace diverse points of view. Whichcote wrote that 'Christian love and affection . . . is a point of such importance . . . that itt is not to be prejudiced, by *supposals* of differences in points of religion',[45] and More and Cudworth pleaded for liberty of conscience. They were not paragons of liberalism—they did not extend their tolerance to Roman Catholics or to the smaller, fragmented sects of the Puritan left, whom they called 'irrational' and 'enthusiasts'. But the anger they could muster—surprisingly little, considering the contentiousness of the times—they preferred to concentrate on non-believers and atheists and on the thinker whom they regarded as the *pontifex maximus* of atheism, namely Thomas Hobbes.

What set the Cambridge Platonists apart from their Christian contemporaries was their special view of reason. Whoever used the term 'reason' in that age took it to mean a source of true knowledge, a way of finding out the truth. But what is the way? The Cambridge Platonists rejected the mediaeval, scholastic method of speculation, 'a thin, aiery knowledge . . . ushered in by Syllogisms' (John Smith, in §S–397: p. 130); and they refused to believe that truth is bound up exclusively in Revelation, in the word of God. Some truth is yielded by logic, and what is in Scripture is certainly true. But the truth that is ultimate, the knowledge of what is most real, is the knowledge of God. That knowledge is attained through a rational process, by which the Cambridge Platonists really meant a spiritual process. 'I oppose not rational to spiritual', said Whichcote, 'for spiritual is most rational'.[46] Reason is thus defined as the presence of God in man enabling man to apprehend spiritual truths. 'The Spirit of a Man is the Candle of the Lord; Lighted *by* God, and lighting us *to* God.'[47]

This conception of human reason as a participation in the Divine Reason is a species of mysticism. But, as C. A. Patrides has observed, it is a mysticism that must be distinguished from the mysticism of other traditions, from 'clouds of unknowing' or the 'negative way' or the 'paroxysms of love' in St Teresa or St John of the Cross (§S–397: p. 17). It is closer to Plotinus, who said that we know God 'by *an Intellectual touch* of him'.[48] It is a paradox—a rational mysticism. Yet it must finally be differentiated from Plotinus too. In Plotinus the ascent of the soul through the realm of Intellect to its union with the One is achieved by means of meditation, and the success of the journey is signalled by a feeling of ineffable joy. In Cambridge Platonism the human soul is 'deified' by moral experience in the present world. The Cambridge philosophers rejected the asceticism of Plotinus. They believed that the Divine Reason is made manifest in human beings by their moral actions, by the practice rather than the mere contemplation of the highest ethical principles. Moral conduct is a source of divine knowledge, a better source than the abstractions of the Schoolmen or the *pilpulism*, the sterile, theological disputations of the Protestant sects. Smith said that Theology is rather 'a *Divine* life then a *Divine* science', and Whichcote that 'the *State* of Religion lyes, in short, in this; A good Mind, and a good Life. All else is *about* Religion' (§S–397: pp. 128, 334).

From the association of reason on the one side with the rational being of God, and on the other with the moral life of man, flowed two corollary beliefs. The first was that morality is absolute and immutable. 'Good and Evil are not by *positive* Institution; Are not things arbitrary' (§S–397: p. 328). Morality is prior to and independent of human institutions and human laws. They depend on it rather than it on they. And the second position is that the will is free, that moral choices are freely taken. If reason is expressed in the moral life of man, then man must make his moral choices freely; if the choices are not under man's control, if they are 'necessitated' or predetermined, then they are by definition not rational. Milton shared this conviction with the Platonists. 'Reason also is choice,' he said in *Paradise Lost* (III, 108); and in *Areopagitica* he wrote that 'When God gave [Adam] reason, he gave him freedom to choose, for reason is but choosing' (*Works*, IV, 319).

All the beliefs so far described and attributed to Whichcote and Smith were held also by Henry More and Ralph Cudworth; but More and Cudworth set themselves the larger task of consciously articulating a philosophical response to what they perceived as challenges to the view of a numinous, ordered, spiritual world. For More and Cudworth that world was compounded intellectually of the elements of the Platonic tradition, including Hermeticism and Cabalism; but an attack on Hermeticism came from an unexpected quarter, from the brilliant scholar Isaac Casaubon, who in 1614 demonstrated that the *Hermetica* were not ancient Egyptian texts but the products of Christian times, in his opinion forgeries by Christian authors. More and Cudworth quibbled over some details of Casaubon's argument, but in the end they accepted it. The prestige of Hermeticism had been undermined, and thus fell one of the pieces of the older world-picture (§S–427).

A greater danger came from Descartes and Hobbes. Descartes published his *Discours de la méthode* in 1637 and the *Meditationes* in 1641. The *Discours* entered England in the year of its publication when a copy was sent to Hobbes from Paris by Sir Kenelm Digby. It is a remarkable book, succinct, lucid, elegantly reasoned. It separates itself from the past more sharply than either Herbert's *De Veritate* or Bacon's *Novum Organum*; even the fact that it was written in French stamps it as a work of modern philosophy, for, as Descartes says, it was 'written in the language of my country, in the hope that those who avail themselves of their natural reason alone, may be better judges of my opinions than those who give heed only to the writings of the ancients'.[49] Like Lord Herbert, Descartes was deeply conscious of the currents of sceptical thought in France, and so he tried to discover a method for establishing absolute truth. He began by exercising his mind in a kind of fictional scepticism, as it were disimagining the world, emptying his mind of all its received contents, and then readmitting only those thoughts whose truth is unexceptional; that is, those thoughts that are apprehended so clearly and distinctly that their truth can no longer be doubted.

Two primary truths that cannot be destroyed by this self-imposed scepticism are the existence of thought itself, and the existence of God. Thought may be true or false, it may arise from the waking or the dreaming state, but that it exists cannot be doubted, and from this it follows that a thinking being must exist. 'Je pense, donc je suis.' Moreover, although it is possible to imagine a world in which physical objects do not exist, it is not possible to imagine a world in which thought does not exist, because the very thought of a non-mental world is itself an instance of thought. This conclusion is the basis of Descartes's celebrated dualism. The world is divided into two separate and distinct realms of being: mind, *res cogitans*, the world of thought, spirit, soul; and body, *res extensae*, the world of extended matter. Mind and body may interact—Cartesianism struggled with the problem of interaction—but they remain essentially different.

The second truth whose certainty cannot be shaken even by a feigned scepticism is the existence of God. Descartes's proof of the existence of God depended upon the prior assertion that thought must imply the existence of a thinking being. Such a being is aware of his imperfections, of the limitations of his power; and these imperfections must imply the existence of perfections against which the imperfections can be measured, and further of a being who possesses these perfections and ultimately of a Being who possesses ultimate perfection and from which all things proceed and upon which they depend. Such an ultimate perfection is God. Descartes summed up the argument by saying 'that it is not possible that my nature should be what it is, and indeed that I should have in myself the idea of a God, if God did not veritably exist'.[50] God is thus a rational abstraction.

This argument for the existence of God is less impressive than the famous 'Cogito ergo sum'—'I think, therefore I am'—but both arguments appealed to Henry More when he first encountered them. He wrote a letter of fulsome praise to Descartes in 1648, calling him a philosophical giant among pygmies.

Although More had some misgivings about Descartes's belief that animals are mere mechanisms, a view that went against his own belief in animate nature, he nevertheless welcomed Descartes as an ally in the defence of spirit. Descartes and he had the same end in view, or so he thought, with Descartes traveling 'the lower Rode of *Democritisme*, amidst the thick dust of Atoms and flying particles of Matter', while More ascended 'the high and airey Hills of *Platonisme*, in that more thin and subtil Region of *Immateriality*'; yet both met together 'at the same Goale, namely at the Entrance of the holy Bible' (§ S–397: pp. 29–30). But this optimism was misplaced. More's early excitement gave way to doubts and ended in outright opposition. The problem was Descartes's dualism and mechanism, his separation of matter and spirit and his belief that the world was a mechanism wholly devoid of spirit. Although More thought at first that mechanism assisted in 'the salving the *Phaenomena* in the world', he came at last to perceive that a thoroughgoing mechanism was destructive of the older picture of an interanimated universe, a world inhabited by spirit and spiritual beings. In

1665 he wrote that 'the phænomena of the world cannot be solved merely mechanically, but that there is a necessity of the assistance of a substance distinct from matter, that is, of a spirit, or being incorporeal'; and in 1669 he said that 'the Mechanical part of the Cartesian Philosophy, which boasts that all Phenomena in the World can be explained only by motion and substance . . . and that there is no extension not material or corporeal, most sweetly misleads scholiasts and half-educated men'.[51]

In his defence of spirit More drew on a variety of arguments. He asserted that spirit is in the world and not out of it, because to say it is out of the world is to affirm what Hobbists and atheists are saying, namely that spirit is nowhere and nothing. Spirit and matter therefore both have the attribute of extension, although, unlike matter, spirit is penetrable. Unless it is granted that spirit has extension, there can be no place in the world for an immanent God. Spirit is in fact analogous to space in that both are extended and incorporeal; and infinite space—the 'spaces incomprehensible', the 'vasty deep' only recently opened up by modern astronomy—shares attributes with God himself.[52] Thus the universe is possessed of 'essential spissitude'; it is a 'vital and spermaticall' universe, alive with spirit; and spirit is not a metaphysical abstraction, no *res cogitans*, but a real, extended substance. To think otherwise is to undermine religion and to destroy the grand intellectual picture, built up over so many centuries, of eternal coherence and cosmic order.

If spirit is a penetrable substance, how is its presence detected? By its effects, said More. He believed that two types of evidence confirm the presence of spirit. The first is evidence drawn from natural science. In one of his letters to Descartes he said that a vase emptied of air retains its shape because of the sustaining pressure of 'divine extension'.[53] And he argued similarly that Robert Boyle's experiments with a vacuum pump demonstrated 'that there is a Principle transcending the nature and power of Matter', a principle which must be equated with spirit, since 'the Mechanick Laws of Matter' cannot by themselves account for the power of a vacuum pump to raise enormous weights.[54]

The second type of 'evidence' was the testimony of witchcraft and occult phenomena. More's argument, in which he was supported by Joseph Glanvill, was that spirit can manifest itself for good or evil, and that the power of witches is an instance of evil spirit. Hence More thought that to disbelieve in witches is to take the first step towards a general denial of spirit and thus to fall into the trap of Hobbist materialism and atheism: 'No Spirit, no God.' The idea was not new. Thomas Browne said that 'they that doubt of [witches], doe not onely deny them, but Spirits; and are obliquely and upon consequence a sort, not of Infidels, but Atheists'.[55] So More and Glanvill, singly and together, collected and published tales of witches and apparitions and personally investigated others, always with the view that 'the Topic is a sensible proof of Spirits and another Life'.[56] They were responding to a scepticism set in motion by Reginald Scot's *Discoverie of Witchcraft* (1584) and repeated with varying degrees of force by writers such as Francis Osborne, John Webster and Hobbes. The effect of this scepticism was, as Browne had said and More understood, 'to destroy the Ladder and scale of creatures'.[57]

CUDWORTH

Behind More's dispute with Descartes lay the spectre of Hobbes. More may have felt that Descartes lacked the 'True Notion of a Spirit', but at least Descartes *had* a notion, whereas Hobbes proclaimed that 'that which is not Body, is no part of the Universe; And because the Universe is All, that which is no part of it, is *Nothing*; and consequently *no where*' (§P–50: p. 371). Even God himself is 'a most pure, simple, invisible spirit corporeal'.[58] Hobbes's materialism was radical and complete. There was no place in it for magic, witchcraft, angels, demons or for a mystical theology or for absolute ideas or Platonic forms. It was the boldest attack yet made on traditional ways of thinking and therefore had to be repulsed if the tradition was to survive. Thus the main task Cudworth set for himself in *The True Intellectual System of the Universe*, completed in 1670 but not published till 1678, was the refutation of Hobbes.

Cudworth did not repudiate dualism. What he argued was that matter is passive, incapable of self-activity. It is 'a bulky extension and tremourous magnitude' and nothing more. If the world consisted entirely of matter, then the world would be eternally at rest. 'There could be no motion or action at all in it; no life, cogitation, consciousness; no intellection, appetite, or volition (which things do yet make up the greatest part of the universe), but all would be a dead lump.'[59] It follows that there is an entity besides matter, and this is Mind. Mind is an incorporeal principle in animate beings. It accounts for consciousness, thought, reflection, awareness, none of which can be accounted for by the movement of matter alone. Hobbes believed that sense-perception is a mechanical process resulting from the pressure of external objects on the organs of sense, and consciousness is the product of 'internal [corporeal] motions in the head', to which Cudworth replied that if such a theory of sensation and consciousness is accepted, 'then would every thing that suffered and reacted motion, such as looking-glasses, have something both of sense and of understanding in them'.[60] Sensation may begin as a physical process, but it ends in a mental perception which is non-material. Matter is 'brute and senseless'; only Mind has the power to think, to reflect on what it has thought, to imagine, to create, to will, and to apprehend things not found in physical nature, such as proportions, relations, contextures, perfect mathematical figures. In fact, relational knowledge, knowledge not conveyed by the senses, is true knowledge, whereas sensory knowledge is merely 'phantasmal'. A watch does not consist of its parts nor even of its parts working together but of a *mental understanding* of the relationship of its parts.[61] In the same way we can understand the true nature of the universe created by God. It is an intellectual system because it is an aspect of Mind. What we know of it truly is its harmony and order, the fitness of its parts.

But what is it that 'makes all things, thus to conspire everywhere, and agree together into one Harmony'? Cudworth said that it is not necessary to assume that God, the author of universal order, intervenes in every intimate operation of nature. Such intervention would render God's task 'operose, solicitous, and distractious', and it would make God responsible for occasional minor imperfections in the system, 'errors and bungles' such as monstrous births, flies, gnats,

etc. Instead, God delegated the day-to-day operation of the system to subordinate agencies, called by Cudworth 'plastic natures'. These are instinctive
non-material powers which influence the behaviour of all natural things. They
carry out God's purposes, but because they work by instinct rather than by
reflection they are capable of making mistakes. Cudworth thought that his
doctrine of 'plastic natures' avoided the extremes of Hobbesian mechanism and
Cartesian Occasionalism on the one hand, and the continuous miraculous
intervention of God on the other.

What Cudworth insisted on above all was that, notwithstanding insignificant
lapses, the universe is a structure of order, charged with God's purposes,
animated and moved by non-material Mind. It is a network of concatenations
arranged according to a system of values, with God at the top and 'senseless
matter' at the bottom. If man were what Hobbes claimed, a mechanism, then he
would be no different from 'senseless matter'. 'He that does not perceive any
higher degree of perfection in a man than in an oyster, nay, than in a clod of
earth or lump of ice, in a piece of paste or piecrust, hath not the reason or
understanding of a man in him.' But, said Cudworth, 'there is unquestionably a
scale or ladder of nature, and degrees of perfection and entity one above
another, as of life, sense, and cogitation, above dead, senseless, and unthinking
matter; of reason and understanding above sense . . .'.[62]

HOBBES

The main target of More and Cudworth's wrath, the philosopher who in their
view (and in the view of many of their contemporaries) did the greatest violence
to the traditional belief in cosmic and moral order, was Hobbes.[63] This does not
mean that Hobbes took nothing from the past. No philosopher has ever been
totally immune from the tradition. But Hobbes took from the past what sorted
best with his scientific and naturalist bias. He admired Plato for the appreciation
of geometry, though he rejected utterly Plato's theory of forms. From the late
mediaeval thinker Ockham he derived his nominalism, that is, his belief that
when we speak of universals we are speaking only of names rather than of real
things. From the fifteenth- and sixteenth-century school of Aristotelian
philosophers in Padua he developed his theory of scientific method, which
states that for its solution a scientific problem must first be broken down and
studied in its constituent parts and then be recomposed into a whole.[64] The
resolutive-compositive method forms the structure of Hobbes's theory of the
commonwealth in Leviathan.

Yet it is as a modern that Hobbes must be understood. T. S. Eliot, who disliked
Hobbes intensely, called him an 'upstart', and there is a sense, disallowing the
pejorative meaning of that term, in which Eliot was right. Whenever Hobbes
employed the tradition, it was in the service of a modern outlook. Consider the
opening of Leviathan. Hobbes says that the State is an artificial man whose parts
are analogous to the anatomy of a natural man.

... the *Soveraignty* is an Artificial *Soul* ... The *Magistrates,* and other *Officers* of Judicature and Execution, artificial *Joynts*; *Reward* and Punishment ... are the *Nerves,* that do the same in the Body Natural; The *Wealth* and *Riches* of all the particular members, are the *Strength*; *Salus Populi* (the *peoples safety*) its *Businesse*; *Councellours,* by whom all things needfull for it to know, are suggested unto it, are the *Memory*; *Equity* and *Lawes,* an artificiall *Reason* and *Will*; *Concord, Health*; *Sedition, Sicknesse*; and *Civill War, Death*.

The 'Body Politique' metaphor is a commonplace of political thought in the sixteenth and early seventeenth centuries. It is an instance of the theory of correspondences between the macrocosm and the microcosm.[65] Thomas Starkey, writing in the 1530s, said that 'this [politic] body hath his parts, which resemble also the parts of the body of man, of which the most general to our purpose be these: the heart, head, hands, and feet. The heart is the king, prince and ruler or the state', etc.; and Edward Forset wrote in 1606 that 'the Commonweale with all her parts ... is ... set forth by sundry fit resemblances ... but by none more properly than eyther by the uniuersall masse of the whole world ... or else by the body of a whole man, being the lesser world, even the diminutiue and modell of that wide extending uniuersall'.[66] Hobbes's use of the metaphor appears to place him in the tradition of the theory of correspondences; but Hobbes used the metaphor because he felt that he had to address the presuppositions of his audience. As far as he was concerned the metaphor was a convenient illustration rather than an assumption of truth about correspondences. Finding similitudes merely exercises one's wit, whereas 'they that observe differences ... are said to have a *good Judgment*'. In 'all rigorous search of Truth', metaphors 'are utterly excluded' (§P–50: pp. 33, 34). And the assumption behind the doctrine of correspondences, namely that the 'marking and matching of the workes of the uniuerse' reveal 'the finger of God', that, as Thomas Browne said, 'to call our selves a microcosme, or little world' was not merely 'a pleasant trope of Rhetorick' but 'a reall truth'[67]—that assumption Hobbes regarded as simply false. The cosmos and the human world are not linked in an ordered structure. They are not guided by divine purposes, and human institutions are shaped by strictly human wills.

It is in this secular, naturalistic spirit that Hobbes developed his political philosophy. The portrayal of human nature in *Leviathan* is realistic, not in a modern psychological sense, but in the sense that it is freed of theological preconceptions and moral admonitions. It is what Hobbes thought man really is, rather than what he ought to be.

What was Hobbes's view of human nature? He began by saying that all men are naturally equal, both in their physical and mental capacities. It is true that there are individual differences in strength, stature, etc., but these may be compensated for by the shorter man getting a longer sword or by weaker men joining in a confederacy against the stronger man. And as to intellectual abilities, these (setting aside injuries to the brain) are but the products of experience, 'which equal time, equally bestows on all men, in those things they equally apply themselves unto' (§P–50: pp. 60–1). Although Hobbes did not explicitly

state that women participate in this equality, neither did he exclude them, and
as he said he was writing about 'the Natural Condition of Mankind' it is not
improper to conclude that he rejected the tradition that stretched from antiquity
to his own time and beyond of the mental inferiority of women.

From this equality of ability, said Hobbes, arises equality of hope in achieving
one's goals. All men desire roughly the same things and in as much as they have
roughly the same capacities to get what they want, they must, in the absence of
external restraints, find themselves in a perpetual competition and warfare. In
this state of nature ego will clash with ego; art, industry, commerce will be
impossible; the hand of every man will be against every other; and the life of
man will be 'solitary, poor, nasty, brutish, and short' (§P–50: p. 62). The picture
of the state of nature is hypothetical, not historical, although Hobbes did make a
feeble attempt to confirm it from experience by referring to the fact that people
arm themselves against intruders, lock their doors and chests at night, etc.; and
he said (employing his characteristic irony) that the state of nature is approxi-
mated in two places: America and the universities.

Hobbes drew two important inferences from the picture of the state of nature.
The first is that aggression in the state of nature is no sin. 'The notions of Right
and Wrong, Justice and Injustice have there no place. Where there is no
common Power, there is no Law: where no Law, no Injustice' (§P–50: p. 62).
And law for Hobbes was positive law, made by men in society and enforced by
the magistrate or sovereign. Gone is the absolute and immutable morality of the
Platonic and Christian tradition, so passionately defended by Cudworth, so
intimately associated with everything Milton thought and felt about ethics.
Swept away is the traditional doctrine of natural law, of innate morality planted
by God in the hearts of men. 'Of law,' Richard Hooker had said, 'there can be no
less acknowledged than that her seat is the bosom of God, her voice the
harmony of the world.'[68] Morality is binding even in the absence of positive law,
even in the absence of civil society. To which Hobbes replied: 'Justice, and
Injustice are none of the Faculties neither of the Body nor Mind. If they were,
they might be in a man that were alone in the world, as well as his Senses, and
Passions. They are Qualities, that relate to men in Society, not in Solitude'
(§P–50: p. 63). When Hobbes speaks of the laws of nature, which he does
frequently, he is referring to moral precepts discovered by reason, and when he
calls these laws eternal he means the timelessness of logical propositions; but
they are not morally binding: in fact they carry no obligation at all until they are
enacted into positive law.[69]

The second inference Hobbes drew from his theory of human nature was that
both the 'passionate'—i.e. emotional—and the rational side of men's natures
will suggest to them a way out of the dilemma of the state of nature. The most
fundamental emotion is fear, chiefly fear of death. Moved by this fear, and
instructed by their reason, men must come to realise that they need a power
greater than the power of any individual, a power to which individual power
must be subjected for the security of all individuals. This power is the sovereign
of a commonwealth. Hobbes preferred that the power be monarchical, but he

said the actual system of government is not crucial: the sovereign may be a king, or a parliament, or a 'king-in-parliament', or even an elected head. The only requirement is that the sovereign's power be absolute, else the security of the citizens will be eroded by their natural tendency to invade one another's persons and property. If for some reason the sovereign cannot protect the security of the citizens, then they may remove him; but Hobbes spoke softly on this point, because he had a greater fear of civil war than he had of tyranny. Never, however, did he advocate tyranny.

Everything Hobbes said about politics breathes the new spirit of rationalism and utility. He replaced the traditional philosophy of natural, cosmic order with a philosophy of artificial, man-made order based on a doctrine of self-interest. Religion, scriptural texts, ancient philosophy—his powerful mind touched them all and bent them to his new purpose. He stands in contrast to the other colossus of the age, Milton. All that Hobbes upheld, Milton opposed. Hobbes was a materialist; Milton believed in a world of spirit. Hobbes denied that morality is absolute and immutable; Milton affirmed it. Hobbes was a determinist; Milton believed that the will is free, and made morality depend on it. Hobbes rejected the traditional assumption of cosmic unity and eternal coherence, whether it came from Platonic, Neoplatonic, Cabalist or Hermetic sources. Milton accepted the idea in its broad outline and made use of many of its details. In the words of Christopher Hill, Milton was 'trying to hold the universe together' (§S–69: p. 401)—and I think we can say that the effect of Hobbesian thought was to cut it asunder.

NOTES

1 *The Anatomie of Melancholy* (§P–392), 5th ed. (Oxford, 1638), 'Democritus to the Reader', p. 13.

2 *Works*, XIV, 27. The best discussion of Milton's idea of nature is §S–486: Ch. III. A standard, influential study of the contrast between the old and the new outlook is §S–549. For a discussion see §S–366: a lucid and penetrating book, its emphasis on political thought but drawing freely on the whole range of seventeenth-century ideas.

3 More, *The Second Lash of Alazonomastix* (Cambridge, 1651), p. 85.

4 *Two Treatises of Government*, ed. Peter Laslett (Cambridge, 1960), p. 202.

5 *The Republic*, VII; in *The Works of Plato*, trans. B. Jowett (1937), II, 269.

6 Some modern critics of Plato believe that the Socratic questions hover on the edge of intellectual bullying; see, for instance, Bertrand Russell, *History of Western Philosophy* (1945), p. 93. But cf. John Herman Randall, *Plato: Dramatist of the Life of Reason* (1973).

7 'Plato', in *Encyclopedia of Philosophy*, gen. ed. Paul Edwards (1967), VI, 324–25. See also Ryle, *Plato's Progress* (Cambridge, 1966).

8 The standard commentary is by H. A. Wolfson, *Philo*, rev. ed. (Cambridge, Mass., 1948), 2 vols.

9   The most widely used translation is by Stephen MacKenna, 3rd ed., revised by B. S. Page (1956). There is a translation of selected portions, with an introduction, by Elmer O'Brien, *The Essential Plotinus* (1964).

10 So we are informed by his biographer, Porphyry (*ibid.*, p. 1).

11 VI, ix, 11. The phrase 'the flight of the alone to the alone' is the rendering by the Cambridge Platonist John Smith of the last words of the *Enneads* [in MacKenna: 'the passing of solitary to solitary']. See §S–397: pp. 18n and 180.

12 An exception is W. R. Inge, *The Philosophy of Plotinus*, 3rd ed. (1948), 2 vols.

13 Russell (as above, note 6), pp. 285–6. He says that Milton's 'At a Solemn Musick' evokes memories of Plotinus.

14 R. Klibansky, *The Continuity of the Platonic Tradition during the Middle Ages* (1950).

15 Ficino's *Opera Omnia* (Basel, 1576) is available in a facsimile reprint (Torino, 1959), 2 vols. The best commentary is by Paul O. Kristeller, *The Philosophy of Marsilio Ficino*, trans. Virginia Conant (1943); see also his shorter exposition in §S–382: Ch. III.

16 Kristeller, in §S–382: p. 45; see also his longer study (in the previous note), pp. 332–4. The immortality of the soul is the principal theme of Ficino's *Theologia platonica*.

17 *Commentarium in convivium Platonis*, trans. Sears Jayne, University of Missouri Studies, XIX (1944), 140.

18 See §S–426: Ch. III; also J. C. Nelson, *Renaissance Theory of Love* (1958). For a further bibliography of this much-discussed subject, see *Major Poets of the Earlier Seventeenth Century*, ed. B. Lewalski and A. Sabol (1973), pp. 16–17.

19 *English Literature in the Sixteenth Century* (Oxford, 1954), p. 6; Shumaker reaches a similar conclusion (§S–408: p. 54). Keith Thomas (§S–147: p. 361) has some penetrating remarks on 'astral determinism'. Pico's attack on astrology is his *Disputationes adversus astrologiam* (1494); for a good study of this work, see §S–408: pp. 16–27.

20 *Heptaplus*, trans. Douglas Carmichael (Indianapolis, 1965), p. 69.

21 Other related though not precisely numerological techniques were *Notarikon*, a system of acrostics including the joining of two words to form a single word of new meaning (a method not unlike the portmanteau words of Joyce's *Finnegans Wake*), and *Themurah*, the transposing of consonants to form new words.

22 See his *Of Learned Ignorance*, trans. Germain Heron (1954). The Cusan's 'mathematicism' is discussed by Ernst Cassirer in §S–354: pp. 7 ff., and in *Das Erkenntnisproblem* (Hildesheim, 1971), I, 45–54.

23 From Dee's 'Mathematicall Preface' to Billingsley's translation of Euclid (§P–408), sig. 1. For a treatment of Renaissance numerology, see C. A. Patrides, 'The Numerological Approach to Cosmic Order during the English Renaissance', *Isis*, XLIX (1958), 391–7; and, for a lucid account of Dee's theory of number, Peter J. French, *John Dee* (1972), pp. 103–9.

24 In 'A Song of Marke Anthony', l. 42.

25 *The Major Works*, ed. C. A. Patrides (Harmondsworth, 1977), pp. 387 and 356 (also pp. 27 and 37).

26 *Ibid.*, p. 74 (also p. 31).

27 The etymology is set forth in Fludd's *Mosaicall Philosophy* (1659).

28 See Reynolds's *Mythomystes* (§ P-666), a mystical-allegorical theory of poetry; More's *A Conjectural Essay of Interpreting the Minde of Moses, according to a Threefold Cabbala* (1662); and Cudworth's *System* (§ P-186).

29 The claim mentioned was advanced by Denis Saurat in *Milton: l'homme et le penseur* (Paris, 1924); for an assessment, see Joseph Blau, 'The Diffusion of the Christian Interpretation of the Cabala in English Literature', *Review of Religion*, VI (1942), 163-4.

30 'Milton and the *Conjectura Cabbalistica*', *Philological Quarterly*, VI (1927), 1-2.

31 Blau (as above, note 29), p. 162.

32 *Argumentum* prefixed to Ficino's *Pimander*, quoted in § S-427: p. 14.

33 *La Révélation d'Hermès Trismégiste* (Paris, 1950-54), I, 84; II, x-xi.

34 Shumaker (§ S-408: pp. 240-1) has collected Burton's references to the *Hermetica*. Hermeticism can also be detected in Chapman's poetry, especially *The Tears of Peace* (1609).

35 *Works*, ed. J. Spedding *et al.* (1857-74), IV, 57.

36 *The English Moralists* (1964), p. 126.

37 In his *De magnete* (1600), quoted in § S-553: p. 181.

38 *Sylva sylvarum*, in Spedding (as above, note 35), II, 381.

39 *Ibid.*, II, 94. For the Hermetic and traditional aspects of Bacon's thought, see the pioneering study of C. W. Lemmi, *The Classic Deities in Bacon* (Baltimore, 1933); Virgil K. Whitaker, 'Francis Bacon's Intellectual Milieu' (Los Angeles: Clark Library Lecture, 1962); Paolo Rossi, *Francis Bacon: From Magic to Science*, trans. S. Rabinovitch (Chicago, 1968); and Brian Vickers's valuable introduction to his edition of *Essential Articles for the Study of Francis Bacon* (Hamden, Conn., 1968).

40 *Autobiography*, ed. Sidney Lee, 2nd ed. (1906), pp. 133-4. Herbert's anxiety about his book was justified: Gassendi and Descartes wrote to express their disagreement, and, much later, it was savaged by Locke. For a delightful evocation of Lord Herbert, see Basil Willey in *Essays and Studies by Members of the English Association*, XXVII (1942).

41 *De Veritate*, trans. M. H. Carré (Bristol, 1937), p. 83. The ensuing quotations are from pp. 86, 116, 139, 119, 111 and 169.

42 *Ibid.*, pp. 289-307. These Notions are: God exists; he must be worshipped; virtue and piety are essential features of religion; sin must be expiated by repentence; death is followed by reward or punishment.

43 In Patrides (as above, note 25), pp. 455 and 439.

44 For selected texts from representative members of the Cambridge school, with an excellent introduction and full bibliography, see the edition by Patrides (§ S-397). Patrides omits Nathanael Culverwell, frequently associated with the group, because Culverwell depreciated the Cambridge view of Reason and therefore never penetrated to the centre of Cambridge Platonism (p. xxvi). But he is included in the edition by G. A. Cragg, *The Cambridge Platonists* (1968), also furnished with a good introduction. Of earlier books on the group, the best is by Tulloch (§ S-502).

45 Letter to Dr Antony Tuckney, appended to Whichcote's *Moral and Religious Aphorisms*, ed. Samuel Salter (1753), p. 118.

46 *Ibid.*, p. 108 (§S–397: p. 10).

47 Whichcote, in §S–397: p. 334. The source of this famous metaphor, frequently quoted by the Cambridge Platonists, is Proverbs 20:27.

48 Quoted by John Smith from the *Enneads* (§S–397: p. 129).

49 *The Philosophical Works of Descartes*, trans. E. S. Haldane and G. R. T. Ross (Cambridge, 1973), I, 97.

50 *Ibid.*, Third Meditation, I, 171.

51 Letter to Robert Boyle, in the latter's *Works* (1772), VI, 515, and letter to Philippus van Limborch, quoted by Rosalie L. Colie, *Light and Enlightenment* (Cambridge, 1957), p. 53.

52 More in *Enchiridion metaphysicum* (1671) enumerated twenty such attributes, including incorporeality, infinitude, eternity, omnipresence, etc. The idea of associating space with God influenced Newton. More may have come upon it in his rabbinical and cabalist reading.

53 *Oeuvres des Descartes*, ed. Victor Cousin (Paris, 1825), X, 184.

54 *An Antidote against Atheisme* (§P–205), 3rd ed. (1662), pp. 46, 40. Boyle did not draw the same conclusion from his experiment: see Mintz (§S–392), pp. 86–8.

55 In Patrides (as above, note 25), p. 98.

56 Glanvill, *Saducismus triumphatus*, 3rd ed. (1688), p. 268.

57 In Patrides (as above, note 25), pp. 97–8. For the best modern study of seventeenth-century attitudes towards witchcraft, see §S–147: Ch. XIV–XVIII. See also K. M. Briggs, *Pale Hecate's Team* (1962); Alan Macfarlane, *Witchcraft in Tudor and Stuart England* (1970); and Barbara Rosen's collection of documents, *Witchcraft* (1972). For a fuller bibliography, consult §S–147: pp. 435–6.

58 Hobbes, *An Answer to Bishop Bramhall*, in *Works*, ed. Sir William Molesworth (1840), IV, 313.

59 *The True Intellectual System of the Universe* (§P–186), ed. J. L. Mosheim (1845), III, 394.

60 *Ibid.*, III, 422.

61 *A Treatise concerning Eternal and Immutable Morality* (1731), Bk. IV, Ch. II, Sect. 8.

62 In Mosheim (as above, note 59), IV, 434–5. For Cudworth's attitude to Descartes, see J. A. Passmore, *Ralph Cudworth* (Cambridge, 1951), pp. 7–11; on Cartesian dualism, pp. 23–5.

63 For seventeenth-century reactions to the materialism and moral philosophy of Hobbes, see Mintz (§S–392). A valuable study of contemporary criticism of Hobbes's political thought is John Bowle, *Hobbes and his Critics* (1951). Although Hobbes generated more opposition than any other English thinker (excepting possibly Darwin), he has also a number of supporters: see §S–137b.

64 John Herman Randall, *The School of Padua and the Emergence of Modern Science* (Padua, 1961). For a more general treatment of the Aristotelian element in Hobbes's thought, see Thomas A. Spragens, *The Politics of Motion* (1973).

65 See §S–366: pp. 22–4, 68–79; also, *The Frame of Order*, ed. J. Winny (1957).

66 Starkey, *A Dialogue between Reginald Pole and Thomas Lupset*, ed. K. M. Burton (1948), p. 57, and Forset (§P–44), sig. iij.

67 Forset (previous note), and Browne, in Patrides (as above, note 25), p. 103; respectively.

68 *Of the Laws of Ecclesiastical Polity* (§P–261), ed. George Edelen (Cambridge, Mass., 1977), I, 142.

69 See Michael Oakeshott's introduction to *Leviathan* (Oxford, 1946), pp. lviii–lxi. Cf. Howard Warrender, *The Political Philosophy of Hobbes: his Theory of Obligation* (Oxford, 1957).

6

The experience of Otherness: theology as a means of life

The seventeenth-century landscape has many prominent features, each impressive in itself. But theology dominates them all, its mighty shadow falling on the political dimension as on the social, and on the literary as on the scientific. Omnipresent in the intellectual and emotional life of the seventeenth century, theology exerted a salutary influence in several directions—and no less adverse in others.

'Theology', it should be made clear at the outset, does not encompass only the aggregate of strictly defined dogmas, nor even the diverse interpretations attendant upon them. Theology also encompasses emotional engagements with modes of experience illumined, in one form or another, by an order of ideas whose ultimate appeal is to Otherness. The reference here is not to the faculty peculiar to the mystic. It is to the sustained awareness of the realist who recognises the need to respond to demands of authorities beyond himself and of quarters beyond the visible. Such an attitude could lead, and did lead, to fanaticism; and so far it can only be deplored. But where the experience was properly channelled, it yielded a commitment to life in all its manifestations. The terminal points are well attested even where they were not attained: socially, the ambition to reform the existing patterns within the State at large and the family in particular; and personally, the dedication to an impressive purity in moral behaviour. Inevitably reflected in the period's literature, these thrusts are demonstrably present not only in explicitly political poems such as Marvell's 'Horatian Ode' but, equally, in any number of major literary works similarly informed by a socially oriented fervour, be they Shakespeare's *The Tempest* (1611) or Ben Jonson's *Epigrammes* (1616) or Herbert's *The Temple* (1633)—and of course the sum total of Milton's endeavours in poetry as in prose.

But if cognisance of Otherness led the period's major minds superbly to articulate issues of perennial import, the same cognisance induced in minor minds the deplorable fanaticism already noted. Risible in itself, such fanaticism should be marked because its demonic proportions loom large in the background against which Shakespeare and Jonson and Milton wrote. Self-appointed moralists abounded, hysterically denouncing 'this hard iron age' with its 'monstrous pride of apparell, of [at]tyres, of bracelets, of Iewels, ouerflowing our nation like a generall deluge', the maidens 'standyng tootyng twoo howers by the Clocke, lookyng now on this side, now on that, least any thyng should bee lackyng needefull to further Pride', while the 'proud plumed gallants . . . do seeme as if they scornde both heauen and hell'—and all indulging, it was said, in 'practices of wantonnesse, as stage-playes, which serve for nothing but to nourish filthinesse'.[1] Indignation of this order was not addressed solely to a few social issues, nor was it voiced by a handful of self-righteous individuals. It covered, on the contrary, the entire circumference of thought and behaviour, and was often sanctioned by formally instituted agents. One example is the ruthless theocracy sustained by Calvin in Geneva from 1541; another, the intolerance displayed by conservative Catholicism through the Counter-Reformation which the Council of Trent launched from 1545. True, both Calvinism and the Counter-Reformation contributed much of enormous and lasting benefit; yet it is advisable to remember in what ensues that the two movements were at times alike vicious, witness the burning at the stake for 'heresy' of Michael Servetus in Geneva (1553) and of Giordano Bruno in Rome (1600), the one condemned for his anti-trinitarian views, the other for his wild flights of fancy. Earlier, at Münster in Westphalia, an extreme group of extreme Anabaptists had indulged in frenetic activities which, distinguished as they were by their lunacy and brutality, were justly condemned by Protestants and Catholics alike. But Protestants and Catholics were themselves no less barbarous, not only in their mutually fervent dedication to censorship but in their manifest zeal in the significantly increased persecution of 'witches'.

To what extent were such activities theologically oriented? The persecution of 'witches', for instance, has been attributed rather to social than to expressly theological reasons in that the hapless victims were dissidents whose extermination was dictated by the need to find 'a scapegoat for social frustration' (§S–277). Even more sweepingly, the controversies of the seventeenth century inclusive of the Civil War have been declared to be primarily social and political in their orientation, the theological language commonly deployed being incidental and ultimately of slight relevance (§S–71). Such efforts to demythologise the Age of Milton must be approached with caution, however. In our secular age, theology is manifestly suspect; and we seek, with an excess of sophistication, to neutralise the force of theological thrusts. The potency of the political, social and economic motives behind the seventeenth century's metaphysical claims can scarcely be denied; yet to question the earnestness and the significance of those claims *as claims* were to risk an imbalance likely to terminate in gross misrepresentation. The vast literature directed against witchcraft, however incredible the arguments and terrifying their application, may not be reduced to so many instances of 'social frustration' so long as it enlisted the support of the misguided but otherwise brilliant Jean Bodin (*De la démonomanie des sorciers*, Paris, 1580) and of the brilliant but otherwise misguided King James (*Daemonologie*, Edinburgh, 1597). We should consider that even the very few sceptics who dared oppose the prevalent views—Johann Wier in 1563 or Reginald Scot in 1584—adamantly refused to deny the reality of witches. The irenic Sir Thomas Browne was in the 1630s to agree:

> I have ever beleeved, and doe now know, that there are Witches; they that doubt
> of these, doe not onely deny them, but Spirits; and are obliquely and upon
> consequence a sort, not of Infidels, but Atheists.
>
> (*Religio Medici*, I, 30)

Browne was certainly not inclined to harden hearts against the victims of fanatics. As his statement makes clear, he was primarily concerned lest a negation of the demonic would involve a negation of the spiritual—and thence a negation of God. As Henry More, the Cambridge Platonist, succinctly observed in 1653, '*No Spirit, no God.*'[2] The thrust is the same; and so is the cognisance of Otherness.

By the same token, our tendency to displace the theological by the purely political and economic in the controversies of the seventeenth century disturbs the balance sought even by a substantial number of the Levellers, the period's most obviously 'secular' political party. But the habitual appeal to Otherness was not a mere rhetorical flourish. It was the foundation which sustained much of the idealism in the seventeenth century's political contexts, whether we focus on the Levellers' view of the Christian brotherhood of all men or on the Diggers' independence under the sovereignty of the ultimate taskmaster ('We have chosen the Lord God Almighty to be our king and protector'). So, too, the Anabaptists—not the religious fanatics at Münster but the pacifists of the communes whether in Moravia (Hutterites) or the Netherlands and north Germany (Mennonites)—in severing themselves from conventional social life aspired to change society politically; yet they remain, as their most recent historian concludes, 'primarily a religious movement rather than a political one' (§S–437: p. 425). We may add that they were also, like the countless other minor groups of the period, specifically Protestant. Their common appeal was, after all, to the Bible, which the Reformation elevated into the foremost if not the exclusive authority in all matters of doctrine as of conduct.

PROTESTANT EMPHASES AND CATHOLIC RESPONSES

The Reformation is supposed to have begun on 31 October 1517, when Luther fastened to the door of the castle church at Wittenberg his ninety-five theses against papal abuses. Like all vulgar suppositions, however, this one is also untenable. At the time, none of the doctrines characteristic of Protestantism had been formulated; the German princes had not yet perceived Luther's usefulness in furthering their political autonomy from Rome; and Rome's eventually militant conservatism was a development reserved for the future. In 1517, certainly, Luther was not even remotely inclined to question his loyalty to the Catholic Church. He was only indulging in the widespread clamour to reform the Church from within, much like the scholarly Lorenzo Valla (d. 1457), who questioned the authenticity of documents such as the 'Donation of Constantine' upon which the papal claims to temporal power rested, or the saintly John Colet (d. 1519), who attacked abuses on several fronts by living the very pattern of the upright Christian humanist, or the fervently moral Juan Luis Vives (d. 1540), who in each of his brilliant works palpitated with an unqualified devotion to 'puritanism'. Twenty years before the episode at Wittenberg, indeed, another 'reformer' had tellingly denounced the 'pseudo-theologians of our time, whose brains are rotten, their language barbarous, their intellects dull, their learning a bed of thorns, their manners rough, their life hypocritical, their talk full of venom, and their hearts as black as ink'. The zeal is similar to Luther's; but the voice is that of the mighty Erasmus.[3]

There were, in other words, numerous efforts at reformation before the Reformation. Even so, however, the Reformation is fully a re-formation in the sense that it proved a radical revolution which recast the religious map of Europe and affected the commitment to Otherness as much outside the Catholic Church as within it. But we must guard against perilous generalisations. In terms of the individual's devotional life, for instance, there was a difference not in kind but in degree: while Protestantism commended the worship capitally of Christ, Catholicism had already intensified that worship—and after the Council of Trent intensified it even further—to include the Virgin in the first instance and the pantheon of saints in the second. Expectations to the contrary, moreover, Protestants did not substantially increase the quality of biblical and theological studies: biblical scholarship reached its apogee with two major contributions by Catholics—the edition of the Greek New Testament by Erasmus (1516) and the Polyglot Bible supervised by Cardinal Ximénez (1522)—while Catholic theology responded to the challenge of the Reformation with impressive spokesmen of the order of Robert Bellarmine and Edmund Campion, both of whom we shall encounter again later. Finally, Protestantism may not be claimed as a liberal force in a world of monkish papists bent on confining the free spirit of man. As before noted, the Catholic Church was by no means the solitary guardian of illiberal conduct.

Positively, we expect, the quintessence of Protestantism should be sought in the writings of Luther. But alas! he wrote rather too much, and the modern reader must be equipped with patience to withstand his histrionics, tact to overlook his lack of coherence, and sympathy to understand the issues he articulates with enormous passion. However, three of his treatises may be commended as still readable: the address *To the Christian Nobility of the German Nation*, which urges the secular authorities to support the Reformation; *The Babylonish Captivity of the Church*, which attacks the seven sacraments; and *The Liberty of a Christian Man*, which expounds his central conviction about 'justification by faith'. But as none of these treatises testifies to Luther's reckless courage, a fourth may also be commended as the foremost of the many blunders he committed during his turbulent life: his espousal of the absolute primacy of Divine Grace in response to Erasmus's reasoned defence of man's free will. Stylistically and philosophically, Luther was annihilated by the infinitely superior grace and intelligence of his opponent. But as *felt* theology—theology as a means of life—Luther's thesis convinces because his commitment to Otherness was so total. His celebrated view of man's will may offend or, at best, amuse;[4] but as Luther himself ruefully observed on one occasion, if the province of Erasmus was style without the truth, that of Luther was the truth without style.[5]

It was a question not of the single truth, however, but of two diametrically opposed attitudes to Otherness. Where Luther proclaimed man's total dependence on God, Erasmus gloried in man's initiative under God. Where Luther condemned the earthbound works of independent man, Erasmus saw in those same works evidence of past achievements and future promise. Where Luther vehemently insisted on the primary authority of the Bible, Erasmus serenely commended the authority even of non-Christians (e.g. 'from Cicero's enchiridion alone flows forth a divine source of virtue which suffices for all our spiritual need').[6] Even more tellingly, where Luther like all Protestants favoured among the early Fathers especially St Augustine, Erasmus reserved his respect particularly for St Jerome.[7] St Augustine appealed to Luther and became the guiding spirit of the Reformation partly because of his providential vision of history in *The City of God*, partly because of his affirmation of the primacy of Divine Grace in opposition to Pelagius—an early if crude prototype of Erasmus—but especially because of his sense of personal sinfulness as detailed in his remarkable *Confessions*. St Jerome appealed to Erasmus, on the other hand, for equally personal reasons; for alike humanists, alike great scholars, they were also alike in that their commitment to the Christian faith was an intellectual exercise, an experience not of the heart but of the mind. Zeal was not absent from the horizons of St Jerome, much less of Erasmus; yet it was a zeal circumscribed habitually by their concern with the learned few, and ultimately determined more by their response to the outward text than to the inner life of the Scriptures: the word, that is to say, in decisive preference to the Word.

Protestantism as moulded by Luther was, then, directly personal, explicitly Augustinian, and ultimately biblical. But its biblical orientation was not nearly as comprehensive as we might expect. The Epistle of James, for instance, was thoroughly disliked by Luther because of its emphasis on works ('by works a man is justified, and not by faith alone').[8] At the other extreme, St Paul's epistles were allotted such a central place in Protestant thought and experience that we may describe the Reformation as fundamentally Pauline. Here the crucial factor was Paul's insistence on the primacy of faith, which eventually yielded the expressly Protestant theological dogma of 'justification by faith'. Rightly proclaimed by Catholics like Campion to be 'the verie Soule of Protestancie',[9] the dogma asserted the individual's salvation not through any good works he might undertake or any external acts of worship he might perform but solely through faith in the redeeming powers of Christ (*sola fide*). In the ensuing controversy, Catholics charged that Protestants dismissed works as irrelevant. Not quite. The 'justified' individual was impelled to an active life, not paralysed into a passive one. 'The life of a Christian is his faith,' it was said in 1623, but 'the life of his faith, is his good workes.' Even more perceptively, John Donne annexed the theological terms to the two commandments: 'love God, and love thy Neighbour, that is, faith and works'.[10]

The Protestant declaration of the primacy of faith had as an inevitable consequence the formulation of another fundamental dogma, the priesthood of all believers. Intended as a redefinition of 'the church' in radical opposition to Catholic claims, it redefined also the nature of universality:

> the Churche is called the whole societie of people that acknowledge the Gospell of Christe and beleue in him. And this Churche not to be of one time only but of all tymes & ages, as Adam with Eue hys wife, his son Abel & his familie was the church, Noah with his familie was the churche, Melchizedek with his familie was the Churche, Abraham also with his familie. Likewyse Isaac, Iacob, Dauid, the Prophetes and Apostles with their Auditours that belceued in the Gospell of Christ were the churche, and where soeuer at this daye the Gospel of Christ is receyued and beleued there is also the church of Christ.[11]

The sweeping enlistment of the Hebrew patriarchs under the Christian banner may surprise; but it was, for all that, a natural corollary to the dogma of justification *sola fide*. The widespread acceptance of Adam as a Christian, for instance, centred on the premise that he believed in Christ and was thereby justified 'by faith only'. The evidence? The prophecy in Genesis (3:15) that Satan would be crushed by 'the seed of the woman', which Protestants consistently interpreted as a reference to the Christ-to-come. In the words of the popular Swiss theologian Rudolf Gwalter,

> It is euident that [Adam] put his whole hope and trust in Jesus Chryst alone, which was that promised seede of the woman. Therefore *Adam* was a christian man, and beleeued that he and his posteritie should be deliuered and saued from the tyrannie of the Diuell, through the merite of Chryst onely.[12]

Consenting, Milton elevated the prophecy of the 'seed' into the single most important pattern of the last two books of *Paradise Lost*, the vision of the future unfolded by Michael terminating in Adam's moving acceptance of the 'seed' as his 'Redeemer ever blest' (XII, 573). For Milton, as for Protestants generally, Adam was indeed 'a christian man'—and more particularly, a Protestant.

The primacy of faith presupposed, for all Protestants, a deeply felt conviction of personal sinfulness reminiscent at its most intense of the experiences of Luther. Whatever the psychological motivation behind such a conviction, the purely theological dimension appealed in the first instance to 'original sin' and, in the second, to its re-enactment in daily life. Original sin is scarcely comprehensible to the modern mind, since it involves the hereditary transmission of Adam's guilt to the sum total of his descendants. Passionately experienced, however, it was with equal passion described as 'an hereditary vitiousnesse' or '*epidemicall* contagion' issuing from Adam and reducing all men into so many 'vngracious bastards' or, less flatteringly still, 'nothing else but a filthy dunghill of all abominable vices'.[13] Should the total terms, so totally uncompromising, distress us by their extravagance, we may consider that in positing man's 'fallenness' they assent to a fact of experience we can hardly question ourselves, namely, that man's conduct is habitually less than perfect. This universal proclivity, translated into theological language, confronts us also in Donne: 'man was sour'd in the whole lump, poysoned in the fountain, perished at the chore, withered in the root, in the fall of *Adam*'.[14]

The consequences were generally agreed upon: man tends invariably toward a re-enactment of the primal disobedience, much as the narrator in Herbert's 'The Collar' duplicates both the experience of Adam ('there is fruit, / And thou hast hands') and its immediate after-life ('I rav'd and grew more fierce and wilde'). Variations upon the same theme abound. Milton in *Paradise Lost* delineated the prototype of the Fall, sombrely warning of its effects on the universe at large. Donne in the *Holy Sonnets* lashed about wildly, confirming a general principle repeatedly echoed across the seventeenth century '(the *Essence* of *sinne* [is] meerely ἀταξία: *Disorder*').[15] Others—Donne once again among them—marked with mounting despair the way the macrocosm mirrors the restlessness of man:

> all the creatures are upon a wheele, and in motion; there is not a creature since *Adam* sinned, sleepeth sound. Wearinesse and motion is laid on *Moon* and *Sunne*, and all *creatures* on this side of the *Moon*. *Seas* ebbe and flow, and that's trouble; *winds* blow, *rivers* move, *heavens* and *stars* these five thousand yeares, except one time,[16] have not had six minutes rest; living creatures walk apace toward death; Kingdomes, Cities, are on the wheele of changes, up, and downe . . . The great *All* of heaven and earth, since *God* laid the first stone of this wide Hall, hath been groning, and weeping . . .[17]

Still others, more militantly disposed, issued a call to arms; and borrowing St Paul's recurrent martial imagery—especially in the Epistle to the Ephesians—they provided massive treatises like John Downame's *The Christian warfare Against the Deuill World and Flesh Wherein is described their nature, the maner of their fight and meanes to obtaine victorye*, which by its fourth edition (1633–34) exceeded eleven hundred folio pages. Enterprises of this order may appear unlikely, and at best useless, until we recall that their tediously spun imagery was essential to the purposes of more refined spirits. Erasmus in his exceedingly popular *Enchiridion* (1503), similarly addressed to Christ's soldiers, had already enlisted St Paul's armoury to the services of Christian 'philosophy'. But the same images had also been deployed to advantage by Spenser in *The Faerie Queene*, and were to be deployed yet again not only in *Paradise Lost* and *The Pilgrim's Progress* but also in Marvell's redaction of the same tradition in 'A Dialogue between The Resolved Soul, and Created Pleasure'.

The war against the devil, the world and the flesh was an experience which Luther lived in delicious agony and Calvin mapped with relentless logic.

Personally most unattractive as he was intellectually most impressive, Calvin had by the late 1530s hammered the flexible views of Luther into the rigid framework of his awe-inspiring *Institutes*.[18] Original sin was magnified into a total experience with total consequences, reducing man to a creature capable of thoughts and deeds strictly evil in both intent and execution. The absolute primacy of faith was moreover made subordinate to the absolute primacy of Grace, transforming 'justification' from a promise into an improbability except where the offended and alienated Deity inscrutably elected ('predestined') some to salvation and the rest to eternal damnation. Not surprisingly, man's free will was abrogated altogether, the Divine Wisdom retaining unqualified priority not only in that the Fall was foreseen but that it was indeed decreed. Could such a scheme have appealed to anyone? And where accepted, was it not bound to paralyse its partisans into inaction? Our expectations to the contrary, however, the scheme generated a remarkable energy as Calvinists under the assumption of their own 'election' propelled themselves into action with missionary zeal. Self-confidence, not the lack of it, accounts for Calvinism's widespread appeal, which by the middle of the sixteenth century had seized the initiative from Lutheranism and for well-nigh a hundred years affected the manner of life and the mode of thinking throughout northern Europe inclusive of England and especially Scotland.

There were changes, certainly. The more uncompromising aspects of Calvin's thought were in reiteration much qualified, less perhaps by Theodore Beza, who succeeded him as head of Geneva's theocracy (from 1564) than by the numerous theologians who constructed Protestant equivalents of the massive 'cathedrals of the mind' characteristic of mediaeval Catholicism. These theologians drew liberally on Calvin's *Institutes*, yet they were equally influenced by the less rigid framework of a work Luther regarded as second in importance to the Bible: the *Common Places* of his genial friend, the humanist Philipp Melanchthon.[19] The most noteworthy consequence was the manual of the theology compiled by the successor to Zurich's great reformer Zwingli, the moderate Heinrich Bullinger (d. 1575), and translated into English as *Common Places* (1572). Other labours included Wolfgang Musculus's *Common Places*, which in its English version (1563) exceeded one thousand folio pages, Peter Martyr Vermigli's *Common Places* (1583), Zacharias Ursinus's *Summe of Christian Religion* (1587), Gulielmus Bucanus's *Institutions* (1606), Lucas Trelcatius's *Common Places* (1610), Hieronymus Zanchius's *Body of Christian Religion* (1659)—and a host of still other works variously designated as 'system', 'exposition', 'body', 'anatomy', 'apology', 'model', 'sum', and the like. Protestants in England as on the Continent were well enough equipped for any eventuality.

But so were Catholics. The Council of Trent (in three sessions in 1545–48, 1551–52, and 1562–63) may have been a victory for the conservative elements within the Catholic Church, and its decrees may have been inflexibly authoritarian. But it signalled the recovery of Catholic self-confidence, which in the ensuing Counter-Reformation strengthened spirituality by emphasising the very aspects so thoroughly detested by Protestants: the intense veneration of saints, the increased celebration of the sacraments, the elaborate liturgy, the exuberant music, the explosive baroque in the ornate churches and in the sensuous arts both visual and plastic. Mariolatry proliferated, its sheer physicality ('Her sacred breasts, were as two Pearly-bottels, tipped with rich rubies')[20] mirrored in the palpable experiences which St Teresa of Avila (d. 1582, canonised 1622) testifies in her celebrated confrontation with the angel 'in corporall forme':

> he was not great but litle, very beautifull, his face so glorious, that he seemed to
> be one of the higher angells . . . I did see in his hand a long darte of gold, and
> the end of the yron head of it seemed to haue a litle fyre, this he seemed to passe
> thorough my heart sometimes, and that it pierced to my entrayles, which me
> thoght he drew from mee, when he pulled it out agayne, & he left me whole
> enflamed in great loue of God, the payne was so great that it made me
> complayne greeuously, & the sweetnesse was so excessiue, which this exceed-
> ing great payne causeth, that I could not desyre to haue it takē away . . .[21]

Catholic self-confidence is also evident in the refusal of Elizabethan England's foremost Catholic poet, Robert Southwell (d. 1595), to compromise his excessive language. Crashaw in the next generation was to prove even more confident, his rousing lyricism centred not on expostulation as on meditation, nor on analysis as on celebration.

Two other developments strengthened Catholic resolve even further. One was the introduction of Catholicism into the Far East by the Portuguese and into the Americas by the Spaniards, in the latter case under exceptionally vicious circumstances which very few—notably the Dominican Bartolomeo de Las Casas—were prepared to question. The other development was the advent of the Jesuits under Ignatius Loyola (d. 1556, canonised 1622), whose efforts in every direction were so brilliantly successful that their very mention among Protestants induced a torrent of virulent denunciations. The violent response is understandable, especially among Calvinists, who unerringly perceived that the Jesuits had by the outset of the seventeenth century regained the initiative for the Catholic Church precisely as Calvinism had already seized the initiative within Protestantism. Typically, in consequence, the English Jesuit Robert Parsons was described on his death (1610) as 'a most Diabolicall, unnaturall, and barbarous butcherlie fellow' (§ S–485: p. 1)—an estimate which in his case was not altogether misplaced, even if he did compose the most popular work of devotion produced by the Counter-Reformation in England (§ P–283). Partisan hysterics apart, however, Jesuits like Campion (d. 1581, canonised 1970) and Bellarmine (d. 1621, canonised 1930) command the highest possible respect. Campion in addition to his personal courage was responsible for one of the most succinct defences of Catholicism (§ P–230), while Bellarmine was the period's most brilliant controversialist, all the more effective because he was so irritatingly courteous to his opponents. His worthiest antagonist in England, William Whitaker, Regius Professor of Divinity at Cambridge, freely acknowledged that Bellarmine was 'unquestionably learned, possessed of a happy genius, a penetrating judgment, and multifarious reading'. In turn, Bellarmine kept a picture of Whitaker in his study because, he said, the English divine was 'the most learned Heretick that ever he read'.[22] The compliments, it should be emphasised, are an exception to the usual manner of engaging in controversies, since Protestants normally attacked Catholic spokesmen as so many 'Bastards borne of one Whore', and Catholics with equal zeal claimed that 'neuer any man writ more filthily, more vnciuilly, more lewdly, and that beyond all boundes of Christian modesty and temperance &c. then did *Luther'*.[23]

Of the major Catholic theologians, the one least accommodated by either side was St Thomas Aquinas. True, his magisterial exposition of the God-descended hierarchy of laws exerted a lasting influence on every Christian writer, including Richard Hooker in Elizabethan England and the Cambridge Platonists in the mid-seventeenth century (§S–486: pp. 81 ff., and §S–397: pp. 149–50). Generally speaking, however, Catholics preferred the aggregate of their theological tradition to any single spokesman, quite unlike Protestants, who so highly favoured St Augustine, as before noted. The reputation of Thomism is adequately represented by John Colet's response to the suggestion of Erasmus that St Thomas was the best of the mediaeval theologians:

> Why do you praise to me a man who, had he not had so much arrogance, would never have defined everything in such a rash and supercilious way, and who, had he not had a worldly spirit, would never have contaminated the teaching of Christ with his profane philosophy?[24]

THE BIBLE: CLAIMS AND THEIR CONSEQUENCES

Protestants appealed to but a single authority, the Bible. In practice, as we have seen, they invoked with readiness St Augustine, as indeed they also resorted to St Bernard of Clairvaux (d. 1153), in whom they respected his passionately expressed pleas for moral purity, and to St John Crysostom (d. 407), in whom they admired his strikingly articulated expositions of Christianity's quintessence. Notwithstanding, the Bible remained for Protestants the court of constant appeal, dictated as it was believed to have been by the Holy Spirit, and indeed 'licensed by the Omnipotent', as Thomas Dekker proclaimed in his preface to *The Seven Deadly Sinnes of London* (1606). The accessibility of the Bible became, in consequence, a characteristic Protestant commitment. Here the way was again led by Luther, who translated the entire Bible into German by 1534. The corresponding achievement in England, the King James ('Authorised') Version of 1611, was prepared with royal approval by a committee of the best available experts, who laboured for nearly seven years. Generous use was made of all previous translations, notably the decisive versions by Wycliffe and Tyndale, witness the evolution of four verses from St Paul's 'hymn to charity' (1 Corinthians 13:4–7):

> Charite is pacient, it is benyngne, charite enuyeth not, it doth not wickidli it is not blowun it is not coueitous, it sekith not the thingis that ben his owne, it is

not stired to wraththe, it thenkith not yuel, it ioieth not on wickidnesse, but it ioieth to gidre to truthe, it suffrith alle thingis: it bileueth alle thingis, it hopith alle thingis it susteyneth alle thingis.   (John Wycliffe, 1380s)

Love suffreth longe, and is corteous. Love envieth not. Love doth not frowardly, swelleth not dealeth not dishonestly, asketh not her awne, is not provoked to anger, thynketh not evyll, reioyseth not in iniquite: but reioyseth in the trueth, suffreth all thynge, beleveth all thynges, hopeth all thynges, endureth in all thynges.   (William Tyndale, 1525 ff.)

Loue suffreth longe, and is curteous. Loue enuyeth not. Loue doth not frowardly, swelleth not, dealeth not dishonestly seketh not her awne, is not prouoked to anger, thinketh no euyll, reioyseth not in iniquitie: but reioyseth in the trueth, suffreth all thynges, beleueth all thynges, hopeth all thynges, endureth all thynges.   (Thomas Cranmer ['The Great Bible'], 1539)

Loue suffreth long, is courteous: loue enuieth not: loue doth not boast it selfe, swelleth not, Disdaineth nothing as vnbeseming, seketh not her owne things, is not prouoked to anger, thinketh not euil, Reioyseth not in iniquitie, but reioyseth in the trueth. Suffreth all thinges, beleueth all thinges, hopeth all thinges, endureth all thinges.   (The Geneva Bible, 1st complete ed., 1560)

Charitie is patient, is benigne: Charitie enuieth not, dealeth not peruersly: is not puffed vp, is not ambitious, seeketh not her owne, is not prouoked to anger, thinketh not euil: reioyseth not upon iniquitie, but reioyseth with the truth: suffereth al things, beleeueth al things, hopeth al things, beareth al things.
                                    (The Rheims New Testament [Catholic version], 1582)

Charitie suffereth long, and is kinde: charitie enuieth not: charitie vaunteth not it selfe, is not puffed vp, Doeth not beuaue it selfe vnseemly, seeketh not her owne, is not easily prouoked, thinketh no euill, Reioyseth not in iniquitie, but reioyseth in the trueth: Beareth all things, beleeueth all things, hopeth all things, endureth all things.   (The King James Version, 1611)

It should be noted that one of the Protestant versions, the extremely popular Geneva Bible, carried marginal notes for the edification of the elect. Even more nervously, the Catholic version of the New Testament published at Rheims—eventually merged with the version of the Old Testament published at Douai (1609–10)—provided marginal notes as well as extensive 'annotations', often longer than the verses and chapters annotated. Comparison is invariably illuminating, even where only the text itself is involved. For example, the 'prophecy' in Genesis concerning 'the seed of the woman' (above, p. 175) reads in the Geneva Bible thus:

I wil also put enimitie betwene thee and the woman, and betwene thy sede and her sede. He shal breake thine head, and thou shalt bruise his heele.

In the Douai Bible, however, the second sentence reads: 'she shall bruise thy head in peeces, & thou shalt lye in waite of her heele'. An accompanying annotation, lengthy as usual, remarks on *She shall bruise*: 'Protestants wil not admitte this reading, . . . lest our Blessed Ladie should be said anie way to bruise the serpents head . . .' The different readings, it is clear, support radically different doctrines: in the Protestant version, 'justification by faith'; and in the Catholic, the status of Mary as co-redemptrix with Christ. Such issues loomed very large in the horizons of the Age of Milton, arousing passions whose intensity we can scarcely begin to comprehend. We may remind ourselves that the Bible was not a minor appendix to life. Easily the foremost 'best seller' of the period, its English versions alone are estimated to have appeared in over six hundred thousand copies by 1640, and as many again by the end of the century.[25]

So far as the interpretation of the Bible is concerned, Protestants commonly endorsed 'the literal sense'. As Donne categorically maintained, 'the word of God is not the word of God in any other sense than literall'.[26] The emphasis was especially voiced in connection with the Book of Genesis, since a denial of its historicity might have mythologised the Christian claims about the presence of God—even of the God-man Jesus—within history. Hence the reiterated warnings that

> Histories in scripture, as that of creation, of paradise, of mans fall, of *Adams* progenie, *Abraham* his leauing his country, and many such are vttered in plaine wordes and proper without allegories, or other figures. Because that would make the scriptures to bee laughed at, and breede infinite absurdities, if one should attempt to make all tropicall [i.e. figurative], and turne every thing into Allegoricall senses, as some wanton unsanctified wittes too much do endeauor it.[27]

Foremost among the 'wanton unsactified wittes' was the brilliant Origen (d. *c.* 254), whose allegorical interpretations continued through the seventeenth century to vex theologians into nightmares. Later, radicals such as Samuel Fisher would in works like *The Rustics Alarm* (1660) additionally demonstrate how the mythologisation of the Bible could be used as a powerful weapon against authority in general (§S–71: pp. 142 ff., 261 ff.). Aware of the dangers, 'orthodox' Protestants maintained with William Tyndale that the literal sense includes all other senses ('the scripture hath but one sence which is ye literall sence. And ye literall sence is ye rote and groūde of all'), much as in the sacraments the outward ceremony and the inner spiritual truth are two indivisible aspects of the same unity.[28] 'The literall sense,' as Donne explained, 'is always to be preserved . . . But the literall sense of every place, is the principall intention of the Holy Ghost, in that place: And his principall intention in many places, is to expresse things by allegories, by figures; so that in many places in Scripture, a figurative sense is the literall sense.'[29]

The sense which is at once literal and figurative is most apparent in the domain of typology. A time-honoured approach to the Bible, typology—to be exact, historical typology—was deployed as early as the New Testament to assert the linearity of the onward-moving, non-recurring historical process in terms of the Messiah's prefiguration in the activities of numerous predecessors ('types'). As elaborated over the centuries, typology designated the extensive

anticipatory 'premonstration' of Christ delineated among others by Bishop
Griffith Williams in 1624:

> [Christ] is the *First*, hee is the *Last* . . . Veyled and shadowed in the Old, reueiled
> and exhibited in the New Testament; *promised* in that, *preached* in this; there
> *shewed* into the Fathers in *Types*, here *manifested* vnto vs in *Truths*: for the *Tree* of
> *Life*, the *Arke* of *Noah*, the *Ladder* of *Iacob*, the *Mercy Seat*, the *Brazen Serpent*, and
> all such mysticall *Types*, and typicall *Figures* that we reade of in the Old
> *Testament*; what were they else but *Christ*; obscurely *shadowed* before he was fully
> *reueiled*; and so all the men of Note, *Noah, Isaac, Ioseph, Moses, Aaron, Iosua,*
> *Sampson, Dauid, Salomon*, Kings, Priests, Prophets, Titles of Dignities, *Names of*
> *Honour*, . . . belong vnto this *King of Kings*.[30]

Poetic adaptations are legion. Explicitly formulated, typology underlies in
Paradise Lost the progressive revelation of Christ's advent in terms of 'types and
shadowes' (XII, 239 f.), and in Crashaw the lyrical celebration of the single
moment in history when 'Types yield to TRUTHES':

> Lo, the full, finall SACRIFICE
> On which all figures fix't their eyes.
> The ransom'd ISACK, and his ramme;
> The MANNA, and the PASCHAL Lamb . . .
>
> ('Lauda Sion Salvatorem', st. XII)

But typology will also be discerned to have affected the total fabric of poems, as
in *Paradise Lost* the 'types and shadowes' encompass not only 'historical figures'
but the very sound patterns and clusters of images which constantly anticipate
other patterns and other images until, thus juxtaposed, they complete Milton's
aesthetic vision. In *The Temple*, too, Herbert deploys a strategy whose eucharistic
burden is, like Grace, omnipresent and 'prevenient' or anticipatory, witness the
way that the lengthy poem 'The Sacrifice' anticipates through its liturgical
stanzas each given narrator's emergent anguish by placing it—in advance of its
articulation—within the context of Christ's Passion.[31]

The figurative nature of much of the Bible could hardly have escaped the
scrutiny even of the most committed partisan of the literal sense. That portions
of the Bible are poems—for example the Psalms and the Proverbs in their
entirety, the Book of Job exclusive of its prologue and epilogue, and shorter
units such as the Song of Moses (Exodus 15) and the Song of Deborah (Judges
5)—was fully recognised during the seventeenth century.[32] Donne, in fact, did
not hesitate to describe God as 'a *figurative*, a *metaphoricall God*':

> A *God* in whose words there is such a height of *figures*, such *voyages*, such
> *peregrinations* to fetch remote and precious *metaphors*, such *extensions*, such
> *spreadings*, such *Curtaines* of *Allegories*, such *third Heavens* of *Hyperboles*, so
> *harmonious eloquutions*, so *retired* and so *reserved expressions*, so *commanding*
> *perswasions*, so *perswading commandments*, such *sinewes* even in thy *milke*, and
> such *things* in thy *words*, as all *prophane Authors*, seeme of the seed of the *Serpent*,
> that *creepes*, thou art the *Dove*, that *flies*.[33]

There was moreover the recognition that the language of the parables in the New Testament, in itself concrete enough to satisfy 'the literal sense', is ultimately symbolic, iconic, emblematic, hieroglyphical. The link was averred, for instance, by Valeriano at the outset of his *Hieroglyphica* (1575). But it also informs the definition of an emblem by Francis Quarles:

> An *Embleme* is but a silent Parable. Let not the tender Eye check, to see the allusion to our blessed Saviour figured in these Types. In holy Scripture, he is sometimes called a Sower; sometimes, a Fisher; sometimes a Physician: and why not presented so as well to the eye as to the ear? Before the knowledge of letters God was known by *Hieroglyphicks*: And indeed, what are the Heavens, the Earth, nay every Creature, but *Hieroglyphicks* and *Emblemes* of His Glory.[34]

The impact of such an attitude on literature was decisive. The creative form which Milton and Herbert and Donne imposed on words appealed in the end to the prototypical activities of the creative Word. For the poets of the seventeenth century, and for prose-writers like Sir Thomas Browne, the universe was 'historical' yet figurative, 'literal' yet emblematic—and essentially sacramental.

The interpretation of the Bible might have presented very few problems had it not been for the enigmatic material comprising the Book of Revelation. It could hardly be 'history' since it appertained to the future. If 'prophecy', however, in what sense was it to be interpreted? Donne valiantly resorted to a distinction:

> In the first book of the Scriptures, that of Genesis, there is danger in departing from the letter; In this last book, this of the Revelation, there is much danger in adhering too close to the letter . . . As then to depart from the literall sense, that sense which the very letter presents, in the book of Genesis, is dangerous, because if we do so there, we have no history of the Creation of the world in any other place to stick to; so to binde our selves to such a literall sense in this book, will take from us the consolation of many spirituall happinesses, and bury us in the carnall things of this world.[35]

Undeterred, numerous commentators ventured to 'open vp the mysteries of this Revelation, . . . both Paraphrastically expounded and Historically applyed'. I quote from John Napier, who, as the discoverer of logarithms, reminds us that the Book of Revelation was by no means the province solely of theologians, witness *inter alia* the subsequent labours of Sir Isaac Newton. Napier's own effort, first published in 1593 (§ P–274), enjoyed by 1645 four editions as well as an *Epitome* (1641). Other expositions were no less popular (§§ P–226, 239, 269, 281), their ambition endorsed by none other than King James ('of all the scriptures, the buik of the Reuelatioun is maist meit for this our last age, as ane prophecie of the letter tyme').[36] The book is a prophecy, it was widely claimed among Protestants, in that it details the victory of the elect over the sinister forces of impiety, inclusive of the activities of the Antichrist (Rev. 13:11 ff., cf. 1 John 2:18) who was habitually identified with the Pope.[37] It is also a prophecy, according to an increasing number of clamorous militants, in that its promise of Christ's temporal reign of a thousand years (Rev. 20:6) was about to be realised.

In short, the literal meaning once enforced, the Book of Revelation yielded as many interpretations of history as there were spokesmen prepared to entertain them.

Donne pretended not to be concerned. Since several of the early Fathers had also accepted the prophecy of Christ's millenarian reign 'in all temporall abundances', any parallel belief in the seventeenth century was not a heresy so much as 'an opinion, which is no word of heavy detestation'. With equal assurance Bishop Joseph Hall averred that the 'opinion' of the latter-day millenarians was not 'so deadly and pernicious in it selfe, as to make ship-wrack of their own or others faith'.[38] In fact, however, millenarianism—chiliasm, according to its alternative designation—was potentially a very serious threat indeed. Millenarian expectations, for one, informed the questionable theoretical premises of the events at Münster. Within the seventeenth century, moreover, a partiality to the number 666—fraught with supernatural import on the basis of the Book of Revelation (13:18)—resulted in a veritable 'Itch of prophecying' ('*O Sixty-six*! Thou center of human Prophecies! Thou Ocean, into which all the Rivers of Conjectural Predictions did run!') which at the approach of 1666 unleashed a phenomenal hysteria as London was struck first by the devastating plague of the year before and then, in the apocalyptic year itself, by the Great Fire.[39] As the Book of Revelation was additionally read in connection with the Book of Daniel—both contain, it was widely believed, 'historicall prophecies'[40]—the thousand years' temporal reign of Christ in the one was identified with the 'fifth monarchy' at the end of history in the other (Daniel 2:44). The political consequences were formidable. At the risible level, violent disputes often centred on whether the beast in Revelation was Charles I or Parliament, and whether the 'fifth monarchy' was to be established by Christ or—an improbable candidate at best—Charles II.[41] The actuality, of course, was far different, involving as it did political ambitions fired by emotional commitments on the part of radicals generally (§S–71) and the Fifth Monarchy men in particular (§S–25), who alike embraced millenarianism with revolutionary fervour. In the moment's 'enthusiasm'—to use the word in the strictly pejorative sense it had assumed by the later seventeenth century—the Book of Revelation was further conflated with extra-biblical 'prophecies'. The most notable of these, first propounded by Joachim of Fiore (d. 1202) and codified by his wilder disciples into the *Evangelium aeternum*, divided history into three temporal Ages of which the third and last, expected to endure for a thousand years, was said to have begun under the supervision of the Holy Ghost. Attacked as a 'most detestable and blasphemous book' by John Foxe during the Elizabethan era as by Donne during the Jacobean, the 'everlasting gospel' was resuscitated by the radicals of the mid-seventeenth century—and beyond, stripped of its theological attire, by Hitler's Third Reich, which was also expected to last a thousand years.[42]

Is it at all credible that such promiscuous interpretations of the Book of Revelation had any influence on literature? Yet the central Protestant view of the battle between the elect and the Antichrist is demonstrably basic to Spenser's design in the first book of *The Faerie Queene*, where Archimago represents the Antichrist, Duessa 'the great whore' arrayed in scarlet (Rev. 17:1 ff.), and Una the woman clothed with the sun as well as the Bride of the Lamb (Rev. 12:1 and 21:2–9).[43] No less demonstrably, Milton in *Paradise Lost* also drew heavily on the Book of Revelation, especially in his apocalyptic account of the War in Heaven which in the poem's 'prevenient' time-scheme anticipates the Son of God's ultimate victory during his second advent at the end of history (§S–448). The Protestant poets of the English Renaissance, it is clear, confirm all too generously the Protestant claim of the Bible's all-encompassing authority. The student of the period's literature will in consequence wish to regard the Bible as his single most important companion. For just as to study the Book of Revelation is to appreciate the apocalyptic orientation of *Paradise Lost*, so *inter alia* to study the Book of Job is to enrich one's understanding of both *Paradise Regained* and *Samson Agonistes*—or indeed Milton's prose inclusive of *Eikonoklastes* (§S–146)—and to study the Psalms is to penetrate deeply into the emotional world of Herbert in *The Temple* and Donne in the *Holy Sonnets*. The literature of the English Renaissance is in its commitment to Otherness essentially biblical.

THE LIFE WITHIN: SERMONS AND SACRAMENTS

The experiential life of Protestantism centred on the proclamation of the Word through preaching and its symbolic confirmation through the sacrament of the Lord's Supper, the Eucharist. Preaching was the capital medium of evangelisation, and though frequently used for expressly political purposes, it consisted by and large of expositions of doctrine and counsel for behaviour. Several manuals provided generous advice on technical details such as the sermon's length and form, and on substantive matters such as procedure (§§P–333, 339, 344, 349). Least heeded, alas, was the advice appertaining to length ('Euery Sermon ought to be briefe' [§P–344: fol. 15v]). Otherwise, however, the most responsible preachers elevated their sermons to the level of art fully commensurate to their noble aims. The principal aim was best set forth by Donne in 1627:

> The Preacher doth so infuse the feare of God into his Auditory, that first, they shall feare nothing but God, and then they shall feare God, but so, as he is God; and God is Mercy; God is Love; and his Minister shall so spread his wings over his people, as to defend them from all inordinate feare, from all suspition and jealousie, from all diffidence and distrust in the mercie of God.[44]

So far as the mode of articulation was concerned, the Marburg theologian Andreas Gerardus (Hyperius) invoked St Augustine's endorsement of the sermon as a studied oration: 'the whole craft of varienge the Oration by *Schemes and Tropes*, pertaineth indifferently to the Preacher and Orator' (§P–344: fol. 9). In England, the highly respected William Perkins in *The Arte of Prophecying. Or a Treatise concerning the Sacred and Onely Trve Manner and Method of Preach-*

ing—translated from its original Latin in 1606 by Thomas Tuke—advanced a vital consideration no less relevant to poetry such as Herbert's:

> *Humane wisedome* must be concealed, whether it be in the matter of the sermon, or in the setting forth of the words: because the preaching of the word is the *Testimonie of God, and the Profession of the knowledge of Christ*, and not of humane skill . . . If any man thinke that by this meanes barbarisme should be brought into pulpits; he must vnderstand that the Minister may, yea & must priuately vse at his libertie the artes, philosophy, and varietie of reading, whilest he is in framing his sermon: but he ought in publike to conceale all these from the people, and not to make the least ostentation. *Artis etiam est celare artem; it is also a point of Art to conceale Art.*   (§P–284: II, 759)

A widely credited misconception accepts that 'Anglicans' and 'Puritans'—designations which themselves call for annotation—delivered sermons 'eloquent' in the former instance, 'plain' in the latter. Perkins, who commended the deployment of implicit eloquence, however, was a Puritan. In actual practice, moreover, eloquence was by no means the exclusive province of celebrated Anglican preachers like Lancelot Andrewes, Donne, Humphrey Sydenham, Jeremy Taylor, or Thomas Fuller, in that the same quality manifests itself throughout the evocative sermons of the Puritan Thomas Adams no less than in one of the period's greatest performances by the equally Puritan Ralph Cudworth (§P–334, repr. in §S–397: pp. 90 ff.). By the same token, 'plainness' is very much in evidence among Anglican preachers, not only Archbishop James Ussher of Armagh but—the ultimate evidence!—that arch-enemy of all Puritans, Archbishop William Laud of Canterbury. The most categorical affirmation of the virtues of 'plainness' in opposition to the elaborately structured sermon, finally, was also ventured by an Anglican. In Herbert's words,

> The Parsons Method in handling of a text consists of two parts; first, a plain and evident declaration of the meaning of the text; and secondly, some choyce Observations drawn out of the whole text, as it lyes entire, and unbroken in the Scripture it self. This he thinks naturall, and sweet, and grave. Whereas the other way of crumbling a text into small parts, as, the Person speaking, or spoken to, the subject, and object, and the like, hath neither in it sweetnesse, nor gravity, nor variety, since the words apart are not Scripture, but a dictionary . . .[45]

Response to preaching by the believing Protestant led to the symbolic confirmation of his faith through the Eucharist. One of the two sacraments recognised by Protestants as warranted by the Bible,[46] the Eucharist occasioned acrimonious controversies which turned Protestant against Protestant and permanently affected the divisions among the Reformers. But the central issue—the precise nature of the 'Real Presence' of Christ in the sacrament—need concern us less than the emphasis which Protestants upheld in opposition to Catholics. For where Catholics regarded the sacrament as dispensing grace irrespective of the attitude of the minister or the recipient, Protestants insisted on the prior condition of the recipient's faith. Equally important, where Catholics maintained that the sacrament as 'an efficacious sign of sanctifying grace' imparts salvation of itself, Protestants claimed that as 'the visible sign of an invisible grace' it is but symbolic of the actual blessings.[47] Translated into literature, the Protestant interpretation figures diversely in *The Faerie Queene* during the spiritual arming of the Redcross Knight for his ensuing victory over Orgoglio (I, xi, 36 and 46), and in *Samson Agonistes* during the gradual transformation of its protagonist into the believer who, inwardly illumined, correctly perceives 'the visible sign of an invisible grace'. But when all is said the poet who responded most fully to the sacramental life was Herbert. No single word which even remotely relates to the Eucharist—not only 'blood' or 'altar' but 'table', 'board', 'repast', 'banquet', 'store', and the like—is ever irrelevant; for, jointly drawn into the diverse experiences recounted in *The Temple*, they yield a cumulative unity which is fundamentally eucharistic.

Whatever our preconceptions, then, the importance of the Eucharist in Protestantism should not be underestimated. True, the devotional life of Protestants appears minimal when compared to that of Catholics; and so indeed it is, but rather in its extent than in its intensity. Mariolatry, as before noted (p. 178), was intensified in Catholicism especially after the Council of Trent. Mariology, on the other hand, was by no means ostracised from Protestantism, the Reformers themselves commending it in no uncertain terms, and Anglicans even more explicitly.[48] We also expect Anglicans to have been far more devotional than Puritans; and we point to the very dimensions so violently denounced at the time by Puritans: the fulsome celebration of the Virgin in Anthony Stafford's *The Femall Glory* (1635), the 'monastic' community at Little Gidding dedicated under Nicholas Ferrar to sustained prayers and ritualistic night-long vigils, the introduction of distinctly 'popish' elements into the liturgy by Archbishop Laud—and beyond, the powerful influence which the devotional writings of St Ignatius Loyola and St Francis of Sales are said to have exerted on Anglican poets (§S–950, but cf. §S–943), or the composition of a fervent poem like Joseph Beaumont's *Psyche* (1648) under the shadow of St Teresa.[49] Yet extreme forms of devotion were not unknown among Puritans. Thus a leading Cromwellian, Francis Rous, indulged in prayers for 'heavenly excesse', 'divine extasie', and the like (in §S–673: pp. 47–51; §P–290), even as Samuel Petto described his 'witnessings of the spirit' in *The Voice of the Spirit*, adding for good measure several 'sweet experiences' under the title *Roses from Sharon* (1654). Significantly, too, a virulent anti-Catholic like William Crashaw—the Catholic poet's most Protestant father—managed to attack the papal Antichrist even in his will,[50] yet he was not at all disinclined creditably to translate several devotional Catholic hymns and meditations in his *Manvall Catholicorum* (1611). Just as telling, finally, is the report of a parliamentary committee which visited Cambridge probably early in 1641 to investigate the suspect new chapel at Peterhouse (consecrated in 1634), which, they discovered, 'hath bene so dressed vp and ordered soe Ceremoniously, that it hath become ye gaze of ye Vniversity & greate invitation to strangers'. Worse still, students from that pre-eminent

Puritan stronghold, Emmanuel College, responded to the sinister practices at Peterhouse with distressing eagerness:

> Some of yᵉ Schollers have received harme by theire frequent goeing to Peterhowse chapp[ell] . . . as appeareth by theire Novel gestures in the Chappell [of Emmanuel], as bowing at their rising vp at *gloria patri* or yᵉ Gospell as also by crucifixe[s] wᶜʰ have bene occasionally discovered in two or three of theire Chambers . . .[51]

Details of this order are imperative if we ever hope to appreciate the frequent confluence of apparently opposed attitudes. Yet these same details should not prevent us from recognising several clear tendencies which differentiate Anglican poets like Donne and Herbert from Puritan ones like Milton. The Passion, for instance, elicited the response of Donne and Herbert in measure equal to its absence from the emotional world of Milton. Not a defect in Milton but a mark of his particular sensibility, his response was reserved for the effects of divine omnipotence within history, whether he celebrates in the Nativity Ode the impact of Christ on the universe at large, in *Comus* the joyous dance of the created order, in 'Lycidas' the actual harmony within the apparent dissonance, or in *Paradise Lost* the constant displacement of demonic disorder by effectual Grace—the Eucharist projected, as it were, on a cosmic canvas.

'ANGLICANS' AND 'PURITANS'

Theology as a commitment to Otherness is clearly not an abstraction. It partakes fully of multifoliate life, however diverse the experiences recounted and the literary forms deployed. We should therefore regard with scepticism any generalisation which channels responses in a single direction at the expense of reality's infinite complexity. The terms 'Anglican' and 'Puritan', for instance, are often used—and have been used even here—as if they were absolute entities that do not admit qualification. Yet we may consider that 'Anglican' is anachronistic in that it is a term of later vintage, while 'Puritan' is misleading in that it was by the early seventeenth century already a term of abuse, 'for the most part held a *name of infamie*', 'used (most commonly) for any Zealous Person'.[52] More to the point, the two terms are not in fact opposed, since they do not designate modes of thought and experience alike theological. 'Anglican' is indeed descriptive of the theology and ecclesiology of the Church of England, but 'Puritan' appertains rather to anti-ritualism in church services and dedication to moral uprightness than to any specific theological tenet. In theology as such, 'Anglican' is properly opposed by 'Calvinist'—save that most Anglicans during Elizabeth's reign (but not later) were very sympathetic to Calvinist theology, just as many Calvinists like William Perkins were sufficiently flexible to have been admired by Anglicans. In matters of Church government, 'Anglican'—here, more accurately, 'episcopalian'—initially stood in opposition to 'Presbyterian', itself a term whose theological horizons terminated in Calvin;

but when the presbyters on displacing the bishops proved no less obsessed with ecclesiastical hierarchy ('New *Presbyter* is but old *Priest* writ large,' Milton protested),[53] the lines of demarcation shifted yet again so that by the 1640s decentralised Church government was in the main espoused by the Independents or Congregationalists. Throughout these configurations the term 'Puritan' remained at its best suggestive of personal experiences centred on 'immediacy in relation to God' (§ S–481). As such, it is an essentially Protestant phenomenon; and William Bradshaw quite rightly observed in 1605 that Puritanism includes the rejection of 'all Ecclesiasticall actions invented & deuised by man', the acknowledgement solely of the Bible's 'absolute perfection', and the participation through faith in the priesthood of all believers ('euery Companie, Congregation or Assemblie of man, ordinarilie joyneing together in the true worship of God, is a true *visible church* of Christ' (§ P–38). The perceptive student of Puritanism will seek its Protestant roots in basic principles equally as much as in the categorical language, the confident poise, the tone of finality.

Developments in the early seventeenth century involve yet another expressly theological term, 'Arminian'. Deriving from the doctrinal positions of the Dutch Protestant theologian Jacobus Arminius (d. 1609), the term was accurately used at the time to represent anti-Calvinism at its most sustained. Alarmed, the Calvinists who monopolised the Synod of Dort (Dordrecht) in 1618–19 condemned Arminianism with predictable indignation. Their anxiety is best attested by their rhetoric. 'I desire,' Francis Rous warned in 1629,

> I desire we may consider the increase of Arminianism, an error that makes the grace of God lackey after the will of man. I desire we may look into the belly and bowels of this Trojan horse, to see if there be not men in it ready to open the gates to Romish tyranny, for an Arminian is the spawn of a Papist, and if the warmth of favour come upon him, you shall see him turn into one of these frogs that rise out of the bottomless pit.   (§ S–454: p. 140)

Not in the least intimidated, however, the 'ever-memorable' John Hales of Eton decided during the Synod of Dort to bid Calvin good night.[54] It was by no means a solitary decision. Anglicans were already forsaking their erstwhile flirtation with Calvinist theology; so much so that when Bishop George Morley of Winchester was asked what the Arminians held, he could blandly reply that they held the best bishoprics and deaneries in the country. Yet the liberal theology represented by Arminianism decisively influenced even 'Puritans' like John Goodwin. It is also mirrored in *Paradise Lost*, whose reiterated proclamations of man's free will (III, 98 ff.; V, 234 ff., 524 ff.,; IX, 343 ff.; X, 43 ff.) would have been condemned early in the seventeenth century as Arminian at best, 'the spawn of a Papist' at worst. By 1667, when the poem was published, however, Calvinism had by and large ceased to be the most pronounced influence on English theology.

Here as elsewhere the change may be measured in terms of the rhetoric deployed. Earlier in the seventeenth century the articulation of the prevalent views differed but in degree from Gabriel Powel's language in *The Resolved Christian* (1616):

> Man is made of the earth, conceiued in sinne, and borne to paine, Man is *euill, wretched, corrupt and abhominable, doing nothing that is good, mortall, vaine* and *wicked, vnprofitable, vanity, altogether lighter than vanitie, sinfull, miserable, dust and ashes, sown in corruption, dishonour and weaknes, deceitfull, naked, subiect to death, dead in sin, a liar, an hypocrite, an enemy vnto God*, a creature that *drinketh iniquity like water, a pilgrime, grasse, ignorant, a stranger & soiorner*, of *no continuance, compassed with the snares of death, water spilt on the ground*. By birth *vncleane*, a *child of wrath*, a *worker of iniquity, an open sepulchre*, a *worm, the meat of wormes, dung and wormes, depriued of Gods glory* . . . True it is, that some few sparks of the Image of God doe yet remaine in Man, but they are few indeede, very small, and of no strength . . .
>
> (pp. 5, 7)

By the middle of the century, however, attitudes were already inclining towards Milton's eventual efforts to justify the ways of God. Typically, Jeremy Taylor in his *Deus justificatus* (1656) could in measured tones firmly deny that 'when we all fell in *Adam*, we fell into the dirt', 'broken all in pieces'. He added:

> We by [Adam's] fall received evill enough to undoe us, and ruine us all; but yet the evill did so descend upon us, that we were left in powers & capacities to serve and glorifie God; Gods service was made much harder, but not impossible; mankind was made miserable, but not desperate, we contracted an actuall mortality, but we were redeemable from the power of Death; sinne was easie and ready at the door, but it was resistable; Our *Will* was abused, but yet not destroyed; our Understanding was cosened, but yet still capable of the best instructions; and though the Devill had wounded us, yet God sent his Son, who like the good Samaritan poured Oyle and Wine into our wounds . . .
>
> (pp. 15–16)

Milton's concurrent partiality to the demands of Divine Justice after the fall of man—'Die he or Justice must' (III, 210)—is also characteristic of the period's evolving thought. Alexander Gil the elder, High Master of St Paul's School when Milton was there in the early 1620s, anticipated the militancy of Milton's God by providing the following 'gloss':

> Either the whole race of mankinde must be lost and perish being tainted with the sinne of *Adam*, or the infinite justice against which the sinne was done, must for ever stand violated and broken, or else a Mediator must bee found who was able to satisfie the infinite justice that was offended. The first is against the wisdome, goodnesse, and love of God to his creatures; either to make mankinde in vaine, that is to destroy it againe, or to make it unto eternall punishment. The second is impossible, that an infinite justice infinitely able to avenge it selfe should endure it selfe for ever to remaine violate and offended: for so should it prize a thing finite, and wicked, before it selfe infinite in justice: therefore there behoves to be a Mediatour who should fully satisfie the justice offended, and utterly blot out the guilt of sinne. Now an infinite justice offended must be satisfied by a punishment answerable, that is infinite: but no finite creature could any way be,

or be accounted infinite. Therefore *when none was found worthy either in heaven, or in earth, or under the earth; the Lambe slaine from the beginning of the world tooke upon him our flesh*, to satisfie for the sinne of his creature, and so by his infinite obedience . . . was the infinite justice satisfied.[55]

The statement is an adequate summary of the Protestant theory of the Atonement. Yet it is significant that its burden was so qualified by Milton that the more brutal aspects of Calvinist logic were eschewed in favour of the gentler theology increasingly characteristic of English thought.

The decline and fall of Calvinism owed much to purely political factors. Yet theological considerations once again dominate the scene. The advent of Arminianism is crucial, certainly. But most thinkers, Milton among them, could as readily have adapted the liberal strain in Christian theology which reaches through Erasmus back to early Fathers like the enticing St Clement of Alexandria (d. *c.* 215). The line of descent is best attested by the Cambridge Platonists, notably Benjamin Whichcote, John Smith, Henry More and Ralph Cudworth. In all essentials 'Puritan', they shared an undeviating commitment to the ancient philosophers and the early Fathers, 'the Greek especially', as it was perceptively noted some time after the Restoration.[56] Of the Greek philosophers, Aristotle was dismissed unceremoniously because he was not 'over-zealous of Religion' (§P–355: p. 48), while Plato was welcomed because his philosophy seemed to be 'the most consistent and coherent Metaphysicall *Hypothesis*, that has yet been found out by the wit of man'.[57] Plotinus was even more favoured in that the Cambridge Platonists share his rational mysticism and endorse especially his experimental knowledge that the vision of God is attained νοερᾷ ἐπαφῇ, 'by an *Intellectual touch*' (Plotinus, *Enneads*, I, ii, 6, quoted in §P–355: p. 2). Pointedly, however, they opposed the Plotinian claim that man achieves union with the Divine unaided, and refused to accept that such a union involves man's translation into another region. It involves rather a transmutation into another state, the state wherein the soul is 'inebriated as it were, with the delicious sense of the Divine life' (§P–205: sig. A5). At no time is the soul 'out of nature'. Aware of its responsibilities within the arena of this world, it utilises the insights gained by 'ecstasy' to propel man from contemplation into action. Hence Whichcote's transfer of the Cartesian *Cogito ergo sum*—'I think, therefore I am'—from a philosophical context to an ethical one: 'I act, therefore I am'.[58]

But action presupposes the reality of man's unimpeded will. The approval that the Cambridge Platonists extended to Eastern theologians like Origen at the expense of Western ones like St Augustine and especially Calvin was based on the conviction that the latter upheld a dichotomy between the natural and the supernatural, the rational and the spiritual, the will of man and the grace of God. In opposition it was now argued that man was not created to be denigrated, nor redeemed to be restrained. 'God hath left us,' declared Whichcote, 'as *Free* as we may be' (§P–361: p. 342); so much so, added More, that it is impossible for any Christian properly so called to 'swallow down that hard Doctrine concerning *Fate* . . . *or Calvinistick Predestination*'.[59] Such premises once established, it remained for Cudworth to place them within the sophisticated philosophical context of his colossal *System*, described by himself as 'A Discourse concerning *Liberty* and *Necessity*, or to speak out more plainly, *Against the Fatall Necessity* of all *Actions* and *Events*' (§P–186: sig. A3). The cumulative result was a dramatic change in the attitudes to Otherness. Peter Sterry, for instance, penned *A Discourse of the Freedom of the Will* (1675), which is not so much a discourse as an extravagantly lyrical hymn to 'all the Beauties, all the Sweetnesses of the Divine Holiness, the Divine Love and Goodness'. 'The Wrath and the Contrariety now ceaseth,' he sang, 'being reconciled and charmed by these Divine Harmonies into the Unity of eternal Love' (p. 220).

It may nevertheless be doubted whether the Cambridge Platonists would have approved of Sterry's lyricism, suspicious as they were of any form of 'enthusiasm'. Their efforts were, after all, directed towards the eradication of fanaticism, which in effect meant an assault both on extreme principles as such and on their presentation in extreme language. The extreme principles were frontally attacked by Henry More in *Enthusiasmus triumphatus* (1656), the blueprint as it were of the Restoration's consistently adverse attitude toward 'enthusiasts'. The extreme language, on the other hand, was most effectively censured through the controlled tone used in particular by Whichcote and Smith to demonstrate the advantages of reasonableness. Style, indeed, became an indispensable weapon against 'enthusiasm' as related writers resorted to a variety of strategies, none more devastating in its immediate consequences than the satire which Marvell in *The Rehearsal Transpros'd* (1672–73) directed against the Anglican 'enthusiast' Samuel Parker.[60]

The fall of Calvinism may or may not have been a felicitous development. But the concurrent annihilation of 'enthusiasm'—not only of the irrational but of the prophetic in religious experience and of the radical in political thought—was eventually to be regarded with passionate regret. One's thoughts race beyond 'the peace of the Augustans' to Blake. But that, as they say, is another story.

NOTES

1   *Seriatim*: John Swift, *The Divine Eccho* (1612), sig. M2; Matthew Brookes, *The House of God* (1627), p. 29; Thomas Salter, *A Mirrhor mete for all Mothers* (1579), sigs. A6–A6v; Robert Pricket, *Times Anotomie* (1606), The Epistle to the Reader; and John Dod with Robert Cleaver, *Exposition of the Ten Commandements*, 19th ed. (1635), p. 269.

2   In the concluding line of *An Antidote against Atheism*.

3   *The Epistles of Erasmus*, trans. Francis M. Nichols (1901), I, 144 (Ep. 59).

4   'Man's will is like a beast standing between two riders. If God rides, it wills and goes where God wills . . . If Satan rides, it wills and goes where Satan wills. Nor may it choose to which rider it will run, or which it will seek; but the riders themselves fight to decide who shall have and hold it' (*De servo arbitrio* [1525], trans J. I. Packer and O. R. Johnston [1957], pp. 103–4). Erasmus's treatise *De servo arbitrio* (1524) is available in the translation by Ernst F. Winter (1961).

5 'Verba sine re Erasmus; res sine verbis Lutherus' (*apud* Wilhelm Pauck in *Luther and Melanchthon*, ed. Vilmos Vajta [Philadelphia, 1961], p. 26).

6 *Apud* Albert Hyma, 'The Continental Origins of English Humanism', *Huntington Library Quarterly*, IV (1940), 17.

7 'I consider Jerome,' wrote Luther, 'as much inferior to Augustine as Erasmus thinks he is superior' (*Luther's Correspondence*, trans. Preserved Smith [Philadelphia, 1913], I, 43 [Ep. 21]; in §S–368: p. 106). The fundamental opposition I posit between Erasmus and Luther is also endorsed—as I discovered subsequently—in the sophisticated core of Richard McKeon's 'Renaissance and Method in Philosophy', in *Studies in the History of Ideas* (1935), III, especially pp. 71–107.

8 James 2:24. Consult Luther's *Reformation Writings*, trans. B. L. Woolf (1956), II, 306–8, and the observations by Willem J. Kooiman, *Luther and the Bible*, trans. John Schmidt (Philadelphia, 1961), pp. 110–15.

9 §P–230: p. 134. A useful way to approach the dogma is through *A Reformation Debate*, ed. John C. Olin (1966), which contains the exchanges between Jacopo Cardinal Sadoleto and Calvin (1539) as well as the formal statements by the Council of Trent (1547) and Calvin in his *Institutes*, III, xi (1559).

10 Jerome Phillips, *The Fisherman* (1623), p. 7, and Donne, *Sermons*, ed. E. M. Simpson and G. R. Potter (Berkeley, 1953–62), II, 256.

11 John Dawes, in the dedicatory address of his translation of Bullinger's *Sermons* (§P–331).

12 *Homelyes . . . uppon Actes*, trans. John Bridges (1572), pp. 852–3.

13 *Seriatim:* Trelcatius (§P–304), p. 509; Anthony White, *Truth and Error* (Oxford, 1628), p. 41; Thomas Morton, *The Three-fold State of Man* (1629), p. 209 (211); and William Whately, *The New Birth* (1618), p. 7.

14 As above (note 10), VIII, 176.

15 Anthony Fawkner, Εἰρηνογονία (1630), p. 17.

16 I.e. the time of Christ's birth, when it was said that nature was exceptionally peaceful (cf. Milton's account in the Nativity Ode, ll. 61 ff.). The 'five thousand yeares' designates the agreed span of time since the world was created some time within the millennium ending this side of 4000 B.C.

17 Samuel Rutherford, *Christ Dying and Drawing Sinners to Himselfe* (1647), p. 12. Cf. Donne's *Anatomy of the World* ('The First Anniversary').

18 *Christianae religionis institutio* was first published in 1536, revised in 1539, and translated into French by Calvin himself in 1541. The student of Calvin's thought should also consult his variable *Tracts and Treatises*, trans. Henry Beveridge (Edinburgh, 1844–51; repr. Grand Rapids, Mich., 1958), 3 vols.

19 *Loci communes* (1521), available in the translation by Clyde L. Manschreck (1965).

20 John Falconer, *The Mirrour of Created Perfection* ([Saint–Omer], 1632), p. 136. Most Catholic books in English were during this period printed by the seminary for English Catholic scholars at Douai in Flanders and the Jesuit College of Saint-Omer in Artois.

21 *The Lyf of the Mother Teresa of Iesvs*, trans. W. M. (Antwerp, 1611), p. 239 (Ch. XXIX).

22 Whitaker, *Disputatio de Sacra Scriptura* (1588, trans. William Fitzgerald, Cambridge,

1849), p. 6, and Anthony á Wood, *Athenae Oxonienses* (1691), I, 303; respectively. On Whitaker's treatise see below, note 28. Bellarmine's major work was his *Disputations against the Heretics of our Time* (Ingolstadt, 1586–93), 3 vols.; but he also wrote numerous devotional and expository works, including the cogent *Dottrina christiana*, translated by Richard Gibbons as *A Short Catechisme* and illustrated with exquisite plates (Augsburg, 1614).

23 John Weemes, *The Christian Synagogue* (1623), p. 271, and Lawrence Anderton (?), *Epigrammes* ([Rouen, c. 1630]), p. 61. Weemes is specifically referring to 'the three pillars of popery', all of the twelfth century: Gratian, the father of canon law; Peter Lombard, author of the *Sentences*, the standard textbook of theology during the Middle Ages; and Peter Comestor, author of *Historia scholastica*, the standard work on biblical history.

24 *Opvs epistolarvm Des. Erasmi*, ed. P. S. and H. M. Allen (Oxford, 1922), IV, 520 (Ep. 1211); trans. in §S–368: p. 75. Even of the panegyrics in honour of St Thomas, one—Lorenzo Valla's *Encomium* of 1457—was in fact a critical anti-panegyric, an anti-eulogy (see John W. O'Malley, 'Some Renaissance Panegyrics of Aquinas', *Renaissance Quarterly*, XXVII [1947], 174–92, and Hanna H. Gray's remarks on Valla's performance in *Essays in History and Literature*, ed. Heinz Bluhm [Chicago, 1965], pp. 37–51). In consequence, John K. Ryan's enthusiastic study of 'The Reputation of St. Thomas Aquinas among English Protestant Thinkers of the Seventeenth Century', *New Scholasticism*, XXII (1948), 1–33, 126–208, is strictly unreliable, given in particular the author's absurd claim that St Thomas is 'the peer of Plato and Aristotle and Augustine'.

25 C. John Somerville, 'On the Distribution of Religious and Occult Literature in Seventeenth-Century England', *The Library*, 5th series, XXIX (1974), 220–5.

26 *Essays in Divinity*, ed. E. M. Simpson (Oxford, 1952), p. 39. By way of contrast, cf. Erasmus's commendation of the 'hidden' sense at the expense of the literal (*Enchiridion*, trans. Raymond Himelick [Bloomington, Ind., 1963], p. 105).

27 Thomas Wilson, *Theologicall Rules* (1615), p. 26.

28 Tyndale, 'The iiii. sences of yᵉ scripture', in *The Obedience of a Christen Man* (Antwerp, 1528), fols. 129–37. The analogy with the sacraments, argued by Whitaker (as above, note 22), is discussed by Charles K. Cannon in *Huntington Library Quarterly*, XXV (1962), 129–38.

29 As above (note 10), VI, 62. See also Helen Gardner, *The Limits of Criticism* (1956), pp. 40–63 ('The Historical Sense').

30 *Seven Goulden Candlestickes* (1624), p. 258. For some of the most detailed expositions of typology see §§P–253 and 254. Modern studies include G. W. H. Lampe and K. J. Woollcombe, *Essays in Typology* (1957), and Jean Daniélou, *From Shadows to Reality*, trans. Wulstan Hibberd (1960).

31 See further the introduction to my edition of *The English Poems of George Herbert* (1974).

32 See, for instance, the sufficiently accurate list in Ferdinando Parkhurst, *Masorah* (1660), p. 128. Consult also the standard essays by Baroway (§S–894).

33 *Devotions* (1624), ed. John Sparrow (Cambridge, 1923), p. 113.

34 *Emblemes* (1658), 'To the Reader'. Valeriano's view of the esoteric language of

hieroglyphics as of parables is noted by D. P. Walker, 'Esoteric Symbolism', in *Poetry and Poetics*, ed. G. M. Kirkwood (Ithaca, N.Y., 1975), p. 227.

35 As before (note 29).

36 *Ane frvitfvll meditatioun . . . of the 20 chap. of the Reuelatioun* (Edinburgh, 1588), fol. A3. The allusion to the 'last age' partakes of the widespread expectation that the end of the world was imminent. Milton in 1641 also held that Christ was 'shortly-expected' (*CE*, III, 78).

37 'The Papists hold the contrary,' John Downame remarked with some astonishment (§P–241: p. 2). But then the Protestant identification of the Pope with the Antichrist had been endorsed even by major Reformers like Melanchthon ('the marks of the Antichrist coincide with those of the pope's kingdom' [§S–497: p. 327]). See especially §S–458.

38 Donne, as above (note 10), IV, 77–8; cf. VI, 62–3, VII, 122, VIII, 81, etc.; and Hall, *The Revelation Unrevealed: Concerning the Thousand-Yeares Reigne of the Saints with Christ upon Earth* (1650), p. 6.

39 The sentiments quoted are by Samuel Rolls, *The Burning of London in the Year 1666* (1667), II, 90 and 96. See further Edward N. Hooker, 'The Purpose of Dryden's *Annus Mirabilis*', *Huntington Library Quarterly*, X (1946–47), 49–67.

40 As above (note 27), p. 62.

41 William Aspinwall, *A Brief Description of the Fifth Monarchy* (1653), and Arise Evans, *The Bloudy Vision . . . also a refutation of . . . Aspinwall* (1653). See also above, Ch. II, *passim*.

42 On the Joachimist tradition see §S–109. Foxe and Donne were quoted, at my instigation, in §S–492: pp. 108–9. On the radicals consult §S–71: pp. 147–8, 390, and §S–99: pp. 126 ff. On the period's eschatological expectations generally, see in particular §S–430.

43 Consult Josephine W. Bennett, *The Evolution of 'The Faerie Queene'* (Chicago, 1942), Ch. IX, and John E. Hankins, *Source and Meaning in Spenser's Allegory* (Oxford, 1971), pp. 99–119. See also J. F. Kermode in *Bulletin of the John Rylands Library*, XLVII (1964), especially pp. 130 ff.

44 As above (note 10), VIII, 44.

45 *A Priest to the Temple, or, The Countrey Parson* (first published posthumously, 1652), Ch. VII; in *The Works of George Herbert*, ed. F. E. Hutchinson (Oxford, 1941), pp. 234–5.

46 The other is baptism. Catholics accept an additional five: confirmation, penance, orders, matrimony, and extreme unction.

47 The former statement is by Peter Lombard; the latter, by St Augustine (quoted in §S–486: p. 218).

48 See A. M. Allchin, 'Our Lady in Seventeenth-Century Anglican Devotion and Theology', in *The Blessed Virgin Mary*, ed. E. L. Mascall and H. S. Box (1963), Ch. IV; and so far as the Reformers are concerned: the texts collected, and the further studies cited, in *Das Marienlob der Reformatoren*, ed. Walter Tappolet (Tübingen, 1962).

49 See Paul G. Stanwood, 'St. Teresa and Joseph Beaumont's *Psyche*', *Journal of English and Germanic Philology*, LXII (1963), 533–50.

50 'I accoûnte Poperie (as howe it is) the Heape and Chaos of all Heresies and the Channell whereinto the fowlest impieties and Heresies that have bene in the Christian world have runne and closelye emptied themselves. I beleeve the Popes seale and power to be the power of the great Antichriste . . .' (P. J. Wallis, 'The Library of William Crashawe', *Transactions of the Cambridge Bibliographical Society*, II [1954–58], 216). See also Crashaw's view of the Catholic Church ('a spirituall leprosie') in *The Sermon preached at the Crosse, Feb. xiiij. 1607* (1608).

51 Allan Pritchard, 'Puritan Charges against Crashaw and Beaumont', *The Times Literary Supplement*, 2 July 1964 (p. 578).

52 Owen Felltham, *Resolves*, 5th ed. (1634), p. 10, and Moses Capell, *Gods Valuation of Mans Soule* (1632), p. 36; respectively.

53 In 'On the New Forcers of Conscience under the Long Parliament'. See especially §S–144.

54 Consult James H. Elson, *John Hales of Eton* (1948), Ch. IV, 'The Synod of Dort'.

55 §P–250: Art. II, pp, 136–7. See further §S–486: Ch. V.

56 John Worthington, *Select Discourses* (1826), p. 36. On Cambridge Platonism, see especially the selections and bibliography in §S–397. On 'the eclipse of Calvinism' generally, consult §S–441: Ch. II.

57 Henry More, *The Second Lash of Alazonomastix* (Cambridge, 1651), p. 85. This tract forms part of More's quarrel with the uncontrollable Thomas Vaughan, the brother of the poet.

58 *Several Discourses* (1701–07), III, 328.

59 Richard Ward, *The Life of . . . Henry More* (1710), p. 6.

60 Raymond A. Anselment, 'Satiric Strategy in Marvell's *The Rehearsal Transpros'd*', *Modern Philology*, LXVIII (1970), 137–50. On the larger context, see George Williamson, 'The Restoration Revolt against Enthusiasm', *Studies in Philology*, XXX (1933), 571–603.

7

The scientific background

Robert Burton, in a digression appended to the second part of his *Anatomy of Melancholy* in 1621 (II, ii, 3), discussed the disquieting consequences of astronomical controversies in his time. The 'main paradox' was Copernicus's rejection of the ancient geostatic world-picture, and his substitution of a rotating and revolving earth, orbiting the sun in the company of the planets (§ S–548: pp. 272–3). Burton assumed that such a system had been accepted among the ancients by Aristarchus of Samos, the Pythagorean. He mistakenly believed Copernicus had revived the belief 'not as a truth, but a supposition'. It was now maintained 'in good earnest' by Kepler, Galileo, Campanella, the Englishmen Digges and Gilbert, and others.

The system's advantages were easy to appreciate. The Aristotelian belief that heavenly bodies were set in and carried around by spheres made of the celestial element, the ether or quintessence, had been vehemently disputed since the sixteenth century. Astronomers pointed out that in their various motions the planets would cut or interfere with each other's spheres. The closing years of the sixteenth century had been particularly rich in cometary visitations. It was simpler to dispense with the spheres. If there were no spheres, what fury made the heavens revolve around the earth 'with such incomprehensible celerity' in twenty-four hours, as the old astronomy assumed? Astronomical calculations now made that speed more vivid to the imagination: 'A man could not ride so much ground, going forty miles a day, in 2904 years, as the firmament goes in twenty-three hours . . . .' It seemed too fantastic to be true. The Copernicans therefore assumed that the earth rotated on its axis to make night and day, and around the sun in a year to produce the cycle of the seasons. The monstrously complex geometrical devices used by astronomers to account for irregularities in planetary motions then became superfluous.

But these conveniences were counterbalanced by very strong disadvantages.

One powerful objection to a moving earth orbiting the sun was that it must result in a 'stellar parallax'. A telescope would have to be turned through a certain angle to observe a particular star, say, during summer. When the earth was on the opposite side of the sun, in winter, it must be turned through a different angle to observe the same star. Yet the much more precise observational astronomy then practised had failed to detect any such difference. To explain it the Copernicans argued that the stars must be much farther away than ever thought and the earth's circuit round the sun was like a tiny speck in the vast expanse of space. The universe must be bigger and much emptier than anyone had ever imagined in the past. An 'incredible and vast space' yawned between the outermost planet, Saturn, and the firmament: according to Tycho Brahe a distance equal to seven million semi-diameters of the earth. New difficulties then arose. To account for the apparent diameter of the stars, now removed to unimaginable distances, each fixed star must be so enormous that, as Burton thought, it was 'quite opposite to reason, to natural philosophy, and all out as absurd as disproportional (so some will) as prodigious, as that of the sun's swift motion of heavens'.

Besides technical problems, the new system raised cosmological and theological perplexities. Previous systems had sharply differentiated the earth from celestial bodies, which were made of the most perfect substances. But if the earth moved, it was a planet. Galileo had shown that the earth, too, shone like the moon. His telescope had revealed a moon rough and rugged as the earth, with seas and mountains. The planets, too, were probably no more 'celestial' or 'etheral' than the earth. Then the earth would be like a moon to the planets: 'per consequence, the rest of the planets are inhabited, as well as the moon', and there must be Lunar, Jovial and Saturnian inhabitants besides earthly ones. If our sun was a star, surrounded by inhabited planets, then every star must be the centre of a similar system. Since Galileo had vastly increased the number of stars with his telescope, ancient ideas of infinite worlds in the infinite ether must again be taken seriously. But then, as Kepler had asked, what sort of creatures inhabited those distant parts of space? Were they rational and did they have souls to be saved? Did they dwell in a better part of the universe? 'Are we or they Lords of the World?' asked Burton, citing Kepler. 'And how are all things made for man?' Thus 'prodigious paradoxes, inferences' followed, if it was once conceded that the earth was a planet and shone like the moon, and that the moon had both land and seas. To avoid such paradoxes, and after the Church of Rome's condemnation of the Copernican system in 1616, a number of alternatives had been suggested. One of them was Tycho Brahe's compromise system in which the planets orbited the sun, which in turn orbited the earth. 'In the mean time the World is tossed in a blanket amongst them, they hoist the Earth up and down like a ball, make it stand and go at their pleasures . . .'

Burton's breathless and somewhat chaotic summary of arguments and implications, and his piling of ancient and mediaeval authorities on contemporary ones, illustrates the upheavals caused by the astronomical theories and discoveries of his time. Even when Copernicanism was considered unacceptable because it seemed to lead to absurdities, compromise systems like that of Tycho Brahe and the telescopic discoveries of Galileo had no less destructive consequences for the world-picture inherited from the ancients. The heavenly spheres disappeared. No sharp line divided terrestial or 'sublunary' from celestial. If comets were celestial objects, then a fiery sphere in which exhalations wafted from the earth took fire was superfluous, and—as Donne said in 'The First Anniversary'—'the Element of Fire is quite put out' (1. 206).

THE ARISTOTELIAN HERITAGE

The old astronomy was found in its most systematic form in the *Syntaxis* of Claudius Ptolemy, the Alexandrian Greek who had synthesised Greek astronomical achievement, and whose *Geography* had given Columbus a false confidence in his ability to reach Cathay by sailing west. But it was Aristotle who, already in the fourth century B.C., had made the geostatic system part of a comprehensive and systematic scientific account of nature that still formed the basis of academic teaching in England (as elsewhere in Europe) well into the seventeenth century. Francis Bacon (1561–1626) had compared the systems of Plato and Aristotle to 'planks of lighter and less solid material', which had floated out on to the waves of time, when Gothic destruction caused human learning to suffer a shipwreck (§P–176: I, Aphor. 77). By 1676 Joseph Glanvill condemned the Aristotelian philosophy taught at the universities as 'but monkery, and moorish ignorance, formed into idle and unintelligible whimsies', having 'no ground, either from sense or reason', serving 'no purpose of knowledge or life' (§P–193). To accept such verdicts is to overlook the cogent reasons which gave Aristotle, the mediaevals' 'master of those that know', primacy in higher education and intellectual culture in the West since the thirteenth century.

When Raphael, in his fresco of the 'School of Athens', painted early in the sixteenth century, made Plato point towards the heavens and Aristotle towards the earth, he symbolised an important contrast between their philosophies. The otherworldly cast of Plato's thought, his Demiurge who fashioned and watched over his creation, and his assertion of the immortality of the soul made it congenial to Christianity and a preparation for it to such notable early converts as St Augustine. There was a flat contradiction, on the other hand, between Aristotelian principles and some fundamental Christian dogmas. Aristotle affirmed the eternity of the universe, denied special creation and providence, and rejected the immortality of the individual soul. His God was the logical terminus of the chain of causes and as such an intellectual principle excluded from intervening in the universe. Nevertheless, like mediaeval Islam and Judaism, at a certain level of intellectual development and sophistication the Christian world had found the treasures of ancient learning integrated into the Aristotelian system irresistible.

The system of Aristotle was perhaps the most audacious attempt ever made to encompass the whole of human knowledge in one coherent scheme. It set up a basic framework of logic and metaphysics, and applied the fundamental concepts to physics, biology, cosmology, ethics, politics, mental life and aesthetics. For a culture living no longer under the shadow of an imminent Second Coming, but endeavouring to reconcile religious authority with the claims of a highly developed secular sphere of life, Aristotle offered an intellectual structure of unrivalled range and subtlety, oriented towards the concerns of a hierarchically organised society and universe. In the thirteenth century St Thomas Aquinas succeeded in reconciling Aristotle and Christian dogma so that the assertion of the primacy of sensible reality, instead of threatening a religious vision of the world, became for a time its most powerful support.

Aristotle denied his master Plato's doctrine that the sensible universe consisted of the debased copies of eternal Forms or Ideas, and the injunction that the wise would not linger among them but contemplate the disembodied essences which the soul had known before it was imprisoned in the body. Forms had no existence apart from the matter in which they realised themselves. They were, indeed, the objects of true knowledge, but the mind could find and disengage them only from sense-experience. Despite his emphasis on sensible knowledge and the dignity of the empirical world, Aristotle was not a materialist. His own viewpoint is nearest to what may be regarded as a (pre-Darwinian) biological world-view. Aristotle was a founder of biology as a scientific discipline, and his own greatest scientific contributions were to the study of the structures and life-histories of a large class of living things.[1]

Neither Pythagorean-Platonic mathematism nor Democritean atomism seemed to Aristotle to do justice to the richness of the world that sense-experience disclosed to us. Mathematics studied abstract entities, like a 'concave curve' instead of a 'snub-nose', but in dealing with the real world both form *and* matter had to be considered together. To reduce everything, on the other hand, to the dance of atoms with the ancient Greek atomists was equally to explain nature in a quantitative and non-directive manner and to do violence to the order and harmony which the universe clearly exhibited. The true nature of things was disclosed far more by their tendency or development towards a goal when unconstrained: the acorn became an oak, the child a man. Objects moved towards the possession of their characteristic forms and their potentialities were actualised. The atomists had reduced all change to change of place. Aristotle treated change of place, or locomotion, itself within a larger framework which may appear to us better adapted to the study of organisms, and in so doing made it into a *process*, through his related doctrine of elements and his cosmology.

Aristotle was not the first to suggest that all objects were made of a combination of four primary elements. His originality lay in grounding their existence in metaphysical necessity and in integrating them with the geocentric cosmology elaborated by earlier thinkers. The universal matter underlying all things was differentiated into Earth, Air, Fire and Water, corresponding to the solid, gaseous, fiery or radiant, and liquid. Each element, in turn, was associated with two of four basic qualities: hot, cold, wet and dry. Each element had its characteristic place in the universe. The 'elementary' nature of an object was disclosed by the place to which it moved when unconstrained. A stone fell down towards the centre of the universe, which was the natural place for earthy objects; steam and flame tended upwards. An object could be moved away from its natural place only through unnatural or 'violent' motion, requiring an agent in immediate and continuous contact with it. Bodies moved towards or away from a centre in a straight line. By contrast, celestial objects in the heavens revolved in uniform, circular paths. They were made of a pure fifth element, the ether, and the motion appropriate to it had neither beginning nor end. The centre of the universe was occupied, therefore, by an immobile earth, around which revolved the heavenly bodies in stately uniform motion in circular orbits.

Aristotle's concepts of elements and their associated qualities, each with an assigned natural place in the universe, were the ruling ideas by which educated men perceived and understood the world of nature. Their hold was made even more powerful and pervasive through their role in the dominant medical system, descending from Galen (*c*. 130–201), who was, like Ptolemy, a Hellenistic Greek thinker who had synthesised and systematised earlier doctrines.[2] Molière satirised Galenic explanations when, in *Le Malade imaginaire* (1673), a candidate physician told his examiners that opium induced sleep through its 'dormitive virtue'. But Galen was a great pioneer anatomist and physiologist who had expressly warned against using his 'faculties' as ultimate explanations. His use of experiment in physiology did not find worthy and systematic successors until William Harvey in the seventeenth century.

But experiments put questions to nature. Galen necessarily depended upon the scientific and philosophical tradition of his period for the scientific language in which questions were posed and the kinds of explanation regarded as satisfactory. Building upon the work of the Hippocratic physicians, Galen adopted a theory in which the four elements were associated with four 'humours' in the human body: fire with blood, water with phlegm, air with yellow bile, and earth with black bile. Since the characteristic balance varied from one individual to another, there was a variety of temperaments. Though Galen himself distinguished thirteen types of temperament, a popular and influential later version simplified them to four: the sanguinous (predominance of blood), the phlegmatic, the choleric (yellow bile), and the melancholic (black bile). Health resulted from the maintenance of the balance of four humours characteristic of a particular individual, and disease from an unbalance. There were, strictly speaking, not diseases, but just disease or distemper, which manifested itself in a small number of groups or symptoms, as in fevers, plague, or the falling sickness. The physician's task, as Hippocrates had tersely framed it, was 'to remove excess and supply deficiency'. *Natura medicatrix* herself did that, cooking the excess humour by fever, and removing it (as in colds). The physician assisted her through bleeding, purging, inducing sweating or vomiting. Since the four-element theory offered a way of classifying all vegetable and animal substance by their predominant qualities, the physician could reasonably choose a suitable therapeutic substance to supply the deficiency of various humours. Particular excesses of humour were plausibly linked to particular places, seasons and ages. Colds and catarrh were more likely in moist than in dry places, in winter rather than in summer, in old age rather than in youth.

Aristotle's vision thus shaped not only the educated man's ideas of right method and valid discourse, but those with which he thought of cosmology, physics, mental life, temperament, as well as health and disease. By the seventeenth century the philosophy of Aristotle had been subtly modified. It bore the impress of the Stoic and Neoplatonic syncretisms of the Hellenistic period, as well as the Judaic, Islamic and mediaeval Christian attempts to harmonise it with their sacred writings. One fruit of these endeavours was the conviction of an order in the universe, sustained by God in the pattern of a Chain of Being whose links formed a graded hierarchy of all things.

As Lovejoy has pointed out, Platonic and Aristotelian ideas were combined in the Great Chain (§S–388). While utterly self-sufficient, Plato's God necessarily gave existence to a world filled with every grade of being, since, being 'good', he was free of envy and must sanction the existence of everything possible. The beings were classified according to a scheme of which there were hints in Aristotle. From stones, endowed only with cohesion, to plants, possessing nutritive powers in addition, to animals (sensibility) and man (rationality), the chain stretched through angels and the intelligences moving the heavenly spheres to the throne of God himself. The Great Chain linked God to his creation, while safeguarding his transcendence. It explained why the one became many, and why God would not have removed evil from a perfect universe. It sanctioned social and ecclesiastical hierarchies and inequalities.

Great changes had altered the landscape of natural philosophy by the end of the sixteenth century.[3] There was a more intensive effort to systematise and consolidate the predominantly Aristotelian-scholastic tradition, to which both halves of the now divided Christian Europe had contributed. So immense was the labour devoted to that enterprise that one authority has suggested that it is the sixteenth century rather than the high Middle Ages which deserve the appelation 'scholastic'. At the same time, the first clear challenges to the inherited world-picture were formulated after many centuries.

COPERNICUS AND NEOPLATONISM

In the early seventeenth century the two foremost and rather different challenges appeared to be those of the Pole Copernicus and the Swiss-German Paracelsus. They were the men of science in the *dramatis personae* of Donne's *Ignatius his Conclave* (1611), where Lucifer judged the claims of innovators who 'gave an affront to all antiquitie, and induced doubts, and anxieties, and scruples, and . . . at length established opinions, directly contrary to all established before'. His Copernicus proclaimed that he had 'turned the whole frame of the world, and [was] thereby almost a new Creator'. His Paracelsus confessed having 'brought all *Methodicall Phisitians*, and the art it selfe into so much contempt, that that kind of phisick is almost lost'. For Burton, Copernicus was 'Atlas his successor', while Paracelsus and 'his chemistical followers' were 'as so many Promethei, [who] will fetch fire from heaven, will cure all manner of diseases with minerals . . . . And though some condemn their skill and magnetical cures as tending to magical superstition, witchery, charms etc., yet they admire, stiffly vindicate, nevertheless, and infinitely prefer them.' In the last decade of the century, Sir William Temple confirmed in his works which began the English 'Ancients *v.* Moderns' controversy that scarcely anyone had challenged the authority of the ancients until the previous century, when such troublesome spirits as Copernicus and Paracelsus tried to overthrow it in the sciences.[4]

Besides these frontal challenges, the scientific landscape was altered in a less spectacular way by the steady and rapid assimilation of ancient doctrines, tradition and methods which enabled men from many culturally diverse regions of Europe to develop, correct and even question them. The massive illustrated tomes of Conrad Gesner of Zurich and Ulysses Aldrovandi of Bologna exemplify the patient accumulation of botanical and zoological information to supplement the ancient inheritance. The emblematic view of nature, which made natural objects significant primarily as aids to scriptural interpretation or reminders of eternal verities, gave way to the delight in nature which Petrarch's 'Ascent of Mount Ventoux' (1336) had foreshadowed. Underlying the work of the German 'fathers of botany and natural history' was a new sense of the worth and dignity of the immediate environment of contemporary Europeans which spurred its imaginative repossession through artistic representation as well as scientific study. The shocked humanist discovery of 'errors' in ancient authorities was succeeded by a realisation that Theophrastus, Dioscorides and Pliny had described Mediterranean fauna and flora. It led to comparative study which gained further stimulus from the discovery of previously unknown plants and animals in the New World.

Since accurate pictorial representation could compensate for deficiencies in the existing vocabulary of technical description, the revolution effected in the diffusion of ideas by the invention of printing by movable type had a special importance for these sciences. The same was true of anatomy, where the Fleming Vesalius's masterpiece, *De humani corporis fabrica* (1543), displayed an art of dissection which equalled Galen's but was able to correct a whole range of errors in the Hellenistic master, since it was not limited, as he was, by the Roman prohibition on the dissection of human cadavers.

Behind Copernicus's achievement lay a quickened rate of mastery of the Greek and Arabic astronomical tradition which advanced European understanding beyond simplified mediaeval epitomes to a comprehension of Ptolemy's complex technical treatise and inspired Copernicus to attempt its radical revision. In mathematics a renaissance was advanced especially by a great school of Bolognese mathematicians, raising the proficiency of methods and techniques in the Greek, Indian and Islamic traditions, inventing a new notation, and laying the foundations of a powerful new algebra.

The nature and scope of the influence that the expanding horizons of economic activity may have exerted on the growth of science in the sixteenth century has been much debated.[5] Neither a crude determinism, which conceives science as a genie at the beck and call of an economically dominant class, nor that view which places the man of science in a lofty tower, insulated from the clamour of the market place, appears satisfactory. The relationship is subtle and complex, since whatever influence the social and economic environment exercises on scientific thought is mediated through on-going traditions and systems of ideas.

The flourishing state of astronomy in Copernicus's day owed a great deal to practical needs.[6] The great voyages of discovery which began in the late fifteenth century depended on astronomical methods of position-finding at sea. The craft-practice of pilotage, based on long-accumulated and detailed knowledge of coastlines, landmarks, tides and sea beds, could not serve the oceanic voyager, who had to depend for latitude-sailing on 'taking' the sun or pole star. Mathematical practitioners, selling astronomical instruments adapted to the needs of sailors and offering instruction in their use, had set up shop in many parts of Europe. Pope Alexander VI's division of newly discovered lands between Portugal and Spain in 1493 east and west of a meridional line of partition gave the search for a method of finding longitude greater urgency.

Scholars were also drawn to astronomical problems by the deficiencies of the calendar inaugurated by Julius Caesar.[7] The vernal equinox came too soon, and the computation of Easter was all wrong by the early sixteenth century. The problem was already evident in the thirteenth century, but consolidation and centralisation in secular as well as ecclesiastical administration made uniformity and efficiency in date keeping appear far more important. Another 'technical need' which demanded greater accuracy in astronomical prediction was that of astrological forecasting.[8] The advent of printing 'democratised' astrology, and much of the output of the early printing presses consisted of ephemerides. Many astrologers were convinced that errors in the existing astronomical tables required urgent correction in order to place their science on a sounder footing.

Copernicus himself was invited to assist in 1514 on the calendar reform then being considered by the Lateran Council, but declined because he felt the positions of sun and moon had to be known with far greater accuracy before any progress could be made. His dissatisfaction was really about the fundamentals of astronomy and well illustrates the deficiencies of any attempt to explain his innovation as an almost predetermined response to a sufficiently strong economic or technological stimulus. The inaccuracy of the calendar was cited by Copernicus in the preface to *De revolutionibus* (1543) as a reason for his dissatisfaction, and a fruit of his work was new tables which improved matters and became the basis of the Gregorian reform in 1582. But his treating it as a symptom of a much more fundamental deficiency which required a total recasting of the received cosmology cannot be understood apart from a consideration of the development of the ancient classical astronomical tradition, as modified by Islamic and mediaeval Christian influences, or without taking account of Renaissance humanism, and especially Neoplatonism and Neo-Pythagoreanism (§S–555: Ch. IV).

No novel observational facts compelled Copernicus to reject the geostatic cosmology and adopt a heliostatic one. Dissatisfaction with the received cosmology had been almost continually voiced since late antiquity for diverse reasons. Eccentric orbits and epicycles were difficult to reconcile with Aristotle's insistence that natural circular motion must occur around an immovable central body. Islamic Peripatetics had unsuccessfully attempted to set up astronomical systems doing away with compounded circles. Such Renaissance Aristotelian objections to a moving earth had to some extent been undermined by theoretical discussions among fourteenth-century scholastics, notably the French Terminists Nicolas Oresme and Jean Buridan.

Copernicus's fierce rejection of the Ptolemaic system seems initially to have been aroused by the Alexandrian master's use of a particular mathematical device, the equant, which violated the axiom of uniform circular motion around a central body more flagrantly than other such devices. More generally, while Ptolemy had systematically dealt with all the astronomical phenomena revealed to the naked eye, and furnished devices and tables for prediction in each case, he had not considered it necessary to make those various devices concordant. Copernicus denounced that as analogous to an artist's combining limbs which had been gathered from different models, each excellently drawn but not matching each other: 'the result would be monster rather than man' (in §S–555: p.   139). In an early sketch of his own system he had condemned Ptolemy's as 'neither sufficiently absolute nor sufficiently pleasing to the mind'.[9]

The very violence of Copernicus's rejection argues a deep commitment to the Pythagorean-Platonic vision of the universe revived especially in the late fifteenth century. He recalled the Pythagorean injunction to silence when explaining why he had kept his system secret for many years. He claimed that a search for ancient alternatives had led him to the Platonists and Pythagoreans who had granted movement to the earth. His disciple Rheticus narrated that Copernicus had followed 'Plato and the Pythagoreans, the greatest mathematicians of that divine age'.[10] Its marginal predictive advantage over Ptolemy and its admitted contradiction of the senses was to confine the appeal of Copernicus's system as a true description of nature to those who, like Kepler and Galileo, accepted the Copernican conception of 'order' and 'harmony' as fundamentally mathematical.

It has been claimed that to abandon the impressive Aristotelian scientific structure for the sake of a more harmonious geometrical astronomy was to return to a Platonic view of nature. But in the *Timaeus* Plato had distinguished between the world of pure Forms and the formless Receptacle on which the Demiurgos had imposed them in creating the universe. The irreducible resistance in the Receptacle prevented the complete imposition of Forms, and a gulf persisted between any mathematical account of nature and its perfect realisation in nature. No such opposition could be granted by the Christian, for whom the Creator was an omnipotent God who made a world which manifested the greatest harmony and orderliness. But, despite the pervasive influence of the ideas of a harmonically structured universe and of its manifestation as much in astronomy as in music, the overriding emphasis during the mediaeval period was on the chasm dividing appearance from reality.

In the Renaissance, architects in particular reached out for and propagated the Pythagorean-Platonic ideal of harmony and strove to give it visible embodiment in the churches they built. Leone Battista Alberti based on the Roman Vitruvius his influential definition of beauty as the rational integration of all parts of a structure in such a way that every part had a fixed shape and size, and nothing could be added or removed without destroying the harmony of the whole. No geometrical form was more adapted to fulfil that demand than the circle (§S–826: pp. 27–30, 33). Copernicus similarly claimed for his system the supreme virtue of reestablishing the 'unchangeable symmetry' of the parts of the universe: for the first time, it was possible to determine the order and relative sizes of all planetary orbits so that 'the heavens themselves become so bound together that nothing in any part thereof could be moved from its place without producing confusion of all the other parts and of the Universe as a whole'.[11] Rheticus asked if we must not attribute 'to God, the Creator of Nature, that skill which we observe in the common makers of clocks'? The masters of astronomy should have imitated the musicians 'who, when one string has either tightened or loosened, with great care and skill regulate and adjust the tones of all the other strings, until all together produce the desired harmony, and no dissonance is heard in any'. Since the significance of Neoplatonism as the carrier of humanistic ideas to northern lands beyond the Alps depended on a difference in cultural as well as socio-economic 'tone', the complex interweaving of what is sometimes artificially separated as an 'internal' and 'external' history is patent.

PARACELSUS

Similar considerations apply when evaluating the significance of Paracelsus.[12] He turned alchemy from the search for transmutation to the compounding of chemical remedies. He rejected the four-element theory which was linked to the humoral theory on which Galenic diagnosis and therapy were based. Modern scholars have traced in his work the origin of the novel conception of 'diseases' in place of the ancient concept of 'distemper'. Diseases were caused by specific entities which invaded a particular site in the body and disturbed its functioning. They were to be countered by chemical medicines, not by the Galenic correction of a supposed imbalance of humours. Paracelsus promoted a chemical interpretation of nature. Not only bodily functions but meteorological occurrences like thunderstorms or geological processes could be understood by analogy with chemical changes which could be duplicated in the laboratory. Nature could not be understood by the logical and dialectical methods of the scholastics, but only by experience and 'experiment', including the practical 'work of the fire'.

But such a bare summary of his achievements fails to recapture what they meant to him and his followers, since they were embedded in an outlook profoundly different from what would now be regarded as chemical or scientific. They must be placed in the context of the society and economy of Germany in the age of the Reformation and of the great changes in the climate of ideas which enabled a transformed alchemy to advance its claims as a replacement for 'heathen' Aristotelian science.

Frightful problems confronted the physician in sixteenth-century Europe. Recovering from the Black Death, most countries entered a period of pronounced and sustained population growth from about 1450 onwards. It was reflected in the 'headlong growth and large multiplication' of towns and cities (§S–254: I, 81). Society was ill equipped to cope with the problems of providing more housing, food, water and fuel, and the increased demands on disposal of garbage and sewage. The decline of corporate regulations made the enforcement of hygienic regulations even more difficult. The mushrooming urban centres were far more vulnerable to epidemic diseases like plague and typhus which swept through them in wave after wave. Consolidated and centralised States could field much larger armies, and campaigns extended into the winter months, laying troops, too, open to epidemics which increasingly began to decide the fate of many battles. More destructive siege cannon and the commoner use of hand guns inflicted more horrible wounds. The movement of troops could spread diseases more easily, as in the eruption of a particularly virulent form of syphilis after the French invasion of Italy in 1494. In the new age of oceanic navigation, ships sought steady winds on the high seas, away from the land, and the mortal disease of scurvy began to attack mariners deprived of fresh fruit and vegetables (§S–254: I, 106–8).

The bewilderment and helplessness of the academically trained physicians in the face of these new medical needs aroused the fury and contempt of Paracelsus. Rejecting their limited and perhaps more realistic view of the therapeutic measures at their command, he voiced his conviction that God in his mercy had planted through nature a cure for every disease which struck specific populations at particular times. In his optimism he was a child of the Renaissance as well as the Reformation. He had a passionate and boundless curiosity that not only embraced the earth and the myriad creatures inhabiting it but extended to stars, constellations and the firmament, together with the confidence that such knowledge and understanding lay within his compass. He affirmed the dignity and importance of man in countering a deterministic astrology which made him merely the passive recipient of celestial influences from a superior world. The world of nature was to him not merely a symbol of God, but rather a necessary manifestation of him. His sympathies lay not with the humanistic Renaissance and the revival of classical culture but with the Florentine Platonism and its associated 'natural magic' as it crossed the Alps and influenced German culture.[13]

Though Paracelsus never became a convert to Protestantism, the currents which nourished the Reformation were powerfully represented in his ideas. Book learning and subtle systems were to be rejected as much in things natural as about matters supernatural. The deepest knowledge came from a form of understanding far deeper than that of the reasoning faculty corrupted by the Fall, and was akin to mystical illumination. The Book of Genesis said man was made of *limus terrae*. All the constituents of the universe was therefore to be found in him, and he could understand, say, the secret workings of plants and herbs by an act of sympathy between the outside object and its inner representative within him. Viewing man as a 'quintessence' of the universe gave a new meaning to the ancient concept of man as a microcosm. Man was at the centre of a web of correspondences and was as capable of influencing the stars as they were of influencing him. By tracing the correspondences between the macrocosm of the universe and the microcosm of man it was possible to learn about the functioning of the human body and the nature of diseases.

It was vain to believe that such knowledge could be articulated and systematised in the neat terms and categories of the scholasticism of the schools. The Fall of Man initiated the work of 'separation', of a falling away from the original divine unity. All was now divided into the individual and specific, bound to particular times and places. Diseases, too, invaded the harmoniously functioning organism to produce separation and corruption. As a *magus*, man was not merely a contemplator of nature. He actively manipulated it to bring things more quickly to their maturity. All who engaged in that activity merited the name of alchemist, whether the baker who turned wheat into bread, the miner who extracted the pure shining metal from the ore, or the true physician who used distillation to exalt the secret working power of vegetables, herbs or minerals to their highest pitch.

On Paracelsus's reformed alchemy lay the stamp of the millennial link between the alchemical art and mining. German prosperity in his century rested in large part on rich mines. Paracelsus and his father were both connected with the mining school of the Fuggers at Hutenberg, near Villach. Mining experience seemed daily to confirm alchemical beliefs. Metals 'grow' in the womb of the earth towards their mature form of gold. Precious metals have to be purged of the less mature ones by the refiner's fire, which transforms ore into lustrous metal and accelerates the leaden tempo of nature. The process seemed analogous to the initiatory rites of mystery cults in which 'death' was followed by resurrection in a purer and more perfect form. Christian alchemists regarded it as typifying the mystic pattern of the death and resurrection of Christ.[14]

The alchemical cosmology differed radically from the scholastic-Aristotelian one in its vision of the universe and ways of comprehending it. Nature was pervaded by secret sympathies and antipathies between things, and they could act at a distance without intermediaries, as the moon influenced the tides, the sun the sunflower, or the loadstone iron. The characteristic properties or powers of a terrestrial object sprang from the quintessence, originating in a star, as it became 'specificated' within it. An act of sympathetic interaction, as Paracelsus had insisted, was necessary between an external object and its inner representative in man, the microcosm. It transcended reasoning, a corrupted and delusive faculty since the Fall. Although alchemists and natural magicians repeatedly emphasised their reliance on 'observation' and 'manual experiments', these mental operations were for them akin to mystical illumination and sharply contrasted to logical induction from particulars. Implicit in Paracelsus's concept of knowledge is something of the craftsman's conviction that he grasps the inner working of a thing or process at a far deeper level than intellectual cognition or apprehension. That conviction could find powerful legitimation in the religious emphasis on grace and illumination. Alchemists had traditionally prided themselves on their way of studying nature by practical manual operations, 'the work of the fire', and Paracelsus, too, stressed the chymist's ability to demonstrate the three principles by direct sensory experience, through smell, taste, touch and sight.

By contrast, scholastic Aristotelianism insisted on the power of human reason to understand nature through rational analysis in terms of the four elements and the associated four qualities. In opposition to the rising tide of magical ideas, fourteenth-century defenders of high scholasticism like Nicole Oresme and Henry of Hesse had sought to bring alleged sympathies and antipathies, the power of constellations, 'signatures' of plants and gems indicating curative properties, and even the mysterious power of beauty, whether of shape or of musical tones, within a theory of intension and remission of forms as a refinement of Aristotelian doctrine. It was significant that Oresme pointed out the impossibility of distinguishing between divine miracles—due to a suspension of ordinary laws of nature—and the settled order of nature if the claims of the alchemists and natural magicians were conceded.[15]

It is popularly assumed that one of the most important distinguishing characteristics of the 'New Science' of the seventeenth century was its reliance on experience and experiment in place of the logic-chopping and excessive theorising of the Aristotelians. Since Paracelsus and his followers insisted on sensory and ocular demonstration, can we regard them as having paved the way for the empiricism of the 'New Science'? Historians now commonly regard the fundamental modern change in scientific thought not so much as a substitution of experiment for theory as an alteration in basic conceptual frameworks which had the consequence of granting experiments a novel importance. The Paracelsians marshalled sensory evidence in support of a view of the operations of nature opposed to that of the Aristotelians. The *tria prima*, the *archeus*, sympathies and antipathies, the relation between microcosm and macrocosm, and the assumption that fire analysis reduced substances to their original constituents and distillation uncovered their 'essences'—all these formed part of that alternative account which could scarcely have arisen from the immediate testimony of the senses. According to Paracelsus, rational methods of comprehending nature had led only to error since the Fall. The evident falseness of the teachings of Aristotle, Galen and the Islamic physicians amply demonstrated that. Reliance on experience was the only way to truth. The importance of experience was reinforced by Paracelsus's insistence on the individuality, specificity and diversity of things, which doomed any attempt to subsume the richness of nature under a few well defined categories, principles or laws. But if valid knowledge of nature was like mystical experience, then it could not be communicated through language. If the abundance of nature defied any attempt intellectually to order it, then a system of natural philosophy to rival Aristotle and Galen could not be conceived.

That was the dilemma confronted by the followers of Paracelsus. Although by the seventeenth century a Paracelsian was usually distinguished from an Aristotelian by his use of three-element theory in place of the Peripatetic four elements, Paracelsus himself, characteristically, stated that the three elements differed from one thing to another, and thus seemed to nullify their value as a tool of analysis. The labours of the first generation of Paracelsians were devoted to the search for a consistent, coherent and intellectually respectable body of doctrine from the writings of Paracelsus, while remaining faithful to his vision of authentic knowledge of nature.[16]

The novelty of the Paracelsian commitment to practical usefulness can easily be overlooked and can only be fully appreciated by contrasting it with the classical and mediaeval conceptions of knowledge. Paracelsian doctrine claimed to be a body of knowledge superior to existing systems, but offered to satisfy certain important mundane needs more fully than ever before. It thereby implied a different sort of relationship between theoretical sciences and practical arts than that definitively formulated by Aristotle. He had conceived the sciences as studying the demonstrative knowledge of causes belonging to the realm of the necessary, while art applied that knowledge to the realm of the contingent. The Galenic physician, for example, applied a rational system of medicine, integrated with Aristotelian cosmology, to that contingent world where pure essences were involved in matter. But the Paracelsian conception challenged such a distinction between sciences and arts. Knowledge meant essentially the knowledge of the powers and virtues of things. It grasped the nature of things and, at the same time, indicated how they could minister to human needs. The Paracelsian conception also (as already noted) abolished the ancient gulf between nature and art. Man was not a contemplator of nature but an 'alchemist', meaning one who brought the things of nature to their full maturity. All these claims marked a significant departure from the dominant traditions of classical and mediaeval thought.

BACON AND NATURAL MAGIC

The Paracelsian philosophy was one among a variety of philosophies of nature which advanced their claims as a replacement for Aristotelianism during the sixteenth century, and shared a basic commitment to the Neoplatonic apparatus of concepts. The three men who most helped to propagate late Italian humanism in their native countries north of the Alps had imbibed the Neoplatonism of the

Florentine thinkers, Marsilio Ficino (1433–99) and Pico della Mirandola (1463 94), in which 'natural magic' had a prominent place. Particularly attractive for the northerners was the place the Florentines had found for the dignity of a man within a christianised Neoplatonism. Man became a mean between all created things in a chain of being which was held together by active forces and affinities (§ S–382: Ch. III–IV). Through Lefèvre d'Étaples (c. 1455–1537), Johannes Reuchlin (1455–1522) and John Colet (1466–1519) their ideas were carried to France, Germany and England.

Colet used the doctrine of the world-soul primarily to expound his ideas on Church reforms, and Lefèvre remained cautious about the magical ideas. Reuchlin was a more wholehearted enthusiast for Pico's Cabalistic ideas. Ficino's concept of a cosmic spirit as the basis for 'natural' or non-demonic magic was repeated by many authors, including Cornelius Agrippa of Nettesheim, to whose great magical handbook, De occulta philosophia (1510: § P–365), Marlowe's Faustus seems to turn when he bids divinity adieu. In England Dr John Dee (1527–1608), mathematical adviser to Queen Elizabeth I, dabbled in angel-magic and an alchemy with Cabalistic number-mystical overtones, even while he was pioneering the promotion of navigational, geographical and mathematical studies in the country.[17]

The resurgence of 'natural magic' and its widespread influence may appear paradoxical in the age of the Reformation. The Reformers were determined to purge religious belief and Church practice of all magical elements. According to Max Weber, the Reformation marked an important stage in the 'disenchantment of the world'.[18] How are we to explain the 're-enchantment' resulting from abandonment of the scholastic Aristotelianism for the doctrines of the Florentine Neoplatonists, Agrippa of Nettesheim or Paracelsus?

The dismantling of ecclesiastical magic, when the explanation and consolation it offered in the face of hunger, disease and misfortune were necessary to many in a technologically backward society, seems to have encouraged continuing resort to 'cunning' men in villages and astrologers in towns, and may have contributed to the growth of witchcraft accusations (§ S–147). Among intellectuals, Neoplatonism offered an attractive alternative to the 'arid subtleties' of Aristotle, and the late-antique framework of magic changed and adapted itself to many of the dominant currents of the period. In Pico's pious humanism, man's dignity resided in his power as a wonder-working magus.[19] Such power was no longer confined to the priest.

The Paracelsian approach reconciled 'natural magic' with powerful Reformation tendencies in its biblicism, its stress on hard work and labour in nature instead of 'lazy' scholastic hair-splitting, and its dedication of fruits to general social and Christian ends. It reflected the will-theology which had led to the Protestant assertion that priestly magic was incompatible with divine omnipotence. For Paracelsians the power of God was exemplified in the world as the infused virtues of things. Since they expressed God's unsearchable will, things and processes could be understood not by logical analysis, but only by illuminated experience and 'experiment'. Finally, Paracelsian doctrine incorporated the premise that the knowledge and power over creatures possessed by the prelapsarian Adam would be restored to man as the millennium approached. A proliferation of useful inventions and discoveries and the increasing perfection of the arts and sciences were confidently to be expected. All this was in sharp contrast to the individual and particular goals, ritualism and technological conservatism usually characteristic of magic.[20]

In *The History of the World* (1614), written while he was imprisoned in the Tower, Sir Walter Ralegh classified various kinds of magic. The first and highest was no other than 'the Art of worshipping God', while the third kind

> containeth the whole Philosophie of Nature; not the brablings of the *Aristotelians*, but that which bringeth to light the inmost vertues, and draweth them out of Natures hidden bosome to humane use . . . *Vertues hidden in the center of the center*, according to the *Chymists*. Of this sort were *Albertus*, *Arnoldus de villa nova*, *Raymond*, [*Roger*] *Bacon*, and many others . . . The *Magick* which these men profest, is thus defined: . . . *Magick is the connexion of naturall agents and patients, answerable each to other, wrought by a wise man, to the bringing forth of such effects as are wonderfull to those that know not their causes*.
>
> (§P–24: I, xi, 2)

Such views, widespread in the early seventeenth century, were perhaps developed and disseminated most widely in the Germanic lands. However, three Catholic thinkers in the late sixteenth century fashioned schemes for social and religious reform, which would heal the division within the Christian world, on a natural-magical basis. One of them was Giordano Bruno (1548–1600), burnt at the stake in Rome for heresies including the assertion of the infinity of worlds, magic as licit and good, the Holy Spirit as an *anima mundi* and Christ as *magus*. It was not his championing of the Copernican system which secured his condemnation, but rather the consequences he drew from it. Copernicus had halted too soon. There was no need to assume spheres to carry the planets around, since they had a principle of life and motion in themselves, as did all things. Nor was it necessary to limit the universe to a tenth sphere. An infinite God required an infinitely extended universe. 'Up' and 'down' and 'heavy' and 'light' could have no absolute significance in such a world. Bruno's realisation of the full implications of Copernicus gives him 'a very important place in the history of the human mind'.[21] The others were Francesco Patrizi (1529–97) and Tommaso Campanella (1568–1639), who sketched a 'City of the Sun' ruled by priest-magicians, and himself spent long years in prison after a disastrous Calabrian revolt.[22]

But in the closing decades of the sixteenth century and the early part of the seventeenth, a counter-attack began to be mounted on the varieties of natural-magical doctrines. Traditionalists like Erastus (in 1572) and the Medical Faculty at Paris defended Galen against the Paracelsians. In Germany, Libavius defended in 1606 the 'chemiatri' who added pharmaceutical chemistry to the traditional *materia medica* but he condemned the Paracelsians. Paracelsus's work was full of illegitimate and demonic magic. His macrocosm–microcosm analogy was false, for there could be no mixture of terrestrial and celestial, and there could be no celestial substance in man. The three principles were valuable, but they really came from Aristotle. Thirteen years later Daniel Sennert, while critically accepting the three principles, agreed there was dangerous magic in Paracelsus and accused him of mixing profane and holy things. Religion and natural philosophy must be kept distinct. In any event, the chemist must renounce overweening ambitions. He could only contribute some observations and experiments, and it was the task of physicians and philosophers to draw conclusions (§S–524: I, Ch. III).

In England, the young Francis Bacon (1561–1626), seeking the patronage of his relative, Lord Treasurer Burghley, wrote to him in 1591 that, having taken 'all knowledge to be my province', he hoped to purge it of 'two sorts of rovers'. One sort had spoiled it 'with frivolous disputations, confutations, and verbosities; the other with blind experiments and auricular traditions and impostures'. By the first he meant the Aristotelians, by the other the Paracelsians and natural magicians. Instead, it was his ambition to bring in 'industrious observations, grounded conclusions, and profitable inventions and discoveries'.[23]

Bacon was an influential propagandist of a new vision of science, but it is evident that in redefining the aims of science, in giving the study of nature a central place in human knowledge, and in the methods and explanations he urged, he owed a great deal to the 'natural magicians' whom he attacked. He took it for granted that nature should be studied 'with a view to work', and recognised that it was an aim shared by mechanic, mathematician, physician, alchemist and magician. Like the last two, he regarded the world as 'a rich storehouse for the glory of the Creator and the relief of man's estate'. Although astrology, natural magic and alchemy had greater 'confederacy' with imagination than reason, their 'ends or pretences are noble'.[24] In rejecting the contemplative ideal of knowledge he too appealed to Protestant themes. Only God and the angels were spectators of the theatre of the world; men were to earn their bread in the sweat of their brows ('by their fruits shall ye know them'). Assuming that fruits meant technologically useful discoveries, Bacon convicted the Greeks of failure: they had contributed hardly 'a single experiment which tends to relieve and benefit the condition of mankind and which can with truth be referred to the speculations and theories of philosophy' (*Novum organum*, I, 63). The highest ambition a man could have was 'to establish and extend the power and domain of the human race itself over the universe'. Who could deny the significance of technical inventions? Printing, gunpowder and the magnet had changed 'the whole face and state of things throughout the world: the first in literature, the second in warfare, the third in navigation', so that 'no empire, no sect, no star seems to have exerted greater power and influence in human affairs than these mechanical discoveries' (*ibid.*, I, 129).

He condemned the view that 'the dignity of the human mind is impaired by long and close intercourse with experiments and particulars', and compared the manual arts, which were continually growing and becoming perfect, with the sciences, which 'stand almost at stay'. It was a cardinal deficiency of natural history, both ancient and modern, that the experiences of the mechanical arts had not been included in it (*ibid.*, Preface and 'The Plan'). Even after the Fall, true and solid arts had enabled man to retain 'some dominion over rebellious nature', but that had been mostly forfeited because Greeks like Aristotle had sought the truth of nature in logic rather than in the patient study of the Book of Nature (*The History of the Winds* [1623], Preface). By making 'his natural philosophy a mere bond servant to his logic' Aristotle had rendered it 'contentious and well-night useless' (*Nov. org.*, I, 54). His philosophy persuaded men 'that nothing difficult, nothing by which nature may be commanded or subdued can be expected from art or human labour' (*ibid.*, I, 88).

Bacon shared, too, the belief that the greatest flourishing of arts and sciences had been reserved for the 'last ages of the world'. Not to be forgotten was the prophecy of Daniel, 'Many shall go to and fro, and knowledge shall be increased'. To Bacon that was a clear intimation that 'the thorough passages of the world (which now by so many distant voyages seems to be accomplished, or in the course of accomplishment), and the advancement of the sciences, are destined by fate, that is by Divine Providence, to meet in the same age' (*ibid.*, I, 124).

His adoption of the aims and standpoint of the 'natural magicians' and Paracelsians led Bacon radically to alter the 'intellectual globe'. 'Metaphysics' now became a supreme theoretical study of nature. Contemplative and operative knowledge was indissolubly united, since in Bacon's conception 'truth . . . and utility are here the very same things, and works themselves are of greater value as pledges of truth than as contributing to the comforts of life'. Humanistic studies were devalued. Rhetoric had turned into a hunt 'more after words than matter' (*The Advancement of Learning*, I, iv, 2). Most of the knotty questions of moral philosophy could be settled by the Holy Faith. Poetry did elevate the mind, but at the price of 'submitting the shows of things to the desires of the mind; whereas reason doth buckle and bow the mind unto the nature of things'. Theology was grounded 'only upon the word and oracle of God'. The scholastics had reduced divinity into an art, and sought in 'a summary brevity, a compacted strength, and a complete perfection; whereof the two first they fail to find, and the last they ought not to seek'. Natural philosophy emerged as the dominant study, and the principles derived by the inquisition of nature offered hope of application even to fields like ethics.

At the same time, Bacon violently attacked some fundamental tenets of the magicians and Paracelsians. He himself wished to 'revive and reintegrate the misapplied and abused name of natural magic . . . purged from vanity and superstition'. For that which passed by that name in books and containing 'certain credulous and superstitious conceits and observances of sympathies and antipathies, and hidden properties, and some frivolous experiments . . . is as far differing in truth of nature from such a knowledge as we require, as the story of King Arthur of Britain . . . differs from Caesar's Commentaries in truth of story'. By mixing religion and natural philosophy they had created 'an heretical religion, and an imaginary and fabulous philosophy'. Paracelsus and the alchemists had 'fantastically strained' the ancient opinion of man as a micro-cosm. They had 'pretended to find the truth of all natural philosophy in the Scriptures; scandalising and traducing all other philosophy as heathenish and profane'. But the 'scope and purpose of the spirit of God is not to express matters of nature in the Scriptures, otherwise than in passage'.

When they were judged by the test of fruits, there was some little of worth among the chemists 'but accidentally and in passing . . . not by any art or theory', their theory rather confusing than aiding them. It was difficult to know whether to laugh or weep at the works of alchemists and natural magicians. The former made useful discoveries as a by-product of a quest their methods could never attain; if the latter had ever done so, they were such as aimed 'rather at admiration and novelty than at utility and fruit'. Indeed, by having 'loaded mankind with promises' of longevity, retardation of age, repair of natural defects, improved intellectual faculties, transmutation, marvellous machines, capturing celestial substances, divining the future, and bringing distant things nearer, the credulous and fraudulent had discredited such enterprises and strengthened the credit and hold of ancient systems of thought.

How, then, did Bacon propose to reform a natural philosophy dominated by the ideas of 'the Grecians and the Alchemists'? He rejected the powerful currents of scepticism of his time, although he fully acknowledged that 'certain it is that the senses deceive' and that no confidence was to be placed 'in the natural and spontaneous process of the mind'. These were the impairments resulting from the Fall. However, the senses also supplied 'the means of discovering their own errors'. Moreover, Bacon had devised a method which did not leave the mind to take its own course but guided it at every step, so that 'the business be done as if by machinery'. Distrust of the human mind had led sceptics to assert that nothing could be known, thereby doing 'philosophy and the sciences great injury'. Abjuring 'carnal reason', the Paracelsians had resorted to the Scriptures and imported extra-rational modes of cognition, appropriate to divine mys-teries, into inquiries into nature. Sternly Protestant moral qualities were required of the practitioner of Bacon's method, but the work consisted of the methodical sifting of experience in a co-operative endeavour. 'For my way of discovering goes far to level men's wit and leaves but little to individual excellence, because it performs everything by the surest rules and demonstra-tions'.

Bacon's aim did not differ essentially from Aristotle in striving for the most general definitions in natural philosophy. For him, too, the universe was a collection of substances with properties and powers, with relations to each other that did not affect their real 'nature'. What he objected to was the total inadequacy of the means offered by Aristotle for grasping the true essences of things (§ S–855: pp. 76–119). His own method was modelled on the way in which he believed the human mind formed true conclusions. The senses transmitted impressions to the mind, which were stored as singular images in memory. Imagination depicted in the mind images from that store. By itself it was apt to yoke them together to form unnatural composites, or fashion systems 'according to the pleasure of the mind'. But reason, which dealt not with images but concepts, compared and combined past impressions according to the rules of nature.

In the study of nature, the counterpart to memory and sense-experience was the compilation of a great 'history natural and experimental', which would markedly differ from ordinary natural histories in the attention to the experiences of the mechanical arts. Neither the mean nor the common was to be excluded from this great arsenal of facts. Once an ample stock of raw material was ready, it would be examined for 'simple natures', for bodies could be regarded as a 'troop or collection' of these. They formed 'an alphabet of nature'. Gold, for example, was yellow in colour, comparatively heavy and ductile to a certain extent. Fire did not volatise it, but it could be liquefied. So a knowledge of 'the forms of yellow, weight, ductility, fixity, fluidity, solution, and so on, and the methods for superinducing them and their gradations and modes' could achieve the alchemist's goal.[25] These simple natures would be educed from the natural histories by drawing up 'tables of discovery'. Although induction—that is, generalisation from particular experiences—was employed, it was not induction by simple enumeration as used by Aristotle, but induction by elimination. Thus, if the form of heat was to be investigated, a Table of Presence recorded circumstances where heat was manifested, while a Table of Absence recorded similar instances where heat was lacking, and a Table of Comparison tabulated variations in its intensity.

Bacon called upon others to emulate him and to dwell 'purely and constantly among the facts of nature' (Preface to *The Great Instauration*). Those who did not wish to devise fabulous worlds but 'to examine and dissect the nature of this very world itself, must go to the facts themselves for everything'. To Bacon, the mind was like a mirror. When cleansed, it would reflect the true nature of things.

But Bacon's conception of the human mind, of 'facts', and of scientific method, was radically defective. The administrator's dream of constructing a machine to routinise the making of scientific discoveries proved a failure. No manipulation of observations could yield a theory to bind the facts. He emphasised the necessity of 'experiments', meaning natural or contrived experience, but did not systematically employ them to test whether a given theory was true or false.

GILBERT

Experiments were far more fruitfully conducted by Bacon's contemporary, William Gilbert (1540–1603), physician to Elizabeth I. Particularly remarkable about Gilbert's 'new style of philosophising' in *De magnete*[26] was his consistent and systematic use of experiments to explore a particular class of natural phenomena. He appealed to those 'who not only in books, but in things themselves look for knowledge', rejected 'any graces of rhetoric, any verbal ornateness', and wrote scathingly about recent authors who 'not being practical in the research of objects in nature, being acquainted only with books, being led astray by certain erroneous physical systems, and having made no magnetical experiments . . ., old-womanishly dreamt of things that were not' (pp. 1, 6). Honour was due to Aristotle, Ptolemy and Galen, 'but our age has discovered and brought to light very many things which they too, were they among the living, would cheerfully adopt' (p. li).

Gilbert's treatise proved to be an inspiring demonstration of the fertility of the experimental approach. He was the first clearly to distinguish electrical from magnetic phenomena. He classified the basic magnetic actions, and announced that the earth itself was a magnet and that the north-pointing property of the compass needle must be referred to it. He urged his readers, even if they disagreed with some of his 'paradoxes', to note the wealth of experiments he had bought at the cost of 'much pains, sleepless nights and great money expenses': 'these it is chiefly that cause all philosophy to flourish' (p. xiix).

That Bacon found no kindred spirit in Gilbert and failed to appreciate his achievement is not as perplexing as historians have sometimes made it out to be. Gilbert's solid accomplishment rested on a flagrant disregard of the method Bacon had urged for the advancement of the sciences. He did not renounce 'anticipations of nature' nor derive his conclusions by pressing out successive 'vintages' from observations. Bacon complained that just as the alchemists had 'made a philosophy out of a few experiments of the furnace', so 'Gilbertus our countryman hath made a philosophy out of the observations of a loadstone' (Adv. Learn.' I, v. 7). Gilbert's example illustrated the dangerous pitfalls lying in wait even for those took to experiments, if they yielded to the temptation to leap immediately to general principles through 'the premature hurry of the understanding' (Nov. org., I, 64). Bacon wanted a sharp separation between 'facts' and the conclusions legitimately educed from them, but theories, experiments and interpretations were intertwined in Gilbert's work. Experiments were used to eliminate rival theories and, guided by models and analogies based on a grand hypothesis, to develop and test his own. Bacon was to detect affinities between Gilbert and certain ancient pre-Socratic thinkers, and like them Gilbert certainly anchored his detailed explanations in a more general account of the basic stuff or elements of which things are made, and of the fundamental processes operating in nature.

All physical objects were ultimately composed of an earth element or its 'effusion', water (De magnete, pp. 83–84). The earth element was found in its purest state in the loadstone and in weaker form in iron. Amber jet and all shining gems were concretions of water. Other bodies were made of a mixture of the two. Gilbert's element theory made sense of the differences he first clearly showed between electrical and magnetic attraction. Electric attraction had to be roused by friction, could easily be choked by a breath of moist air or stopped by a sheet of fine linen or paper, and acted on all light objects indifferently. The loadstone required no rubbing, and attracted only 'magnetic bodies', whether it was itself wet or dry, placed in air or water, and through 'solidest bodies . . . or thick slabs of stone, or plates of metal' (pp. 85–86). Gilbert concluded from these experiments that something material was exuded from the rubbed electric. It was in the form of subtle effluvia which, like material rods, seized straw, chaff and twigs in the vicinity until their force was spent. Since electrics were concretions of water, they shared the power of moisture to cement things together. But the action of the loadstone, since it acted through solid screens, could not be due to something corporeal given off by the loadstone and implied the presence of a 'soul' in it. That soul or form was present in a deformed state in iron, but was instantly recalled by the presence of a loadstone and caused it to leap and unite with it. Here was no tyrannical or unilateral compulsion exercised by the loadstone, but an example of the harmony ruling the universe, a mutual coming together with must be described not as attraction but as 'coition' (pp. 97, 108–13). Since the earth's core was made of loadstone, it was itself a magnet. The north-pointing property of the compass needle, which others had explained by the attraction of the pole star or magnetic mountains at the north pole, could simply be explained by the tendency of the earth-substance to orient itself the way the earth did in space. Moreover, the analogy between the loadstone and the earth opened up the possibility of experimentally investigating the various forms of action of the compass needle by using a spherical loadstone and a specially mounted magnetised needle. Gilbert accordingly investigated exhaustively the orientation of the needle, its declination from the geographical north and its dip in various latitudes.

Guiding Gilbert's experimental investigations were his deep cosmological preoccupations. He accepted the Copernican idea at least of the diurnal rotation of the earth and believed his magnetical discoveries answered all objections to it. Since the earth was not the cold and dry element of Aristotle but displayed life and animation, it possessed a soul and was capable and worthy of self-motion. Since the magnetic power kept the parts of the earth firmly togher, the fear of Ptolemy and his modern followers that a rotating earth would fly to pieces was baseless. The magnetic power maintained the orientation of the earth's axis during its rotation. Since parts of the earth would cohere with it, the atmosphere, and all things shot into it, would 'advance simultaneously and uniformly with the earth' and would not be left behind, as opponents of Copernicus contended. Bacon, on the contrary, believed that the diurnal motion of the earth was 'most false' and invented by Copernicus merely for ease of calculation and 'for the sake of that pretty notion of explaining celestial motions by perfect circles'.[27] A true account would have to wait until 'the substance, motion, and influence of the heavenly bodies as they really are' became known, presumably by the application of his method. Gilbert had not offered that, 'in working out some one experiment'.[28]

Bacon was perceptive in remarking that Copernicus's great innovation was rooted in the backward-looking notion of explaining celestial motions as 'perfect circles', a 'pretty notion' itself open to doubt. It was in keeping with his disdain for mathematics, which seemed to him to have seduced men into vainly attempting to find perfect geometric patterns in nature. However, the first modern to break with the 'pretty notion' of perfect circles by ascribing elliptical orbits to the planets, Johannes Kepler (1571–1630), was sustained in his great astronomical labours by his early conviction that planetary orbits were related to the five perfect Platonic solids.[29] Kepler warmly praised Gilbert's *De magnete*, and went beyond Gilbert in accounting for the revolution of planets around the sun by magnetic forces seated in sun and planets.

Kepler's overriding concern with mathematical harmonies in nature involved a break with the Aristotelian explanation of nature by the purposes thought to constitute the essential nature of things. Bacon, too, believed final causes corrupted rather than advanced the sciences, and had bred 'a vastness and solitude' in the tract of physical causes.[30] Gilbert, for all his strictures on Aristotle, was far more closely bound to fundamental Aristotelian concepts and ways of explaining nature. Motion was a process in which potentiality was being actualised: iron moved to the loadstone because its disordered potential form was 'recalled' by the loadstone; the earth rotated because rotation was ordained for its own good through the change of seasons, and it was therefore unreasonable that the fictional sphere of stars should do that. Gilbert cited 'Hermes Zoroaster, Orpheus' when arguing that the whole universe was animated (*De magn.*, p. 309). He had gained much from natural-magical authors and laid continual emphasis on the harmony which was the ruling principle of the universe. But while he rejected the Aristotelian nest of heavenly spheres because it would turn the universe into a clockwork, he was equally contemptuous of explanations by sympathies and antipathies, which threatened 'the ruin of true philosophy' (pp. 175, 6, 11, 146). With the hard critical sense of the Aristotelian tradition Gilbert combined an experimental testing of theories which, within medicine, had been practised expertly by ancient masters like Galen.

HARVEY

It was another English physician, William Harvey (1568–1657), whose experimental investigations, guided by fundamentally Aristotelian concepts and methods, led to the greatest physiological discovery of the period, the circulation of the blood in the animal body. His approach, in which theory, observation and experiment were inseparable, would hardly have won Bacon's commendation. Harvey had acted as physician to Bacon and, according to John Aubrey, admired him for 'his witt and style but would not allow him to be a great philosopher. Said he to me: He writes philosophy like a Ld. Chancellor, speaking in derision.'[31]

Like many other medical students, Harvey had overcome the deficiencies of English medical education by qualifying as physician at the celebrated university of Padua, where a succession of outstanding anatomists and physiologists had stimulated a great revival of biological sciences. His Paduan years seem to have imprinted on Harvey the Aristotelian outlook which some of his teachers favoured over the generally prevalent Galenism. In his masterpiece, *De motu cordis et sanguinis*, published at Frankfurt in 1628, he proclaimed himself the first 'to oppose tradition and to assert that blood travelled along a previously unrecognised circular pathway of its own'.[32]

It was not a discovery made by or capable of demonstration by direct observation. What Harvey offered was a sequence of arguments, supported by experimental evidence and quantitative considerations. The received and mainly Galenic account of the lungs, left side of the heart, and arteries, made it a separate functional system. Quite separate was the venous system, conveying nutritive blood (made in the liver from ingested food) to all parts of the body. Thus only part of the blood went to the heart, and the blood was used up in nourishing the tissues. There were two centres for the formation and direction of blood, the liver and the heart, and two kinds of blood: the nutritive blood made by the liver, and the arterial blood to transmit vital spirits from inhaled air.

These ideas were modified in the course of the sixteenth century by discoveries and criticisms. Vesalius in the second edition of *De fabrica* (1555) asserted the imporosity of the fleshy wall dividing the two halves of the heart, and the passage of venous blood from the right to the left side solely through the lungs was accepted by the martyred Servetus (1511–53) as well as the Paduan physician Realdo Colombo (1516–59). Another Paduan teacher, Fabrici d' Aquapendente (1537–1619), discovered the valves in the veins, although he assumed their function was to prevent collection of blood in the inferior parts.

The Paduan discoveries were to play an important role in Harvey's novel conception. When, in his old age, he was asked by Robert Boyle what first led him to his idea of circulation, he replied that it was consideration of the purpose of the valves in the veins. They existed not merely to prevent the blood from falling down to the feet but to promote a one-way blood flow from the veins towards the heart on the left side of the body. It is characteristic that it was meditation on the Aristotelian 'final cause'—'that so provident a cause as Nature not so plac'd many valves without design' (§ P–385: p. 157)—that he should have recalled as his starting-point. But many other components of the Aristotelian outlook seem to have been of great significance for his discovery, notably the conception of the blood as a single fluid with immanent vital properties rather than as varying through properties derived from superadded 'spirits', and the image of the circle as the pattern of perfection in the heavens as on earth. By regarding the blood as a single fluid Harvey arrived at an argument of crucial importance for proving the circulation of the blood: if the blood passes in even minimal amount through the lungs and the heart, it is carried to the arteries and to the whole of the body in a far richer amount than can be supplied from the ingestion of foodstuffs or, in general, without making a circuitous return. In half an hour perhaps 500 ounces of blood passed through the heart into the arteries, if the heart made over a thousand beats in that time; that is, 'blood in greater amount than can be found in the whole of the body'. His other proofs were based on experiments using ligatures, and on evidence from the comparative anatomy and embryology which, following Aristotle's example, some of his

Paduan teachers had greatly promoted.

Harvey's Aristotelianism cannot be regarded as an anachronistic survival which fortunately did not impede his momentous discovery. It is truer to say that discovery sprang out of his acceptance of Aristotelian concepts and methods. It is easy enough to transform Harvey into a caricature of a 'modern scientist', supposedly relying entirely on observation and experience, by plucking suitable quotations from his literary remains. Dedicating his *De motu cordis* to the London physicians, he praised the true philosophers who 'suffer not themselves to become enslaved and lose their freedom in bondage to the traditions and precepts of any, except their own eyes convince them'. Answering those who thought it impious to overturn opinions accepted for many centuries, he wrote: 'To all these let my reply be that the facts of Nature wait upon no antiquity: for there is nothing older or of greater authority than nature.' 'I give merely the facts and add no physiological speculation or extra causes,' he wrote to his critic Caspar Hofmann. But for Harvey these professions were by no means incompatible with a basic adherence to Aristotelian guiding principles. Nor did that adherence rule out criticism or rejection of many specific Aristotelian doctrines.

Attempts to preserve the 'modernity' of Harvey by dismissing his Aristotelianism as an anachronistic survival break against his *De generatione animalium* (1651), just as storm-driven waves in the Sicilian sea—to use the metaphor he once chose—'break in pieces and are repelled in a mass of foam' by the rocks inside Charybdis.[33] The work, which Harvey perhaps regarded as his crowning achievement, was unabashedly Aristotelian, indeed 'more Aristotelian than Aristotle himself'[34] in some of its most important opinions. It equally expressed fundamental opposition to the mechanistic and atomistic currents of thought which we now identify with the emergence of modern science in the seventeenth century. Harvey believed, like Aristotle, that the workings of nature were revealed most clearly in the mysteries of animal generation: 'All things are full of deity: so also in the little edifice of a chicken, and all its actions and operations, the Finger of God, or the God of Nature doth reveal himself.'[35] It was wrong to judge nature by arts or artificers, as was done when mechanistic analogies were employed. Rather, the untaught natural action by which the spider wove his web, birds hatched eggs and built their nests, and the foetus took shape within the maternal womb, revealed the pattern by which the operations of the arts were to be judged.[36]

The characteristic originality and independence of Harvey is as evident in *De generatione* as it was in *De motu cordis*. He criticised and revised or rejected the received views of his own time, supported by a great mass of observations, experiments and arguments, guided by an Aristotelian approach. Aristotle believed that in generation the female contributed the matter and the male the initiating and formative power. Generation was clearly to be distinguished from any mere putting together of parts. The parts existed only potentially 'preformed' in the female material, and developed successively. The first part to be actualised was the heart. That was necessary since the formation of other parts required the blood which the foetal heart obtained from the mother through the umbilical vessels. His masterly study of the chick embryo was believed by Aristotle to have confirmed that, as the first noticeable movement was the pulsation of the heart.

Following Galen's teachings on generation, the prevalent view in Harvey's own day differed significantly from Aristotle's opinion. Galen believed the female material was differentiated by the 'alterative faculties' in the male semen, which separated the hard from the soft particles. Veins, arteries and nerves already existed in the semen, which was not a simple and homogeneous fluid, as Aristotle had believed. In the influential textbook version of Jean Fernel (1485–1558), the 'formative spirit' in the semen was said to make the parts 'step out into visibility'.[37] That the parts pre-existed in the material, and were separated and arranged by the activity of a 'soul' within the semen, was asserted much more unequivocally by those reviving atomistic ideas in Harvey's time, such as Daniel Sennert (1572–1637) and Pierre Gassendi (1592–1655).[38] Faithful to Aristotle's monistic viewpoint, Harvey opposed the proliferation of 'spirits' in Fernel and other Renaissance medical authors because they distinguished between a material substratum and superadded powers. Those spirits were 'a common subterfuge of ignorance': 'For smatterers, not knowing what causes to assign to a happening, promptly say that the spirits are responsible and introduce them as general *factota*. And, like bad poets, they call this *deus ex machina* on to their stage to explain their plot and catastrophe.'[39] Instead, Harvey insisted that vital substances like semen and blood were to be thought of as having inseparable material and vital features. At the same time, he declared his total opposition to the views on generation of the revivers of atomism because they confounded generation with a mere mixture or putting together of existing parts.

Harvey came to the conclusion that Aristotle himself had compromised his monism and opened the way to the 'spirits' by admitting that something 'analogous to the element of the stars' was present in semen. Instead of conceding that semen and blood were endowed with a physical substance of finest corporeality hailing from the stars, he insisted on the integrity of their material and vital aspects. Repeating Aristotle's classic studies of the chick embryo, what impressed Harvey was the fact that the first to appear in it could be described as the heart only if by heart was meant 'the blood to wit, with its containing parts—the pulsating vesicles and veins, as one and the same organ'.[40] The blood was in motion and reacted if pricked, and hence must possess sensation even before the formation of the brain. Why not then recognise the blood as intrinsically possessing a power transcending that of the elements? It did not borrow its innate heat from the heart, but rather was superior in importance and dignity to that organ. Besides breaking with Aristotle in giving primacy to the blood over the heart, Harvey differed from him in believing that semen did not enter the female matter, which was fertilised by the male geniture through a 'magnetic' impulse acting at a distance, just as was the case in contagion, magnetic attraction, and indeed all sympathy and antipathy in nature.[41]

When Harvey referred to a 'soul' acting in the blood, he did not mean the immortal soul, any more than did Gilbert when asserting the presence of a 'soul' in the magnetic earth-substance. It was the Aristotelian nutritive and sensitive soul, an immanent vital principle directing the substance with which it was indissolubly united. Gilbert had rejected the adamantine planetary and starry spheres of the ancients because they would turn the universe into a 'clockwork', and Harvey believed that those 'who make all things out of atoms, as Democritus, or out of the elements, as Empedocles', were equally deceived: 'As if generation were nothing in the world, but a mere separation, or collection, or order of things'.[42] Harvey and Gilbert were alike far from accepting atomistic or mechanical explanations or rejecting a vitalistic view which refused to reduce all phenomena to matter and motion. It has often been said that Harvey thought of the body as a mechanical system, since he compared the heart to a pump and the circulation of the blood to a hydraulic system. In fact, he never used the pump analogy in *De motu cordis*, and it appears only once in the 'Second Essay to Riolan', in order to make the point that the blood spurting from a cut artery was like that from a bellows pump. He certainly did not think of the heart as a machine but rather as a muscle with a vital pulsific power, while the blood as a vital fluid gained increasing importance in his thought until it assumed superiority to the heart. Like Gilbert, Harvey found the ideas of the chemists and natural magicians uncongenial. He upheld Aristotelian monism against those who introduced 'highly subtle, extremely penetrative, and mobile' spirits, or assumed that 'these sublime, bright, ethereal, celestial and divine spirits are the bonds of the soul'.[43]

It is unnecessary and misleading to contrast the 'mechanistic' Harvey of *De motu cordis* with the Aristotelian Harvey of *De generatione*. The Aristotelian approach in the latter treatise paved the way for what we recognise as the brilliant success of the former. Fidelity to that approach, together with the limited optical means at Harvey's disposal and his choice of an unsuitable species for his investigations (the deer in royal parks), led to other results that now appear obscure and 'unprogressive'.[44] Nevertheless, the rival atomistic and mechanistic accounts of generation were no more successful. Writing much later in the century, John Ray noted that 'mechanical Philosophers . . . very cautiously and prudently broke off their Systems of Natural Philosophy here'; and, he added, 'those Accounts which some of them have attempted to give of the Formation of a few of the Parts, are so excessively absurd and ridiculous, that they need no other Confutation, than *ha, ha, he*'.[45]

MATHEMATICS: KEPLER AND FLUDD

Mechanistic explanations of animal generation aroused Ray's contemptuous laughter. Yet already by the mid-seventeenth century the mathematical-mechanistic mode of conceiving and explaining nature had scored great successes in natural philosophy. It provided the basis for a fundamental revision of ancient physics which for the first time furnished a mechanics compatible with a rotating and revolving earth. Instead of serving as a warning example (as it was to Francis Bacon) of the absurdities committed by astronomers in order to 'save appearances', the Copernican system could now be regarded as an essential feature of the new world-picture.

Through a shift in aesthetic sensibility, geometric harmonies had gained increasing significance since the fifteenth century. In the churches they designed and built, Italian architects gave expression to a new ideal, based on the circle and its derivatives, and inspired by the Pythagoreans and Plato's *Timaeus*. Pacioli even doubted the efficacy of divine offices performed in a church not built 'with correct proportions' (§ S–826: p. 27). Music had enjoyed the dignity of a *quadrivium* subject since antiquity because it was regarded as having a mathematical basis. In propagating the ideal of an architecture whose mathematical ratios expressed the same harmonies that pervaded music, Italian architects were doubtless also striving to raise the social status of their *métier* from a 'manual' to a 'liberal' art. Painting was, analogously, described by Leonardo da Vinci as sister to music, because each conveyed harmonies, and the same numerical ratios governed musical intervals and the linear perspective whose discovery was an important Renaissance achievement (§ S–826: p. 117).

Copernicus, as has already been noted, couched the advantages of his own system in terms which appealed to the aesthetic ideal made a commonplace in his own time by Renaissance artists and architects. To make the physical truth of a cosmology inhere in its mathematical harmony was to fly in the face of the Aristotelian tradition. Aristotle had viewed mathematics as abstracting from natural bodies a limited and dependent aspect. To use his favourite example, it studied not so much the 'snub' nose of Socrates as a 'concave' geometrical shape. Various Renaissance Aristotelians reaffirmed Aristotle's strictures on the Pythagoreans. Fracastoro warned that although crises in fevers came on the fourth, seventh or other specified days, it would be quite wrong to ascribe potencies to those numbers, since numbers could never be principles of action.[46] A deep consciousness of the gulf between the divine mind and the impaired human intellect prompted Bacon to regard the search for ideal mathematical forms and harmonies in nature as one of the most dangerous snares for explorers of nature.

Bacon's distaste for mathematics may have owed something to the magic with which they became associated in the revival of Neoplatonic and Pythagorean doctrines throughout the sixteenth century. That tendency was strengthened by Pico della Mirandola's 'Christianisation' of the Jewish Cabala, which claimed to be part of a secret tradition going back to biblical times.[47] Every letter in Hebrew has a numerical value, and the esoteric meaning underlying every word in Scripture was thought to be derived by substituting another word of the same numerical value. Pico wished through his fantastic permutations to demonstrate that underlying the separate revelations to Orpheus, Pythagoras, Zoroaster, Moses, Plato and Christ was the same *philosophia perennis*. Reuchlin (1455–1522), a leading figure of the northern Renaissance, embraced these ideas and believed Pythagoras had derived his wisdom from Moses. No simple and clear line can be drawn between those addicted to number mysticism and those advancing 'genuine' mathematics for much of that century. It has been contended that one of the great achievements of the period was a transformation of the Greek concept of number, which always meant a definite number of definite things, to a symbolic conception of number, which led to the emergence of a true algebra in the work of Vieta in the late sixteenth century.[48] The precise role of those various currents in the development of the new conception still awaits historical assessment.

The difficulties of making sharp distinctions in that period between 'mystical' and 'genuine' mathematics are well illustrated by a controversy involving two celebrated *savants* between 1619 and 1622. One of them was Johannes Kepler (1571–1630), recognised today as one of the founders of modern astronomy. The other was Robert Fludd (1574–1637), an English physician and occultist who had championed the mysterious 'Rosicrucian brotherhood'.

Kepler, ravished by the mathematical harmony which he believed Copernicus had restored to the universe, was an early convert to his system of the world. He dedicated his lifelong astronomical work to the search for the rational mathematical order in God's handiwork, especially as manifested in the number of planets and in the size and motion of their orbits. Why had God created solid matter at the beginning? Because he had intended to create quantity, which made manifest the contrast between the curve and the straight line, since (as Nicholas of Cusa had boldly asserted) the curve could be assigned to God and the straight line to that which he created. But a more important reason was the manifestation of the Divine Trinity in the spherical universe. The sphere was a fitting image of the Triune God, with the Father at the centre, the Son on the surface, and the Holy Ghost midway between the central point and the circumference. The contrast between curve and straight line was seen in the sphere, in the connection between the curvature of the surface and the rectitude of the diameter. In the universe, the sun symbolised the Father, the world-sphere the Son, and space filled with celestial aura the Holy Ghost.

Why had God chosen to make a particular number of planets and arrange them in a certain order? Plato in his *Timaeus* had already made his artisan-creator choose to fashion the elements out of four 'perfect solids', while the fifth itself supplied the geometric form for the whole universe. A rational creator would have chosen those solids because an elegant geometric proof had shown in Plato's time that only five of them could possibly be constructed, using triangles and pentagons to form their faces. Kepler, too, believed in their special significance in creation, but conceived it in a different fashion in order to buttress the Copernican cosmology. The five regular solids were related to spheres, since they could be inscribed in spheres, while spheres could be inscribed in them. If the five solids and the corresponding spheres were inserted in one another, then there would be precisely six spheres. 'There,' he wrote, 'you have the reason for the number of the planets.'[49]

Kepler tested out his speculations, relating the radii of the spheres as calculated according to his arrangement with the distances as supplied by Copernicus. The agreement was only approximate and, indeed, very approximate for the innermost and outermost planets. But he thought it too significant to be due merely to chance. Various reasons could be given for the discrepancies, most important of all the defects in astronomical data, which he hoped would be repaired by the labours of the Danish astronomer Tycho Brahe (1546–1601), who was developing naked-eye observational astronomy to a degree of precision never before achieved.

Although Kepler rejected numerological speculations such as those of Rheticus, who had praised Copernicus's reduction of the numbers of planets from seven to six because six was the 'most perfect' of numbers, his opposition was based on theological considerations. Before creation there was only the number of the three Persons of the Trinity. The number six attained its special status only *after* creation, because God had chosen to make six planets. When accounting for the structure of the universe, 'one's demonstration should not be based on numbers which have acquired a particular significance only in relation to things engendered since the creation of the world'.[50] Rather, it should refer to the relation between solid figures, such as the perfection of the five 'Platonic' solids. A system which placed six moving spheres around the sun had imparted the true astronomy because of the way solids and spheres could then be arranged. Kepler was therefore hardly sympathetic to Tycho's counsel, in their first exchange of letters, that he should try to find numerical relations in the universe since God had ordered it in such a way 'that it may be represented just as well by numbers as by forms, as was foreseen formerly to some extent by the Pythagoreans and Platonists'.[51]

Kepler searched not only for 'archetypal' laws but also for the dynamic ones which governed the motions of the planets. He speculated on the 'motive soul' seated in the sun, which, as the image of the Father, moved the planets around it with a force whose attenuation could be shown to be governed by a certain mathematical relationship. His fundamental intellectual orientation never changed, even though the details of his cosmology changed in important ways later on. He was to reject planetary spheres, and in his quest for the most precise fit between theory and observation was led for the first time to substitute elliptical planetary orbits for circular ones. In his *Harmonice mundi* (1619), he supplemented the purely geometrical or spatial relations God had expressed in the universe by harmonic relations which he now thought God had also embedded in the motions of the planets and of which the Pythagoreans had an inkling in their notion of the 'music of the spheres'. A universe in motion could not be explained solely by the static model based on the 'Platonic' solids. God could have made planets revolve eternally on concentric circles, without ever changing their speeds or distances from the sun. But each planet would then eternally produce the same 'note', and at best a monotonous concord. God must therefore have given each planet its individual note from which a polyphonic and contrapuntal harmony would result, even if it was necessary to depart from strict geometrical ratios to achieve it. The regular solids merely prescribed the 'rough external quantity' of the mass of the universe: the harmonies provided the eccentricities which gave 'so to speak, nose, eyes, and other members to the statue'.[52] Kepler's idea of an animate force seated in the sun and planets also underwent significant changes and became a 'corporeal' force. Borrowing from Gilbert, he imagined the sun and the planets as magnets, elliptical orbits resulting from the varying attraction and repulsion between planets and sun as their like or unlike poles acted on each other. But the sun, earth and planets continued, in his thought, to be endowed with at least motive 'souls'.

While inspired by a fundamentally Platonic and Pythagorean approach, Kepler made important changes in the tradition with which it was associated. He regarded astronomy as the science of the 'real' world. There was no unbridgeable gulf between astronomical theories and the findings of the most precise astronomical observation. The metaphysical reasons which had guided God's arrangement of his creation had precisely been realised in a universe whose material, unlike Plato's 'receptacle', could not exercise any resistance to them. Kepler rejected the Platonic dichotomy between the celestial and the terrestrial. Like the earth itself, celestial bodies were animated as well as *material*, and therefore required a motive force to overcome their resistance to motion. The matter of the world was cold, dead and heavy. In keeping with Neoplatonic tenets, Kepler attributed heat, motion and life to a higher principle, a soul or *spiritus*, which pervaded body. Besides the universal aetherial spirit, the earth was endowed with its own spirit which generated metals, released hidden vapours as streams, founts or vapours, and stored its heat. As heat resulted from the action of the *spiritus*, fire could not count as an element, and the fiery sphere surrounding the earth became superfluous. The Aristotelian four elements were reduced to the Trinity Kepler saw reflected in the constitution of the universe. In his study of optics, Kepler considered light an intimate constituent of all physical phenomena: like magnetism, it was a power without which material bodies, confined within the limit of their surfaces, were unable to express their influence in space. While the power was not material, like corporeal bodies, it consisted of a certain kind of matter with geometric dimensions. The theological model of the relation between the Trinity and the relations in a sphere was also invoked here to support the idea that the sphere was the most apt figure for studying the propagation of power.[53]

At first sight, Fludd's ideas may appear very similar to those of Kepler.[54] Fludd believed that the study of numbers and ratios had given the Pythagoreans the greatest secrets of the universe. Their music was about the harmonic consensus and proportions manifest in the whole world. The image of the triune God was revealed in creation by the equilateral triangle as God's symbol, and its mirror image, an inverted triangle, for creation. There was a 'trinity' of elements, derivable from the Genesis account: darkness, light and the primaeval waters. The waters separated out into the heavenly or fiery portion and the earthly portion, which became the spheres of air, water and earth. The proportion of light to dark in each thing, from angels down to stones, determined their worth and dignity. The two principles were involved in continual struggle. The material pyramid grew upward from the earth like a tree, matter becoming finer towards the top. The formal pyramid of light grew downward, with the apex on the earth. These opposing principles just counterbalanced in the sphere of the sun, where by a 'chymic wedding' the *infans solaris* or freed world-soul was generated. Being the seat of the *spiritus*, the sun was placed in a central position among the planets, just as the earth was at the centre of the universe. From the proportions and ratios of the parts of the two pyramids arose a cosmic music, whose understanding was inaccessible without a knowledge of alchemical and Rosicrucian mysteries.

In an appendix to *Harmonice mundi* Kepler strongly objected to Fludd's mode of reasoning. Fludd had claimed that the mathematics of his own time, dominated in geometry by Euclid, contributed nothing to the understanding of Pythagorean mysteries. Kepler objected that the accurate certainty of mathematical demonstration, as exemplified in Euclid's proofs, was indispensable if supposedly mathematical explanations were not to degenerate into wild speculations. Fludd, in his reply, left 'vulgar mathematicians to concern themselves with quantitative shadows', while alchemists and Hermetic philosophers comprehended 'the core of the natural bodies'. Kepler retorted that 'you deny that your purpose is subject to mathematical demonstration, without which I am like a blind man'.[55] He pointed out that the dimensions of Fludd's planetary spheres did not agree with their true dimensions. Fludd was undismayed, claiming that among philosophers there was no agreement on them and, finally, they were of little importance for his purposes. When Kepler responded that quantitative precision was essential where music was concerned, Fludd consigned everything quantitative to the dark principle in the universe. Where Kepler had postulated a sort of instinct which enabled the human soul to respond to mathematical harmony, Fludd ascribed such sensitivity to the soul's unfortunate entanglement in the physical world. Kepler sharply contrasted his procedures, which brought 'facts of Nature into the light', to Fludd's delight in 'mysterious puzzle-pictures of reality'.[56] He claimed that he himself dealt only with movements visible and demonstrable to the senses, contented with the effects manifested in the motion of the planets.

The situation was not really as simple as Kepler made it out to be. As should be evident by now, his procedure was not the 'Baconian' one of starting with observations and arriving at very general conclusions. Speculation, mathematical reasoning and observation went in hand in hand in his investigations. Unlike Fludd, he insisted that speculations had to be confirmed by observation, for example, in the case of his hypothesis of the five Platonic solids by 'determination of the distances of astronomical orbits, and proceeding to geometrical demonstrations',[57] even though he often tended to attribute the mismatch to inaccuracies in the available data or introduced saving hypotheses. The results of his great labours issued in many other numerical harmonies besides those recognised today as his 'three laws', and to him were just as important.[58]

GALILEO

While Kepler may appear to have had some difficulty in distinguishing his own Neoplatonist and Pythagorean attitude to mathematical harmonies in the universe from that of Fludd, a clear break with number mysticism was announced in the work of Galileo Galilei (1564–1642). 'Philosophy,' Galileo proclaimed, 'is written in this grand book, the universe, which stands continually open to our gaze. But the book cannot be understood unless one first learns to comprehend the language and read the letters in which it is composed. It is written in the language of mathematics, and its characters are triangles, circles, and other geometric figures without which it is humanly impossible to understand a single word of it; without these one wanders about in a dark labyrinth.'[59] But although Galileo insisted that the world could only be understood in mathematical terms, he refused to endow mathematical forms with ontological dignity:

> For my part, never having read the pedigrees and patents of nobility of shapes, I do not know which are more and which are less noble, nor do I know their rank in perfection. I believe that in a way all shapes are ancient and noble; or, to put it better, that none of them are noble and perfect, or ignoble and imperfect, except in so far as for building a wall a square shape is more perfect than a circular, and for wagon wheels, the circle is more perfect than the triangle.[60]

It may seem ironical, then, that Kepler's elliptical orbits had no appeal for Galileo, because he believed that 'for the maintenance of perfect order among the parts of the universe, it is necessary to say that movable bodies are movable only circularly',[61] and not because any perfection resided in circular motion as such.

Galileo's early notebooks at Pisa show him steeped in scholastic Aristotelian natural philosophy. But his study of Euclid and then of Archimedes led him radically to revise his opinions. In 1589 he became Professor of Mathematics at Pisa. In a dialogue written about two years later, Aristotle's arguments on local motion were criticised as childish and fantastic. One particular issue, with crucial bearing on the credibility of the Aristotelian approach to the study of nature, was that of the lightness and heaviness of bodies. Nowhere was Aristotle's view of qualities as irreducible and truly existing characteristics of things better illustrated. Plato had said that a body was heavy or light, depending on a greater or lesser number of identical parts. Aristotle objected that in that case a large enough quantity of fire would be heavier than a small quantity of air, and would fall; or a large quantity of air would take its place below a small quantity of water. Lightness and heaviness were absolute qualities of the elements, and made them strive to return to their 'natural places'. Locomotion, after all, was only one aspect of 'motion' as he had conceived it. Motion meant the actualisation of potentiality and thus a process manifested as much in a stone attempting to return to the centre of the universe as in an acorn becoming an oak or an unlettered man becoming literate. By making locomotion a process, and by insisting that such a change could not itself be thought of as changing, Aristotle deflected attention from its quantitative aspects. But in the fourteenth and fifteenth centuries a veritable mania for quantifying qualities—such as hot, cold, dryness, wetness, colour and brightness—manifested itself among some thinkers. It was in time recognised that such analysis of the 'intention' and 'remission' of forms could also be applied to velocity, and so the idea of changes in velocity was given a precise meaning, leading on to attempts to analyse non-uniform motions. Although the achievements of these thinkers have only recently been recognised, it must be stressed that the analysis was carried out within the framework of the Aristotelian conception of 'motion' and, in a theological milieu, involved consideration of such qualities as the theological virtues. It is only by leaving out such problems that the mediaeval *scientia de motu* can be made to seem like the science of mechanics to which Galileo was to contribute.[62] Galileo was well acquainted with the new language of concepts they had developed, but the Archimedean influence provided him with a novel approach and model.

As Archimedes's work became better known through printed editions beginning in 1543, various Italian thinkers recognised in it a model of a truly mathematical science of nature. Peripatetics regarded it as furnishing a purely mathematical account of certain mathematical problems. It dealt with abstracted 'forms', while natural philosophy was concerned with bodies made up of form *and* matter. The levers with which Archimedes dealt were weightless and possessed no dimensions except length, and in their movements encountered neither friction nor air resistance. The weights attached to them were plane geometric figures, possessing only the quality of weight. It provided an impressive demonstration of the degree of abstraction required if physical problems were to be clearly expressed in mathematical terms. But it was necessary to determine and justify the conditions under which it was legitimate to ignore certain factors in concrete situations if the ideal of a mathematical science of nature was to be established.

Galileo drew upon the work of 'the most divine Archimedes' in a dialogue, *De motu*, written about 1590, to furnish a truer account of free fall and projectile motion in place of those of Aristotle, whom he accused of having written 'the opposite of truth' in everything to do with local motion.[63] By careful reasoning Galileo showed inconsistencies in Aristotle's own arguments, or demonstrated how they conflicted with facts from ordinary experience, or with simple 'thought-experiments'. A thought-experiment, for example, showed contradictions in Aristotle's 'commonsensical' assumption that, of two bodies made of the same material, the heavier would descend faster. Heavy and light were relative qualities, reflected in the specific weight of substances in a given medium. All substances were heavy, in the sense that there was 'a single matter in all bodies, which is heavy in all of them'. Natural motion was, therefore, downward, towards the centre, and all upward motion was violent. The old cosmology, with the earth at the centre, could be explained by the distinct specific weight of bodies which arranged themselves around it, instead of appealing to a doctrine of natural places. In building an alternative account, Galileo adapted concepts from Archimedean statics and hydrostatics, and extended the approach in *Le mechaniche*, about five years later.

The promise and the challenge of mathematisation in natural philosophy became clearer to Galileo through his work on these treatises. He attempted to substitute quantitative for qualitative concepts, and to model physics on the deductive order of Euclidean geometry. In order to do so, naive sense-experience must be rejected. Indeed, Aristotle's mistakes were usually rooted in reliance on ordinary experience, although 'we seek the causes of effects, and these are not revealed by experience'.[64] Aspects amenable to mathematical treatment must be selected from the complexity of a concrete situation. But that did not involve falsification, as Peripatetics alleged. It was a 'geometric license' which the protecting wings of 'superhuman Archimedes' had encouraged him to undertake.[65] Galileo has popularly been regarded as having destroyed Aristotelian physics by dropping objects from the Leaning Tower of Pisa and as establishing new laws of motion by rolling balls down an inclined plane. He himself looked on experiments principally as aids to the clear conceptualisation which was the most creative and difficult part of scientific study. They gained a new importance because, instead of the changes in forms and qualities with which Peripatetics were primarily concerned and which were supposed to disclose themselves directly in observation, the mathematical aspects on which Galileo wished to focus attention demanded carefully contrived experimental situations.

By 1597 Galileo acknowledged his conversion to the truth of Copernicanism. When in 1609 he heard of the Fleming invention of the telescope, he constructed one himself. Pointing it at the heavens, he made a series of sensational discoveries which were brilliantly deployed as arguments for the Copernican system in his *Starry Messenger* (1610). The telescope revealed the moon as 'not robed in a smooth and polished surface but . . . rough and uneven, covered everywhere, just like the earth's surface, with huge prominences, deep valleys, and chasms'.[66] It was even possible to estimate the height of mountains on the moon by a simple method. The Aristotelian contrast between the celestial and the terrestrial could not hold. Galileo's later discovery of sunspots, which he regarded as being clouds or smoke, showed even generation and corruption in the supposedly immutable heavens. Traditionally, the dark earth was contrasted with the luminous and resplendent celestial bodies. Galileo ingeniously explained certain observed changes in the 'secondary light' of the moon as due to sunlight scattered into space by the earth. Moreover, Venus showed phases just like the moon, and borrowed its light from the sun, like all other planets. Since Venus could not show phases if it circled the earth together with the sun, it was a decisive argument against Ptolemy's system. The Milky Way was shown by the telescope to consist of a vast array of stars, unknown to the ancients. Galileo observed around Jupiter no fewer than four circling moons. In all known cosmologies Jupiter had always been placed in motion around a central body. If such motion did not deprive it of its moons, then the earth could surely continue to retain its own single moon even if it went around the sun.

Galilèo's discoveries were hailed by Italian astronomers, and he was feted by those of the Collegium Romanum. But while his discoveries seemed incompatible with Ptolemy's theories, they were equally compatible with the compromise system of Tycho, in which the planets circled the sun, which itself circled the central earth. In order to establish the truth of the Copernican system, Galileo occupied himself with stating the objections to a moving earth in the language of mechanics and systematically refuting them. His enthusiasm inspired him to seek the acceptance of the Copernican cosmology by the Roman Catholic Church. Cardinal Bellarmine of the Collegium Romanum, replying to Foscarini, a Carmelite Provincial who supported Galileo's efforts, wrote in April 1615 that acceptance of Copernicus's innovation as a useful calculating device was perfectly acceptable. But to affirm it as a truth was 'not only to arouse all Scholastic philosophers and theologians but also to injure our holy faith by contradicting the Scriptures'. If 'real proof' of the Copernican scheme was indeed forthcoming, then the Church would have to move with great circumspection in explaining Scriptural teaching to the contrary. 'But, as for myself, I shall not believe that there are such proofs until they are shown to me.'[67]

Persisting in his efforts, Galileo undertook a 'Copernican pilgrimage' to Rome in 1615. He was by then 'Chief Mathematician and Philosopher' to the Grand Duke of Tuscany, and the alarmed Florentine ambassador reported to his master about Galileo being 'all afire in his opinions', vehement and 'all fixed and impassioned in this affair', not realising the dangers he ran with a Pope who could not stand 'novelties and subtleties'. 'This is a business,' added the ambassador, 'which is not a joke but may become of great consequence, and this man is here under our protection and responsibility.'[68] The Inquisition in fact obtained in February 1616 papal consent to a censure of Galileo for holding the opinion of the motion of the earth. He was asked to abandon it, and 'to abstain altogether from teaching or defending this opinion and doctrine and even from discussing it' on pain of imprisonment.[69] The following month Foscarini's published letter, defending the view, was prohibited, and Copernicus's *De revolutionibus* was suspended until it has been 'corrected'.

The election eight years later of Maffeo Barberini as Pope Urban VIII revived Galileo's hopes of gaining the Church's acceptance of Copernicus. Barberini had written adulatory verses in honour of Galileo. After his accession, he had Galileo's *Il Saggiatore* (1623) read to him at meal times. He told a German cardinal that the Church had never condemned Copernican doctrine as heretical, only as rash. Galileo himself visited Rome in 1624 and was granted six audiences with Urban VIII in the course of six weeks. But the only concession he was able to win from him was his approbation of Galileo's project of writing a dialogue dispassionately examining the Ptolemaic and Copernican systems. According to the Pope, there was no way of deciding between them, because God could bring about effects in many, perhaps an infinite number of ways as long as they did not involve a logical contradiction. Galileo, by contrast, imagined he had now a physical proof of the motion of the earth in a new theory of the occurrence of tides, and even wished to describe his completed work as 'On the Flux and Reflux of the Sea'. But on a further visit to Rome in 1630 he accepted Urban's advice that it should be called 'On the Two Chief World Systems'.

The preface to Galileo's great *Dialogue*, published in 1632, asserted that from it foreigners would learn that in Italy 'it is not from failing to take count of what others have thought that we have yielded to asserting that the earth is motionless, and holding the contrary to be a mere mathematical caprice, but . . . for those reasons that are supplied by piety, religion, the knowledge of Divine Omnipotence, and a consciousness of the limitations of the human mind'.[70] However, Galileo found it difficult to maintain the fiction of posing as an agnostic which papal insistence had imposed upon him. Since he believed, quite mistakenly, that he had found a physical proof of the motion of the earth in a new theory of the tides, he could meet the demand that Bellarmine had made. Urban, however, had forbidden him to advance it as a clinching argument. In the *Dialogue*, Galileo devoted the whole of the last Day to his theory of tides, and placed the Pope's reservations in the mouth of Simplicio, the dogmatic and continually outwitted Peripatetic.

The Pope's fury was unbounded. 'I have used him better than he used me,' he told the Florentine ambassador, who had come to plead on Galileo's behalf, 'for he deceived me.' The printer was ordered to suspend sales, and in October Galileo was ordered to Rome to submit himself to examination by the Holy Office. In February of 1633 he arrived in Rome, was examined by the Inquisitors in April and in June, and finally capitulated to their demands, swearing that he had not held and did not hold as true the condemned opinion 'of the motion of the earth and the stability of the sun'. He even offered to add more 'days' to the Dialogue to confute arguments in favour of Copernicus 'in such most effectual manner as by the blessing of God may be supplied to me'.[71] He spent the rest of his life, under permanent house arrest, in his villa at Arcetri, near Florence. Instead of the promised new Peripatetic arguments, he produced a new dialogue, *Two New Sciences*, published at Leyden in 1638.

Galileo's combativeness and lack of prudence in advancing radically novel opinions, the enmity and intrigues of certain Dominicans and Jesuits, and the Pope's anxieties about the course of the Thirty Years War: all these are said to have played some part in the tragedy of Galileo's trial and humiliating abjuration. Certainly it would be misleading to see it as symbolising the relation between science and religion in the seventeenth century. Nevertheless, the condemnation of Galileo appeared a serious setback to other Catholic thinkers who were also inspired by the vision of building up a mathematical science of nature to replace Peripatetic natural philosophy.

MECHANICAL PHILOSOPHERS

By the 1640s, with Galileo's *Discorsi* already published at Leyden, a number of other thinkers advocated the mechanistic approach as the only intelligible way of explaining nature. They included the Frenchmen Descartes, Gassendi and Mersenne, and the Englishmen Hobbes, Thomas White and Sir Kenelm Digby.[72] Some of these acknowledged the great influence of Galileo on their own thought. Mersenne's early writings expressed alarm at the diverse currents of occultism, Paduan 'Averroism', scepticism and libertinism in France. He found a model of certainty in mathematics, discovered the work of Galileo, and gradually came to see in mechanistic science a new way of safeguarding religion from the animated universe of 'naturalists'. Gassendi began with anti-scholastic polemic and came to recognise in Epicurus, whose ethical views were influential in some French circles, the model for a new atomistic explanation of all nature. He corresponded with Galileo and performed the experiments on shipboard as imagined in Galileo's *Dialogue*. Hobbes discovered Euclid at the age of forty, and later acknowledged motion as the key to nature, finding in Galileo 'the first that opened to us the gate of natural philosophy universal, which is the knowledge of *motion*'. Unlike Galileo, these thinkers attempted to provide a mechanical explanation of *all* phenomena in nature, and thus hoped to supplant the Aristotelian science taught at the universities.

They differed, however, on such questions as the relations between theory, observations and experiment, the role of mathematics, the explanation of biological and chemical problems, and the acceptance of atoms and void in nature. Gassendi's telescopic work reinforced his view that true scientific knowledge could be derived from 'experience and the appearance of things'. Descartes distrusted sensory knowledge because it could not satisfy the criteria which alone distinguished truth: of being 'clear and distinct'. Explanations were to be framed, based only on the geometric properties of small parts of bodies, and tested by observation and experiment. Descartes believed that living bodies could be studied just as if they were machines, while Gassendi included 'seminal atoms' to explain the stability of species in the animal, plant and mineral kingdoms. Gassendi accepted the atoms and void of the ancient atomists. Descartes identified space with matter and regarded a void as inconceivable. In the end, the ingenious explanations with which the works of the two men were filled did not differ greatly. Both were vulnerable to the charge of displaying a fertile imagination but of violating the scientific ideals proclaimed by their authors, whether of experimental test or mathematical formulation. However, they helped to illustrate the fact that it was possible, in principle, to offer mechanistic explanations of every phenomenon in nature.

In England the ideas of Gassendi and Descartes began to influence English thinkers in a climate which, at first, might not appear very conducive to their favourable acceptance. In 1640 the financial problems of Charles I forced him to summon the Long Parliament, regarded by many as an instrument through which a fundamental transformation of society and religion, in preparation for the millennium, could be realised. Among them was the group around the Prussian refugee, Samuel Hartlib. Their apocalyptic utilitarianism made them sympathetic to the Paracelsian and natural-magical tradition. The Bohemian educationist, J. A. Comenius, who briefly visited England at their instigation, admired Bacon, but found the basic principles of science in the text of Genesis.[73]

While sects proliferated, claiming the sanction of private illumination, finding the true pattern of Church and society in Scripture, and drawing their following from the labouring classes, various approaches to natural philosophy acquired an ideological resonance. Moderates and conservatives saw an affinity between sectarians and the Paracelsian and natural-magical reliance on illuminated experience and the Genesis account for a truer science. The mechanistic approach, as exemplified in the works of Descartes and Gassendi, reduced the animated nature of Renaissance philosophies to a dead automaton to be studied by sober and rational methods. Henry More, the Cambridge Platonist, in 1651 counselled the mystical chemist Thomas Vaughan to calm his fancy by reading Descartes, since it was too common then 'to be driven by heedlesse intoxicating imaginations under pretense of higher strains of Religion and supernaturall light'.[74]

In London and at Oxford groups of men began to discuss and investigate experimentally the problems in mechanics, mathematics, astronomy, chemistry and physiology arising from the work of Galileo, Descartes, Gassendi and Harvey. One of their members, Seth Ward, appointed Savilian Professor of Astronomy in 1649, refuted radical critics of the universities, and set off his group's mechanical and mathematical approach against schemes which would turn them to 'studying Magical signatures, Astrology, and Jacob Behmen'.[75] Robert Boyle, who, together with John Milton, had earlier shared the 'pan-sophic' dreams of the Hartlib circle, settled in Oxford in about 1654, and began to dedicate himself to his lifelong labour of outlining a non-contentious 'Corpuscular or Mechanical Philosophy'. He strove to lend it support by masses of experiments which were usually more serviceable in demolishing rival Peripatetic or Paracelsian explanations than in vindicating the mechanistic theories (§S–550: pp. 93–105).

The acceptance of the 'Mechanical Philosophy' was, however, rendered problematical by its association through Hobbes's *Leviathan* (1651) with the materialism and determinism which had made atomism a suspect doctrine for many centuries. Hobbes extended its scope to psychology and politics and ruthlessly drew out its destructive implications for traditional religious, ethical and political doctrines. The Oxford group tried to counter him, for the most part by attempting to discredit his scientific and mathematical competence. The Cambridge Platonists, on the other hand, responded by including the mechanistic approach within a novel restatement of Renaissance Platonism.

Henry More held that Cartesianism and Platonism were once part of a 'Mosaic Cabbala'—hinted at in the Book of Genesis—of which the physical part alone passed to the 'atheistic' Greek atomists, while the metaphysical one was taken over by Plato. Mechanical explanations were not to be renounced, but their chief advantage was in teaching the limitations of mere matter and motion, as was evident, for example, in Cartesian explanations of magnetism and gravity. They could only be explained by invoking the 'Spirit of Nature', a new version of the Platonic World-Soul. Moreover, in opposition to Hobbes, who grounded his materialism on the argument that everything that is, is extended in space, and that 'immaterial' or spiritual beings are therefore a contradiction in terms, More asserted that souls and God are alike extended beings. Ultimately he developed the conception of infinite space as an organ in and through which God creates and maintains the world: a finite world, limited in space and time, exists within the infinite extension and duration of God. These ideas were to prove of great significance through their influence upon Newton.

At the Restoration the various tendencies in the London, Oxford and Cambridge thinkers interested in new scientific currents came together in the 'Royal Society for the Improving of Natural Knowledge', founded in 1662. It was primarily a body of amateurs, compared with the French Académie des Sciences which, established in 1666, was a body of professionals, funded by the Crown.

NEWTON

When Newton came as an undergraduate to Cambridge in 1661, he was required to study science from neo-scholastic textbooks, but he had also begun to read Descartes, Boyle and Henry More. The unfolding of his scientific and mathematical genius within the broad framework of the Cambridge Platonist interpretation of the mechanical philosophy helps to explain much that is baffling in his life and thought.

Newton shared with them the belief that the conception of a finite material world, made of hard immutable atoms and existing in an infinite void constituted by the extension of God, was part of an ancient philosophical revelation. He accepted their contention that the idea of the universe as a machine, fabricated by God in the beginning and running thereafter by itself with only his general providence, was derogatory of the divine attributes and paved the way for materialism and atheism. As his scientific work progressed, Newton came to the conclusion that the mere operation of mechanical action would lead to a continual diminution of the total quantity of motion, to the desiccation of the earth and the eventual collapse of the planets into the sun. 'Active Principles' were planted by God in nature to generate new motion: comets periodically replenished earthly reserves of water. Newton believed that his greatest discovery, that of a gravitational attraction between all parts of matter operating according to a precisely quantifiable law, could perhaps never be explained mechanically. It operated 'not according to the quantity of the surfaces of the particles upon which it acts (as mechanical causes do), but according to the quantity of solid matter which they contain'.[76] Some 'agent' was involved in it, but instead of invoking a Platonic 'Spirit of Nature', Newton preferred to think of it as the direct action of God, who had never abandoned his direct superintendence over his creation.

For Newton the intervention of immaterial agencies and forces was not a reason for renouncing scientific labours. Rather, since those powers acted according to precisely quantifiable laws, it was the main business of 'experimental philosophy' to bring them to light. The 'feigning' of plausible explanations in terms of picturable mechanisms, as attempted by the general run of mechanical philosophers, had no real place in such a philosophy. With the publication of his *Principia mathematica* (1687) the dream of a new science of nature, compatible with a rotating and revolving earth, seemed to have been realised. The same laws were shown to regulate the fall of an apple towards the earth as of the planets towards the sun. Yet Continental Cartesians, while admiring it as a stupendous achievement, regarded it as a betrayal of the programme of explaining nature purely in terms of matter and motion.

The 'paradox' of Copernicus that had so perplexed Burton was by the end of the century established as the true system of the universe. Its vindication required a conceptual revolution, 'substituting for our world of quality and sense perception, the world in which we live, and love, and die, another world—the world of quantity, of reified geometry, a world in which, though there is a place for everything, there is no place for man'.[77]

NOTES

1 See G. E. R. Lloyd, *Aristotle* (1968), and M. Grene, *A Portrait of Aristotle* (1963).

2 On Galen, see §S–573, and L. S. King, *The Growth of Medical Thought* (Chicago, 1963), Ch. II.

3 See §§S–539 and S–567; also W. P. D. Wightman, *Science in a Renaissance Society* (1972).

4 'Some Thoughts upon Reviewing the Essay of Ancient and Modern Learning', in *Works* (1731), I, 290.

5 See G. Basalla, ed., *The Rise of Modern Science: Internal or External Factors* (Lexington, Mass., 1968), for the older controversy. More recent discussions are in B. Barnes, *Scientific Knowledge and Sociology Theory* (1974), Ch. V, and M. A. Finocchiaro, *History of Science as Explanation* (Detroit, 1973), Ch. XVIII.

6 Consult §S–576 and E. G. R. Taylor, *The Haven-finding Art* (1956).

7 See A. Pannekoek, *A History of Astronomy* (1961), pp. 217–21.

8 Thorndike (§S–574), Vol. V, Ch. X, XII, XV; Vol. VI, Ch. XXXIII and XXXV.

9 'Commentariolus', in *Three Copernican Treatises*, trans. E. Rosen (1959), p. 58.

10 'Narratio Prima' (1540), *ibid.*, p. 147.

11 *Ibid.*, pp. 137–8.

12 See Walter Pagel, *Paracelsus: An Introduction to Philosophical Medicine in the Era of the Renaissance* (1958); also A. Koyré, 'Paracelse', in *Mystiques, spirituels, alchimistes* (Paris, 1955).

13 *Ibid.*, pp. 126 ff.

14 See Mircea Eliade, *The Forge and the Crucible*, trans. Stephen Corrin (1962), and F. Sherwood Taylor, *The Alchemists* (1949).

15 M. Clagett, ed. and trans., *Nicole Oresme and the Medieval Geometry of Qualities of Motion* (1968); Thorndike (§S–574), Vol. III, Ch. XXVII.

16 §S–524: I, 57, and Pagel (as above, note 12), pp. 82–104.

17 On Colet and Reuchlin, see L. Miles, *John Colet and the Platonic Tradition* (1962), especially Ch. III and VI, and D. P. Walker, 'The "Prisca Theologia" in France', *Journal of the Warburg and Courtauld Institutes*, XVII (1954), 205–59; on Agrippa: D. P. Walker, *Spiritual and Demonic Magic from Ficino to Campanella* (1958), pp. 90–5; and on Dee: Walker, *ibid.*, pp. 95–6 and 113–14, and C. H. Josten, 'A Translation of Dee's "Monas Hieroglyphica" (1564)', *Ambix*, XII (1964).

18 Discussed in R. Bendix, *Max Weber: An Intellectual Portrait* (1960), especially Ch. III and VIII.

19 'Oration of the Dignity of Man' (*c.* 1486), trans. E. L. Forbes in §S–356: Ch. IV.

20 See W. J. Goode, *Religion among the Primitives* (1964), pp. 50–5; Max Weber, *General Economic History*, trans. Frank H. Knight (1961), pp. 264–70; and §S–147: pp. 656–7.

21 §S–554: p. 54. See also §S–427 and P.-H. Michel, *The Cosmology of Giordano Bruno*, trans. R. E. W. Maddison (Ithaca, N.Y., 1973).

22 On Patrizi, see §S–427: pp. 181–4, and §S–382: Ch. VII. On Bruno, consult §S–427: Ch. XX.

23 *Life and Letters*, ed. J. Spedding (1861), I, 109.

24 From the *Novum Organum* (1620), trans. J. Spedding *et al.*, I, and *The Advancement of Learning* (1605), I, v, 2. Quotations are from Bacon's *Works*, ed. J. Spedding *et al.* (1857–59).

25 *Nov. org.*, II, aph. 6; *Adv. Lear.*, II, viii, 3.

26 'Author's Preface' to *De magnete*, trans. P. F. Mottelay (1893), p. xlix. Quotations are throughout from this translation.

27 *Works* (as above, note 24), II, 140 and 287; VI, 132; VIII, 504.

28 Ibid., IV, 348; and *Nov. org.*, II, aph. 36, and I, aph. 70.

29 See A. Koyré, *The Astronomical Revolution*, trans. R. E. W. Maddison (Ithaca, N.Y., 1973), pp. 117–64, and A. Koestler, *The Sleepwalkers* (1959), Part IV.

30 *Nov. org.*, II, aph. 2; *Adv. Lear.*, II, vi, 6.

31 *Brief Lives*, ed. A. Powell (1949), pp. 229–30.

32 *The Circulation of the Blood and Other Writings*, trans. K. J. Franklin (1963), p. 6.

33 *Ibid.*, 'Second Essay to Riolan', pp. 166–7.

34 Walter Pagel, *Harvey's Biological Ideas* (1967), p. 332. See also his study cited below, note 38.

35 *Works*, trans. R. Willis (1847), Excert. LIV, pp. 401–2.

36 *ibid.*, Excert. I, p. 369.

37 Pagel (as above, note 34), p. 237.

38 Walter Pagel, *New Light on William Harvey* (1976), pp. 23–5.

39 *Writings* (as above, note 32), 'Second Essay to Riolan', p. 149.

40 *Ibid.*, Excert. LII, p. 387.

41 Pagel (as above, note 38), p. 27.

42 *Works* (note 35), Excert. XI, p. 207.

43 As above, note 39.

44 Pagel (as above, note 34), pp. 327–33.

45 *The Wisdom of God manifested in the Works of the Creation* (1691; 9th ed., 1717), p. 295.

46 'De causis criticorum dierum libellus', in *Opera omnia*, 2nd ed. (Venice, 1574), pp. 45–56.

47 See above, pp. 148 ff.; also §S–382: pp. 61–2, and F. Secret, *Les Kabbalistes chrétien de la Renaissance* (Paris, 1964).

48 Jacob Klein, *Greek Mathematical Thought and the Origin of Algebra*, trans. Eva Brann (Cambridge, Mass., 1968).

49 Cited in *ibid.*, p. 146.

50 Cited in *ibid.*, p. 139.

51 *Ibid.*, p. 160 (letter of 11 April 1598).

52 *Ibid.*, p. 342.

53 Gerd Buchdahl, 'Methodological Aspects of Kepler's Theory of Refraction', *Studies in the History and Philosophy of Science*, III (1972), 265–98.

54 W. Pauli, 'The Influence of Archetypal Ideas on the Scientific Theories of Kepler', in *The Interpretation of Nature and the Psyche*, by C. G. Jung and W. Pauli (1955), pp. 147–240; also §S–524: I, 205–93.

55 Cited by Pauli, *ibid.*, pp. 196–7.

56 *Harmonice[s] mundi*, Appendix to Book V; in *Gesammelte Werke*, ed. M. Caspar (Munich, 1940), VI, 374.

57 *Ibid.*, I, 43.

58 §S–517: pp. 59–60; see also Robert S. Westman, 'Kepler's Theory of Hypothesis and the "Realist Dilemma" ', in *Studies* (as above, note 53), pp. 233–64.

59 From *The Assayer* (1623), trans. in Stillman Drake, *Discoveries and Opinions of Galileo* (1957), pp. 237–8.

60 *Ibid.*, p. 263.

61 *Dialogue* (as below, note 70), p. 56.

62 John Murdoch, 'Philosophy and the Enterprise of Science in the Later Middle Ages'. in *The Interaction between Science and Philosophy*, ed. Y. Elkans (Atlantic Highlands, N.J., 1974), pp. 51–74; M. Clavelin, *The Natural Philosophy of Galileo*, trans. A. J. Pomerans (Cambridge, Mass., 1974), pp. 61–117.

63 S. Drake and I. E. Drabkin, *Mechanics in Sixteenth-Century Italy* (Madison, 1969), pp. 331–77.

64 Cited and discussed in William R. Shea, *Galileo's Intellectual Revolution* (1872), p. 72.

65 Clavelin (as above, note 62), pp. 173–4.

66 In Drake (as above, note 59), p. 28.

67 Cited in Giorgio di Santillana, *The Crime of Galileo* (1961), pp. 99–100.

68 *Ibid.*, pp. 116–17.

69 *Ibid.*, p. 122.

70 *Dialogue concerning the Two Chief World Systems*, trans. Stillman Drake (Berkeley, 1962), p. 6.

71 Santillana (as above, note 67), pp. 193 and 256.

72 See J. F. Scott, *The Scientific Work of René Descartes* (1952); R. Lenoble, *Mersenne où la naissance du mécanisme* (Paris, 1971); B. Rochot, *Les travaux de Gassendi sur Epicure et sur l'atomisme 1619—1658* (Paris, 1944), and O. R. Bloch, *La Philosophie de Gassendi* (The Hague, 1971); and §S–550.

73 See §S–277: pp. 237–93; §S–338; and §S–577.

74 *The Second Lash of Alazonomastix* (Cambridge, 1651), p. 68.

75 *Vindiciae academiarum* (1654), p. 41 (facsimile in §S–302).

76 'General Scholium', added to the 2nd edition of his *Principia mathematica* (1713), trans. A. Motte and F. Cajori (Berkeley, 1934), p. 546.

77 A. Koyré, 'The Significance of the Newtonian Synthesis', in his *Newtonian Studies* (1965), p. 23.

8

*The fair musick
that all creatures made*

MUSIC'S STATUS

John Milton, father and son, lived through one of the most remarkable and fruitful periods in English musical history. Between 1590 or thereabouts and the time of the Civil War, English composers created a wealth of music in every conceivable form, from the solemn Latin motet to the humble dance tune. The abundance of allusions to music in contemporary literature, the subtlety with which musical imagery is so frequently handled and the almost casual way in which complex musical terms are so often bandied about in contemporary drama suggest that audiences were highly responsive to and thus extraordinarily knowledgeable about music.

But just how musical was England at this time? 'During the long reign of Elizabeth,' William Chappell wrote enthusiastically, 'music seems to have been in universal cultivation, as well as in universal esteem . . . They had music at dinner; music at supper; music at weddings; music at funerals; music at night; music at dawn; music at work; and music at play.'[1] Had this really been so, however, would the distinguished Oxford don, John Case, have gone to the considerable expense and trouble of publishing a lengthy defence of music, first in English under the title *The praise of musicke* (Oxford, 1586), and then two years later in Latin?[2] Would, moreover, Case's book have drawn such an immediate response from William Byrd, England's most distinguished composer? For as a tribute to Case, Byrd composed an elaborate six-part setting of Thomas Watson's verses, in praise of music, and he took the unprecedented step of publishing it as a single, self-contained hand-out. Watson's words certainly have a defiant ring about them:

Let others praise what likes them best
I like his lines above the rest,
Whose pen hath painted music's praise.
By nature's law, by wisdom's rule
He soundly blames the senseless fool,
And barbarous Scythian of our days.

In his book Case questions not so much the innate musicality of the English as the narrowness of their musical vision. As he readily admitted, 'there be none but few men so senseless and blockish by nature, or of disposition so peevish and wayward, that taking no delight in Music themselves do account it as a thing either vain or unlawful, or idle and unprofitable' (Ch. IX). At the time he was writing, however, there was considerable hostility to church music (other than of the simplest kind), to theatrical entertainments and theatre music, and indeed to any music that did not have an overtly didactic function. Since the accession of Elizabeth I practically no secular music of any kind had been printed, the only active trade being in metrical psalters in which were to be found the 'church tunes', 'set forth for the increase of virtue; and abolishing of other vain and trifling ballads'.

To the serious Elizabethan scholar who lacked an ear, music must certainly have seemed but a trifling distraction. Such a distinguished bibliophile as Sir Thomas Bodley had little regard even for superlative English literature, and dismissed plays as mere 'baggage books' and 'riffe-raffes'. It is hardly surprising, then, that no music books are listed in his library catalogue, or that there are so few references to music in library catalogues of the period.[3] The 1609 catalogue of the Arundel–Lumley library is a rare exception. The collection had been started by Archbishop Cranmer; it subsequently passed into the hands of the Earl of Arundel, and was managed for more than fifty years by his son-in-law, John Lumley. It was a practical, general-purpose library, closely conforming to Sir Thomas Bodley's ideal; all but 500 of the 2,800 volumes were in Latin (fewer than 200 were in English, the rest being in French and Italian). Surprisingly enough, though, at the very end of the catalogue some forty sets of music books are listed, ranging from Petrucci's beautifully printed edition of Masses by Josquin (dated 1516) to William Byrd's three Masses (1592–95) and an assortment of manuscripts of sacred and secular music. (It was to Lumley, incidentally, that Byrd dedicated his 1591 collection of Latin motets.) The serious collector of music books, however, would not normally have been the gentleman amateur, but the well-to-do professional, and it is to the library of such a man as William Heather—founder of the Oxford Chair in Music—that we must later turn to gain the clearest idea of the influences that were shaping the work of English composers at the time.[4]

The gap that had always existed between the world of scholarship and the world of practical music was if anything widening during the late sixteenth and early seventeenth centuries. In earlier times music had had a certain academic standing as one of the four 'quadrivium' sciences, and it was studied at the university, together with mathematics, geometry and astronomy as a dimension of universal 'proportion'. By now, however, the mediaeval structure of university studies had been greatly eroded. Boethian abstractions had fallen out of favour, and as far as music was concerned there was nothing equivalent to take their place.

It is in this context that Thomas Morley's great book, curiously named *A Plaine and Easie Introduction to Practicall Musicke* (1597), is most usefully viewed. Morley published it just nine years after Case's *Apologia musices* had appeared. By then he had shown himself to be the leading composer of the younger generation. He had been the first to publish original music in the lighter Italian forms of the ballett and canzonet; he had edited two anthologies of Italian madrigals, providing them with English texts; he had published a further two volumes of reworked Italian madrigals; and he had composed some outstanding cathedral music, in the very latest style. Something of this innovatory spirit comes through in the third and final section of the book. Much of the work, though, is an impressive monument to historical scholarship. It is written in English, to be sure, and it does have the appearance in its opening pages of being a popular tutor for the amateur who wishes to acquire a reasonable competence in practical music, but its simple opening is deceptive. Philomathes is recounting to a friend a dreadful experience that he had had the previous evening at a dinner given by Master Sophobulus. Before the meal, conversation had got round to music, and the assembled company had simply refused to believe that Philomathes was ignorant of what was being discussed; they had in fact interpreted his silence as evidence of stand-offishness and ill breeding. Worse, however, was to follow!

> Supper being ended and music books (according to the custom) being brought to the table, the mistress of the house presented me with a part, earnestly requesting me to sing; but when, after many excuses, I protested unfeignedly that I could not, every one began to wonder; yea, some whispered to others demanding how I was brought up, so that upon shame of my ignorance I go now to seek out my old friend Master Gnorimus, to make myself his scholar.

The obvious point that Morley is making is of course that the well educated man really must have a grasp of the practicalities of music. There is, however, more to it than this. The practical music came as relaxation after supper and it was supervised by the lady of the house. The discussion, on the other hand, took place before the meal, when wits were still sharp, and it was conducted by the menfolk. Morley shows, by the way he sets out his book, that he is quite as concerned to impress the reader with the weight of his scholarship as he is to instruct him on plain and easy practicalities. During the course of the book he cites nearly every major authority of classical antiquity, and many of the leading European composers and theorists of the fifteenth and early sixteenth centuries as well. And he devotes an altogether disproportionate amount of space—more than a third of the book, in fact—to the exposition of a wholly outdated, highly mathematical and extraordinarily abstruse system of rhythmic notation.

Nor was Morley alone in his concern to impress. His eminent lutenist colleague, John Dowland, went to the lengths of translating an early sixteenth-century treatise by the German theorist Andreas Ornithoparcus, publishing it in 1609 with a dedicatory preface to the Earl of Salisbury. Ornithoparcus's *Micrologus* is none other than a full-blooded restatement of the Boethian position, in which music is treated as a threefold science comprising 'the world's music, humane music and instrumental music', or in other words, the music of the spheres, the harmony of the soul, and practical music, both vocal and instrumental. In his opening chapter, Ornithoparcus reviews the various kinds of musical activity that come under the third heading: there are instrument makers and performers, who are 'but servants, using no reason'; there are also 'poets', the composers who rely more on 'natural instinct' than 'speculation'; but the true musician is the man 'who hath the faculty of speculation and reason', for only he will have the skill 'to judge and discern good ayres from bad'. That Dowland saw fit to devote his time to so reactionary a treatise (and he was, after all, one of the more forward-looking composers of the day) lends further weight to the idea that music somehow lacked status.

This surely explains why Thomas Ravenscroft brought out some five years later his own extraordinarily outdated book on notation, the *Briefe Discourse*, in which he argued for a return to the antique system that Morley had so exhaustively described in his *Plaine and Easie Introduction*. The book in itself is remarkable enough. Even more extraordinary is the fact that several distinguished and forward-looking colleagues lent their support to it, including Nathaniel Giles, Master of the Chapel Royal choristers, Thomas Campion, poet and musician, whose masques provided such a challenging vehicle for musical innovation, John Dowland, foremost of England's lutenists, whose compositions reveal more than a passing acquaintance with the new Italian music, and Martin Peerson, whose *Private Musicke* (1620) was the first collection of ensemble music by an English composer to employ the new Italian method of 'basso continuo' accompaniment.

The translation and publication of Castiglione's *The Courtier* by Sir Thomas Hoby in 1561 was undoubtedly an event of some musical significance, for it did serve to spread abroad the idea of music as a social accomplishment, if at the same time one that was not to be taken too seriously. Its influence may perhaps be detected in such a work as Thomas Palmer's *Essay of the Meanes how to make our Travails into foreign countries the more profitable and honorable* (1606). That music was an ornament to a man of breeding—an 'ornation', as Palmer put it—was never in question, and it was axiomatic that a gentleman when on his travels should inform himself about the music of other nations. He might even study for a while with some foreign virtuoso. Palmer insisted, nonetheless, that expertise in music was to be considered a 'quality of ornation' and not a 'science', a 'grace' to be cultivated at convenient times and places, 'to be sociable' but not 'a science, whereof men make profession'. Though Palmer represents the Renaissance tradition of Castiglione, he has at least this in common with Boethius, a mistrust of overmuch practical skill in music.

One of music's most ardent advocates in the field of education was Richard Mulcaster, who after twenty-five years as headmaster of the Merchant Taylors

School in London became High Master of St Paul's School, a post which he held until his retirement in 1608. He arrived there as 'one of the best informed men in England', and in the light of his earlier teaching experience he reintroduced acting into the school curriculum, together with a number of less conventional subjects, including music. His general philosophy of education is set out in a substantial book, the *Positions*, which he published in 1581. Although Mulcaster allotted comparatively little space to music, he evidently held the highest opinion of its general educational value, realising at the same time that this view was a somewhat unusual one. There were those, he admitted, who felt that music was altogether 'too sweet', and that it should therefore be 'quite forborn' or 'not so much followed'. For his own part, though, he 'dare not dispraise it which hath so great defenders'; indeed, he esteemed it as 'one of the chief principles for training up of youth'. The unmusical person, he argued, 'must needs have a head out of proportion which cannot perceive, or doth not delight in the proportion of number'. And yet, he remarked, 'there groweth some miscontent with it, though it be never so good, and that not only in personages of small account, but in some very good, honest, and well disposed natures'. Certainly, he agreed, music can be misused, but 'which of our principles shall stand if the person's blame shall blemish the thing?'.

COURT PATRONAGE

Whatever doubts Case and Mulcaster may have had, the omens for the future of English music were nonetheless good, and musicians were to enjoy liberal patronage from the court, the aristocracy and gentry, the Church and the State. Of these, the court undoubtedly exercised the greatest influence, and, as we shall later see, many of the more striking musical developments of the age originated there. The musical establishment at court comprised a secular arm, under the care of the Lord Chamberlain (for convenience this will be described as the 'King's Music'),[5] and a chapel choir (the choristers and Gentlemen of the Chapel) under the direction of a dean (who normally held a bishopric) and a sub-dean. During Elizabeth's reign the two establishments were wholly independent of each other, but during the 1620s and 1630s there was an increasing interchange of personnel, 'Gentlemen' taking part in masques and other court entertainments, and instrumentalists of the King's Music accompanying the choir on important occasions. Elizabeth seems to have employed on average some twenty-five musicians, the number increasing slightly perhaps towards the end of her reign; in 1603 allowances for 'mourning livery' were paid to thirty-three musicians: seven string players (viols, and violins), seven recorders, seven flutes, six oboes and sackbuts (trombones) and six lutenists and singers. By 1628 the number had increased to close on sixty, the most substantial additions being to 'violins', 'lutes and voices', all of which were particularly associated with the masque.

Wages were good. During the reigns of James I and Charles I a top-ranking

English singer or instrumentalst could expect to get a basic minimum of £40 a year, plus a livery allowance of £16 2s 6d (distinguished foreigners seem to have been able to improve considerably on this). Within the secular establishment, moreover, there was an elite of some half-dozen or so musicians, who were known as the king's own 'private' musicians. They attended the 'privy-chamber', and perhaps even the innermost of the royal living rooms, the bed-chamber, to which only a very select group of courtiers was admitted. These musicians often held two or more appointments concurrently, and were thus earning very substantial sums: Orlando Gibbons, 'privy-organist' to James I, was also an organist of the Chapel Royal and of Westminster Abbey; his annual income therefore cannot have been much below £120. Alfonso Ferrabosco, son of one of Elizabeth's most favoured musicians, continued to enjoy the fruits of three places that his father had held, 'a musician's place in general, a composer's place, a viol's place and he also held an instructor's place to the prince in the art of music'. It can hardly be wondered at, then, that many gifted musicians (including some who had been brought back from Italy and France in private service) found the attraction of the court too strong to resist.

The court, too, was the Mecca for church musicians. During the late sixteenth and early seventeenth centuries daily services in English were sung by profes-sional choirs of men and boys in some forty cathedrals and chapels up and down the country. These choirs ranged in size from the one of sixteen or so men and boys at St David's, where for a while Thomas Tomkins's father was precentor, to thirty or more, as at Durham and Winchester (the Chapel Royal choir was easily the largest, with forty-four men and boys). All except the Chapel Royal were severely hit by inflation. The salaries they could offer were insufficient to attract musicians of the highest calibre, and moreover some deans and chapters seem to have had very little time for choral music of any kind (§ S–616: pp. 14–17 and Ch. II). The most highly paid lay clerk was earning little more than £16 per annum, and in some establishments—those of Carlisle and Gloucester, for instance—this figure was as low as £7. A 'Gentleman' of the Chapel Royal earned between £30 and £40, and furthermore was allowed to hold a position in a choir elsewhere: this was possible because duties were so arranged that the men were required for no more than two-thirds of the year. It is hardly surprising, then, that practically every major church composer was a member at some time in his career of the Chapel Royal, and that quite a few continued, as did Thomas Tomkins and Orlando Gibbons, to play an active role in two choirs.

PRIVATE AND CIVIC PATRONAGE

Some of the larger households of the aristocracy and the gentry were also sources of liberal musical patronage, and in many cases the musicians of these households provided music from time to time in other large and neighbouring houses. The account books of the Earl of Rutland record payments to many such groups of visiting musicians at the turn of the sixteenth century, including 'My

Lord Willoughby's men' from Wollaton Hall, 'Sir Thomas Stanhope his musicians', 'My Lord Cumberland's musicians', and 'Sir Henry Cavendish's musicians' (§S–655: App. B and C). A wealth of information yet remains to be co-ordinated concerning the musical activities of the larger country houses, but there can be no doubt that there was a good deal of movement from house to house, one represented on the largest scale by the dreaded royal Progress; it is also clear that in most aristocratic establishments a few of the servants at least were engaged with a particular eye to their musical accomplishments.

Cities and towns were yet another important source of musical patronage. There is evidence that no fewer than seventy different towns employed 'waits' in a primarily musical capacity, their role as city watchmen having by this time greatly diminished. The larger companies of waits, notably those of the cathedral cities, were able to furnish music for all occasions: for civic and guild banquets, for public outdoor events, for important Church festivals, when they would have accompanied the cathedral choir on cornets and sackbuts, and for private functions: the Rutlands, for instance, engaged the waits of Newark, Pontefract, Gravesend, Scarborough, Huntingdon, Grantham and Lincoln, all within the space of a dozen years. The City of London waits were even required to give public concerts, playing from 'the turret at the Royal Exchange every Sunday and holiday towards the evening' (§S–655: p. 50).

MUSIC PUBLISHING

From 1588 until the mid-1620s there was a phenomenal increase in music publishing activity. During the previous twenty-five years no more than fifteen works had been published: four of these were books on music and another six were of comparatively slight musical interest, containing simple settings of versified biblical texts. In the next twenty-five there were printed almost a hundred sets of music books and books on music, many of the very highest calibre. Just how widely this music would have been disseminated, however, is a matter that deserves some discussion. The music that concerns us here can of course only be enjoyed by a literate population. In fact literacy was rather more widespread than had once been imagined, the ratio of grammar schools to children being rather better than it was to be in early Victorian times—and to gain admission to such a school, incidentally, a child had already to be proficient in reading and writing. The effective barrier was not so much educational as financial.[6] Bess of Hardwick paid her most skilled stonemason no more than £13 6s 8d a year during the building of Hardwick Hall in the 1590s; for a six-day week her unskilled labourers received no more than £5 4s a year. To buy John Dowland's *The seconde Booke of songes and ayres* Bess's humble labourer would have to sacrifice two weeks' pay, and a further two weeks' work would have been needed to pay for a new set of lute strings. A lute on which to accompany himself would perhaps have cost as much as a year's wages. Clearly, then, complex art music was beyond the reach of the common man. What he would have been able to afford was the simple ballad sheet. These, as Robert Burton tells us in his *Anatomy of Melancholy* (1621), were immensely popular, and as soon as a new song was published you could hear 'carmen, boys, and prentices go singing that new tune still in the streets'. William Chappell, incidentally, lists well over a hundred such ballad tunes and dances that found their way into 'serious' contemporary music of all kinds.

The slowness with which English music publishing developed will never be fully explained, nor indeed the extraordinary explosion of activity that occurred in 1588. The control of music printing (other than that connected with metrical psalters) had been in the hands of Tallis and Byrd, two of the Queen's most distinguished musicians, since 1575. Their one serious venture, a set of Latin motets (*Cantiones*, 1575), was not a commercial success. There is probably a good deal of truth in the suggestion that their printer, the earnest, godly Vautrollier, was not particularly interested in secular music. Certainly it was only after his death in 1587 that music publishing prospered.

Surprisingly little is known about the publishing business: how many copies were run off, what price they were sold at, and how much the composer benefited. Some insight into these matters, however, is afforded by a study of legal proceedings that John Dowland took against his English agent, George Eastland, in connection with his *Second Booke of Songs* (1600).[7] As Dowland was resident in Denmark at the time, he sold Eastland the right to print a thousand copies; the two were to share any contribution that their dedicatee, the Countess of Bedford, should give them, and Eastland was to pay Dowland £20. Thomas East was to get £10 for the actual work of printing and £7 16s 6d for the paper, whilst Thomas Morley and Christopher Heybourne (successors to Byrd and Tallis as holders of the patent to print music) took a royalty £2, and a further 6s for every ream of paper that was used. Eastland planned to sell the work for 4s 6d and thus to make a handsome profit; he sold some copies nonetheless for as little as 2s. Eastland may have chosen to print rather more copies than would normally have been printed, for Dowland's *The First Booke of Songes* (1597) was much in demand and had already reached a second edition. That larger editions of other kinds of music were published is most unlikely, and it may be assumed that a thousand copies satisfied the demand from a population of between four and a half to five million. Few books were successful enough to merit reprinting, and these tended to be of the lighter forms of sacred and secular music; for every six volumes of music that were published, no more than one was reprinted. On the other hand, Sternhold and Hopkins's enormously popular psalter was reprinted more than three hundred times during the same period. Practically all these reprints contained selections of unharmonised, hymn-like melodies, to which the metrical psalms could be sung. Only four editions, however, supplied harmonised settings of these tunes. This suggests that a great many people may have been able to pick their way through a simple unharmonised hymn tune, but that very few indeed were up to holding their own in even the simplest part-music, despite Morley's suggestions to the contrary in his *Plaine and Easie Introduction*.

It was equally the custom in music as in literature, up to the time of the Civil War, for an author or composer to seek the protection of some influential and wealthy patron whose approval would be guaranteed to silence unwelcome criticism. Remarkably few musicians dispensed with this convention, and those who did were the editors and composers of works that had few musical pretensions: Barley's *Pathway to Music*, Hale's *Parthenia Inviolata*, Thomas Ravenscroft's three books of popular songs and catches—*Pammelia, Deuteromelia* and *Melismata*—and his anthology of harmonised psalm tunes.

Not surprisingly, patrons of provincial composers (none of whom was a match for his London contemporaries, Weelkes and Wilbye excepted) were comparatively minor figures. Composers such as Bennet, Bateson, Carlton, Kirby, Lichfield and Pilkington, all of whom spent their time in the relative peace and security of the country, had to content themselves with minor, local dignitaries. The major composers, however, called upon an impressively large circle of distinguished patrons, and if at times the patron was evidently not approached before his name was placed at the head of the dedicatory epistle, it is clear enough that composers felt sufficiently sure of the reactions of their victims to chance their arm. In all, the members of some seventy families were honoured in this way; remarkably few were untitled, and many held high rank and office in government. There was, too, a hard core of dedicatees, comprising families which had come from the 'rising' gentry and who provided the backbone of Elizabethan and early Jacobean commerce, politics and court society (§S–256). Among these may be numbered the Cecils (the Burghley and Salisbury households), the Cliffords (Earls of Cumberland), the Herberts (Earls of Pembroke), the Sidneys and the Talbots (Earls of Shrewsbury). It was Sir William Cecil who first obtained for William Seres his patent to print music books, as far back as 1552; and it was Sir Robert Cecil who obtained a similar patent for Morley in 1598. To various Cecils were dedicated Damon's 1591 psalms, Morley's 1595 *Ballets*, John Dowland's translation of Ornithoparcus (1609) and Robert Jones's first set of madrigals (1607). Francis Clifford fourth Earl of Cumberland, who spent part of 1610 at 'M. Pluvenal's' in Paris learning the lute, was the dedicatee of Byrd's last anthology of English music (1611), Campion's first and second books of ayres, and the music that Mason and Earsden wrote for the entertainment at Brougham Castle of James I in 1618. The closely interlinked Herberts, Sidneys and Walsinghams were named in no fewer than eight dedications.

Successive Lords Chamberlain, understandably enough, were highly prized; William Byrd addressed his 1589 *Songs of Sundrie Natures* to Sir Henry Carey, Baron of Hunsdon (first cousin to the Queen), by whom, as he put it, 'through the honorable office which you exercise about her Majesty's person, both myself (for my place of service) and all other her Highness's musicians are to be commanded, and under your high authority to be protected'. Many musicians besides Byrd must have been 'deeply bound' to the Lord Chamberlain for favours shown, including Morley and John Dowland.

Royalty itself was not wholly immune from such exploitation, though in view of the interest that Elizabeth and her successors took in music it is perhaps surprising that more of the royal musicians at least did not take advantage of their position. Tallis and Byrd dedicated their 1575 anthology of Latin motets to the Queen. The Queen's Master of the Chapel Royal children, William Hunnis, addressed his very popular *Poore Widows Mite* (part of the *Seven Sobs* of 1583) to her; he was at the time very hard-up, claiming that he had spent a good deal of his own money keeping the boys in food and clothing. It is, then, to be hoped that Elizabeth took his poetic dig at her in good part!

> Great gifts of gold, and gems of price,
>   poore *Hunnis* would present,
> If he them had, in stead whereof
>   he prays this may content
> New Year, and may God you send,
>   in health with peace to reign,
> And after when your spirit departs,
>   with Christ it may remain.

(It will be seen that these last lines form the conclusion of the device, Elizabeth Regina, and that the *Poore Widows Mite* is his New Year's gift to her.)

James I was the dedicatee of only one work, Robinson's *Schoole of Musicke* (1603), and then on the grounds that Robinson had taught Anne, his Queen. Anne herself attracted some attention due no doubt to her obvious enjoyment in masquing, and it was to her that Captain Hume dedicated in 1607 his *Poeticall Musicke* (the contents of which may well have been arranged from the music that was performed during the riotous few days that James spent with the King of Denmark at Theobalds in 1606) and John Dowland in 1605 his *Lachrimae*. The Princes Henry and Charles were each called on twice, whilst King Charles and Henrietta Maria were the dedicatees of three very varied publications: Filmer's *French Court-aires* (1629), Henry Lawes's psalms (1638), and his later *Choice Psalmes* (1648).

THE RELATIONSHIP BETWEEN PATRON AND PROFESSIONAL MUSICIAN

If royal example was needed to lend respectability to music as a social art, then example was certainly not lacking. Elizabeth enjoyed playing the virginals 'when she was solitary, to shun melancholy', and she was not averse even to being 'secretly' overheard by visiting ambassadors.[8] She also sang to the lute, and greatly enjoyed dancing. On coming to the throne in 1603, James I immediately raised the morale of the Chapel choir by a substantial increase in pay (he also seems to have increased the pay of the secular establishment, though no firm instruction to this end is known: see §S–616: Ch. III). The royal children were all taught music. Prince Henry, the heir apparent, even maintained a sizeable musical establishment of his own, and his tragic death in 1612 brought forth a response from composers that far exceeded the bounds of mere decorum (see §S–616: pp. 149–50, for an extract from Thomas Tomkins's funeral anthem for the Prince of Wales). King Charles took delight in playing consort music 'exactly well' on the bass viol, with Orlando Gibbons and Giovanni Coperario.[9]

In view of this, more extensive references might have been expected in dedicatory prefaces to the practical interests and skills of the dedicatees. For the most part, however, the tone of these prefaces closely follows that set by William Byrd in his 1588 *Psalmes*, where he extols in only the most general terms Sir Christopher Hatton's 'judgement and love' of music. There seems to have been a hesitance, indeed, to admit that degree of commitment to music which might imply an unconcern for more important things, a 'courtly' attitude that was as implicit in Castiglione's *The Courtier* as it was in Henry Peacham's *The Compleat Gentleman* (1622). Thus Morley in his address to Sir Robert Cecil in the 1595 *Ballets* extolled the 'many brave and excellent qualities' of his patron, including a deep love of music, 'a ladder to the intelligence of higher things'. The whole question of music's status is in fact never far below the surface in these prefatory dedications. As John Wilbye put it to Lady Arabella Stuart in his 1609 *Madrigales*, the need for a distinguished patron who professed an especial interest in music was particularly pressing at a time 'when music sits solitary among her sister sciences, and (but for your Honour) often wants the fortune to be esteemed (for so she is worthy even among the worthiest)'. That is why Thomas Robinson in *The Schoole of Musicke* (1603) makes the knight say in his opening discussion with Timotheus, his new lute master, that it is 'impossible to be a good musician except a man be seen in all the seven liberal sciences, for I know many great clerks in Divinity, Physic, Law, Philosophy, etc., that have small or no knowledge at all in music; nay some that quite reject it'. The implication is, of course, that a musician will only win respect if he can show a competence in other studies.

The relationship between composer and dedicatee varied from one in which there was no personal contact at all to the rare one in which there was a close bond of friendship. The casual approach is exemplified by William Hunnis, who committed his *Seven sobs* (1583) to the Countess of Sussex with the cheerful admission that he had been much 'at fault' in making her the patroness 'of so slender a piece without her knowledge'. Whether or not Morley asked permission of Sir Stephen Some, Lord Mayor of London, and the 'right worshipful the Aldermen of the same' before he dedicated his *First Booke of Consort Lessons* to them is an open question, too. For the Mayor and Corporation were no friends to the theatre, and it was in the theatre that much of Morley's consort music was played.[10] Possibly Morley was hoping to convert them by flattery, as perhaps was Stephen Gosson when he dedicated his *Schoole of Abuse* to Sir Philip Sidney and his *Plaies Confuted* to Sir Francis Walsingham.

In most cases, however, there is a clear connection between composer and dedicatee. Many prefaces express indebtedness for education or employment. Very occasionally the relationship between composer and patron was much closer; Sir Robert Sidney, for instance, was godfather to John Dowland's son

Robert; Sir Robert Hatton was Gibbons's 'much honoured friend' (in the 1612 *Madrigals*). Gibbons was certainly not on the same terms, though, with Edward Wray, Groom of His Majesty's Bedchamber (*Fantasies*, *c*. 1621), and in general the tone of the prefaces suggests an unbridgeable social gulf between composer and patron. For though literature and drama could boast many titled practitioners, composers almost without exception came from comparatively humble stock.

The names of members of distinguished families also came to be associated with specific pieces. There are many named dances in almost every manuscript and printed collection of the time; in Hume's *Poeticall Musicke* we find The Duke of Lennox's Delight, The Earl of Salisbury's Delight, The Earl of Worcester's Favour, The Lady Arabella [Stuart]'s Favour, The Earl of Montgomery's Favour, The Earl of Pembroke's Galliard, Sir Christopher Hatton's Choice, and The Lord Derby's Favour—all names of families that took a prominent part in the early Jacobean court masque. The custom suggests that the pieces were at least approved, if not actually commissioned, by the people concerned.

THE CONSORT SONG

It was in the context of the court, as I have said, that the more striking musical developments of the age originated. There were the choirboy plays, in which Elizabeth took especial delight; there were masques, which reached a peak of opulent splendour during the reigns of James I and Charles I; and endless 'revels, triumphs and entertainments' of various kinds which contributed so much to court life and to the pageantry of royal Progresses. Music was an important ingredient of all these events, and composers, writers, designers, dancers and actors were constantly setting themselves new and exciting challenges. During the period, there developed a particular interest in solo song; new melodic styles and new methods of instrumental accompaniment were evolved to meet the various situation. The choirboy play was the most important outlet for musical inventiveness during the early years of Elizabeth's reign. This late extension of a long-standing tradition engaged the energies of all of Elizabeth's Chapel Royal choirmasters—Richard Edwardes, Richard Farrant, William Hunnis and Nathaniel Giles—and plays were regularly performed at court, not only by the Chapel Royal boys but also by those of St Paul's Cathedral, Westminster School and St George's Chapel, Windsor.[11] Richard Farrant, seeing the commercial possibilities of the genre, took premises at Blackfriars, ostensibly as rehearsal rooms in which the Windsor and Chapel Royal boys could jointly prepare their plays for the court. Soon, however, expensive tickets were on sale for the 'rehearsals' there, and the rooms came to be frequented by the best London society.

In no sense, of course, were such plays operas or musicals, with fully written out musical scores. Special music would have been composed for the songs within the play, but there would have been much incidental music besides.

Enough of the specifically dramatic music has survived to give a fair idea of its range and calibre.[12] Not surprisingly, this music is almost wholly scored for solo boys, both 'meane' (low compass) and 'treble' (high compass), and an accompaniment of unspecified melody instruments. The boys played a variety of instruments, but viols would have formed the core of the ensemble. Already in 1561 the boys of St Paul's Cathedral and Westminster Abbey were in demand at City banquets. At the annual dinner of the Grocers' Company, the diarist Henry Machyn tells us, 'the singing children of St Paul's played upon their viols and sung very pleasant songs to the great delectation of the whole company (§ S–616: pp. 217–25).

There can be little doubt that much of the attraction of the choirboy play was the music that was performed, not only during the play but beforehand as well. Evidently the Duke of Stettin-Pomerania was greatly taken with it when he attended a play given by the Queen's boys in 1602:

> All the performances are by candlelight, and the effect is indeed spectacular. For a whole hour before the play begins there is a concert of music for organs, lutes, pandoras, citterns, viols and recorders [that is, for Thomas Morley's 'broken consort' instrumentation].[13] When we were there a boy 'cum voce tremula' [Could this possibly mean that he was skilled in the new Italian style of singing? See Caccini, below, p. 258] sang so charmingly to the accompaniment of a bass viol that we have heard nothing to equal him anywhere, except possibly the Nuns at Milan.[14]

The early consort song for solo voice (almost all for a boy) and four viols belongs broadly to one of two types; the simpler of the two was stanzaic, the music for the first stanza being repeated for subsequent ones. In style this type of consort song is akin to the harmonical metrical psalm: there are few expressive harmonies and the musical rhythms ponderously outline the verbal accentuation. The second type is through-composed, there is a good deal of imitation (the passing of melodic phrases from part to part), the vocal line, though still ponderous, is somewhat more flexible, and there is a good deal of motivic interchange between voice and instruments. Nathaniel Giles's 'Cease sorrows now' well represents the more dramatic song of the early seventeenth century. There are no abrupt changes of texture and rhythm, as there are in the madrigal, though madrigalian harmonic effects are here and there exploited. Further on in the song the music 'modulates' very effectively to a cadence on E flat major and then abruptly to D minor, in response to the words 'then yield to sad despair'. The tonal scheme of the song is in fact well managed, and in this respect it measures up to the later work of Henry Lawes. The melodic line, however, by no means has the rhythmic flexibility of the continuo song at its best.[15]

William Byrd wrote much of his early secular music in this idiom, and he published a selection of these pieces in his first English anthology of sacred and secular music, the 1588 *Psalmes*,[16] adding words rather crudely to the original instrumental lines and identifying the original vocal line by the phrase 'first singing part'. The quality of the poetry, as Dr Fellowes has observed, is excellent, including as it does verse by Sir Philip Sidney, Edward Earl of Oxford, Edward Dyer and Thomas Deloney. Despite a passing fashion first for the madrigal and then for the lute song, the consort song never entirely disappeared; it had a natural solemnity and gravity that made it the ideal idiom for sacred words, and in the hands of such composers as Amner, Gibbons, East, Nicholson, Peerson, Ravenscroft and Wilkinson it was reshaped into the 'consort anthem', in which 'verses' (solos) were sung by various groupings of voices to the accompaniment of viols, choruses being interspersed for vocal ensembles of four, five and six parts.[17] The influence of the consort song is very apparent in the elder Milton's extant anthems, and there can be little doubt that the young Milton must frequently have listened to and taken part in grave and solemn music of this kind, particularly as two of the most prolific composers of consort anthems were at St Paul's: Thomas Ravenscroft and Martin Peerson. School plays, moreover, were still very much part of the curriculum when young Milton was at the school there—plays that involved a good deal of music, as the account books show.

THE MADRIGAL

Probably the music that comes most readily to mind as characteristic of England's 'Golden Age' is the madrigal and the lighter madrigalian forms of the ballet and canzonet. And yet in certain respects the native madrigal was the most ephemeral achievement of the age. It had an effective life of little more than twenty years; it was in European terms almost an anachronism; and it had little direct influence on the future development of English music. This is not to suggest, even so, that the best English madrigals are anything but impressive by the best Italian standards. There can be no better description of the genre than Morley's:

> As for music, it is next to the motet, the most artificial and, to men of understanding, most delightful. If therefore you will compose in this kind you must possess yourself with an amorous humour (for in no composition shall you prove admirable except you put on and possess yourself wholly with that vein wherein you compose), so that you must in your music be wavering like the wind, sometime wanton, sometime drooping, sometime grave and staid, otherwhile effeminate: you may . . . show the very utterance of your variety, and the more variety you show the better you shall please.[18]

It is curious perhaps that English composers waited so long before attempting the madrigal forms. Nicholas Yonge's *Musica Transalpina* (1588) is usually cited as early evidence of the Italian madrigal in England. Yonge, a singingman at St Paul's, had for some time before 1588 been organising daily music meetings at his house, to which 'Gentlemen and Merchants of good accompt' repaired to sing Italian madrigals. There can be little doubt, though, that Italian madrigal books had been coming into the country for twenty or more years before that. In the comparatively small Lumley catalogue, for instance, no fewer than fifteen sets of Italian madrigals are listed, including a 1541 print by one of the very earliest madrigalists, Arcadelt. William Heyther's very considerable collection of printed books and manuscripts abounds with sixteenth-century Italian compositions. Five anthologies of Italian madrigals were actually published in England between 1588 and 1598 (none after, only excepting Croce's 1606 set of sacred madrigals), including two by Morley. Morley also published two books, in which original Italian compositions were considerably reworked.[19] The native madrigal dates from Morley's *Canzonets, or little short songs to three voyces* (1593), and its chief exponents were (apart from Morley) Weelkes and Wilbye (the secular music of Byrd, Gibbons and Tomkins belongs rather to the English consort song tradition, in which the textures are by no means so sectionalised). In one respect at least the consort song exerted an increasing influence on the English madrigal from 1600 onwards, Weelkes's *Madrigals of 5. and 6. parts* being the first to advertise its contents as 'apt for voices and viols'.[20]

The true madrigal, however, needed no instrumental support and it made its effect by means of rapid changes of texture and rhythm; chromaticism was also used, to express the darker moods. Of the thirty-five or so published sets of madrigals, the composite volume including a piece by the elder John Milton compiled by Thomas Morley—*The Triumphes of Oriana*—is particularly fascinating. All the Oriana pieces effectively illustrate that 'very utterance of variety' that Morley considered to be the essence of the madrigal. If Thurston Dart is right in supposing the madrigals to have been first performed before the Queen as a diversion after Essex's tragic execution, the elder Milton must have been more than flattered to find himself in such august company, and the equal of such brilliant young professionals as Thomas Tomkins, Thomas Weelkes and John Wilbye. His madrigal may lack the sheer exuberance of Wilbye's 'The Lady Oriana' or the cumulative splendour of Weelkes's 'As Vesta was from Latmos hill descending', but it is a thoroughly capable piece of work, exhibiting a firm if limited sense of tonal direction and a good ear for vocal colour; every ounce of variety, moreover, is wrung from a not particularly emotive text:

JOHN MILTON, SR: from 'Fair Oriana in the morn'
(in *The Triumphes of Oriana*, 1601; *The English Madrigalists*, ed. E. H. Fellowes,
rev. R. T. Dart [1962], No. 18)

In this extract 'O stay, thou shepherds maid' is placed in parentheses by the introductory chordal 'The roses, blushing, said'; the idea of 'staying', moreover, is illustrated by a change of speed and by the use of suspensions (ties in which a harmony note is held into the following chord). After this the music speeds up in response to 'And on a sudden' (the impact is increased by the vertical alignment of the words), and it moves into a lengthy section based on the imitative point 'Thus sang those shepherds'; this is passed backwards and forwards, from voice to voice, from nymph to nymph. We may be sure that 'Fair Oriana in the morn' was often called for during the musical evenings at the Miltons' house in Bread Street.

THE MASQUE

Upon the accession of James I the masque rapidly achieved an altogether new and overriding importance at court. Historians of music have in the past paid insufficient attention to the genre, for the reason perhaps that there is no readily accessible repertory of music to study. The court masque was a ceremonial event of considerable splendour; it was rarely repeated, and it had little relevance outside court circles. As moreover the musical forces that it employed were considerably greater than those that were likely to be available anywhere else, there can be no surprise that so little of it was published or carefully preserved in score. Yet the masque continued to offer exciting musical challenges to the imaginative composer up to the very time of the Civil War. It invited him, moreover, to take note of developments abroad, notably in France, where the

Ballet de cour offered something of a parallel to the masque, and in Italy, where the Renaissance *Intermedio* had blossomed into full-scale opera.[21]

During the early years of the seventeenth century there was considerable musical interchange between England and the Continent, especially between England and Italy.[22] A few musicians were lucky enough to travel abroad in the entourage of some distinguished diplomat (§S–264: pp. 459–63). Some went abroad to study: Walter Porter, Gentleman of the Chapel Royal, claimed that he had actually studied with Monteverdi; John Cooper, less fortunate perhaps, made up for it by becoming Signor Giovanni Coperario on his return to England, where he subsequently became composer in the King's 'private music'. Others went abroad as travelling virtuosi; the viol players William Brade and Thomas Simpson headed a group of English instrumentalists who spent much of their time on the Continent, and who did much to establish the high reputation of English consort music abroad. Robert Dowland was engaged by the Danish court to instruct Anne, the future Queen of James I. John Dowland was welcomed as far north as Elsinore, and as far south as Rome.

Those composers who were not lucky enough to travel yet had an excellent chance to find out what was happening abroad, for many foreign musicians came to settle in England. There was Signor Lugario, musician to Queen Anne, a former colleague of Monteverdi's at Mantua, who arrived in London in 1607. There was the Venetian Angelo Notari who by 1610 was lutenist to Prince Henry. He was evidently well acquainted with the work of the Florentine Camerata, and particularly with Caccini's *Le Nuove musiche* (1602), the leading textbook on the new monodic style of composition and singing.[23] In 1613 he published in London his own *Prime Musiche Nuove*, containing monodies, duets, trios and canzonette, and described as 'one of the most interesting collections of madrigals and airs published in England during the reign of James I'. There also exists an autograph collection of Notari's, dating from the early 1620s, which includes a good deal of contemporary Italian music, and in particular a substantial part of Monteverdi's seventh book of madrigals (1619).[24] According to the publisher, John Playford, who printed a translation of the singing instructions from Caccini's *Le Nuove musiche* in his *Introduction to the Skill of Music* (1655 ff.),[25] the Gentlemen of the Chapel Royal—many of whom took part in court masques during the 1630s—were already by 1620 skilled in the new Italian style of singing that Caccini had described. Further evidence of familiarity with the new Italian music is provided by Robert Dowland's *Musicall Banquet* (1610), in which there is Caccini's famous 'Amarilli mia bella', and by a number of English manuscripts, notably Tenbury 1018–19, in which are to be found Italian monodies by Alfonso Ferrabosco, 'instructor to the Prince of Wales'.[26] It seems, too, that Nicholas Lanier, who was to become Master of the King's Music to Charles I, set the whole of Jonson's masque, *The Vision of Delight*, 'after the Italian manner, stylo recitativo'. If, however, the one surviving section of the masque is anything to go by, Lanier's music was more akin to the English declamatory ayre than to the Italian recitative (see §S–647: p. 47, ex. 15).

There were ample opportunities, too, for the King's musicians to learn about

French music. Four of Queen Anne's private musicians were Frenchmen; in 1617 a group of French musicians staged a *Ballet* at court; and a number of English masques seem to owe something at least to earlier French models. The signs are nonetheless that French music aroused comparatively little interest, at least before the opening of Queen Henrietta Maria's Catholic chapel in 1636 (§ S–616: pp. 86–8). Thomas Campion ventured an English adaptation of *Musique mesurée à l'antique* in his setting of 'Come, let us sound with melody';[27] interesting as the *vers mesurée* attempts were to relate musical and verbal stress more intimately, they carried with them severe musical limitations. Lack of English interest, then, is hardly surprising.[28] If Edward Filmer is to be believed, the English were still very ignorant of French music in 1629, the year in which he published his *French court-aires*. English tailors and English dancing masters, he argued, had long been modelling themselves on French practices; it was time therefore that English composers did likewise 'for pleasing novelty's sake' and 'for life of air'.

Since the only significant studies of the masque so far have been the work of literary scholars, it may be worth emphasising, as we were reminded some years ago,[29] that in content the masque is in the first place dance (and thus dance music), in the second place spectacular entertainment, and only thirdly literature. Even as literature the masque was rather more sung than spoken text. Francis Bacon's essay 'Of Masques and Triumphs' leaves no doubt, moreover, that this is how the masque was seen at the time; indeed, Bacon hardly refers to literature or drama at all. In his words,

> Dancing to song is a thing of great state and pleasure. I understand it that the song be in quire, placed aloft, and accompanied with some broken music [colourful music, that is, for a variety of instruments]; and the ditty [text] fitted to the device . . . Several quires, placed one over against the other, and taking the voice by catches, anthem-wise [presumably singing imitatively and anti-phonally], give great pleasure. Let the scenes abound with light, specially coloured and varied, and let the masquers or any other that are come down from the scene, have some motions upon the scene itself before their coming down, for it draws the eye strangely.

The core of the masque had been, and was to remain up to the time of the Interregnum, the involvement of distinguished personages in specially prepared dances. The Jacobean masque was an extension of the form that had been developed towards the end of the previous reign and which was rep-resented by two Christmas pieces produced by the Gentlemen of the Inns of Court in 1594. These were built around three central events: the formal entry and entry dance of the masquers; the social dances (revels) in which the audience participated at the invitation of the masquers (these could last indefinitely, and many a court masque seems to have gone on until dawn); and to end with, the recall and final dance of the masquers. The spoken dialogue was in the hands of professionals (the masquers neither sang nor spoke); dialogue generally preceded the initial entry of the masquers to place the masque in some sort of dramatic or allegorical context, and there was normally some further dialogue between the dances. Two developments of some musical importance subsequently took place. The first was the addition of a main masquing dance, commonly separated from the entry dance by a song and by instrumental music (particularly in the later masques), after the pattern of the 'grand ballet' of the French *Ballet de cour*. Ben Jonson's *Hymenaei* (1606) was one of the first to be extended in this way. The second development involved the creation of an introductory antimasque, to act as a 'false masque' or 'foil' to the high seriousness of the main masque. An early example of this is to be found in Jonson's *Masque of Queens* (1609). The antimasque rapidly assumed considerable importance, and for some people it became the main event. 'How many antimasques have they? Of what nature?' asks Fancy, at the beginning of Shirley's *Triumph of Peace* (1634), 'for these are fancies that take most: your dull and phlegmatic inventions [the main masques] are exploded. Give me a nimble antimasque.'[30]

Ben Jonson, the principal author of the court masque, was concerned that it should not degenerate through insensitive handling of the antimasque into a string of disconnected and merely amusing episodes. His *Oberon*, in which Prince Henry danced the title role, is an excellent example of the masque as an integrated whole. The antimasque characters do not disappear when the main masque begins, but continue to weave a thread of 'plot' around the masque dances and the final recall. The work comprises three scenes, forming a visual crescendo. The first is 'all obscure, and nothing perceiv'd but a darke Rocke, with trees beyond it; and all wildnesse, that could be presented'. The satyrs are awaiting the coming of Oberon who

> doth fill with grace,
> Every season, ev'ry place;
> Beautie dwels, but in his face:
> H'is the height of all our race.

(ll. 62–5)

The scene next opens to reveal 'the Frontispice of a bright and glorious Palace' with transparent walls and gates; sylvans, or watchmen, are sleeping at the gates: it is their task to guard the palace by day. This is the setting for the antimasque dance of the satyrs. At the first light of dawn the whole palace opens to reveal a 'nation' of fairies, 'some bearing lights; others singing; and within a farre off in perspective [are to be seen] the knights masquers sitting . . .: At the further end of all, Oberon, in a chariot'. The masquers then enter to 'lowd triumphant musique', and Oberon's chariot slowly moves to the front of the stage, drawn by two white bears and attended by seven sylvans. Excited by so splendid a sight, the fairies burst into song, and the satyrs begin to dance excitedly around. All is quickly silenced by the chief guard, however, with the timely reminder that this is an occasion

> of greatnesse, and of state;
> Not to be mixt with light, and skipping sport:

A night of homage to the British court,
An ceremony, due to Arthurs chaire.

(ll. 320–3)

The dancers then descend to the masquing floor to the sound of a fairy duet and chorus and to the accompaniment of a further antimasque dance. After the entry dance, a musical interlude, and the main dance, the masquers invite the audience to join in the revels or social dances. The evening is thereupon brought to a close with Alfonso Ferrabosco's 'Gentle knights, know some measure of your nights'.[31]

No music at all has yet been located for some twenty of the thirty-five or so Jacobean masques that are known to have been produced. Music for the other fifteen comprises individual masque songs—some of which found their way into the printed lutenist song collections of the period—and a vast quantity of miscellaneous dance music, notably in Adson's *Courtly masquing ayres* (1621), John Playford's collection of the same title (1662), and British Library MS Add. 10444. Most of this dance music carries no precise identification, and it was probably used for the revels. These sources do nonetheless contain pieces from at least half a dozen antimasques, some of which definitely call for imaginative music. Much of music's effect in the more curious antimasques would undoubtedly have derived from the scoring, which, in so far as it is known at all, is known only through very generalised verbal descriptions. But composers did experiment with rhythms, melodies and harmonies in their search for the unusual. The anonymous Second Witches dance from Jonson's *Masque of Queens* (§S–641: p. 123) well illustrates this: the first eccentric device is to set a 4/4 melody against a 3/4 bass: this does not really come off, for the strongest harmonic changes fall on to the strongest 4/4 beats of the melody (on the first and third beats of the bar, that is). The second device (bars 8–9) shifts the bar line one beat backwards, in order to confuse the rhythmic flow: the confusion is worse confounded by an ensuing three bars of 3/4 metre, and a very fast and bumpy two bars of 4/4. The dance ends in compound ternary metre, in which 6/4 and 3/2 metre conflict. Most of the dance music, though, is of the simplest kind; melodies are stepwise, the harmonic progressions smooth, and the phrases four-square. This in fact is the idiom of the popular ballad tune, and it is here (as in the splendid virginal music of the period) that courtly and popular music most effectively meet.

The early masque songs range in style from Campion's simple and tuneful lute songs to Alfonso Ferrabosco's declamatory ayres,[32] which match the increasingly theatrical grandeur of the masque. Spink (§S–647: pp. 44–5) points above all to Lanier's 'Bring away this sacred tree', from Campion's *Squires Masque*, as the archetype of the future English continuo song, in which the declamatory solo line is set to a simple chordal accompaniment.

It would be a happy coincidence if Milton's *A Mask* (1634)—commonly called *Comus*—and Henry Lawes's incidental music to it were to represent the peak of achievement in the Caroline masque. *Comus*, however, is more properly a poetic entertainment, since it lacks the central element of masque dance. The collaboration of poet and musician resulted not in any new musico-literary forms but in a poetic sequence, in the course of which there occurred isolated and self-contained songs. These Henry Lawes set competently, if somewhat stiffly, in the declamatory manner of Lanier's 'Bring away this sacred tree'.

It was not in fact Milton's 'Harry' but the younger brother William who was working, in his music for *The Triumph of Peace* (1634), *The Triumph of the Prince d'Amour* (1636) and *Britannia Triumphans* (1638), towards the creation of much more continuous musical structures within the masque.[33] Significantly perhaps, Lawes did not try to emulate Lanier's attempts at a through-composed 'stylo recitativo'. The fact that Lanier seems not to have tried this more than twice[34] suggests that the masque was unsuitable for it. Recitative originated in a desire, on the part of members of the Florentine Camerata (notably Caccini and Peri), to develop a new musical style that would ensure maximum word audibility and a natural, speech-like delivery. It was ideally suited to carry the action of an opera, but far less appropriate for the comparatively undramatic masque.[35] Sensing this, perhaps, Lawes chose an alternative solution, in which a variety of comparatively short and formal sections are fused together into a coherent whole. Thus the first masque group in *Britannia Triumphans* comprises a dance-like five-part chorus, a free declamatory aria for solo treble, a further song for the treble constructed on the bass line of the opening chorus (entitled 'ciacona'), and a quartet for solo treble, alto, tenor and bass which expands into a concluding full chorus *à cinq*. Lawes creates moreover a large-scale tonal plan for the masque which serves to enhance the coherence of the separate groups: the pieces that have just been described centre on A minor and its relative key of C major; the second group are in C minor and E flat major, the third and 'Valedictory' group in C major. The idea was not wholly new. Alfonso Ferrabosco was evidently feeling his way to it in *The Masque of Beauty*, though on a much smaller scale.[36]

THE LUTE SONG AND CONTINUO SONG

If the masque afforded the composer a broad canvas on which to work, if it invited grand musical gestures, striking effects and bold declamation, it was solo song that inspired the deepest and subtlest musical response to words. The history of English song is a continuous one, extending through the Elizabethan consort song to the lute song (of which Dowland's *Booke of Songes* in 1597 is the first published collection), and into the so-called 'continuo song' of the early seventeenth century (§S–647: pp. 13–127). The process of transformation from lute song to solo song was a subtle one, a process that has been much obscured by the gap of thirty years or so between the publication of the last collection of lute songs (Attey's *Booke of ayres*, 1622) and the first books of solo songs (*Select Musicall Ayres*, ed. Playford, 1652, and Henry Lawes's *Ayres and Dialogues*, 1653). During these thirty years, however, there was no slackening of song-writing activity, and a vast repertory has survived in well over thirty manuscripts, the contents of which are not precisely datable.

The most obvious, if at the same time the most superficial, difference between lute song and continuo song is that the accompaniment to the lute song is fully written out, whereas in the later form only the vocal line and a bass are supplied from which the accompaniment must be improvised. The seeds of 'continuo' accompaniment are already present in the lute song, however, for most published collections of lute songs require the lowest line of the accompaniment to be reinforced by a bass viol.

That a difference was clearly felt at the time between lute song and continuo song is undeniable. It is equally clear that of the many song writers who were active between 1620 and 1660, Milton's 'Harry' Lawes was considered to be pre-eminent. Cartwright, Carew, Lovelace, Suckling and Waller all went out of their way in their published collections of poems to mention that Henry Lawes had set their verse to music. The greatest tribute of all, perhaps, was paid by Milton himself, whose sonnet prefaces the Lawes brothers' *Choice Psalmes* of 1648:

> To Mr. H. Lawes, on his Aires
>
> Harry whose tuneful and well measur'd Song
>   First taught our English Musick how to span
>   Words with just note and accent, not to scan
> With Midas Ears, committing short and long;
> Thy worth and skill exempts thee from the throng,
>   With praise enough for Envy to look wan;
>   To after age thou shalt be writ the man,
> That with smooth aire couldst humor best our tongue . . .

Milton's claim is a bold one, for earlier composers had by no means been unalive to the desirability of 'just note and accent'. Was Milton perhaps moved to an exaggerated regard for a close friend? If not, can the particular qualities that he admired be more precisely defined? It is clear to begin with that Milton's sonnet was no momentary impulse or hasty formality but the product of careful revision over a period of time. Some inkling of Milton's particular regard for Lawes may be gathered from a comparison of the printed sonnet with an earlier manuscript version.[37] The revisions show that Milton had focused his comment more precisely on Lawes's sensitivity to words, making less, at the same time, of Lawes's purely musical achievement. The original version of the second and third lines, for instance, reads as follows:

> First taught our English Music how to span
> words with just notes which till then us'd to scan
> with Midas eares . . .

whilst lines 7 and 8 made no explicit reference to the setting of words:

> To after age thou shalt be writ a man
> That did reform thy art

Just how Henry Lawes, and to a lesser extent his song-writing contemporaries, achieved this closer union with poetry is best studied in the music itself. A comparison between Lawes's setting of Donne's 'Sweet, stay awhile' and John Dowland's setting of the same poem may serve to focus the main issues.[38]

JOHN DOWLAND, from 'Sweet, stay awhile'
(in *A Pilgrimes Solace*, 1612)

HENRY LAWES, from 'Sweet, stay awhile'
(in British Library Add. MS 53723: f. 10v)

As 'just accent' the two have much in common. Both composers accentuate 'sweet', 'do' (will), 'rise', 'light' and 'O' by means of pitch—the higher the note, the more accentuated it is. Where the two differ, Lawes more effectively underlines the declamatory shape of the verse, notably in the line 'To think that I from you must part'; possibly, however, he handles the final 'in' less sensitively. The two settings are closely comparable, too, in rhythmic accentuation and phrase structure; but Dowland continues with only the briefest pause right through line 3 of the first stanza. At first sight this would seem to be the correct thing to do. The structure of the verse is complex, however, for 'it' refers not to 'day' but to 'break'. Lawes's solution allows more time for the meaning to be unravelled, and it is possibly therefore the one to be preferred. The melodic structure differs most strikingly in the fifth and sixth lines, where Dowland interrupts the flow of the verse for the sake of a purely musical effect, and in doing so makes nonsense of the second stanza. Lawes, on the other hand, studiously avoids word repetition.

There yet remains the more subtle matter of cadence structure. Renaissance composers were keenly aware of the need to marry musical 'punctuation' (cadence) with verbal punctuation. As Morley put it, 'you must not make a close (especially a full close) till the full sense of the words be perfect. So that keeping these rules you shall have a perfect agreement and, as it were, an harmonical consent betwixt the matter and the music'.[39] Charles Butler in *The Principles of Musick* (1636) further elaborated Morley's instructions. The relative finality of punctuation, he explained, was determined by both musical rhythm and cadence. 'Periods' (full stops) and colons required long rests in the melodic line of a semibreve or more. Semicolons, commas or other brief articulations such as 'breathings and sighs' called for short rests of no longer than a minim. 'Primary cadences' were to be linked to the period and colon: these were chord progressions involving successively the chord on the fifth or dominant of the scale, and the tonic, or root. Cadences involving chords on other notes of the scale—'secondary cadences', as Butler called them—were to be used for other less emphatic points of verbal punctuation, whilst 'imperfect cadences'—ones that actually did not come to a rest—were to mark 'points of imperfect sense'.

It is in the matter of cadence structure that the settings of Dowland and Lawes most significantly differ. Despite Donne's punctuation, his first stanza naturally falls into three interlinked sections: the first relates to the beloved (ll. 1–2), the second to the lover (3–4), and the third to their future relationship (5–6). By the judicious use of secondary and imperfect cadences Lawes achieves a forward-moving tonal structure that at the same time reflects the poetic argument:

	Dowland		Lawes	
	begins on:	and ends on:	begins on:	and ends on:
Line 1	a	E–A	a	a–F
2	E	d–E	C	d–a**
3	a	G–C	a	a–E
4	F	E–A	E	E–B–e
5	G	B–E*	C	a–E**
6	a	a–A	C	E–a

* Ending on the first inversion of E, and thus imperfect.
** Other imperfect cadences.
CAPS = major chord.

Dowland's comparative insensitivity to cadence in this song is most obvious in his treatment of the first line, for he sets the question 'Will you rise?' to the most conclusive cadence of all, the dominant (E) to tonic (A). Lawes, on the other hand, ends the first line with a very weak chordal movement that stops inconclusively on the very 'secondary' chord of F major. He avoids the tonic a minor, until the end of the stanza's first 'section', though as four more lines are to follow, he uses the rather less conclusive 'plagal' form of cadence here from d to a. At the beginning of the third line both settings are in the tonic: Lawes, however, moves away into E minor by way of a dominant chord (B major) in the new key. By this time Dowland has long again reached the home key of a minor, and in terms of musical logic his song could very well end here. In the fifth line he does modulate into E minor, and by the use of an unstable 'first inversion' on

E major at the end of that line he projects the music forward into the last line of verse. Lawes, with greater subtlety still, manages to avoid the home tonic chord altogether until the very end, when it is firmly prepared for by an extended E major dominant. It is the combination of these various techniques that Milton surely must have appreciated in the best songs of his contemporaries.

Further evidence of Lawes's sensitivity to words is to be found in his strophic variation songs. Dowland, as we have seen, left the second stanza of 'Sweet, stay awhile' to fend for itself. Lawes was not above doing this from time to time, but where verbal rhythm and articulation varied from stanza to stanza he often readjusted the rhythm of the melodic line, and even the harmonic flow, in order to preserve 'just accent'. Such songs as 'Come my sweet, while every strain' and 'No, no, fair heretic' well illustrate the technique.[40]

A comparison of Henry Lawes's 'It is but a frown' with Walter Porter's setting of the same text[41] may help to explain more fully why Lawes was so much more highly esteemed than any of his contemporaries (see p. 268). The anonymous poem takes the form of a monologue from a lover to the mistress who despises him. The words do not invite expansive musical development, for they involve a conceit, one that is simple enough in the reading or speaking but which could easily be obscured by an over-elaborate musical setting. The opening lines, moreover, are very direct, and are best declaimed, succinctly and unlyrically. Lawes's skilfully varied and balanced tonal structure will at once be appreciated, as will Porter's lack of tonal direction. The conceit itself is the idea of the snowball, at once comforted and destroyed by the warmth of the sun. Lawes manages by the sensitive use of cadence to project the music forward, pausing momentarily and aptly on 'the while', but avoiding the dominant–tonic progression until the final 'dies'. Porter succeeds in making nonsense of this passage, firstly by setting 'you only warm a ball of snow' so slowly that the sense of musical continuity is badly strained, then by inserting a rest after 'which, whilst it gathers', by repeating the phrase and separating it by a further rest from 'comfort from your eyes'. A pointless five bars of instrumental interlude intervene before the conclusion of the conceit, at which point the listener will be lucky not to have lost the thread of the argument entirely. The ineptitude of the verbal accentuation needs no comment. In all, this is not an impressive example from one who claimed to have been a Monteverdi pupil!

Whether Milton would have had much acquaintance with continuo song before he met Henry Lawes is an open question. His father's music belongs in style to the age of Morley and Gibbons; much of it, for Sir William Leighton's *Teares or Lamentacions*, and for Myriell's *Tristitiae Remedium*,[42] is elaborately imitative, and full of high seriousness. To him, the new continuo song must have seemed a very lightweight and inferior product.

That the young Milton was more than usually musical is a fair assumption. According to Aubrey[43] he had a 'delicate, tunable voice' and, thanks to his father's teaching, 'good skill' in practical music. He played the organ, and in later years 'he would be cheerful even in his gout fits, and sing'. He had a warm regard for his father's musical skills ('Ad Patrem', 1630) and in his tract *Of*

HENRY LAWES (in British Library Add. MS 53723: f. 50)

You on-ly warm a ball of snow the while; which, whilst it gathers comfort from your eyes, With that same com-fort melts a - way, and dies.

WALTER PORTER (in *Madrigales and ayres*, 1632)

You on - ly warm a ball of snow the whilst, Which whilst it ga-thers, which whilst it ga-thers com-fort from your eyes, With that same com - fort melts a - way, [a - way] and dies.

Education (1644) he acknowledges music's 'great power over dispositions and manners, to smooth and make them gentle from rustick harshness and distemper'd passions' (*CE*, IV, 289). We know, too, that on taking over responsibility for educating his two young nephews, Edward and John Phillips, he made them 'songsters, and sing, from the time they were with him'. And yet, oddly enough, in his own letters and essays there is precious little evidence of any very serious concern for music.

John Arthos (§ S–173) gives an impressive account of what Milton might have seen on his travels; he refers to the 'theatrical' nature of church services in Italy, he outlines the operatic productions that Milton might have attended in Venice, he reminds us that Monteverdi was then Maestro di Cappella of St Mark's in Venice. Of all this, however, Milton wrote not a word. He was, to be sure, much flattered by the warm reception he was accorded by Francesco Cardinal Barberini when he attended the cardinal's sumptuous musical entertainment in Rome. It is true, too, that one of the more alluring qualities of the Italian girl about whom he wrote so warmly to Charles Diodati was her 'song, which might lure from her middle hemisphere the labouring moon'. Nothing emerges, however, to show that at any time during the Italian journey music was uppermost in his mind. Rarely, too, can a warm, personal response to music be sensed in Milton's own poetry. There is, of course, that marvellous passage from 'Il Penseroso' (1632–33) which affords us a precious glimpse of an experience that must have made a deep impression on him: cathedral service in some majestic and reverberant building—perhaps the chapel of King's College, Cambridge, or St Paul's Cathedral in London. Few other musical lines that Milton penned, however, come across with such intense commitments:

> There let the pealing Organ blow,
> To the full voic'd Quire below,
> In Service high, and Anthems cleer,
> As may with sweetnes, through mine ear,
> Dissolve me into exstasies,
> And bring all Heav'n before mine eyes.
>
> (ll. 161–6)

The music in Milton's poetry is for the most part the music of nature, the music of the spheres, the music of the heavenly host, in which explicit reference to contemporary musical experience is studiously avoided. Milton names not viols, citterns, lutes and orpharions, but unfashionable (and antique) harps and dulcimers. His musicians do not play virginals, clavichords or harpsichords, but the remote and majestic king of instruments, the organ, an instrument of impeccable classical pedigree. His singers are unaware of the existence of ballet, canzonet, madrigal, lute song or dialogue, nor do they dance pavans, galliards, almains or corantos. His descriptions of music are involved; the use of technical terms is deliberately blurred. The visionary organist in *Paradise Lost* (XI, 560–3) has a 'volant touch / Instinct' which, 'through all proportions low and high / Fled and pursu'd transverse the resonant fugue'. Such juxtapositions of technical terminology would have come strangely to the lips of a professional. Musicians simply did not describe 'proportions' as 'low' and 'high', nor would they have employed the term 'transverse' in connection with fugal procedures. Buildings or instruments might well have been described as 'resonant', but never a fugue. Milton is here, as in so many other places, keeping 'musica instrumentalis' at a distance.

The impression remains, rightly or wrongly, that Milton found steadily less time for music as the years progressed. By 1654 he was looking back to the happy years that he had spent with his father at the country house at Horton, and he was writing of his past love of music.[44] Certainly, total blindness would have cut him off from the serious study of new music, and he would surely have looked back, more and more, to those early years when he had the inclination and leisure to keep abreast of contemporary developments. Not, indeed, that there proved to be a great deal in the 1650s and 1660s that was truly new. The demand for musical instruction grew apace, if the extraordinary popularity of Playford's *Brief Introduction* is anything to go by. But the music that the public wanted, as Playford astutely realised, was not the latest sonata or cantata from abroad, but singable, tuneful songs, duets and trios, undemandingly scored for whatever continuo instruments happened to be available. The music of the Lawes brothers, Lanier, Wilson and Hilton that fills the pages of Playford's song collections met the need admirably, nor would it have seemed at all extraordinary had it been published some twenty or thirty years earlier. The debt that the leading Restoration composers (notably Blow and Purcell) owed to their immediate predecessors has never sufficiently been recognised. But it was only in the 1670s that the younger men began to acquire a distinctively and fully assured 'Restoration' accent. And of this, the ageing Milton would have known nothing.

NOTES

1 *Old English Popular Music*, revised by H. E. Wooldridge (1893), I, 59.

2 Howard B. Barnett, 'John Case: An Elizabethan Music Scholar', *Music and Letters*, L (1969), 252–6.

3 See *The Lumley Library: The Catalogue of 1609*, ed. Sears Jayne and F. R. Johnson (1956).

4 See Margaret Crum, 'Early Lists of the Oxford Music School Collection', *Music and Letters*, XLVIII (1967), 23 ff.

5 Entries relating to music in the Lord Chamberlain's accounts are printed in H. D. De Lafontaine, *The King's Musick* (1909).

6 See L. Stone (§S–264), Ch. XII. The chapters on 'Conspicuous Expenditure', and 'Office and the Court', will also well repay attention.

7 See Margaret Dowling, 'The Printing of John Dowland's *Second Booke of Songs or Ayres*', *The Library*, 4th series, XII (1932), 365–80.

8 Sir James Melville, *Memoirs*, ed. S. F. Stewart (1929), p. 95.

9 See R. T. Dart, 'The Printed Fantasias of Orlando Gibbons', *Music and Letters*, XXXVII (1956), 342–9, and 'Jacobean Court Music', *Musica Britannica*, IX (1955), ed. Thurston Dart and William Coates, especially pp. 171–91, for the kind of music he would have played.

10 See *The First Book of Consort Lessons collected by Thomas Morley*, reconstructed by Sidney Beck (1959). Beck's extensive preface provides a fascinating background to instrumental consort music of the period; see also 'Music for Mixed Consort', ed.

Warwick Edwards, *Musica Britannica*, XL (1977), for further information and music. Both studies discuss the interrelationship between the Walsinghams, Sidneys, Hattons and Untons.

11 See H. M. Hillebrand, 'The Child Actors: A Chapter in Elizabethan Stage History', *University of Illinois Studies in Language and Literature*, XI (Urbana, 1926).

12 See 'Consort Songs', ed. Philip Brett, *Musica Britannica*, XXII (1967), for music and commentary; also his 'The English Consort Song', *Proceedings of the Royal Musical Association*, LXXXVIII (1961–2), 73–88.

13 See Morley's *Consort Lessons* (above, note 10).

14 'The Diary of Philip Julius, Duke of Stettin-Pomerania', ed. G. Von Bulow, *Transactions of the Royal Historical Society*, VI (1892).

15 The two settings are in *Musica Britannica*, XXII (1967), 30 and 37.

16 *The Collected Works of William Byrd*, ed. E. H. Fellowes, revised by Philip Brett, XII (1963).

17 See *The Treasury of English Church Music*, II: *1545—1650*, ed. Peter le Huray: Mundy, 'Ah, helpless wretch' (p. 28); Byrd, 'Teach me, O Lord' (p. 60); Morley, 'Out of the deep' (p. 114); Weelkes, 'Give me ear, O Lord' (p. 166); Gibbons, 'See, see, the Word is incarnate' (p. 198). The accompaniments for all but 'See, see, the Word' are for organ (the cathedral 'verse anthem' for organ and voices originates from the same root as the 'consort anthem').

18 *A Plain and Easy Introduction to Practical Music*, ed. R. A. Harman (1952), pp. 294–5.

19 The history of the English madrigal is best studied in §S–613; for the music, see *The English Madrigalists*, I–XXXVIII, ed. E. H. Fellowes, revised by Thurston Dart (1956 ff.). For studies of individual composers, see especially §S–587 and §S–588.

20 From East's 1604 collection the subtitle is attached to almost every set of madrigals.

21 The European context of the masque is best studied in *The New Oxford History of Music*, IV (1968), pp. 784–820 [Ch. XIV: 'Music and Drama'].

22 See Sir Jack Westrup, 'Foreign Musicians in Stuart England', *Musical Quarterly*, XXVII (1941), ii, 70–89; also 'Domestic Music under the Stuarts', *Proceedings of the Royal Musical Association*, LXVIII (1942), 19–53.

23 Substantial extracts are given in *Source Readings in Music History*, ed. Oliver Strunk (1950), pp. 377 ff.

24 See Ian Spink, 'Angelo Notari and his *Prime Musiche Nuove*', *Monthly Musical Record* (1957), pp. 168–77; also §S–647: pp. 42–4; and Pamela J. Willetts, 'The Autographs of Angelo Notari', *Music and Letters*, L (1969), 124–6.

25 The section entitled 'A brief discourse of the Italian manner of singing; wherein is set down the use of those graces in singing, as the Trill and Gruppo, used in Italy, and now in England: written some years since by an English Gentleman, who had lived long in Italy, and being returned, taught the same here'.

26 The music is in *The English Lute-Songs*, 1st series, XVII (John Coperario); 2nd series, XVII (Robert Johnson), XVIII (Greaves, Mason and Earsden), and XIX (Alfonso Ferrabosco II).

27 *Ibid.*, 1st series, IV, 'Songs from Rosseter's *Booke of Ayres* (1601)'.

28 For a brief sketch of this French style, see *The New Oxford History of Music*, IV (1968), 29–31.

29 By Otto Gombosi, 'Some Musical Aspects of the English Court Masque', *Journal of the American Musicological Society* (1949), pp. 3–19. For a chronological list of masques extant in print, see *English Masques*, ed. Herbert A. Evans (1897), and §S–641; and for a general discussion of the masque: Enid Welsford, *The Court Masque* (Cambridge, 1927). Cf. §S–598.

30 Mary S. Steele, *Plays and Masques at Court during the Reigns of Elizabeth, James and Charles* (New Haven, 1926), p. 198. This annotated calendar gives a useful summary of the various dramatic entertainments for which music would have been needed.

31 *The English Lute-Songs*, 2nd series, XIX, 16; the texts of Jonson are in *The Complete Masques*, ed. Stephen Orgel (New Haven, 1969).

32 Compare, for instance, Campion's 'Move, now, with measured sound' (*Lord Hay's Masque*, 1607) with Ferrabosco's 'Gentle knights' (*Oberon*, 1611); in §S–641.

33 An admirably detailed account of every aspect of these three masques is in Murray Lefkowitz, *Trois Masques a la Cour de Charles Ier d'Angleterre* (Paris, 1970), together with scholarly editions of all the extant music.

34 In *Lovers made Men* and *Vision of Delight* (both 1617); §S–647: p. 46.

35 See *The New Oxford History of Music*, IV (1968), pp. 151–9; substantial extracts from writings by members of the Camerata are in Strunk (as above, note 23): see especially V. Galilei, *Dialogo . . . della musica antica e della moderna* (pp. 302–22) and Pietro Baldi's letter to G. B. Doni (pp. 363–6).

36 See §S–641: pp. 34–9, and *The English Lute-Songs*, 2nd series, XVI, 'Alfonso Ferrabosco: Ayres, 1609'.

37 McD. Emslie, 'Milton on Lawes; The Trinity MS Revisions', in §S–617: pp. 96–102.

38 See, for Lawes: 'English Songs, 1625–1660', ed. Ian Spink, *Musica Britannica*, XXXIII (1971), 61; for Dowland: *English School of Lutenist Song Writers*, ed. E. H. Fellowes (1920), p. 6.

39 Morley (as above, note 18), p. 292.

40 *Musica Britannica*, XXXIII (1971), 70 and 81.

41 For Lawes: *ibid.*, n. 80; for Porter: his *Madrigals and Ayres*, ed. D. Greer (facsimile: Menston, Yorks., 1969).

42 'The Tears or Lamentations of a Sorrowful Soul', ed. Cecil Hill, *Early English Church Music*, XI, 27, 107, 155 and 183; Pamela J. Willetts, 'The Musical Connections of Thomas Myriell', *Music and Letters*, XLIX (1968), 36–42.

43 *Aubrey's Brief Lives*, ed. Oliver L. Dick, 3rd ed. (1958), pp. 200–2. Aubrey claimed to be quoting the words of Milton's brother Christopher.

44 In the *Defensio Secunda*. For the more important musical passages in Milton's works, see §S–646: pp. 100–51; but in other respects this work is out of date.

PHILIPP P. FEHL

9

Poetry and the entry of the fine arts into England: ut pictura poesis

PREMISES: CASTIGLIONE ON ART

When Milton was young, Britain was teeming with the love of art. Never before had gentlemen been so encouraged to sponsor the arts, to try their hands at drawing, to travel in order to see works of art, to collect them, and to build magnanimously. Standards were set by the King and the first lords of the realm, most notable among whom (as a collector and patron) was Thomas Howard Earl of Arundel.

As with all love, the love of art is a passionate thing. It therefore readily succumbs to vice, notably luxury, pride and envy. To enemies of the King his love of art only demonstrated corruption; but, of course, the King and his court saw the matter differently. His pleasure in the arts was not only condoned as a royal prerogative but also extolled as a royal virtue. It advanced good government, elevated the manners of the nation, set the stage for the practice of noble living, and was the ornament of the State. The course of history proved that this interpretation was only flattery or wishful thinking, wrapped in the form of a compliment; but the fiction of the compliment was not idle and bears investigation. It is made of the very fabric of moral cogitation which justifies the love of art as a force in the improvement of mankind through the exercise of the imagination.

Poets in Milton's England had ample reason to claim the moral distinction of their art as a birthright. It was a given attribute of poetry, as classical antiquity taught by example and precept. To be in the living presence of their masters, writers had but to open the books that had been their steady companions from schooldays on; and, if they looked upon the works of the moderns, they were assured of the same truth with the same, or even greater, splendour in the English as in the Italian or the French tongue. We need but name Sir Philip

Sidney, both as a poet and, in the *Defence of Poesie*, as a critic, and Shakespeare to be touched by the justice of such a conviction.

The dignity of the visual arts, on the other hand, was a concept rather new to Britain even though certain elements of it were perceived from the early sixteenth century on and Holbein and Torrigiano (the sculptor of the tomb of Henry VII) were received in England with a welcome, and with salaries, befitting celebrities. Their works were cherished, and influenced local production to the extent that a craft was improved, above all in the production of reliable portraits. The practical in their art was separated from the grand and triumphed in good-natured complacency. In architecture too the fashions of the Continent, ever nursed by references to classical antiquity and the new productions in the Italian manner, were variously adapted in the building of stately and commodious homes, some of which (such as Knole) are still the joy of the English countryside. The wonder of these buildings, however, is not so much that they are works of art—though they are decorated artfully—as that they are rich and agreeable, relaxed in the profusion of their often classicising ornaments, and by and large sensible; country houses, literally, rather than palaces. They also have a dignity of their own, but it is not so much that of art as of good common sense; they do not fuss about art. '*Houses* are built to Liue in,' says Bacon in defence of this tradition when it was already threatened, 'and not to Looke on: Therefore let Vse bee preferred before Vniformitie; Except where both may be had. Leaue the Goodly Fabrickes of *Houses*, for Beautie only, to the *Enchanted Pallaces* of the *Poets*: Who build them with small Cost' ('Of Building', *Essayes*, 1625).

Characteristically, the first printed books on architecture in English were pattern books adapted from foreign sources which offered practical and fashionable Italianate designs for the use of the builder and not explanations of the art. It was, in essence, the master of the house who was its builder, and not his architect. Even Robert Peake's translation of Serlio (1611; §P–544) did not, by itself, effect a change. The book, which depends chiefly on its plates, does not really speak when it is consulted away from the environment in which the experience of architectural beauty is alive; and in the hand of the private builder it turns into but another pattern book.

But a better understanding and a progress to a nobler practice of the arts, in which beauty was served with a more reflective zeal than the pursuit of immediately practical ends and the mere heaping of ornament could afford, was waiting in the wings. Foreign example invited imitation. Moreover, the principles of the education of a gentleman predisposed an influential public of worthies and schoolmen towards a respectful concern for the cultivation of the visual arts, such as had been practised for well over two hundred years in Italy. With Sir Thomas Hoby's translation of Castiglione's *Courtier* (1561; §P–85), the worthiness of the subject was presented in England:

> I will talke of an other thing, whiche for that it is of importaunce (in my judgemente) I beleve our Courtyer ought in no wise to leave it out. And that is

the cunning in drawyng, and the knowledge in the very arte of peincting. And wonder ye not if I wish this feat in him, whiche now a dayes perhappes is counted an handycraft and ful litle to become a gentleman, for I remember I have read that the men of olde time, and especially in all Greece would have Gentlemens children in the schooles to apply peincting, as a matter both honest and necessary. (p. 81)

And in verye dede who so esteameth not this arte, is (to my seemyng) farre wyde from all reason: forsomuche as the engine of the worlde that we behoulde with a large sky, so bright with shining sterres, & in the middes, the earth environed with the Seas, severed in partes wyth Hylles, Dales, and Rivers, & so decked with suche diverse trees, beawtifull flowres and herbes, a man maye saye it to be a noble and a great peincting, drawen wyth the hande of nature & of God: the whych whoso can folow in myne opinion he is woorthye much commendacion. Neyther can a man atteyne to thys wythout the knoweledge of manye thinges, as he well knoweth that trieth it. Therefore had they of olde time in verye great estimation both the art and the artificers, so that it came to the toppe of all excellencye. And of this maye a man gather a sufficient argument at the autient ymages of marble and metall, whyche at thys daye are to be seene. And though peincting be a diverse matter from carving, yet do they both arise of one self fountayne (namelye) of a good patterne. And even as the ymages are divine & excellent, so it is to be thought peinctinges were also, & so much the more, for that they conteine in them a greater workemanshipp. (p. 82)[1]

A quality which Castiglione greatly treasures in a gentleman is *sprezzatura*, 'Reckelesnes' (as Hoby translates), or artful negligence:

. . . to cover art withall, and seeme whatsoever he doth and sayeth to do it wythout pain, and (as it were) not myndyng it. And of thys do I beleve grace is muche deryved, for in rare matters & wel brought to passe every man knoweth the hardnes of them, so that a redines therein maketh great wonder.
. . . . Therefore that may be said to be a very art that appeereth not to be art. (p. 49)

Castiglione develops his definition of *sprezzatura* with examples from music (where a certain surfeit of perfection 'engendereth urkesomnesse and betokenth a to curious harmonye') and from painting:

Behould ye then, answered the *Count*, that curiousnesse hurteth in thys as well as in other thynges. They say also that it hath bene a proverbe emonge some most excellent peincters of old time, that To muche diligence is hurtfull, & that Apelles found fault with Protogenes because he coulde not keepe his handes from the table [*tabula*, i.e. 'his picture']. (p. 51)

The example is taken from Pliny's *Natural History* (XXXV.80), where it is directly preceded by the account of Apelles's own estimate of the value of his work. Apelles, says Pliny, would speak with admiration of the work of other great painters who were his contemporaries, 'praising every beauty [*venustas*] and yet observing that they failed in that grace [*Venus*] called Charis in Greek, which was distinctly his own; everything else they had attained, but in this alone none equalled him'.[2] Apelles's criticism of Protogenes, when it is seen in regard to his conception of grace, suggests a moral definition of beauty. Ceaseless application betrays the illiberality of the practitioner who may indeed produce a work of many beauties but his very insistence on the perfection of his picture prevents it from becoming perfect. Grace is the charm of beauty which joins it to the life of the soul. It escapes measurement and lives in freedom only.

The truly perfect courtier, the gentleman whose grace is a natural attribute of his wisdom, Castiglione advisedly shows us only at the end of his book when Pietro Bembo gives his inspired oration in praise of perfect love. Here we no longer 'appreciate' perfection, we are touched by it, as is the speaker himself, to the point almost of being transported into the better world of which he sings. Seeming and being now are united. The true artist, then—to return to our discussion of art at its noblest—must have within himself just that perfection which, in *The Courtier*, distinguishes Bembo. Renaissance art theory points out with conviction that in the modern age such a joining of the artist and gentleman was achieved in the art and life of Raphael and with pride and sorrow quotes the epitaph which the very same Bembo composed upon the untimely death of Raphael in 1520. The epitaph pays tribute to his 'almost-breathing likenesses [which] if thou beholdest, thou shalt straightway see Nature and Art in league', concluding:

> This is that Raphael, by whom in life
> Our mighty mother Nature fear'd defeat;
> And in whose death did fear herself to die.
> (Vasari, *Lives*, trans. George Bull, p. 323)

It is from an appreciation of such a view of the artist's calling that Popes and princes came to bestow knighthoods on artists whom they considered excellent. In England it took a long time before this occurred: not until Charles I dubbed Rubens a knight in 1630; and even then, to avoid scandal, the King employed a subterfuge. Rubens was knighted not for his art but for his excellence as a diplomat, i.e., a courtier. Two years later, however, the King knighted van Dyck, who was not a diplomat, simply for being van Dyck the artist.

THEORY: LOMAZZO AND HAYDOCKE

The first and, for a long time, the only book on the theory of art in English was Richard Haydocke's translation of a complex work by the Milanese painter Gian Paolo Lomazzo, *A Tracte Containing the Artes of curious Paintinge Caruing Building* (1598).[3] Haydocke, a student of medicine at Oxford, had an amateur's interest in the arts. He had travelled on the Continent and he dabbled in painting and engraving and occasional poetry. He was altogether smitten with Lomazzo's book, which, like a *summa* of knowledge in the field, is built on earlier Italian treatises, notably Leone Battista Alberti's books on architecture, painting and sculpture; Vasari's *Lives*; and the (unpublished) notebooks of Leonardo da Vinci. Lomazzo suffered the misfortune of becoming blind in his thirty-third year. His fame rests on his writing. Haydocke wished to bring the knowledge of this rare book not only to a few but 'to have divulged it to all. Wherefore intending a common good: I have taught a good Italian to speake a bad english phrase, yet such a one as I hope shall not bee offensive to the learned, and beneficiall I am sure to the ignorant.'

Lomazzo was a passionate academician. He attempted to produce a book which would contain 'the whole perfection of painting', a systematic survey of the theory to guide and elevate the practice of the painter, to instruct the layman, and to show the interrelation of all the visual arts (including architecture) and their dependence on the art of drawing (*disegno*). Drawing, in the sense in which it is used here, not only denotes accuracy in the rendition of visual likeness but also the exercise of the designing, measuring and organising faculty of the mind. It controls the imagination and overcomes the limitations of the artists' materials; it is the chief ornament—and the principal tool—of the educated painter.

The work is divided into seven books. The first, appropriately in keeping with Lomazzo's high design, concerns itself with *Proportion*, that most important branch of all the arts which connects them with order, measurement and the interrelation of parts and the whole. It is, one might say, the heart of *disegno*. In a stirring chapter, 'Vertue and praise of Proportion', Lomazzo sums up the advantages of intellectual charm and moral beauty which are bestowed on a painting that observes the rules of proportion:

> Now the effectes proceeding from *proportion* are vnspeakeable: the principall whereof, is that *maiestie and beautie*, which is founde in bodies, called by *Vitruvius, Eurithmia*. And hence it is, that when we beholde a well proportioned thing, wee call it *beautifull*; as if wee shoulde saie, indued with that exact and comely grace, whereby all the perfection of sweete delightes belonging to the sight, are communicated to the eye, and so conueyed to the vnderstanding.
>
> But if we shall enter into a farther consideration of this beauty, it wil appeare most euidently, in things appertaining to Ciuile discipline. For it is strange to consider, what effects of *piety, reuerence*, and *religion*, are stirred vp in mens mindes, by meanes of this sutable comelinesse of apte proportion.

Like his predecessors, Lomazzo constantly refers to the authority of the writers of classical antiquity, above all to Vitruvius, whose *De architectura*—as interpreted in the light of Alberti's *Ten Books on Architecture*—is also a guide to the moral significance of art, and to Pliny the Elder's *Natural History*, our chief documentary source on the lives and works of the Greek and Roman artists. Pliny's accounts in turn abound with rather dryly told anecdotes that often point a moral lesson or demonstrate the high regard accorded in classical antiquity to artists and their works.

Lomazzo's 'first booke of Proportion' talks not only of the various proportions of humans (we are led from 'proportion of a tall mans body of 10 faces' to

'Proportion of a childe of 4 faces') but also of horses 'before and behind'. Then we come to the Proportions of the orders of architecture and, eventually, to a chapter on 'How the measures of Ships, Temples, Buildings and other thinges are drawn from mans body' which explores (darkly) the harmonic relation that, in a state of perfection, should govern man and man-made things. In the last chapter Lomazzo speaks 'Of the power of proportion, and how by the helpe thereof the greatnesse of the Colossi might be wrought'. The point of this seemingly disproportionate conclusion is that optical distortions in tall statuary should be compensated for so that the effect of the work will be natural and its beauty perfect: the seeming of art is the source of its truth.

The second book, 'of Motion', discusses the representation of action and the emotions or 'passions of the minde'. As in life so in art the life of the soul is expressed in motion. This leads us directly to the contemplation of the painter's noblest task in the hierarchy of genres: history painting—the representation of actions that are grand, memorable and instructive. What Lomazzo means becomes, perhaps, as self-evident to us as it was to him when we listen to his praise of a great work of art:

> Whereof amongst all other of his [Leonardo da Vinci's] works, that admirable last supper of *Christ* in *Refect: S. Maria de Gratia* in *Milane*, maketh most euident proofe, in which he hath so liuely expressed, the passions of the Apostles mindes in their countenances, and the rest of their body, that a man may boldly say: the truth was nothing superiour to his representation: and neede not be afraide, to reckon it amongst the best workes of *Oyle-painting*; (of which kinde of painting Iohn de Bruges was the first inuentor.) For in those Apostles, you might distinctly perceiue admiration, feare, griefe, suspition, loue, &c: all which were sometimes to be seene together in one of them; and finally in Iudas a treason-plotting countenance, as it were the very true counterfeit of a Traitor. So that therein, he hath left a sufficient argument, of his rare perfection, in the true vnderstanding of the passions of the minde, exemplified outwardly in the bodie.

Lomazzo rehearses the various 'passions' in a number of chapters which show how learned in psychology the painter must become through observation. His guides are the poets who paint pictures with words:

> Sadnesse (differing very little from Melancholy) cannot (in my iudgement) be better described, then as *Ariosto* doth it in *Angelica Cant. 8.* saying:

> > Heere shee remaining helpelesse and alone,
> > Amonge the fruitlesse trees and senslesse rockes,
> > Standing her selfe all like a marble stone,
> > Saue that sometimes shee tare her golden lockes,
> > At last her eies to teares, her tongue to mone
> > Shee doth resolue, her faire white brest shee knockes,
> >   Blaming the God of heaven, and powre devine,
> >   That did the Fates vnto her fall incline.

> > > > > > (*Orlando Furioso*, VIII.30.1–8)

The third and fourth books talk of colour, light and shadows, that is, of the fundamentals of seeing and the resources of the painter's art for representing nature truthfully, even to the point of deceiving the eyes of men as well as beasts. Birds pecked at the grapes painted by Zeuxis, and 'Andreas Mantegna of our time deluded his maister with a *flie*, which he had drawne uppon the eielid of a Lyon'. The discussion is concerned in some detail with the theory of vision and then goes on to its practical application in painting, book four reinforcing and amplifying what has been said in book three. 'Light hath so great force in pictures, that (in my judgment) therein consisteth the whole grace thereof, if it be wel vnderstood; and contrariwise, the disgrace if it be not perceived.' He finds beautiful words for the effect upon the heart that Correggio or Titian can produce by the painting of light, that of the sun and of the heavens and on clouds, and of darknesses illuminated by fire.

The fifth book, which ends the theoretical instruction of Lomazzo, considers perspective, the most mathematical branch of the art which unites it unequivocally with the world of philosphical truth. Lomazzo takes care, however, to point out that the painter must make allowances for the beauty of figures which perspective, when employed too rigorously, will distort:

> . . . although the Images stand neere the eie, yet we must not wholly obserue the naturall, but wee must regard the grace of the figure; And that proportion which is most decent to the eye must bee followed, as *Raphael* and all other good workemen vsed in all their workes, wherein we shall find feete in pictures something too little, and legges longer then the life.

Haydocke gives us the titles of the last two books—'Of practice' and 'Of History'—and their chapter headings but he does not include them in his translation. It was more important to him that the theoretical part of the book reach the public speedily. Should the volume receive a friendly welcome, he promises to add the missing books as well as a catalogue of artists, both ancient and modern, which would include the lives of the British artists. However, this continuation never appeared.

A look at the title page of Haydocke's translation will show us some of his strengths and his limitations. (Plate 1). He invented, drew and engraved the title page himself. It is clearly the work of an amateur. The proportions of the two goddesses on the top of the page are, however, so unnatural that we must attribute them to a mistaken application of precept rather than to the artist's relative inexperience in drawing. They reflect Lomazzo's teaching regarding the height of the statues of gods[4]—but what in statues makes great figures appear taller, in miniature only makes them look uncannily thin. The *disegno* of the page is a mere symmetry of forms; two axes intersect and in their centre hold a shield. All other units are accommodated in the cubby-holes thus carved out from the page; and each hole is neatly bordered by a rather heavy pattern of scrollwork. The pictures themselves, however, tell a story, a lesson regarding the purpose and the greatness of art—even if that lesson is contradicted in the attempt to demonstrate it through art. In fairness to Haydocke (who never claimed the status of an artist), let us look at his invention rather than his execution.

Above the central shield is the portrait of Lomazzo taken from the title page of the Italian text;[5] and, below it, the matching portrait of Haydocke, possibly after a miniature by Hilliard and certainly in his manner. Author and translator thus are on the same axis about which the picture story is arranged. The two goddesses above are patrons of the art of painting. Juno, with her eye-topped sceptre and her peacock, represents air, colour and vision but also justice and cognition. Minerva represents wisdom; the dragon by her side is in fact the serpent which Phidias placed next to his statue of the Athena Parthenos. In her left hand she holds a cloth, the tapestry she wove in her contest with Arachne; and behind her we see spiders and spiders' webs, signs of Arachne's transformation for daring to challenge the goddess with her art. The elegantly woven web on the right may be an allusion to the art of *disegno*.

The two coats of arms which mark the horizontal axis of the page are, respectively, that of Oxford University and of St Mary College (New College), of which Haydocke was a fellow. In the niches below we see, on the left, Prometheus and, on the right, Daedalus, both shown in their capacity as artists. Prometheus, according to Lomazzo (who cites St Augustine and Eusebius as his authorities), was the first to make statues of men in clay; and by certain arts he made them move as if they were alive. Haydocke shows just that. Prometheus has stolen the fire from the gods and preserved it in a hollow reed. He now blows it towards his 'golem' figures and makes them move. He is, indeed, the first sculptor, but he has also abused his art. Above him, we see the punishment the gods send to men: Pandora approaching with her covered chalice (or 'box'), and that meted out to Prometheus who, in the lower right, is shown chained in Tartarus, the eagle feeding on his liver. Daedalus is shown as the architect of the Labyrinth and the sculptor of the cow he made for Pasiphae to enter so that she could receive the bull whose love she craved. His punishment is indicated above him. His son Icarus, for whom he had invented wings, did not steer a just middle course but flew too high, too close to the sun. He now falls from the sky.

Both arch-artists have done stupendous deeds with their art; but they also have been presumptuous and heedless of the gods. Haydocke shows us the range both of art and of its abuse. The motto from Ecclesiastes which he places at the bottom of his title inscription reads: 'In the handes of the skilfull shall the worke be approved'. This refers not only to the work of Lomazzo and the value of his own translation, but to the worth of art altogether. The gods above—in his pictorial language, Juno and Minerva; in his sense, God himself—shall be the judges and the guides of artists and of art. Without regard for the gods, the imagination leads us to devise extravagant and shameful acts; under them our works become godlike themselves.

Haydocke's art, then, if we will view it once more, does not exemplify what Lomazzo teaches or means to teach; but, such as words translated into pictures can do it, praises it. Characteristically we can comprehend his praise better when we retranslate it into words.

DIFFUSION: HENRY PEACHAM

As the seventeenth century progressed, it became a commonplace in tracts on manners and polite education—all of which descend from Castiglione's *Courtier*—to endorse the practice of drawing and the study of the visual arts as at once noble and useful accomplishments in the life of a gentleman. The most far-reaching and perhaps most amiable of these didactic works is Henry Peacham's *The Compleat Gentleman* (1622). Peacham writes at the court of the art-loving Earl of Arundel (the book is dedicated to one of Arundel's grandsons whose tutor Peacham had been) and in full view of Arundel's great collections. In 1634 Peacham added a new chapter 'Of Antiquities' to his book. In it we find a graphic description of the Earl's activity as a collector:

> And here I cannot but with much reverence, mention the every way Right Honourable *Thomas Howard* Lord high Marshall of *England*, as great for his noble Patronage of Arts and ancient learning, as for his birth and place. To whose liberall charges and magnificence, this angle of the world oweth the first sight of Greeke and Romane Statues, with whose admired presence he began to honour the Gardens and Galleries of Arundel-House about twentie yeeres agoe, and hath ever since continued to transplant old Greece into *England*.
>
> (*The Compleat Gentleman*, 1634, p. 107)

Other chapters which pertain to our study are 'Of Drawing and Painting in Oyle' and 'Of Travaile'. Both, as is the whole book, are full of good advice. The chapter on drawing and painting also contains hints of elementary instruction in the practice of the arts (Peacham was himself an amateur) and, in the form of anecdotes, in the history of Renaissance art. Peacham makes a point of telling us that he was unable to consult Vasari's *Lives*, 'which I have not seene, as being hard to come by: yet in the Libraries of two my especiall and worthy friends, M. Doctor *Mountford*, the late Prebend of *Pauls* and M. *Inigo Iones*, Surveyer of his Majesties workes for building and *Calvin* [i.e. Carel van] *Mander* in high *Dutch*, unto whom I am beholden, for the greater part what I have here written, of some of their lives' (p. 154).

But with all his proximity to Inigo Jones and the Earl of Arundel and the charm of his anecdotes of the lives of the painters, Peacham's work only shows a mechanical appreciation of the fine arts. The chapter 'Of Drawing and Painting in Oyle' is followed by two on armorial devices. They, more than anything, in Peacham's view, demonstrate the usefulness of painting to a nobleman.[6] Let us sum up with an earlier brave exhortation Peacham addresses to noblemen in doubt about the honour of painting. It is, he says, 'no more disgrace to a Lord to draw a fair picture then to cut his Hawk's meat, or play footeball with his men' (§ P–539: p. 3).

SCHOLARSHIP: FRANCISCUS JUNIUS

Altogether different, unique and resplendent in a noble learning, is the work of the Dutch humanist Franciscus Junius the Younger, *De pictura veterum*.[7] Junius, who spent the best years of his life in England, was the librarian of the Earl of Arundel (who was as great a collector of books and manuscripts as of works of art) and, intermittently, the tutor of his sons and grandsons.

The Earl had begun about 1614 to bring works of Greek and Roman sculpture, inscriptions as well as statuary, to England. Not content with what he could buy on the market or excavate in Rome, he also sent agents to Turkey to negotiate purchases on a large scale and to excavate in the Levant, an enterprise as impressive for its daring as in its results. Remnants of the collection still exist and testify to the grandeur and the comprehensive nature of Arundel's taste.[8]

Like every responsible collector of antiquities, the Earl longed to study and identify the works in his possession in the light of ancient literature. He therefore commissioned Junius to identify, review and put in order all pertinent texts. The project, which would intimidate even a computer-equipped modern research team, did not daunt Junius, whose patience and good nature matched his vast erudition. He soon realised that his material tended towards two *foci* of collecting, one which illuminated the theory of art in classical antiquity and the other the lives and works of the ancient artists. In short, he had two books to prepare, instead of the one the Earl had commissioned.

The book on theory, which is the exposition of an idea, had to be persuasive but not exhaustive in its documentation. Junius therefore relatively soon considered it ready for publication. This is the *De pictura veterum* of 1637 (printed in Rotterdam). He continued, however, to enlarge the book with notes and additions throughout his long life as he went about completing the second work. The latter, by the nature of its purpose, required the greatest possible completeness. It was published posthumously in Rotterdam in 1694, together with a new edition of *De pictura veterum*. The title of the work perfectly defines its contents: *A Lexicon of Architects and Engineers, but especially of Painters, Sculptors, Engravers, Turners and other Artists, and of their works, culled from the Sources of Ancient Literature*.[9] It is the first and, as far as literary sources are concerned, the most comprehensive dictionary of the lives and works of the artists of the ancient world (including the artists mentioned in the Bible). Even though it was not published until the end of the century, the ever-growing manuscript must have been a steady source of reference for the Arundel household and other users of the Earl's library.

De pictura veterum dealt not only with what art once was but what it ought to be; and it spoke to its audience in the language of antiquity. *Pictura*, we must remember, is not only painting but altogether the art of representation and expression, in sculpture as well as in painting and drawing. It is axiomatic for Junius that poetry, oratory and *pictura* all serve the same ends, the instruction and the delectation of the audience.

From countless Greek and Latin fragments Junius pieced together a huge mosaic of quotations that, seen as a whole, returns to us in the language of the ancients their lost theory of art. It is presented in three books or orations:

I. On the origins and the nature of *pictura*.

II. On the causes which advance or arrest the arts and their progress.
III. On the perfection of the fine arts.

Junius achieves in these orations a coherence of language which speaks as a thousand voices in one, just as the knowledge of art in classical antiquity is a concord of many discussions, conflicts and laws forming one grand whole. This body of true knowledge, Junius believes, can best be comprehended under the guiding light of revelation, just as the study of scripture may profit from the wisdom to be gleaned from classical texts. Thus, for Junius, Greek, Latin and even Hebrew words may be joined in a common etymology if there is a common meaning, the parallel words jointly expounding the significance of each.

The most cogent and enlightening sources cited by Junius are only marginally taken from what strictly constitutes literature of the visual arts. All art, to the Renaissance reader and—as Junius shows repeatedly—to the classical reader as well, was one. Junius took an acknowledged and constructive liberty with his sources. When it suits the occasion he lets writers on oratory or poetry speak as if they were talking about *pictura*. In his eyes this is not a distortion, but a form of documentation, the quotation being comprehended by its meaning rather than by its specific application.

Junius's book, then, is as much a theory of poetry and rhetoric as it is of the visual arts. Particularly, he dwells on the power of the imagination, its importance in the creation of works of art, and the need to manage it by reason and decorum. He was, in fact, the first among the moderns who wrote on art to speak of Longinus's *On the Sublime* with considered emphasis.

In 1638 Junius brought out an English version of *De pictura veterum*: 'The PAINTING OF THE ANCIENTS in Three Bookes Declaring by Historicall Observations and Examples, The BEGINNING PROGRESSE AND CONSVMMATION OF that most Noble Art. And how those ancient ARTIFICERS attained to their still so much admired Excellencie' (§P–535). The translation is also to some extent a revision. It is dedicated to the Countess of Arundel and designed to serve the amateur and the artist, rather than the scholar. Some new elements of learning are added, others are dropped, and the argument is tightened. In a significant change, when Junius speaks of grace, a quotation from a modern, English poet replaces one by Martial in the Latin edition, aptly illustrating the point and seeming to merge modern with classical literature. 'A certain grace' pulls all the other elements together and gives the work its life through an ease of representation, 'a sweet concent' which is the very breath of beauty in art:

> Like divers flowers whose divers beauties serve
> To deck the earth with his well-coloured weed,
> Though each of them his privat form preserve
> Yet joyning forms, one sight of beauty breed.
> > (Sidney, *Arcadia*, III, Pamela's song to Musidorus)

We may wonder, did Milton read *De pictura veterum*? He may have been acquainted with the author (§S–709: p. 60); the book would make perfect literature for a Latinist preparing to visit Italy, and it appeared just in time to be readily available. There is no record showing that he did, but a sheet of notes possibly by Milton, entitled 'Of Statues of Antiquities' (CE, XVIII, 258–61), which lists in some detail how one goes about buying and judging antiquities, reads as if he had received advice from one of Arundel's agents. But whether Milton read Junius or not is not really very important. Junius's work is as much a *summa* of poetical as of artistic theory. The terms, as we have seen, are often interchangeable. Milton already possessed this theory in the very life of his art and used it not just for the sake of ordering his poetry but for viewing the world. Poetry and the study of nature and history coincide, whether the medium by which we explore, consider and represent our experience be words that make us see or images that speak.

For those of us who are trying to find Milton, however, the work of Junius is of great importance, for he teaches us to read the ancient sources (from which Milton drew his knowledge of poetry) generously and hopefully. If we follow Junius we shall see, better than in any other work, that the study of poetry and the fine arts is one and that classical antiquity leads the way.[10]

PARTICIPATION: SIR HENRY WOTTON

THE ELEMENTS OF ARCHITECTURE, *Collected by* HENRY WOTTON *Knight, from the best Authors and Examples* (§P–545) first appeared in 1624, thirteen years before Junius's De pictura veterum. We present it at the end of our discussion of theory because the book takes us directly to Italy and into the realm of practice. It is magisterial, short, written *con brio* and in the spirit and the life of *sprezzatura*; the work of a diplomat and poet who lived for many years as King James I's ambassador in Venice, the home of Palladian building and the art of Titian, Veronese and Tintoretto. Among his friends were Sir Francis Bacon, Isaac Casaubon and Izaac Walton, to whom we owe one of the most touching memorials of friendship, the *Reliquiae Wottonianae* (§P–685).[11] His life straddles the generations into which we so neatly like to divide history. Wotton's eldest brother, Sir Edward Wotton, was a friend of Sir Philip Sidney, who mentions him in the very beginning of his *Defence of Poesie*. Wotton, as did Sidney, knew Junius's father. He met him when he stayed in Heidelberg, in 1589, and henceforth, as he put it, 'held his acquaintance dear'. As Wotton's life was drawing to a close, young Milton, who was getting ready for his Italian journey, called on Wotton and then sent a copy of *Comus*, declaring himself the author of the still anonymous work. Wotton, the first great man so to encourage the poet, responded to the gift with unstinting praise:

> Wherein I should much commend the Tragical part, if the Lyrical did not ravish me with a certain Dorique delicacy in your Songs and Odes, where unto I must plainly confess to have seen yet nothing parallel in our Language, *ipsa mollities* ['tenderness itself'].
>
> (CE, I, 476)

He also gives him good advice on his journey and especially on how to behave in Rome without incurring danger and yet not to compromise his religion: ' "*i pensieri stretti e il viso sciolto*" [i.e. 'Your thoughts close and your countenance loose'] will go safely over the whole world'.

No one at court knew Italy and its art better than Sir Henry Wotton. He was himself a collector of art, and a purchaser for others, especially for the Duke of Buckingham, who was assembling a gallery of great paintings in rivalry with the Earl of Arundel. Wotton's taste was altogether free from affectation. He delights as much in the naturalism of art as in the grand style; in fact he sees no conflict between the two: correctness is a matter of emphasis and decorum, a choice of the right style in the right place. Consider the tomb of Sir Francis Bacon in the choir of St Michael's church at St Albans, for which Wotton composed the epitaph (Plate 2). Bacon sits in a chair, clad in modern dress, ruffles, buttons and all. The arm of the statue is propped on the arm-rest of the chair; his head gently reclines into his opened palm; '*Sic sedebat,*' so he used to sit, says the principal inscription on the tomb. The text is in Latin, and the sculpture in its plain portrait likeness is Roman. But a Roman dress for Bacon would not have been Roman at all, rather an estrangement from the very *romanitas* that Bacon himself perfected, through Christ and in the travails of his own time.[12]

Wotton well remembered the pose of Bacon's monument. There survives at Eton College, where he spent the last years of his life as provost of the school, a portrait painting of himself, his elbow resting on a table, his lower arm reaching up, and his head in a thinking pose, propped against his hand. Wotton looks straight at us; the word PHILOSOPHEMVR is inscribed next to his head. 'Let us philosophise,' or, equally, 'Let us love wisdom together,' is the exhortation to his Etonians which is also his memorial. Wotton left to each of the fellows 'a plain ring of gold enamelled black, all save the verge, with this Motto within, *Amor vincit omnia*'.[13] The conceit is a visual one. Even though, on the outside, the rings were black, the letters on the inside (which were cut through the enamel) shone brightly in imperishable gold. Love conquers Death and turns sorrow to joy.

Wotton's love of art, joined— as in *The Courtier*—to the art of leading a good life, shows itself in sudden flashes in his poems and letters, in apophthegms, and in anecdotes about him. *The Elements of Architecture* is a polite essay, not a treatise. Though it gives advice, it offers no precepts; there are no illustrations, nor are we badgered with measurements. That is but the mechanical part of the art. Wotton acknowledges its importance, but this is not what the book is about. He expounds the art of architecture, not its tricks.

The preface begins with a declaration of independence from pedantry and apologetics: 'For *Architecture* can want no commendation, where there are *Noble Men* or *Noble* minds, I will therefore spend this *Preface*, rather about those, from whom I have gathered my knowledge. For I am but a gatherer and disposer of other mens stuffe at my best value.' Wotton names Vitruvius, 'Our principall *Master*', and some of his expounders: Alberti, Philandrier, Rivius, and—in the text proper—Philibert de l'Orme, Vignola, Daniele Barbaro and Palladio. Wotton's master among these is unquestionably Palladio. In fact, *The Elements* is to some extent a musing paraphrase and commentary on the first two books of Palladio's *I quattro libri dell' architettura*.

There are two ways, Wotton says, by which he could have treated of the art of building. Historically, by a presentation of examples—but that was 'performed already in good part, by *Giorgio Vassari* in the lives of *Architects*'—or logically, 'by casting the *rules* and cautions of the Art, into some comportable *Methode*'. He chose the latter as the soundest, for '*rules* should precead, that we may by them, be made to judge of *examples*'.

'Well building hath three Conditions. *Commoditie, Firmenes*, and *Delight*.' So begins Wotton's text (as does the first chapter of Palladio) in agreement with Alberti's clear focus on three terms offered by Vitruvius: *firmitas, utilitas, venustas*. Alberti's *De re aedificatoria* is arranged in three parts, in accordance with these principles: *firmitas* for the soundness of structure, *utilitas* for function, and *venustas* for ornament. Wotton, loosely, follows suit, all along stressing appropriateness in the work, the sense of natural correspondences. He refers us to the human body, handiwork of 'the *High Architect*', to exemplify his primary maxim, 'the *place* of every part is to be determined by the Vse'.

Among his 'chambers of *Delight*' Wotton includes the *Pinacothecia*—a term found in Vitruvius—'by which he intendeth (if I may guess at his Greeke, as wee must doe often euen at his Latine) certain *Repositories* for workes of rarity in Picture or other Arts, by the Italians called *Studioli*'. They should face north, for 'at any other Quarter, where the course of the *Sunne* doth diversifie the *Shadowes*, [they] would loose much of their grace'. By no means, however, should we follow antique precedent or prescription blindly. We must consider 'the nature of the *Region*: Euery Nation, being tyed aboue al Rules whatsoever, to a discretion, of prouiding against their owne *Inconueniences*. And therefore a good *Parler* in Aegypt would perchance make a good *Celler* in England' (pp. 9–10).

Having instructed us in the choice of the site of a building and the placement of its parts on the site ('The *Seate*'), he proceeds to the building itself, 'the *Worke*'. There is first 'the Preparation of the *Materials*', which is the mechanical part of the art of building, and 'the Disposition which is the *Forme*'. The former is the work of artisans, who should be overseen by a second superintendent of the work. The latter is the task of the architect proper, 'whose glory doth more consist, in the *Designement* and *Idea* of the whole *Worke*, and his truest ambition should be to make the *Forme*, which is the nobler Part (as it were) triumph over the *Matter*'. The interior of the church of Santa Giustina in Padua, for example, cannot boast of any material splendour or decoration 'being but ordinarie stone, without any garnishment of sculpture', but its art 'doe yet ravish the Beholder, (and hee knowes not how) by a secrete *Harmony* in the Proportions'.[14]

For houses it is best to choose a rectangular plan 'prouided that the Length doe not exceede the *Latitude* aboue one third part, which would diminish the beauty of the *Aspect*'. Insistence on the one produces dullness, on the other, extravagance. 'Enormous heights of six or seuen Stories, as well as irregular

Formes, and the contrary fault of low-distended *Fronts,* is Vnseemely.' Extremes must be avoided. 'And so much for the generall *Figuration,* or *Aspect of the Worke'* (p. 22).

And now, following Alberti, Wotton moves to the act of building itself, from the foundation to the roof. 'As I passe along, I will touch also the naturall Reasons of *Art,* that my discourse may be the lesse *Mechanicall.'* Wotton keeps his word; his opportunity comes when he speaks of columns. He names 'fiue *Orders* of *Pillers',* and no more. One of them, the *'Compound Order',* he dismisses as 'nothing in effect, but a *Medlie,* or an *Amasse* of all the precedent *Ornaments,* making a new kinde by stealth, and though the most richly tricked, yet the poorest in this, that he is a borrower of all his *Beautie'* (p. 38).

His argument, like that of all other writers on the orders, is moral. It is Vitruvius's gift to the understanding of classical architecture. Wotton, the amateur, however, is more outspoken on the subject and much more critical of the Compound Order than the architect-writers who as a rule content them-selves with drawings but few words on this difficult subject. He addresses himself to the sense of the system of orders, not its laws and by-laws. This, then, is the constitution of the orders—one might almost say their character. 'First therefore the *Tuscan* is a plain, massie, rurall Pillar, resembling some sturdy well-limmed Labourer, homely clad, in which kinde of comparisons *Vitruvius* himselfe seemeth to take pleasure' (p. 33).

Wotton gives us, as he will in all the other instances, the distinctive symmetry of the order, its relation of diameter to height, the appropriate distance between the columns and the *'Architraues, Frizes,* and *Cornices,* as they are vsually handled'. The Tuscan order 'is of all the rudest Pillar, and his principall Character *Simplicity'.* The Doric, the gravest of the orders, has a *'Masculine Aspect,* and [is] a little trimmer than the *Tuscan* that went before, saue a sober garnishment now and then . . .' By contrast 'The *Ionique Order* doth represent a kinde of Feminine slendernesse, yet saith *Vitruvius,* not like a light Housewife, but in a decent dressing, hath much of the Matrone'. These three orders—the simple, the grave, the decent—are, Wotton maintains, Vitruvius's 'best *Charac-ters'.* The Corinthian column, however, is seductive, 'laciuiously decked like a Curtezane'. Even though dangerous, the order still is deserving of praise: 'As *Plainesse* did Characterize the *Tuscan,* so must *Delicacie* and *Varietie* the *Corinthian Pillar,* besides hight of his Ranke' (p. 38).

He now offers 'Cautions', in which again he follows Palladio, with an interesting aside concerning the relations of fact and fiction in architecture. Englishmen might feel they cannot build in the classical style because marble is too costly in England. It is not the marble that matters but the spirit of the work. Wotton refers us to Palladio's Corinthian atrium in the convent of the Carità (now the Academy) in Venice (Plate 3):

> Then which, mine Eye, hath neuer yet beheld any *Columnes,* more stately of Stone or Marble. For the Bricks, hauing first beene formed in a *Circular Mould,* and then cut before their burning into foure quarters or more, the sides

afterwards ioyne so closely, and the points concenter so exactly, that the *Pillars* appeare one *entire Peece*, which short description I could not omit, that thereby may appeare, how in truth wee want rather *Art* than stuffe, to satisfie our greatest *Fancies*.[15]

After columns, Wotton considers pilasters and the articulation of walls, then arches and vaults, and lastly *'Appertions'* or *'Ouertures'*, that is, doors and windows, staircases, chimneys and pipes (for heat and sewage). *'Ouertures'* allow Wotton once more to speak of what is dearest to him, proportion, or a musical harmony in building. Again he stresses that this is not just a matter of measurement but of a justice which regards function, propriety and decorum: '. . . we must take heede not to make a House (though but for ciuill vse) all *Eyes*, like *Argus*: which in Northerne *Climes* would be too could, In *Southerne*, too hot: And therefore the matter indeede imparteth more than a merry comparison' (p. 56).

We proceed to *Compartition*, 'the art of a *gracefull* and *vsefull* distribution, of the whole *Ground plot* both for roomes of *Office*, and of *Reception* or *Entertainement*, as farre as the *Capacity* thereof, and the nature of the *Countrey* will comport'. Again, there are no absolute rules; Wotton deliberately qualifies. In so far as he gives a rule, it is an allegory: *'Gracefulnesse* . . . will consist in double *Analogie* or coorespondencie,' a suiting of both parts to the whole and part to part.

'Vsefulnesse' is introduced next to underline the concord between what is true, good, natural and beautiful, if we will but be practical in a high-minded manner. *'Vsefulnesse* which will consist in a sufficient *Number* of Roomes, of all sorts, and in their apt *Coherence*, without *distraction*, without *confusion*, so as the beholder may not onely call it, *Vna Fabrica ben raccolta*: as *Italians* vse to speake of well vnited *Workes*, but likewise that it may appeare *airie* and *spiritous*, and fit for the welcome of cheerfull Guests' (p. 68).

Part II of Wotton's book is much shorter, but brings us to a discussion of painting and sculpture, that is, *'Ornaments* within, or without the *Fabrique'*. It begins by defining the English country house in relation to truth of character:

Every Mans proper *Mansion* House and *Home*, being the *Theater* of his *Hospitality*, the *Seate* of *Selfe-fruition*, the *Comfortablest part* of his own *Life*, the *Noblest* of his Sonnes *Inheritance*, A kind of priuate *Princedome*; Nay, to the *Possessors* thereof, an *Epitomie* of the whole *World*: may well deserue by these *Attributes*, according to the degree of the *Master*, to be *decently* and *delightfully* adorned. (p. 82)

Wotton wants to teach no more than this. He links domestic architecture to our sense of liberty and decorum, and even to the ordering of the universe. What there is to be said about the other genres of architecture—churches, public buildings, city planning—will follow from understanding the nobility of the home.

Painting and sculpture are 'two *Arts* attending on *Architecture*' to *'dresse* and *trimme* their *Mistresse'*. Wotton compares the two, in the tradition of the *paragone*, the contest between the two arts which arrives at a better understanding of each. And indeed 'wee haue a *Rule* somewhere (I well remember) in *Pliny*, and it is a prettie obseruation: that they doe mutually helpe to censure one another'. Painting is best when it gives the illusion of three-dimensional reality 'as if it were carued', and sculpture, conversely, 'when it appeareth so *tender*, as if it were *painted*'. The comparison reminds us of Horace's *ut pictura poesis* as we have met it in Junius: *pictura* and *poesia* are one; and sculpture is *pictura* as much as is painting.

How does one judge of a 'Piece of *Art*?' Italians have three categories to describe the excellence of works of art. It could be made '*Con Diligenza, Con Studio*, and *Con Amore*'. The progression is in the spirit of Castiglione's *Courtier*. '*Con Amore*', Wotton qualifies, is not with love 'to the *Bespeaker* of the *Worke* but with a loue and delight in the *Worke* it selfe, vpon some speciall *Fancie* to this or that *Storie*'. Thus we turn to the praise of history painting, and to the question of what matters in the rendering of a picture.

'In well *Designing*, there must bee *Truth* and *Grace*, in well *Colouring*, *Force* and *Affection*; all other *Praises*, are but Consequences of these.' *Affection* is defined as 'the *Liuely Representment* of any *passion* whatsoeuer, as if the *Figures* stood not vpon a *Cloth* or *Boorde*, but as if they were acting vpon a *Stage*'. So great is the subtlety of representation that 'the least touch of a *Pensill* will translate a *Crying*, into a *Laughing* Face'. Psychological complexity of this order makes painting poetry's equal: 'This coincidence of extreame affections I obserue represented by *Homer*, in the person of *Hector's* wife, as Painters and Poets haue alwaies had a kinde of Congenialitie.' He quotes and translates *Iliad*, VI, 483–4, 'She tooke her childe into her fragrant bosome: weepingly laughing.'[16]

In the end of his discussion Wotton invokes Quintilian's penultimate chapter of the *Institutio oratoria* (XII.10.5) and lets it speak for him. The chapter, which is also a mainstay of Junius's argument for the dignity of art, offers a brief history of painting and sculpture in moral terms. '*Zeuxes* did make *Limbes*, bigger than the *life*; deeming his *Figures*, thereby the more *stately* and *Majesticall*; & therein (as some thinke) imitating *Homer*, whom the stoutest forme doth please, euen in *Women*.' Here we may think of Rubens, 'that Homer of painting' as a later age called him, who himself said that he found it easier to paint large pictures than small ones.[17] We tend to be genteelly scandalised by his big women, but are they not grand? And if grand, how could they be slim? They are Zeuxian, might be Wotton's retort, and thus Homeric. Without the evidence of Rubens's paintings could we ever imagine what the ancients meant by calling a painter 'Homeric'? And had Rubens not been touched by what Quintilian wrote of Zeuxis, would he so unabashedly have sought out models for his heroines that were so Homeric? The question is perhaps mute; still, it gives us access to the vocabulary of art which joins Wotton, Junius, Quintilian and Rubens.[18]

Wotton's observations on painting return us to the starting-point in our review of the theory of art. But where in Haydocke and Lomazzo a certain pedantry ruled, even in the praise of *sprezzatura*, here we meet the *sprezzatura* Wotton praises in his very manner of praising. It would be absurd to call him an English Bembo; but Wotton has brought the language of the love of art, fully alive, out of Italy and made it speak English and be at home anywhere.

TRAVEL TO ITALY

Gentlemen travellers had many reasons for going to Italy which were not at all, or only marginally, connected with the arts (see §S–268). To name but a few of the many obvious attractions: excellent teachers of fencing and riding, famous courts in which to gather experience, instruction in anatomy and physical science by the greatest masters of the age, and, for the dissolute and reckless, the lure of the courtesans of Venice. But, for the poetically responsive, Italy was the stage of ancient history, literature and art. Its very air was charged with the reality that formed the substance of such a traveller's youthful dreams. The steps of heroes and the love songs and lamentations of nymphs and shepherds yet resounded in echoes from a noble past; there he still found the gentle climate, the meadows, streams and brooks that he knew only from his longing. There also the landscape was strewn with ruins that inspired admiration and melancholy; there broken statuary, some just recently released from a thousand years or more of confinement in the earth, breathed again and, no matter how poorly mended, showed its beauty.

The visitor to Rome, particularly, would be moved at once to regret and exaltation. He saw the one-time capital of the ancient world, fallen and yet still grand, it ruins embraced by a protective Nature. Much of what had been the ancient city was now countryside, and even in the Forum cows were pasturing. Engravings of the antiquities of Rome, ever popular with travellers, perfectly record the melancholy glory of these ruins in a landscape that was a city (Plate 4). Many of the engravings were published to form a series, the *Speculum Romanae magnificentiae* (Rome, 1555 *et seq.* See §S–744). The traveller could select what suited him and bind the pictures in a book of his own making. These pictures come to life and speak out loud in Joachim Du Bellay's *Antiquités*, translated by Spenser as *The Ruins of Rome* (1591).

Rome was not only a city of ruins, however, nor Italy such a land. Venice, Florence, Bologna, Mantua, Genoa and the other great cities, smaller towns such as Vicenza, and countless country villas were now bristling with activity in all the arts or had been very active in the recent past. The remains of classical antiquity were the standard of the artists' instruction and the measure of their success. This does not mean that these remains were idly copied but, rather, that they served as models to be emulated and developed in keeping with the truth of revelation and the needs of the modern world. Both artists and patrons thus hoped, by constructively imitating the ancients, not only to equal but even to surpass them.

Of all the cities, Rome especially was a centre of great artistic life. Finally recovering from the terrible ruin of the sack in 1527, it became a great and wonderful and well-run city, a new Rome that prided itself on its ancientness, the proper capital (in the view of the Popes) of the Christian world. Its new buildings and their ornaments now spoke, as did its ancient ruins, a timeless Latin, while the language of the Church itself was being recast into a corresponding new–old *latinitas*. Pope Urban VIII, one of the greatest patrons of art of all time, was also a Latin poet of considerable renown who found it perfectly in order that his impeccably classical poems—some idyllic or playful or heroic, others in veneration of the Eucharist or lovingly dedicated to the Virgin Mary—should be illustrated by Bernini (see Maffeo Barberini, *Poemata*, 1631). Seventeenth-century architecture in Rome was not, for the people who commissioned it, made it and lived with it, 'baroque' (as we like to call the period in a perhaps futile search for grand developmental vistas in history), but classical, in a variety of styles—as was ancient art itself. The same held true, *mutatis mutandis*, for painting and sculpture, except that in these arts the study of nature and its direct imitation was a constant corrective and a spur to an ever more imaginative art of imitating the antique.

Painting, furthermore, was in a peculiar position because, except for the *grotteschi* in the underground ruins of the Golden House of Nero and the humble paintings in the catacombs, there was virtually nothing left that could bear witness to the practice in antiquity. Neither survival had anything to do with the grand style of painting of which the ancient literary sources spoke with such admiration. The masters to whom one turned for inspiration and study were the great painters of the sixteenth century, who had developed history painting—the highest form of the art—through the study of nature and classical sculpture to an art that was immediately persuasive and corresponded in naturalness and grandeur to anything that the literary sources could claim for the excellence of painting in classical antiquity.

It would be presumptious here to attempt to survey the teeming life of seventeenth-century art in Italy that always, with a view to timelessness, discussed and weighed its purposes and accomplishments and temptations on the scale of antiquity and sixteenth-century precedent. Nor is there a need for it. Names like Caravaggio and the Carracci, Guido Reni, Domenichino, Bernini, Borromini, Algardi, and—among the non-Italians who owed the perfection of their art to their Italian connection—Rubens, van Dyck and Poussin are known well enough to evoke an image of the splendour of this art and the variety of its practice and influence. Not so well known, however, or perhaps not considered with the respect we believe it deserves, is the climate of moral cogitation in which these artists' works were produced and judged and made a lasting effect upon the hearts of responsive viewers.

Protestant Englishmen who came to Rome with a knowledge of the classics were perhaps particularly susceptible to the charm and the challenge of this climate. As much as they longed for perfection and even obtained a view of it through the study and measuring of the surviving statuary and ruins of antiquity, so would they be on guard in Rome against the possible blandishments of a modern art that, wherever they saw it, was in the service of popery. There was a whole range of possible responses to the dilemma, from a facile bigotry to the finest sophistication in the judgement of works of art.

PANDAEMONIUM

It has long been thought that Milton's famous descriptions of Pandaemonium, 'the high Capitol / Of Satan and his Peers' (*Par. Lost*, I, 756–7), reverberates with echoes of his Roman visit, as does of course its companion passage, the description of the city of Rome itself in *Paradise Regained* (but see §S–709: pp. 134–5, 325–9). The latter is presented topographically; in *Paradise Lost* Milton reconstructs a real city. Pandaemonium, however, is in Hell, a triumph of building at once so sublime in its beauty (it is built by angels, even if fallen ones) and so horrific in the vast extravagance of its size and the pride of its ornaments that we can never encompass it with our understanding. Our view of the work, as it rises before our eyes, keeps growing away from us into space and darkness lit by starry lamps; we can only attend in quiet fascination, with a shudder. Yet the dark immensity of the resplendent work has its own propriety, for not only does vanity—which here is expressed to perfection—suit Hell, but the vast structure is functional, designed to contain the myriads of daemons (who make themselves quite small as they enter) and, in gigantic shape, the Lords of Hell, who occupy a separate council chamber.

Anyone who has been to Rome will recognise in Pandaemonium touches of the Pantheon, the Colosseum, and above all—estranged into a daemonic likeness—St Peter's as we see it on certain feast days when both the church and the piazza are so crowded with worshippers that none can move: 'in narrow room / Throng numberless' (I, 779–80). How much greater must have been the effect of the building when the church was new, the piety of the crowds more fervent, and the pomp of the clergy resplendent! At the time of Milton's visit the building, which had been begun by Bramante—who said he was going to put the dome of the Pantheon on top of the Temple of Peace (i.e. the Basilica of Maxentius: Plate 4)—was barely finished; and the church, with the nave by Maderno, was even larger than originally had been contemplated. The inscription celebrating the completion of the work was placed in 1612. In 1633 the interior of the church was crowned with Bernini's *baldacchino*, four gigantic, twisted columns in gilded bronze, a phantastic triumph of casting. The height of the *baldacchino*, guides are fond of pointing out, is that of the Palazzo Farnese; but one can hardly believe it, as the size of the *baldacchino* is so much in keeping with the scale of the church.

The description of the construction of Pandaemonium begins with a mining operation for gold, which is then refined and cast in the ground in one great engineering operation. Mammon, Hell's architect, leads multitudes of spirits who finish the work instantaneously. (I, 688–709). It would be a mistake, however, to equate Pandaemonium with St Peter's or even to draw inferences of comparison. We are too fascinated, awestruck by what we see as we read the account of the building of this ghostly palace, ever to leave the realm of Hell. Rather than point outside the poem, the poet leads us, by echoes of the known—as he was led himself—to fathom the unimaginable reality of Hell's heaven, the *kosmos* of immoderation. We behold a gigantic perfection of limitlessness into which are absorbed and thus perverted the accomplishments of the art of containment and harmony—a rape of beauty in the name of beauty.

Milton tells us enough about the building (I, 710–30) to show that Pandaemonium is built in the classical style. There are Doric columns, pilasters, architraves and arches. There is even sweet music to which the work rises from the ground, as once Thebes did to Amphion's lyre. Still, Milton compares the structure only to the temples of barbarian nations. Mammon, as an architect in Heaven, had known perfection; but he abused what here we may call the heavenly orders by improving upon them, turning the consonance of harmony to chaos luxuriating in splendour. To support the arches he chose the Doric column, Wotton's 'grauest [order] that hath been received into ciuil vse'—a right choice, surely, for such an immense structure—but he decked it with an architrave so richly carved that it would suit the plenty of the Corinthian style rather than Doric simplicity. To make matters worse—or hellishly right—the medley of forms is wrought in gold. What Wotton finds offensive in the Composite Order here triumphs in its archetype; and the poet, in awe, beholds the grandeur of evil.

INIGO JONES AND ITALIAN ARCHITECTURE

Milton did not need Wotton's instruction to invent Pandaemonium. He views architecture, and the blessings and abuses of its harmonies, as he views poetry. Milton and his readers, as well as Wotton, could see the art of building well marvellously exemplified in England in the works of Inigo Jones. A master of decorum in architecture, Jones was inventive and fastidious at once. We need only look at the porch of his church of St Paul's in Covent Garden (1631), in the perfection of the Tuscan style which Jones developed for the purpose, to see what harmony can be wrought on the theme of the 'rudest pillar', as Wotton called it, whose 'principall character [is] *Simplicity*' (Plate 5). Jones, like Wotton, discovered the *exempla* of his art when he travelled in Italy, viewing, drawing and listening to the ever-continuing discussions on the nature of beauty in art and the conditions of its decadence and revival.

It is perhaps not an accident that Palladio, the great master of fine and morally attuned distinctions in modern architecture, was from the Veneto. Venice, 'the second Rome', engendered a scepticism about modern Rome which, from the vantage point of the Republic, seemed extravagant, erratic and despotic in matters of state and monkishly enthusiastic in religion. The English and the Venetians were drawn to each other not only for political reasons, but also by the sharing of this scepticism. Reticence, irony, and an appreciation of the value of elegance in meeting the forces of nature, human as well as physical, seem to flourish particularly well among seafaring nations. The Venetians had long developed a style of government and civil life in which the demands of religion and the State were balanced intelligently and the individual citizen was both free and bound by law and custom. Historical writing, such as Pietro Bembo's famous *Storia di Venezia*, added the refinements of hindsight to memory and endowed this art of the practical with an ideal form.

The Protestant English, concerned in their own right with the perfection of a balance between Church and State, were appreciative students of the government of Venice. Feeling more at home in the Veneto than anywhere else in Italy, they were also more cordially welcomed. A gentleman's education in the classics, furthermore, predisposed him to a comprehension of Venetian fine distinctions, in art as in politics. Ever since Erasmus's visit to England, the study of Greek and Latin was advanced there with a particular emphasis upon the virtues of precision, variation and well considered simplicity of expression. Since the Reformation these qualities, joined to a fine irony, prospered among certain ranks of the clergy and sweetened the influence of its *latinitas* and *graecitas* with sophistication.

It is therefore no wonder that Wotton, Jones and the Earl of Arundel, each in his own ways and circumstances, as well as others among the English travellers and residents in Italy, were attracted to the art of Palladio, even though—or perhaps exactly because—Palladio was not then in the forefront of architectural fashion. If Palladio and Jones treasured a noble simplicity in architecture, it does not mean that they disdained wealth of expression. It was entirely a matter of propriety. Jones's St Paul's at Covent Garden was the first Protestant church built on a new site in London, a parish church that served as the focus of a speculative housing development, the Covent Garden Piazza, which would, at a minimum of building expense, introduce dignity and commodiousness to city dwellers who could not command palaces. The church is simple, and distinguished in its simplicity, in keeping with the fundamentals of the faith and the exigencies of the development of the entire piazza.

The case is quite different, and yet the observance of architectural decorum the same, when we look at Jones's resurfacing of the exterior of the old cathedral church of St Paul's and the new porch that he added to its west façade (1633–42: Plate 6). The porch is majestic as befits the entrance to the grandest church of Protestant England, rich in the Corinthian style but restrained, a well measured, great overture in timeless art to the Norman ancientness that ruled within. This wealth within bounds is further stressed by the rich reticence of the Doric measure about the exterior walls, which does not disguise but, in accents of symmetry, expresses the structure it conceals.

When, finally, we turn to Jones's Banqueting House at Whitehall (1619–22), we have before us a joyous and dignified structure, rising in noble ease above the Gothic buildings which surround it (Plate 7). Two rows of columns, echoed by pilasters in proper sequence, define the height and width of the façade, giving it a weighty weightlessness, an articulation of pure being that is stately, predictable and festive. The surface of the wall itself is rusticated in Tuscan simplicity. The lowest storey, unadorned, creates a pedestal for the ornately developed part of the façade. The two orders of columns are Ionic and Composite; but the Composite is restrained and elegant, not the monstrous exuberance that Wotton chastised. Where the connoisseur, even so genial a one as Wotton, was absolute in his condemnation, the artist rejoiced in developing the chaste potential of exuberance. The friezes of both orders maintain and impose a quiet reserve. There is no carving on them, but from the capitals of the

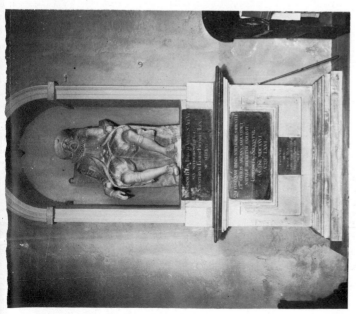

2 *Tomb of Sir Francis Bacon,* St Michael's, St Albans, Herts.

1 (*right*) Richard Haydocke, title page for his translation of Giovanni Paolo Lomazzo, *A Tracte containing the Artes of curious Paintinge Caruinge Buildinge* (Oxford, 1598).

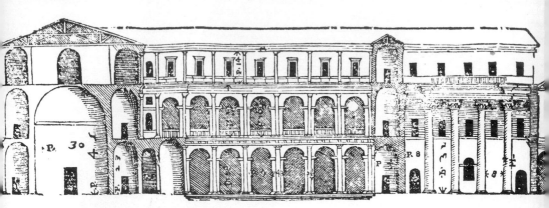

3 Palladio, Convent of the Carità, Venice. Detail: Atrium. From Palladio, *I Quattro Libri dell'Architettura* (Venice, 1570).

4 Etienne Dupérac, *Vestigij del Tempio della pace* [Basilica of Maxentius]. Folio 5 of the series of 1575.

5 Inigo Jones, *St Paul's Church*, Covent Garden. Engraving by Wenceslaus Hollar.

6 Inigo Jones, *Porch of St Paul's Cathedral*, London. Engraving by Wenceslaus Hollar.

7 *Whitehall as seen from the Thames* (c. 1640). Engraving by Wenceslaus Hollar.

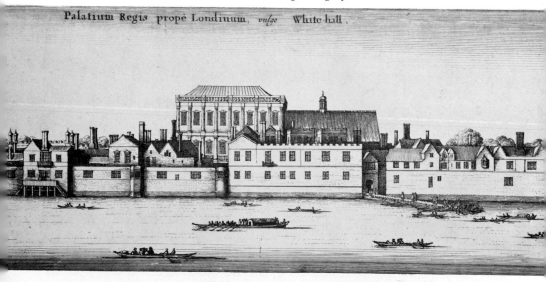

CELEBERRIMVS VIR INIGO IONES   PRÆFECTVS ARCHITECTVRÆ

MAGNÆ BRITTANIÆ   REGIS ETC.

Ant.van Dyck pinxit
R V Voest sculp.

Cum priuilegio

8 Van Dyck, *Inigo Jones*. Engraving by Robert van Voerst for van Dyck's *Centum Icones*.

9 Rubens, *Fall of the Rebel Angels*. Engraving (after Rubens) by Lucas Vorsterman.

10 Rubens, *Peace and War* (now called *Minerva protects Pax from Mars*).

11 Rubens, *Apotheosis of James I*, centre panel, Banqueting House ceiling, Whitehall, London.

12 Van Dyck, *Lord John and Lord Bernard Stuart*.

Composite Order hang festoons and masks, bestowing upon the wealth of the order a becoming function. The wreaths join the capitals to each other in an articulated sub-frieze; but they hang freely, seeming to play in the breeze, a quotation of nature and its echo. On top the whole is crowned with an airy balustrade. The house looks every inch a royal building in the service of a king's serenity.

The classical structure of the interior, all of painted wood, corresponds to the promise of the façade. Its life is intimate and delicate—yet, within the frame of this intimacy, formal: a courteous processional chamber. On special days it was rich in its trimmings,[19] but never overbearing. Even the fields on the ceiling, which enclose Rubens's celebration of the glory of Stuart monarchy, are contained in a simple division of matching rectangles, a deliberate correction, in which perhaps Jones and Rubens co-operated, of the precedent of artfully convoluted frames that hold the famous ceiling paintings in the Doge's Palace at Venice.

In speaking of Palladio and Jones as masters of decorum and fine distinction in architecture, we do not intend to denounce the architects of St Peter's and other masters of the time as enemies of the system that we have described, or even as less attentive to the problems which Palladio and Jones solved so superbly.[20] On the contrary, although they worked in different modes and were, perhaps even happily, more carefree about perfection than Palladio and Jones, they addressed—and some, with equal genius, solved—the same problems that we have been discussing throughout. The justice of our view depends upon our understanding of the building task involved and the pattern of propriety that suits it. There are also certain variations of degree in the conventions which determine the difference between what is just enough and what is too much in the measure of ornament that an architect must bestow on a building to make it beautiful and, in keeping with its task, eloquent or nobly silent, as the case may be.

Bramante's grand statement of intent to place the Pantheon on top of the Temple of Peace has shocked many a reader, as if Bramante had intended to build the tower of Babel once more in a Roman style. But, if we look at his plans and consider the nature of the task he approached, we may see that he set out to reconcile greatness of size with a sense of restraint and so to arrive at true greatness in his work. Palladio recognised and honoured the true classicist in Bramante. Of the works of modern architects, besides his own, he shows but one in his *Quattro libri*: Bramante's *tempietto* at San Pietro in Montorio in Rome; and he calls it worthy of being included among the works of the ancients.

Bernini himself, whom we like to call 'baroque' as if he represented a movement away from the harmonies Jones found in Palladio, recognised Palladio as his master. The restrained Tuscan colonnade of the Piazza of St Peter's (which Milton did not see), wide in its sweep, a prelude of grandeur and simplicity to the glory of the interior of the church and Michelangelo's dome above, bears this out on a scale of overwhelming rightness. The *baldacchino* itself—if it will be seen, as it should be, as the focal point of the immense assembly of the church, wherein the disparity of dome and nave are reconciled in one great accent of celebration—speaks, in a different temperament and on a different occasion and in a unique place, still the same language as did Palladio. There are variations, of course, occasioned by these different circumstances and by the need to respond constructively to the challenge of an ever-enlarging corpus of established precedent; but these variations only indicate a change in accent patterns, even a possible enrichment of the language and by no means necessarily its corruption. The search for the appropriate and the desire to demonstrate appropriateness seek the comparison of opposites, which some-times results in bitter quarrels; but these are feuds within a family sharing the same vocabulary of praise and blame, of perfection and failure; the same vocabulary, in fact, which we have seen Junius patiently collect and interpret from the literary sources of classical antiquity.

What is 'mannered' or 'bizzare' ('baroque' was not employed as a critical term in the seventeenth century) and what is meant by 'classical' in the debates on beauty in works of art, or in the quarrels to which we have alluded, is not a matter of period style but rather of good taste. The confrontation is a way of exploring the moral significance or the dignity of the visual arts. There are strict constructionists of the law of decorum and the observance of canonical forms and there are genial, permissive ones. The discussion tends to focus upon the interpretation of grace, of *sprezzatura*; and what is *sprezzatura* in one view may be licence in another. It is the difference in the old quarrel in classical rhetoric between Attic and Asian, the exact and the copious style.

Artists who created their works without a consideration of the points scrutinised in the debates were outside the fold. For them the arts were not 'fine' but mechanical. Their works were 'Gothick', either from ignorance, as when the artists worked in darkness in the times before the invention or the rediscovery of true art, or, worse, when contemporaries deliberately chose to ignore the hierarchy of values and decorum in art. In so doing they acted from malice or frivolity and abused beauty for the sake of luxury, vanity and pride. These are the sins of art, and they triumph in the temple of Hell. The architecture of Pan-daemonium is the exact negation, not merely the opposite but the complete distortion of everything that is expressed and represented by the Pan-theon, the temple of supreme perfection such as men can achieve, 'imitating the celestiall Orbes, and the universall Forme' (Wotton, *Elements*, p. 17).

COLLECTING

It is impossible to read without astonishment the count of famous paintings that in the lifetime of Charles I had gone to England. The nucleus of important possessions was, of course, the King's own collection. Henry Wotton, in a Latin panegyric upon Charles's return from Oxford in 1633, praises the king's noble pleasures:

. . . the most splendid of all your entertainments is your love of excellent

Artificers; and works: wherewith in either Art, both of picture and sculpture, you have so adorned your palaces, that Italy (the greatest Mother of Elegant Arts) or at least (next to the Grecians) the principal Nursery may seem by your magnificence to be translated into England.

('A Panegyrick to King Charles,' trans. in §P–685)

Next to the King, and almost equally lavish, the outstanding collectors were the Duke of Buckingham and the Earl of Arundel, whom Rubens once described as 'uno delli quarto evangelisti e soportator del nostro arte' (§S–726: p. 175). Both, in rivalry, had already advised Charles and purchased works for him when he was still Prince of Wales; and even earlier Arundel had advised and aided Prince Henry, Charles's elder brother who died in 1612, in the collecting of works of art. It was an aspect of the prince's preparation to become the perfect prince.

The great men in the realm necessarily often had to rely upon others to do their buying, to negotiate and make selections for them, and in varying degrees even to instruct them. Among the diplomat-connoisseurs who were so engaged, we have already met Henry Wotton. We must add the names of Dudley Carleton, Endymion Porter, a spirit straight from *The Courtier*, and Balthasar Gerbier, by profession a miniature painter but also a secret agent and diplomat in the service of Buckingham. And, of course, there were Rubens and van Dyck.

The most wonderful influence upon the development of collecting and patronage in England was the all-embracing genius of Inigo Jones. In 1606 we find Jones described as the man 'through whom there is hope that sculpture, modelling, architecture, painting, acting and all that is praiseworthy in the elegant arts of the ancients, may one day find their way across the Alps into England' (§S–756: p. 43). Jones had studied in Italy and prepared himself for this mission for possibly six years; he, therefore, could and would speak of antiquities and Italian art with authority. In a second Italian journey (1613–15) he accompanied the twenty-seven-year-old Arundel on a triumphal tour of study, excavation and collecting that was the most decisive event of Arundel's career as a lover of art.[21] As Jones was Arundel's mentor, so Arundel himself—by the very example of his collecting and patronage—became the mentor of others.

The great English collectors shared, by and large, the same interests. There is a lavishness and a magnificence in the representation of the great masters of the Italian Renaissance, the Zeuxises and Apelleses of the modern world, with a particular interest in the Venetian painters; also an appreciation for the tradition of realism, exemplified particularly by Holbein and Dürer; and, of course, a concern for the masters of modern art. Living artists were valued not because they were modern but because some—notably Rubens, van Dyck and, in sculpture, Bernini—were considered true successors to the masters of antiquity, perfectly capable of holding their own and their works well suited to unite with the voices of the past in a chorus of beauty and truth.

A glance at the splendour of the King's collection must suffice to remind us of the kind of treasures which the great collectors looked for and often found. To name but a few of the famous works which Charles owned at the height of his collecting: the Raphael cartoons for the Vatican Tapestries; Mantegna's cartoons of *The Triumph of Caesar*; Raphael's *St George and the Dragon* (National Gallery, Washington), his *Holy Family*, called *La Perla* (Prado); Giorgione's *Judith* (Hermitage), his *Concert Champêtre* (Louvre); Leonardo's *St John the Baptist* (Louvre); Correggio's *Venus, Mercury and Cupid* (National Gallery, London), his *Jupiter and Antiope*, his allegories of *Virtue* and *Vice* (all in the Louvre). Among the Titians were the full-length portrait of *Charles V, Venus and the Organ Player* (both in the Prado), *Girl in a Fur Cloak* (Vienna), *The Twelve Caesars* (lost), *The Pardo Venus*, *Allegory of Alonso d'Avalos, Supper at Emmaus*, and *The Entombment* (all in the Louvre). But this was only one aspect of the glory. The King also owned works by Holbein, Dürer and Cranach; and, among near-contemporaries, works by the Carracci, Caravaggio, Domenico Feti, Guido Reni; and, finally, the works of the artists he sponsored: Daniel Mytens, Gerrit van Honthorst, Orazio and Artemisia Gentileschi, Rubens, van Dyck. These pictures were displayed not in a historical sequence or grouped by artists, but, rather, in keeping with their themes and the requirements of their size, the nature of the *tout ensemble*, and the functions of the rooms in which they were hung.[22]

What all the joy of these pictures meant, beyond the amassment of treasure and the connoisseur's delight in authentication, evaluation and distinction of hands, what *Pictura* herself could teach and how she could delight as a liberal art, we may see most readily when we look at Rubens and van Dyck escorting her into England.

TWO ENGRAVINGS

Van Dyck's portrait of Inigo Jones is realistic and ennobled at once. He draws the soul as well as the man (Plate 8). Van Dyck knows the limits of his mute art and transcends them by respecting them. He will not foolishly pretend to show *what* Jones is thinking; but he shows him thinking, contemplating high things, not as a seer but as a practical man and a quick one, very likely. We see not only what Jones looks like, but the man he is and what is characteristic of him. The gesture of a moment is seized and transformed to represent him for all time. We justifiedly feel that we may trust the artist and are glad to have met Inigo Jones. Our knowledge of him has been expanded through portraiture as a fine art. The picture, obviously, cannot teach us architecture, but it may help us to improve our idea of what it means to be a great architect. Realism and ideal statement in such an art are inextricably united, the one depending for the fullness of its convincing truth upon the background provided by the other. English lovers of art likened van Dyck to Titian; for both, it was not the colours that mattered but the truth they could represent and reveal.

Van Dyck's drawing of Inigo Jones still exists in the original at Chatsworth (reproduced in § S–720). We have here presented an engraving which was made in accord with van Dyck's purpose; he had intended to publish a volume of portraits of famous artists and lovers of art.[23] The engraving is more stylised than the intimate drawing, more deliberately Jones's pictorial monument, a public statement which enshrines rather than exhibits the privacy of his being.

Engraving in the age of Rubens had become a reliable medium for the reproduction of works of art. In England Arundel employed the gifted Bohemian artist Wenceslaus Hollar to make copies of the paintings and sculptures in his collection, with a view towards eventually establishing a complete pictorial catalogue. But it was Rubens in particular who sponsored and developed the art of engraving as a reliable and pictorially convincing reproductive medium.[24] Touched especially by the example of Dürer, he looked upon engraving as a form of publication which would communicate to a large public and to posterity both the invention and—translated appropriately into black and white and adapted to the paper format—the poetry of his painting. Artists, with the help of engraving and etching, thus came to join poets and influence them, as conversely they were influenced by them, in the expanding and shaping of the imagination through print—in the joy of the library.

We turn now to Rubens's *Fall of the Rebel Angels* (original now lost) as it is represented in an engraving by Lucas Vorsterman (Plate 9). The stupendous event is before us in the action of a moment that does not pass. It is nourished in its motion, and suspended in time, by what we see has just happened and by what will happen next. The rebel angels are being transformed as they tumble in a stream of fire headlong into the abyss. Their convulsions and gestures—and even their very fall, however much they struggle against it—express their hatred, terror, lust and envy. In their fall their evil finds its proper outward shape in bestial forms. Satan has already turned into the dragon that he is. Another rebel, fully extended downwards, still shows the glory of the angelic likeness, but is convulsed with the passions which consume him. He looks with fear and desperate longing at the sign and manifestation of the perfection that he betrayed: the name of God inscribed in blazing light on Michael's shield. Thus Envy ever is attracted to Beauty and hates it. On the daemon's head snakes now sprout forth; in a rage, both formidable and impotent, he tears them out and attempts to hurl them at Michael. Michael himself and his attendant angels, however, in all the intensity of battle do not lose their beauty. The force of their motions resounds in music and defines their victory: Light overcomes Darkness.

Clearly Rubens does not propose that what he painted is a pictorial record, like a newsreel, of what actually happened when the daemons fell. Instead, he invites us to a leap of the imagination. The better we understand that a true account of the event is inaccessible to either vision or speech, the more vividly do we see it happen in truth, before our eyes, in his picture. Rubens makes the invisible visible through images of truth, likely likenesses which gain an absolute reality of their own because they are extensions of forms and actions that we know and understand. Reaching into a world of greatness both positive and negative, they are patterned on certain standard works of classical and Renaissance art which established a commonly shared vocabulary for the representation of the world beyond the experience of the mortal eye.

In painting *The Fall of the Rebel Angels* Rubens recalled Raphael's *St Michael* and his *Expulsion of Heliodorus*, as well as antiques such as the *Fallen Niobid*, the *Laocoön* and perhaps *The Fall of Phaeton* from a sarcophagus. To give shape to the unpaintable, he also had recourse to Schongauer's *Temptation of St Anthony*. Each of the works that he touched upon he used for its own kind of sublimity or terror.[25] All of them are transformed in the fire of his vision, assuming the sense they uniquely have in this work. Taking the work apart will not help us to see it better. Rubens's genius has assimilated the art of antiquity and of his Renaissance forebears. He does not quote it, he lives it. And his viewers, if they are properly responsive, will do so with him.

Milton, although he may well have seen it, did not need this picture to paint his own fall of Satan. Certainly he knew some of its sources, however, and was affected by the same sense of truth that made them dear to Rubens, just as he knew (as did Rubens) an array of comparable passages in literature. It was through this knowledge—and not through a link to a given image—that his imagination was enlarged and that he was as able as the painter to take the measure of this extraordinary topic.

TRIUMPH

When Rubens came to England in 1629 he was on a diplomatic mission in the service of the Infanta Isabella, who governed the Spanish Netherlands, and of Philip IV of Spain. The purpose was to establish a lasting peace between Spain and England. The peace was desired by both parties and, with the help of Rubens's tact and perseverance, was secured in 1630. Not long after his arrival, Rubens painted as a present for the King the picture that we know by the title *Peace and War* (Plate 10). It celebrates the King's statecraft and armed preparedness as the preserver of England's peace. But, if the subject is timely, the language of the allegory is timeless. The occasion which caused it to be painted recedes in importance; it frames the sense of the picture but does not determine it.

We see before us a landscape rejoicing in peace, a blessed island. The nude goddess presiding over it gently, with a gesture of compassion, offers the abundance of her milk to an infant who lovingly approaches her. Since Mars and Minerva are close to her, we may see her as Venus in the role of a protectress of peace and prosperity. On the right is the realm of war. Mars has rushed madly towards the island, threatening to invade it, but is repelled by Minerva. Her action is defensive, firm and intelligent. Mars casts a last crazed look at the blessed landscape and follows the course of least resistance. The Fury of war, her torch lit, will lead him through the darkness, across the unhappy Europe of the Thirty Years War or anywhere, at any time.

On the left a little cupid hovers over Venus ever so importantly. In his right hand is an olive wreath, denoting peace, with which he is about to crown the goddess. With his left hand he waves a caduceus, a sign of the prosperity of trade and the arts but also of diplomacy, concord, union and peace. On the right two children are nearing the island of peace. They are members of our world, coming from the side governed by Mars and his Fury, refugees, it would seem, from war-torn Europe. The children are timid and yet rejoice in their reception. The figure between them is difficult to identify—perhaps a protective genius or guide, supporting the children and urging them to be at ease.

The satyr at the feet of Venus holds a cornucopia abounding with the gifts of Bacchus and Ceres. Bacchus's leopard playfully claws at them; but the satyr, a figure full of a singular and sensuous goodness, proffers the fruit of the harvest to the children. Cupid himself offers an apple and points out the splendour of the yellow and red grapes to the approaching children: 'Come and eat!' The older girl, to whom Cupid seems specifically to be addressing himself, holds up the hem of her skirt, as if to improvise an apron in which to receive the fruit. The little girl has already taken a bite of it and looks at us with her big eyes, happy but serious. Next to her a little genius holds a torch in one hand; with the other he places a wreath on the head of the older girl. He is Hymen, the god of wedlock. In short, the children are welcomed by the land of plenty and the older girl soon will be honourably wed. The nymph or bacchante on the left, with her tray of golden cups and vessels and string of pearls, may even hold gifts for her dowry. The whole island is concerned with welcoming the children.

The two girls and Hymen have long been identified as portraits. They are children of Sir Balthasar Gerbier, at whose house Rubens was staying when he painted the picture. A group portrait, now in the National Gallery in Washington, includes the children's mother, showing a fourth child, a baby boy still in her arms. Is it too much to identify him as the infant being nursed by Venus? Gerbier came to England in 1616 from Holland, where his parents had lived as Protestant refugees from France. Gerbier worked for Buckingham, thereby incurring the distrust of the Commons, who in the summer of 1628 very nearly threw out a Bill for his naturalisation. After Buckingham's assassination he entered the King's service and was knighted soon after, in December 1628. The King thus gave Gerbier and his progeny a permanent home. The picture surely alludes to that.[26] It is Rubens's compliment both to the King and to Sir Balthasar Gerbier.

Rubens's joining of the precarious world of the children's portraits with the timeless life of the allegories lifts the picture into a world of drama. We too, like the figures on the side of peace, are moved to pity and generosity; we tremble as we see how peace and war are weighed in the balance of fortune and statecraft; and we are glad that the little children, for once, are safe.

Perhaps this view of *Peace and War* will help the reader find a virtuous delight in his own contemplation of what is surely one of Rubens's most resplendent and audaciously conceived works, the ceiling of Inigo Jones's Banqueting Hall. Wherever we look, gods and allegories move to and fro, occupied with the bidding of James I. The King, although dressed in a garb better than royal, still looks sufficiently like the real and not altogether prepossessing James I. Enthroned in splendour and responded to by divinities, he remains a figure readily identified as belonging to the world of men. The centre picture, which rules the entire ceiling, represents James's apotheosis: he now himself becomes a god (Plate 11).[27]

Did James deserve this elevation? Surely not in the eyes of history; but the language of panegyric vision does not pretend to that sort of truth. It shows a likeness not of what is but of what should be. We see what is reflected in the mirror of princes, not what is written on the tablets of Clio. The ceiling celebrates good government under a good king and shows the rewards of his labours.[28] It offers, to the trumpet sounds of fame and in the language of fiction, a political programme which is guaranteed by the unchanging reliability of the character of the gods and the myth of the perfect aspirations of the first Stuart monarch. James himself had been at pains to propagate this myth, and even to believe it. It was up to the painter to give it reality through a fiction that never lies.

Did Rubens succeed? The opinions have always been divided. To this writer it seems infinitely moving that Rubens, working in a medium of story-telling that is easily corrupted by flattery, carefully protected the integrity of his gods and allegorical figures. They are presented with respect and appear in glory. When they do the King's bidding, he also does theirs; they serve him because he serves them. If he who styled himself 'the Prince of Peace' bids peace, it is not he who chases Mars from the realm but Minerva. Plenty and Justice then embrace and the kingdom prospers in their blessings. The joys and sorrows of the allegories depend on the actions of men, notably kings; but men perish and allegories rule in their appointed spheres. Great and noble actions set them in motion and they will reward mankind. James, to the moment of his death, remains a man, a member of our world. Only when he comes to die does he achieve immortality, not by conquering death but by the support of the eternal figures who approve the completed course of his reign. They lift off his earthly crown and replace it with wreaths of glory. Religion offers her prayer and takes him by the arm; she half carries and half escorts him up to the invisible realm that is the residence of the gods. The last and perfect look we get of the King, his head already shining with the light he is to join, is that of a man surprised. He deserved immortality because to the last he knew he was mortal.

EPILOGUE

Rubens sent the finished paintings for the Banqueting House ceiling to London for installation in 1635. Not quite fourteen years later, the Banqueting House served as Charles I's last place of confinement and as the backdrop for his execution. The King's collection of art was sold shortly afterwards for the good of the realm.[29] Arundel had earlier taken most of his valuable pictures to the safety of Amsterdam. He lived on in melancholy retirement at Padua until 1646. When the young John Evelyn called on him, shortly before his death, Arundel told Evelyn to go to Vicenza and see the works of Palladio. The advice was

Arundel's artistic legacy. After his death his pictures were sold in Amsterdam. Most of England's great collections were dispersed and the visual arts languished. The Earl of Clarendon writes with justified bitterness of the princes of Europe, who failed to assist Charles I when he was in mortal danger and after his death greedily competed for the possession of his pictures:

> And that which is stranger than all this, and more wonderful, (since most men by recovering their fortunes use to recover most of what they were before robbed of,) many who joined in the robbery pretending that they took care to preserve it for the true owner, not one of these princes ever restored any of the unlawful purchases to the King [Charles II] after his blessed restoration.[30]

So much, then, for the effectiveness of the much vaunted mission of the fine arts: to instruct their lovers in the life of just delights and to improve men by the purging of their passions. But this, the ridiculous failure of the arts—or perhaps of all humanistic education—to influence the affairs of the practical world, takes the measure of only one side, the ugly side of the coin of truth in history. If we flip it again, it may show us its other side, upon which fiction rules, greed is powerless, and truth beautiful. There we are offered not the promise of success in the world but the more lasting gift of consolation. Sometimes, ever so rarely and more to reward our loyalty than to prove a point, fiction works a miracle, improving in an objectively measurable way the quality of practical life by bestowing upon it the mirage of good manners.

Jacob Burckhardt, a self-respecting citizen of a free republic, was no lover of aristocracy; but he had memorable words in praise of van Dyck's aristocratic portraits, most notably those of the English nobility. These portraits show van Dyck's subjects in so refined and accurate a likeness of what was best in them that the pictures obtain validity as a standard for true nobility. We recognise in this art of portrayal Castiglione's argument for the feigning of *sprezzatura* as a first step in the education of the true courtier. Like Bembo's oration at the conclusion of *The Courtier*, however, the double portrait of Lord John and Lord Bernard Stuart shows what it means when reserve and freedom are united in the perfection of a noble resolve (Plate 12). As ever in the young who are beautiful and pose, nothing here is feigned.

Burckhardt's final words are quite firmly pessimistic; but they are also touched by wonder that art, any art, ever could have transcended its frame and through fiction affected the manners of men for the better. In Burckhardt's time the results of the change were still evident. We gratefully join him in his astonishment, for the gestures of the airy nothings about which we have written come to life only if we endow them with our own lives and fondest hopes:

> The aristocracy of the entire seventeenth century and its descendants in all lands owe the master their deepest gratitude because he firmly established the general prejudice in favor of a distinction of the upper classes. But in the end mankind in general is obliged to him for this prejudice.[31]

NOTES

This chapter is based upon a longer study, with fuller documentation and a somewhat different emphasis, to be published separately.

1 This passage paraphrases the beginning of Philostratus the Elder, *Imagines*. See J. J. Pollitt, trans., *The Art of Rome* (Englewood Cliffs, N.J., 1966), p. 220.

2 Trans. K. Jex-Blake and Eugenie Sellers, *The Elder Pliny's Chapters on the History of Art* (Chicago, 1896), p. 121.

3 §P–536. The original *Trattato dell' Arte de la pittura* first appeared in 1584; Haydocke based his translation on the second of the enlarged editions of 1585. See Lomazzo, *Scritti sulle arti*, ed. R. P. Ciardi (Florence, 1973), I, 1xxxiii–iv, notes 19–28. The most extensive account of the translator is Karl Josef Höltgen, 'Richard Haydocke: Translator, Engraver, Physician', *The Library*, XXXIII (1978), 15–32. For a reconstruction of Lomazzo's original programme, see §S–657; and, for his indebtedness to Ficino, see §S–772.

4 The proportions which Haydocke uses are nine lengths of the face for the full height of Juno and nine lengths of the head for Minerva. See Lomazzo, I, 14–15.

5 For this and other details regarding the title page, see Höltgen (as above, n. 3). For the sources of Haydocke's mythological invention, described in this and the next paragraph, see Lomazzo, ed. Ciardi, II, pp. 387, 504–7, 572, 555, 568, 19; I, p. 121; II, p. 576. Minerva's serpent and Prometheus's hollow reed are not in Lomazzo; but Haydocke could have found them in Vincenzo Cartari, *Le imagini degli Dei antichi*, or a comparable pictorial source. For a fuller discussion of Haydocke's title page, see Margery Corbett and R. W. Lightbown, *The Comely Frontispiece: the Emblematic Title Page in England 1550–1660* (1979), pp. 67–78.

6 The emphasis is not surprising, given Peacham's interest in *imprese* which resulted in his own emblem book (§P–654). His 'how to do it' approach to art is most fully exemplified in *The Gentlemans Exercise* (1634), intended as a supplement to *The Compleat Gentleman*.

7 Born in Heidelberg, 1598, died at Windsor, 1677. His father, Franciscus Junius the Elder, a French Huguenot, was a famous theologian and Hebrew scholar. Junius the Younger is now best remembered as a philologist, the founder of Anglo-Saxon studies and decipherer of the Gothic language. On his activities and reputation, see §S–702, and the introduction to Franciscus Junius, *The Literature of Classical Art*, ed. Keith Aldrich and Philipp and Raina Fehl (Berkeley, 1980); for his association with the Arundel family, see §S–726.

8 The bulk of the surviving collection is in the Ashmolean Museum, Oxford. See D. E. L. Haynes, *The Arundel Marbles* (Oxford, 1975).

9 *Catalogus architectorum, mechanicorum, sed praecipue pictorum, statuariorum, caelatorium, tornatorum, aliorumque artificum et operum quae fecerunt . . . secundum seriem litterarum digestus . . . .*

10 Rubens sent to Junius a congratulatory letter upon the publication of *De pictura verterum* in which he also expresses the wish that it were possible to compose a comparable treatise on Italian paintings that provide tangible illustration of the theory. The passage has been considered as a veiled criticism of Junius (see Lawrence Lipking, *The Ordering of the Arts in Eighteenth-Century England* [Princeton, 1970] pp.

25–6); but it also may be read as a tribute both to Junius and to the Italians whose works revived the art of antiquity.

11 On Wotton's life and writings, see also Logan Pearsall Smith, *The Life and Letters of Sir Henry Wotton* (Oxford, 1907). On *The Elements*, see Frederick Hard's introduction to the facsimile reprint (Charlottesville, 1968); and Marilyn Perry Caldwell, 'Sir Henry Wotton: Aspects of English Taste in the Early Seventeenth Century', M.Phil. thesis, London University (The Warburg Institute, 1968).

12 For the text of Wotton's epitaph (which is separate from the 'sic sedebat'), see William Rawley's life of Bacon, *Resuscitatio* (1657) and Aubrey's *Brief Lives*.

13 Smith, *Life and Letters*, I, p. 218.

14 Page 21 (misprint for 12). Several architects were involved with the church. The construction was completed by Orazio da Urbino in 1584. The facade remains unfinished. See Caldwell (as above, n. 11), p. 62.

15 Page 44. The atrium was never completed and much of what was built was destroyed in a fire. But even the remaining fragment earned Goethe's heartfelt praise: 'I am convinced I am right when I say that I never saw anything more sublime, more perfect, in my life' (*Italienische Reise*, 2 October 1786).

16 This passage was originally omitted by a printer's error; Wotton inserted it in the dedication copies in longhand (see p. 88).

17 See R. S. Magurn, ed., *The Letters of Peter Paul Rubens* (Cambridge, Mass., 1955), p. 77 ('To William Trumbull', 13 September 1621).

18 On Rubens's experiments in painting in antique styles, see Elizabeth McGrath, 'The Painted Decoration of Rubens's House', *Journal of the Warburg and Courtauld Institutes*, XLI (1978), 245–77.

19 These probably included tapestries from the Mortlake factory, designed after the Raphael cartoons for the history of the Apostles (then in the King's collection and now at the Victoria and Albert Museum).

20 Jones himself was not, in fact, a 'Palladian', but—like Palladio—an eclectic artist within the confines of classical and Renaissance precedent. For Jones's indebtedness to the ornate art of Serlio, see §S–809: pp. 36, 42, 92–4. (The present discussion owes much to this study.) On Palladio's own relaxed eclecticism, see §S–659.

21 See §S–809: pp. 35–7; and Jacob Hess, 'Lord Arundel in Rome', *English Miscellany*, I (Rome, 1950), 197–220. On Arundel and Buckingham as collectors, see §S–756: pp. 5–25; and, on Arundel, §S 726 and §S–802.

22 For a detailed account, see Oliver Millar, ed., 'Abraham van der Doort's Catalogue of the Collections of Charles I', *Walpole Society*, XXXVII (1960); also 'The Inventories and Valuations of the King's Goods, 1649–1651', *Walpole Society*, XLIII (1972).

23 The series of engravings was eventually published as *Icones virorum doctorum pictorum, chalcographorum, statuariorum necnon amatorum pictoriae artis ad vivum expressae* (Antwerp, 1645). Van Dyck also planned to include a portrait of Junius; an oil sketch now at Oxford (Bodleian Library) would have been the engraver's model.

24 Cf. Henri Hymans, *Histoire de la gravure dans l'école de Rubens* (Brussels, 1897) and Konrad Renger, ed., *Rubens in der Grafik* (exhibition catalogue, Göttingen, 1977).

25 For other sources, the history of the work, and Rubens's other versions of this

subject, see *Corpus Rubenianum Ludwig Burchard, VIII*: Hans Vlieghe, *Saints*, II (1973), 124–31.

26 For Gerbier, see *Dictionary of National Biography*. Rubens's concern for refugees is developed more fully in a matching picture, now in Munich (see Rudolf Oldenburg, *Peter Paul Rubens*, Berlin, 1921, pl. 313). Wolfgang Stechow, 'Peter Paul Rubens's "Deborah Kip, Wife of Sir Balthasar Gerbier, and her Children" ', *Studies in the History of Art*, V (Washington, D.C., 1973), 7–22, describes in detail the National Gallery group portrait. Stechow rejects previous identifications of the older girl in *Peace and War* with Elizabeth Gerbier—a judgment with which I disagree. See also Ludwig Burchard and R.-A. d'Hulst, *Rubens Drawings* (Brussels, 1963), I, 229–30, 266–7; and *Corpus Rubenianum Ludwig Burchard, XIX*: Frances Huemer, *Portraits*, I (1977), 95–8, 120–7.

27 The apotheosis is in the image of Julius Caesar's. For an emblematic version, cf. Rubens's title page for *Icones imperatorum Romanorum* (Antwerp, 1645), in which Caesar's star shines between sun and moon. For· a modern counterpart, see the engraved portrait of the Infanta Isabella for the title page of *La peinture de la serenissime princesse Isabelle Claire Eugenie* (Antwerp, 1634). See *Corpus Rubenianum Ludwig Burchard, XXI*: J. Richard Judson and Carl van de Velde, *Book Illustrations and Title-Pages* (1978), I, 277–80, 340–3; II, 222–4, 279–82.

28 Cf. Wither's emblem '*Sapiens Dominabitur Astris*'. The motto reads, 'Hee, over all the *Starres* doth raigne, / That unto *Wisdome* can attaine', and the verse concludes: 'The *Soule* of *Man* is nobler then the *Sphaeres*: / And, if it gaine the Place which may be had, / Not here alone on Earth, the Rule it beares, / But, is the *Lord*, of all that *God* hath made. / Be *wise in him*; and, if just cause there bee, / The *Sunne* and *Moone*, shall stand and wayt on thee' (§P–684: p. 31). See also Wither's dedicatory verse epistle to Charles I, which offers all the complimentary platitudes relevant to the programme of Rubens's ceiling, but with none of the art that infuses it with truth.

29 See Oliver Millar, *The Queen's Pictures* (1977), pp. 55–63; also Hugh Trevor Roper, *The Plunder of the Arts in the Seventeenth Century* (1970), and §S–779.

30 Edward, Earl of Clarendon, *The History of the Rebellion and the Civil Wars in England*, ed. W. D. Macray (Oxford, 1888), IV, 499 (Book XI, 251).

31 Jacob Burckhardt, 'Anton van Dyck', *Vorträge*, ed. Emil Dürr (Basel, 1918), p. 342 (my translation).
     As an envoi to our subject, see Wither's emblem upon 'Pegasus, the Muses Horse': 'this old *Emblem* (worthy veneration) / Doth figure out, that *winged contemplation*, / On which the *Learned* mount their best *Invention*, / And, climbe the *Hills* of highest Apprehension. This is the nimble *Gennet*, which doth carry, / Their *Fancie*, thorow *Worlds* imaginary; / And, by *idaeas* feigned, shewes them there, / The nature of those *Truths*, that reall are. / By meanes of *this*, our *Soules* doe come to know / A thousand secrets, in the *Deeps* below; / Things, here on *Earth*, and, things above the *Skyes*, / On which, we never fixed, yet, our eyes' (§P–684: p. 105).

THOMAS O. SLOANE

10

Rhetoric, 'logic' and poetry: the formal cause

Form is an argument. That statement may seem extraordinary to students of literature. For when we think of literary form we tend to think of neutral containers or appealing transparencies, like the acts of a play or rhyme schemes. If these are 'outer' forms, then 'inner' forms are surely such principles of organisation as chronology or metre. Neither seems argumentative; both seem more conventional than controversial. Moreover, simply to conceive of form itself as an isolable feature requires effort, for to do so we must abandon that doctrine drummed into us by a generation of literary critics concerning the inseparability of 'form' from 'content'. But rhetoricians, not aestheticians, still set the major tone for literary interpretation in Milton's day, although their dominance was being challenged, and in the rhetorical view form is a detachable element in any discourse, one that should be carefully examined for its own special efficacy and impact. Because the concept of form as argument is singularly appropriate to that view, it shall serve as our path into the nexus of seventeenth-century argumentative theory and poetry. Understanding that nexus should in turn help us understand some of the attitudes in Milton's audience as well as some of the special qualities of discourse in the period.

In addition to 'form', another word must be re-thought: 'argumentative', which for us is a type of discourse, one that is much more easily isolable than it was for Milton's contemporaries. Most of us have been taught that 'argumentative' is only one type of discourse, the others being 'expository', 'descriptive', and perhaps even 'narrative' and 'aesthetic'. Though efforts were begun anew in Milton's age to draw neat and clean lines between the various language arts, the creation and interpretation of all discourse generally belonged to argumentation, which as most Renaissance theorists taught always had three purposes: to teach, to please and to move. The three purposes usually coalesced. Plays, poems, sermons, speeches, treatises, all were to be fashioned and understood according to the canons of argument.

As we might suppose, given its breadth, 'argument' had special meaning. It was typically defined in a maddening tautology: 'An argument is any severall conceipt apt to argue that whereunto in reason it is referred'.[1] Fire could be an argument; when referred to heat it is a *cause*, whereas heat referred to fire is an *effect*. The tautology of the definition merely emphasises the verbal coherence of the underlying view of the world, whether on the simple physical level or the complex metaphysical one: man referred to sickness is a *subject*, or to his dwelling is an *adjunct*; or man referred to God is an *effect*, God is man's *efficient cause*, man's soul is his internal *formal cause*. Fire argues heat; man argues God. Cause, effect, subject, adjunct—these were the names of some of the argumentative instruments known as 'places', the reference-points in 'reason' which showed how one 'conceipt' related to another. 'Argument', then, pertained to the verbal 'relatableness' of things, forces, phenomena.[2]

Teaching, pleasing and moving, which were the Ciceronian ends of discourse, were somewhat sombrely updated in Milton's age by the doctrine that arguments were to be used 'for showing, explaining, or proving something'.[3] But though apparently narrower in meaning, these terms did not signify what we might think of as scientific demonstration, a distinction which was itself just getting firmly established in Milton's day. A closer modern paraphrase would be: 'observing, acknowledging, and/or experiencing the existence of something'. Form, too, as argument had those ends. That is, the form of a discourse could be used not simply to show the reader the content, or to get him to perceive it in a certain way, but also to 'prove' it, to get him to experience it. For example, a statement of a poem's 'argument' would be a disclosure of the core of relationships at its centre plus the speaker's intention:

> *This first book proposes, first in brief, the whole Subject*, Man's disobedience, and the loss thereupon of Paradise wherein he was plac't: *Then touches* the prime cause of his fall, the Serpent, or rather *Satan* in the Serpent; who revolting from God, and drawing to his side many Legions of Angels, was by the command of God driven out of Heaven with all his Crew into the great Deep. *Which action past over, the Poem hasts into the midst of things, presenting* Satan with his Angels now fallen into Hell, *describ'd here*, not in the Center (*for Heaven and Earth may be suppos'd as yet not made, certainly not yet accurst*) but in a place of utter darkness, fitliest call'd Chaos . . ..
>
> (*Paradise Lost*, Book I: 'The Argument')

These relationships are in turn organised, set forth and 'proved' by the poem's form. What that form may be and how it, too, functions as argument, in its host of complex interconnections with the poem's subject and audience, are the themes of this survey. We must be alert to the fact that a poem's argument is not that which is 'commonly call'd the Plot',[4] however much the statement of its argument looks like a 'plot summary'. Nor is 'plot' a sufficiently comprehensive synonym for 'form', though certain of Milton's contemporaries were eager to equate the two. And, in studying form as argument, we must continually recognise that 'argument' is always a combative concept; its overriding goal, then as now, is to make points in a controversy or to win assent.

From Plato to Milton, two theories of argumentation were recognised. One, for disputation among experts, was known as dialectic. Only remotely resembling our modern 'dialogue', and far more combative than logic, whose traditional systems of formal validity it had subsumed by Milton's day, dialectic was a systematic means of reasoning in which both speaker or writer and audience were more or less on the same level of expertise in an adversary situation. The other theory of argumentation, rhetoric, was for a situation in which the advocate's audience consisted of laymen as well as experts. Note that the distinction lay in the audiences, not in the subjects. From ancient times, dialectic was spoken of metaphorically as a closed fist, rhetoric as an open palm (§S–854: p. 4); the difference between the two signified the tight, tough reasoning required in dialectic for an audience of experts and the expansive adaptation to a mixed audience required in rhetoric. Imagine a time in which dialectic and rhetoric encompassed *all* modes of thought and reasoning whatsoever, and you will imagine the situation in the age just preceding Milton's, whose own time was engaged in the momentous struggle to free thought and reason from their verbal confines and to construct modes of discourse whose sole purpose was rational demonstration. One step in this direction was taken by an intellectual movement which Milton, to a certain extent, abetted. Dialectic became *widely* regarded as intellectually more serious than rhetoric and was proposed as the central discipline for instructing men in how to think and reason, whether they were constructing epic poems, presenting speeches before Parliament or writing treatises. It was called 'logic'—though that was nothing new, for 'logic' and 'dialectic' had been used casually as synonyms for at least a century before Milton. Though verbal in its orientation and not even so rigorous as the logic known to the ancients, the newly emerging dialectic had a kind of plainness and ostensibly revisionary or modern look which appeased the restless scientists of the age. As its star rose, traditional rhetoric fell into disfavour.

But the antecedents of that intellectual revolution, however modern in appearance, actually reach from the early seventeenth century into antiquity. In ancient times, the art of composing discourse was thought of as having (at most) five offices: *invention, arrangement, style, memory* and *delivery*. Cicero described the function of these offices in the following way: the speaker 'must first hit upon what to say; then manage and marshal his discoveries, not merely in orderly fashion, but with a discriminating eye for the exact weight . . . of each argument; next go on to array them in the adornments of style; after that keep them guarded in his memory; and in the end deliver them with effect and charm'.[5] The same instruction was given to writers, though with less emphasis on *delivery*. In so far as *memory* pertained to storing and recalling knowledge, not simply storing and recalling the structure of a speech, it was an art of almost universal application.[6] Cicero, of course, was describing the offices of rhetoric. It was largely *his* rhetoric, or what he had to say about the subject, that enjoyed a resurgence in the writings of Renaissance humanists. But *invention* and *arrangement* in the renewed Ciceronian rhetoric so closely resembled *invention* and judgement in the dialectic inherited from the Middle Ages that the stage was set for combining the two. When they were combined, the newly revised dialectic contained the most important offices of composition, and rhetoric was made to consist of instruction in ornament and *delivery*. But no one was particularly interested in teaching delivery. And ornament, which enjoyed wide popularity in the sixteenth century, was regarded with suspicion in the seventeenth. In sum, as the controversialist of the sixteenth century gave way to the scientist of the seventeenth, traditional rhetorical theory was fragmented, and many of its offices were dispersed to other disciplines. But, as we shall see, its attitudes towards language (and 'argument') continued for a time to prevail.

Form as argument was taught in each one of the traditional offices of composition. The notion lies in a 'place' of *invention*, the four causes: efficient, material, formal and final. Consider a statue. Its efficient cause is the sculptor; marble or stone is the material cause; its formal cause is its shape; its final cause is the artist's intention to produce a certain effect on his audience.[7] All causes are apparent in any one and are demonstrated by the effect. That is, we may sort out our response to a statue by considering the effect as a composite result of its causes: the sculptor, the material, the shape and the artist's intention. The formal cause is a compound of two principles, one external and the other internal, which are themselves closely linked. To apply in this instance the modification of the doctrine as adapted for use in theology: the external form is an outward and visible sign of an inward and invisible force. That force, in the case of a statue, would be reflected externally in the statue's 'attitude', stance, gesture or demeanour, which are themselves fused with the internal operation of the artist's intentions and skill within the limitations imposed by his materials.

Writers in Milton's period agree that form is the *sine qua non* of the created object. Take away the form, the thing ceases to be. It is form which gives anything its existence and individuality. Viewed as argument, form becomes a means whereby the causes of a thing are related to the effect it produces, and vice versa. In the study of discourse, this view leads to the notion of structure as a manifestation of the speaker, his materials and his intention. It would appear, then, that the office of *arrangement* is crucial to our present survey. But, as noted, the concept of form as argument pervaded all the offices of composition: *style*, in the bodying forth of relationships through tropes and figures; *memory*, in the containment of concepts within relevant images; and *delivery*, in the congruence of action, speech and gesture to idea and emotion. However, *arrangement*—usually called 'disposition' in the seventeenth century, after the Latin *dispositio*—offers the most direct instruction on major formal, organisational principles. Moreover, it was in this office, particularly in 'logic', that some of the most heated intellectual battles of the time centred (see §§S–848 and S–869). Here traditional concepts of form as argument were directly challenged.

Such, in sum, is the argument of this survey. A word now about its arrangement. In the seventeenth century, anyone who proposed to write didactic discourse was usually advised to arrange his material so that it proceeded from the most general or best known to the most specific or least known. Occasionally certain variations were allowed *en route*, such as chronological development. If a discourse were organised so that it began with a general statement—'form is an argument'—and proceeded through definition and division to discuss the ostensibly relevant parts of the proffered whole, then the speaker's primary intention, so a seventeenth-century reader or listener believed, was *to teach*. That would be the intention such a form would declare. It must be noted that *persuasion* was not quite so isolable as it tends to be in modern concepts. Persuasion would be involved whether one's primary intention were to teach, to please *or* to move. But in Milton's age the new dialecticians were insisting that it is possible, and advisable, to divorce teaching from the other two functions of discourse. The insistence was something of a half-way house *en route* to the position that mathematics, or symbolic logic, is the language of rational discourse. It would seem appropriate in a survey such as the one I have undertaken to use a form similar to the one recommended, though perhaps without the impersonal barrenness its fiercest advocates urged—perhaps, too, without its desiccated pedagogy. Having begun (I) with a general position, we will now proceed to develop it in two ways, (A) through a brief exposition of its background and (B) through an examination of some details in Milton's day. And the second division will be developed in two ways, through an examination (1) of certain contexts for which (2) Ramism and Baconianism will be our texts. Finally, all these matters become parts of our general survey, which will be applied (II) specifically towards a consideration of form in Milton's writing.

BACKGROUND

To *philosophers* through the ages, dialectic has always been a more serious mode of communication than rhetoric: dialectic did not involve appeals to the passions, which so concerned Plato, nor did it involve catering to the needs of a mixed audience, that 'beast of many heads' as Aristotle called it. So most rhetorical theorising was done not by philosophers but by *practitioners*. One sign of apparently irreconcilable difference between philosophers and rhetoricians is life style. The philosopher's life is contemplative and withdrawn, the rhetorician's engaged and public. Renaissance humanists, who tried to combine philosophy and rhetoric, held the correlative life styles in uneasy balance, preaching engagement while practising contemplation. In their efforts to revive rhetorical theory their acknowledged master was Cicero, who provided the most applicable footnote to Plato and Aristotle and whose life seemed successfully to combine oratory and contemplation. Besides, Cicero was also eminently useful to humanist efforts in reforming Latin studies. To those humanists who had Greek, Isocrates was another great orator-contemplator; long before Cicero, Isocrates had demonstrated the function of moral character (*ethos*) as formal cause and thereby exemplified a rhetorical quality which was to become a central, motivating concern in all humanist writing. But when the uneasy balance of sixteenth-century humanism was tipped in favour of the 'New Philosophy' of the seventeenth century, the entire heritage of classical rhetorical theory was reinterpreted and drastically altered.

There are three characteristics of classical rhetorical theory which are instructive of developments in rhetoric, 'logic' and poetry in the Age of Milton. To make such a statement we are of course implying that there is something monolithic about classical rhetorical theory, an implication that, alas, a rapid survey must allow, though in this case not inappropriately. It is my effort to view these matters as they might be seen by a seventeenth-century Englishman. But let us at least begin with a reminder that a generation separated Aristotle from Plato and Isocrates, and almost three centuries intervene between Aristotle and Cicero. Between Cicero and Milton there are over seventeen centuries, the latter decades of which were marked by a great revival of classical learning, which at first, before the sophistication of historical methods of research, viewed antiquity as immutable. There was the recent past, which was largely in error. There was the remote past, which was to be prized and sought after. Then there was the future, which the great humanist reformers insisted should be built upon the best lessons from the remote past. Eventually, however, the seventeenth-century Englishman began to seek the new and different; if he sought the old it was neither to copy nor to idolise it but to revise or update it or view its errors in the light of new scientism. In the process, at least three characteristics of ancient rhetoric were drastically altered: rhetoric, though discrete, was considered by the ancients, at times proudly, a derivative subject; it was a faculty of speaking inherent in all genres; and it was pleasurable.

To be facile and glib, never at a loss for something to say, able to dilate on any subject at a moment's notice—such speakers were the cause of Plato's ire, for they easily swayed the hearts and minds of men and were the true corrupters of youth. The arts of speaking, he believed, must be based upon knowledge, not of language merely and how it works but substantive knowledge of all the humane arts—as Socrates states in the recapitulation of his argument to Phaedrus:

> First you must know the truth about the subject that you speak or write about; that is to say, you must be able to isolate it in definition, and having so defined it you must next understand how to divide it into kinds, until you reach the limit of division; secondly, you must have a corresponding discernment of the nature of the soul, discover the type of speech appropriate to each nature, and order and arrange your discourse accordingly, addressing a variegated soul in a variegated style that ranges over the whole gamut of tones, and a simple soul in a simple style.[8]

Though the speaker had to understand the psychology of audiences, above all he had to know whereof he spoke, and this substantive knowledge was to be derived from other disciplines.

Rhetoric as a derivative subject was interpreted differently by Aristotle. The arts were to be divided, more strictly than by Plato, into their various kinds. Rhetoric, an object of this columbarian effort, fell within that division of the arts Aristotle named the *probable* or contingent, as opposed to the *demonstrable* or necessary; the former dealt with matters of opinion, the latter with matters of certitude. A modern rhetorician, attempting to give rhetoric some serious philosophic consideration, has described a realm not unlike Aristotle's *probable*:

> Instead of basing our philosophy on definitive, unquestionable truths, our starting point is that men and groups of men adhere to opinions of all sorts with a variable intensity, which we can only know by putting it to the test. These beliefs are not always self-evident, and they rarely deal with clear and distinct ideas. The most generally accepted beliefs remain implicit and unformulated for a long time, for more often than not it is only on the occasion of a disagreement as to the consequences resulting from them that the problem of their formulation or more precise definition arises.[9]

Within this realm, for Aristotle, rhetoric was to be the counterpart of dialectic, the two differing not simply in the audiences of each but also in the modes of thought appropriate to each undertaking. The *Topics*—a treatise on 'places'—was largely for dialectical reasoning, spare, lean and tough. A different, looser set of places more dependent upon prior analysis of the audience was constructed for the *Rhetoric*. With these places the speaker could analyse almost any subject appropriate to his speech. Knowledge of the subject, though gained through other disciplines, was to be analysed by rhetorical means. Thus rhetoric was both discrete and derivative.

So it was for Cicero, who specifies the kinds of knowledge which the orator must have besides rhetoric: logic, moral philosophy, natural philosophy, civil law and history. For Cicero the discipline of rhetoric, whose product was the man of eloquence, was at the very pinnacle of humane learning, a place reserved by Plato for philosophy, the two positing a hierarchical arrangement of the arts differing from Aristotle's rather more horizontal arrangement.

By contrast, hierarchies and horizons seem not to fit Isocrates's conceptual model of rhetorical education. For this contemporary of Socrates the *goal* of education was apparently far more important than either a hierarchy or a discretising of the arts. That goal was practical wisdom. Rhetoric—not so much the theory but the practice of speaking and writing—was its instrument. It stood therefore at the centre of the curriculum, neither on top nor at the side. Perhaps because of his emphasis on substantive knowledge, Isocrates alone of all the Sophists drew Plato's praise—the highest praise, for having a mind with 'an innate tincture of philosophy'.[10] And partly because his long and very full life appeared to be a model of wisdom practically applied, he drew Milton's praise as 'that Old man eloquent'.[11] We shall take a closer look at Isocrates's accomplishments at the conclusion of this section. A point which we must note here is that, while placing rhetoric at the centre of the curriculum—and at the centre of each subject—Isocrates insisted, as Aristotle did later, that it was an art not simply of speaking but of thinking: 'for the same arguments which we use in persuading others when we speak in public, we employ also when we deliberate in our own thoughts'.[12] But by the time of Cicero a break had occurred that remained irreparable until the Renaissance, when it was corrected only to become irreparably broken again for centuries:

> Socrates . . . in his discussions separated the science of wise thinking from that of elegant speaking, though in reality they are closely linked together . . . . This is the source from which has sprung the undoubtedly absurd and unprofitable and reprehensible severance between the tongue and the brain, leading to our having one set of professors to teach us to think and another to teach us to speak.[13]

In this respect Cicero's doctrines are aimed at maintaining a valuable wholeness. More like Isocrates and Aristotle than Plato, he insists on the interconnectedness of expression and thought—or, to put the matter in Ciceronian terms, he would preserve the rhetorical integrity of *invention* and *arrangement* and foil their divorce from the other offices of composition. The spirit of pedagogical reform, however, continually assaults that integrity.

Second, ancient doctrine saw rhetoric as inherent in all genres. Rhetoric was not identified simply as an art of persuasion. Indeed, persuasion could be better, more long-lastingly accomplished by other means. Nor was it the only art of argumentation. Dialecticians argued. But the first aim of rhetoric was immediate victory over the minds of one's auditors in a commemorative rite or of one's judges in a controversy. Its time was always the present; its subject the real, even the quotidian; its audience a slice of the populace; its long-lasting effects, including those we might conceive of as 'aesthetic', were fortuitous. Thus rhetoric could be a factor in any genre—a Platonic dialogue between unequals (who is ever the equal of Socrates?) on, say, how to judge a certain speech; it could be in a poem or play, as the reader of the *Poetics* realises when Aristotle advises him to consult 'the art of Rhetoric' for instruction in the possibilities of thought and speech by a character in 'modern' drama. True, Aristotle defined rhetoric in his treatise on the subject as the faculty for discovering in a particular case the available means of persuasion. But the word 'persuasion' and the emphasis in the ensuing treatise on forms of reasoning show that Aristotle intended to reform rhetoric, in part by narrowing its purview. Moreover, the attempted narrowing is in turn somewhat offset by Aristotle's insistence that 'everybody to some extent makes use of both Dialectic and Rhetoric; for all make some attempt to sift or to support theses, and to defend or attack persons'.[14] In short, probably the most elemental, the most identifiable characteristics of ancient rhetoric were its goal of immediate victory and the particularity of its speaking situations. These characteristics in turn would seem to account for rhetoric's association with oratory and public address, funeral elegies and forensic speeches. Because these types of speaking pervade literary genres, the eventual assimilation of *all* literature to rhetoric was anticipated by ancient doctrine—an assimilation which was sealed by early systems of Roman education and rarely questioned in England before the Age of Milton.

Third, as the ancients taught and demonstrated, rhetorical efficacy to a large extent inheres in the motives of pleasure. Indeed, rhetoricians have taught for centuries that taking pleasure in speaking and hearing is a worthy human trait and only increases the speaker's control of the moment. Cicero, above all others, updated and transmitted to the centuries the ancient equation of pleasure with stylistic devices, an equation which had earned for the Sophists some disrepute among early philosophers.

To teach, to please and to move were, as we have noted, the purposes Cicero set for the orator. And style is one sure way to please, because style appeals not simply to the ear but to the mind. In an eloquent oration, Cicero argued, there should 'be metaphors of all sorts in great abundance, because these figures by virtue of the comparison involved transport the mind and bring it back, and move it hither and thither; and this rapid stimulation of thought in itself produces pleasure'.[15] Moreover, when compared with the philosopher's plain discourse, the highly figurative speech of the orator is more efficacious because of its appeals to the passions:

> It is therefore easy to distinguish the eloquence which we are treating in this work from the style of the philosophers. The latter is gentle and academic; it has no equipment of words or phrases that catch the popular fancy; it is not arranged in rhythmical periods, but is loose in structure; there is no anger in it, no hatred, no ferocity, no pathos, no shrewdness; it might be called a chaste, pure and modest virgin.[16]

Cicero's fervent admirers in the Renaissance frequently argued about what constituted the true 'Ciceronianism' in theory and practice. At times they were misled by that schematised approach to problems of style offered in the *Rhetorica ad Herrenium*, for centuries erroneously thought to be a work of Cicero's. Furthermore, the stylistic dimensions of 'Ciceronianism' at times linked with another heritage, this one from the Middle Ages, which taught that effective rhetoric actually centred in figurative language. Nonetheless, for whatever reasons and through whatever sanctions, delight in creating and identifying the figures was a strong motivation for the Renaissance Englishman.[17]

We may be certain that he had been taught through the revived rhetorical traditions that pleasure is itself a significantly human motivation. The Ciceronian theorist of education, Quintilian (first century A.D.), whose writings were to enjoy widespread, approving attention in the Renaissance, put the matter plainly: 'the end which the orator must keep in view is not persuasion but speaking well'.[18] That meant not only grammatical correctness, or adequate volume and clarity, but also speaking or writing impressively so that one's mastery over the beauty and complexities of language gave pleasure to his audience. The teaching lies behind the multitudinous definitions of rhetoric as *ars bene dicendi*. Isocrates's voice belongs in that chorus. But, again judging largely from his 'written speeches', Isocrates had a somewhat different and rather more specific approach to the matter of pleasure, however much it is at least partially incorporated within Cicero's view: pleasure arises from the rhythmical blending of parts into a whole. By means of that blending, the written oration potentially outlives its particular moment and finds a wider audience, so long as the blended whole is deeply reflective of the speaker's moral character.

That observation leads us once again to our path through this thicket: form. Plato, in the quotation from the *Phaedrus*, indicates that there are two forms to be considered: one, a logical progression of definition and division, through which the speaker or writer is to marshal his thoughts; the other, a public form for those thoughts dependent upon what the rhetor knows of his audience's emotions. Aristotle, who in the *Topics* distinguished the four 'causes' noted at the outset of this survey, has very little to say on form in the *Rhetoric*. The rhetor, he believed, need divide his discourse into only two parts, statement and proof. The implication is strong that the formal cause of the oration depends less on the moral character of the speaker (*ethos*), less on emotional appeals to his audience (*pathos*), and more on his materials—*logos*, specifically the enthymeme. In the *Poetics* Aristotle addresses directly the formal cause of poetry, which was meant to be the imitation of a human action. The lesson, however, was lost until the late sixteenth century, when, as we shall see, it was revived, only to become initially absorbed by established rhetorical doctrine. Cicero, the *Rhetorica ad Herrenium* and Quintilian had definite schemes of dividing an oration into various parts. The divisions were externally imposed and were believed to suit the needs of any audience. Generally, the discourse was to begin with an exordium, then proceed with appropriate digressions through narration (background), proposition, division, proof, refutation and peroration—a progressive concept of form which pervaded all arts of discourse in the English Renaissance, including poems and plays as well as prose meant for distribution in writing or print, such as Sidney's *Defence of Poesie* or Bacon's *Of the Advancement of Learning*. External principles of form became conventional; the internal, in rhetorical theory, were largely neglected.

Isocrates is usually given credit for first making skilful use of those oratorical parts later described in Ciceronian theory. But it was his great stroke in practice to show that the wellsprings of rhetorical form—that is, form as argument—lie not in external conventions, not in *pathos*, nor in *logos*, but above all in *ethos*.

Unique among the Attic orators, Isocrates lived in a philosopher's retirement from the world and wrote his arguments. He shunned actually appearing before an audience—perhaps because of his weak voice, his shyness, or his confessed love of 'peace and tranquillity'. But through his writing he created a manner of speaking for which he became famous: he avoided the excesses of style through which his own master, Gorgias, acquired such fame, and showed how pleasures with language may be achieved through other means. Striking phrases and local effects were less important for Isocrates than the overall structure of the work itself. The major principle of that structure lay within the character of a certain kind of speaker, the product of an educational scheme centrally concerned with rhetoric and directed towards the practical application of wisdom. Isocrates described the unity of an argument as making 'all parts consonant with one another', but he indicated that this consonance arose not from an application of rules and not simply from nature or practice but from that refinement of moral character which is the greatest achievement of a liberal education.[19] The force of *ethos* as a mode of proof was skilfully demonstrated by a contemporary, Lisias, in his speeches written for courts of law. But Isocrates wrote most of his speeches for larger audiences on topics that were pan-Athenian, at times panhellenic in scope, and the character he fashioned as his communicative instrument in his later speeches was not variable like the dramatic *ethopoeia* of Lisias but derived from a willed synthesis of morality and politics. The lesson was to be of great significance for the seventeenth century in England, when the moral rhetor would cast his printed orations before an immense, unseen public:

> The problem of Isocrates in inventing journalism (and the problem of anyone attempting to make use of his invention) was to create *on paper* a figure whose being is totally defined by the passion, the energies, and the logic of his will . . . We all know . . . that this fiction, this ideal, charismatic illusion of pure *Voluntas* does not exist for itself; its function is to create the illusion that we, all the scattered, infinitely varied individuals to whom it speaks, are members of the creature's vast, invisible, unified audience. (§S–856: p. 225)

Like all rhetorical elements, *ethos* is constructed on the particularities of the speaking situation and aimed at immediate victory or assent. But as Isocrates showed, the final effects of this implied authorial voice can be universal and long-lasting.

This was a lesson that, like so many others from antiquity, was available more through revived discourse than through reborn theory.

SEVENTEENTH-CENTURY CONTEXTS

The depreciatory sense of the word *rhetoric* in English—as speech possibly delightful but certainly deceptive—was firmly established by the beginning of the seventeenth century. As the century progressed, the subject was regarded in some quarters as tainted with immorality. Writers turned on it with feelings akin to disappointment and betrayal. Milton's description of Belial is an epitome of the moralist's case against rhetoric:

> A fairer person lost not Heav'n; he seemed
> For dignity compos'd and high exploit:
> But all was false and hollow; though his Tongue
> Dropt Manna, and could make the worse appear
> The better reason, to perplex and dash
> Maturest Counsels: for his thoughts were low . . .
> (*Paradise Lost*, II, 110–15)

'To make the worse appear the better reason' was a 'commonplace' (in the technical meaning of the word, to be discussed later) charge against rhetoric—a charge as old as Isocrates (see *Antidosis*, 15). But we must be careful in our assessment of the seventeenth-century Englishman's depreciation of rhetoric: we must understand that he applied the word primarily to the misuse of *style* and *delivery*, two offices which in his day were theoretically cut off from the true rhetorical tradition and mainstream. Satan's intricate style in both *Paradise* poems exemplifies just this misuse, and his ingenious delivery in tempting Eve invites a contrast not only with the great orators of Greece and Rome but also between modern and ancient rhetoric.[20]

It used to be common among modern scholars to speak of an 'anti-rhetorical' movement which developed first in the late sixteenth century. Now, because of recent work in the history of rhetoric, we understand that what occurred was more likely a movement away from one kind of rhetoric towards another. Yet the word 'anti-rhetorical' is at least dramatically accurate. It conveys a sense of the strong feelings of seventeenth-century language reformers, who believed that they were at long last correcting the errors of pagan rhetoric, which seemed at times predicated on curiously amoral attitudes (even Cicero was guilty of the charge, and Isocrates could appear inconsistent), and which seemed overly titillated by the wickedly sensuous delights of language, and which was above all vaguely defined and unscientifically taught.

In the meantime, however, poetry had become associated with some of rhetoric's earlier eminence. In fact, prior to the 'anti-rhetorical' movement, poetry was widely regarded in sixteenth-century England as rhetoric *par excellence*—a view which, when compared with classical attitudes, underscores the ascendance of poetry over oratory.[21] When rhetoric's fortunes changed, so did poetry's. In the midst of the change, the fortunes of dialectic as the plain and honest purveyor of truth re-ascended. But this 'logic' was not exactly centred on the contemplative intellect so prized in the centuries between Cicero and the humanist revival of classical rhetoric. It was, rather, a means for a naked, bolder assault on truth as well as on the intellectual indolence and intransigence of other men. It was, in short, rhetoric in a new guise.

In reviewing these developments we have touched only on surface characteristics. Below the surface lies the complex intellectual turmoil which is approached by different paths in every chapter of this book. Without endeavouring to trace cause-and-effect relationships precisely, perhaps in the space of this essay three closely related developments may be described. These will correlate with the three characteristics of classical rhetorical theory described earlier.

First, whereas ancient rhetoric had maintained a wholeness of concept and offered a unique approach to analysis and thought, Renaissance rhetoric became fragmented in the seventeenth century. Classical rhetoric had a clearly assigned place in the practical affairs of men. It had an integrated system, from *invention* to *delivery*. Even the rhetoric revived by the humanists offered instruction not merely in how to speak but in how to *think* of certain problems in terms of the available means of persuasion. But in the seventeenth century most matters of *invention* and *judgement* or *arrangement* or 'method' in general were considered beyond the proper scope of rhetorical theory. *Memory* was regarded by a few theorists as no longer necessary in an age of literacy and print; by others as a mystifyingly occult art; and by still others as an epistemological issue at the very heart of radical concepts of man's reason. Thus rhetorical theory in the most prominent system of the early seventeenth century was left only with *style* and *delivery*. But so deeply ingrained had rhetoric become as a conceptual model that the old system was a paradigm for all theorising about the language arts. It pervaded dialectic, which was increasingly thought of as a communicative mode effective for *all* men. Literary theory was virtually old rhetoric without *memory* or *delivery*.[22]

To understand how it was possible for this fragmentation and dispersal to come about, we need to review the intellectual milieu within which it occurred, at least to the extent that the milieu reveals characteristic attitudes towards language, the mind, and the uses of knowledge. Let us return to that definition of argument as 'relatableness' with which this survey began. If we were to analyse discourse in terms of that definition, two questions might present themselves: (1) does this language signify relations actually present in the world? or (2) does it represent certain possibilities for agreement, common ground, or persuasiveness in a controversy? The second question had always marked out the realm of rhetoric, whose claims to truth, we would say, were not objective but subjective. However, in the seventeenth century the first question, to the inevitable disparagement of traditional rhetoric as productive inquiry, received the more excited attention by intellectuals, breathless with a feeling that they were on the brink of discovering immutable, universal truths.

They had been led to that brink partly because of the vast expanse of knowledge made available by the printing press. Used at first by the humanists to disseminate those classical manuscripts whose reappearance marks the age we call the Renaissance, the press showed an insatiable hunger. Into its maw went manuscripts forged and fraudulent as well as authentic. The process quickly became one of discovery, an antiquarian thrust towards the ancient frontiers of man's knowledge, whereon some believed lay the ur-book of wisdom and the *lingua humana*, the primitive language of man before Babel.[23] Or, to use the metaphor employed by Milton for the same subject (in *Areopagitica*): as if the body of Truth had been broken and scattered into a hundred places, man had to continue his efforts to rejoin the fragments against their perfect rejoining in the Second Coming. By Milton's time, however, the search had already begun to proceed in a different direction, no longer towards discovering the dispersed truths of antiquity but towards developing the utterly new.

The original nature of this search had been largely determined by humanist insistence on practical application of knowledge. A disinterested pursuit of ideas formed only a minor part of humanist motives. Knowledge was to be *used*. But as that knowledge became vast, one of its uses became specific: to some latter-day humanists and new scientists, discoveries in literature as well as in lands seemed to show that all men, everywhere and throughout the ages, had a certain 'natural' reason. Associated with this idea was the equally forceful one

that what was 'natural' was both 'naked' and 'plain'. Rhetorical ornamentation
was ostentatious. It was unnatural. By comparison, mathematics offered a
language closer to the needs of natural reason—as implied in Thomas Sprat's
famous praise of the members of the Royal Society (1667); 'They [the Royal
Society] have exacted from all their members, a close, naked, natural way of
speaking; positive expression, clear senses; a native easiness: bringing all things
as near the Mathematical plainness, as they can . . .' (§P–443: p. 113). The
doctrines of the humanists, like the rhetorical theories they had revived, were
being discarded.

In the sixteenth century, traditionally based rhetorical theories usually began
with the premises that man alone had been elevated by God above brutishness
by virtue of speech and reason, and that eloquent—gracefully ornamented—
speech is the surest way to move anyone's will. Little wonder that on these
premises poetry could be regarded as the supreme rhetoric—or that for a
profoundly humanist poet like Milton a major difference between pre- and
post-lapsarian eloquence is that the former was 'prompt', the latter deliberate,
studied or forced, but both were natural and necessary (§S–875). However, the
premises were scorned by the new intellectuals and scientists of the seventeenth
century, the anti-humanists, who rejected all 'eloquence' as interferences with
the operation of natural reason and so disparaged even *style* and *delivery* which
then comprised virtually all that remained of traditional rhetoric.

Second, it was equally apparent to the ancients and to the sixteenth-century
Englishman that rhetoric was a factor in all modes and genres of public
discourse, but it was not so apparent to the latter *at first* that the new means of
'public speaking' called for a rhetorical theory radically different in its orientation. Ancient rhetorical theory was oriented towards oral performance, though it
was aimed at written as well as spoken communication. This oral orientation is
seen not merely in the ancient inclusion of *delivery* as an integral part of rhetoric,
and not merely in the insistence in ancient rhetorical theory on *copia* and on aural
schemes of style, but above all in ancient rhetoric's overriding concern with the
particularity of the rhetorical situation, the *specific* motives of speech: an
audience, a time, a place, a motive. Only one mode of oratory—the epideictic—veered away from the specific and toward the universal, but even these
commemorative speeches were designed for impact within a specific situation.
Oral orientation is evident in the written speeches as well. After all, Isocrates
and Cicero wrote for particular audiences of men like themselves who would
most likely *hear* the speech read aloud. It would have been inconceivable to
them, as it was inconceivable within the rhetorical theories and orations which
their ages transmitted through the humanists, to prepare an oration for an
audience accessible through a 'mass medium' like print.

In reviving classical rhetoric and basing their educational reforms—particularly instruction in Latin—on it, the humanists in effect fostered principles of
composition at odds with the needs of their age, not simply because that age was
an age of print and literacy but also because it was an age of expansiveness and
exploration. Ironically, whereas classical rhetoric had emphasised the varieties

of personalities who might be present in any one audience, one correlative effect of the knowledge explosion, as we have seen, was to view all men as potentially accessible through a uniform quality known as 'natural reason'. These mark two extremes on a continuum. Obviously, successful communication was achieved without adherence to either concept, of the variegated particularity of an audience or of a reductive though universalised concept of its 'nature'.

But many documents of the age bear the marks of one concept or the other. Milton's *Areopagitica* is an especially pertinent example. Even a cursory reading of that written oration will reveal a point near the beginning when a major shift in style seems to occur. Actually, the shift is marked by a change in mode of address. Milton forgets about his particular audience, in effect putting aside doctrines he had been taught through classical rhetoric. The opening paragraphs are laboured, at times awkward, convoluted in their efforts to reach a particular group of men, Parliament in 1644. The moves which Milton makes are conventional ones for the *exordium*.[24] But then his attention seems to drift from his audience. The speech becomes smoother, more graceful, easier to follow. Another principle of composition, which the first had only interfered with, takes over. That principle, one scholar has argued, is that Milton switches his audience in midstream, turning from members of Parliament to a morally fit audience though few, consisting not only of his countrymen but people in other lands as well.[25] But the central lesson of Isocrates's example is apt to be overlooked in that view. For however much Milton uses the *Areopagiticus* of Isocrates as his foil, the lesson of the master rhetorician remains: how to reach a remote audience by creating a certain *ethos* 'on paper'. The lesson was an integral part of the rhetorical tradition, though subject to interference by superficial doctrines of form in traditional rhetorical theory. Moreover, that theory, as I have tried to suggest, was in turn singularly unsuited to the communicative challenges of an age of print. Nor, as Milton must have realised, were those challenges likely to be met at the other extreme by new theories of universal reason.

In addition to the developments we have discussed—the fragmentation and dispersal of rhetoric, the theoretical fostering of principles of composition at odds with the needs of the age—there was a third development which like the first two emphasised universal reason but even more directly than the first two propelled the 'anti-rhetorical' movement: linguistic sensuousness was viewed as interfering with serious thought. The impact of this development was necessarily strong, since the 'material cause' of any discourse depends largely upon the speaker's notions of the kinds of uses to which language may be put. Let us recall that for the ancients pleasurability was an integral part of rhetoric and that, for them, language could be made to yield delights. These delights might be of an imaginative order, challenging the audience to mental gymnastics, or of a purely linguistic order, constructing schemes of echoing sounds. Of all the features integral to rhetoric from ancient days, this one bore the brunt of greatest disapproval in the seventeenth century, reaching its pinnacle in Locke's condemnation: figurative language is an 'abuse' and must be disallowed in all serious efforts to convey truth and knowledge; 'if we would speak of Things as they are, we must allow, that all the Art of Rhetorick, besides Order and Clearness, all the artificial and figurative application of Words Eloquence hath invented, are for nothing else, but to insinuate wrong Ideas, move the Passions, and thereby mislead the Judgment; and so indeed are perfect cheat'.[26] In the new quest for truth, order and clarity are to be prized; other pleasures of language are to be rejected.

This deep suspicion of 'eloquent' style would seem to be a necessary consequence of certain forces which led as well to the other developments we have discussed. Several interpretations have been offered of those forces. Some sort of 'dissociation of sensibility' had occurred in the seventeenth century, T. S. Eliot suggested in a famous essay, which divorced feeling from thinking and nullified that 'direct sensuous apprehension of thought' which distinguishes Elizabethan and Jacobean verse.[27] To Walter Ong, that dissociation is more precisely and causally viewed in terms of the convergence, in logical and rhetorical systems of the time, of oral- and print-oriented sensibilities (§§S–869 and S–870). Recently, Richard Lanham offered an interpretation whose scope exceeds both: 'The Western self has from the beginning been composed of a shifting and perpetually uneasy combination of *homo rhetoricus* and *homo seriosus*, of a social self and a central self' (§S–859: p. 6). With Lanham's dichotomy, we should describe developments in the seventeenth century as the total undermining of the rhetorical tradition and a new elevation of seriousness.

However intriguing these interpretations, we may with fewer cosmic gestures note a patent truth: rhetoric did not die, only fashions in eloquence changed. The change occurred on extremist fringes of intellectual circles, and had a sobering effect on literature.[28] Language was to become transparent. The self was to become not merely centralised and rigorously consistent but effaced and objective—an obliteration of *ethos*. The passionate aspects of man's nature (elements of *pathos*) were not simply to be neglected, they were to be avoided. Naked reason, unadorned *logos* was to be supreme.

Before touching on examples, let us return more firmly to our path. All the matters just reviewed have implications for form. Form, as the embodiment of the speaker's thought, is complexly sensuous. Since according to increasingly rigid doctrine appeals to the senses are tantamount to appeals to the emotions and so deflect the mind from seriousness, a logical consequent would seem to be that form itself should be made systematic and mechanical, after the pattern of 'natural reason'. This new concept, as in the quotation from Locke, is better called 'order' than 'form'. But when not confused by theoretical fashions of the day, speakers and writers yet found the oldest, humanist solution to problems of form deeply embedded within rhetorical practice:

> I see thou know'st what is of use to know,
> What best to say canst say, to do canst do;
> Thy actions to thy words accord, thy words

To thy large heart give utterance due, thy heart
Conteins of good, wise, just the perfect shape.
                                        (*Paradise Regained*, III, 7–11)

An ancient rhetorical ideal is here set forth: the orator must be a man of knowledge as well as a man of action; he must be able to suit his gestures to his speech, and he must from his own character and passions impress the suitable form on his discourse. The praise is authentic, though spoken by Satan to flatter Christ, Satan having collected 'all his Serpent wiles' and in the flattery created a perfect *gradatio*.

RAMISM

Ramism is a fitful abridgement of the most urgent forces at work in the theories of rhetoric, 'logic' and poetry of Milton's day—fitful in its militant claims of innovative reform, though it was only a kind of précis of ideas offered by Continental theorists in their efforts to construct a clearer, more nearly Aristotelian division between the language arts, which from their point of view had become almost hopelessly entangled. For example, Aristotle had taught that the doctrine of the four causes (described earlier in this chapter) belonged to dialectic; his rhetoric did not treat of causes. But by the sixteenth century the doctrine of the four causes had become thoroughly rhetoricised and taught in 'logic' as well as in rhetoric. Ramism assayed to straighten out this overlapping—but, ludicrously, without attempting to reform the concept of 'argument', which as suggested at the outset of this survey had already expanded beyond its Aristotelian bounds. Taking its name from a French educational reformer, Pierre de la Ramée (Petrus Ramus), Ramism received considerable impetus from the circumstances of Ramus's death in the St Bartholomew's Day Massacre in 1572, causing him to be widely regarded as the first Protestant martyr. It is as unlikely that Milton was a Ramist as it is that he was totally unaffected by the movement.

Most of the Ramists' efforts were aimed at improving logic, and to accomplish this they plundered rhetoric of its systems of thought. *Invention* and *disposition/judgement* were to belong solely to 'logic'. Rhetoric alone was to have *style* and *delivery*. That is, even orators were to learn the subtle arts of thinking and verbalising in the new 'logic', as Ramus himself wrote in a preface to Talon's *Rhetorica* in 1567, and only ornaments and vocal expression were to be solely the matter of rhetoric, even when needed for philosophical disputation. Of course, the necessity for ornamenting and delivering a philosophical argument had drastically diminished in an age of print and science. Poetry, the Ramists believed—as they inevitably had to, given their system—had no special requirements in thinking and speaking; it was merely metred prose.

Our present discussion of Ramism need not be lengthy. The Ramists stood at the extreme of every radical, ostensibly anti-traditional and clearly anti-humanist attitude already described in this survey: Ramism fragmented the arts, it offered a concept of 'natural reason' as a kind of universalised audience for communication, it was devoted to high seriousness and was deeply suspicious of the passions as enemies of thought, it rejected the sensuousness of tropes and figures as instruments of reason. One might also add that in its impulse to abridge knowledge it fitted perfectly the Renaissance love of epitomising, providing how-to-do-it manuals for the autodidact.[29] All of this was revisionary, not innovative—as Bacon notes in his opaque reference to Ramus as a 'man of bold disposition, and famous for methods and short ways which people like, who has in appearance reduced them to an art, while he has in fact only spoiled all that the others had done'.[30] What must occupy our attention here is the Ramist approach to problems of form: there was a natural form, according to the Ramists, which is the counterpart of natural reason.

Within each man, the Ramists taught, are sparks of natural reason. This natural reason is best able to intuit the connections between things in the orderly universe—in short, to construct 'arguments' of the sort defined at the outset of this survey. The concept of 'argument' is indeed typical of the age. What is uniquely Ramist is the insistence that the argumentative ability is intuitive and natural. All one needs is a systematic education to sharpen its use. Moreover, truth is truth, the Ramists believed, and does not require further sophistication through constructing canons appropriate to judging the contingent as opposed to the necessary; consequently, emphasis fell on the axiomatic, the self-evident (cf. the quotation offered earlier explaining Aristotle's *probable*), arrived at by those very sparks of natural reason *intuiting* the interconnectedness of all phenomena within an order that was itself chartable.

To chart this order, one constructed a dichotomised diagram, a series of brackets breaking into natural components a thesis or definition, proceeding from the most general or best known to the most specific or least known. 'Man is a rational animal'; the definition can be dichotomised: 'rational' and 'animal', and bracketing divisions of these two elements are also possible. This is, as it were, the path of natural reason. The efficacy of any communication—say, a Virgilian eclogue—is diagrammatically demonstrable. The brackets make visible the 'logical' relations between elements of a successful discourse; as if, in a modern essay, the writer were to allow the numbering and lettering of his sections to serve as a visible if crude substitute for transitions and connectives, so the brackets could make visible the interconnectedness of all parts of the discourse. Good poetry is metred prose which follows the order of the dichotomised diagram, a lesson the Ramists continued to offer though they admitted that besides 'natural method' there is also 'prudential method', which was merely the traditional rhetorical systems of arrangement.

But in their zeal the Ramists proposed the natural method for *all* kinds of discourse, and they insisted it was present in the best discourse through the ages, including speeches, poems and the Bible. Being 'natural', it would have to be. Truth was to be found, and spoken, and judged by a single means; that is, in technical terms, there was one art of *invention* and there was no distinction between the arts of *arrangement* (*dispositio*) and *judgement* (*iudicium*). With that one move the Ramists considerably thickened a centuries-old confusion. Moreover, however grudgingly prudential method was allowed for oratory and poetry, natural method and only natural method was to be used for any discourse which had teaching as its aim. But that move was a crude, not a discriminating effort at separating the ends of discourse (which had been virtually indistinguishable for centuries), for the Ramists imagined that any speaker or writer had one of two purposes, either to teach or to deceive.

Milton wrote his *Art of Logic* (published 1672, but apparently written in his youth) as a recension of Ramus's *Dialectique*. It was ostensibly a tribute to the master, but it undercuts extreme doctrines of form allied with the Ramist movement. Certainly it is possible neatly to outline Milton's *Logic*: its 'order' is so dichotomised that one may cast all its main heads on to bracketed diagrams. But the 'fuller institution' of Milton's intention, stated in the title (*Artis logicae plenior institutio*), loosely expands the discussion and offers the sort of audience assistance which contradicts a reliance on intuitive reasoning.[31] In that regard, too, Milton discusses the syllogism at much greater length than do most Ramists; in fact, he emphasises it as an aid to reason when intuition fails to see the truth of an axiom. Further, there can be, as he notes at least twice, a formal validity apart from 'truth',[32] a distinction painful to most Ramists. Finally, a most telling contrast between Milton and the Ramists is his relinquishment of 'prudential method' to the arts of 'oratory' and 'poetics'. For the Ramists, method of either sort was to be taught only in 'logic'; but their 'logic' generally left the 'prudential method' to be discovered in the actual practice of orators and poets, whose 'method', according to the first Englishing of Ramus's logic in 1574, by contrast with the 'natural method' seems not only 'imperfect' but 'preposterous and out of all good fashion and order'.[33]

BACONIANISM

Of all the many movements in reformed rhetoric and logic of the time, such as the neo-Ciceronians and the Systematics, another must receive at least passing attention in this survey, for it offers a contrasting and in many ways much longer-lasting approach to the problem of form. This is the movement associated with Francis Bacon. Because of the vastness and complexity of this movement, it may be best to begin by narrowing our scope to the subject of poetry, fictive writing in general. This we may do by looking first at Sidney's *Defence of Poesie*, an almost antediluvian defence. The real deluge came a few decades later.

The occasion of Sidney's apologia (1583) was the likelihood of increased attacks on poetry from the new moralists, especially the Puritans, with their high seriousness. However occasioned, the work stands as the first sustained English criticism of poetry, including the dramatic. Almost every theme which was to be sounded in attacks on and defences of poetry through the ensuing century are to be found in Sidney's essay. For example: eloquence is a necessary ingredient which allows the discourse to enter 'into the gates of popular judgments', and it turns otherwise dull lessons into 'hart-ravishing knowledge'. Certainly the ability of poetry to ravish the heart is conceded by Puritans and members of the Royal Society alike, who took a rather different view of the necessity for eloquence. Eloquence, moreover, says Sidney, has 'some dyvine force in it', and the poet at work is 'lifted up with the vigor of his owne intention'. This was spoken of as inspiration or madness in ancient theory and was admitted into Baconianism.[34] Poetry, such as drama, according to Sidney, should not be scorned for its presentation of wicked characters, for man learns virtuous action through 'making known his enemie vice, which must be destroyed, and his combersome servant Passion, which must be maistered'. The theme is echoed in Milton's *Areopagitica*, where the subject is not poetry but freedom to publish all books. Most characteristic of pro-poetry opinion in his day, Sidney argues that poetry is superior rhetoric and as such is the supreme purveyor of all knowledge. Finally, as if in answer to Ramist insensitivity, Sidney insists that poetry is not simply metred prose; in fact, 'one may be a Poet without versing, and a versifier without Poetry'.

A striking feature of Sidney's work, so far as poetic form is concerned, is that he conflates Aristotelian *mimesis* with a Plutarchan metaphor and Horatian and Ciceronian ends: 'Poesie therefore is an arte of imitation, for so *Aristotle* termeth it in his word *Mimesis*, that is to say, a representing, counterfetting, or figuring foorth: to speake metaphorically, a speaking picture: with this end, to teach and delight . . .'[35] As Aristotle taught, in his recently revived *Poetics*, the imitation of a human action is the motive of plot, which is in turn the formal cause of poetry. But Sidney takes also from Plutarch the idea that a poem is a speaking picture and, in later passages, extends the Horatian ends of teaching and delighting to include the Ciceronian one of moving as well. A poem as imitation still fell within the category of argumentative discourse.

The stance was itself defiantly moralistic. Man needs the powers of poetry to move him to virtue. The poet does this not simply by copying nature but by setting before us a second nature, one in which virtue and vice are purposefully exaggerated. Poetry is thus an object of our reason aimed at our will through our imagination—both possible and necessary, 'sith our erected wit, maketh us know what perfection is, and yet our infected will, keepeth us from reaching unto it'.

The danger of the Sidneyan position is that most of it can be readily co-opted by disputants who would devalue poetry's worth. A poet can be allowed his identity as a 'popular persuader'. But that identity will not count for much in times of linguistic reform within the circles of what we have later come to call 'hard science'. Scientists engaged in inductive reasoning, experimentation and creating a mode of communication appropriate to the limits of their work can easily, with Sidney's position, keep poetry from having any claims on seriousness whatsoever.

Bacon assigned to rhetoric a function not unlike the one Sidney gave poetry: the application of '*Reason to Imagination* for the better moving of the will'.[36] That is, reason is to be applied to the speaker's imagination as well as, in turn, by him to his audience's. The comparative 'better' in Bacon's statement should not be ignored. Imagination alone could move and mislead the will through inciting the passions. But if imagination is brought under the dominion of reason, as it is to be in Bacon's reformed rhetoric, it is less likely that the will would be misled. Poetry, however, in Bacon's view, is not hampered by reason and so it is granted more imaginative freedom than rhetoric. The core of the lesson keeps both arts well on the fringes of the emerging seriousness.

There is some reason to believe, moreover, that the lesson was used to poetry's harsh disparagement more by Baconians than by Bacon himself. In a passage similar to one in Sidney, Bacon argues that man after the Fall cannot find in nature the order he desires and that in so far as poetry represents an ideal pattern it potentially stimulates man to strive for knowledge and virtue.[37] Thus, like Sidney, Bacon gives poetry rhetorical ends. All questions of seriousness aside, the two arts are mixed. Moreover, before summarising Baconian doctrine of form, which is radically non-rhetorical, it may be well to review yet another feature of Bacon's work which was also profoundly rhetorical, his use of commonplaces.

Technically, commonplaces were sources of argument suitable for all compositions. The different types of oratory—deliberative, forensic, epideictic—each had its own source of argument, set of topics, or 'places'. The orator composing a deliberative oration would turn in the office of *invention* to those places suitable for deliberative argumentation. The commonplaces, on the other hand, as the name suggests, cut across all rhetorical genres. To supply these commonplaces, the rhetor was encouraged to collect (or copy from others) apophthegms, gnomic statements, epigrams, short disquisitions on various themes—'kingship', 'love', 'war', 'friendship', 'marriage', *ad infinitum*—as a treasury on which he might draw to enhance any argument. With the commonplace material so collected and copied, he would always have on hand an example or something with which to avoid dead silence or stammering in oral composition—or thinness in written argumentation, which until the Ramists was always regarded as a fault. In sum, commonplaces provided copiousness of expression, *copia*, 'copie' as the Englishman called it, who often called collections of commonplaces 'copybooks'. That this relict of ancient modes of oral composition was very much alive in Milton's age is shown by the widespread practice among intellectuals of maintaining copybooks and by the popularity throughout the seventeenth century of Thomas Farnaby's *Index Rhetoricus*, over half of which is devoted to instruction in gathering material for commonplace books.[38]

The ambiguity of the word 'copy', when seen from our perspective, is functional. Abundance, not originality, was the goal. After all, art under the dominance of traditional rhetoric does not prize originality. The aim of the rhetorical artist was to be not an originator but a 'consummately expert retooler of thought and expression' (§S–870: p. 80). Thus Bacon notes that 'to invent' rhetorically only means 'to recover or resummon that which we already know'.[39] The ambiguity of 'copy' may also help us sense its important association with *memory* and in turn the place of the concept within the most ancient traditions of composition. By contrast, the Ramist reformers' truly anti-traditional (and, from the humanist standpoint, anti-intellectual) stance can be gauged: they dropped all attention to *memory*, believing that once a concept, argument or discourse had been arranged in the mind after the patterning of 'natural method' it would be easy to recall, and believing that there was no need to rely on copybooks for the commonplaces of invention, for the Ramist

> thought of himself as securing his arguments from the 'nature of things', with which his mind somehow came into direct contact. Thus he felt he would find arguments against disloyalty by simply understanding disloyalty and 'analyz-ing' its genus, species, conjugates, and the rest, rather than by finding under the headings of the various 'places' what had been said about it.
>
> (§S–870: p. 84)

Intuition, with a little systematic prodding, would provide all that was neces-sary, whether one was searching out arguments to use on others or meditating on God's creation as a private lesson for oneself.

That this was hardly Bacon's view is shown not only by the rigours through which his 'new organon' would test the product and procedures of intuition but also by his own commonplace book and by his *Essays*. The relationship between copybooks and essays was noted early by Ben Jonson, who in typically irascible fashion faulted the essayists for offering little more than commonplace collec-tions, suitable for arguing on either side of a question.[40] But Bacon's essays hardly suffer from such categorisation. They need be neither faulted nor praised for being other than what they are: virtuoso performances in rhetorical *invention*. Each essay dilates a topic through stringing together pithy observations, which themselves had been taken from a certain 'promptuary' collection, as Bacon shows in the commonplace book he inserts into *De augmentis scientarum*,[41] and which may be—in fact, have been—removed and applied elsewhere in other discourses.

What is most important about the commonplace tradition is the associational habit of composition which it reveals. Composing by means of commonplaces produces a rhapsodic method of composing, which the Ramists so abhorred, a stitching together of pieces of the already known. Usually these were given shape by a superimposed principle of form, such as the parts of an oration noted earlier. Inexpertly done, the result merely revealed the unburnished common-places, as we still note today in our use of 'commonplace' pejoratively for the obvious, trite and ordinary. That Milton kept a copybook could be significant, particularly since he kept it for his own use and not for publication as essays. In some of his prose pieces and poems the commonplace habit of composition with superimposed external form can be observed (§S–864). As in Bacon, it reveals a traditional turn of mind. But in Milton a certain principle of *internal* form welds these commonplaces into a cohesive whole; for that principle we must look elsewhere, outside theory—including Bacon's.

For however much Bacon appears to be 'inextricably tangled in the rhetorical tradition',[42] the reform of language which is associated with his work produced distinctly and, on the surface at least, curiously non-rhetorical results. Bacon's entanglement with the rhetorical tradition led him not merely into rhetoricising science, seeing the functions of science in terms of the offices of rhetoric, but into urging a scientising of rhetoric as well, a divorcing of its offices from one another for the sake of scientific investigation. Thus, resulting from Bacon's work, John Bulwer's *Chirologia* appeared in 1644, the first scientific work on *delivery*, a study of hand gestures as part of the universal language of the body.[43]

Like delivery, *style* too was to be scientised—this time in ways directly marked out by Bacon himself. Language was to be not merely examined but purified. It was to be made useful for the objective needs of scientific communication, language purged of its 'vulgar' conceptions, 'juggleries' and 'charms', free of what Bacon called the 'idols of the marketplace'.[44] It was in these remarks in the *Novum organum* and in the *De augmentis scientarum* that 'the seventeenth-century critique of language had its roots' (§S–858: p. 36). Earlier we touched on some features of this critique, particularly the insistence that language was to be transparent. Virtually the whole thrust of Bacon's language reform, especially the reform carried out by his followers, lay in that insistence. In a characteristic move, Bacon himself points out that the poet composes and divides mental impressions 'according to the pleasure of the mind', whereas the scientist composes and divides them 'according to the nature of things as it exists in fact'.[45] The comparison became increasingly invidious as the century proceeded. Scientific language was to be purified and tested, Bacon insisted, so that it could reveal an objectified apprehension of the formal cause of any object or phenomenon.[46] In short, scientific language was not to call attention to itself. Its own form was to be virtually indistinguishable from its 'content', as we might say. Or, to recast the observation with which I began this survey, linguistic form was to be neutral, and the old idea of 'argument' was to make way for a newer, more objective or at least ostensibly self-evident mode of reportage. Mathematical plainness, as we have seen, was to become the model of order and clarity.

TOWARDS THE STUDY OF FORM IN MILTON

In this chapter I have touched only on major developments in rhetoric, 'logic' and literary theory, with most attention given to rhetoric as the central art of language. Throughout the sixteenth and early seventeenth centuries the centrality of rhetoric was not challenged by initial attempts to reform logic; the real challenge could come only when the traditional concept of 'argument' was radically altered. Nor was rhetoric's centrality challenged initially by the revival of Aristotle's *Poetics*.

At first, the potentially strong differences between rhetoric and the *Poetics* were either ignored or applied to the advantage of the firmly established rhetorical doctrines. Humanists in Italy, where the *Poetics* was revived in the middle of the sixteenth century, and in England seemed to regard Aristotle's treatise as a way of expanding literary doctrines already being taught within rhetoric; thus, as I observed earlier, literary theory even up to the time of Milton remained old rhetoric without *memory* or *delivery*. Sidney's essay exemplifies this fusion, just as the forces associated with Bacon show the coming need to create a different, philosophically serious ground for the criticism of poetry. Establishing that ground by bordering off the *Poetics* from the purview of a steadily weakening rhetoric, in the face of increasingly potent science, became the effort of the movement now known as 'neo-classical'.[47] That this movement was well under way in Milton's time is observable within the materials of this survey. But that Milton was not himself a part of that movement is a point I would offer. Though in many respects Milton was a man of his age, he was as rhetorician very much a man of the preceding century. In fact, as I shall try to suggest in this conclusion, so far as artistic form is concerned he was very much a man of the most ancient rhetorical traditions. That is, he was profoundly humanistic and not a neo-classicist—nor, as some recent scholars would have him be, an early romantic.

In his treatise *Of Education* Milton acknowledges that the principal sources of his critical thinking about poetry were the *Poetics*, Horace, and the commentaries on Aristotle and Cicero provided by the great Italian humanists of the sixteenth century. However, when we turn to the two short commentaries Milton himself wrote directly on his own work, the effects of Horace and the humanists seem slight, for his comments are imbued with narrowly Aristotelian, neo-classical concerns: his 'Note on the Verse of *Paradise Lost*' is a justification of blank verse, his preface to *Samson Agonistes* is a discussion of the genre of tragedy. But in the light of his achievement these critical concerns are superficial. When we turn to the matter of formal cause we see clearly where Milton parts company with the *Poetics*.

For Aristotle, the central inner principle of a drama—or, as the neo-classicists and some modern aestheticians have argued, all discourse deserving the name of poetry—is *mimesis*, or imitation: the formal cause of 'poetry' is the imitation of a human action, such as the actions of a man thinking aloud to himself in soliloquy, or the progression of actions which lead to the destruction of a tragic hero. In general, mimetic discourse is a linguistic structure which in its completeness has something of the beginning–middle–end integrity of a human experience. The doctrine had a counterpart in rhetoric. But for the rhetorician *imitatio* meant following rhetorical models, revivifying the best which had been thought and said by the masters of the past, not in dull, slavish copying, though that was necessarily the effect at times, but in skilful re-creation of the thought, forms, means, methods and intentions of the major orators and poets of antiquity. Aristotelian *mimesis* can be—and was, by the humanists—absorbed within the larger ends of rhetorical *imitatio*. In that case the imitation of a human action became only one of the means of achieving rhetorical imitation, which was always 'an attempt', as Hardison puts it, 'to reproduce in one's own age the greatness of the classics. It is not opposed to originality so much as to the idea that one can achieve literary excellence while ignoring the past. Its supreme justifications in English literature are *Paradise Lost* and *Samson Agonistes*' (§ S–850:

p. 7). For humanists, rhetorical imitation shaped the final causes of a work even when Aristotelian *mimesis* shaped part of the formal causes.

But formal and final causes are not disparate in an artistic achievement. To find the central formal causes in humanist art, one must look deeply within the rhetorical traditions, beyond the age's critical battles over the 'true' Aristotelianism, which began to replace the older battles over the 'true' Ciceronianism. Let us return to one of the developments mentioned in this survey, the controversy over traditional rhetorical delight in the sensuousness of language. It is a point at which many of the most impassioned critics of the time—the puritans with their charges of immorality and lying against imaginative writing as well as the scientists with their concerns about all linguistic obfuscation—met and agreed.

It is patently observable that rhetoricians from Gorgias to Henry Peacham taught that language should be self-consciously used so that it would delight the senses. But a certain concomitant pleasure in opacity grew extreme towards the end of the sixteenth century. When the emphasis fell on plainness and seriousness, the reform in language came initially through logic. Poetry and the other kinds of discourse were subject to all these currents, within which were two radically differing doctrines of form: the first is traditional, that form is detachable and may even be conspicuous; the second is revolutionary, that form should be transparent and neutral. Deep within that first doctrine there was a teaching—as old as Isocrates, and far more subtle than late sixteenth-century fashions—which locates the springs of language and form not in diction but in the character of the man speaking, not in *arrangement* alone but in *ethos*:

> doubtless that indeed according to art is most eloquent, which returnes and approaches neerest to nature from whence it came; and they expresse nature best, who in their lives least wander from her safe leading, which may be call'd regenerate reason. So that how he should be truly eloquent who is not withall a good man, I see not.

So wrote Milton in the *Apology for Smectymnuus*. The statement is part of an argument, of course, and has local reference. But that quality in no way diminishes its force of application to Milton's work itself; neither does its quality of Ramistic naturalism with a heavily moral cast. The same discourse later observes that

> whose mind so ever is fully possest with a fervent desire to know good things, and with the dearest charity to infuse the knowledge of them into others, when such a man would speak, his words . . . like so many nimble and airy servitors trip about him at command, and in well order'd files, as he would wish, fall aptly into their own places. (CE, III, 362)

It is the heart of such a man, as Satan told Christ, which provides the fittest shape to his discourse, nor would such a man find his eloquence merely in *style* or *arrangement* or the other offices of rhetoric. True eloquence, Milton wrote, lies not alone in 'those rules which best Rhetoricians have giv'n' but in a character distinguished by his 'serious and hearty love of truth'. The centre is ultimately at a far remove from concerns for the sensuousness of language.

'The good man skilled in speaking' had been a commonplace definition of the rhetor since the time of Cato the Elder. Isocrates's system of education, centuries before Cato, and Quintilian's, centuries after, were built upon achieving that goal. And, though by differing methods, so was Milton's ideal, as enunciated in his treatise *Of Education*: he would place logic and rhetoric, with poetry in between, as the ultimate arts in the curriculum, not as 'trivial' arts for the beginner but as highly sophisticated disciplines to be attempted after the student has acquired, along with knowledge, moral and political character. Whatever we might think now of the morals and politics Milton might have had in mind, we cannot deny that the educational goal expresses his own deep oratorical orientation; moral consciousness is to be honed in rhetorical practice. This, I have tried to suggest, is the commitment which 'informs' Milton's writing—a thoroughly humanist idea, with the precariously balanced scales tipped for one last time more towards the 'social self', as Lanham would call it, the public man, the arguer and controversialist, and less towards the isolated, pre-romantic, private or 'central self'. One need not confuse, as some scholars have done, the *ethos* projected in Milton's writings with egocentrism, nor the role he spent years creating as rhetor with the self-absorbed speaker.

Something like that latter role may be heard within the meditative fashions of the seventeenth century, a mediaeval resurgence which at first served to intensify the contemplative impulse in humanism and then became a separate mode of thought and expression. As a rhetorical genre, meditation offered a distinctly non-rhetorical kind of strategy: the audience was placed in an 'overhearing' relationship to the speaker, who addressed God or the divisions within his own soul.[48] It differed on all levels from the other older, equally literate, and far more humanistic strategy available through such ancient rhetorical traditions as the practice of Isocrates, who showed speakers how to create on paper 'an ideal fiction of pure will as a means of unifying his audience' (§S–856: p. 229). Unlike the meditator, the Isocratean writer speaks openly and directly with his audience—in the case of the Christian humanist, as an observer[49] or messenger of God's grace. Louis Martz, who has described in depth the emerging meditative tradition in the poetry of the seventeenth century (§S–950), has argued that Milton was being less oratorical than meditative in *Paradise Lost* and *Paradise Regained*. He was, according to Martz, following an Augustinian mode of meditation, clearly non-oratorical but perhaps not so intensely solitary as other meditative modes. But though the approach illuminates certain local effects in the poems, Martz nonetheless posits a false dilemma: Milton either 'manipulates' his audience or lets them 'discover' with him in the course of his utterance 'the true, developing nature of his own response'.[50] The present essay has suggested another alternative: Milton allows his audience to confront his *ethos* directly; his communicative strategy lies in creating a fictive *Voluntas* speaking in a mode more closely akin to oratory than to any process wherein the audience became passive onlookers to an act of private devotion. How much 'manipulation' is involved would seem to depend upon the skill with which the *ethos* was invented and its will acts.

Certainly Augustinianism, in all its complex manifestations through such Puritan doctrines as 'the inner light', is present in Milton. In fact, it has been argued that most classical rhetorical lessons were filtered through St Augustine on their way to Milton.[51] Since the influence of Isocrates on St Augustine has also been proposed (§S–856), perhaps one could counterbalance arguments concerning Milton as an Augustinian meditator with a view of his Isocratean–Augustinian oratory. But such specific influences could be merely incidental. After all, problems of *ethos* were at the very core of Continental and English humanism, which was pervaded by Ciceronian as well as Isocratean examples of translating character into writing, however much the examples were clouded by revived theories. Grappling with problems of public character on the one hand and private realities on the other was the foremost challenge of any humanist writer, whether he sought advancement at court or fulfilment of Christian obligations; solutions resulted in that 'uneasy balance' mentioned earlier. Moreover, in Christian humanism generally, it was not enough that moral character be publicly perceptible; it must also be efficacious in exemplifying and in persuading others to adopt an appropriate stance towards God and man.

A direct confrontation of moral character would seem to be integral to the intention, the final cause, of Milton's writing, whose formal cause—in addition to such external conventions as epic or dramatic structure, or the traditional parts of an oration—is the character he shaped for himself on paper as a Christian rhetor, one whose hope was to perform an office 'neither unacceptable to God, unsalutary to the Church, nor without its utility to the commonwealth'.[52] Such is the fundamental identity of the speaker, 'the ideal fiction of pure will', the individuating voice, heard within Milton's writing. This *ethos* could change subtly to accord with external conventions and traditions and to suit the final causes of any one work, just as its changes would also naturally reflect the writer's own growth within or accommodations to time or personal circumstance; but always the voice is profoundly oratorical, profoundly humanist and Christian in its efforts to achieve change in others. As a principle of form, it is the fulfilment of that opinion affirmed in Milton's youth, 'that he who would not be frustrate of his hope to write well hereafter in laudable things, ought him selfe to bee a true Poem, that is, a composition, and patterne of the best and honourablest things'.[53] A cohesive element which is exemplary of or attractive to its argument, it is a voice yet audible to our ears.

Thus, although humanism with its unreconciled union of oratory and contemplation was among Milton's contemporaries all but displaced by a rage for newer modes of thought and expression, the study of form in Milton's writings should be approached through the rhetorical ideals and practices which precede his age, in some instances by millennia. Humanists would note that the internal form of Milton's work 'argues' the writer's *ethos*. Considering the intellectual developments I have surveyed, we might additionally note that the *ethos* so argued 'proves' the writer's steadfastness to tradition.[54]

NOTES

1 Abraham Fraunce, *The Lawiers Logike* (1588), fol. 4^v.

2 Rosemond Tuve has an illuminating discussion of the term as a technical word in the Ramist handbooks: 'The best I can do with it is to say that it seems to indicate the relatableness of a word or thing; that aspect by which we conceive of it as relatable to another word or thing' (§S–988. pp. 344–5).

3 Milton, *A fuller Institution of the Art of Logic arranged after the Method of Peter Ramus* (1672), in CE, XI, 23–5.

4 Milton, in the Preface to *Samson Agonistes*.

5 *De oratore*, I, xxxi, 142; trans. E. W. Sutton and H. Rackham, Loeb Classical Library (Cambridge, Mass., 1959), I, 99.

6 Moreover, the assimilation of memory by systems of religion and occult sciences only served to increase its pervasiveness in the Renaissance. See §S–889.

7 Fraunce (above, note 1), fol. 25: 'the finall cause, the end, purpose, intent, drift, marke, or scope, as it were of the whole action, is propounded to the efficient, and so urgeth and moveth him to prepare the matter, and apply the forme thereunto for the full accomplishing of the enterprise'.

8 *Phaedrus*, 277; trans. R. Hackworth, in *The Collected Dialogues of Plato*, ed. Edith Hamilton and Huntington Cairns (Princeton, 1961), pp. 522–3.

9 Ch. Perelman and L. Olbrechts-Tyteca, *The New Rhetoric*, trans. John Wilkinson and Purcell Weaver (Notre Dame and London, 1969), p. 511.

10 *Phaedrus*, 279; trans. Hackforth (as above, note 8), p. 524.

11 Sonnet X ('Daughter of that good Earle, once President').

12 *Antidosis*, 256; trans. George Norlin, *Isocrates*, Loeb Classical Library (Cambridge, Mass., 1962), II, 327.

13 *De oratore*, III, xvi, 60–1; trans. H. Rackham, Loeb Classical Library (Cambridge, Mass., 1960), II, 49.

14 *Rhetoric*, i, 1; trans. Lane Cooper (1932), p. 1.

15 *Orator*, xxxix, 134; trans. H. M. Hubbel, Loeb Classical Library (Cambridge, Mass., 1960), p. 407.

16 *Orator*, xix, 64; *ibid.*, p. 353.

17 'We get the impression that the process of naming the ornaments was something to be enjoyed in its own right' (Peter Dixon, *Rhetoric* [1971], p. 35). This surely is the motivation for that 'passion for formal rhetoric' which C. S. Lewis found integral to the Renaissance Englishman's enjoyment of literature (*English Literature in the Sixteenth Century excluding Drama* [Oxford, 1954], p. 61).

18 *Institutio oratoria*, XI, i, 11; trans. H. E. Butter, Loeb Classical Library (Cambridge, Mass., 1961), IV, 161.

19 *Antidosis*, 274–8. As George Kennedy notes, 'Peculiar to Isocrates, perhaps, is the insistence upon moral consciousness as actually growing out of the process of rhetorical composition' (*The Art of Persuasion in Greece* [Princeton, 1963], p. 178). Kennedy argues that Isocrates was a political opportunist, whose speeches were

partly advertisements for his school. The interpretation would have seemed strange to Milton.

20 *Paradise Lost*, IX, 665–78:

> The Tempter, but with shew of Zeal and Love
> To Man, and indignation at his wrong,
> New parts puts on, and as to passion mov'd,
> Fluctuates disturb'd, yet comely, and in act
> Rais'd, as of some great matter to begin.
> As when of old som Orator renound
> In *Athens* of free *Rome*, where Eloquence
> Flourishd, since mute, to som great cause addrest,
> Stood in himself collected, while each part,
> Motion, each act won audience ere his tongue,
> Somtimes in highth began, as no delay
> Of Preface brooking through his Zeal of Right.

21 Cicero, for example, wrote, 'The truth is that the poet is a very near kinsman of the orator, rather more heavily fettered as regards rhythm, but with ampler freedom in his choice of words, while in the use of many sorts of ornament he is his ally and almost his counterpart' (*De oratore*, I, xvi, 70; trans. Sutton and Rackham [as above, note 5], I, 51). Thomas Lodge in 1579 reversed the judgement: 'It is a pretye sentence, yet not so prety as pithy, *Poeta nascitur, Orator fit*: as who should say, Poetrye commeth from above, from a heavenly seate of a glorious God, unto an excellent creature man; an Orator is but made by exercise' (*Defense of Poetry*, in G. Gregory Smith, ed., *Elizabethan Critical Essays* [1904], I, 71). Over a generation later, Ben Jonson parodied Cicero direct: 'The *Poet* is the neerest Borderer upon the Orator, and expresseth all his vertues, though he be tyed more to numbers, is his equall in ornament, and above him in his strengths' (*Timber, or Discoveries*, in §S–850: p. 284).

22 John Dryden, for example, in a letter to Sir Robert Howard, states, 'So then the first happiness of the poet's imagination is properly invention, or finding the thought; the second is fancy, or the variation, deriving, or moulding, of that thought, as the judgment represents it proper to the subject; the third is elocution, or the art of clothing and adorning that thought, so found and varied, in apt, significant, and sounding words' (*Works*, ed. Sir Walter Scott [Edinburgh, 1821], IX, 98).

23 The role of the printing press in the search for the ur-book of wisdom is well discussed in §S–843; see also §S–844. Knowlson discusses the search for the *lingua humana* in §S–858.

24 As Milton reminded his classmates in one of his youthful 'Prolusions': 'All of the most distinguished teachers of rhetoric far and wide have left behind the opinion—a fact which has not escaped your notice, my fellow students—that in every kind of speaking, whether demonstrative or deliberative or judicial, the exordium ought to be occupied with securing the goodwill of the listeners' (CE, XII, 119).

25 Wittreich, in §S–888. Elsewhere (§S–887) he develops the argument that Milton uses not simply the *Areopagiticus* but the character of Isocrates as his foil; the reading is

cogent, if at times overly inventive in positing a fit audience though (necessarily only an ingenious) few who would fully understand what Wittreich believes Milton was really up to in this ostensibly public oration. The point I seek to raise concerns rhetorical strategy, in particular the presentation of moral character, and not dissimilarities or differences between Milton's *ethos* and that of Isocrates, or of any other rhetorician in antiquity.

26 *An Essay concerning Human Understanding* (1690), III, x, 251.

27 'The Metaphysical Poets', in *Homage to John Dryden* (1924), pp. 30–1.

28 For the extent of this sobering effect and its centre in scientific circles, see §S–924; Richard F. Jones, 'Science and Language in England of the Mid-Seventeenth Century', in §S–378; and §S–425.

29 For instance, 'Roll. Makylmenaeum' states in his 'Epistle to the Reader' prefacing *The Logike of the Most Excellent Philosopher P. Ramus Martyr* (1574), pp. 7–8: 'thou shalt understand that there is nothing appartayning to dialecticke eyther in Aristotles xvii booke of logike, in his eight bookes of Phisicke, or in his xiii bookes of Philosophie, in Cicero his bookes of Oratorie, or in Quintilian (in the which there is almost nothing that doth not eyther appartayne to the invention or arguments or disposition of the same), but that shalt finde it shortlie and after a perfect methode in this book declared'. Thereupon follow only eighty-five octavo pages of text.

30 Preface, *The Great Instauration*, in *Works*, ed. James Spedding *et al*. (1858–75), IV, 15.

31 This major difference is discussed in §S–842.

32 See *CE*, XI, 363, 373. Another non-Ramist feature is Milton's belief in the force of the 'middle term' in argument: see p. 339, and §S–842.

33 'Roll. Makylmenaeum' (as above, note 29), p. 101.

34 *Of the Advancement of Learning*, II, ed. Spedding, III, 343; *De augmentis scientarum*, II, xiii, ed. Spedding, IV, 316.

35 Quotations are from the text by Hardison (§S–850).

36 *Adv. of L.*, II; ed. Spedding, III, 409.

37 *De aug.*, xiii; ed. Spedding, IV, 315–16.

38 For a discussion of Farnaby's work see §S–867. For a study of the commonplace tradition see §S–861.

39 *Adv. of L.*, II; ed. Spedding, III, 389.

40 '*Some* that turne over all bookes, and are equally searching in all papers; that write out of what they presently find or meet, without choice; by which meanes it happens that what they have descredited and impugned in one worke, they have before or after extolled the same in another. Such are the Essayists, even their Master Mountaigne . . .' (§S–850: pp. 272–3).

41 See *Works*, ed. Spedding, IV, 472–92. The point may be seen by comparing Bacon's essay 'Of Marriage and Single Life' with a couple of entries under his commonplace list of antitheses:

V. Wife and Children

For	*Against*
A wife and children are a kind of discipline of humanity; whereas unmarried men are harsh and severe.	He that has wife and children has given hostages to fortune.

42 §S–870: p. 102. Gilbert, too, discusses Bacon's entanglement in the rhetorical tradition: 'Bacon transformed the debating procedure of the Topics into a transaction in which Nature replaced the respondent and the challenger became the scientist' (§S–848: p. 224).

43 In his preface (sig. A5), Bulwer cites a passage in *De augmentis scientarum* as the inspiration for his work.

44 *Novum organum*, I, lix; *De aug.*, V, iv; ed. Spedding, IV, 60–1, 433–4.

45 'Description of the Intellectual Globe', ed. Spedding, V, 504. See §S–851.

46 §S–885: pp. 126–7. See also §S–855: Ch. V, for Bacon's doctrine of 'forms' in nature and suggestion of its implication for linguistic form.

47 Baxter Hathaway has so described the effects of this Aristotelianism that it seems almost a direct response to Baconianism as delineated in the present survey: 'we must realize that with the growth of the influence of Aristotle, the study of literature became more rationalistic, finite-minded, or scientific' (§S–852: p. 19).

48 This is part of the thesis I propose in §S–877.

49 Shawcross (§S–874) describes Milton's *ethos* as observer in a re-presentation of the Creation.

50 Martz, *The Paradise Within: Studies in Vaughan, Traherne, and Milton* (New Haven, 1964), p. 109. A similar dilemma is posited by Hardison; see note 54, below. The local effects which Martz's approach illuminates uncover Augustinian theology in these two poems. The examples he cites of Milton's voice and role are more accurately those of the rhetor than the meditator.

51 That Milton was strongly influenced by St Augustine is part of John M. Major's argument in §S–862.

52 *Pro se defensio*, in *CE*, IX, 227.

53 *Apology for Smectymnuus*, in *CE*, III, 303.

54 Wittreich, too, sees *ethos* in Milton as partly a structural principle, partly a mode of proof (§S–888), though he does not see it as the major component of the internal formal cause of discourse. The present essay, like Wittreich's, sees Milton's *ethos* as profoundly oratorical even in his later works, contrary to the argument developed by O. B. Hardison, Jr., in 'The Orator and Poet: The Dilemma of Humanist Literature', *Medieval and Renaissance Studies*, I (1971), 33–44. Milton may have rejected contemporary humanism but, as I have tried to show, there was another alternative besides self-absorbed meditation or early romanticism, and it lay deep within rhetorical tradition.

RAYMOND B. WADDINGTON

11

Milton among the Carolines

Born into the first decade of a new century as the country adjusted to the death of a great queen, the precocious boy attended private school and university, gaining some notice as a learned and witty poet. Later he travelled on the Continent, returning to support himself as a teacher. The experience of civil war directed the thrust of his writings to politics; but the passage of time brought a disillusionment with the political process. One might say that from seeking political solutions to religious problems he turned to seeking religious solutions to political problems. Spending his post-war years in intellectual exile, he nonetheless wrote steadily and abundantly. Over the course of his career he worked in a variety of forms—prose, poetry, drama, even libretti for musical dramas. Although as a poet he often seemed an anomaly, an odd anachronism developing between the dominant movements of the age, by the time of his death, in his sixty-sixth year, his position as a major poet was established. John Milton? No, W. H. Auden.

I offer this sleight of hand not merely to start the familiar hare of a special affinity between the seventeenth and the twentieth centuries, although I think such an argument valid; rather, I want to underscore the radical difference in the state of our knowledge of comparable poetic figures in the two periods. Primed by post-romantic conceptions of poetic genius and the uniqueness of the individual, fed by modern journalism, confessional writings and information retrieval systems, advantaged by simple proximity, we know so much *more* about Auden. We have his private allusions elucidated by Spender and Isherwood; we can track the impact of the ideas of Homer Lane and Freud; we can examine his reaction to *The Waste Land*. Despite the fact that we know more about the life of Milton than that of any earlier English poet, there are distinct limitations to that knowledge. Milton's confessional remarks and autobiographical references are always conventional, an orator's proof of character; his poetics, grounded upon imitation, looks to classical models, or, more contemporaneously, to poets of a previous generation. We simply do not know if, say, the publication of Herbert's *The Temple* fired the twenty-five year old Milton's creative enthusiasm; we do not know if he shared the popular view that Edmund Waller was the finest poet of his generation; we do not know if he mourned Jonson, admired Pascal, was as captivated as Henry More by the poetics of infinity.

In most respects such absences of response are no handicap, but, rather, a healthy corrective. Milton was as much a classicist in his poetic, as in his rhetorical, taste (see above, pp. 329 ff.); and his dismissal of modern educational theory, 'to search what many modern *Janua's* and *Didactics*, more than ever I shall read, have projected, my inclination leads me not' (*Of Education*, in *CE, IV*, 276), probably ought to be heeded as general injunction. Even so, we should distinguish between Milton's settled opinions and the process of formulating those opinions; between his preference for the classic and his range of inquiry and knowledge of the modern. Given his omnivorous reading, his ardent controversialism in prose, his sense of poetic vocation and awareness of his own public image, it violates our sense of the man's character to assume that he did not know intimately the literary activities of his contemporaries. With his Christ he might respond, 'Think not but that I know these things, or think / I know them not (*Par. Regained*, IV, 286–7). In the same breath with which he denies having read 'modern *Janua's* and *Didactics*' he assures us that he alludes to Comenius and attests his familiarity with Comenius's major works. We might hypothesise, similarly, that his knowledge of contemporary literature must be detected allusively, through unnamed referents which both reveal and conceal. In *Samson Agonistes*, for instance, the Chorus's flat-footed insistence that the hero is no suicide—'self-kill'd / Not willingly, but tangl'd in the fold / Of dire necessity' (1664–6)—perhaps owes its existence to John Donne's paradoxical consideration of Samson as a suicide in *Biathanatos* (first published posthumously in 1646–47), a calumny Milton surely would challenge. If so, the reference functions like the one in *Areopagitica* to Bishop Hall—'him who went about to impaire your merits with a triviall and malignant *Encomium*' (*CE, IV*, 294). Milton does not deign to name an opponent who would probably be unmistakable to a contemporary audience. It becomes necessary, therefore, to recreate something of the contemporaneity of that perspective.

The present chapter attempts two things. It looks at Milton as a developing Caroline poet, sketching his position and poetics against those of the times in which he actually evolved to poetic maturity—that is, the two decades approximately from the accession of Charles to the publication of the 1645 *Poems*. It has been more usual, perhaps, to discuss Milton as a belated peer of the late Elizabethan giants or, remembering the publication dates of the major poems, sometimes determinedly to examine his work in a Restoration context. Both of these approaches have admitted virtues. But I wish here to consider Milton's reaction to poetic events, movements, fashions in the formative stage of his own career; even if only by negation such contemporary activity affected his own development. And, while the major poems would be unpublished, presumably unwritten, for many years to come, the 1645 *Poems* exhibit a technical and formal mastery of craft which puts the epics within reach. In this sense the Caroline period is crucial and deserving of closer scrutiny. And, secondly, putting aside the obvious truth that Tasso and Spenser are the modern poets who meant the most to Milton (§S–965), the essay will try to read between the lines of Milton's own poetry to suggest what he might have learned from lesser contemporaries.[1] After highlighting certain issues by comparing Milton's first volume of poetry to a rival's, the chapter will progress through poetic persona, genre, symbolism and style.

'HIMSELF . . . A TRUE POEM': PERSONA AND GENRE

In the effort to discriminate Milton's position in the context of Caroline poetry, it is enlightening to juxtapose his 1645 *Poems* to those of a then more notable contemporary, Edmund Waller.[2] The comparison would have been a natural one, stemming from the superficial similarity of lives as well as volumes. Only two years older than Milton, Waller preceded him at Cambridge before studying law and entering Parliament. Their books at first glance would have seemed virtual twins: both published by Humphrey Moseley with the same title formula (*Poems of Mr . . .*) and the same acknowledgement of song settings by Henry Lawes. Indeed, Moseley's preface to the Milton *Poems* declares that the success of '*Mr Wallers* late choice Peeces' prompted the subsequent venture, implying the kinship; and the casual reader might respond to a basic similarity in the expansive, descriptive mode with its predominance of adjectives, nouns and participals, its 'ceremony of vocabulary', in fact the common Spenserian heritage (§S–952: pp. 61–102). But there the similarity ends.

Milton's double volume of English and Latin verse presents generic groupings arranged internally by approximate order of composition. As has been remarked, 'Milton's attention to genre makes a difference, for it asks us to view the poet's development according to the principles of poetry'.[3] The chronological ordering, possibly reflecting the influence of Puritan spiritual autobiographies,[4] coalesces with the emphasis upon poetic development to present the theme of 'the growth toward maturity': 'the whole volume has been arranged to convey a sense of the predestined bard's rising powers' (§S–984: pp. 20, 12). The arrangement of Waller's book, too, consciously projects an image of the poet. Whereas the Milton volume commences with a set of religious poems, thereby establishing the priority of the poet-priest, Waller's signals that its author is a courtier-poet. The opening set of poems in praise of the King are not so much a defiant gesture by the disgraced and exiled royalist as—in view of their celebration of occasions from the '20s and '30s—an apologetic and nostalgic glance at happier political times. Following the religious poems, Milton offers sets of poems associated with his schooldays as scholar and poet. Waller modulates from the political to the social with a poem 'To the Queen, occasioned upon sight of her Majesties Picture'; the attributes and qualities of Henrietta Maria are largely indistinguishable from those of his frequently to be praised Sacharissa. Thereafter, any generic grouping or sequencing seems deliberately avoided; Waller presents himself as a court poet—social, amorous, occasional.

This difference in attitude towards the importance of poetic genres itself is of a piece with the larger attitudes towards their craft. Writing as a courtier, Waller makes the conventional derogation by which one disclaims any seriousness of purpose: 'not so much to have made verses, as not to give over in time, leaves a man without excuse: the former presenting us with an opportunity at least of doing wisely: that is to conceale those we have made, which I shall yet doe, if my humble request may be of as much force with your Ladiship' (sigs. A2v–A3). With the volume already set in type presumably her ladyship had little opportunity to revoke her 'command' to publish. For Milton, however, the poet's vocation takes second place to none and requires no apology, only a certain amount of explanation to one's father ('Ad Patrem'). The keynote of the divinely inspired poet is sounded in the Nativity Ode: whereas the pagan oracles are 'dum' in the presence of the Christ child, the poet joins his voice 'unto the Angel Quire'. Infused with the power of the heavenly muse, the Christian poet may attain a perfect literary recreation of God's original. Such perfection of utterance, Andrew Marvell later was to judge, Milton achieved in *Paradise Lost*: 'Thy Verse created like thy Theme sublime, / In Number, Weight, and Measure, needs not Rhime'.[5] Possibly it was recognition of this role of the vatic poet, and not simply the stylistic influence, which caused Moseley to herald 'as true a Birth, as the Muses have brought forth since our famous Spencer wrote'. Milton's proper provenance is in the line of visionary poets including Spenser and Chapman and extending to Blake.[6]

Within the design of the 1645 *Poems* exceptions to the chronological principle of arrangement supply an important clue to intention.[7] The alpha and omega of the English poems are the Nativity Ode and 'Lycidas', the design implicitly announcing Milton's calling with the former and displaying his finest early achievement as poet-prophet with the latter (§S–1009: pp. 111–29). The chronological blocks of religious poems, 'Elizabethan' poems, and sonnets contrive to show how the writing of 'Lycidas' came to be possible, in terms of both technical and spiritual development. Milton's chosen persona of prophet and priest dictates a rhetorical situation which distinguishes his poetry from that of most of his contemporaries.

Basic discriminations in poetic 'mode' may be made in the range of audience addressed: in the private mode a poet talks to himself or another individual; in the social mode the context of a limited society (e.g. Waller's court circle) is assumed; only in the public mode is a general audience addressed (§S–953a). The question of audience firmly dissevers Milton from Waller once again, despite their affinity in language and sentence structure. A shared social ambiance establishes between Waller and, say, Jonson a basic alliance which overrides the differences in language and structure. Standing outside the poetic movements with more restricted audience ranges ('private' and 'social' are equivalents to the traditional 'metaphysical' and 'cavalier'), Milton presents an anomalous figure even among public poets in that the notable public poetry of the mid-century—for instance, that by Denham, Marvell, Dryden—tends to be political rather than religious (§S–997).

A massive shift to devotional poetry characterises the first half of the seventeenth century (§S–952: p. 101); and we have learned to call such poetry 'meditational' in recognition of the influence of the techniques of formal religious meditation. Characteristically, meditational poetry exhibits a three-stage sequence–composition of place, analysis and colloquy–which corresponds to the actions of three mental faculties, memory, understanding and will. In so far as the 'methods of meditation are in themselves adaptations of ancient principles of logic and rhetoric', however, it is not always possible to make a clear-cut distinction between the rhetorical and the specifically meditational in religious poetry.[8] Furthermore, the heavy recourse to the liturgy as a source of structures, themes, allusions and imagery in poetry of private devotion as well as public worship creates a strong commonality in religious verse of this period, also serving to complicate the task of distinguishing between kinds.[9] Once again, however, definition of intended audience provides a useful differentia. Meditation 'has as its primary aim personal, private devotion, and only secondarily the aim of moving an overhearing audience' (§S–878: p. 230).

Attending to the implied audience permits us to understand why the Nativity Ode is not a meditational poem, even though its general objective—comprehending the meaning of the Nativity—is the same as that of a meditation upon the Nativity. The rhetoric of meditation is insinuative; it seeks to raise the meditator up to a higher plane of understanding or spiritual illumination. Conversely, the rhetoric of prophecy is accommodative: the prophet attempts to bring his truth down to a level at which it can be comprehended by his audience, or at least those members of his audience capable of responding. Milton's 'fit audience . . . though few' (*Par. Lost*, VII, 31) expresses his sense of the traditional prophetic dilemma with its attendant probability of being ignored or misunderstood.[10] The Nativity Ode works in a number of ways to project the implication that its contemplation of the consequences of Christ's birth is externally directed. The poet lays overt claim to the prophetic mantle at the conclusion of the Proem—'And joyn thy voice unto the Angel Quire, / From out his secret Altar toucht with hallow'd fire'—evoking Isaiah's account of his purification and prophetic mission (6: 1–10). The biblical context is complemented by the resonances of Virgil's 'Messianic Eclogue' (§S–989: p. 60) and reinforced by the Spenserian qualities of the language and prosody, which point to this novice's descent from the major prophetic poet of the preceding century (§S–965: pp. 60–1; §S–1009: pp. 25–55).

With the distinction of audience in mind, we may understand how Milton's poem differs from such meditational poems as Donne's 'Goodfriday, 1613. Riding Westward' and Vaughan's 'Christs Nativity' in its adaptation of liturgical materials. Whereas Donne and Vaughan commence their poems in the historical present, emphasising chronological disparity before progressing to 'symbolic simultaneity', Milton inverts the process, moving from temporal simultaneity to disparity. As in the Advent liturgy, he establishes a symbolic time or timelessness which itself subsumes the three modes of past, present and future (§S–905: pp. 145–9). Milton's willingness to overleap the historical present for the directly symbolic suggests, again, that the focus of examination is not the speaker's own situation but the interpretation of the event for mankind generally.

Yet another way through which Milton reveals his intention is by his use of the kinds. The generic range of the 1645 *Poems* acts as an assertion of Milton's poetic development. Having completed his apprenticeship in the lower genres—pastoral, satire, Ovidian elegy, Italian sonnet—he displays his attainments in each and announces his readiness to move on to more ambitious kinds. The gestures here are classical: as a Renaissance poet he has done his basic training in the Ovidian genres; as a poet with serious ambitions he follows the 'Virgilian progression' from lesser to greater kinds, alluding to his transitional state in both 'Lycidas' and 'Epitaphium Damonis', the concluding English and Latin poems. In one sense, then, the genres proclaim the poet, Milton's seriousness opposed to Waller's casualness; in another they proclaim the meaning of the poems. To any public poet, whether political or religious, the question of genre is an important one, for genre is the conventionalised vessel which contains his word, thereby giving it a form by which his audience may understand it (§S–991: pp. 10–11). The concept of greater and lesser kinds, of a hierarchy of genres, is a literary expression of a vision of life ordering human experience into a hierarchy. The kind of truth which the religious poet seeks to express sounds the upper range of the hierarchy. 'On the morning of Christs Nativity' (to give the poem its proper title) is both 'ode' and 'hymn', the poet informs us, the two 'high' poetic kinds conventionally used to praise a God (§S–989: pp. 43 ff.), a fitting overture to a volume which announces Milton's vocation as a religious poet.

His early adaptation of prophetic stance and vatic voice has aesthetic and generic consequences which conspire to place Milton outside the mainstream of Caroline poetic fashion in other ways as well. The whole passion for the charming miniature with the concomitant *multum in parvo* aesthetic—e.g. Herrick's 'A Ternarie of Littles' or Marvell's 'On a Drop of Dew'—did not affect him (§S–974: pp. 38–117). Aside from exercises such as the Latin epigrams and the lyric 'On May Morning', consequently, the genres designed for littleness meant little to him (§S–908: pp. 32–75). Significantly, the most notable emblem occurring in *Paradise Lost*, the golden scales by which God gives Satan a sign of his weakness (IV, 990–1005), is inflated to cosmic proportions.

Milton's poetry exhibits all the late Renaissance tendencies towards generic mixture and inclusiveness; but, however much he modifies the conventional limits of a poetic kind, his works have a firm, governing generic identity. *Paradise Lost*, as a simulacrum of God's own creation, contains all things; and literary inclusiveness is a strategy of the poet's plenitude. But while we recognise the local effects of emblem and hymn, Petrarchan love lyric and Platonic dialogue, and respond to the larger modal movements of pastoral to tragedy, all this is firmly contained by the enveloping epic form. The Nativity Ode is a case in point: it strongly draws upon the native tradition of Nativity poems; the personification of 'meek-ey'd Peace' seemingly reflects the influence of the masque; and the expulsion of the pagan gods is an inverse progress poem, reversing the expected geographical and chronological movements from east to west, past to present. Yet, despite this inclusiveness, the dominant generic identity remains firm: it is a praise of his God and, as such, 'the greatest ode in the English language' (§S–949: p. 321).

Frequently in Milton's early poetry we can observe a pattern of, first, scrupulous adherence to the conventions of a form; then, with that standard mastered to his satisfaction, a willingness to experiment, to extend the boundaries to suit his particular requirements. Thus the Latin elegies on the Cambridge Vice-Chancellor and Beadle are relentlessly conventional, the one on Lancelot Andrewes impudently witty, and the English elegy 'On the Death of a Fair Infant' (first published in 1673) astonishingly innovative in its rhetorical and mythological invention.[11] 'Arcades' is a conventional masque in the subordination of poetry to the visual and musical elements; A Mask (or Comus) so radically alters the proportions that earlier generations of critics had difficulty accepting it as a masque, although the accuracy of Milton's own title has now been affirmed.[12] The early sonnets punctiliously observe the formal requirements of complimentary and heroic Italian sonnets; such post-1645 sonnets as 'On the Late Massacre in Piemont' virtually obliterate the orthodox form (§S–965: pp. 89–107). Undoubtedly the subtlest generic achievement of the early period is 'Lycidas', with its formal adaptations of the *canzone* and the Italian eclogues, its vast assimilation of the entire tradition of pastoral elegy, its infusion with the language and structure of biblical prophecy derived from commentaries upon the Book of Revelation.[13] Milton chose simply to call it a 'Monody', and, despite the presence of several voices in the poem, the dominant impression which lingers is that of the solitary singer's modulating voice.

In one other respect Milton's sense of vocation as a religious poet importantly affected his response to genre. Most of the minor poems were written too early to reflect it, but by the early 1640s Milton was evolving a biblical poetics which extends to the notion that the Bible itself constitutes an anthology of literary forms, providing divine models for the godly poet. This generic conception seems a logical extension of the familiar Renaissance veneration for Moses as the first literary creator, who, when inspired by God to write the Pentateuch, was given the paradigm for all subsequent literary creations.[14] The poet of *Paradise Lost* thus invokes the muse 'that on the secret top / Of *Oreb*, or of *Sinai*, didst inspire / That Shepherd, who first taught the chosen Seed, / In the Beginning how the Heav'ns and Earth / Rose out of *Chaos*' (I, 6–10). In 1642 Milton is working out his concept of sacred genres:

> The Scripture also affords us a divine pastoral Drama in the Song of *Salomon* consisting of two persons and a double *Chorus*, as *Origen* rightly judges. And the Apocalyps of Saint *John* is the majestick image of a high and stately Tragedy,

shutting up and intermingling her solemn Scenes and Acts with a sevenfold *chorus* of halleluja's and harping symphonies: and this my opinion the grave authority of *Pareus*, commenting that booke, is sufficient to confirm. Or if occasion shall lead to imitat those magnifick Odes and Hymns wherein *Pindarus* and *Callimachus* are in most things worthy, some others in their frame judicious, in their matter most an end faulty. But those frequent songs throughout the law and prophets beyond all these, not in their divine argument alone, but in the very critical art of composition, may be easily made appear over all the kinds of lyrick poesy to be incomparable.

(*The Reason of Church Government*, in CE, III, 237–8)

It is impossible to know exactly when Milton brought this conception to fruition; there seems little doubt, however, that biblical genres, whether comprehended directly or through the *vade mecum* of the commentators, shaped his own major poems. The traditions underlying *Paradise Regained* as a 'brief epic' modelled upon the book of Job have been explored; and Milton's observations about Revelation as a tragedy have been pursued in relation to *Samson Agonistes*.[15] However directly it is possible to correlate formal and structural features of biblical genres to Milton's own poetry, his argument that the Bible is the formal manifestation of the Logos is both seriously intended and an appropriate rhetorical stance. The reader who has given due attention to *The Reason of Church Government* will not be surprised by Christ's rejoinder to Satan that all he needs or cares to know about oratory, music and poetry may be found in the Scriptures.[16] Generic choice is the first embodiment of the poet's identity and theme, the visible image, as it were, of the voice which he has elected to assume. When the assumed identity is that of a religious prophet it follows as naturally that the media of expression will be biblical genres as it does that Waller's courtier poet will speak through casually structured lyrics and praises.[17]

'FROM SHADOWY TYPES TO TRUTH': SYMBOLISM AND PERSONA REVISITED

All Milton's writings have a double structure, rhetorical and imagistic. By this statement I do not mean to deny that his images function logically and fulfil a part of the rhetorical design, as is typical of English poetry at least from the time of Wyatt (§S–988); rather I wish to assert that Milton's imagery has an importance and development quite beyond its rhetorical significance. As Rosemond Tuve once observed, 'All poems use figurative language, and all say what they mean through images, but only certain kinds organize themselves with exquisite economy around great central figurative conceptions' (§S–989: p. 4). Her fine essays on the 'radically figurative' nature of the minor poems, coupled with a number of studies reading *Paradise Lost* essentially from the same premise,[18] serve to document a point of fundamental importance: Milton is a symbolic artist; as such, a failure to respond to the symbolic dimensions of any one of of his poems, early or late, is to risk badly misunderstanding that poem. This is not to argue that his poems can be understood properly by a 'New

Critical' tracing of image patterns. The control of imagery through genre, the tradition behind figures, the rhetorical discrimination of kinds of figures and their purposes, all contribute to our comprehension of imagery as an affective embodiment of Milton's themes (§S–989: pp. 3–14; §S–890).

Although Milton's verse is characteristically symbolic throughout his career, the conception of his symbolism undergoes an evolution; and that change expresses itself in his poetic persona. The early phase of Milton's thought profoundly reflects the influence of Christian Platonism, an aesthetic-philosophic movement which burgeoned a century and a half earlier in Florence under the aegis of Marsilio Ficino and moved steadily northward.[19] Milton displays his Platonic disposition directly in such Cambridge exercises as *Prolusion II* and *De Idea Platonica*, indirectly, and probably unconsciously, in certain linguistic traits so habitual as to seem innate: the pervasive imagery of darkness and light, which extends from *Prolusion I* to the poetry early and late,[20] or the persistent use of negative constructions. The latter may be illustrated brilliantly by *Areopagitica*: 'I cannot praise a fugitive and cloister'd vertue, unexercis'd and unbreath'd, that never sallies out and sees her adversary, but slinks out of the race, where that immortall garland is to be run for, not without dust and heat' (*CE*, IV, 311). Or, from the same work, much more awkwardly and so interesting for its wilfulness:

> there wanted not among them long since, who suggested such a cours; which
> they not following, leave us a pattern of their judgment, that it was not the not
> knowing, but the not approving, which was the cause of their not using it.
>
> (*CE*, IV, 316)

Both of these characteristics, the imagery and the syntactic negations, reveal a Platonic vision of reality. This world which we inhabit is a realm of negation, falsehood, darkness and corruption (since the Fall, the Christian must add); at best a mere shadow of reality. Given this mortal condition, Milton's epistemology works by negation: 'And perhaps this is that doom which *Adam* fell into of knowing good and evill, that is to say, of knowing good by evill' (*CE*, IV, 311). Man experiences evil and learns to know good, what is not in order to know what is, the false to arrive at the true. Thus *Comus*'s antimasque logically precedes the 'victorious dance / O're sensual Folly, and Intemperance' (973–4); so Hell in *Paradise Lost* precedes the Book III vision of God in his Heaven. The Attendant Spirit's disdainful contrast of his mansion 'where those immortal shapes / Of bright aerial Spirits live inspher'd / In Regions milde of calm and serene Air' to 'the smoak and stirr of this dim spot, / Which men call Earth' (2–6) describes his position from the perspective opposite to that of the blind, night-foundered bard who seeks to express 'holy Light' unblamed (*Par. Lost*, III, 1–3); but the perception of the human condition remains unaltered.

Commitment to a Platonic view of reality has a number of significant consequences for the poet. It was the Platonists who disseminated the conception, previously mentioned, that the artist is not a superior craftsman but a

God-like creator who communicates an intimation of the divine reality through his art. The purpose of such art is instructional, appealing to the rational soul and the faculty of understanding or judgement rather than to the senses and passions. The sensualist Comus urges the Lady 'to please, and sate [her] curious taste', describing her denial as 'a pet of temperance' (713, 720). But the Lady understands that 'this Jugler' seeks 'to charm my judgement, as mine eyes, / Obtruding false rules pranckt in reasons garb' (756–8). The reader of *Paradise Lost*, put in a situation analogous to the Lady's, is required to choose between Satan's flashy rhetoric, with its enthemymes and appeals to *pathos*, and God's tightly logical, schematically plain declamations, solidly based on the speaker's *ethos*.[21] Even where such art is not overtly instructive, it was understood to appeal to the rational soul through its form; the Platonists believed the higher reality to consist of such qualities as harmony, order, proportion, symmetry, beauty, qualities which are adumbrated in the Divine Artist's creation and again in the creations of human artists (§S–611: pp. 18–19: §S–372: pp. 325–93).

'At a Solemn Music' serves to illustrate the theory in both form and argument. The poet explains how the 'Sphear-born harmonious Sisters, Voice and Vers, / Wed [their] divine sounds' (2–3) to uplift the earth-bound faculties of sinful man, giving him a perception of the ultimate reality, symbolised as total visual and aural harmony—simultaneously an 'undisturbed Song of pure concent' and an 'endles morn of light'. The vision of this lost harmony awakens in man the ardent desire to reform his 'disproportion d' sinfulness and "keep in tune with Heav'n" ' (6, 28). Similarly, the intricately varied harmonies of syntax, rhythm and rhyme within the unity of one sustained sentence formally present an image of the 'perfect Diapason' which is the theme of the poem. The Platonic notion that music instructs through the mathematical proportions of its form conjoins with the tradition that music and poetry, both being constructed upon 'numbers', are sister arts (§S–605: pp. 32–40). This complementarity feeds the constant image parallels of the minor poems: darkness and dissonance, harmony and light, music and poetry.[22] Although the aesthetic principle of *concordia discors*, itself revelatory of the strain to perceive essential order in an increasingly disparate universe, was a major force in pre-Restoration poetry, clearly it had a special importance to Milton.[23]

In circular fashion this leads us again to poetic persona. The Isaiah-like prophet of the Nativity Ode is not wholly representative of Milton's early verse. An extraordinary passage in *The Reason of Church Government* links Milton's 'covenant' to produce great poems when released from religious tyranny with an assertion of the proper sources of poetic inspiration:

> . . . nor to be obtain'd by the invocation of Dame Memory and her Siren daughters, but by devout prayer to that eternall Spirit who can enrich with all utterance and knowledge, and sends out his Seraphim with the hallow'd fire of his Altar, to touch and purify the lips of whom he pleases.   (*CE*, III, 241)

The statement suggests several things. The adaptation of the covenant metaphor[24] to poetic vocation implies that, as Milton's religious position evolves towards more thoroughgoing Puritanism, so his poetics is reformulated in more strictly religious terms, e.g. the biblical genres and the persona of the Old Testament prophet. Further, in so far as Platonic poetics are based upon divine inspiration and memory,[25] his spurning the invocation of 'Dame Memory' suggests a turning away from the Platonism which had nurtured the 'major' minor poems. This change ought to be seen as a shift in emphasis, not a 'root and branch' extirpation;[26] but *The Reason of Church Government* does mark a significant milestone in Milton's thought. That he would thus define the new conception of his poetic covenant by the Isaiah allusion in 1642 and choose to give the Nativity Ode pride of place in 1645 indicates not what he has been but the way he wishes to be perceived as he embarks upon the major stage of his career. Isaiah 6, in the episode to which Milton recurrently alludes, has been accurately described as 'the most vivid and detailed account given in the Bible of the making of a prophet'.[27] It is this sense of newly confirmed vocation which the design and persona of the 1645 *Poems* are meant to convey.

Through the 1630s, however, the figure of the poet which obsessed Milton and best expressed the Platonism of his poetics was Orpheus. A culture hero to Ficino and the Florentine Platonists, Orpheus was celebrated as an 'ancient theologian' in the line of descent from the legendary Hermes Trismegistus to Moses; the founder of a mystery religion with parallels to Christianity; a legendary civiliser, poet-musician, philosopher, and prophet. Indeed, his descent to the underworld to rescue Eurydice caused him to be understood as a pagan type of Christ; and the mythology of the Orphic poet had been used importantly by Milton's vatic predecessors, Chapman and Spenser.[28] Allusions to the Orphic poet constitute a motif which threads through the early prose and verse, most importantly 'L'Allegro' and 'Il Penseroso', *A Mask* and 'Lycidas'.

The period of study for the M.A. at Cambridge and the private, postgraduate course at Hammersmith and at Horton was a time of strenuous learning and self-discipline; and Milton expressed the objective of the regimen in language reminiscent of Pico della Mirandola's famous *Oration on the Dignity of Man*. According to Pico, the distinguishing mark of man's nature is his indeterminateness, his freedom to metamorphose his nature to the heights of divinity or the depth of bestiality. Milton agrees with Pico that the means to attain that angelic height is philosophy, learning, wisdom:

> . . . nothing in life can happen quite unexpectedly, nothing by chance to one who has gained possession of this stronghold of wisdom. He will seem to be one whose power and authority the stars will obey, the land and the sea will follow implicitly, the winds and the storms will strive to please. Mother Nature even will hand over herself in surrender, quite as if some god, having abdicated power on earth, had delegated to him his court, his laws, his executive power, as though to some prefect.   (*Prolusion VII*; in CE, XII, 267)

The most familiar portrait of the magus, the ascetic wiseman who through occult study has achieved god-like power over lower nature and expresses this power in a benevolent white magic, is Shakespeare's Prospero. We may forget that he is a poet, since his songs, pageants and masques are delegated to Ariel; but the harmonies of spirit and nature symbolised in literary creation are as much a sign of the magus as his powers over the natural world. The famous tale of nature's response to the Orphic music makes a myth of the concept: 'The trees themselves, the very bushes and every grove once on a time, unfettered by roots, hastened after the most skilled songs of Orpheus' (*Prolusion VII*; in CE, XII, 283). Thus for Milton the touchstone of poetic achievement, transforming the vision attained by arduous study and religious devotion, is the power to animate inanimate nature: 'Wed your divine sounds, and mixt power employ / Dead things with imbreath'd sense able to pierce' ('At A Solemn Music'. 3–4).

Thyrsis, the shepherd-tutor of *A Mask*, similarly is praised by his charges for his Orphic powers of harmony: 'Whose artful strains have oft delaid / The hudling brook to hear his madrigal, / And sweeten'd every muskrose of the dale' (493–5). Presumably it is Thyrsis who has taught the Elder Brother to understand the positive and negative metamorphoses of the human soul (452–74), a lesson which the Second Brother appreciates Orphically: 'How charming is divine Philosophy! . . . musical as is *Apollo*'s lute' (476–8). If *A Mask* shows the accomplished Orphic musician-singer demonstrating his powers in a contest of magicians, the white magic of the Attendant Spirit (Thyrsis) against the black magic of Comus, 'Il Penseroso' illustrates the training programme through which such powers are attained.[29] Like Ficino, who popularised the concept of the melancholic as saturnine, contemplative genius in an effort to ameliorate his own temperament,[30] the poet banishes the crippling Galenic melancholy of 'L'Allegro' to invoke the 'sage and holy' Goddess, 'divinest Melancholy'. Through silence, contemplation and religious devotion he will study the teachings of Plato and 'thrice great Hermes' (i.e. Hermes Trismegistus) to gain mastery over the secret harmonies of nature; in so doing he can attain Orphic powers of immortality through art and 'something like Prophetic strain'. The Orphic personae of 'Il Penseroso' and *A Mask* represent the height of Milton's optimistic belief that great poetry can be created through a simple combination of individual talent and a Platonic-humanistic faith in the efficacy of education. Although the Orpheus myth figures prominently in 'Lycidas',[31] the usage is already transitional; the emphasis here upon Orpheus as a type of Christ had been far less overt in the earlier poems; and the fusion of Orpheus, Apollo and Christ in the image of the rising sun dispels the Orphic night of 'Il Penseroso' to greet the Son of Righteousness.

Milton's projection of his philosophic attitude through the persona of Orphic poet finds formal expression in the poetics of harmony and a complementary realisation in its mode of symbolism. E. H. Gombrich has explained cogently the Platonic theory of visual symbols:

They are the forms which the invisible entities can assume to make themselves understood to the limited human mind. In other words, the Idea of Justice—be it conceived as a member of the celestial Hierarchy or as an abstract entity—is

> inaccessible to the senses. At best we can hope to grasp it in a moment of ecstasis
> and intellectual intuition. But God has decreed in His mercy . . . that these
> entities may accommodate themselves to our understanding and assume visible
> shape. Strictly speaking these allegorical images neither symbolize nor represent
> the Platonic idea. It is the Idea itself, conceived as an entity, which through these
> images tries to signal us and thus to penetrate through our eyes into our mind.
>
> (*Symbolic Images* [§S–713], p. 177)

This theory of symbolic images as the accommodation of Ideas to our sense-bound understanding is precisely analogous to the central mystery of the Christian faith: just as Jesus Christ is not a figure for divinity but the incarnate God, so the image is the Idea itself taken on flesh. Gombrich points out that the notion arises as an extension of the habit of reading significances in the book of nature; the creations of art and literature reveal meaning as surely as the created world. Whereas Plato had denigrated art as the imitation of an imitation, Plotinus redefined the objective of art as the communication of divine reality, putting the realms of art and nature on an equal footing. The Platonic view thus presupposes that art, like nature, should be perceived as coherent and systematic, the assumption of system finding most convenient expression in mythology. Classical myth therefore becomes the subject-matter or supplies the 'grammar' of much larger-scale Renaissance art and literature; in smaller forms the attributes, iconography, hieroglyphs and emblems so frequently derived from the myths synecdochically serve the same purpose. It is this tradition of symbolic images which underlies the great thematic figures elucidated by Tuve: the 'structural figures' of Mirth and Melancholy in 'L'Allegro' and 'Il Penseroso', 'the great hinge of the Circe–Comus myth' in *A Mask*, the 'Good Shepherd' of 'Lycidas'.

The minor poems display a full commitment to the mythological syncretism so characteristic of Christian Platonism. Since the entire movement founded by Ficino was predicated upon the principle of intellectual harmony—between Platonism and Christianity, between the metaphysics of Plato and Aristotle, between Christianity and the Cabala—a concomitant of this tradition is the acceptance of classical myths as types of biblical figures and events without the prudential qualifiers: 'crooked', 'imperfect', 'distorted' truths.[32] This influence upon English poetry peaked during Milton's nonage, at which time Chapman could write a 'Hymn to the Saviour' deriving its material more directly from Ficino's discussion of the Narcissus myth than from the Bible, and underwent a decline as the shades of Puritanism gathered, promulgating a literal approach to the Bible and a stricter separation of revealed and feigned word. Milton's contemporary Henry Reynolds can still quote Pico della Mirandola in *Mythomystes* (1632), and in 1647 Alexander Ross can still assert, 'Our blessed Saviour is the true Hercules' (§P–669: p. 169), but already they are slightly anachronistic-sounding voices in the wilderness. The Nativity Ode can image the Christ child as 'the mighty *Pan*' and the serpent-strangling infant Hercules, remembering from Macrobius, Servius and Selden that both Pan and Hercules were sun gods and therefore fit images for the Son of Righteousness;[33] in

'Lycidas', Orpheus, Apollo, St Peter and Christ become interchanging and fusing figures of the sacrificed shepherd as both pastor and poet.

In the major poems, however, the reliance upon classical myth is both more sparing and more stringent. Without recourse to a consideration of Milton's theological views, it seems possible to adduce two poetic reasons for such a change: first, the abandonment of the Orphic persona with the rejection of the Muse Calliope as 'an empty dream' (*Par. Lost*, VIII, 39); and, second, a principle of decorum seemingly at work when he amplifies directly sacred writ, not merely expounding upon the meaning of an event occurring in the Bible, as is the case with the Nativity Ode, 'On the Circumcision', and 'On the Passion'. Thus a study of the precision with which Milton discriminates between 'fabled' and 'feigned' pagan myths demonstrates that, rather than the rejection of mythology, *Paradise Lost* exhibits a more skilful control and mature appreciation of this material than do the minor poems.[34]

When the pagan prophet Orpheus gives place to Isaiah as embodiment of the poet's new sense of vocation, so the mode of symbolic utterance modulates, as well. No longer dominated by the symbolic images characteristic of the Platonic Renaissance, the figural bedrock of the major poems is typological symbolism, derived from the tradition of typological exegesis of the Bible (see above, pp. 181 ff.). Modulation, again, is the key term. Since typology takes its origins from the platonising commentaries of the Alexandrian Church Fathers, it would be perilous to insist upon too strict a distinction in modes of symbolism.[35] The touchstone of biblical typology is the literal and historical reality of the type (whether person, object or event) in conjunction with its spiritual significance as prefiguration, however limited or incomplete, of the greater antitype. Milton, however, employs typological symbolism both strictly and more flexibly.

In *Paradise Lost* Moses must be understood as a type of Christ the Mediator, 'whose high Office now / *Moses* in figure bears, to introduce / One greater, of whose day he shall foretell' (XII, 240–2); and, accordingly, he informs his people 'by types / And shadows' (XII, 232–3) of his own antitype. Selecting his poetic persona for this greatest of epics, Milton therefore discards the voice of Isaiah, no longer needing the role of the novice prophet, to envelop himself in the mantle of Moses, 'That Shepherd, who first taught the chosen Seed'. In so doing, the poet reminds us that success in this audacious enterprise, which seeks to encompass the larger order of God's entire creation within the heterocosm of the poem, requires the same inspiration as that through which Moses achieved a verbal mimesis of Creation in the Book of Genesis. Simultaneously the emphasis evokes Moses's typological role as precursor of the Good Shepherd, himself the 'destind Seed to bruise / The Serpent' (XII, 233–4). That Milton's choice of persona should initially establish the typological presence of Christ in poet and everyman is a strikingly appropriate anticipation of his theme and action. The epic which that persona narrates is, in the largest sense, a progressive revelation of the mystery of mankind's redemption through Christ; the poem stands as type to the antitype of its meaning. In just this way, whether Orphic fashioner of symbolic images or Mosaic expounder of types, Milton's choices of persona and symbolic mode reveal an intimate connectedness with the modulations of difference themselves determined by the requirements of theme and genre.

'AND WOV'N CLOSE, BOTH MATTER, FORM AND STYLE'

> If one considers Milton's English verse as a whole up to 1638, it shows that his chief purpose was to assimilate as much of the English poetic heritage as he found worthy and capable of being turned to his own use . . . build[ing] a more lofty, polished, and condensed poetic style than had yet been achieved in English (§S–965: pp. 58–9).

F. T. Prince's summation has the deleterious effect of limning a Miltonic monster of inhuman calculation and ego. Aside from the unintentional caricature, however, the comment points to a way out of the influence conundrum. Milton's stylistic models in the earliest English poems are Spenser primarily in the religious poems, and Jonson in the more courtly or social poems: on the one hand, the softened and therefore distanced pictorialism of the Nativity Ode or 'A Fair Infant'; on the other, the chiselled clarity of 'An Epitaph on the Marchioness of Winchester' or 'Arcades'. In 'L'Allegro' and 'Il Penseroso', however, and even more startlingly in *A Mask*, Milton ceases to be merely the servant of two masters, impersonating instead the entire Elizabethan poetic pantheon. In the companion poems the echoes of a dozen English poets have been tabulated;[36] and for the masque,

> Consider the fact that *Comus* is so 'indebted' to earlier poems that it might be called, not just a transcendental form, but a transcendental pastiche. Echoes of Shakespeare's voice predominate . . . . But there is also the spectral presence of Marlowe, Spenser, Sylvester, Drayton, Jonson, Peele, John Fletcher, and William Browne, among the more notable English authors.[37]

What is one to make of such outrageous eclecticism? Is the poet an entrapped Proteus, fatally bound by his facile virtuosity, or simply a distractible magpie? The problem suggests a need to examine in the aggregate the technique of stylistic echoing.

The most sophisticated response to this need has been Angus Fletcher's formulation of the 'principle of echo'. Discussing 'subliminal' (stylistic) echo as the structural complement to 'mimetic' (dramatic and musical) echo scenes, he perceives a collective function in the masque's variousness that is the farthest thing from simply patchwork composition: 'Its verbal echoing is a radical process, a going to the bottom of language. By recollecting so many poets dead and gone, Milton revives their voices and their ghostly persons' (§S–919: p. 203) Rosalie Colie has described well the process in which generic conventions become reduced to topoi and motifs, transmuting to metaphors which—like musical key signatures—have the effect of evoking in brief the entire set of values and attitudes associated with that genre (§ S–908: pp. 103–28). The 'principle of echo' defines a stylistic analogue to Colie's principle of generic inclusiveness. Through the verbal echoing Milton similarly evokes the social and ideational context, the entire mind-set of Elizabethan pastoralism, summoning up a literary style of life which social events of the 1630s impugn as obsolescent escapism. The purpose of this stylistic recreation is neither a Walleresque nostalgia nor a Puritanical satire upon defeated illusions. Rather, the figurative ambiance of the style functions as a structural counterpart to the action and dialogue of the masque which radically test the assumptions and values associated with the style.

One entire aspect of the echo principle which does not respond to this formulation, however, is Milton's addiction to what has been called self-plagiarism.[38] That the granaries of the mind which Milton so assiduously stocked in the Hammersmith and Horton years included local harvestings has been amply documented; and the habit of self-quotation, his consistency in choice of images and verbal motifs, his Miltonic echoings must be evident to any careful reader. Whether the process is the result of conscious technique, compositional habit, or merely psychological idiosyncracy, awareness of the self-quotations enriches by connotative extensions our receptiveness to nuances of meaning or responsiveness to thematic discriminations.

The 'yet once more' of 'Lycidas' has been tracked plausibly to Hebrews 12:26, but the phrase resonates from the apprentice's reluctant assumption of poet's mantle through the sightless husband's anguished vision of his late espoused saint (Sonnet XXIII, 7) to the prophetic obviation of sin in God's explanation of grace (*Par. Lost*, III. 173–84).[39] Sometimes such repetitions can serve to define the primary implications of a half-obscured line. To draw again upon 'Lycidas': the trembling of the poet's ears at the touch of Phoebus Apollo (77) is elucidated by Sonnet XIII, in which we learn how it is that Henry Lawes avoided the ass's ears assigned to Midas by the same musical arbiter. Sonnet XII—with its theme of licence versus liberty, the motif of metamorphosis, the imagistic oppositions of 'barbarous noise' to harmony and 'roav[ing]' to following the 'mark'—is a microcosmic reprise of *A Mask*, written at least eleven years before. The usefulness in identifying the connection might be found in the relation between Milton's concepts of marriage and divorce, defended in the sonnet, and the ideal of chastity projected in the masque. Some of these examples surely are conscious reworkings of material; others, the habitual light and dark imagery, for instance, seem to arise from the well-springs of the poet's psyche.

Whether intentional or unconscious, however, the general phenomenon of Milton's tendency to treat his own earlier work as a literary tradition to be plundered and adapted at will creates a new kind of reading experience. Milton may be the first English poet whose work needs to be read as a canon with individual images, lines and poems expanding and deepening in implication through the extended context of an *oeuvre*. Shakespeare, Donne and even Herbert, although they all have their idiosyncratic preoccupations, are poets drawing upon traditions of symbolism which remain in the public domain. A

Shakespeare metaphor can usually be well comprehended by consulting the currency in that public treasury and not necessarily enriched by pondering similar metaphors elsewhere in Shakespeare's writings. While Milton is obviously a traditionalist in respect to metaphoric values, his work stands as a body which encourages and rewards the evolving and cross-referential understanding regularly accorded to a Blake or a Wordsworth, poets whose symbolism is more dominantly private and self-defining.[40]

The reason for this particular quality of Milton's writing would seem related to his distinct image of himself as poet, a concern about which earlier English poets tended to be much more self-effacing, and to his compulsion to create a style accurately mirroring that self-image. As a stylist, throughout his career, Milton writes with two seemingly contradictory objectives: to establish his own stylistic identity and to subordinate that identity to the generic requirements of the work at hand.[41] The earliest fully achieved realisation of Milton's mature poetic style—most, perhaps all, readers might agree—occurs with 'Lycidas'. Josephine Miles has defined the particular innovation of 'Lycidas' as the infusion and articulation through repetition of the language of natural description with thematic, ethical and emotive referential values. The poem thereby charts a new course in English poetry:

> To us today, the integration of sense-imagery with sound-pattern and emotional
> harmonic structure is natural to poetry. The imagists and symbolists have called
> for such an integration, and we find it in Keats, in Dylan Thomas, in Hart Crane;
> these are poets in the tradition of *Lycidas*. (§S–963: p. 100)

This could be achieved in 1637 through the fruition of talent and training; but it might be suggested as well that it occurred in this poem and not another because the subject and theme of 'Lycidas' permitted the personal and generic requirements of style to coalesce perfectly.

'Lycidas' is a lyric version of *Paradise Lost*, a young man's personal vision of the fall from innocence to experience with the knowledge of evil particularised, not as teleological and sexual betrayal, but through mortality, corruption and injustice. While the dilation from one to all mankind's epitome is immense, awareness that the mythic substructure remains a constant may have eased the problem of adapting the stylistic strategy of 'Lycidas' to the larger poem. Too simply expressed, the value-infused pastoral descriptions of the elegy are blown up to macrocosmic proportions with the 'moral geography' of *Paradise Lost*. Constantly in the epic, descriptions of place, movement and spatial relation intimate moral status and psychological tendency to the extent that virtually every local episode becomes a microcosm of the central themes.[42] The sustained, resonant density of descriptive language in *Paradise Lost* is far the more awesome achievement, but the technique in itself recognisably extends from that of 'Lycidas'.

Unlike 'Lycidas', however, *Paradise Lost* so expands the perspective on man's fate that it permits no easy collaboration between rival stylistic demands. There is as much internal stylistic variation in the poem as there is generic inclusiveness; however, 'for all its sub-genres, passages in various styles, sometimes as much as a book long, *Paradise Lost* is unmistakably an epic, and an epic in the official mode; though astonishingly flexible, its style is fundamentally "grand" '.[43] But to recognise Milton's orthodoxy in following the decorum which assigns the grand style to epic without also attempting to reconcile it to his heterodoxy in the handling of epic genre is to ignore one of his subtlest authorial dilemmas. The traditional epic celebrates a complex of values and behaviour which, taken seriously, can only be perceived as fundamentally un-Christian; in choosing to assay a genuinely Christian epic, Milton also had to undertake a radical reassessment of the epic tradition:

> *Paradise Lost* is to the tradition of heroic poetry what the 'anti-novel' is to the conventional novel . . . Undermining the established epic tradition by destroying its ethical foundations, *Paradise Lost* is at once both epic and counter-epic. If it imitates the established models of heroic poetry, it also refutes them. In its own way it achieves an intellectual revolution no less extraordinary than that of Copernicus and Kant.   (§S–981: p. xx)

How, then, can Milton simply use the conventional grand style as an uncritical expression of meaning? The answer, of course, is that he does nothing so obvious in his effort to obtain 'answerable style'. Chiefly, Milton finesses the problem, turning this difficulty to one of the poem's extraordinary strengths, by exploiting the differences in person and voice which the narrative afforded him. Not least of these was the duality of his own persona as narrator. Simultaneously the bard's blindness connotes fallen man's mortal imperfection, the stigma of original sin, and the precondition to his prophetic illumination by which he can 'see and tell / Of things invisible to mortal sight' (*Par. Lost*, III, 54–5).[44] At any particular moment in the narrative, epic grandeur of style may serve to suggest the attainment of Mosaic inspiration or, veering in the other direction, the Satanic solipsism of 'heroic' confidence and pride. As Satan's role and actions conform to the pattern of the traditional epic hero in a superficial way,[45] so, too, do his speeches exaggerate and burlesque the style associated with that hero, thereby providing one standard of measure for the other speakers. The contrastive style of God's plain, non-figurative speech comes as a sharp corrective. The reader, it has been argued, re-enacts Adam's errors of choice and is educated into their correction.[46] His easy empathy with Satan's pathos and initial antipathy to God's uncomfortable accuracy are equally wrong responses which must be modified. This 'affective response' thesis works best in the sections of the poem where moral absolutes are most clearly opposed; it becomes problematic in the more neutral—'innocent' would be a better word—territory of Paradise, the created world itself. Here Milton solves the problem of narrative authority by the implied conflation of persons. Standing in the same tutorial relation to reader as do the angels Raphael and Michael to Adam, in effect he assumes the voices of the seraphic guides who speak the better part of these books.

In all the varied styles of *Paradise Lost*, perhaps the most boldly innovative occurs in Books XI and XII, as the voice of Michael revealing to Adam the future of mankind. Such adjectives as 'disappointing', 'tired' and 'perfunctory', which have been levied against the execution of these books, only indicate failure to comprehend how radically Milton rethought the problem of decorum of presentation. Here presenting direct what previously had been only promised or implied in the poem, the providential course of history and man's redemption through the mysteries of the Incarnation and Atonement, Milton confronted the question of a style fit to celebrate the true Christian hero. In this respect the concluding books of *Paradise Lost* constitute a trial run for *Paradise Regained*,[47] the opening line of which, with its allusion to the completed Virgilian progression, inflicts the final undercutting of its predecessor: not epic after all, merely a bitter pastoral of 'the happy Garden'.[48] The later poem, requiring inspiration 'With prosperous wing full summ'd to tell of deeds / Above Heroic, though in secret done', is the true Christian epic. And the style faithfully reflects this. As every reader notices, *Paradise Regained* is written in a simpler, more direct, modest and monotonal style than the 'grand' epic style of *Paradise Lost*. The new style is not the classical middle style, nor is it a Miltonic invention *ex nihilo*. Rather, it is his attempt to adapt to poetics the aesthetic of the *sermo humilis*, the Augustinian tradition of an expanded low style characterising the humility of the Incarnation itself and the *humilitas* of biblical style.[49] Mediating between the humble and the heroic, the style evokes a sense of both gospel plainness and a severely restrained epic line, the paradoxical combination which the poet conceived as the fittest instrument to sing 'the better fortitude / Of Patience and Heroic Martyrdom' (*Par. Lost*, IX, 31–2). As such it also suggests the secured subordination of poetic identity to religious purpose, Milton's characteristically public solution to the personal poetic dilemma in Herbert's 'The Garland' and Marvell's 'The Coronet'.

Through all the modifications of Miltonic style from early to late, the Nativity Ode to *Samson Agonistes*, we may determine a constant: form and style are 'wov'n close' to subject matter, observing 'the grand master-piece' decorum. That is to say, the chain of relations that we have been following runs thus: subject and theme dictate genre, genre regulates persona and voice, which in turn seek the appropriate garment of style.[50]

'THY WORTH AND SKILL EXEMPTS THEE FROM THE THRONG'

As the preceding explorations are likely to have made Milton seem even more than ever isolated from his poetic milieu—a gnarled oak verging on a grove of stunted pines—the exasperated audience may be tempted to ask me, paraphrasing Milton's Satan, What dost thou in this Caroline World? I would reply in conclusion with an unabashed speculation, a return to the principle of reading between the lines. It has always been difficult for us to swallow Milton's purported admiration for Cowley as the greatest of his contemporaries.[51] One could imagine him respecting the critical intelligence underlying the poetic

choices in *Davideis*, even if all the while deploring the execution; a demonstration of the influence Cowley's English Pindarics exerted upon the choral
strophes of *Samson Agonistes* has made the whole business far more intelligible.[52]
Prosody is one area wherein poetic genius might well learn from the careful,
uninspired technician. In a less constricted question of influence, however, we
rightly expect that genius will respond to genius. Recollecting Wordsworth and
Coleridge, Pound and Eliot, Jonson and Inigo Jones, we expect that a two-way
interchange will occur in despite of superficial differences in, say, age, politics
and temperament. That being the case, I shall offer some utterly unprovable
speculations about Milton's relationship with the one undisputed poetic genius
to emerge in the interval between the 1645 *Poems* and the major works.

On 21 February 1653 Milton wrote to John Bradshaw, President of the Council
of State:

> there will be wth: you tomorrow upon some occasion of busines a Gentleman
> whose name is Mr: Marvile; a man whom both by report, & ye: converse I have
> had wth: him, of singular desert for ye: state to make use of; who alsoe offers
> himselfe, if yere: be any imployment for him. His father was ye: Minister of Hull
> & he hath spent foure yeares abroad in Holland, ffrance, Italy, & Spaine, to very
> good purpose, as I beleeve, & ye: gaineing of those 4 languages; besides he is a
> scholler & well read in ye: latin & Greeke authors, & noe doubt of an approved
> conversation, for he com's now lately out of ye: house of ye: Lord ffairefax who
> was Generall, where he was intrusted to give some instructions in ye: Lan-
> guages to ye: Lady his Daughter.[53]

How extraordinary! And how mythically true that Marvell, after wrestling with
his conscience those years in contemplative retirement at Appleton House,
should elect the active life and place his future unerringly in the hands of that
arch-activist poet, John Milton. There is no doubt that Milton thoroughly
approves the decision. '[If the] Councell shall thinke it I shall need any assistant
in ye: performance of my place . . . it would be hard for them to find a Man soe
fit every way for its purpose as this Gentleman.'

Unfortunately, from the standpoint of poetic truth, the recommendation did
not pay off immediately, but Marvell continued to cultivate the older man's
acquaintance, calling on him in London and gaining a reputation as one of
Milton's 'particular friends', a 'learned familiar acquaintance'.[54] Three days after
the publication of Milton's *Second Defence of the English People*, Marvell wrote:

> I shall now Studie it even to the getting of it by Heart: esteeming it according to
> my poor Iudgement (which yet I wish it were so right in all Things else) as the
> most compendious Scale, for so much, to the Height of the Roman Eloquence.
> When I consider how equally it turns and rises with so many figures, it seems to
> me a Trajans Columne in whose winding ascent we see imboss'd the severall
> Monuments of your learned victoryes.[55]

On 2 September 1657 Marvell finally was appointed Latin Secretary to the
Council of State, apparently co-equal to Milton, the Secretary of Foreign

Tongues; and a bare year later the two, sober public men, swelling the scene of a tragic action, walked together in Cromwell's funeral procession.

With the Restoration the balance of the relationship shifted, the younger man becoming protector and advocate. Marvell successfully defended Milton in Parliament, obtaining clemency for the defender of regicides; he got both Milton released from prison and the jailer's fee reduced.[56] Thereafter, happily, he had only to defend Milton in print, as he did against Samuel Parker in *The Rehearsal Transpros'd* (*The Second Part*, 1673). Finally, in the year of Milton's death, Marvell performed what may have been his most important service to his friend, writing the first intelligent, critical appreciation of *Paradise Lost* as a prefatory poem for the second edition.[57]

My outline of the friendship presents nothing new in fact, only a certain shifting of emphasis. The presumption seems always to have been that any resulting influence could only have passed from the older and greater to the younger and lesser poet; thus, Marvell's poems have been searched for Miltonic echoes, which not surprisingly have appeared.[58] But to admit that Marvell is not Milton's equal hardly makes his verse contemptible; the respect and affection between the two seems to have been mutual; and where else among Milton's contemporaries could he have found such a keen poetic intelligence at work upon themes which obsessed him? Would not manuscripts have been produced and verses recited during those visits to Milton's house in the mid-1650s? Is it only coincidental that *The Second Defence*, which Marvell intended to learn by heart, justifies Cromwell's leadership by his first acquiring government over himself? This is an argument which Marvell had used in the 'Horatian Ode' and to which Milton would return again in describing the antitype of the Christian king in the process of refusing, as Cromwell did, an unjust crown: 'Yet he who reigns within himself, and rules / Passions, Desires, and Fears, is more a King; / Which every wise and vertuous man attains: / And who attains not, ill aspires to rule' (*Par. Regained*, II, 466–9). When Milton sent *The Second Defence* to Marvell immediately upon publication on 30 May 1654, would not Marvell have reciprocated on 17 January 1655 with a copy of 'The First Anniversary of the Government under O.C.'? Marvell's Cromwell poems, like the later *Paradise Lost*—while written out of reaction to what the two men for very different reasons would have perceived as the wreckage of a glorious achievement—are the epic's precursor in their efforts to 'assert Eternal Providence' in the face of an often cruelly baffling history (§S–962: pp. 19 ff.).

Rather than merely throwing up a sequence of such speculative parallels, I wish to close by focusing upon the relation between two important and singularly elusive poems. In Marvell's *Upon Appleton House* one man's unexpected retirement from the active life is sympathetically explored, another man's nature probed and tested in rustic retreat as preparation for his return to the world and the active life. In *Paradise Regained* the actions which Marvell, rational amphibian, divides between Fairfax and himself are united in the desert temptations of Christ. Looking at Marvell's poem as Milton might have perceived it, we find a man undergoing an *imitatio Christi*, a withdrawal into self to learn who he is and thereby better to comprehend the nature of his mission in the world. Concomitant to this action are the themes which Milton associated with its original: contemplative retirement and active engagement, governance over the self and governance in the world, the rejection of military solutions to political governance, the rejection of sensual and intellectual self-indulgence, truth to one's own nature, and the freedom of individual choice as the fulfilment of providential destiny.[59]

If these constitute matter and themes, what sort of container did Marvell contrive for them? What can be said generically about this most chameleon-like of poems? *Upon Appleton House* includes a multitude of kinds—country-house poem, the praise of a patron, Ovidian metamorphosis, pastoral, masque, perspective, what you will.[60] The critical question upon which to fix is whether, like *Paradise Lost*, it has a dominant generic identity controlling and subordinating the other kinds or whether Marvell has created a totally mixed form, a hybrid undercutting the singleness and stability of a containing point of view. A suggestive case has been made that the generic norm of the poem is epic, in part a response to Davenant's simplistic advocacy of the active life as the truly heroic: 'Fairfax had retired to practise the better fortitude of patience, and it is this version of Christian heroism that the poem celebrates, without denigrating the active life which Davenant held to be the only subject of epic verse.'[61] In this view Marvell's public life follows the standard of Christian virtue practised in retirement by Fairfax; patron and poet share a code of values embodied equally by the house and the poem. Exemplary of a Christian heroism, the poem stands as a Christian epic.

This formulation stops only a half-step from my own point: not Christian epic in Davenant's sense—nor, indeed, Tasso's and Spenser's—but a Miltonic brief epic. Marvell signals the scaling down from 'diffuse' epic to *genus humilis* with his initial contrast between the grand and the simple house: '*Humility* alone designs / Those short but admirable lines / By which, ungirt and unconstrain'd / Things greater are in less contain'd'. In doing so he articulates an aesthetic which applies exactly to the poem that his friend would later undertake. A number of short, biblical narrative poems have been examined as progenitors to Milton's brief epic (§S–944: pp. 36–101); but they seem to contribute less to *Paradise Regained* that he would have learned from a single reading of *Upon Appleton House*. From Dante, Ariosto and Spenser we know that the epic poet conventionally figures his perilous enterprise as a voyage across the sea in a grand ship, by dint of heroic effort at last bringing his vessel to safe harbour.[62] In his closing stanza Marvell reminds us again what his poem is and is not with a wonderful lowering of the epic metaphor to the modest, domesticated image of the 'Salmon-Fishers' carrying home their 'Leathern Boats' in the gathering darkness, a reduction which yet contains the greater in less: 'for the dark *Hemisphere* / Does now like one of them appear'. With such an example of implicational understatement and modesty (a forerunner of the quiet minor-key conclusion to *Paradise Regained*) one only dares follow Marvell: 'Let's in'.

NOTES

1 In no sense is this chapter intended as a systematic survey of Milton's literary milieu. For that one should consult Bush (§S–900), as well as more specialised studies, such as George W. Whiting, *Milton's Literary Milieu* (Chapel Hill, 1939).

2 William R. Parker concludes that Milton had no significant public reputation until after the publication in 1650 of *Pro populo anglicano defensio* and that only in the Restoration did he become known as a poet. See *Milton's Contemporary Reputation* (Columbus, Ohio, 1940).

3 Louis L. Martz, 'The Rising Poet, 1645', in §S–984: pp. 3–4. As Martz notes (pp. 5–6), however inept as portraiture, William Marshall's engraved frontispiece emphasises the generic range of the volume. For a view contrary to Martz's and my own, see George W. Nitchie, 'Milton and his Muses', *Journal of English Literary History*, XLIV (1977), 77–84. Nitchie projects a lifelong Miltonic psychomachia between playful artist and possessed prophet, with the 1645 *Poems* a record of abandoned artist's roles. There is a grain of truth in this perception of ambivalence, but it is exaggerated almost beyond recognition.

4 See William B. Hunter, Jr., 'John Milton: Autobiographer', *Milton Quarterly*, VIII (1974), 100–4.

5 'On *Paradise Lost*', 53–4 (in *CE*, II, 5). On the tradition Marvell evokes, see Røstvig (§S–970).

6 See Kathleen Williams, 'Milton, Greatest Spenserian', and Joseph A. Wittreich, Jr., ' "A Poet amongst Poets": Milton and the Tradition of Prophecy', in §S–1009: pp. 25–55, 97–142; also William Kerrigan, *The Prophetic Milton* (Charlottesville, 1974).

7 I am not here concerned with problems of strict chronology, such as exactly when the decision to become a poet was arrived at or the date at which 'Ad Patrem' was written. Instead my concern is with the image which Milton elected to project in 1645 by the selection and arrangement of previously written materials.

   The chronological displacement of *A Mask* requires separate mention. Following 'Lycidas', like the Latin poems it has a separate title page and therefore stands as an independent unit between English and Latin sections. Probably length is the primary determinant for this positioning—'Arcades' can pass as lyric—but a secondary consideration may be generic. As works projecting an image of the poet in search of patrons, the masques may have seemed to represent a dead end or a miscalculation in his development. 'Mansus' explores another kind of poet-and-patron relationship, but one that Milton also eventually rejected.

8 Martz (§S–950), p. 38. On the problem of distinction, see R. B. Waddington, 'Shakespeare's Sonnet 15 and the Art of Memory', and T. O. Sloan, 'The Crossing of Rhetoric and Poetry', in §S–878: pp. 117–22 and 226–31.

9 On liturgical elements in poetry, see, e.g., Rosemond Tuve, *A Reading of George Herbert* (Chicago, 1954), and Chambers (§S–905).

10 See Michael Murrin, *The Veil of Allegory* (Chicago, 1969), pp. 21–53.

11 See D. C. Allen, *The Harmonious Vision* (Baltimore, 1954), pp. 47–52, and Jackson I. Cope, 'Fortunate Falls as Form in Milton's "Fair Infant"', *Journal of English and Germanic Philology*, LXIII (1964), 660–74.

12 Contrast Allen (previous note), pp. 31–3, with C. L. Barber, 'The Masque as a Masque', in §S–984: pp. 35–66, and Fletcher (§S–919).

13 On these elements, see, respectively, Prince (§S–965), pp. 70–88; J. H. Hanford, 'The Pastoral Elegy and Milton's "Lycidas"', in §S–963: pp. 27–55; and Wittreich (§S–1009), pp. 119–27.

14 On this see, e.g., R. B. Waddington, 'The Sun at the Center: Structure as Meaning in Pico della Mirandola's *Heptaplus*', *Journal of Medieval and Renaissance Studies*, III (1973), 69–86.

15 Lewalski (§S–944), and her '*Samson Agonistes* and the "Tragedy" of the Apocalypse', *Publications of the Modern Language Association*, LXXXV (1970), 1050–62.

16 For a view of Milton's poetics emphasising the disparaties between *The Reason of Church Government* and *Paradise Lost*, see John F. Huntley, 'The Images of Poet and Poetry in Milton's *Reason of Church Government*', in §S–947: pp. 83–120.

17 On the importance of biblical personae to seventeenth-century devotional poetry, see Lewalski (§S–945). For the forms of Waller's verse, see Warren L. Chernaik, *The Poetry of Limitation* (New Haven, 1968).

18 See, particularly, Jackson I. Cope, *The Metaphoric Structure of 'Paradise Lost'* (Baltimore, 1962), and Isabel G. MacCaffrey, *'Paradise Lost' as Myth* (Cambridge, Mass., 1959).

19 See above, pp. 146 ff.: also P. O. Kristeller, *The Philosophy of Marsilio Ficino*, trans. Virginia Conant (1943); André Chastel, *Marsile Ficin et l'art* (Geneva, 1954); D. P. Walker, *The Ancient Theology* (1972); and Yates (§S–427).

20 See, e.g., D. C. Allen, 'Milton and the Descent to Light', *Journal of English and Germanic Philology*, LX (1961), 614–30, and Cope (as above, note 18), pp. 72–148.

21 See Stanley E. Fish, *'Surprised by Sin'* (1967), pp. 57–91, and John M. Steadman, *Milton's Epic Characters* (Chapel Hill, 1968), pp. 227–77.

22 Allen (as above, note 11), pp. xi–xx.

23 On *concordia discors* in seventeenth-century poetry, see §S–997: pp. 53–61, and §S–991: pp. 35–44, 166–70; for Milton, see H. V. S. Ogden, 'The Principles of Variety and Contrast in Seventeenth-Century Aesthetics and Milton's Poetry', *Journal of the History of Ideas*, X (1949), 159–82.

24 §S–999: pp. 197–99. For covenant theology, see Perry Miller, *The New England Mind: The Seventeenth Century* (Cambridge, Mass., 1954), pp. 365–462.

25 See Murrin (as above, note 10), pp. 85–97.

26 Indeed, recently Michael Fixler has maintained that a precisely Platonic theory of inspiration underlies the invocations in *Paradise Lost*; however, the argument is conducted at too abstract a plane to be fully persuasive. See 'Plato's Four Furors and the Real Structure of *Paradise Lost*', *Publications of the Modern Language Association*, XCII (1977), 952–62.

27 G. G. D. Kilpatrick, in *The Interpreter's Bible* (1956), V, 204. Although Milton later relinquished this role, his fondness for the text remained constant. Deborah, his youngest daughter, later recounted that 'she and her sisters used to read to their father in eight languages, which by practice they were capable of doing with great readiness and accuracy, though they understood what they read in no other language

but English; and their father used often to say in their hearing, *one tongue was enough for a woman*. None of them were ever sent to school, but all taught at home by a mistress kept for that purpose. *Isaiah, Homer,* and Ovid's *Metamorphoses* were books, which they were often called to read to their father; and at my desire she repeated a considerable number of verses from the beginning of both those Poets with great readiness' (Pierre Bayle, *A General Dictionary, Historical and Critical,* enlarged ed., trans. John Peter Bernard *et al.* (1738), VV, 588).

28 See, respectively, Chastel (as above, note 19), pp. 173–6; Walker (§S–418), pp. 22–41; Allen (as above, note 44), pp. 614–30; and Waddington (§S–991), pp. 45–9.

29 On Thyrsis as 'the Orphic persona', see §S–919: pp. 186–94; the best account of the Orphic dimension in the companion poems is Michael Fixler, 'The Orphic Technique of "L'Allegro" and "Il Penseroso"', *English Literary Renaissance,* I (1971), 165–77.

30 See Chastel (as above, note 19), pp. 163–9; and Rudolf and Margot Wittkower, *Born under Saturn* (1969), pp. 98–104.

31 See Caroline W. Mayerson, 'The Orpheus Image in *Lycidas'*, *Publications of the Modern Language Association,* LXIV (1949), 189–207; condensed in §S–963.

32 Some basic guides to this large subject are: §§S–342, S–796, S–825, S–901; D. T. Starnes and E. W. Talbert, *Classical Myth and Legend in Renaissance Dictionaries* (Chapel Hill, 1955); and Douglas Bush, *Pagan Myth and Christian Tradition in English Poetry* (Philadelphia, 1968).

33 See Mary Christopher Pecheux, 'The Image of the Sun in Milton's "Nativity Ode"', *Huntington Library Quarterly,* XXXVIII (1975), 315–33.

34 See Jonathan H. Collett, 'Milton's Use of Classical Mythology in *Paradise Lost'*, *Publications of the Modern Language Association,* LXXXV (1970), 88–96.

35 As does William G. Madsen, *From Shadowy Types to Truth* (New Haven, 1968); more balanced approaches are taken by, e.g., Allen (as above, note 20), and Geoffrey Hartman, 'Adam on the Grass with Balsamum', *Journal of English Literary History,* XXXVI (1969), 168–92. Barbara K. Lewalski attempts to discriminate the particular character of Protestant typology: see 'Typology and Poetry', in *Illustrious Evidence,* ed. Earl Miner (Berkeley, 1975), pp. 42–3.

36 See J. B. Leishman, '"L'Allegro" and "Il Penseroso" in their Relation to Seventeenth-Century Poetry', *Essays and Studies 1951,* pp. 1–36.

37 Fletcher (§S–919), pp. 201–2, See also Joan Grundy, *The Spenserian Poets* (1969), pp. 206–10, and Joan Klein, 'Some Spenserian Influences on Milton's *Comus'*, *Annuale Mediaevale,* V (1964), 27–47.

38 Edward S. LeComte, *Yet Once More* (1953).

39 See David S. Berkeley, 'A Possible Biblical Echo of *Lycidas,* l. 1', *Notes and Queries,* new series, VIII (1961), 178. The implicit common element among these occurrences is the prophetic situation; cf. §S–1009: pp. 117–18.

40 For an excellent concise statement of the differences between Renaissance and Romantic poetics, see Wasserman's chapter, 'Metaphors for Poetry', in §S–997: pp. 169–88.

41 Cf. Nitchie (as above, note 3), who extends the conflict from the stylistic to the psychological.

42 Cope (as above, note 18), pp. 72–148.

43 Rosalie L. Colie, 'My Echoing Song': Andrew Marvell's Poetry of Criticism (Princeton, 1970), p. 277; she expands upon the remark in §S–908: pp. 119–23. For a succinct account of why epic style must be grand, see Arnold Stein, Answerable Style (Minneapolis, 1953), pp. 120–2. Christopher Ricks, Milton's Grand Style (Oxford, 1963), lacks historical definition.

44 Cf. Anne Davidson Ferry, Milton's Epic Voice (Cambridge, Mass., 1963).

45 Steadman (§S–981), pp. 17–20, 28–30, 49–51, 79–83, 140–4.

46 Fish (as above, note 21).

47 Cf. R. B. Waddington, 'The Death of Adam: Vision and Voice in Paradise Lost, Books XI and XII', Modern Philology, LXIX (1972), 9–21.

48 See Arnold Stein, Heroic Knowledge (Minneapolis, 1957), pp. 6–7.

49 See Erich Auerbach, Literary Language and its Public in Late Latin Antiquity, trans. Ralph Manheim (1965), pp. 24–66, especially pp. 40–52.

50 On poetic decorum, see Tuve (§S–988), pp. 192–247. The decorum of Milton's prose has been studied by Kranidas (§S–937).

51 So reported by Milton's third wife, Elizabeth Minshull; see J. M. French, The Life Records of John Milton (New Brunswick, N.J., 1949–58), V, 322–3.

52 Edward Weismiller, 'The "Dry" and "Rugged" Verse', in §S–984: pp. 115–52.

53 Complete Prose Works, gen. ed. Don M. Wolfe (New Haven, 1966), IV, ii, 859–60.

54 The phrases are from Edward Phillips and John Aubrey, in the texts given by Merritt Y. Hughes, ed., John Milton: Complete Poems and Major Prose (1957), pp. 1023, 1035. Phillips's comment refers to the period 1652–60; Aubrey's cannot be dated so precisely. See also Christopher Hill, 'Milton and Marvell' (in §S–962), who argues for a close relationship through the 1650s; but I cannot follow Hill's thesis that Milton, Marvell and Marchamont Nedham were active republican conspirators in the 1660s and 1670s.

55 Prose Works (as above, note 53), IV, ii, 864.

56 See the summary of associations in ibid., IV, ii, 862.

57 On Marvell's poem, see Joseph A. Wittreich, Jr., 'Perplexing the Explanation: Marvell's "On Mr. Milton's Paradise Lost" ' (in §S–962); also H. F. Lippincott, Jr., 'Marvell's "On Paradise Lost" ', English Language Notes, IX (1972), 265–72.

58 H. M. Margoliouth suggests several echoings of 'Lycidas': see his notes to Upon Appleton House and 'A Poem upon the Death of O.C.' in The Poems and Letters of Andrew Marvell, revised by Pierre Legouis and E. E. Duncan-Jones (Oxford, 1971). Professor John M. Wallace informs me that he credits Marvell with the earliest printed allusion to Paradise Lost.

59 On the themes of Marvell's poems, see John M. Wallace, Destiny his Choice (Cambridge, 1968), pp. 232–57; and Colie (as above, note 43), pp. 219–49.

60 Colie (as above, note 43), pp. 277–94.

61 Wallace (as above, note 59), p. 242. Significantly, for my argument, Wallace uses scholarship upon *Paradise Regained* to establish the standard of Christian heroism.

62 See E. R. Curtius, *European Literature and the Latin Middle Ages*, trans. W. R. Trask (1953), pp. 128–30.

A chronological outline

Developments on the Continent are listed within brackets. A question mark indicates that the date given is doubtful.

Significant events prior to the accession of the Stuarts from 1603 include: the defeat of the Spanish Armada (1588); the war in Ulster (1595); [the Edict of Nantes (1596);] the death of Burghley (1598 [and, on the Continent, the peace between France and Spain, and the death of Philip II of Spain]); the Essex rebellion, Elizabeth's last Parliament, and the battle of Kinsale (1601).

THE REIGN OF JAMES I (1603–25)

1603 Peace in Ireland. Death of Elizabeth I; accession of James I. The Millenary Petition. [Accession of the sultan Osman (to 1622).]

1604 James's first Parliament. Peace with Spain. Richard Bancroft appointed Archbishop of Canterbury. The Hampton Court Conference. *Othello* first acted.

1605 The Gunpowder Plot. *King Lear* first (?) acted. Bacon's *Advancement of Learning* published. Sir Thomas Browne born. [Pope Clement VIII died; election of Leo XI, then Paul V (to 1621). Tsar Boris Godunov died; 'Time of the Troubles' to 1613. Cervantes's *Don Quixote*, Part I, published; Part II in 1615.].

1606 Bate's Case (Impositions). *Macbeth*, Jonson's *Volpone* and Tourneur's *Revenger's Tragedy* first (?) acted. Waller born. [Rembrandt, Corneille born.]

1607 *Antony and Cleopatra* first acted (1606?); also *Coriolanus* (1608?). Bishops imposed on the Scots. First successful English colony founded, in Virginia. Flight of the Earls from Ireland. [Monteverdi's first opera, *Orfeo*, performed.]

1608 Robert Cecil created Earl of Salisbury and appointed Lord Treasurer. Shakespeare's *Pericles* first (?) acted. Sylvester's translation of Du Bartas: first complete edition. Milton, Thomas Fuller, Clarendon born.

1609 Spenser's *Faerie Queene*: first folio edition. Shakespeare's *Sonnets* published; his *Cymbeline* first acted (1610?). Sir John Suckling, Benjamin Whichcote born. [Dutch-Spanish truce.]

1610   The Great Contract; end of James's first Parliament. Jonson's *Alchemist* first acted;
       also Shakespeare's *Winter's Tale* (1611?). [Galileo reports on his telescopic view of
       the·heavens. Henry IV of France assassinated; accession of Louis XIII (Marie de'
       Medici regent). Caravaggio died.]
1611   George Abbot appointed Archbishop of Canterbury. The King James ('Authorised')
       Version of the Bible published. Shakespeare's *Tempest* first (?) acted. Donne's
       Anatomy of the World published. Chapman's *Iliad* completed, followed by the
       Odyssey (1614–15). [Charles IX of Sweden died; accession of Gustavus Adolphus (to
       1632).]
1612   Robert Carr, later Earl of Somerset, in favour. Death of the heir apparent Prince
       Henry; also of Salisbury. Last burning of a heretic in England. Donne's *Second
       Anniversary* published. [Emperor Rudolf II died; accession of Matthias.]
1613   Princess Elizabeth marries Frederick Elector Palatine. Sir Thomas Overbury mur-
       dered. Cleveland, Crashaw, Jeremy Taylor born. [La Rochefoucauld born. Rise of
       the Romanov dynasty: Michael elected tsar (to 1645).]
1614   The Addled Parliament. Ralegh's *History of the World* published; also *Characters* by
       Overbury *et al*. Jonson's *Bartholomew Fair* first acted; also (?) Webster's *Duchess of
       Malfi*. Henry More born. [El Greco died.]
1615   George Villiers, later Duke of Buckingham, in favour. Denham, Lilburne born.
       Donne ordained.
1616   Jonson's *Works*, Chapman's *Whole Works of Homer* and John Napier's *Description of
       Logarithmes* published. John Smith the Cambridge Platonist born (?). Shakespeare
       and Francis Beaumont died. [Cervantes died.]
1617   Ralph Cudworth born. [Murillo born.]
1618   Supremacy of Villiers. Sir Walter Ralegh executed. Bacon appointed Lord Chancel-
       lor. Abraham Cowley, Richard Lovelace born. [The Synod of Dort. The Thirty Years
       War (to 1648).]
1619   Inigo Jones begins the Whitehall Banqueting House (completed 1622). Nicholas
       Hilliard died. [Emperor Matthias died; accession of Ferdinand II (to 1637). Kepler's
       De harmonice mundi published.]
1620   The Pilgrim Fathers sail in the *Mayflower* and found Plymouth Colony in New
       England. Milton at St Paul's School (to 1624). Bacon's *Novum Organum* published.
       Thomas Campion died. [Battle at White Mountain.]
1621   James's third Parliament. Bacon impeached. Cranfield appointed Lord Treasurer.
       Donne appointed Dean of St Paul's. Burton's *Anatomy of Melancholy* published.
       Marvell born. [Philip III of Spain died; accession of Philip IV (to 1665). Dutch-
       Spanish war resumed. Gregory XV, Pope (to 1623). La Fontaine born.]
1622   Henry Vaughan born (?). [Molière born.]
1623   Prince Charles and Buckingham visit Madrid. The first Shakespeare Folio pub-
       lished. Giles Fletcher, John Dowland, William Byrd died. [Urban VIII, Pope (to 1644).
       Pascal born. Accession of the sultan Murad IV (to 1640).]
1624   James's last Parliament; fall of Cranfield, Earl of Middlesex; war with Spain (to
       1630). Donne's *Devotions* published. [Lord Herbert of Cherbury's *De veritate*
       published in Paris. Cardinal Richelieu chief Minister in France.]

THE REIGN OF CHARLES I (1625–49)

1625   Death of James I; accession of Charles I, who marries Henrietta Maria of France. His
       first Parliament. Outbreak of the plague. Milton admitted to Christ's College,
       Cambridge. Orlando Gibbons died; also (?) John Webster. [Maurice of Nassau died;
       Frederick Henry stadtholder of the Netherlands (to 1647). Jan Breughel died.]

1626 Charles's second Parliament attempts to impeach Buckingham, and is dissolved. Forced Loan. Lancelot Andrewes, Bacon died. John Aubrey born.

1627 War with France (to 1629). Five Knights' Case.

1628 Charles's third Parliament. The Petition of Right. Richard Weston appointed Lord Treasurer; and Thomas Weston, a peer. Buckingham assassinated. Wentworth President of the North. William Harvey's discovery of the circulation of the blood published. Fulke Greville died. John Bunyan born. [Malherbe died].

1629 Dissolution of Charles's third Parliament. Visit of Rubens to England. Lancelot Andrewes's *XCVI Sermons* published. Milton admitted to the B.A.

1630 The Great Migration to Massachusetts begins; Boston founded. Prince Charles (later Charles II) born. Herbert at Bemerton. [Kepler died.]

1631 Donne died. Dryden born.

1632 Van Dyck settles in England. Milton admitted to the M.A. Sir Christopher Wren, John Locke born. [Galileo's *Dialogues concerning the Two Principal Systems of the World* published. Gustavus Adolphus of Sweden killed; accession of Christina (under regent to 1644). Sigismund III of Poland died; accession of Wladyslaw IV. Vermeer, Spinoza born.]

1633 William Laud appointed Archbishop of Canterbury. Wentworth in Ireland. Death of George Herbert: *The Temple* published; also Donne's *Poems*. Pepys born. [The trial of Galileo.]

1634 Ship money levied on maritime areas. Milton's *Comus* performed. Chapman, Marston died.

1635 Ship money extended to inland counties and towns. Thomas Sprat born.

1636 Bishop Juxon appointed Lord Treasurer. Advent of Cambridge Platonism (1636 ff.). Joseph Glanvill born.

1637 Censorship enforced. New Scottish Prayer Book. Milton's *Comus* published. Jonson, Nicholas Ferrar, Robert Fludd died. Thomas Traherne born. Hampden's Case. [Descartes's *Discourse on Method* published. Emperor Ferdinand II died; accession of Ferdinand III (to 1657).]

1638 The National Covenant signed in Scotland. Milton abroad; his 'Lycidas' published. [Cyril Lucaris, the 'Protestant' Patriarch of Constantinople, died.]

1639 First Bishops' War. Viscount Wentworth (Earl of Strafford, 1640) adviser to King Charles. Sir Henry Wotton died. [Racine born.]

1640 The Short Parliament; Second Bishops' War. The Long Parliament (to 1660); Laud and Strafford impeached. The Root and Branch Petition. Donne's *LXXX Sermons* published. Robert Burton, Thomas Carew died. Wycherley born. [The Portuguese war of independence (to 1668); accession of John IV (to 1656). Revolt of the Catalans. Accession of the sultan Ibrahim I (to 1648); decline of Ottoman power. Rubens died.]

1641 The Triennial Act; Strafford's attainder and execution. Irish Rebellion. The Grand Remonstrance. Milton's anti-prelatical tracts begin. Comenius in England. Van Dyck died. [Domenichino died.]

1642 Attempt on Five Members; the Militia Ordinance. Charles I raises his standard at Nottingham; the Civil War begins. The battle of Edgehill. Theatres closed. Milton marries Mary Powell (who dies in 1652). Newton born. Sir John Suckling died. [Galileo died. Richelieu died; Cardinal Mazarin named chief Minister in France.]

1643 The Westminster Assembly of Divines. The Solemn League and Covenant. Bill for the abolition of episcopacy passed. Sir Thomas Browne's *Religio Medici* published (authorised edn.). Joseph Mede's *Key of Revelation* published (Latin original, 1627). Hampden, Falkland, Godolphin, killed in action; Pym died. [Louis XIII of France died; accession of Louis XIV (Anne of Austria regent). Monteverdi died.]

1644 The battle of Marston Moor. Milton's *Areopagitica* published. Chillingworth, Francis

Quarles, George Sandys died. [Innocent X, Pope (to 1655).]

1645   Laud executed. The Self-Denying Ordinance; the New Model Army formed. The battle of Naseby. Beginnings of the Leveller movement. Milton's 'minor poems' published. [Tsar Michael died; accession of Alexis (to 1676).]

1646   Charles I surrenders to the Scots. End of First Civil War. Crashaw's *Steps to the Temple* and Sir Thomas Browne's *Pseudodoxia Epidemica* published.

1647   The Scots hand Charles over to the English Parliament; he is seized by the army, which occupies London. The Putney Debates. Charles flees to the Isle of Wight. Lilly's *Christian Astrology* and Henry More's *Philosophical Poems* published. [Frederick Henry of the Netherlands died; William II stadtholder.]

1648   Charles's treaty with the Scots; the Second Civil War. The battle of Preston. Pride's Purge. Charles brought to London. The Whitehall Debates. Herrick's poems published. Lord Herbert of Cherbury died. [Peace of Westphalia: end of the Thirty Years War. The Fronde (to 1653). Wladyslaw IV of Poland died; accession of John Cassimir (to 1668). Christian IV of Denmark died; accession of Frederick III (to 1670). Accession of the sultan Mohammed IV (to 1687).]

1649   Trial and execution of Charles I. Monarchy and the House of Lords abolished. Charles II proclaimed in Scotland.

THE INTERREGNUM (1649–60)

1649   The Commonwealth established; rule of the Rump Parliament (to April 1653). The Irish Rebellion crushed by Cromwell. Milton appointed Secretary of Foreign Tongues. Crashaw died.

1650   Fairfax retired. Invasion of Scotland. The battle of Dunbar. Vaughan's *Silex scintillans* published (Part II in 1655). Phineas Fletcher died. [William II of the Netherlands died; Jan de Witt assumes power (to 1672). Davenant's *Gondibert* published in Paris. Descartes died.]

1651   Battle of Worcester finally ends royalist resistance; Charles II escapes to France. Henry Ireton died; also (?) Nathaniel Culverwell. Hobbes's *Leviathan* published.

1652   Conquest of Ireland and of Scotland completed. Act for the Settlement of Ireland. The first Anglo-Dutch War (to 1654). Inigo Jones and John Smith the Cambridge Platonist died. [Crashaw's *Carmen Deo Nostro* published in Paris. Nikon appointed Patriarch of Moscow, introduces liturgical reforms.]

1653   Expulsion of the Rump. Barebone's Parliament. Instrument of Government; the Protectorate established under Cromwell. Izaac Walton's *Compleat Angler* published. [Corelli born.]

1654   First Protectorate Parliament. [Jamaica occupied by British forces. Christina of Sweden abdicated; accession of Charles X.]

1655   Regime of the Major-Generals established (to January 1657). Jews readmitted to England. War with Spain (to 1660). Denham's *Coopers Hill* (authorised edn.) and Thomas Stanley's *History of Philosophy* (1655–62) published. [Alexander VII, Pope (to 1667).]

1656   Second Protectorate Parliament. James Harrington's *Commonwealth of Oceana* and Cowley's poems published. Milton marries Katherine Woodcock (who dies in 1658). Joseph Hall died. [John IV of Portugal died; accession of Alfonso VI.]

1657   The Humble Petition and Advice; Cromwell refuses the crown. Anglo-French alliance. William Harvey died; also Lilburne and (?) Richard Lovelace. [Emperor Ferdinand III died; accession of Leopold I.]

1658   Battle of the Dunes. Death of Cromwell; the Protectorate passes to his son Richard. Sir Thomas Browne's *Hydriotaphia* and *Garden of Cyrus* published. Cleveland died.

1659   Richard Cromwell obliged to abdicate; the Rump and the Commonwealth restored.

The Rump expelled, and restored again. General Monck's march south. Purcell born. [Franco-Spanish war ended.]

1660 Pepys begins his Diary (to 1669). Monck reaches London; return of Secluded Members; the Long Parliament dissolves itself. The Declaration of Breda; the Convention Parliament recalls Charles II. Monarchy restored.

THE RESTORATION (from 1660)

1660 The House of Lords restored. Clarendon chief Minister. Theatres reopened. Defoe born. [Charles X of Sweden died; accession of Charles XI, regency until 1670. Velásquez died.]

1661 The Cavalier Parliament (to 1679). Thomas Fuller died. [Mazarin died; Louis XIV assumes full powers. Saint-Aman died.]

1662 Charter of the Royal Society. The Licensing Act. The Act of Uniformity. [Pascal died.]

1663 Milton marries Elizabeth Minshull.

1664 Second Anglo-Dutch War (to 1667). Vanbrugh born.

1665 Outbreak of the Great Plague (to early 1666). Robert Hooke's *Micrographia* published. [Philip IV of Spain died; accession of Charles II. Poussin died.]

1666 The Great Fire of London.

1667 The Dutch in the Medway; the Triple Alliance. Fall of Clarendon; rise of the so-called Cabal Ministry. Milton's *Paradise Lost* and Thomas Sprat's *History of the Royal Society* published. Abraham Cowley, Jeremy Taylor died. Swift born. [Alfonso VI of Portugal abdicated; his brother becomes regent, then king from 1683 as Peter II. Borromini died.]

1668 [Giambattista Vico born.]

1669 Denham died.

1670 Charles concludes open and secret Treaties of Dover with Louis XIV. Congreve born.

1671 Milton's *Paradise Regained* and *Samson Agonistes* published. Third Earl of Shaftesbury born.

1672 Third Anglo-Dutch War (to 1674). The Declaration of Indulgence offers religious toleration. [French invasion of the Netherlands; fall of de Witt's regime; William III saves the Netherlands.]

1673 The First Test Act. James Duke of York resigns Admiralty; break-up of Cabal. Wren begins St Paul's Cathedral.

1674 Danby chief Minister. Second revised edition of *Paradise Lost* published; also Bunyan's *Pilgrim's Progress* (Part II in 1684).

1677 Dryden's *All for Love* first performed. Marriage of William III and James's daughter, Mary.

1678 The fictitious 'Popish Plot'. Farquhar born. [Peace between France and the Netherlands.]

1679 The Exclusion Crisis; appearance of Whigs and Tories (1679–81). Habeas Corpus Act.

1681 Marvell's *Poems* published.

The era closes with the deaths of Milton, Robert Herrick, Thomas Traherne and Clarendon (1674); Harrington (1677); Marvell (1678); Hobbes (1679); Joseph Glanvill (1680); Sir Thomas Browne (1682); Edmund Waller, Izaak Walton and Benjamin Whichcote (1687); Bunyan (1688) [and on the Continent: Rembrandt (1669), Molière (1673), Vermeer (1675), Spinoza (1677), La Rochefoucauld (1680), Corneille (1684)].

An introduction to the
Short-Title Catalogue

CONTENTS

Throughout, places of publication are given only if they are other than London or New York.

The abbreviation 'P' designates a Primary source, while 'S' in the next bibliography (pp. 393–427) designates a Secondary source.

PREFACE

The indispensable starting point for serious research in seventeenth-century studies is the *Short-Title Catalogue of Books printed in England, Scotland, & Ireland, and of English Books printed abroad, 1475–1640*, compiled by A. W. Pollard and G. R. Redgrave (Oxford, 1926). Essentially a book-list arranged alphabetically, the *STC* provides the following information for each entry: first the assigned reference number (important both as the unique mark of identity within the *STC* and because many secondary works now use *STC* numbers as a brief form of citation); author and title; translator and/or editor (if relevant); edition, format (i.e. folio, quarto, etc.), printer, publisher and/or bookseller (if known), year of publication; and copies located in major libraries. The principle of inclusion is any book printed in the British Isles—in whatever language—or English-language books and Latin service-books for the British market printed abroad. The time span commences with the advent of mechanical printing in England and terminates at the point at which George Thomason began his formidable collection (see below). The efforts of Pollard and Redgrave have been complemented by Donald Wing, *A Short-Title Catalogue of Books printed in England, Scotland, Ireland, Wales and British America and of English Books printed in other countries, 1641–1700* (1945–51), 3 vols., and *A Gallery of Ghosts: Books published between 1641–1700 not found in the STC* (1967).

The fiftieth anniversary of the publication of the *STC*, appropriately, was marked by the appearance of Volume 2 (I–Z) of the long-awaited revised edition; it was begun by W. A. Jackson and F. S. Ferguson and completed by Katherine F. Pantzer. Volume 1 (A–H) may be expected to follow within a few years. The significance of the revised *STC* lies in the fact that the 26,000 entries of the Pollard and Redgrave edition will be increased by as much as thirty per cent; moreover, the citation of libraries holding *STC* books has been vastly expanded, as well as the apparatus (e.g. cross-referencing and subject groupings). For a thoughtful, non-technical review of the new *STC*, one may consult the essay by David Rogers in the *Times Literary Supplement* (27 August 1976, p. 1061). A revision of the Wing *STC* also is in progress; the first volume (A1–E2926) was published in 1972.

In addition to the Wing continuation, the work of Pollard and Redgrave inspired a number of other *STCs*—of other nations, of specific subjects (e.g. history of science), or simply *STC* holdings in a particular library. Of more immediate significance to our purposes is a group of research tools created by complete or selective rearrangement of the *STC*, thereby making it possible to use its entries in a number of different ways. First in importance is the rearrangement of the alphabetical ordering of the *STC* into chronological sequence, which enables the student to examine the aggregate of publication in any given year. The chronological index to the *STC* originated at the Huntington Library (San Marino, California); but such card catalogues are now available at a number of major libraries. Paul G. Morrison has compiled an *Index of Printers, Publishers and Booksellers* (Charlottesville, Virginia, 1950) with a companion index to Wing (Charlottesville, 1955). F. B. Williams has compiled an *Index of dedications and commendatory verses in English books before 1641* (1962). M. A. Shaaber recently supplemented the coverage of foreign-language publication with his *Check-list of works of British authors printed abroad, in languages other than English, to 1641* (1975). The problem of secret or disguised publications by and for recusants may be approached through A. F. Allison and D. M. Rogers, *A Catalogue of Catholic Books in English printed abroad or secretly in England 1558–1640* (Bognor Regis, 1956). Finally, the student needs to remember that, except for contemporary translations, the *STC* does not concern itself with the vast area of Continental publications by Continental authors. The local accessibility of such publications may be studied through, e.g., H. M. Adams, *Catalogue of Books Printed on the Continent of Europe, 1501–1600, in Cambridge Libraries* (Cambridge, 1967).

While somewhat out of date, William Bishop, *A Checklist of American Copies of 'S–TC' Books* (2nd ed., Ann Arbor, 1950), remains useful. Two older guides of particular value may be mentioned: Jacque C. Brunet, *Manuel du libraire et de l'amateur de livres* (Paris, 1860–65; supplement, 1878–80); and W. T. Lowndes, *The bibliographer's manual of English literature; an account of rare, curious, and useful books, published in or relating to Great Britain and Ireland from the invention of printing*, rev. ed. by H. G. Bohn (1885–89). The catalogues of two great national libraries are rich in seventeenth-century holdings: *Catalogue of Printed Books in the British Museum* (1881–1900; supplement, 1900–05; rev. ed., 1931 ff.); and *Catalogue Général des Livres Imprimés de la Bibliothèque Nationale* (Paris, 1897 ff.).

A collection of extraordinary importance for the Civil War and Interregnum was undertaken by the seventeenth-century bookseller George Thomason. Now reposing in the British Library, the Thomason Tracts comprise 22,255 individual items bound in 2,008 volumes, with each item dated, numbered, and annotated by Thomason (see a *Catalogue of the pamphlets, books, newspapers, and manuscripts relating to the civil war, the commonwealth, and restoration, collected by George Thomason, 1640–61*, ed. G. K. Fortescue, 1908, 2 vols.). Recently University Microfilms International has commenced publishing on film all the Tracts, volume by volume, as Thomason compiled them.

Until comparatively recently, using the *STC* perhaps seemed an entirely academic exercise to all but those students fortunate enough to have access to one of the half-dozen major research libraries or to a major university library. Now, thanks to several ambitious projects, we have the promise that every *STC* title will eventually be available to virtually any university student. University Microfilms International has well in progress its effort to film complete both the Pollard and Redgrave *STC* and the Wing *STC*, for the current status of which one should consult the annual catalogues: *Early English Books, 1475–1640, Selected from Pollard & Redgrave's S–TC: A Guide to Year 42 of the Microfilm Collection, Reels 1505–1536* (Ann Arbor, 1977); and *Early English Books, 1641–1700, Selected from Donald Wing's S–TC: A Guide to Year 18 of the Microfilm Collection, Reels 621—649* (Ann Arbor, 1976). As the microfilm reels are selective, it should be noted that titles which have been by-passed will be filmed in later years.

In 1967 Theatrum Orbis Terrarum (Amsterdam) and Walter J. Johnson, Inc. (Norwood, New Jersey) jointly began *The English Experience*, a series which undertakes to publish facsimile editions of books printed in England before 1640. At present nearly a thousand titles are available. Indeed, the rapid proliferation of facsimile reprint publication has resulted in a number of presses and series which reprint seventeenth-century editions: The Rota (Exeter), Scholars' Facsimiles & Reprints, The Scolar Press, Johnson Reprint Corporation's *Sources of Science*, the Augustan Reprint Society (despite the name, the series reprints titles from as early as the 1640s), and Garland Publishing Inc., *The Renaissance and the Gods* (largely devoted to Continental books).

The following selection is designed as a sampling of the riches listed in Pollard and Redgrave, and in Wing. It presents a cross-section of major works, landmark editions, and representative secondary works. For the convenience of the reader these titles have been grouped according to the topics of the preceding chapters (although, obviously, many titles could justifiably be placed under several headings). The novice should remember that such a listing invariably discriminates against shorter works, whether poems or political pamphlets; that, because of the latinity of the age, many extremely important foreign publications were never translated; and that many significant writings were published only in later times. Clarendon's *History of the Rebellion* and *Life*, Burnet's *History of His Own Time*, and Lord Herbert's *Autobiography* were all published in the eighteenth century; the diaries of Evelyn and Pepys and Aubrey's *Brief Lives*, were printed first in the nineteenth century, during which Cromwell's scattered writings also were collected by Carlyle; and Traherne's *Poems* and *Centuries of Meditation* remained in manuscript until the twentieth. Because Latin was the recognised international language of scholarship until past the mid-century, much important writing is inaccessible to the Latinless modern student. Robert Fludd's major works, for instance, remain encased in Latin folios.

The omnipresence of theology poses a special challenge to the modern student. He should study, in addition to the Continental manuals of theology (cited above, pp. 177 f.), the basic documents of the Protestant movement such as the Augsburg Confession of 1530 together with its 'Apology' by Melanchthon in 1531 and the Smalcald Articles prepared by Luther in 1537 (in §S–497: pp. 23–318). He should also scan the major 'confessions of faith' from the Arminian 'Remonstrance' of 1610 (in §S–494: III, 545–9) to the Presbyterian 'Westminster Confession' approved by Parliament in 1648 (§P–314) and the Independents'

Savoy Declaration of 1658 (§P–294); and he should consider Anglican thought in terms of the Thirty-nine Articles as annotated strictly by Thomas Rogers in 1607 (§P–289) as well as the magniloquent sermons of Andrewes and Donne (§P–328, §P–337). He should moreover investigate commentaries on the Bible from its first book of Genesis to its last of Revelation; examine the philosophical premises of treatises such as Philippe de Mornay's *Trewnesse of the Christian Religion* (§P–271); consider the practical directions in manuals on household affairs such as Perkins's *Christian Oeconomie* (§P–121); study the heated exchanges between 'Fencers in Religion'—in Ben Jonson's phrase—since their very violence often clarifies the issue debated, for example the nature of 'enthusiasm' in the case of Henry More against Thomas Vaughan (§P–270); and ponder the reasons for the extravagant popularity of works such as Samuel Smith's sermons on a few verses of Revelation (§P–356), Arthur Dent's 'dialogue-wise' *Plaine Mans Path-way to Heaven* (§P–238), Baxter's *Call to the Unconverted* (§P–218), and the books of conduct by Bishop Bayly and Richard Allestree (§P–220, §P–77).

A number of Milton's publications have been included in our selection; but for a complete listing, as well as an enumeration of surviving seventeenth-century copies, see Parker, *Milton* (§S–244), Vol. II, Appendices 1–2. Finally, we trust that any irritation with our selection will only have the salutary effect of turning the reader back directly to the *STC*.

HISTORY AND HISTORIOGRAPHY

P–1 ALLEN, THOMAS: *Chain of Scripture Chronology* (1659).

P–2 BLUNDEVILLE, THOMAS: *The True Order and Methode of Wrytyng and reading Hystories* (1574).

P–3 CAMDEN, WILLIAM: *Annales. The True and Royall History of the famous Empresse Elizabeth*, trans. A. Darcie (1625) and T. Browne (Oxford, 1629).

P–4 CAMDEN, WILLIAM: *Britain*, trans. Philemon Holland (1610).

P–5 DANIEL, SAMUEL: *Collection of the Historie of England* (1618).

P–6 FOXE, JOHN: *Actes and Monuments* (1563); retitled, *The Ecclesiastical History* (1570) [Foxe's 'Book of Martyrs'].

P–7 FULLER, THOMAS: *The Church-History of Britain* (1655).

P–8 FULLER, THOMAS: *The History of the Worthies of England* (1662).

P–9 GRAFTON, RICHARD: *A Chronicle . . . of the Affayres of Englunde* (1569).

P–10 EDWARD, LORD HERBERT of Cherbury: *The Life and Reign of King Henry the Eighth* (1649).

P–11 HOLINSHED, RAPHAEL: *The Chronicles of England, Scotland, and Irelande* (1577).

P–12 HOWELL, WILLIAM: *An Institution of General History* (1661).

P–13 ISAACSON, HENRY: *Saturni Ephemerides* (1633).

P–14 KNOLLES, RICHARD: *Generall Historie of the Turkes* (1603).

P–15 LLOYD, DAVID: *Memoires of the Lives . . . of those . . . that suffered in our late Intestine Wars* (1668).

P–16 LUCINGE, RENÉ DE: *The Beginning, Continuance, and Decay of Estates*, trans. John Finet (1606).

P–17 MAY, THOMAS: *History of the Parliament in England* (1647).

P–18 MAYERNE-TURQUET, LOUIS DE: *The Generall Historie of Spain*, trans. Edward Grimeston (1612).

P–19 MILTON, JOHN: *History of Britain* (1670).

P–20 MORE, JOHN: *A Table from the Beginning of the World* (1593).

P–21 MUNDAY, ANTHONY: *A Briefe Chronicle . . . from the Creation* (1611).

P–22 OSBORN, FRANCIS: *Historical Memoires* (Oxford, 1658).

P–23 PRIDEAUX, MATHIAS: *An . . . Introduction for Reading . . . Histories* (Oxford, 1648).
P–24 RALEGH, SIR WALTER: *The History of the World* (1614).
P–25 SERRES, JEAN DE: *A General Inventorie of the Historie of France*, trans. Edward Grimeston (1607).
P–26 SLEIDANUS, JOHANN PHILLIPPSON: *A Briefe Chronicle of the Foure Principall Empyres*, trans. Stephen Wythers (1563).
P–27 SPEED, JOHN: *History of Great Britaine* (1611).
P–28 SPRIGGE, JOSHUA: *Anglia Redivia* (1647).
P–29 STOW, JOHN: *A Summarie of Englyshe Chronicles* (1565); retitled, *Annales* (1592); continued by E. Howes (1615).
P–30 USSHER, JAMES: *The Annals of the Old and New Testament* (1658).
P–31 VERGIL, POLYDORE: *Historia Anglica* (1534).
P–32 WHEARE, DIGGORY: *The Method and Order of Reading . . . Histories*, trans. Edmund Bohun (1685).
P–33 WINSTANLEY, WILLIAM: *England's Worthies* (1660).
P–34 WINSTANLEY, WILLIAM: *The Lives of the Most Famous English Poets* (1687).
P–35 WOOD, ANTHONY À: *Athenae Oxonienses* (1691).
P–36 XENOPHON: *Cyrupaedia*, trans. Philemon Holland (1632).

POLITICS AND POLITICAL THEORY

P–37 [ASCHAM, ANTHONY]: *The Bounds and Bonds of Publique Obedience* (1649).
P–38 BRADSHAW, WILLIAM: *English Puritanisme* (Amsterdam [?], 1605).
P–39 FILMER, SIR ROBERT: *The Anarchy of a Limited or Mixed Monarchy* (1648).
P–40 FILMER, SIR ROBERT: *The Necessity of the Absolute Power of all Kings* (1648).
P–41 FILMER, SIR ROBERT: *Observations concerning the Originall of Government* (1652).
P–42 FILMER, SIR ROBERT: *Observations upon Aristotles Politiques* (1652).
P–43 FILMER, SIR ROBERT: *Patriarcha: or the Natural Power of Kings* (1680).
P–44 FORSETT, EDWARD: *A comparative discourse of the bodies natural and politique* (1606).
P–45 GAUDEN, JOHN: *Eikon Basilike: The Pourtraicture of his Sacred Majestie in his Solitude and Sufferings* (1649).
P–46 GEE, EDWARD: *The Divine Right and Originall of the Civill Magistrate from God* (1658).
P–47 GOODWIN, JOHN: *Right and Might Well Met* (1648).
P–48 HARRINGTON, JAMES: *The Common-Wealth of Oceana* (1656).
P–49 HARTLIB, SAMUEL: *A Description of the famous Kingdome of Macaria* (1641).
P–50 HOBBES, THOMAS: *Leviathian* (1651).
P–51 HOBBES, THOMAS: *Philosophical Rudiments concerning Government and Society* (1651).
P–52 HUNTON, PHILIP: *A Treatise of Monarchie* (1643).
P–53 JAMES I: *Basilikon Doron* (Edinburgh, 1599).
P–54 JAMES I: *The True Law of Free Monarchies* (Edinburgh, 1598).
P–55 LILBURNE, JOHN: *Free-mans Freedome Vindicated* (1646).
P–56 LILBURNE, JOHN: *The Legall Fundamentall Liberties of the People* (1649).
P–57 MACHIAVELLI, NICCOLÒ: *Discourses*, trans. Edward Dacres (1636).
P–58 MACHIAVELLI, NICCOLÒ: *The Prince*, trans. Edward Dacres (1640).
P–59 MILTON, JOHN: *The Tenure of Kings and Magistrates* (1649).
P–60 MILTON, JOHN: *Eikonoklastes* (1649).
P–61 MILTON, JOHN: *A Treatise of Civil Power* (1659).
P–62 MILTON, JOHN: *The Ready and Easy Way to Establish a Free Commonwealth* (1660).

P–63 NALSON, JOHN: *The common interest of king and people* (1678).

P–64 NEDHAM, MARCHAMONT: *The Case of the Common-Wealth of England stated* (1650).

P–65 NEDHAM, MARCHAMONT: *The Excellencie of a Free-State* (1656).

P–66 NEVILLE, HENRY: *Plato redivivus, or a dialogue concerning government* (1681).

P–67 OVERTON, RICHARD: *A Remonstrance of Many Thousand Citizens* (1646).

P–68 PARKER, HENRY: *Observations upon some of his Majesties late Answers and Expresses* (1642).

P–69 PRYNNE, WILLIAM: *The Sword of Christian Magistracy supported* (1647).

P–70 ROUS, FRANCIS: *The Lawfulness of obeying the Present Government* (1649).

P–71 RUTHERFORD, SAMUEL: *Lex, Rex* (1644).

P–72 SANCROFT, WILLIAM: *Modern policies taken from Machiavel, Borgia, and other choise authors* (1652).

P–73 SELDEN, JOHN: *The Historie of Tithes* (1618).

P–74 SELDEN, JOHN: *Of the Dominion, Or, Ownership of the Sea*, trans. Marchamont Nedham (1652).

P–75 WILLIAMS, ROGER: *The Bloudy Tenet of Persecution for Cause of Conscience* (1644).

P–76 WINSTANLEY, GERRARD: *The Law of Freedom in a Platform* (1652).

SOCIAL AND ECONOMIC

P–77 ALLESTREE, RICHARD: *The Whole Duty of Man* (1659).

P–78 BLAXTON, JOHN: *The English usurer, or, usury condemned* (Oxford, 1634).

P–79 BLOUNT, SIR HENRY: *Voyage into the Levant* (1636).

P–80 BRATHWAIT, RICHARD: *The English gentleman* (1630).

P–81 BRATHWAIT, RICHARD: *The English gentlewoman* (1631).

P–82 BULLINGER, HEINRICH: *The Christen state of matrimonye*, trans. Miles Coverdale (1541).

P–83 CALTHORPE, CHARLES: *The relation betweene the lord of a mannor and the coppyholder his tenant* (1635).

P–84 CARR, ROGER: *A Godly Form of Household Government* (1598).

P–85 CASTIGLIONE, COUNT BALDASSARE: *The Courtyer of Count Baldessar Castilio*, trans. Sir Thomas Hoby (1561).

P–86 CLEAVER, ROBERT: *A Godly Form of Householde Government* (1598).

P–87 CORYATE, THOMAS: *Coryats Crudities; Hastily gobled up in five Moneths travells* (1611).

P–88 COTTA, JOHN: *The triall of witch-craft shewing the true methode of the discovery* (1616).

P–89 DALTON, MICHAEL: *The countrey Justice, conteyning the practise of the justices of the peace out of their sessions* (1618).

P–90 DEKKER, THOMAS: *The Wonderfull Yeare* (1603).

P–91 DIGGES, SIR DUDLEY: *The defence of trade* (1615).

P–92 DU BOSC, JAQUES: *The compleat woman*, trans. N. N. (1639).

P–93 DUGDALE, SIR WILLIAM: *History of imbanking and drayning of divers fennes and marshes* (1662).

P–94 FENTON, ROGER: *A treatise of usurie* (1611).

P–95 FERNE, SIR JOHN: *The blazon of gentrie* (1586).

P–96 GAGE, THOMAS: *New Survey of the West Indies* (1648).

P–97 GARDINER, RICHARD: *Profitable instructions for manuring, sowing and planting of Kitchin gardens* (1603).

P–98 GOUGE, WILLIAM: *Of Domesticall Duties* (1622 [?]).

P–99   HAKLUYT, RICHARD: *The principal Navigations, Voyages, and Discoveries made by the English Nation* (1589).

P–100 HALL, JOSEPH: *Quo Vadis? A just censure of travell* (1617).

P–101 HARTLIB, SAMUEL: *A Discours of Husbandrie* (1650).

P–102 HARTLIB, SAMUEL: *London's Charitie stilling the Poore Orphan's Cry* (1649).

P–103 HERRING, FRANCIS: *Mischeefes mysterie; or treasons masterpeece. The Powder-plot truly related*, trans. J. Vicars (1617).

P–104 HITCHCOCK, ROBERT: *A pollitique platt, for the honour of the prince* (1580).

P–105 JAMES I: *A Counter-blaste to Tobacco* (1604).

P–106 JAMES I: *Daemonologie, in forme of a dialogue* (Edinburgh, 1597).

P–107 JAMES, THOMAS: *The strange and dangerous voyage of captaine T. James* (1633).

P–108 JOBSON, RICHARD: *The golden trade, or a discovery of the river Gambra* (1623).

P–109 LAMBARD, WILLIAM: *Eirenarcha: or the office of the justices of peace* (1581).

P–110 LILLY, WILLIAM: *The Worlds Catastrophe, or Europes many mutations until 1666* (1647).

P–111 LITHGOW, WILLIAM: *The Totall Discourse, Of the Rare Adventures, and painefull Peregrinations of long nineteene Yeares Travalyes* (1632).

P–112 MARKHAM, GERVASE: *Countrey contentments* (1615).

P–113 MAY, JOHN: *A declaration of the estate of clothing now used* (1613).

P–114 MIÈGE, GUY: *A Relation of Three Embassies from his Sacred Majestie Charles II to the Great Duke of Muscovie, the King of Sweden, and the King of Denmark* (1669).

P–115 MILTON, JOHN: *The Doctrine and Discipline of Divorce* (1643).

P–116 MISSELDEN, EDWARD: *Free trade, or, the means to make trade flourish* (1622).

P–117 MORYSON, FYNES: *An Itinerary . . . Containing His Ten Yeeres Travell* (1617).

P–118 NICCHOLES, ALEXANDER: *A Discourse of Marriage and Wiving* (1615).

P–119 PEACHAM, HENRY: *The Art of Living in London* (1642).

P–120 PEACHAM, HENRY: *The Compleat Gentleman* (1622).

P–121 PERKINS, WILLIAM: *Christian Oecomonie*, trans. Thomas Pickering (1609).

P–122 POWELL, ROBERT: *Depopulation arraigned, convicted, and condemned* (1636).

P–123 PURCHAS, SAMUEL: *Purchas his Pilgrimage. Or Relations of the World and The Religions Observed* (1613).

P–124 PURCHAS, SAMUEL: *Hakluytus Posthumus or Purchas His Pilgrimes* (1625).

P–125 RALEGH, SIR WALTER: *The discouverie of the large, rich, and bewtiful empire of Guiana* (1595).

P–126 ROBERTS, LEWIS: *The merchants mappe of commerce* (1638).

P–127 SANDYS, GEORGE: *A Relation of a Journey begun An: Dom: 1610* (1615).

P–128 SCOT, REGINALD: *The discoverie of witchcraft* (1584).

P–129 SMITH, JOHN: *Advertisements for the unexperienced planters of New England* (1631).

P–130 SWETNAM, JOSEPH: *Arraignment of Lewde, Idle, Froward, and Unconstant Women* (1615).

P–131 VIOLET, THOMAS: *An appeal to Caesar, wherein gold and silver is proved to be the kings* (1660).

P–132 VIVES, JUAN LUIS: *The Instruction of a Christian Woman*, trans. Richard Hyde (1529).

P–133 VIVES, JUAN LUIS: *The Office and Duetie of an Husband*, trans. Thomas Paynell (1553).

P–134 WEBSTER, JOHN: *The Displaying of Supposed Witchcraft* (1677).

EDUCATION

P–135 ASCHAM, ROGER: *The scholemaster* (1570).

P–136 BALES, PETER: *The writing schoolemaster* (1590).

P–137 BLOUNT, THOMAS: *Glossographia* (1656).

P–138 BRINSLEY, JOHN, the Elder: *A consolation for our grammar schooles* (1622).

P–139 BULLOKAR, JOHN: *An English Expositor: teaching the interpretation of the hardest words used in our language* (1616).

P–140 BULLOKAR, WILLIAM: *Bullokars booke at large for the amendment of orthographie for English speech* (1580).

P–141 CALVIN, JEAN: *The catechisme or manner to teache children the Christian religion*, trans. Anon. (1556).

P–142 CAWDREY, ROBERT: *A Table Alphabetical of Hard Used English Words* (1604).

P–143 CLELAND, JOHN: *Hero-paideia: or the Institution of a Young Noble Man* (1607).

P–144 CLEMENT, FRANCIS: *The Petie Schole* (1587).

P–145 COMENIUS, JOHANNES AMOS: *A Reformation of Schooles*, trans. Samuel Hartlib (1642).

P–146 COMENIUS, JOHANNES AMOS: *Orbis Sensualium pictus*, trans. Charles Hoole (1659).

P–147 COMENIUS, JOHANNES AMOS: *The Gate of Languages*, trans. Thomas Horn (1650).

P–148 COWLEY, ABRAHAM: *A Proposition for the Advancement of Experimental Philosophy* (1661).

P–149 DURY, JOHN: *The Reformed School* (1649).

P–150 DURY, JOHN: *The Reformed Librarie-Keeper* (1650).

P–151 ELYOT, SIR THOMAS: *The boke named The Governour* (1531).

P–152 ELYOT, SIR THOMAS: *Dictionary* (1538).

P–153 ELYOT, SIR THOMAS: *Bibliotheca Eliotae: Eliotis Librarie*, augmented by Thomas Cooper (1548).

P–154 ERASMUS, DESIDERIUS: *The Education . . . of Children*, trans. Sir Thomas Elyot (1533).

P–155 ERASMUS, DESIDERIUS: *One dialogue or colloquy entitled Diuersoria*, trans. E. H. (1566).

P–156 FLORIO, JOHN: *A Worlde of Wordes* (1598).

P–157 GETHING, RICHARD: *Calligraphotechnica, or, the art of faire writing* (1619).

P–158 GIL, ALEXANDER: *Logonomia Anglica* (1619).

P–159 HART, JOHN: *An orthographie* (1569).

P–160 HOOLE, CHARLES: *New Discovery of the Old Art of Teaching schoole* (1660).

P–161 KEMPE, WILLIAM: *The Education of Children* (1588).

P–162 LEVINS, PETER: *Manipulus vocabulorum. A dictionarie of English and Latine wordes* (1570).

P–163 LILY, WILLIAM: *A Shorte Introduction of Grammar* (1549).

P–164 MILTON, JOHN: *Accidence Commenc't Grammar* (1669).

P–165 MILTON, JOHN: *Of Education* (1644).

P–166 MULCASTER, RICHARD: *The first part of the Elementarie* (1582).

P–167 MULCASTER, RICHARD: *Positions where those circumstances be examined necessarie for the training up of children* (1581).

P–168 PLUTARCH: *The education or bringing up of children*, trans. Sir Thomas Elyot (1535).

P–169 POOLE, JOSHUA: *English Academe* (1655).

P–170   RAMUS, PETRUS: *The Latine grammar of P. Ramus*, trans. Anon. (1585).
P–171   RECORD, ROBERT: *The grounde of artes, teachyng the worke and practise of arithmetike* (1542).
P–172   WALKER, OBADIAH: *Of education especially of young gentlemen* (1673).
P–173   WEBSTER, JOHN: *Academarium Examen* (1653).
P–174   WHARTON, JOHN: *A New English Grammar* (1655).

PHILOSOPHY

P–175   BACON, SIR FRANCIS: *The Twoo Bookes . . . Of the proficience and advancement of Learning, divine and humane* (1605).
P–176   BACON, SIR FRANCIS: *Novum Organum* (1620).
P–177   BACON, SIR FRANCIS: *Of the Advancement and Proficience of Learning, or the Partitions of Sciences*, trans. Gilbert Watts (Oxford, 1640).
P–178   BARCKLEY, SIR RICHARD: *A Discourse of the Felicitie of Man* (1598).
P–179   BOETHIUS: *Five Bookes of Philosophicall Comfort*, trans. J. T. (1609).
P–180   BRAMHALL, JOHN: *Castigations of Mr. Hobbes* (1657).
P–181   BRYSKETT, LODOWICK: *A discourse of civill life; containing the ethike part of morall philosophie* (1606).
P–182   CARDANO, GIROLAMO: *Cardanus comforte*, trans. T. Bedingfield (1573).
P–183   CHARLETON, WALTER: *The Darkness of Atheism* (1652).
P–184   CHARRON, PIERRE: *Of Wisdome*, trans. Samson Lennard (1612).
P–185   COMENIUS, JONANNES AMOS: *A Patterne of Universall Knowledge*, trans. Jeremy Collier (1651).
P–186   CUDWORTH, RALPH: *The True Intellectual System of the Universe* (1678).
P–187   CULVERWELL, NATHANIEL: *An Elegant and Learned Discourse of the Light of Nature* (1652).
P–188   DANEAU, LAMBERT: *The Wonderful woorkmanship of the world*, trans. Thomas Twyne (1578).
P–189   DOVE, JOHN: *A Confutation of Atheisme* (1605).
P–190   DU VAIR, GUILLAUME: *A Buckler against Adversitie*, trans. Andrew Court (1622).
P–191   DU VAIR, GUILLAUME: *The Moral Philosophie of the Stoicks*, trans. Thomas James (1598).
P–192   GLANVILL, JOSEPH: *The Vanity of Dogmatizing* (1661).
P–193   GLANVILL, JOSEPH: *Plus Ultra, or the Progress and Advancement of Knowledge* (1668).
P–194   GREVILLE, ROBERT, LORD BROOKE: *The Nature of Truth* (1642).
P–195   HAKEWILL, GEORGE: *An Apologie of the Power and Providence of God* (Oxford, 1627).
P–196   EDWARD LORD HERBERT OF CHERBURY: *De Veritate* (Paris, 1624).
P–197   'HERMES TRISMEGISTUS': *Divine pymander, in seventeen books. Together with his . . . Asclepius*, trans. John Everard (1657).
P–198   HOBBES, THOMAS: *De Corpore politico or the Elements of Law* (1650).
P–199   HOBBES, THOMAS: *Elements of Philosophy* (1656).
P–200   HOBBES, THOMAS: *Questions concerning Liberty, Necessity, and Chance* (1656).
P–201   LA PRIMAUDAYE, PIERRE DE: *The French Academie*, trans. Thomas Bowes and R. Dolman (1586–1618).
P–202   LE ROY, LOUIS: *Of the Interchangeable Course or Variety of Things in the Whole World*, trans. Robert Ashley (1595).
P–203   LIPSIUS, JUSTUS: *Two Bookes of Constancie*, trans. Sir John Stradling (1595).

P–204 LUCRETIUS: *An Essay on the first Book of T. Lucretius Carus, with a metrical Version*, trans. John Evelyn (1656).

P–205 MORE, HENRY: *An Antidote against Atheisme* (1653).

P–206 MORE, HENRY: *An Explanation of the Grand Mystery of Godliness* (1660).

P–207 MORE, HENRY: *The Immortality of the Soul* (1659).

P–208 RUST, GEORGE: *A Letter of Resolution concerning Origen and the chief of his opinions* (1661).

P–209 SENECA: *The Workes*, trans. Thomas Lodge (1614).

P–210 SHERMAN, JOHN: *A Greek in the Temple* (Cambridge, 1641).

P–211 STANLEY, THOMAS: *The History of Philosophy* (1655).

P–212 STERRY, PETER: *A Discourse of the Freedom of the Will* (1675).

THEOLOGY: GENERAL

The principal translations of the Bible, fundamentally important and influential, are cited and briefly discussed above, pp. 179–81.

P–213 AINSWORTH, HENRY: *The Orthodox Foundations of Religion* (1641).

P–214 AMES, WILLIAM: *The Marrow of Sacred Divinity*, trans. Anon. (1642).

P–215 ANDERTON, JAMES: *The Protestants Apologie* (St Omer, 1608).

P–216 ANDREWES, LANCELOT: *A Patterne of Catechisticall Doctrine* (1630).

P–217 ANDREWES, LANCELOT: *The Morall Law Expounded* (1642).

P–218 BAXTER, RICHARD: *A Call to the Unconverted* (1658).

P–219 BAXTER, RICHARD: *The Safe Religion. Or Three Disputations . . . against Popery* (1657).

P–220 BAYLY, LEWIS: *The Practice of Pietie* (1613?; 35th ed., 1635).

P–221 BEARD, THOMAS: *The Theatre of Gods Judgements* (1597).

P–222 BELLARMINE, ST ROBERT: *An Ample Declaration of the Christian Doctrine*, trans. Richard Haddock (Douai, 1604).

P–223 BERNARD, RICHARD: *The Isle of Man, or the Legall Proceedings in Man-shire against Sinne* (1626).

P–224 BÈZE, THEODORE DE: *A Briefe . . . Summe of the Christian Faith*, trans. Robert Fyll (1565?).

P–225 *Booke of Common Prayer* (1549; revised, 1662).

P–226 BRIGHTMAN, THOMAS: *A Revelation of the Revelation*, 2nd ed. (1615).

P–227 BUCANUS, GULIELMUS: *Institutions of Christian Religion*, trans. Robert Hill (1606).

P–228 BULLINGER, HEINRICH: *Common Places of Christian Religion*, trans. John Stockwood (1572).

P–229 CALVIN, JOHN: *The Institution of Christian Religion*, trans. Thomas Norton (1561).

P–230 CAMPION, EDMUND: *Campian Englished. Or . . . the Ten Reasons*, trans. Anon. (Douai?, 1632).

P–231 CARPENTER, RICHARD: *Experience, Historie, and Divinitie* (1642).

P–232 CASAUBON, MÉRIC: *A Treatise concerning Enthusiasme*, 2nd ed. (1656).

P–233 CHILLINGWORTH, WILLIAM: *The Religion of Protestants a Safe Way to Salvation* (Oxford, 1638).

P–234 COSIN, JOHN: *A Collection of Private Devotions* (1627).

P–235 CRASHAW, WILLIAM: *The Jesuites Gospel* (1610).

P–236 DAILLÉ, JEAN: *THe Right Use of the Fathers*, trans. Thomas Smith (1651).

P–237 DEACON, JOHN, and JOHN WALKER: *Dialogicall Discourses* (1601).

P–238 DENT, ARTHUR: *The Plaine Mans Path-way to Heaven* (1601; 25th ed., 1640).

P–239 DENT, ARTHUR: *The Ruine of Rome: or an Exposition of the whole Revelation* (1603).

P–240 DOD, JOHN, and ROBERT CLEAVER: *Plain and Familiar Exposition of the Ten Commandments* (1604).

P–241 DOWNAME, GEORGE: *A Treatise concerning Antichrist* (1603).

P–242 DOWNAME, JOHN: *The Summe of Sacred Divinitie* (1630?).

P–243 EDWARDS, THOMAS: *Gangraena* (1577).

P–244 ERASMUS: *A Playne . . . Declaration of the Comune Crede*, trans. Anon. (1533).

P–245 FONSECA, CRISTÓBAL DE: *Devout Contemplations*, trans. James Mabbe (1629).

P–246 FOX, GEORGE: *A Journal* (1694).

P–247 FRANCIS DE SALES, ST: *Introduction to a Devout Life*, trans. J. Yakesley (Douai, 1613).

P–248 FRANCIS DE SALES, ST: *A Treatise of the Love of God*, trans. 'Thomas Carr' [i.e. Miles Pinkney] (Douai, 1630).

P–249 GERHARD, JOHANN: *The Summe of Christian Doctrine*, trans. Ralph Winterton (Cambridge, 1640).

P–250 GIL, ALEXANDER: *The Sacred Philosophie of the Holy Scripture* (1635).

P–251 GOODMAN, GODFREY: *The Fall of Man, or the Corruption of Nature Proved* (1616).

P–252 GUILD, WILLIAM: *The Harmony of all the Prophets* (1619).

P–253 GUILD, WILLIAM: *Moses Unveiled* (1620).

P–254 GWALTER (WALTHER), RUDOLF: *Homelyes . . . uppon the Actes*, trans. John Bridges (1572).

P–255 HALL, JOSEPH: *The Invisible World* (1659).

p–256 HAYWARD, SIR JOHN: *The Sanctuary of a Troubled Soule* (1604; 1607).

P–257 HEINSIUS, DANIEL: *The Mirrour of Humilitie*, trans. John Harmar (1618).

P–258 HEMMINGIUS (HEMMINGSEN), NICOLAS: *The Faith of the Church Militant*, trans. Thomas Rogers (1581).

P–259 HEMMINGIUS (HEMMINGSEN), NICOLAS: *A Postill, or Exposition of the Gospels*, trans. Arthur Golding (1574).

P–260 HOLLAND, HENRY: *The Historie of Adam* (1606).

P–261 HOOKER, RICHARD: *Of the lawes of ecclesiasticall politie* (Books I–III, 1593; V, 1597; VI–VIII, 1648 and 1651).

P–262 HYPERIUS, ANDREAS GERARDUS: *The Course of Christianitie*, trans. John Ludham (1579).

P–263 JEWEL, JOHN: *An Apologie . . . of the Church of England*, trans. Anne Lady Bacon (1562).

P–264 KIMEDONCIUS, JACOBUS: *Of the Redemption of Mankind*, trans. Hugh Ince (1598).

P–265 KING, HENRY: *An Exposition upon the Lord's Prayer* (1634).

P–266 LAUD, WILLIAM: *A Relation of the Conference between William Lawd . . . and Mr Fisher the Jesuite* (1639).

P–267 LEIGH, EDWARD: *A System or Body of Divinity* (1654).

P–268 MARLORAT, AUGUSTIN: *A Catholike Exposition upon the Revelation*, trans. Arthur Golding (1574).

P–269 MEDE, JOSEPH: *The Key of the Revelation*, trans. Richard More (1643).

P–270 MORE, HENRY: *Enthusiasmus triumphatus* (1656).

P–271 MORNAY, PHILIPPE DE: *A Woorke concerning the Trewnesse of the Christian Religion*, trans. Sir Philip Sidney and Arthur Golding (1587).

P–272 MOSSOM, ROBERT: *Sion's Prospect* (1651).

P–273 MUSCULUS, WOLFGANG: *Commonplaces of Christian Religion*, trans. John Man (1563).

P–274 NAPIER, JOHN: *A Plaine Discovery of the Whole Revelation of Saint John* (Edinburgh, 1593).

P–275 NORDEN, JOHN: *The Pensive Mans Practise* (1584; 41st impr., 1635).

P–276 NOWELL, ALEXANDER: *A Catechisme*, trans. Thomas Norton (1570).

P–277 P., S. [SIMON PATRICK?]: *A Brief Account of the new Sect of Latitude-Men together with some reflections upon the New Philosophy* (1662).

P–278 PAGITT, EPHRAIM: *Christianographie, or the Description of . . . Christians* (1635).

P–279 PAGITT, EPHRAIM: *Heresiography* (1645).

P–280 PALFREYMAN, THOMAS: *The Treatise of Heavenly Philosophie* (1578).

P–281 PAREUS, DAVID: *A Commentary upon . . . Revelation*, trans. E. Arnold (Amsterdam, 1644).

P–282 PARR, ELNATHAN: *The Grounds of Divinitie* (1614).

P–283 PARSONS, ROBERT: *A Christian Directorie* (Rouen, 1585).

P–284 PERKINS, WILLIAM: *Works* (1600).

P–285 PETTO, SAMUEL: *The Voyce of The Spirit* (1654).

P–286 POLANUS, AMANDUS: *The Substance of Christian Religion*, trans. Elijah Wilcox (1600).

P–287 PRYNNE, WILLIAM: *A Briefe Survay and Censure of Mr. Cozens his Couzening Devotions* (1628).

P–288 PUENTE, LUIS DE LA: *Meditations*, trans. John Heigham (St Omer, 1619).

P–289 ROGERS, THOMAS: *The Faith, Doctrine, and Religion, Professed and Protected in the Realme of England . . . expressed in 39 Articles* (Cambridge, 1607).

P–290 ROUS, FRANCIS, THE ELDER: *The Mysticall Marriage. Experimentall Discoveries of the Heavenly Marriage, betweene a Soule and her Saviour* (1635).

P–291 SALKELD, JOHN: *A Treatise of Angels* (1613).

P–292 SALKELD, JOHN: *A Treatise of Paradise* (1617).

P–293 SANDERS, NICHOLAS: *The Rocke of the Church* (St Omer, 1624).

P–294 SAVOY DECLARATION: *A Declaration of . . . the Congregational Churches in England* (1658).

P–295 SHELFORD, ROBERT: *Five Pious and Learned Discourses* (Cambridge, 1635).

P–296 SMITH, RICHARD: *A Conference of the Catholike and Protestant Doctrine* (Douai, 1631).

P–297 SPARKE, MICHAEL: *Crums of Comfort* (1621).

P–298 TAYLOR, JEREMY: *Deus justificatus* (1656).

P–299 TAYLOR, JEREMY: Θεολογία ἐκλεκτικὴ: *A Discourse of the Liberty of Prophesying* (1647).

P–300 TAYLOR, JEREMY: *The Rule and Exercises of Holy Living* (1650).

P–301 TAYLOR, JEREMY: *Holy Dying* (1651).

P–302 TERESA OF AVILA, ST: *The Flaming Heart or the Life of the Glorious S. Teresa*, trans. Sir Toby Mathew [?] (repr. Antwerp, 1642).

P–303 TRAHERNE, THOMAS: *Christian Ethicks* (1675).

P–304 TRELCATIUS, LUCAS: *. . . Common Places of Sacred Divinitie*, trans. John Gaven (1610).

P–305 URSINUS, ZACHARIUS: *The Summe of Christian Religion*, trans. Henry Parry (Oxford, 1595).

P–306 USSHER, JAMES: *Immanuel, or the Mystery of the Incarnation* (1638).

P–307 VENNING, RALPH: *Orthodoxe Paradoxes* (1647).

P–308 VERMIGLI, PIETRO MARTIRE (PETER MARTYR): *Commentaries . . . upon . . . Romanes*, trans. H. B. (1568).

P–309 VERMIGLI, PIETRO MARTIRE (PETER MARTYR): *Common Places*, trans. Anthony Marten (1574).

P–310 VIREL, MATTHIEU: *A Learned and Excellent Treatise, containing all the Principall Grounds of Christian Religion*, trans. Anon. (1594).

P–311 VIRET, PIERRE: *The Christian Disputations*, trans. John Brooke (1579).

P–312 VIRET, PIERRE: *A Christian Instruction*, trans. John Shute (1573).

P–313 WEEMES, JOHN: *The Portraiture of the Image of God* (1627).

P–314 WESTMINSTER CONFESSION: *The Confession of Faith . . . by the . . . Divines sitting at Westminster* (1648).

P–315 WHITE, ANTHONY: *Truth and Error* (Oxford, 1628).

P–316 WILLET, ANDREW: *Synopsis Papismi: that is a Generall Viewe of Papistry* (1592).

P–317 WILLET, ANDREW: *Hexapla in Genesin: that is, A Sixfold Commentarie upon Genesis* (Cambridge, 1605).

P–318 WILLIAMS, GRIFFITH: *The Best Religion* (1636).

P–319 WILLIAMS, GRIFFITH: *The True Church* (1629).

P–320 WILSON, THOMAS: *A Christian Dictionarie* (1612).

P–321 WITHER, GEORGE: *A Preparation to the Psalter* (1619).

P–322 WOLLEB, JOHANN: *The Abridgment of Christian Divinitie*, trans. Alexander Ross (1650).

P–323 WOOLTON, JOHN: *A Newe Anatomie of Whole Man* (1576).

P–324 YATES, JOHN: *A Modell of Divinitie* (1622).

P–325 ZANCHIUS, HIERONYMUS: *Speculum Christianum*, trans. Henry Nelson (1614).

P–326 ZANCHIUS, HIERONYMUS: *The Whole Body of Christian Religion*, trans. Ralph Winterton (1659).

THEOLOGY: SERMONS, THE ART OF PREACHING, AND DEVOTIONAL WORKS

P–327 ADAMS, THOMAS: *Workes* (1629).

P–328 ANDREWES, LANCELOT: *XCVI Sermons* (1629).

P–329 BAXTER, RICHARD: *The Saints Everlasting Rest* (1650).

P–330 BULLINGER, HEINRICH: *Fiftie . . . Sermons*, trans. H. I. (1577).

P–331 BULLINGER, HEINRICH: *A Hundred Sermons upon the Apocalips*, trans. John Dawes (1561).

P–332 BUNYAN, JOHN: *Grace Abounding* (1666).

P–333 CHAPPELL, WILLIAM: *The Preacher, or the Art and Method of Preaching* (1656).

P–334 CUDWORTH, RALPH: *A Sermon preached before the Honourable House of Commons* (Cambridge, 1647).

P–335 DELL, WILLIAM: *Several Sermons and Discourses* (1652).

P–336 DONNE, JOHN: *Devotions* (1624).

P–337 DONNE, JOHN: *LXXX Sermons* (1640).

P–338 FRANK, MARK: *Sermons* (1672).

P–339 HALL, JOSEPH: *Arte of Divine Meditation* (1606).

P–340 HALL, JOSEPH: *Works* (1625).

P–341 HOOKER, RICHARD: *A Learned Sermon of the Nature of Pride* (Oxford, 1612).

P–342 HOMILIES: *Certayne Sermons, or Homelies, appoynted by the Kynges Majestie* (1547).

P–343 HOMILIES: *The Second Tome of Homelyes* (1563).

P–344 HYPERIUS, ANDREAS GERARDUS: *The Practis of Preaching . . . an excellent Method how to frame Divine Sermons*, trans. John Ludham (1577).

P–345 LAKE, ARTHUR: *Ten Sermons* (1641).

P–346 LAUD, WILLIAM: *Seven Sermons* (1651).

P–347 MAXEY, ANTHONY: *Certaine Sermons* (1619).

P–348 OCHINO, BERNARDINO: *Certayne Sermons*, trans. Richard Argentine (1550?).

P–349 PERKINS, WILLIAM: *The Art of Prophecying Or, a Treatise concerning . . . Preaching* (1606).

P–350 PRESTON, JOHN: *The Breast Plate of Faith and Love* (1630).

P–351 SANDERSON, ROBERT: *Ten Sermons* (1627).

P–352   SIBBES, RICHARD: *The Bruised Reede* (1630).
P–353   SIBBES, RICHARD: *Divine Meditations and Holy Contemplations* (1638).
P–354   SMITH, HENRY: *Gods Arrowe against Atheists* (1593).
P–355   SMITH, JOHN: *Select Discourses* (1660).
P–356   SMITH, SAMUEL: *The Great Assize* (1618).
P–357   STRUTHER, WILLIAM: *Christian Observations and Resolutions* (Edinburgh, 1628).
P–358   SYDENHAM, HUMPHREY: *Five Sermons* (1626).
P–359   TAYLOR, JEREMY: *XXVIII Sermons* (1651).
P–360   USSHER, JAMES: *Eighteen Sermons* (1659).
P–361   WHICHCOTE, BENJAMIN: *Select Discourses* (1698).
P–362   WILSON, THOMAS: *Theological Rules* with *Aenigmata Sacra* (1615).
P–363   WRIGHT, ABRAHAM: *Five Sermons in Five Several Styles* (1656).

SCIENCE

P–364   AGRIPPA VON NETTESHEIM, H. C.: *Of the vanitie and uncertainite of artes and sciences*, trans. J. Sanford (1569).
P–365   AGRIPPA VON NETTESHEIM, H. C.: *Three books of occult philosophy*, trans. J[ohn] F[rench] (1651).
P–366   ANTHONIE, FRANCIS: *The apologie: or defence of . . . a medicine called Aurum Potabile* (1616).
P–367   ASHMOLE, ELIAS (editor): *Theatrum chemicum Britannicum* (1652).
P–368   BABINGTON, JOHN: *A short treatise of geometrie* (1635).
P–369   BACON, SIR FRANCIS: *The historie of life and death*, trans. Anon. (1638).
P–370   BACON, SIR FRANCIS: *The naturall and experimentall history of winds*, trans. R. B. (1653).
P–371   BACON, SIR FRANCIS: *Sylva Sylvarum: or, A Naturall Historie* with *New Atlantis* (1626).
P–372   BACON, ROGER: *The mirror of alchimy*, trans. Anon. (1597).
P–373   BAILEY, WALTER: *Two treatises concerning the preservation of eie-sight* (Oxford, 1616).
P–374   BAINBRIDGE, JOHN: *An astronomicall description of the late comet* (1619).
P–375   BANISTER, JOHN: *The historie of man, sucked from the sappe of the most approved anathomistes* (1578).
P–376   BARLOW, WILLIAM: *Magneticall advertisements* (1616).
P–377   BARROUGH, PHILIP: *The method of phisicke* (1583).
P–378   BARTHOLOMEUS ANGLICUS: *Batman uppon Bartholome his booke De Proprietatibus Rerum*, trans. Stephen Bateman (rev. ed. 1582).
P–379   BIGGS, NOAH: *Mataeotechnia medicinae praxeos. The vanity of the craft of physick* (1651).
P–380   BLAGRAVE, JOHN: *The art of dyalling in two parts* (1609).
P–381   BLAGRAVE, JOHN: *The mathematicall jewell* (1585).
P–382   BLUNDEVILLE, THOMAS: *M. Blundeville his Exercises, containing six treatises* (1594).
P–383   BOSTOCKE, R.: *The difference betwene the auncient Phisicke . . . and the latter Phisicke* (1585).
P–384   BOYLE, ROBERT: *Certain physiological essays* (1661).
P–385   BOYLE, ROBERT: *A disquisition about the final causes of natural things* (1688).
P–386   BOYLE, ROBERT: *Experiments and considerations touching colours* (1664).
P–387   BOYLE, ROBERT: *The sceptical chymist* (1661).

P–388 BOYLE, ROBERT: *Some considerations touching the usefulnesse of experimental naturall philosophy* (Oxford, 1663).

P–389 BRAHE, TYCHO: *Learned Tico Brahe his astronomicall conjecture of the new and much Admired [star]*, trans. 'V.V.S.' (1632).

P–390 BRIGHT, TIMOTHY: *A treatise of melancholie* (1586).

P–391 BROWNE, SIR THOMAS: *Pseudodoxia Epidemica* (1646). Also *Hydriotophia* (§ P–583).

P–392 BURTON, ROBERT: *The Anatomy of Melancholy* (Oxford, 1621).

P–393 CASTLE, GEORGE: *The chymical Galenist* (1667).

P–394 CHARLETON, WALTER: *Natural history of nutrition, life and voluntary motion* (1659).

P–395 COEFFETEAU, NICHOLAS: *A Table of Humane Passions*, trans. Edward Grimeston (1621).

P–396 COGAN, THOMAS: *The haven of health* (1584).

P–397 COLES, WILLIAM: *Adam in Eden: or, Natures paradise. The history of plants, fruits, herbs and flowers* (1657).

P–398 CROLL, OSWALD: *Philosophy reformed & improved in four profound tractates*, trans. H. Pinnell (1657).

P–399 CROOKE, HELKIAH: *Microcosmographia. A description of the body of man* (1615).

P–400 CULPEPPER, NICHOLAS: *The English physitian* (1652).

P–401 CULPEPPER, NICHOLAS: *Pharmacopoeia Londinensis: or The London dispensatory* (1653).

P–402 CUNNINGHAM, WILLIAM: *The cosmographical glasse* (1559).

P–403 DEE, JOHN: *General and rare memorials pertayning to the perfecte arte of navigation* (1577).

P–404 DESCARTES, RENÉ: *The passions of the soule*, trans. Anon. (1650).

P–405 DIGBY, SIR KENELM: *Choice and experimented receipts in physick and chirurgery* (1668).

P–406 DuCHESNE, JOSEPH: *The practise of chymicall, and Hermeticall physicke*, trans. Thomas Timme (1605).

P–407 ELYOT, SIR THOMAS: *The castel of helth* (1539).

P–408 EUCLID: *The Elements of Geometrie*, trans. Sir Henry Billingsley (1570).

P–409 FRENCH, JOHN: *The art of distillation* (1651).

P–410 GERARD, JOHN: *The herball or generall historie of plantes* (1597).

P–411 GILBERT, WILLIAM: *De Magnete* (1600).

P–412 GLASER, CHRISTOPHE: *The compleat chymist*, trans. 'a fellow of the Royal Society' (1677).

P–413 HARVEY, WILLIAM: *The anatomical exercises* (1653).

P–414 HARVEY, WILLIAM: *Anatomical exercitations, concerning the generation of living creatures* (1653).

P–415 HARWARD, SIMON: *Harwards phlebotomy: or a treatise of letting of blood* (1601).

P–416 HELMONT, JEAN BAPTISTE VAN: *Deliramenta catarrhi* with *A ternary of paradoxes*, trans. Walter Charleton (1650).

P–417 HEYDON, SIR CHRISTOPHER: *An Astrological Discourse* (1650).

P–418 HEYDON, JOHN: *The English physitians guide* (1662).

P–419 HEYLYN, PETER: *Microcosmus, or a little description of the great world* (Oxford, 1621).

P–420 HOOKE, ROBERT: *Micrographia: or Some physiological descriptions of minute bodies made by magnifying glasses* (1665).

P–421 HOPTON, ARTHUR: *Speculum Topographicum: or, the topographicall glasses* (1611).

P–422 IRVINE, CHRISTOPHER: *Medicina magnetica: or, The rare and wonderful art of curing by sympathy* (1656).

P–423 JABIR IBN HAIYAN: *The Works of Geber*, trans. R. R. (1678).

P–424 JONSTON, JOHN: *An History of the Wonderful Things of Nature* (1657).

P–425 JOSSELYN, JOHN: *New-Englands rarities discovered* (1672).

P–426 LANGHAM, WILLIAM: *The garden of health* (1597).

P–427 LE FÈVRE, NICOLAS: *A compleat body of chymistry*, trans. P.D.C. (1664).

P–428 LOWE, PETER: *A discourse of the whole art of chyrurgerie* (1612).

P–429 MAPLET, JOHN: *A greene Forest, or a Naturall Historie* (1567).

P–430 MERCATOR, GERALD: *Historia Mundi, or Mercators Atlas*, trans. W. Saltonstall (1635).

P–431 NAPIER, JOHN: *A description of the admirable table of logarithmes*, trans. E. Wright (1616).

P–432 NEDHAM, MARCHAMONT: *Medela medicinae* (1665).

P–433 NOLLIUS, HENRY: *Hermetical Physick*, trans. Henry Vaughan (1655).

P–434 PARACELSUS: *Paracelsus his archidoxes*, trans. Anon. (1660).

P–435 PARACELSUS: *Of the supreme mysteries of nature*, trans. R. Turner (1656).

P–436 PARACELSUS: *The secrets of physick and philosophy*, trans. John Hester (1633).

P–437 PARKINSON, JOHN: *Paradisi in sole, Paradisus Terrestris, or A Garden of all sorts of pleasant flowers* (1629).

P–438 PLATTES, GABRIEL: *A Discovery of subterraneall treasure* (1639).

P–439 PLINY: *The historie of the world*, trans. Philemon Holland (1601).

P–440 PORTA, G. B. DELLA: *Natural magick*, trans. Anon. (1658).

P–441 RECORDE, ROBERT: *The castle of knowledge* (1556).

P–442 REYNOLDS, EDWARD: *A Treatise of the Passions and Faculties of the Soule of Man* (1647).

P–443 SPRAT, THOMAS: *The History of the Royal Society* (1667).

P–444 STURTEVANT, SIMON: *Metallica. Or, the treatise of . . . new metallicall inventions* (1612).

P–445 SWAN, JOHN: *Speculum Mundi* (Cambridge, 1635).

P–446 VAUGHAN, THOMAS: *Magia Adamica* (1650).

P–447 VAUGHAN, WILLIAM: *Naturall and Artificiall Directions for Health* (1600).

P–448 WALKINGTON, THOMAS: *The optick glasse of humors* (1607).

P–449 WARD, SETH: *Vindicae Academiarum* (Oxford, 1654).

P–450 WEBSTER, JOHN: *Academiarum Examen* (1654).

P–451 WILKINS, JOHN: *The discovery of a world in the moone* (1638).

P–452 WRIGHT, EDWARD: *The description and use of the sphaere* (1613).

MUSIC: BOOKS ON MUSIC

P–453 BUTLER, CHARLES: *The principles of musik, in singing and setting* (1626).

P–454 CASE, JOHN: *The praise of musicke* (Oxford, 1586).

P–455 CAMPION, THOMAS: *A new way of making fowre parts in counter-point* (1614 [?]).

P–456 HOLBORNE, ANTONY: *The Cittharn-Schoole* (1597).

P–457 MACE, THOMAS: *Musick's Monument* (1676).

P–458 MORLEY, THOMAS: *A plaine and easie introduction to practicall musicke* (1597).

P–459 ORNITHOPARCUS, ANDREAS: *A. Ornithoparcus his micrologus, or introduction containing the art of singing*, trans. J. Douland [John Dowland] (1609).

P–460 PLAYFORD, JOHN: *A breefe introduction to the skill of musick for song and violl* (1654; and numerous expanded editions).

P–461 RAVENSCROFT, THOMAS: *A briefe discourse of the true use of charact'ring the degrees in measurable musicke* (1614).

P–462 ROBINSON, THOMAS: *The schoole of musicke* (1603).

P–463 ROBINSON, THOMAS: *New citharen lessons* (1609).

P–464 SIMPSON, CHRISTOPHER: *The principles of practical musicke* (1665).

P–465 SIMPSON, CHRISTOPHER: *The division-violist* (1659).

MUSIC: PUBLISHED COLLECTIONS AND INDIVIDUAL COMPOSER COLLECTIONS

P–466 ADSON, JOHN: *Courtly masquing ayres* (1621).

P–467 ATTEY, JOHN: *The first booke of ayres* (1622).

P–468 BYRD, WILLIAM: *Psalmes, Sonets and Songs* (1588).

P–469 BYRD, WILLIAM: *Liber primus sacrarum cantionum* (1589).

P–470 BYRD, WILLIAM: [*Masses for 3, 4 and 5 voices*] (1600 [?]).

P–471 BYRD, WILLIAM: *Gradulia* (1605, 1607).

P–472 CAMPION, THOMAS: *A booke of ayres* (1601).

P–473 CHILD, WILLIAM: *The first set of psalmes of III voyces* (1639).

P–474 DERING, RICHARD: *Cantica sacra . . . cum basso continuo ad organum* (1662).

P–475 DOWLAND, JOHN: *The first booke of songes or ayres* (1597).

P–476 DOWLAND, JOHN: *Lachrymae, or seaven teares figured in seaven passionate pavans* (1604).

P–477 DOWLAND, JOHN: *A pilgrimes solace* (1612).

P–478 FERRABOSCO, ALFONSO: *Ayres* (1609).

P–479 FERRABOSCO, ALFONSO: *Lessons for 1.2. and 3. viols* (1609).

P–480 GIBBONS, ORLANDO: *The first set of madrigals and mottets* (1612).

P–481 GIBBONS, ORLANDO: *Fantasies of three parts* (1610 [?]).

P–482 HILTON, JOHN: *Ayres, or fa la's for three voyces* (1627).

P–483 HOLBORNE, ANTONY: *Pavans, galliards, allmains, and other short aeirs . . . for viols, violins, or other musicall wind instruments* (1599).

P–484 HUME, TOBIAS: *The first booke of ayres* (1605).

P–485 LAWES, HENRY: *A paraphrase upon the psalmes of David* (1638).

P–486 LAWES, HENRY: *Select musicall ayres and dialogues* (Book I, 1653; II, 1655; III, 1658).

P–487 LAWES, HENRY and WILLIAM: *Choice psalmes* (1648).

P–488 LOCKE, MATTHEW: *Matthew Locke his little consort of three parts* (1656).

P–489 LOCKE, MATTHEW: *The English opera: or the vocal musick in Psyche* (1675).

P–490 MORLEY, THOMAS: *The first booke of ballets to five voyces* (1595).

P–491 MORLEY, THOMAS: *The first booke of ayres, or little short songs, to sing and play to the lute, with the bass viole* (1600).

P–492 NOTARI, ANGELO: *Prime musiche nuove* (1613).

P–493 PEERSON, MARTIN: *Private musicke, or the first booke of ayres and dialogues* (1620).

P–494 PEERSON, MARTIN: *Mottects or grave chamber musique, containing songs of five parts of several sorts, some ful, some verse* (1630).

P–495 TOMKINS, THOMAS: *Songs* (1622).

P–496 WEELKES, THOMAS: *Madrigals of 6 parts* (1600).

P–497 WILBYE, JOHN: *First set of madrigals* (1598).

P–498 WILSON, JOHN: *Cheerful ayres or ballads* (1660).

MUSIC: ANTHOLOGIES

P–499 *Cantica sacra: containing hymns and anthems for two voices to the organ, both Latine and English . . . The Second sett*, ed. J. Playford (1674).

P–500 *Cantus, songs and fancies to three, foure, or five partes, both apt for voices and viols. With a briefe introduction to musick . . .* , ed. T. D. (Aberdeen, 1662).

P–501 *Catch that catch can*, ed. J. Hilton (1652).

P–502 *Choice songs and ayres for one voyce to sing to a theorbolute, or bass-viol . . .* , ed. J. Playford (1673).

P–503 *Court-ayres: or, pavins, almains, corant's, and sarabands, of two parts, treble and basse, for viols or violins*, ed. J. Playford (1655).

P–504 *Courtly masquing ayres: containing almaines, ayres, corants, sarabands, morisco's, jiggs, &. of two parts treble and basse for viols or violins*, ed. J. Playford (1662).

P–505 *The dancing master*, ed. J. Playford (1651).

P–506 *Deuteromelia: or the second part of musicks melodie*, ed. T. Ravenscroft (1609).

P–507 *The first booke of consort lessons . . . for sixe instruments . . .* , ed. Thomas Morley (1599).

P–508 *The first book of selected church musick . . .* , ed. J. Barnard (1641).

P–509 *French court-Aires*, ed. Edward Filmer (1629).

P–510 *Melothesia: or, certain general rules for playing upon a continued-bass*, ed. M. Locke (1673).

P–511 *A Musicall banquet, furnished with varietie of delicious ayres . . .* , ed. Robert Dowland (1610).

P–512 *Musick's delight on the cithren . . .* , ed. J. Playford (1666).

P–513 *Musicks hand-maide . . . . lessons for the virginals or harpsycon*, ed. J. Playford (1663).

P–514 *Musick's recreation: on the lyra viol*, ed. J. Playford (1652).

P–515 *New ayres and dialogues composed for voices and viols. . .* , by John Banister and Thomas Low (1678).

P–516 *Pammelia, musicks miscellanie, or mixed varietie of pleasant roudelayes, and delightfull catches . . .* , ed. T. Ravenscroft (1609).

P–517 *Parthenia or the maydenhead of the first musicke that ever was printed for the virginalls*, by William Byrd, John Bull, and Orlando Gibbons (1613).

P–518 *Parthenia inviolata or Mayden-musicke for the virginalls* (1614 [?]).

P–519 *The pleasant companion: or, new lessons and instructions for the flagelet*, ed. Thomas Greeting (1673).

P–520 *Psalms and hymns in solem musick of foure parts . . .* (1671).

P–521 *Scelta di canzonette italiane de piu autori*, ed. G. Pignani (1679).

P–522 *The triumphes of Oriana, to 5. and 6. voices . . .* , ed. Thomas Morley (1600).

P–523 *Varietie of lute-lessons: viz. fantasies, pavins, galliards, almaines, corantees and volts . . .* , ed. Robert Downland (1610).

THE FINE ARTS

P–524 ANON.: *A Book of Drawing, Limning, Washing or Colouring* (1652).

P–525 B[ATE], J[OHN]: *The Mysteryes of Nature, and Art* (1634).

P–526 BROWNE, ALEXANDER: *The Whole Art of Drawing* (1660).

P–527 BROWNE, ALEXANDER: *Ars Pictoria, or an Academy treating of Drawing, Limning, and Etching* (1669).

P–528 CARTARI, VINCENZO: *The Fountaine of Ancient Fiction*, trans. R. Lynche (1599).

P–529 DE CHAMBRAY, ROLAND FRÉART: *An Idea of the Perfection of Painting*, trans. John Evelyn (1668).

P–530 DU FRESNOY, C. A.: *The Art of Painting*, trans. John Dryden (1695).

P–531 EVELYN, JOHN: *Sculptura: on the History and Art of Chalcography and Engraving in Copper* (1662).

P–532 FAITHORNE, WILLIAM: *The Art of Graveing and Etching* (1662).

P–533 HOLLAR, WENCESLAUS: *A Booke of Drawinges* (1651).

P–534 JONES, INIGO: *The Most notable antiquity of Great Britain vulgarly called . . . Stone-heng* (1655).

P-535   JUNIUS, FRANCISCUS: *The Painting of the Ancients* (1638).
P-536   LOMAZZO, GIOVANNI PAOLO: *A Tracte containing the Artes of curious Paintinge,*
        Carvinge, Buildinge, trans. Richard Haydocke (Oxford, 1598).
P-537   MOXON, JOSEPH: *Practical Perspective* (1670).
P-538   PALLADIO, ANDREA: *The First Book of Architecture,* trans. G. Richards (1668).
P-539   PEACHAM, HENRY: *The art of drawing with the pen, and limming in water colours*
        (1606).
P-540   PLATT, SIR HUGH: *The Jewell House of Art and Nature* (1594).
P-541   SALMON, WILLIAM: *Polygraphice* (1672).
P-542   SANDERSON, SIR WILLIAM: *Graphics, or The Use of the Pen and Pensil* (1658).
P-543   SELDEN, JOHN: *Marmora Arundelliana* (1629).
P-544   SERLIO, SEBASTIANO: *The First [-Fift] Booke of Architecture,* trans. Anon. (1611).
P-545   WOTTON, SIR HENRY: *The Elements of Architecture* (1624).

Given the age's latinity, it was noted above (p. 372), many important foreign works were
not translated until well after the seventeenth century. This is particularly true of the
primary sources relating to the visual arts, save that some crucial works in Latin as well as
in Italian, French, and German, are still not available in English. In consequence, the items
listed above should be supplemented with the following:

(a)   Works not yet translated into English, such as Andrea Alciati, *Emblematum libellus cum*
      commentariis (Padua, 1621; 1st ed., 1531); U. Aldrovandi, *Delle statue antiche che per tutta*
      Roma in diversi luoghi e case particolari si veggono (Venice, 1558); Pietro Aretino, *Lettere*
      sull'arte, ed. F. Pertile and Carlo Cordi (Milan, 1957), 2 vols.; G. P. Bellori, *Le vite de'*
      pittori, scultori ed architteti moderni (Rome, 1672); Domenico Bernini, *Vita del Cavalier*
      Gian Lorenzo Bernini (Rome, 1713); Natale Conti (Natalis Comes), *Mythologiae* (Venice,
      1567); Paul de Fréart, Sieur de Chantelou, *Journal du voyage du Cavalier Bernini en France*
      (Paris, 1930); Giovanni Paolo Lomazzo, *Scritti sulle arti,* ed. Roberto Paolo Ciardi
      (Florence, 1973; cf. §P-536); Pomponius Gauricus, *De sculptura,* ed. André Chastel and
      Robert Klein, with a translation into French (Geneva, 1969); Cesare Ripa, *Iconologia*
      (Padua, 1611; 1st ed., without illustrations, 1593); Joachim von Sandrart, *Teusche*
      Academie de Edlen Bau-Bild-und Mahlerey-Kunst (Nuremberg, 1675; ed. A. R. Peltzer,
      Munich, 1928); Pompilio Totti, *Ritratto di Roma moderna* (Rome, 1638); G. P. Valeriano
      Bolzani, *Hieroglyphica* (Lyons, 1602); Giorgio Vasari the younger, *Città ideale* (1598;
      repr. Warsaw, 1962); etc.

(b)   Works available in later translations, such as Leone Battista Alberti, *On Painting and*
      On Sculpture, trans. Cecil Grayson (1972), and *Ten Books on Architecture,* trans. James
      Leoni (1955); Filippo Baldinucci, *The Life of Bernini,* trans. Catherine Enggass (Univer-
      sity Park, Pa., 1966); Ascanio Condivi, *The Life of Michelangelo,* trans. Alice Wohl
      (Baton Rouge, 1976); Jacopo Giunta, *The Divine Michelangelo: The Florentine Academy's*
      Homage on his Death in 1564, trans. Rudolf and Margot Wittkower (1964); Franciscus
      Junius, *The Literature of Classical Art,* trans. Keith Aldrich, Philipp and Raina Fehl
      (Berkeley, 1980; cf. §P-535); Leonardo da Vinci, *Literary Works,* ed. and trans. Jean
      Paul Richter, 2nd rev. ed. (1939), 2 vols., and *The Notebooks,* trans. Edward MacCurdy
      (1923); Michelangelo, *Letters,* trans. E. H. Ramsden (1963), 2 vols.; Andrea Palladio,
      Four Books on Architecture, trans. Isaac Ware (1738; facsimile, 1965; cf. §P-538); Peter
      Paul Rubens, *Letters,* trans. Ruth S. Magurn (Cambridge, Mass., 1955); Giorgio
      Vasari, *The Lives of the Painters, Sculptors, and Architects,* trans. A. B. Hinds (1963), 4
      vols., and *The Lives of the Artists* (a selection), trans. George Bull (Baltimore, 1965);
      Pollio Vitruvius, *Ten Books on Architecture,* trans. Morris H. Morgan (Cambridge,
      Mass., 1914; repr. 1960); etc.

(c)   Collections and composite editions, such as *Scritti d'arte del Cinquecento* (Milan, 1971)
      and *Trattati d'arte del Cinquecento fra Manierismo e Contro-riforma* (Bari, 1960–61), 3 vols.,

alike edited by Paola Barocchi; *Emblemata*, ed. Arthur Henkel and Albrecht Schöne (Stuttgart, 1967); *The Arte of Limning* attributed to Nicholas Hilliard, ed. Philip Norman, *Walpole Society Annual Volume*, I (1912), 1–54; *Inigo Jones on Palladio, being the notes by Inigo Jones in the copy of 'I quattro libri architettura di Andrea Palladio* (Newcastle upon Tyne, 1970); *The Elder Pliny's Chapters on the History of Art*, ed. E. Sellers, trans. K. Jex-Blake (Chicago, 1968); etc.—as well as several volumes in the Prentice-Hall series 'Sources and Documents in the History of Art' (Englewood Cliffs, N.J.), i.e. Robert Klein and Henri Zerner's *Italian Art, 1500—1600* (1966), Wolfgang Stechow's *Northern Renaissance Art, 1400–1600* (1966), Robert Enggass and Jonathan Brown's *Italy and Spain, 1600—1750* (1970), etc. See also §S–730.

LOGIC AND RHETORIC

P–546 BLOUNT, THOMAS: *The Academie of Eloquence* (1654).
P–547 BLUNDEVILLE, THOMAS: *Art of Logike* (1599).
P–548 BULWER, JOHN: *Chirologia* (1644).
P–549 BUTLER, CHARLES: *Rhetoricae Libri Duo* (1598).
P–550 COX, LEONARD: *The Arte or Crafte of Rhetoryke* (1524).
P–551 DAY, ANGEL: *The English Secretorie* (1586).
P–552 ERASMUS, DESIDERIUS: *Proverbes or Adagies*, trans. Richard Taverner (1539).
P–553 ERASMUS, DESIDERIUS: *Apophthegmes*, trans. Nicholas Udall (1542).
P–554 FARNABY, THOMAS: *Index Rhetoricus* (1625).
P–555 FENNER, DUDLEY: *The Artes of Logike and rethorike* (1584).
P–556 FRAUNCE, ABRAHAM: *The Arcadian Rhetorike* (1588).
P–557 FRAUNCE, ABRAHAM: *The Lawiers Logike* (1588).
P–558 GRATAROLUS, GULIELMUS: *The castel of memorie*, trans. William Fullwood (1562).
P–559 HOSKYNS, JOHN: *Direccions for Speech and Style* (1600).
P–560 LAMY, BERNARD: *The Art of Speaking* (1676).
P–561 LEVER, RALPH: *The Arte of Reason, rightly termed, Witcraft* (1573).
P–562 MILTON, JOHN: *A fuller Institution of the Art of Logic* (1672).
P–563 PEACHAM, HENRY: *The Garden of Eloquence* (1577).
P–564 PRIDEAUX, JOHN: *Sacred Eloquence* (1659).
P–565 RAINOLDE, RICHARD: *The Foundacion of Rhetorike* (1563).
P–566 RAMUS, PETER: *The Logike*, trans. 'Roll. Makylmenaeum' (1574).
P–567 SHERRY, RICHARD: *A Treatise of Schemes and Tropes* (1550).
P–568 SMITH, JOHN: *The Mysterie of Rhetorique Unveil'd* (1659).
P–569 STURMIUS, JOANNES: *A ritch Storehouse or Treasurie . . . called Nobilitas Literata*, trans. T. B.[rowne] (1570).
P–570 WALKER, OBADIAH: *Some Instructions concerning the Art of Oratory* (1659).
P–571 WILLIS, JOHN: *The art of memory* (1621).
P–572 WILSON, SIR THOMAS: *The Arte of Logike* (1551).
P–573 WILSON, SIR THOMAS: *The Arte of Rhetorique* (1553).
P–574 WRIGHT, THOMAS: *The passions of the minde in generall* (1601; expanded 1604).

LITERATURE

P–575 ALLOT, ROBERT (ED.): *Englands Parnassus; or the choysest Flowers of our Moderne Poets* (1600).

P–576   ARIOSTO, LODOVICO: *Orlando Furiso in English heroical verse*, trans. Sir John Harington (1591).

P–577   BACON, SIR FRANCIS: *Essayes* (1597; enlarged 1612, 1625).

P–578   BACON, SIR FRANCIS: *The Wisedom of the Ancients*, trans. Sir Arthur Gorges (1619).

P–579   BEAUMONT, FRANCIS, and JOHN FLETCHER: *Workes . . . being Tragedies and Comedies* (1633); *Fifty Comedies and Tragedies* (1679).

P–580   BEAUMONT, JOSEPH: *Psyche: or Loves Mysterie in XX. Canto's* (1648).

P–581   BENLOWES, EDWARD: *Theophila, or Loves Sacrifice: A Divine Poem* (1652).

P–582   BROWNE, SIR THOMAS: *Religio Medici* (1642).

P–583   BROWNE, SIR THOMAS: *Hydriotaphia* and *The Garden of Cyrus* (1658).

P–584   BROWNE, WILLIAM: *Britannia's Pastorals* (1613, 1616).

P–585   BUNYAN, JOHN: *The Pilgrim's Progress* (Part I, 1678; Part II, 1684).

P–586   BUTLER, SAMUEL: *Hudibras* (Part I, 1662–3; Part II, 1664; Part III, 1678).

P–587   CAMOÊS: *Lusiad*, trans. Sir Richard Fanshawe (1655).

P–588   CAMPION, THOMAS: *Observations in the art of English poesie* (1602).

P–589   CAMPION, THOMAS: *Poemata* (1595).

P–590   CAREW, THOMAS: *Poems* (1640).

P–591   CERVANTES SAAVEDRA, MIGUEL DE: *The History Of . . . Don-Quixote*, trans. Thomas Shelton (1612, 1620).

P–592   CHAMBERLAYNE, WILLIAM: *Pharonnida: A Heroick Poem* (1659).

P–593   CHAPMAN, GEORGE, and CHRISTOPHER MARLOWE: *Hero and Leander* (1598).

P–594   CLEVELAND, JOHN: *Poems* (1651).

P–595   COLONNO, FRANCESCO: *Hypnerotomachia. The strife of love in a dreame*, trans. Sir Robert Dallington (1592).

P–596   CORNWALLIS, SIR WILLIAM: *Essayes* (1600–1).

P–597   COWLEY, ABRAHAM: *Works* (1668).

P–598   CRASHAW, RICHARD: *Steps to the Temple* (1646, 1648).

P–599   CRASHAW, RICHARD: *Carmen Deo nostro* (Paris, 1652).

P–600   DANIEL, SAMUEL: *A Defence of Ryme* (1603).

P–601   DANIEL, SAMUEL: *The Civile Wares* (1609).

P–602   DAVENANT, SIR WILLIAM: *Gondibert* (1651).

P–603   DAVIES, SIR JOHN: *Orchestra or a Poem of Dauncing* (1596).

P–604   DENHAM, SIR JOHN: *Coopers Hill* (1642, 1655).

P–605   DIGBY, SIR KENELM: *Observations on the 22. Stanza in the 9th. Canto of the 2d. Book of Spencers Faery Queen* (1643).

P–606   DIGBY, SIR KENELM: *Observations upon Religio Medici* (1643).

P–607   DONNE, JOHN: *An Anatomy of the World* (1611).

P–608   DONNE, JOHN: *The Second Anniversarie* (1612).

P–609   DONNE, JOHN: *Juvenilia: or Certaine Paradoxes, and Problemes* (1633).

P–610   DONNE, JOHN: *Poems* (1633).

P–611   DRAYTON, MICHAEL: *Poems* (1605–37).

P–612   DRUMMOND of HAWTHORNDEN, WILLIAM: *Flowers of Sion* and *Cypresse Grove* (Edinburgh, 1623).

P–613   DU BARTAS, GUILLAUME SALUSTE: *Bartas His Devine Weekes & Workes*, trans. Josua Sylvester (1605, 1608).

P–614   EARLE, JOHN: *Micro-cosmographie* (1628).

P–615   FARLEY, ROBERT: *Lychnocausia . . . Lights. moral emblems* (1638).

P–616   FELLTHAM, OWEN: *Resolves* (1623–9).

P–617   FLETCHER, GILES: *Christs Victorie, and Triumph* (Cambridge, 1610).

P–618   FLETCHER, PHINEAS: *The Locusts, or Apollyonists* (Cambridge, 1627).

P–619   GAUTRUCHE, PIERRE: *The Poetical Histories: being a compleat collection of all stories necessary for a perfect understanding of the Greek and Latin poets*, trans. Anon. (1671;

6th rev. ed., 1685).

P–620 GOSSON, STEPHEN: *The School of Abuse* (1579).

P–621 GOULART, SIMON: *A Learned Summary upon the famous poeme of . . . Bartas*, trans. Thomas Lodge (1621).

P–622 GREVILLE, FULKE: *Certaine Learned and Elegant Workes* (1633).

P–623 HABINGTON, WILLIAM: *Castara* (1640).

P–624 HALL, JOSEPH: *Characters of Vertues and Vices* (1608).

P–625 HALL, JOSEPH: *Virgidemiarum, sixe bookes* (1597–8).

P–626 HARVEY, CHRISTOPHER: *The Synagogue* (1640).

P–627 HERBERT of CHERBURY, EDWARD LORD: *Occasional Verses* (1665).

P–628 HERBERT, GEORGE: *The Temple* (1633).

P–629 HERRICK, ROBERT: *Hesperides: or, The Works both Humane & Divine* (1648).

P–630 HEYWOOD, THOMAS: *The Hierarchie of the Blessed Angells* (1635).

P–631 HEYWOOD, THOMAS: *Apology for Actors* (1612).

P–632 HOMER: *The Whole Works*, trans. George Chapman (1616).

P–633 HORACE: *His art of poetry*, trans. Ben Jonson in the latter's *Other workes . . . never printed before* (1640).

P–634 HOWARD, HENRY, EARL of SURREY: *Songes and Sonettes* [Totell's *Miscellany*] (1557).

P–635 JAMES I: *The essayes of a prentise in the divine art of poesie* (Edinburgh, 1584).

P–636 JOHNSON, ROBERT: *Essaies, or rather Imperfect Offers* (1601).

P–637 JONSON, BEN: *Workes* (1616–40).

P–638 KING, HENRY: *Poems, Elegies, Paradoxes, and Sonnets* (1657).

P–639 LOVELACE, RICHARD: *Lucasta* (1649).

P–640 LUCAN: *Pharsalia*, trans. Thomas May (1626–7).

P–641 MARMION, SHAKERLEY: *Cupid and Psiche* (1637).

P–642 MARSTON, JOHN: *Tragedies and Comedies* (1633).

P–643 MARVELL, ANDREW: *Miscellaneous Poems* (1681).

P–644 MERES, FRANCIS: *Palladis Tamia. Wits Treasury* (1598).

P–645 MILTON, JOHN: *A Maske Presented At Ludlow Castle* (1637).

P–646 MILTON, JOHN, and others: *Justa Edouardo King naufrago* (1638).

P–647 MILTON, JOHN: *Poems* (1645).

P–648 MILTON, JOHN: *Paradise Lost* (1667, rev., 1674).

P–649 MILTON, JOHN: *Paradise Regained* and *Samson Agonistes* (1671).

P–650 MONTAIGNE, MICHAEL DE: *The Essayes*, trans. John Florio (1603).

P–651 MORE, HENRY: *Philosophicall Poems* (Cambridge, 1647).

P–652 OVID: *The. XV. Bookes of P. Ovidius Naso, entytuled Metamorphosis*, trans. Arthur Golding (1567).

P–653 OVID: *Ovid's Metamorphosis. Englished, Mythologized, and Represented in Figures*, trans. George Sandys (Oxford, 1632).

P–654 PEACHAM, HENRY: *Minerva Britanna* (1612).

P–655 PHILLIPS, EDWARD: *Theatrum Poetarum* (1675).

P–656 PICO DELLA MIRANDOLA, GIOVANNI: *A Platonick Discourse upon Love*, trans. Thomas Stanley in the latter's *Poems* (1651).

P–657 PLUTARCH: *Morals*, trans. Philemon Holland (1603).

P–658 PLUTARCH: *Lives of the noble Grecians and Romanes*, trans. Sir Thomas North (1579).

P–659 POOLE, JOSHUA: *The English Parnassus: or, A Helpe to English Poesie* (1657).

P–660 PRYNNE, WILLIAM: *Histrio-Mastix* (1633).

P–661 PUTTENHAM, GEORGE: *The Arte of English Poesie* (1589).

P–662 QUARLES, FRANCIS: *Divine Fancies* (1632).

P–663 QUARLES, FRANCIS: *Emblemes*, with *Hieroglyphikes of the Life of Man* (1634, 1639).

P–664 RABELAIS, FRANÇOIS: *Works, Books 1—11*, trans. Sir Thomas Urquhart (1653).

P–665   RANDOLPH, THOMAS: *Poems* (1638).

P–666   REYNOLDS, HENRY: *Mythomystes* (1632).

P–667   ROSS, ALEXANDER: *Medicus Medicatus* (1645).

P–668   ROSS, ALEXANDER: *Mel Heliconium* (1642).

P–669   ROSS, ALEXANDER: *Mystagogus Poeticus* (1647).

P–670   SHAKESPEARE, WILLIAM: *Sonnets* (1609).

P–671   SHAKESPEARE, WILLIAM: *Comedies, Histories, and Tragedies* [first folio edition] (1623).

P–672   SIDNEY, SIR PHILIP: *The Countesse of Pembrokes Arcadia . . . with sundry new additions* (1598, 1613).

P–673   SIDNEY, SIR PHILIP: *The Defence of Poesie* (1595: the Ponsonby text) and *An Apologie for Poetrie* (1595: the Olney text).

P–674   SPENSER, EDMUND: *The Faerie Queene* [first folio edition] (1609).

P–675   STANLEY, THOMAS: *Poems and Translations* (1647, 1651).

P–676   SUCKLING, SIR JOHN: *Aglaura* (1638).

P–677   TASSO, TORQUATO: *Godfrey of Bulloigne*, trans. Edward Fairfax (1600).

P–678   VAUGHAN, HENRY: *Silex Scintillans* (1650).

P–679   WALLER, EDMUND: *Poems* (1645).

P–680   WALTON, ISAAC: *The Compleat Angler* (1653).

P–681   WALTON, ISAAC: *The Lives of Dr. John Donne . . . etc.* (1670).

P–682   WATSON, THOMAS: *Hecatompathia; or A Passionate Centurie of Love* (1582).

P–683   WHITNEY, GEOFFREY: *A Choice of Emblemes* (1586).

P–684   WITHER, GEORGE: *A Collection of Emblemes, ancient and modern* (1634–5).

P–685   WOTTON, SIR HENRY: *Reliquiae Wottonianae* (1651).

P–686   WRIGHT, ABRAHAM (ed.): *Parnassus Biceps* (1656).

Bibliography of
secondary sources

CONTENTS

Throughout, places of publication are given only if they are other than London or New York.

The abbreviation 'S' designates a Secondary source, while 'P' in the previous bibliography (pp. 373–92) designates a Primary source.

A BIBLIOGRAPHICAL NOTE

The student of the period's literature and its backgrounds will find extensive bibliographies in C. S. Lewis, *English Literature in the Sixteenth Century excluding Drama* (Oxford, 1954), pp. 594–685, and Douglas Bush (§ S–900), pp. 461–668. The revised first volume of *The New Cambridge Bibliography of English Literature*, ed. George Watson (Cambridge, 1974), is exhaustive but severely noncommittal. More modest bibliographies will be found in the various Folger Booklets on Tudor and Stuart Civilization, and in *A Guide to English Literature*, ed. Boris Ford, II: *The Age of Shakespeare*, and III: *From Donne to Marvell* (rev. eds., 1961–62).

The standard annual bibliographies include: the English Association's *The Year's Work in*

English Studies (1919 ff.), the Modern Humanities Research Association's *Annual Bibliography of English Language and Literature* (1920 ff.), *Publications of the Modern Language Association* (1922 ff.), *Studies in Philology* (1922 ff.), and *Studies in English Literature* (1961 ff.).

Studies of individual authors are available in all the bibliographies cited above. But the interested student should also consult the Goldentree Bibliographies on select authors, including Milton (ed. J. H. Hanford, 1966; rev. 1979), the lists of recent studies of various authors in *English Literary Renaissance* (1971 ff.), and the compilations appended to C. A. Patrides's editions of *Milton's Epic Poetry* (1967), *John Milton: Selected Prose* (1974), *The English Poems of George Herbert* (1974) and *Sir Thomas Browne: The Major Works* (1977).

A vast area of knowledge, with comprehensive bibliographies in each instance, will be found in the *Dictionary of the History of Ideas*, ed. Philip P. Wiener (1973–74), 5 vols. For biographies, consult in the first instance the *Dictionary of National Biography* (1885–1900), 63 vols., with several supplements. *A Milton Encyclopedia*, gen. ed. William B. Hunter, Jr. (Lewisburg, Pa., 1978 ff.), 8 vols., is necessarily of central importance.

THE HISTORICAL AND POLITICAL BACKGROUND

The most indispensable bibliographical guide is *Bibliography of English History: Stuart Period, 1603—1714*, ed. Godfrey Davies, 2nd ed. revised by Mary F. Keeler (Oxford, 1970).

S–1 ALBION, GORDON: *Charles I and the Court of Rome* (1935).

S–2 ALLEN, J. W.: *English Political Thought*, Vol. I: *1603—1644* (1938).

S–3 ASHLEY, MAURICE: *Oliver Cromwell and his World* (1972).

S–4 ASHLEY, MAURICE: *General Monck* (1977).

S–5 AYLMER, G. E.: *The King's Servants: The Civil Service of Charles I, 1625—1642* (1961, rev. ed. 1975), and *The State's Servants: the Civil Service of the English Republic, 1649—1660* (1973).

S–6 AYLMER, G. E.: *The Struggle for the Constitution: England in the Seventeenth Century* (1963; 5th rev. ed., 1975; American ed.: *A Short History of Seventeenth-Century England*).

S–7 AYLMER, G. E. (ed.): *The Interregnum: The Quest for Settlement 1646—60* (1972).

S–8 AYLMER, G. E. (ed.): *The Levellers in the English Revolution* (1975).

S–9 BAKER, HERSCHEL: *The Race of Time: Three Lectures on Renaissance Historiography* (Toronto, 1967).

S–10 BARKER, ARTHUR E.: *Milton and the Puritan Dilemma 1641—1660* (Toronto, 1942).

S–11 BECKETT, J. C.: *The Making of Modern Ireland 1603—1923* (1966).

S–12 BLITZER, C.: *An Immortal Commonwealth: The Political Thought of James Harrington* (1960).

S–13 BONNEY, RICHARD: *Political Change in France under Richelieu and Mazarin, 1624—1661* (Oxford, 1978).

S–14 BOSHER, ROBERT S.: *The Making of the Restoration Settlement . . . 1649—62* (1951).

S–15 BOULENGER, JACQUES: *The Seventeenth Century in France* (1963).

S–16 BOXER, C. R.: *The Dutch Seaborne Empire 1600—1800* (1965).

S–17 BRAILSFORD, HENRY N.: *The Levellers and the English Revolution* (1961).

S–18 BRAUDEL, FERNAND: *The Mediterranean and the Mediterranean World in the Age of Philip II*, trans. Sian Reynolds (1972–73), 2 vols.

S–19 BRINKLEY, ROBERTA F.: *Arthurian Legend in the Seventeenth Century* (Baltimore, 1932).

S–20 BRUNTON, DOUGLAS, and D. H. PENNINGTON: *Members of the Long Parliament* (1954).

S–21 BURKE, PETER: *The Renaissance Sense of the Past* (1969).

S–22 BURY, J. B.: *The Idea of Progress: An Inquiry into its Origin and Growth* (1920).

S–23 CAMPBELL, LILY B.: *Tudor Conceptions of History and Tragedy in 'A Mirror for Magistrates'* (Berkeley, 1936).

S–24 CAMPBELL, WILLIAM M.: *The Triumph of Presbyterianism* (Edinburgh, 1958).

S–25 CAPP, BERNARD: *The Fifth Monarchy Men* (1972).

S–26 CHABOD, FEDERICO: *Machiavelli and the Renaissance*, trans. David Moore (1958).

S–27 CLARK, SIR GEORGE: *The Seventeenth Century*, 2nd ed. (Oxford, 1947).

S–28 COCHRANE, ERIC (ed.): *The Late Italian Renaissance 1525—1630* (1970).

S–29 COLES, PAUL: *The Ottoman Impact on Europe* (1968).

S–30 COLLINSON, PATRICK: *The Elizabethan Puritan Movement* (1967).

S–31 COLTMAN, IRENE: *Private Men and Public Causes: Philosophy and Politics in the English Civil War* (1962).

S–32 CROSS, CLAIRE: *Church and People, 1450—1660: The Triumph of the Laity in the English Church* (1976).

S–33 DAVIES, GODFREY: *The Early Stuarts 1603—1660*, 2nd ed. (Oxford, 1959).

S–34 DAVIES, GODFREY: *The Restoration of Charles II, 1658—60* (San Marino, Calif., 1955).

S–35 DEAN, LEONARD F.: 'Tudor Theories of History Writing', *University of Michigan Contributions in Modern Philology*, I (1947), 1–24.

S–36 DONALDSON, GORDON: *Scotland—James V to James VII* (Edinburgh, 1965).

S–37 ELLIOTT, J. H.: *Europe Divided, 1559—1598* (1968).

S–38 ELLIOTT, J. H.: *Imperial Spain 1469–1716* (1963).

S–39 ELTON, G. R.: *England under the Tudors*, 2nd ed. (1974).

S–40 ELTON, G. R. (Ed.): *The Tudor Constitution: Documents and Commentary* (Cambridge, 1960).

S–41 EVERITT, ALAN M.: 'The Local Community and the Great Rebellion', *Historical Association*, General Series, LXX (1969).

S–42 FERGUSON, WALLACE K.: *The Renaissance in Historical Thought: Five Centuries of Interpretation* (Boston, 1948).

S–43 FIGGIS, J. N.: *The Divine Right of Kings* (1896; repr. with an introduction by G. R. Elton, 1965).

S–44 FINK, ZERA S.: *The Classical Republicans: . . . The Recovery of a Pattern of Thought in Seventeenth Century England*, 2nd ed. (Evanston, Ill., 1962).

S–45 FIRTH, SIR CHARLES: *Essays Historical and Literary* (Oxford, 1938). With essays on Ralegh, Milton, *et al.*

S–46 FIRTH, SIR CHARLES: *The Last Years of the Protectorate, 1656—58* (1909), 2 vols.

S–47 FIRTH, SIR CHARLES: *Oliver Cromwell* (1900; World's Classics ed., 1953).

S–48 FIXLER, MICHAEL: *Milton and the Kingdoms of God* (1964).

S–49 FOX, LEVI (ed.): *English Historical Scholarship in the 16th and 17th Centuries* (1956).

S–50 FRANK, JOSEPH: *The Beginnings of the English Newspapers, 1620–1660* (Cambridge, Mass., 1961).

S–51 FRANK, JOSEPH: *The Levellers: . . . John Lilburne, Richard Overton, William Walwyn* (Cambridge, Mass., 1955).

S–52 FUSSNER, F. SMITH: *The Historical Revolution: English Historical Writing and Thought 1580–1640* (1962).

S–53 GARDINER, S. R.: *History of England 1603–42* (1883–84), 10 vols.; *History of the Great Civil War, 1642–1649*, new ed. (1893), 4 vols.; and *History of the Commonwealth and Protectorate, 1649–1656*, new ed. (1903), 4 vols.

S–54 GEYL, PETER: *The Revolt of the Netherlands, 1555–1609*, 2nd ed. (1958), and *The Netherlands in the Seventeenth Century* (1936–64), 2 vols.

S–55 GOLDSMITH, M. M.: *Hobbes's Science of Politics* (1966).

S–56 GOOCH, G. P., and H. J. LASKI: *English Democratic Ideas in the Seventeenth Century*, 2nd ed. (Cambridge, 1927).

S–57 GOUGH, J. W.: *Fundamental Law in English Constitutional History* (Oxford, 1955).

S–58 GUNN, J. A. W.: *Politics and the Public Interest in the Seventeenth Century* (1969).

S–59 HALEY, K. H. D.: *The Dutch in the Seventeenth Century* (1962).

S–60 HALLER, WILLIAM: *Foxe's Book of Martyrs and the Elect Nation* (1963).

S–61 HALLER, WILLIAM: *The Rise of Puritanism* and *Liberty and Reformation in the Puritan Revolution* (1938 and 1955).

S–62 HALLER, WILLIAM (ed.): *Tracts on Liberty in the Puritan Revolution* (1935), 3 vols. Primary sources.

S–63 HALLER, WILLIAM, and G. DAVIES (eds.): *The Leveller Tracts, 1647–53* (1944). Primary sources.

S–64 HAY, DENYS: *Europe: The Emergence of an Idea* (Edinburgh, 1957).

S–65 HAY, DENYS: 'History and Scholarship in the Seventeenth Century', in his *Annalists and Historians* (1977), Ch. VII.

S–66 HILL, CHRISTOPHER: *The Century of Revolution 1603—1714* (Edinburgh, 1961; repr. 1969).

S–67 HILL, CHRISTOPHER: *God's Englishman: Oliver Cromwell and the English Revolution* (1970; repr. Penguin Books, 1972).

S–68 HILL, CHRISTOPHER: *Intellectual Origins of the English Revolution* (Oxford, 1965; repr. 1966).

S–69 HILL, CHRISTOPHER: *Milton and the English Revolution* (1977).

S–70 HILL, CHRISTOPHER: *Puritanism and Revolution: Studies in Interpretation of the English Revolution of the Seventeenth Century* (1958).

S–71 HILL, CHRISTOPHER: *The World Turned Upside Down: Radical Ideas during the English Revolution* (1972; repr. Penguin Books, 1975).

S–72 HIRST, DEREK: *The Representative of the People? Voters and Voting in England under the Early Stuarts* (Cambridge, 1975).

S–73 HOLDEN, WILLIAM P.: *Anti-Puritan Satire, 1572–1642* (New Haven, 1954).

S–74 HUIZINGA, J. H.: *Dutch Civilisation in the Seventeenth Century, and other essays*, trans. A. J. Pomerans (1968).

S–75 HURSTFIELD, JOEL: *Freedom, Corruption and Government in Elizabethan England* (1973).

S–76 HURSTFIELD, JOEL: *The Queen's Wards: Wardship and Marriage under Elizabeth I* (1958).

S–77 IVES, E. W. (ed.): *The English Revolution 1600–1660* (1968).

S–78 JONES, J. R.: *Britain and Europe in the Seventeenth Century* (1966).

S–79 JORDAN, WILBUR K.: *The Development of Religious Toleration in England*, especially vols. II–IV (1932–40).

S–80 JOSEPH, B. L.: *Shakespeare's Eden: The Commonwealth of England 1558–1629* (1971).

S–81 JUDSON, MARGARET: *The Crisis of the Constitution: An Essay in Constitutional and Political Thought, 1603–1645* (New Brunswick, N.J., 1949).

S–82 KENDRICK, SIR THOMAS: *British Antiquity* (1950).

S–83 KENYON, J. P.: *The Stuarts: A Study in English Kingship* (1958).

S–84 KENYON, J. P. (ed.): *The Stuart Constitution, 1603–1688: Documents and Commentary* (Cambridge, 1966).

S–85 KNAPPEN, M. M.: *Tudor Puritanism: A Chapter in the History of Idealism* (Chicago, 1939).

S–86 KOENIGSBERGER, H. G.: *The Habsburgs and Europe, 1516–1660* (Ithaca, N.Y., 1971).

S–87 KOENIGSBERGER, H. G., and GEORGE L. MOSSE: *Europe in the Sixteenth Century* (1968).

S–88 LEVY, F. J.: *Tudor Historical Thought* (San Marino, Calif., 1967).

S–89   LEWALSKI, BARBARA K.: 'Milton: Political Beliefs and Polemical Methods, 1659–60', *Publications of the Modern Language Association*, LXXIV (1959), 191–202.

S–90   LOADES, D. M.: *Politics and the Nation, 1450–1660: Obedience, Resistance and Public Order* (Brighton, 1974).

S–91   LOUGH, JOHN: *An Introduction to Seventeenth Century France* (1954).

S–92   MACAULAY, THOMAS BABINGTON: *The History of England* (1848), Vol. I.

S–93   MACPHERSON, C. B.: *The Political Theory of Possessive Individualism: Hobbes to Locke* (Oxford, 1962).

S–94   MANNING, BRIAN S. (ed.): *Politics, Religion and the English Civil War* (1974).

S–95   MASSON, DAVID: *The Life of John Milton: Narrated in Connexion with the Political, Ecclesiastical, and Literary History of his Time* (1859–94, repr. 1946), 7 vols.

S–96   MAZZEO, JOSEPH A.: *Renaissance and Revolution: Backgrounds to Seventeenth-Century English Literature* (1965).

S–97   MORRILL, J. S.: *The Revolt of the Provinces : Conservatives and Radicals in the English Civil War, 1630—1650* (1976).

S–98   MORRIS, CHRISTOPHER: *Political Thought in England: Tyndale to Hooker* (1953).

S–99   MORTON, ARTHUR L.: *The World of the Ranters: Religious Radicalism in the English Revolution* (1970).

S–100 MORTON, ARTHUR L. (ed.): *Freedom in Arms: A Selection of Leveller Writings* (1975).

S–101 NEALE, SIR JOHN: *The Elizabethan House of Commons* (1949), and *Elizabeth I and her Parliaments* (1953).

S–102 NEVO, RUTH: *The Dial of Virtue: A Study of Poems on Affairs of State in the Seventeenth Century* (Princeton, 1963).

S–103 *The New Cambridge Modern History*, Vol. III: *The Counter-Reformation and the Price Revolution, 1559–1610*, ed. R. B. Wernham (1968); Vol. IV: *The Decline of Spain and the Thirty Years War, 1609–1648/59*, ed. J. P. Cooper (1970); and Vol. V: *The Ascendancy of France, 1648–1688*, ed. F. L. Carsten (1961).

S–104 NICOLSON, MARJORIE H.: 'Milton and Hobbes', *Studies in Philology*, XXIII (1926), 405–33. See also Don M. Wolfe, 'Milton and Hobbes: A Contrast in Social Temper', *ibid.*, XLI (1944), 410–26.

S–105 OGG, DAVID: *England in the Reign of Charles II*, 2nd ed. (Oxford, 1956), 2 vols.

S–106 OGG, DAVID: *Europe in the Seventeenth Century*, 9th ed. (1971).

S–107 ORTIZ, A. D.: *The Golden Age of Spain, 1516–1659* (1971).

S–108 PARRY, R. H. (ed.): *The English Civil War and After, 1642–58* (1970).

S–109 PATRIDES, C. A.: 'The Grand Design of God': *The Literary Form of the Christian View of History* (1972).

S–110 PEARL, VALERIE: *London and the Outbreak of the Puritan Revolution: City Government and National Politics, 1625–43* (1961).

S–111 PENNINGTON, D. H.: *Seventeenth Century Europe* (1970).

S–112 POCOCK, J. G. A.: *The Ancient Constitution and Feudal Law: A Study of English Historical Thought in the Seventeenth Century* (Cambridge, 1957).

S–113 POCOCK, J. G. A.: *The Machiavellian Moment: Florentine Political Thought and the Atlantic Republican Tradition* (Princeton, 1975).

S–114 POCOCK, J. G. A. (ed.): *The Political Works of James Harrington* (Cambridge, 1977).

S–115 POLIŠENSKÝ, J. V.: *The Thirty Years War*, trans. Robert Evans (1972).

S–116 PULLAPILLY, CYRIAC K.: *Caesar Baronius: Counter-Reformation Historian* (Notre Dame, Ind., 1975).

S–117 QUINN, DAVID B.: *England and the Discovery of America 1481–1620* (1973; 1974).

S–118 QUINN, DAVID B.: *Raleigh and the British Empire* (1947).

S–119 RAAB, FELIX: *The English Face of Machiavelli: A Changing Interpretation, 1500—1700* (1964).

S–120 RABB, THEODORE K. (ed.): *The Thirty Years' War: Problems of Motive, Extent and*

Effect, 2nd ed. (Lexington, 1972).

S–121   RACIN, JOHN: *Sir Walter Raleigh as Historian* (Salzburg, 1974).

S–122   REYNOLDS, BEATRICE R.: 'Latin Historiography: A Survey, 1400–1600', *Studies in the Renaissance*, II (1955), 7–66.

S–123   REYNOLDS, BEATRICE R.: 'Shifting Currents in Historical Criticism', in *Renaissance Essays*, ed. P. O. Kristeller and P. P. Wiener (1968), Ch. V.

S–124   RICHARDSON, R. C.: *The Debate on the English Revolution* (1977).

S–125   ROBERTS, MICHAEL: *Gustavus Adolphus: A History of Sweden, 1611–1632* (1953–58), 2 vols.

S–126   ROBERTS, MICHAEL (ed.): *Sweden's Age of Greatness, 1632–1718* (1973).

S–127   ROOTS, IVAN: *The Great Rebellion 1642–1660* (1966).

S–128   RUSSELL, CONRAD: *The Crisis of Parliaments: English History 1509—1660* (Oxford, 1971).

S–129   RUSSELL, CONRAD: *Parliament and English Politics 1621–29* (1979).

S–130   RUSSELL, CONRAD (ed.): *The Origins of the English Civil War* (1973).

S–131   SABINE, G. H. (ed.): *The Works of Gerrard Winstanley* (Ithaca, N.Y., 1941).

S–132   SALMON, J. H. M.: *The French Religious Wars in English Political Thought* (Oxford, 1959).

S–133   SAMUEL, IRENE: 'Milton and the Ancients on the Writing of History', *Milton Studies*, II (1970), 131–48.

S–134   SEYMOUR, ST JOHN D.: *The Puritans in Ireland 1647–1661* (1912).

S–135   SIEBERT, FREDRICK S.: *Freedom of the Press in England, 1476–1776* (Urbana, 1952). Parts II–III are on the period 1603–60.

S–136   SIMPSON, ALAN: *Puritanism in Old and New England* (Chicago, 1955).

S–137   SKINNER, QUENTIN: (*a*) 'History and Ideology in the English Revolution', *Historical Journal*, VIII (1965), 151–78; (*b*) 'The Ideological Context of Hobbes's Political Thought', *ibid.*, IX (1966), 286–317.

S–138   SKINNER, QUENTIN: *Foundations of Modern Political Thought*, Vol. I: *The Renaissance*, Vol. II: *The Age of Reformation* (Cambridge, 1978).

S–139   SMITH, ALAN G. R. (ed.): *The Reign of James VI and I* (1973).

S–140   STEINBERG, S. H.: *The Thirty Years War and the Conflict for European Hegemony 1600–1660* (1966).

S–141   STONE, LAWRENCE: *The Causes of the English Revolution 1529–1642* (1972).

S–142   STOYE, JOHN W.: *Europe Unfolding, 1648–1688* (1969).

S–143   STRUEVER, NANCY S.: *The Language of History in the Renaissance* (Princeton, 1970).

S–144   SYKES, NORMAN: *Old Priest and New Presbyter* (Cambridge, 1956). On episcopacy and Presbyterianism.

S–145   TATLOCK, J. S. P.: *The Legendary History of Britain* (Berkeley, 1950).

S–146   TEUNISSEN, JOHN J.: 'The Book of Job and Stuart Politics', *University of Toronto Quarterly*, XLIII (1973), 16–31.

S–147   THOMAS, KEITH: *Religion and the Decline of Magic: Studies in Popular Beliefs in Sixteenth and Seventeenth Century England* (1971).

S–148   TREVOR-ROPER, H. R. (ed.): *The Age of Expansion: Europe and the World, 1559–1660* (1968).

S–149   TUVESON, ERNEST L.: *Millennium and Utopia: A Study in the Background of the Idea of Progress* (Berkeley, 1949).

S–150   UNDERDOWN, DAVID: *Pride's Purge: Politics in the Puritan Revolution* (Oxford, 1971).

S–151   WALLACE, JOHN M.: *Destiny his Choice: The Loyalism of Andrew Marvell* (Cambridge, 1968).

S–152   WALZER, MICHAEL: *The Revolution of the Saints: A Study in the Origin of Radical Politics* (Cambridge, Mass., 1965).

S–153   WARRENDER, HOWARD: *The Political Philosophy of Hobbes* (Oxford, 1957).
S–154   WATKINS, OWEN C.: *The Puritan Experience* (1972).
S–155   WEBSTER, CHARLES (ed.): *The Intellectual Revolution of the Seventeenth Century* (1974).
S–156   WEDGWOOD, C. V.: *The Great Rebellion*, Vol. I: *The King's Peace 1637–1641* (1955); Vol. II: *The King's War 1641–1647* (1959).
S–157   WEDGWOOD, C. V.: *Poetry and Politics under the Stuarts* (Cambridge, 1960).
S–158   WEDGWOOD, C. V.: *The Thirty Years War* (1938, repr. 1957).
S–159   WEDGWOOD, C. V.: *The Trial of Charles I* (1964; American ed.: *A Coffin for King Charles*).
S–160   WEISINGER, HERBERT: 'Ideas of History during the Renaissance', in §S–386: Ch. III.
S–161   WILSON, JOHN F.: *Pulpit in Parliament: Puritanism during the English Civil Wars, 1640–1648* (Princeton, 1969).
S–162   WOLFE, DON M.: *Milton in the Puritan Revolution* (1941).
S–163   WOLFE, DON M. (ed.): *Leveller Manifestoes of the Puritan Revolution* (1944). Primary sources.
S–164   WOODHOUSE, A. S. P. (ed.): *Puritanism and Liberty*, 2nd ed. (1938). Extracts on the political thought of the Puritan revolution.
S–165   WORDEN, BLAIR: *The Rump Parliament, 1648–53* (Cambridge, 1974).
S–166   WORMWALD, B. H. G.: *Clarendon: Politics, History and Religion* (1951).
S–167   ZAGORIN, PEREZ: *The Court and the Country: The Beginnings of the English Revolution* (1969).
S–168   ZAGORIN, PEREZ: *A History of Political Thought in the English Revolution* (1954).

Consult in addition the bibliographical surveys by Perez Zagorin and Paul H. Hardacre in *Changing Views on British History*, ed. Elizabeth C. Furber (Cambridge, Mass., 1966), pp. 119–59.

See also §§S–117, 224, 253, 277, 390, 392, 438, 466, 501, 959.

THE SOCIAL AND ECONOMIC BACKGROUND

S–169   ADAM, ANTOINE: *Grandeur and Illusion: French Literature and Society 1600–1715*, trans. Hebert Tint (1972).
S–170   AKRIGG, G. P. V.: *Jacobean Pageant; or the Court of James I* (1962).
S–171   ANGLO, SYDNEY (ed.): *The Damned Art: Essays in the Literature of Witchcraft* (1977).
S–172   APPLEBY, ANDREW: 'Nutrition and Disease: The Case of London, 1550–1750', *Journal of Interdisciplinary History*, VI (1975), 1–22.
S–173   ARTHOS, JOHN: *Milton and the Italian Cities* (1968).
S–174   ASHLEY, MAURICE: *Life in Stuart England* (1964).
S–175   ASHTON, JOHN: *Humour, Wit and Satire of the Seventeenth Century* (1883, repr. 1968).
S–176   ASHTON, ROBERT: *The Crown and the Money Market 1603–1640* (Oxford, 1960).
S–177   ASTON, TREVOR (ed.): *Crisis in Europe 1560–1660* (1965).
S–178   BALL, J. N.: *Merchants and Merchandise: The Expansion of Trade in Europe 1500–1630* (1977).
S–179   BERRY, LLOYD E., and ROBERT O. CRUMNEY (eds.): *Rude and Barbarous Kingdom: Russia in the Accounts of Sixteenth-Century English Voyagers* (Madison, 1968).
S–180   BRETT-JAMES, NORMAN G.: *The Growth of Stuart London* (1935).
S–181   BOSSY, JOHN: *The English Catholic Community, 1570–1850* (1975).
S–182   BOWDEN, P. J.: *The Wool Trade in Tudor and Stuart England* (1962).

S–183 BULLOUGH, GEOFFREY: 'Polygamy among the Reformers', in *Renaissance and Modern Essays*, ed. G. R. Hibbard (1966), pp. 5–23.

S–184 BURTON, ELIZABETH: *The Jacobeans at Home* (1962).

S–185 CAMPBELL, MILDRED: *The English Yeoman under Elizabeth and the Early Stuarts* (New Haven, 1942; repr. 1960).

S–186 CARUS-WILSON, E. M. (ed.): *Essays in Economic History*, Vols. I–II (1954–62).

S–187 CAWLEY, ROBERT R.: *Milton and the Literature of Travel* (Princeton, 1951).

S–188 CHALKLIN, C. W., and M. A. HAVINDEN (eds.): *Rural Change and Urban Growth 1500–1800* (1974).

S–189 CHAMBERLIN, E. R.: *Everyday Life in Renaissance Times* (1965).

S–190 CHAMBERS, J. D.: *Population, Economy and Society in Pre-industrial England* (1972).

S–191 CLARK, SIR GEORGE: *The Wealth of England from 1496 to 1760* (1946).

S–192 CLARK, PETER, and PAUL SLACK: *English Towns in Transition 1500–1700* (Oxford, 1976).

S–193 CLARK, PETER, and PAUL SLACK (eds.): *Crisis and Order in English Towns, 1500–1700* (1972).

S–194 CLARKSON, L. A.: 'The Organization of the English Leather Industry in the Late Sixteenth and Seventeenth Centuries', *Economic History Review*, 2nd Series, XIII (1960).

S–195 CLARKSON, L. A.: *The Pre-industrial Economy in England, 1500–1750* (1971).

S–196 CLIFFE, J. T.: *The Yorkshire Gentry from the Reformation to the Civil War* (1969).

S–197 COLEMAN, D. C.: *The Economy of England, 1450–1750* (1977).

S–198 COLEMAN, D. C.: *Industry in Tudor and Stuart England* (1975).

S–199 DAVIS, NATALIE ZEMON: *Society and Culture in Early Modern France* (Stanford, 1975).

S–200 EVERITT, ALAN (ed.): *Perspectives in English Urban History* (1973).

S–201 FINCH, M. E.: *The Wealth of Five Northamptonshire Families*, Northamptonshire Record Society, XIX (1956).

S–202 FISHER, F. J.: (ed.): *Essays in the Economic and Social History of Tudor and Stuart England* (Cambridge, 1961).

S–203 FRYE, ROLAND M.: *Shakespeare's Life and Times: A Pictorial Record* (Princeton, 1967).

S–204 FRYE, ROLAND M.: 'The Teachings of Classical Puritanism on Conjugal Love', *Studies in the Renaissance*, II (1955), 148–59.

S–205 GEORGE, CHARLES H. and KATHERINE: *The Protestant Mind of the English Reformation, 1570–1640* (Princeton, 1961).

S–206 GODFREY, ELIZABETH: *Home Life under the Stuarts, 1603–1649* (1903).

S–207 HALKETT, JOHN: *Milton and the Idea of Matrimony: A Study of the Divorce Tracts and 'Paradise Lost'* (New Haven, 1970).

S–208 HALL, VERNON, JR.: *Renaissance Literary Criticism: A Study of its Social Context* (1945).

S–209 HALLER, WILLIAM and MALLEVILLE: 'The Puritan Art of Love', *Huntington Library Quarterly*, V (1941–2), 235–72.

S–210 HAMILTON, ELIZABETH: *Henrietta Maria* (1976).

S–211 HAMMERSLEY, G.: 'The Charcoal Iron Industry and its Fuel, 1540–1750', *Economic History Review*, 2nd Series, XXVI (1973).

S–212 HARRISON, G. B. (ed.): *A Late Elizabethan Journal, being a Record of those things most talked about during the years 1599–1603* (1933); *A Jacobean Journal . . . 1603–1606* (1941); and *A Second Jacobean Journal . . . 1607–1610* (1958).

S–213 HART, ROGER: *English Life in the Seventeenth Century* (1970).

S–214 HEXTER, J. H.: 'The Myth of the Middle Class in Tudor England', and 'Storm over the Gentry', in his *Reappraisals in History* (1961), Ch. V–VI.

S–215 HILL, CHRISTOPHER: *Change and Continuity in Seventeenth-Century England* (1974).

S–216 HILL, CHRISTOPHER: *Economic Problems of the Church from Archbishop Whitgift to the Long Parliament* (Oxford, 1956).

S–217 HILL, CHRISTOPHER: *Society and Puritanism in Pre-Revolutionary England* (1964).

S–218 HOSKINS, W. G.: *Provincial England: Essays in Social and Economic History* (1963).

S–219 HOUGHTON, WALTER E.: 'The English Virtuoso in the Seventeenth Century', *Journal of the History of Ideas*, III (1942), 51–73, 190–219.

S–220 HOWARTH, WILLIAM D. (ed.): *The Seventeenth Century* (1965), being Vol. I of the series *Life and Letters in France*, gen. ed. Austin Gill.

S–221 JACK, SYBIL M.: *Trade and Industry in Tudor and Stuart England* (1978).

S–222 JOHNSON, JAMES T.: 'The Covenant Idea and the Puritan View of Marriage', *Journal of the History of Ideas*, XXXII (1971), 107–18.

S–223 JORDAN, WILBUR K.: *Philanthropy in England 1480–1660* (1959).

S–224 KAMEN, HENRY: *The Iron Century: Social Change in Europe 1550–1660* (1971).

S–225 KERRIDGE, ERIC: *The Agricultural Revolution* (1967).

S–226 KNIGHTS, L. C.: *Drama and Society in the Age of Jonson* (1937), and 'On the Social Background of Metaphysical Poetry', *Scrutiny*, XIII (1945), 37–52.

S–227 LANGBEIN, JOHN H.: *Prosecuting Crime in the Renaissance: England, Germany, France* (Cambridge, Mass., 1974).

S–228 LASLETT, PETER: *The World We Have Lost* (1965).

S–229 LEE, SIR SIDNEY, and C. T. ONIONS (eds.): *Shakespeare's England: An Account of the Life and Manners of his Age* (Oxford, 1961), 2 vols.

S–230 MALAND, DAVID: *Culture and Society in Seventeenth Century France* (1970).

S–231 MANNING, BRIAN: *The English People and the English Revolution 1640–1649* (1976).

S–232 MATHEW, DAVID: *The Jacobean Age* and *The Age of Charles I* (1938 and 1951).

S–233 MATHEW, DAVID: *The Social Structure of Caroline England* (Oxford, 1948).

S–234 MINCHINTON, W. E. (ed.): *The Growth of English Overseas Trade in the 17th and 18th Centuries* (1969).

S–235 MONTER, E. WILLIAM: *Witchcraft in France and Switzerland: The Borderlands during the Reformation* (Ithaca, N.Y., 1976).

S–236 MOUSNIER, ROLAND: *Peasant Uprisings in Seventeenth-Century France, Russia, and China*, trans. Brian Pearce (1970).

S–237 MURRAY, JOHN J.: *Amsterdam in the Age of Rembrandt* (1972).

S–238 NOTESTEIN, WALLACE: *The English People on the Eve of Colonization 1603–1630* (1954).

S–239 NOTESTEIN, WALLACE: 'The English Woman, 1580 to 1650', in *Studies in Social History*, ed. J. H. Plumb (1955), Ch. III.

S–240 NOTESTEIN, WALLACE: *A History of Witchcraft in England from 1558 to 1718* (Washington, 1911). Still one of the best surveys.

S–241 OLSEN, V. NORSKOV: *The New Testament Logia on Divorce. A Study of their Interpretation from Erasmus to Milton* (Tübingen, 1971).

S–242 OUTHWAITE, R. B.: *Inflation in Tudor and Stuart England* (1969).

S–243 PARKER, GEOFFREY, and LESLEY M. SMITH (eds.): *The General Crisis of the Seventeenth Century* (1978).

S–244 PARKER, WILLIAM R.: *Milton: A Biography* (Oxford, 1968), 2 vols.

S–245 PARKES, JOAN: *Travel in England in the Seventeenth Century* (1925).

S–246 PARKS, GEORGE B.: 'The Decline and Fall of the English Renaissance Admiration of Italy', *Huntington Library Quarterly*, XXXI (1968), 341–57.

S–247 PARRY, J. W.: *The Age of Reconaissance* (1963).

S–248 PENROSE, BOIES: *Travel and Discovery in the Renaissance 1420–1620* (Cambridge, Mass., 1952).

S–249 PERELLA, NICOLAS J.: *The Kiss Sacred and Profane* (Berkeley, 1969). Ch. V–VI are on Renaissance attitudes.

S–250   POWELL, CHILTON L.: *English Domestic Relations 1487–1653* (1917).

S–251   PRESTWICK, MENNA: *Cranfield Politics and Profits under the Early Stuarts. The Career of Lionel Cranfield Earl of Middlesex* (Oxford, 1966).

S–252   RABB, THEODORE K.: *Enterprise and Empire: Merchant and Gentry Investment in the Expansion of England, 1575–1630* (Cambridge, Mass., 1967).

S–253   RABB, THEODORE K.: *The Struggle for Stability in Early Modern Europe* (1975).

S–254   RICH, E. E., and C. H. WILSON (eds.): *The Cambridge Economic History of Europe*, Vols. IV–V (Cambridge, 1967 and 1977).

S–255   ROTH, CECIL: *The Jews in the Renaissance* (1959).

S–256   ROWSE, A. L.: *The Elizabethan Age*, a trilogy: *The England of Elizabeth: The Structure of Society* (1950); *The Elizabethan Renaissance: The Life of Society* (1971); and *The Elizabethan Renaissance: The Cultural Achievement* (1972).

S–257   RYE, WILLIAM B.: *England as seen by Foreigners in the Days of Elizabeth and James I* (1865). Still the best collection of primary sources.

S–258   SCHÜCKING, LEVIN L.: *The Puritan Family*, trans. B. Battershaw (1969).

S–259   SELLS, ARTHUR L.: *The Paradise of Travellers: The Italian Influence on Englishmen in the Seventeenth Century* (1964).

S–260   SIEGEL, PAUL N.: 'Milton and the Humanistic Attitude toward Women', *Journal of the History of Ideas*, XI (1950), 42–53.

S–261   SIMPSON, ALAN: *The Wealth of the Gentry 1540–1660: East Anglian Studies* (Cambridge, 1961).

S–262   SPUFFORD, MARGARET: *Contrasting Communities: English Villages in the Sixteenth and Seventeenth Centuries* (Cambridge, 1974).

S–263   STEENSGAARD, NIELS: *The Asian Trade Revolution of the Seventeenth Century: The East India Companies and the Decline of the Caravan Trade* (Chicago, 1974).

S–264   STONE, LAWRENCE: *The Crisis of the Aristocracy 1558–1641* (Oxford, 1965).

S–265   STONE, LAWRENCE: *The Family, Sex and Marriage in England 1500–1800* (1977).

S–266   STONE, LAWRENCE (ed.): *Social Change and Revolution in England 1540–1640* (1965).

S–267   STONE, LAWRENCE (ed.): *The University in Society* (Princeton, 1975), Vol. I: 'Oxford and Cambridge from the 14th to the early 19th Century'.

S–268   STOYE, JOHN W.: *English Travellers Abroad: Their Influence in English Society and Politics* (1952).

S–269   SUPPLE, B. E.: *Commercial Crisis and Change in England, 1600–42* (Cambridge, 1959).

S–270   TAWNEY, A. J. and R. H.: 'An Occupational Census of the Seventeenth Century', *Economic History Review*, V (1934).

S–271   TAWNEY, R. H.: *Religion and the Rise of Capitalism* (1926).

S–272   THIRSK, JOAN: *Economic Policy and Projects. The Development of a Consumer Society in Early Modern England* (Oxford, 1978).

S–273   THIRSK, JOAN: *English Peasant Farming* (1957).

S–274   THIRSK, JOAN (ed.): *The Agrarian History of England and Wales . . . 1500–1640* (Cambridge, 1967).

S–275   THIRSK, JOAN, and J. P. COOPER (eds.): *Seventeenth-Century Economic Documents* (Oxford, 1972).

S–276   TREVOR-ROPER, H. R.: 'The Gentry, 1540–1640', *Economic History Review Supplements*, I (1953).

S–277   TREVOR-ROPER, H. R.: *Religion, the Reformation and Social Change, and other essays* (1967). Includes 'The European Witch-Craze of the Sixteenth and Seventeenth Centuries' (also published separately, 1969).

S–278   UNWIN, GEORGE: *Industrial Organization in the 16th and 17th Centuries* (Oxford, 1904).

S–279   VRIES, JAN DE: *The Economy of Europe in an Age of Crisis 1600–1750* (Cambridge,

1976).

S–280 WATSON, D. R.: *The Life and Times of Charles I* (1972).

S–281 WEDGWOOD, C. V.: *Milton and his World* (1969).

S–282 WILLAN, T. S.: *The English Coasting Trade, 1600–1750* (Manchester, 1938).

S–283 WILLAN, T. S.: *River Navigation in England, 1600–1750* (1936).

S–284 WILLIAMSON, JAMES A.: *A Short History of British Expansion. The Old Colonial Empire*, 3rd ed. (1945).

S–285 WILSON, CHARLES: *England's Apprenticeship 1603–1763* (1965).

S–286 WILSON, CHARLES: *Profit and Power: A Study of England and the Dutch Wars* (1957).

S–287 WRIGHT, LOUIS B.: *Middle-Class Culture in Elizabethan England* (Chapel Hill, 1935).

S–288 WRIGHT, LOUIS B., and VIRGINIA A. LaMAR (eds.): *Life and Letters in Tudor and Stuart England* (Ithaca, N.Y., 1962).

S–289 WRIGLEY, E. A. (ed.): *An Introduction to English Historical Demography from the 16th to the 19th Century* (1966).

See also §§S–76, 147, 167, 310, 318, 325, 437, 557, 569, 623, 655, 722, 751, 780.

THE EDUCATIONAL BACKGROUND

S–290 BALDWIN, THOMAS W.: *William Shakespere's Small Latine and Lesse Greeke* (Urbana, Ill., 1944), 2 vols.

S–291 BEALES, A. C. F.: *Education under Penalty 1547–1689* (1963).

S–292 BENNETT, H. S.: *English Books and Readers 1603 to 1640* (Cambridge, 1970).

S–293 BLAGDEN, CYPRIAN: 'Notes on the Ballad Market in the Second Half of the Seventeenth Century', *Studies in Bibliography*, VI (1953–4), 161–80.

S–294 CHARLTON, KENNETH: *Education in Renaissance England* (1965).

S–295 CLARK, DONALD L.: *John Milton at St. Paul's School: A Study of Ancient Rhetoric in English Renaissance Education* (1948).

S–296 CLARK, PETER: 'The Ownership of Books in England 1560–1640: The Example of Some Kentish Townsfolk', in *Schooling and Society: Studies in the History of Education*, ed. L. Stone (Princeton, 1976), pp. 95–114.

S–297 CLARKE, M. L.: *Classical Education in Britain 1500–1900* (Cambridge, 1959).

S–298 CONANT, JAMES B.: 'The Advancement of Learning during the Puritan Commonwealth', *Proceedings of the Massachusetts Historical Society*, LXVI (1936–41), 3–31.

S–299 COSTELLO, WILLIAM T.: *The Scholastic Curriculum at Early Seventeenth Century Cambridge* (Cambridge, Mass., 1958).

S–300 CRESSY, DAVID: 'Educational Opportunity in Tudor and Stuart England', *History of Education Quarterly*, XVI (1976), 301–20.

S–301 CURTIS, MARK H.: *Oxford and Cambridge in Transition, 1558–1642* (Oxford, 1959).

S–302 DEBUS, A. G.: *Science and Education in the Seventeenth Century: The Webster–Ward Debate* (1970).

S–303 FLETCHER, HARRIS F.: *The Intellectual Development of John Milton* (Urbana, Ill., 1956–61), 2 vols.

S–304 GOODY, JACK: *Literacy in Traditional Societies* (Cambridge, 1968).

S–305 GREAVES, RICHARD L.: *The Puritan Revolution and Educational Thought* (New Brunswick, N.J., 1969).

S–306 GUIZBURG, CARLO: 'High and Low: The Theme of Forbidden Knowledge in the Sixteenth and Seventeenth Centuries', *Past and Present*, LXXIII (November 1976), 28–41.

S–307   HARDACRE, P. H.: 'Clarendon and the University of Oxford 1660–67' *British Journal of Educational Studies*, IX (1961), 117–31.

S–308   HEXTER, J. H.: 'The Education of the Aristocracy in the Renaissance', in his *Reappraisals in History* (1961), Ch. IV.

S–309   HILL, CHRISTOPHER: 'The Radical Critics of Oxford and Cambridge in the 1650s', in *Universities in Politics*, ed. John W. Baldwin and Richard A. Goldthwaite (Baltimore, 1972), Ch. IV.

S–310   KEARNEY, HUGH: *Scholars and Gentlemen: Universities and Society in Pre-industrial Britain* (1970).

S–311   LEWALSKI, BARBARA K.: 'Milton on Learning and the Learned Ministry Controversy', *Huntington Library Quarterly*, XXIV (1961), 267–82.

S–312   MACLEAR, J. F.: 'Popular Anti-clericalism in the Puritan Revolution', *Journal of the History of Ideas*, XVII (1956), 443–70.

S–313   MASON, M. G.: 'Literary Sources of John Locke's Educational Thoughts', *Pedagogica Historica*, V (1965), 65–108.

S–314   MAY, P. R.: 'Richard Baxter on Education', *British Journal of Educational Studies*, XV (1967), 60–73.

S–315   MULDER, JOHN R.: *The Temple of the Mind: Education and Literary Taste in Seventeenth-Century England* (1969).

S–316   O'BRIEN, J. J.: 'Commonwealth Schemes for the Advancement of Learning', *British Journal of Educational Studies*, XVI (1968), 30–42.

S–317   PARKER, WILLIAM R.: 'Education: Milton's Ideas and Ours', *College English*, XXIV (1962), 1–14.

S–318   PINCHBECK, IVY, and MARGARET HEWITT: *Children in English Society*: Vol. I: *Tudor Times to the Eighteenth Century* (1969).

S–319   PLUMB, J. H.: 'The New World of Children in Eighteenth Century England', *Past and Present*, LXVII (May 1975), 64–95.

S–320   PREST, W. W. R.: *The Inns of Court under Elizabeth I and the Early Stuarts* (1972).

S–321   SADLER, JOHN E.: *J. A. Comenius and the Concept of Universal Education* (1966).

S–322   SAMUEL, IRENE: 'Milton on Learning and Wisdom', *Publications of the Modern Language Association*, LXIV (1949), 708–23.

S–323   SCHULTZ, HOWARD: 'Philosophy and Vain Deceit: Some Issues in the Learned Ministry Controversy', in his *Milton and Forbidden Knowledge* (1955), pp. 184–93.

S–324   SEAVER, PAUL S.: *The Puritan Lectureships: The Politics of Religious Dissent, 1560–1662* (Stanford, 1970).

S–325   SIMON, JOAN: *Education and Society in Tudor England* (Cambridge, 1966).

S–326   SMITH, S. R.: 'Religion and the Conception of Youth in Seventeenth-Century England', *History of Childhood Quarterly*, II (1974–5), 493–516.

S–327   STARNES, D. T., and E. W. TALBERT: *Classical Myth and Legend in Renaissance Dictionaries* (Chapel Hill, 1955).

S–328   STONE, LAWRENCE: 'The Educational Revolution in England, 1560–1640', *Past and Present*, XXVIII (1964), 41–80.

S–329   STRAUSS, GERALD: *Luther's House of Learning: Indoctrination of the Young in the German Reformation* (Baltimore, 1978).

S–330   STRAUSS, GERALD, and LEWIS W. SPITZ: 'Reformation and Pedagogy: Educational Thought and Practice in the Lutheran Reformation', in §S–414: pp. 272–306.

S–331   SOLT, L. F.: 'Anti-Intellectualism in the Puritan Revolution', *Church History*, XXV (1956), 306–16.

S–332   TAYLOR, ARCHER: *Renaissance Guides to Books* (Berkeley, 1945).

S–333   VINCENT, W. A. L.: *The Grammar Schools: Their Continuing Tradition 1660–1714* (1969).

S–334   VINCENT, W. A. L.: *The State and School Education 1640–1660 in England and Wales* (1950).

S–335   VOSE, G. N.: 'Milton's *Tractate*: An Attempt at Re-assessment', *History of Education Quarterly*, I (1961), 217–36.

S–336   WATSON, FOSTER: *The English Grammar Schools to 1660* (Cambridge, 1908).

S–337   WEBSTER, CHARLES: 'William Dell and the Idea of a University', in *Changing Perspectives in the History of Science*, ed. M. Teich and R. Young (1973), pp. 110–26.

S–338   WEBSTER, CHARLES (ed.): *Samuel Hartlib and the Advancement of Learning* (Cambridge, 1970).

S–339   WOODWARD, WILLIAM H.: *Studies in Education during the Age of the Renaissance, 1400—1600* (Cambridge, 1906, repr. 1967).

See also §§S–223, 260, 267, 277, 513, 577.

THE INTELLECTUAL AND PHILOSOPHICAL BACKGROUND

S–340   ALLEN, DON C.: *Doubt's Boundless Seas: Skepticism and Faith in the Renaissance* (Baltimore, 1964).

S–341   ALLEN, DON C.: *The Legend of Noah: Renaissance Rationalism in Art, Science, and Letters* (Urbana, 1949).

S–342   ALLEN, DON C.: *Mysteriously Meant: The Rediscovery of Pagan Symbolism and Allegorical Interpretation in the Renaissance* (Baltimore, 1970).

S–343   ANDERSON, FULTON H.: *The Philosophy of Francis Bacon* (Chicago, 1948).

S–344   BAKER, HERSCHEL: *The Dignity of Man* (Cambridge, Mass., 1947, repr. as *The Image of Man*, 1961), and *The Wars of Truth* (1952). Companion volumes on the climax and decay of Renaissance Christian humanism.

S–345   BLAU, JOSEPH L.: *The Christian Interpretation of the Cabala in the Renaissance* (1944).

S–346   BOLGAR, R. R.: *The Classical Heritage and its Beneficiaries* (Cambridge, 1954).

S–347   BREDVOLD, LOUIS I: *The Intellectual Milieu of John Dryden* (Ann Arbor, 1934).

S–348   BRÉHIER, EMILE: *The History of Philosophy: The Seventeenth Century*, trans. Wade Baskin (Chicago, 1966).

S–349   BROWN, KEITH (ed.): *Hobbes Studies* (Oxford, 1965).

S–350   BUCKLEY, GEORGE T.: *Atheism in the English Renaissance* (Chicago, 1932).

S–351   BUSH, DOUGLAS: *Prefaces to Renaissance Literature* (Cambridge, Mass., 1965). On classical influences on Renaissance literature, 'God and Nature', 'Time and Man', and 'The Isolation of the Renaissance Hero'.

S–352   BUSH, DOUGLAS: *The Renaissance and English Humanism* (Toronto, 1939).

S–353   CARRÉ, MEYRICK H.: 'The New Philosophy', in his *Phases of Thought in England* (Oxford, 1949), Ch. VII.

S–354   CASSIRER, ERNST: *The Individual and the Cosmos in Renaissance Philosophy*, trans. Mario Domandi (1963).

S–355   CASSIRER, ERNST: *The Platonic Renaissance in England*, trans. J. P. Pettegrove (1953).

S–356   CASSIRER, ERNST, with P. O. KRISTELLER and J. H. RANDALL (eds.): *The Renaissance Philosophy of Man* (Chicago, 1948).

S–357   COCHRANE, ERIC: *Florence in the Forgotten Centuries, 1527–1800* (Chicago, 1973).

S–358   CRAIG, HARDIN: *The Enchanted Glass: The Elizabethan Mind in English Literature* (1936); and its sequel, *New Lamps for Old* (1960).

S–359 CRUICKSHANK, JOHN (ed.): *French Literature and its Background*, Vol. II: *The Seventeenth Century* (Oxford, 1969).

S–360 CURRY, WALTER C.: *Milton's Ontology, Cosmology and Physics* (Lexington, 1957).

S–361 DRESDEN, SAMUEL: *Humanism in the Renaissance*, trans. Margaret King (1968).

S–362 EVANS, ROBERT J. W.: *Rudolf II and his World: A Study in Intellectual History, 1576–1612* (Oxford, 1973).

S–363 FERGUSON, WALLACE K.: *The Renaissance* (1940).

S–364 FERGUSON, WALLACE K., et al.: *The Renaissance* (1953).

S–365 GARIN, EUGENIO: *Italian Humanism*, trans. Peter Munz (1965).

S–366 GREENLEAF, W. H.: *Order, Empiricism and Politics* (Oxford, 1963).

S–367 HALE, J. R.: *England and the Italian Renaissance: The Growth of Interest in its History and Art*, rev. ed. (1963).

S–368 HARBISON, ELMORE H.: *The Christian Scholar in the Age of the Renaissance* (1956).

S–369 HARRIS, VICTOR: *All Coherence Gone* (Chicago, 1949). On the controversy over nature's decay.

S–370 HAYDN, HIRAM: *The Counter-Renaissance* (1950). On the period's 'radical anti-intellectual revolution'.

S–371 HENINGER, S. K., JR.: *The Cosmographical Glass: Renaissance Diagrams of the Universe* (San Marino, Calif., 1977).

S–372 HENINGER, S. K., JR.: *Touches of Sweet Harmony: Pythagorean Cosmology and Renaissance Poetics* (San Marino, Calif., 1974).

S–373 HOOPES, ROBERT: *Right Reason in the English Renaissance* (Cambridge, Mass., 1962).

S–374 HUGHES, MERRITT Y.: *Ten Perspectives on Milton* (New Haven, 1965). Backgrounds to Milton's thought.

S–375 HUNTER, WILLIAM B.: 'The Seventeenth Century Doctrine of Plastic Nature', *Harvard Theological Review*, XLIII (1950), 197–213.

S–376 HYMA, ALBERT: 'The Continental Origins of English Humanism', *Huntington Library Quarterly*, I (1940), 1–25. Largely a bibliographical study.

S–377 JAYNE, SEARS: 'Ficino and the Platonism of the English Renaissance', *Comparative Literature*, IV (1952), 214–38.

S–378 JONES, RICHARD F., et al., *The Seventeenth Century* (Stanford, 1951).

S–379 KEELING, S. V.: *Descartes* (1934).

S–380 KENNY, ANTHONY: *Descartes: A Study of his Philosophy* (1968).

S–381 KINSMAN, ROBERT S. (ed.): *The Darker Vision of the Renaissance: Beyond the Fields of Reason* (Berkeley, 1974).

S–382 KRISTELLER, PAUL O.: *Eight Philosophers of the Italian Renaissance* (Stanford, 1964).

S–383 KRISTELLER, PAUL O.: *Medieval Aspects of Renaissance Learning*, trans. Edward P. Mahoney (Durham, N.C., 1974).

S–384 KRISTELLER, PAUL O.: *Renaissance Thought: I* (1961) and *II* (1965).

S–385 KRISTELLER, PAUL O.: *Studies in Renaissance Thought and Letters* (Rome, 1956).

S–386 KRISTELLER, PAUL O., and PHILIP P. WIENER (eds.): *Renaissance Essays* (1968).

S–387 LAMPRECHT, S. P.: 'The Role of Descartes in Seventeenth-Century England', in *Studies in the History of Ideas* (1935), III, 181–240.

S–388 LOVEJOY, ARTHUR O.: *The Great Chain of Being: A Study in the History of an Idea* (Cambridge, Mass., 1936).

S–389 MAJOR, JOHN M.: *Sir Thomas Elyot and Renaissance Humanism* (Lincoln, 1964).

S–390 McNEILLY, F. S.: *The Anatomy of 'Leviathan'* (1968).

S–391 MEAGHER, JOHN C.: *Method and Meaning in Jonson's Masques* (Notre Dame, Ind., 1966).

S–392 MINTZ, SAMUEL I.: *The Hunting of Leviathan: Seventeenth-Century Reactions to the Materialism and Moral Philosophy of Thomas Hobbes* (Cambridge, 1962).

S–393 NICOLSON, MARJORIE H.: 'The Early Stages of Cartesianism in England', *Studies in Philology*, XXVI (1929), 356–74.

S–394 OBERMAN, HEIKO A., and T. A. BRADY (eds.): *Itinerarium Italicum: The Profile of the Italian Renaissance in the Mirror of its European Transformations* (Leiden, 1975).

S–395 PARTEE, CHARLES: *Calvin and Classical Philosophy* (Leiden, 1977).

S–396 PATRIDES, C. A.: 'Renaissance Thought on the Celestial Hierarchy', *Journal of the History of Ideas*, XX (1959), 155–66, and 'Hierarchy and Order', in *Dictionary of the History of Ideas*, ed. Philip P. Wiener (1973), II, 434–49.

S–397 PATRIDES, C. A. (ed.): *The Cambridge Platonists* (1969). With full bibliography.

S–398 POPKIN, RICHARD H.: *The History of Scepticism from Erasmus to Descartes* (Assen, 1960).

S–399 QUINONES, RICARDO J.: *The Renaissance Discovery of Time* (Cambridge, Mass., 1972).

S–400 RÉE, JONATHAN: *Descartes* (1974).

S–401 RICE, EUGENE F.: *The Renaissance Idea of Wisdom* (Cambridge, Mass., 1958).

S–402 ROBB, NESCA: *Neoplatonism of the Italian Renaissance* (1935).

S–403 ROSS, JAMES B., and MARY M. McLAUGHLIN (eds.): *The Portable Renaissance Reader* (1953).

S–404 RUSSELL, BERTRAND: *History of Western Philosophy* (1946), Part III, 'Modern Philosophy'.

S–405 SAUNDERS, JASON L.: *Justus Lipsius: The Philosophy of Renaissance Stoicism* (1955).

S–406 SCHOLEM, GERSHOM: *Major Trends in Jewish Mysticism*, 2nd rev. ed. (1961). Also *On the Kabbalah and its Symbolism*, trans. Ralph Manheim (1965).

S–407 SESSIONS, WILLIAM A. (ed.): *The Legacy of Francis Bacon*, in *Studies in the Literary Imagination*, IV (Atlanta, 1971).

S–408 SHUMAKER, WAYNE: *The Occult Sciences in the Renaissance* (Berkeley, 1972).

S–409 SPENCER, THEODORE: *Shakespeare and the Nature of Man* (Cambridge, Mass., 1942).

S–410 SPINK, J. S.: *French Free-Thought from Gassendi to Voltaire* (1960).

S–411 SPITZER, LEO: *Classical and Christian Ideas of World Harmony*, ed. A. G. Hatcher (Baltimore, 1963).

S–412 TILLYARD, E. M. W.: *The Elizabethan World Picture* (1943).

S–413 TRAPP, J. B. (Foreword by): *Background to the English Renaissance: Introductory Lectures* (1974).

S–414 TRINKAUS, CHARLES, and HEIKO A. OBERMAN (eds.): *The Pursuit of Holiness in Late Medieval and Renaissance Religion* (Leiden, 1974).

S–415 ULLMANN, WALTER: *Medieval Foundations of Renaissance Humanism* (Ithaca, N.Y., 1977).

S–416 VAN LEEUVEN, HENRY G.: *The Problem of Certainty in English Thought 1630–1690* (The Hague, 1963).

S–418 WALKER, D. P.: 'Orpheus the Theologian', in his *The Ancient Theology* (1972), Ch. I. A reliable study of Orphism.

S–419 WATKINS, J. W. N.: *Hobbes's System of Ideas* (1965).

S–420 WEISS, ROBERTO: *The Renaissance Discovery of Classical Antiquity* (Oxford, 1969).

S–421 WEISS, ROBERTO: *The Spread of Italian Humanism* (1964).

S–422 WERKMEISTER, WILLIAM H. (ed.): *Facets of the Renaissance* (Los Angeles, 1959).

S–423 WIENER, PHILIP P. (ed.): *Dictionary of the History of Ideas* (1973), 3 vols. A wide-ranging collection of authoritative studies.

S–424 WILEY, MARGARET L.: *The Subtle Knot: Creative Scepticism in Seventeenth Century England* (1952).

S–425 WILLEY, BASIL: *The Seventeenth Century Background: Studies in the Thought of the Age in Relation to Poetry and Religion* (1934).

S–426 WILLIAMSON, GEORGE: *Seventeenth Century Contexts* (1960). Includes 'Mutability,

Decay and Jacobean Melancholy', 'Milton and the Mortalist Heresy', 'The
Convention of "The Extasie" ', etc.

S–427 YATES, FRANCES A.: *Giordano Bruno and the Hermetic Tradition* (1964). The best
survey of Hermetic thought.

S–428 YATES, FRANCES A.: *The French Academies of the Sixteenth Century* (1947).

S–429 YATES, FRANCES A.: *The Rosicrucian Enlightenment* (1973).

See also §§S–55, 93, 147, 153, 699, 929.

THE RELIGIOUS AND THEOLOGICAL BACKGROUND

S–430 BALL, BRYAN W.: *A Great Expectation: Eschatological Thought in English Protestantism to 1660* (Leiden, 1975).

S–431 BEARDSLEE, JOHN W. (ed. and trans.): *Reformed Dogmatics* (1965). Extracts from
three treatises.

S–432 BLENCH, J. W.: *Preaching in England in the late Fifteenth and Sixteenth Centuries: A
Study of English Sermons 1450–c.1600* (1964).

S–433 BORNKAMM, HEINRICH: *Luther's World of Thought*, trans. M. H. Bertram (St Louis,
1958).

S–434 CHADWICK, OWEN: *The Reformation* (1964).

S–435 CHANDOS, JOHN (ed.): *In God's Name: Examples of Preaching in England 1534–1662*
(1971).

S–436 CHRISTIANSON, PAUL K.: *Reformers and Babylon: Apocalyptic Visions in England from
the Reformation to the Outbreak of the Civil War* (Toronto, 1977).

S–437 CLASEN, CLAUS-PETER: *Anabaptism: A Social History, 1525–1618* (Ithaca, N.Y.,
1972).

S–438A CLOHN, NORMAN: *The Pursuit of the Millennium: Revolutionary Messianism in
Medieval and Reformation Europe . . .* (1957; rev. ed., 1970).

S–438B CONKLIN, GEORGE N.: *Biblical Criticism and Heresy in Milton* (1949).

S–439 COOLIDGE, JOHN S.: *The Pauline Renaissance in England: Puritanism and the Bible*
(Oxford, 1970).

S–440 CRAGG, G. R.: *The Church and the Age of Reason, 1648–1789* (1962).

S–441 CRAGG, G. R.: *From Puritanism to the Age of Reason: A Study of Changes in Religious
Thought within the Church of England 1660 to 1700* (Cambridge, 1950).

S–442 DAICHES, DAVID: *The King James Version of the English Bible* (Chicago, 1941).

S–443 DANIEL-ROPS, HENRI: *The Church in the Seventeenth Century*, trans. J. J. Buckingham (1963).

S–444 DAVIES, HORTON: *Worship and Theology in England*, Vol. II: *From Andrewes to
Baxter and Fox, 1603–1690* (Princeton, 1975).

S–445 DICKENS, A. G.: *The Counter Reformation* (1968).

S–446 DICKENS, A. G.: *The English Reformation* (1964).

S–447 DICKENS, A. G.: *Reformation and Society in Sixteenth Century Europe* (1966).

S–448 DOBBINS, AUSTIN C.: *Milton and the Book of Revelation: The Heavenly Cycle*
(University, Ala., 1975).

S–449 EVANS, J. M.: *'Paradise Lost' and the Genesis Tradition* (Oxford, 1968).

S–450 EVENNETT, H. OUTRAM: *The Spirit of the Counter-Reformation* (Cambridge, 1968).

S–451 FRYE, ROLAND M.: *God, Man, and Satan: Patterns of Christian Thought and Life in
'Paradise Lost', 'Pilgrim's Progress', and the Great Theologians* (Princeton, 1960).

S–452 GREENSLADE, S. L. (ed.): *The Cambridge History of the Bible: The West from the
Reformation to the Present Day* (Cambridge, 1963). With bibliographies.

S–453 GRIMM, HAROLD J.: *The Reformation Era 1500–1650* (1954).

S–454 HARRISON, A. W.: *Arminianism* (1937).

S–455 HAVRAN, MARTIN J.: *The Catholics in Caroline England* (Stanford, 1962).

S–456 HEPBURN, R. W.: 'Godfrey Goodman: Nature Vilified', *Cambridge Journal*, VII (1954), 424–34, and 'George Hakewill: The Virility of Nature', *Journal of the History of Ideas*, XVI (1955), 135–50. On the protagonists of the controversy over nature's decay.

S–457 HEPPE, HEINRICH (ed.): *Reformed Dogmatics, set out and illustrated from the sources*, ed. Ernst Bizer, trans. G. T. Thomson (1950).

S–458 HILL, CHRISTOPHER: *Antichrist in Seventeenth-Century England* (1971).

S–459 HUGHES, PHILIP: *The Reformation in England* (1950–54), 3 vols. A study from the Catholic point of view.

S–460 HUNTER, WILLIAM B.: 'The Theological Context of Milton's *Christian Doctrine*', in §S–947: pp. 269–87.

S–461 HUNTER, WILLIAM B., and C. A. PATRIDES and J. H. ADAMSON: *Bright Essence: Studies in Milton's Theology* (Salt Lake City, 1971).

S–462 HURSTFIELD, JOEL (ed.): *The Reformation Crisis* (1965).

S–463 JONES, RUFUS M.: *Spiritual Reformers in the 16th and 17th Centuries* (1914).

S–464 KIDD, B. J. (ed.): *Documents illustrative of the Continental Reformation* (Oxford, 1911). Without translations.

S–465 KNOX, R. A.: *Enthusiasm: A Chapter in the History of Religion, with special reference to the 17th and 18th centuries* (Oxford, 1950). See also George Williamson, *Seventeenth Century Contexts* (1960), Ch. IX.

S–466 LAMONT, WILLIAM A.: *Godly Rule: Politics and Religion, 1603–60* (1969).

S–467 LÉONARD, EMILE G.: *A History of Protestantism*, ed. H. H. Rowley, trans. J. M. H. Reid (1965–66), 2 vols.

S–468 LEWIS, C. S.: *The Literary Impact of the Authorized Version* (1950); reprinted with other essays in *The Bible Read as Literature*, ed. Mary E. Reid (Cleveland, 1959).

S–469 McADOO, H. R.: *The Spirit of Anglicanism: A Survey of Anglican Theological Method in the Seventeenth Century* (1965).

S–470 McADOO, H. R.: *The Structure of Caroline Moral Theology* (1949).

S–471 MacCALLUM, HUGH R.: 'Milton and Figurative Interpretation of the Bible', *University of Toronto Quarterly*, XXXI (1962), 397–415.

S–472 MacLURE, MILLAR: *The Paul's Cross Sermons, 1534–1642* (Toronto, 1958).

S–473 McNEILL, JOHN T.: *The History and Character of Calvinism* (1954).

S–474 MATTHEWS, A. G. (ed.): *The Savoy Declaration of Faith and Order 1658* (1959).

S 475 MAYCOCK, A. L.: *Nicholas Ferrar of Little Gidding* (1938).

S–476 MILWARD, PETER: *Religious Controversies of the Jacobean Age: A Survey of Printed Sources* (Lincoln, 1978).

S–477 MITCHELL, W. FRASER: *English Pulpit Oratory from Andrewes to Tillotson: A Study of its Literary Aspects* (1932).

S–478 MORE, PAUL E., and FRANK L. CROSS (eds.): *Anglicanism: The Thought and Practice of the Church of England, illustrated from the religious literature of the 17th Century* (1935).

S–479 MURRAY, IAIN H.: *The Puritan Hope: A Study in Revival and the Interpretation of Prophecy* (1971).

S–480 MURRAY, IAIN H. (ed.): *The Reformation of the Church: A Collection of Reformed and Puritan Documents on Church Issues* (1965).

S–481 NUTTALL, GEOFFREY F.: *The Holy Spirit in Puritan Faith and Experience* (Oxford, 1946).

S–482 NUTTALL, GEOFFREY F.: *Visible Saints: The Congregational Way, 1640–1660* (Oxford, 1957).

S–483 O'CONNELL, MARVIN R.: *The Counter-Reformation, 1560–1610* (1974).

S–484 OZMENT, STEVEN E.: *Mysticism and Dissent: Religious Ideology and Social Unrest in the Sixteenth Century* (New Haven, 1973).

S–485 PARISH, JOHN E.: 'Robert Parsons and the English Counter-Reformation', *Rice University Studies*, LII (1966), §1.

S–486 PATRIDES, C. A.: *Milton and the Christian Tradition* (Oxford, 1966; repr. Hamden, Conn., 1979).

S–487 PATRIDES, C. A.: 'Renaissance and Modern Thought on the Last Things', *Harvard Theological Review*, LI (1958), 169–85.

S–488 PAUCK, WILHELM: *The Heritage of the Reformation*, rev. ed. (1961, 1968).

S–489 PETTIT, NORMAN: *The Heart Prepared: Grace and Conversion in Puritan Spiritual Life* (New Haven, 1966).

S–490 POLLARD, A. W. (ed.): *Records of the Bible: The Documents relating to the Translation and Publication of the Bible in English, 1525–1611* (1911).

S–491 POWICKE, F. M.: *The Reformation in England* (1941).

S–492 REEVES, MARJORIE: *The Influence of Prophecy in the Late Middle Ages: A Study of Joachimism* (Oxford, 1969).

S–493 ROBINSON, H. WHEELER (ed.): *The Bible in its Ancient and English Versions* (Oxford, 1940).

S–494 SCHAFF, PHILIP: *The History of the Creeds*, 2nd ed. (1877–78), 3 vols.

S–495 SLIGHTS, CAMILLE: 'Ingenious Piety: Anglican Casuistry of the Seventeenth Century', *Harvard Theological Review*, LXIII (1970), 409–32.

S–496 SPARROW, JOHN: 'John Donne and Contemporary Preachers', *Essays and Studies by members of the English Association*, XVI (1930), 144–78.

S–497 TAPPERT, THEODORE G. (ed. and trans.): *The Book of Concord: The Confessions of the Evangelical Lutheran Church* (Philadelphia, 1959).

S–498 THOMPSON, ELBERT N. S.: 'Mysticism in Seventeenth Century English Literature', *Studies in Philology*, XVIII (1921), 170–231.

S–499 TOON, PETER (ed.): *Puritans, the Millennium and the Future of Israel: Puritan Eschatology 1600 to 1660* (1970).

S–500 TORRANCE, THOMAS F. (ed. and trans.): *The School of Faith: The Catechisms of the Reformed Church* (1959).

S–501 TREVOR-ROPER, H. R.: *Archbishop Laud 1573–1645*, 2nd ed. (1962).

S–502 TULLOCH, JOHN: *Rational Theology and Christian Philosophy in England in the Seventeenth Century*, rev. ed. (Edinburgh, 1874, repr. 1965–6), 2 vols. Still very useful.

S–503 WALKER, D. P.: *The Decline of Hell: Seventeenth Century Discussions of Eternal Torment* (1964).

S–504 WATKINS, OWEN C.: *The Puritan Experience* (1972).

S–505 WENDEL, FRANÇOIS: *Calvin: The Origins and Development of his Religious Thought*, trans. P. Mairet (1963).

S–506 WEST, ROBERT H.: *The Invisible World: A Study of Pneumatology in Elizabethan Drama*, and *Milton and the Angels* (Athens, Ga., 1939 and 1955).

S–507 WHALE, J. S.: *The Protestant Tradition* (Cambridge, 1955).

S–508 WILLIAMS, ARNOLD: *The Common Expositor: An Account of the Commentaries on Genesis, 1527–1633* (Chapel Hill, 1948).

S–509 WILLIAMS, GEORGE H.: *The Radical Reformation* (Philadelphia, 1962).

S–510 WILLIAMS, GEORGE H., and ANGEL M. MERAL (eds.): *Spiritual and Anabaptist Writers: Documents illustrative of the Radical Reformation* (Philadelphia, 1957).

S–511 WOODHOUSE, H. F.: *The Doctrine of the Church in Anglican Theology 1547–1603* (1954). With a chapter on the period 1603–49.

See also §§S–14, 24, 32, 94, 99, 144, 147, 152, 324, 326, 355, 369, 373, 391, 553, 579, 894, 916, 923, 945, 948, 1001, 1004, 1008.

THE SCIENTIFIC BACKGROUND

S–512 ALLEN, DON C.: *The Star-Crossed Renaissance: The Quarrel about Astrology and its Influence in England* (Durham, N.C., 1941).

S–513 ALLEN, PHYLLIS: 'Medical Education in Seventeenth Century England', *Journal of the History of Medicine*, I (1946), 115–43.

S–514 ANDERSON, PAUL R.: *Science in Defense of Liberal Religion: A Study of Henry More's Attempt to link Seventeenth Century Religion and Science* (1933).

S–515 BAMBOROUGH, J. B.: *The Little World of Man* (1952). On Renaissance psychological theory.

S–516 BRIGGS, ROBIN: *The Scientific Revolution of the Seventeenth Century* (1969).

S–517 BURTT, EDWIN A.: *The Metaphysical Foundations of Modern Physical Science*, 2nd rev. ed. (1932).

S–518 BUSH, DOUGLAS: *Science and English Poetry 1590–1950* (1950). With two chapters on the Renaissance.

S–519 BUTTERFIELD, HERBERT: *The Origins of Modern Science 1300–1800*, new ed. (1957).

S–520 CIPOLLA, CARLO M.: *Public Health and the Medical Profession in the Renaissance* (Cambridge, 1976).

S–521 COFFIN, CHARLES M.: *John Donne and the New Philosophy* (1937).

S–522 CROMBIE, A. C.: *Augustine to Galileo: The History of Science, A.D. 400–1650*, 2nd ed. (1961).

S–523 DEBUS, ALLEN G.: *The Chemical Dream of the Renaissance*, 'Churchill College . . . Lecture Number Three' (Cambridge, 1968).

S–524 DEBUS, ALLEN G.: *The Chemical Philosophy: Paracelsian Science and Medicine in the Sixteenth and Seventeenth Centuries* (1977).

S–525 DEBUS, ALLEN G.: *The English Paracelsians* (1965).

S–526 DEBUS, ALLEN G.: *Man and Nature in the Renaissance* (Cambridge, 1978).

S–527 DEBUS, ALLEN G. (ed.): *Science, Medicine and Society in the Renaissance* (1972), 2 vols.

S–528 DIJKSTERHUIS, E. J.: *The Mechanization of the World Picture*, trans. C. Dikshoorn (Oxford, 1961).

S–529 DOBBS, BETTY J. T.: *The Foundations of Newton's Alchemy* (Cambridge, 1975).

S–530 DUNCAN, F. H.: 'The Natural History of Metals and Minerals in the Universe of Milton's *Paradise Lost*', *Osiris*, XI (1954), 386–421.

S–531 ELLRODT, ROBERT: 'Scientific Curiosity and Metaphysical Poetry in the Seventeenth Century', *Modern Philology*, LXI (1964), 180–97.

S–532 GILLESPIE, CHARLES C. (gen. ed.): *Dictionary of Scientific Biography* (1970–78), 15 vols.

S–533 GREAVES, RICHARD L.: 'Puritanism and Science: The Anatomy of a Controversy', *Journal of the History of Ideas*, XXX (1969), 345–68.

S–534 HALL, A. RUPERT: *From Galileo to Newton, 1630–1720* (1963).

S–535 HALL, A. RUPERT: *The Scientific Revolution 1500–1800: The Formation of the Modern Scientific Attiude*, 2nd ed. (1962).

S–536 HALL, A. RUPERT (ed.): *The Making of Modern Science* (Leicester, 1960).

S–537 [HALL], MARIE BOAS: *Robert Boyle and Seventeenth-Century Chemistry* (Cambridge, 1958).

S–538 [HALL], MARIE BOAS: 'The Establishment of the Mechanical Philosophy', *Osiris*, X (1959), 412–541.

S–539 HALL, MARIE BOAS: *The Scientific Renaissance 1450–1630* (1962).

S–540 HALL, MARIE BOAS (ed.): *Nature and Nature's Laws: Documents of the Scientific Revolution* (1970).

S–541 HARRÉ, R. (ed.): *Early Seventeenth-Century Scientists* (1965).

S–542 HARRISON, CHARLES T.: 'The Ancient Atomists and English Literature of the

Seventeenth Century', *Harvard Studies in Classical Philology*, XLV (1934), 1–79.

S–543 HARTLEY, SIR HAROLD (ed.): *The Royal Society: its Origins and Founders* (1960).

S–544 HENINGER, S. K., JR.: 'Tudor Literature of the Physical Sciences', *Huntington Library Quarterly*, XXXIII (1969), 101–33, 249–70.

S–545 HENREY, BLANCHE: *British Botanical and Horticultural Literature before 1800* (1975), 3 vols.

S–546 HOENINGER, F. D. and J. F. M.: *The Growth of Natural History in Stuart England* ('Folger Booklets on Tudor and Stuart Civilization', 1969).

S–547 JAMMER, MAX: *Concepts of Space: The History of Theories of Space in Physics* (Cambridge, Mass., 1954).

S–548 JOHNSON, FRANCIS R.: *Astronomical Thought in Renaissance England* (Baltimore, 1937).

S–549 JONES, RICHARD F.: *Ancients and Moderns: A Study of the Rise of the Scientific Movement in Seventeenth-Century England*, 2nd ed. (1961).

S–550 KARGON, ROBERT H.: *Atomism in England from Hariot to Newton* (Oxford, 1966).

S–551 KEARNEY, HUGH: *Origins of the Scientific Revolution* (1964).

S–552 KEARNEY, HUGH: *Science and Change, 1500–1700* (1971).

S–553 KOCHER, PAUL: *Science and Religion in Elizabethan England* (San Marino, Calif., 1953).

S–554 KOYRÉ, ALEXANDRE: *From the Closed World to the Infinite Universe* (Baltimore, 1957).

S–555 KUHN, THOMAS S.: *The Copernican Revolution: Planetary Astronomy in the Development of Western Thought* (Cambridge, Mass., 1957).

S–556 MERTON, EGON S.: *Science and Imagination in Sir Thomas Browne* (1949).

S–557 MERTON, R. K.: *Science, Technology and Society in Seventeenth-Century England* (1938, repr. 1970).

S–558 NICOLSON, MARJORIE H.: *Science and Imagination* (Ithaca, N.Y., 1956). On Milton, Donne, *et al.*

S–559 ORNSTEIN, MARTHA: *The Rôle of Scientific Societies in the Seventeenth Century*, 3rd ed. (Chicago, 1938).

S–560 PARKER, DEREK: *Familiar to All: William Lilly and Astrology in the Seventeenth Century* (1975).

S–561 RATTANSI, P. M.: 'Paracelsus and the Puritan Revolution', *Ambix*, XI (1963), 24–32.

S–562 RATTANSI, P. M.: 'The Social Interpretation of Science in the Seventeenth Century', in *Science and Society: 1600–1900*, ed. Peter Mathias (Cambridge, 1972), pp. 1–32.

S–563 RIGHINI BONELLI, M. L., and WILLIAM R. SHEA (eds.): *Reason, Experiment, and Mysticism in the Scientific Revolution* (1975).

S–564 RAVEN, CHARLES E.: *English Naturalists from Neckham to Ray* (Cambridge, 1947).

S–565 ROSE, PAUL L.: *The Italian Renaissance of Mathematics: Studies on Humanists and Mathematicians from Petrarch to Galileo* (Geneva, 1975).

S–566 SARTON, GEORGE: *Appreciation of Ancient and Medieval Science during the Renaissance, 1450–1600* (Philadelphia, 1955).

S–567 SARTON, GEORGE: *Six Wings: Men of Science in the Renaissance* (1957).

S–568 SHIRLEY, JOHN W. (ed.): *Thomas Harriot: Renaissance Scientist* (Oxford, 1974).

S–569 SMITH, A. G. R.: *Science and Society in the Sixteenth and Seventeenth Centuries* (1972).

S–570 STIMSON, DOROTHY: 'Puritanism and the New Philosophy in Seventeenth Century England', *Bulletin of the Institute of the History of Medicine*, III (1935), 321–34.

S–571 STIMSON, DOROTHY: *Scientists and Amateurs: A History of the Royal Society* (1948).

S–572 SVENDSEN, KESTER: *Milton and Science* (Cambridge, Mass., 1956).

S–573 TEMKIN, OWSEI: *Galenism: Rise and Decline of a Medical Philosophy* (Ithaca, N.Y., 1973).

S–574 THORNDIKE, LYNN: *A History of Magic and Experimental Science*, Vols. VII–VIII: *The Seventeenth Century* (1958).

S–575 THORNDIKE, LYNN: 'Newness and Craving for Novelty in Seventeenth-Century Science and Medicine', *Journal of the History of Ideas*, XII (1951), 584–98.

S–576 WATERS, DAVID W.: *The Art of Navigation in England in Elizabethan and Early Stuart Times* (1958).

S–577 WEBSTER, CHARLES: *The Great Instauration: Science, Medicine, and Reform, 1626–1660* (1976).

S–578 WESTFALL, RICHARD S.: *The Construction of Modern Science* (Cambridge, 1978).

S–579 WESTFALL, RICHARD S.: *Science and Religion in Seventeenth-Century England* (New Haven, 1958).

S–580 WESTMAN, ROBERT S. (ed.): *The Copernical Achievement* (Berkeley, 1975).

S–581 WHITEHEAD, ALFRED NORTH: 'The Century of Genius', in his *Science and the Modern World* (Cambridge, 1926), Ch. III.

S–582 WOLF, ABRAHAM: *A History of Science, Technology and Philosophy in the 16th and 17th Centuries*, 2nd rev. ed. (1950).

See also §§S–155, 343, 456, 786, 797, 857, 892.

MUSIC

S–583 ARKWRIGHT, G. E. P.: 'Six Anthems by John Milton; with a biographical memoir', *Old English Edition*, Vol. XXII (Oxford, 1900).

S–584 BLUME, FRIEDRICH: *Renaissance and Baroque Music: A Comprehensive Survey*, trans. M. D. Herter Norton (1967).

S–585 BOYD, M. C.: *Elizabethan Music and Musical Criticism* (Philadelphia, 1940).

S–586 BRIDGE, SIR FREDERICK: *Samuel Pepys, Lover of Musique* (1903).

S–587 BROWN, DAVID: *Thomas Weelkes* (1969).

S–588 BROWN, DAVID: *John Wilbye* (1974).

S–589 BROWN, HOWARD M.: *Music in the Renaissance* (Englewood Cliffs, N.J., 1976).

S–590 BUKOFZER, MANFRED F.: *Music in the Baroque Era from Monteverdi to Bach* (1947).

S–591 BUXTON, JOHN: *Elizabethan Taste* (1963).

S–592 CALDWELL, JOHN: *English Keyboard Music before the Nineteenth Century* (Oxford, 1973).

S–593 CARPENTER, NAN C.: *Music in the Medieval and Renaissance Universities* (Norman, Okla., 1958).

S–594 CUTTS, JOHN P.: *Seventeenth Century Songs and Lyrics* (1959).

S–595 DANIEL, R. T., and PETER LE HURAY: 'The Sources of English Church Music, 1549–1644', *Early English Church Music* (Supplement I, 1972).

S–596 DAVEY, HENRY: *History of Music in England* (1929, repr. 1969), Ch. V, VI, VII [vii].

S–597 DAY, C. L., and E. B. MURRIE: *English Song Books, 1651–1702* (1940, 1972).

S–598 DEMARAY, JOHN G.: *Milton and the Masque Tradition* (Cambridge, Mass., 1968).

S–599 DENT, EDWARD J.: *Foundations of English Opera: A Study of Musical Drama in England during the Seventeenth Century* (Cambridge, 1928).

S–600 DOUGHTIE, EDWARD (ed.): *Lyrics from English Airs, 1596–1622* (Cambridge, Mass., 1970).

S–601 DUCKLES, VINCENT (ed.): *Words to Music: Papers on Seventeenth-Century English Song* (Los Angeles, 1967).

S–602 EVANS, WILLA M.: *Ben Jonson and Elizabethan Music* (Lancaster, Pa., 1929).

S–603 EVANS, WILLA M.: *Henry Lawes: Musician and Friend of Poets* (1941).

S–604 FELLOWES, EDMUND H. (ed.): *English Madrigal Verse*, 3rd ed., revised by F. W. Sternfeld and David Greer (Oxford, 1967).

S–605 FINNEY, GRETCHEN L.: *Musical Backgrounds for English Literature, 1580–1650* (New Brunswick, N.J., 1962).

S–606 FOSS, MICHAEL: *The Age of Patronage in England, 1660–1750* (Ithaca, N.Y., 1971).

S–607 GARVIE, PETER (ed.): *Music and Western Man* (1958).

S–608 HARLEY, JOHN: *Music in Purcell's London: The Social Background* (1968).

S–609 HARMAN, ALEC, with ANTHONY MILNER: *Late Renaissance and Baroque Music*, being Part II of *Man and his Music* (1962; also published separately, 1969).

S–610 HOLLANDER, JOHN: *The Untuning of the Sky: Ideas of Music in English Poetry 1500–1700* (Princeton, 1961).

S–611 JENSEN, H. JAMES: *The Muses' Concord: Literature, Music, and the Visual Arts in the Baroque Age* (Bloomington, Ind., 1977).

S–612 JOHNSON, PAULA: *Form and Transformation in Music and Poetry in the English Renaissance* (New Haven, 1972).

S–613 KERMAN, JOSEPH: *The Elizabethan Madrigal* (1962).

S–614 LAFONTAINE, H. C. de: *The King's Musick* (1909, repr. 1973).

S–615 LEFKOWITZ, MURRAY: *William Lawes* (1960).

S–616 LE HURAY, PETER: *Music and the Reformation in England* (1967, repr. Cambridge, 1978).

S–617 LONG, JOHN H. (ed.): *Music in English Renaissance Drama* (Lexington, 1968).

S–618 LONG, JOHN H. (ed.): *Shakespeare's Use of Music: The Histories and the Tragedies*, I–III (1955, 1961, and 1971).

S–619 LONG, KENNETH R.: *The Music of the English Church* (1972).

S–620 LOWINSKY, EDWARD F.: 'Music in the Culture of the Renaissance', in §S–386: Ch. XIV.

S–621 LOWINSKY, EDWARD F.: 'Music of the Renaissance as Viewed by Renaissance Musicians', in *The Renaissance Image of Man and the World*, ed. B. O'Kelly (Columbus, 1966).

S–622 MacCLINTOCK, CAROL C.: *The Solo Song, 1580–1730* (1973).

S–623 MACKERNESS, E. D.: *A Social History of English Music* (1964).

S–624 McGUINESS, ROSAMOND: *English Court Odes, 1660–1820* (Oxford, 1971).

S–625 MELLERS, WILFRID: *Harmonious Meeting: A Study of the Relationship between English Music, Poetry and Theatre, c. 1600–1900* (1965).

S–626 MEYER, ERNST: *English Chamber Music* (1946).

S–627 MEYER-BAER, KATHI: *Music of the Spheres and the Dance of Death: Studies in Musical Iconology* (Princeton, 1970).

S–628 MOORE, ROBERT E.: *Henry Purcell and the Restoration Theatre* (1961).

S–629 MONTAGU, JEREMY: *The World of Medieval and Renaissance Musical Instruments* (Newton Abbot, 1976).

S–630 NAYLOR, EDWARD W.: *Shakespeare and Music: with illustrations from the music of the 16th and 17th centuries* (1931, repr. 1973).

S–631 *New Oxford History of Music*, Vol. IV (1968), Ch. IX, XI, XII, XIII, XIV; and Vol. V (1975), Ch. V and VIII.

S–632 PALISCA, CLAUDE V.: *Baroque Music* (Englewood Cliffs, N.J., 1968).

S–633 PATTISON, BRUCE: *Music and Poetry of the English Renaissance* (1948).

S–634 POULTON, DIANA: *John Dowland* (1972).

S–635 REDLICH, HANS F.: *Claudio Monteverdi: Life and Works* (1952).

S–636 REESE, GUSTAVE: *Music in the Renaissance*, rev. ed. (1959).

S–637 RIMBAULT, EDWARD F. (ed.): 'The Cheque Book of the Chapel Royal', *Camden Society*, III (1872, repr. 1966).

S–638   ROBERTSON, ALEC, and DENIS STEVENS (eds.): *Renaissance and Baroque*, being Vol. II of *The Pelican History of Music* (1963).

S–639   ROLLINS, HYDER F. (ed.): *A Pepysian Garland: Black-Letter Broadside Ballads of the Years 1595–1639* (Cambridge, Mass., 1971).

S–640   ROLLINS, HYDER F. (ed.): *Old English Ballads, 1553–1625* (1920).

S–641   SABOL, ANDREW J. (ed.): *Songs and Dances for the Stuart Masque* (Providence, R.I., 1959). Also see his *Four Hundred Songs and Dances from the Stuart Masque* (Providence, R.I., 1978).

S–642   SCHOLES, PERCY A.: *The Puritans and Music in England and New England* (Oxford, 1934; repr. 1969).

S–643   SENG, PETER J.: *The Vocal Songs in the Plays of Shakespeare* (Cambridge, Mass., 1967).

S–644   SHIRE, HELEN MENNIE: *Song, Dance and Poetry of the Court of Scotland under King James VI*, ed. K. Elliott (Cambridge, 1969).

S–645   SIMPSON, CLAUDE M.: *The British Broadside Ballad and its Music* (New Brunswick, N.J., 1966).

S–646   SPAETH, SIGMUND G.: *Milton's Knowledge of Music* (Princeton, 1913: repr. 1963).

S–647   SPINK, IAN: *English Song: Dowland to Purcell* (1974).

S–648   STEELE, ROBERT: 'The Earliest English Music Printing', *Bibliographical Society* (1903).

S–649   STERNFELD, F. W.: *Music in Shakespearean Tragedy* (1963).

S–650   STEVENS, DENIS: *Thomas Tomkins* (1957; repr. 1967).

S–651   STRUNK, OLIVER (ed.): *Source Readings in Music History: The Renaissance* (1950).

S–652   THORP, WILLARD (ed.): *Songs from the Restoration Theater* (Princeton, 1934).

S–653   WALKER, D. P.: 'Musical Humanism in the 16th and early 17th Centuries', *Music Review*, II (1941), 1–13, 111–21, 220–7, 288–308, and III (1942), 55–71.

S–654   WILSON, JOHN (ed.): *Roger North on Music* (1959).

S–655   WOODFILL, WALTER L.: *Musicians in English Society from Elizabeth to Charles I* (Princeton, 1953).

S–656   ZIMMERMAN, F. B.: *Henry Purcell, 1659–1695* (1967).

See also §§S–173, 411, 425, 665, 797.

Currently accessible editions of music: a wide spectrum of English music, both instrumental and vocal, is published by the Royal Musical Association in the series *Musica Britannica*. Offprints are available of items in many of the volumes. The following volumes are most directly relevant to the present study: §2, Cupid and Death (Locke and Gibbons); §5, Keyboard Music (Tomkins); §6, Ayres (Dowland); §9, Jacobean Consort Music; §§14 and 19, Keyboard Music (Bull); §15, Music of Scotland, 1500–1700; §20, Keyboard Music (Gibbons); §21, Consort Music (William Lawes); §22, Consort Songs (c. 1560–1640); §23, Anthems (Weelkes); §25, Secular Vocal Music (Dering); §26, Consort Music (Jenkins); §§27 and 28, Keyboard Music (Byrd); §§31 and 32, Chamber Music (Locke); §33, English Songs, 1625–1660; §34, Church Music (Pelham Humfrey); and §37, Motets and Anthems (Locke).

Church music is best secured through the Oxford University Press Octavo Series *Tudor Church Music*; through the publications of the Church Music Society; and through the *Early English Church Music* series, in course of publication by the British Academy. The entire English repertory of madrigals is published by Stainer and Bell in the *English Madrigalists* Series; the same firm also publishes the entire corpus of English lute song (also available in facsimile from the Scolar Press).

THE FINE ARTS

S–657   ACKERMAN, G. M.: 'Lomazzo's Treatise on Painting', *Art Bulletin*, XLIX (1967), 317–26.

S–658   ACKERMAN, JAMES S.: *The Architecture of Michelangelo* (Harmondsworth, 1970).

S–659   ACKERMAN, JAMES S.: *Palladio* (Harmondsworth, 1966).

S–660   ADDLESHAW, G. W. C., and FREDERICK ETCHELLS: *The Architectural Setting of Anglican Worship* (1948).

S–661   AIRS, MALCOLM: *The Making of the English Country House, 1500–1640* (1975).

S–662   ALPERS, SVETLANA: 'Manner and Meaning in some Rubens Mythologies', *Journal of the Warburg and Courtauld Institutes*, XXX (1967), 272–95.

S–663   ALPERS, SVETLANA: 'Ekphrasis and Aesthetic Attitudes in Vasari's *Lives*', *ibid.*, XXIII (1960), 190–215.

S–664   ARTHOS, JOHN: *Dante, Michelangelo and Milton* (1963).

S–665   ARTZ, FREDERICK B.: *From the Renaissance to Romanticism: Trends in Style in Art, Literature, and Music, 1300–1800* (Chicago, 1962).

S–666   BAKER, C. H. COLLINS, and W. G. CONSTABLE: *English Painting of the Sixteenth and Seventeenth Centuries* (Florence, 1930).

S–667   BAXANDALL, MICHAEL: *Giotto and the Orators: Humanist Observers of Painting in Italy and the Discovery of Pictorial Composition 1350–1450* (Oxford, 1971).

S–668   BAXANDALL, MICHAEL: *Painting and Experience in Fifteenth Century Italy* (Oxford, 1972).

S–669   BAZIN, GERMAINE: *The Baroque: Principles, Styles, Modes, Themes* (1968).

S–670   BENESCH, OTTO: *The Art of the Renaissance in Northern Europe*, rev. ed. (1965).

S–671   BENEVOLO, LEONARDO: *The Architecture of the Renaissance*, trans. Judith Landry (1977).

S–672   BERNT, WALTHER: *The Netherlandish Painters of the Seventeenth Century*, rev. ed. (1965).

S–673   BERTONASCO, MARC F.: *Crashaw and the Baroque* (University, Ala., 1971).

S–674   BIALOSTOCKI, JAN: *Art of the Renaissance in Eastern Europe: Hungary, Bohemia and Poland* (1976).

S–675   BIEBER, MARGARET: *Laocoön: The Influence of the Group since its Rediscovery* (1942).

S–676   BLUNT, ANTHONY: *Art and Architecture in France, 1500–1700* (Baltimore, 1957).

S–677   BLUNT, ANTHONY: *Artistic Theory in Italy, 1450–1600* (Oxford, 1940).

S–678   BLUNT, ANTHONY: *Nicholas Poussin* (1967), 2 vols.

S–679   BLUNT, ANTHONY: *Philibert de l'Orme* (1958).

S–680   BRUMMER, H. H.: *The Statue Court of the Vatican Belvedere* (Stockholm, 1970).

S–681   BURCKHARDT, JACOB: *The Civilization of the Renaissance*, trans. S. G. C. Middlemore (1904; frequently repr.).

S–682   BURCKHARDT, JACOB: *Recollections of Rubens*, ed. H. Gerson (1950).

S–683   BURNS, HOWARD: *Andrea Palladio 1508–1580: The Portico and the Farmyard* (1975).

S–684   BUXTON, JOHN: *Elizabethan Taste* (1963).

S–685   CHASTEL, ANDRÈ: *The Age of Humanism*, trans. K. M. Delavenay and E. M. Gruyer (1963).

S–686   CHASTEL, ANDRÈ: *The Crisis of the Renaissance, 1520–1600*, trans. Peter Price (Geneva, 1968).

S–687   CHASTEL, ANDRÈ: *The Flowering of the Italian Renaissance*, trans. Jonathan Friffin (1965).

S–688   CLARK, KENNETH: *Landscape into Art* (1949).

S–689   CLARK, KENNETH: *The Nude* (1956).

S–690   CLEMENTS, R. J.: *Michelangelo's Theory of Art* (Zurich, 1961).

S–691   CLEMENTS, R. J.: *Picta Poesis: Literary and Humanistic Theory in Renaissance Emblem Books* (Rome, 1960).

S–692   COFFIN, DAVID R. (ed.): *The Italian Garden* (Washington, D.C., 1972).

S–693   COMITO, TERRY: *The Idea of the Garden in the Renaissance* (New Brunswick, N.J., 1978).

S–694   CONWAY, WILLIAM M.: *Literary Remains of Albrecth Dürer* (Cambridge, 1899).

S–695   CUST, L.: *Anthony van Dyck: An Historical Study of his Life and Work* (1914).

S–696   DANIELLS, ROY: *Milton, Mannerism and Baroque* (Toronto, 1963).

S–697   DEMARAY, JOHN G.: *Milton and the Masque Tradition* (Cambridge, Mass., 1968).

S–698   DICKINSON, G.: *DuBellay in Rome* (Leiden, 1960).

S–699   DIECKMANN, LISELOTTE: *Hieroglyphics: The History of a Literary Symbol* (St Louis, 1970).

S–700   EDGERTON, SAMUEL Y., JR.: *The Renaissance Discovery of Linear Perspective* (1975).

S–701   EINSTEIN, LEWIS: *Italian Renaissance in England* (1962).

S–702   ELLENIUS, ALLAN: *De Arte Pingendi: Latin Art Literature in Seventeenth Century Sweden* (Uppsala, 1960).

S–703   ETTLINGER, LEO: 'Exemplum doloris: Reflections on the Laocoön Group', in *De Artibus Opuscula XL. Essays in Honour of Erwin Panofsky* (1961), pp. 121–6.

S–704   EYLER, ELLEN C.: *Early English Gardens and Garden Books* (Ithaca, N.Y., 1963).

S–705   FEHL, PHILIPP P.: *The Classical Monument: Reflections on the Connection between Morality and Art in Greek and Roman Sculpture* (1972).

S–706   FEHL, PHILIPP P.: 'On the Representation of Character in Renaissance Sculpture', *Journal of Aesthetics and Art Criticism*, XXXI (1973), 291–307.

S–707   FREEDBERG, S. J.: *Painting in Italy, 1500–1600* (1971).

S–708   FRIEDLÄNDER, MAX J.: *From Van Eyck to Bruegel*, 3rd ed. (1969), 2 vols.

S–709   FRYE, ROLAND M.: *Milton's Imagery and the Visual Arts* (Princeton, 1978).

S–710   GANZ, PAUL: *The Paintings of Hans Holbein*, trans. R. H. Boothroyd (1950).

S–711   GERSON, HORST, and E. H. ter KUILE: *Art and Architecture in Belgium, 1600–1800* (Harmondsworth, 1960).

S–712   GOMBRICH, E. H.: *Art and Illusion: A Study in the Psychology of Pictorial Imagination* (1962).

S–713   GOMBRICH, E. H.: *Studies in the Art of the Renaissance—Norm and Form* (1966); *Symbolic Images* (1972); and *The Heritage of Apelles* (1976).

S–714   GOMBRICH, E. H.: 'The Subject of Poussin's Orion', *Burlington Magazine*, LXXXIV (1944), 37–41.

S–715   GORDON, D. J.: *The Renaissance Imagination: Essays and Lectures*, ed. Stephen Orgel (Berkeley, 1975).

S–716   GREENHALGH, M.: *The Classical Tradition in Art* (1978).

S–717   HAGSTRUM, JEAN M.: *The Sister Arts* (Chicago, 1958).

S–718   HALE, J. R.: *England and the Italian Renaissance: The Growth of Interest in its History and Art* (1954).

S–719   HALE, J. R.: *Italian Renaissance Painting from Masaccio to Titian* (Oxford, 1977).

S–720   HARRIS, JOHN, and STEPHEN ORGEL and ROY STRONG: *The King's Arcadia: Inigo Jones and the Stuart Court*, Exhibition Catalogue, Arts Council of Britain (1973).

S–721   HASKELL, FRANCIS: *Patrons and Painters: A Study of the Relations between Italian Art and Society in the Age of the Baroque* (1963).

S–722   HAUSER, ARNOLD: *Mannerism: The Crisis of the Renaissance and the Origin of Modern Art* (1965), 2 vols.

S–723   HELD, JULIUS, and DONALD POSNER: *Seventeenth and Eighteenth Century Art* (1971).

S–724   HEMPEL, EVERHARD: *Baroque Art and Architecture in Central Europe* (Harmondsworth, 1965).

S–725   HERMANN, FRANK: *The English as Collectors: A Documentary Crestomathy* (1972).

S–726   HERVEY, MARY F.: *The Life, Correspondence and Collections of Thomas Howard, Earl of Arundel, 'Father of Vertu in England'* (Cambridge, 1921).

S–727   HEYDENREICH, L. H., and WOLFGANG LOTZ: *Architecture in Italy, 1400–1600* (Harmondsworth, 1974).

S–728 HIBBARD, G. R.: 'The Country House Poem in the Seventeenth Century', *Journal of the Warburg and Courtauld Institutes*, XIX (1956), 159–74.

S–729 HIBBARD, HOWARD: *Michelangelo* (1975).

S–730 HOLT, ELIZABETH G. (ed.): *Documentary History of Art* (1957), 2 vols.

S–731 HOOK, JUDITH: *The Baroque Age in England* (1976).

S–732 HUNT, JOHN D.: ' "Loose Nature" and the "Garden Square": The Gardenist Background for Marvell's Poetry', in §S–962: pp. 331–51.

S–733 HUNT, JOHN D., and PETER WILLIS (eds.): *The Genius of the Place: The English Landscape Garden, 1620–1820* (1975).

S–734 KENNEDY, RUTH W.: *Novelty and Tradition in Titian's Art* (Northampton, Mass., 1963).

S–735 KEYNES, GEOFFREY: *John Evelyn* (1937).

S–736 KLIBANSKY, R., and F. SAXL and E. PANOFSKY: *Saturn and Melancholy* (1964).

S–737 KRISTELLER, PAUL O.: 'The Modern System of the Arts: A Study in the History of Aesthetics', in *Ideas in Cultural Perspective*, ed. Philip P. Wiener (New Brunswick, N.J., 1962), pp. 145–206.

S–738 LECOAT, GEARD: *The Rhetoric of the Arts, 1550–1650* (Bern and Brankfurt, 1975).

S–739 LEE, RENSSELAER W.: *Ut Pictura Poesis: The Humanistic Theory of Painting* (1967).

S–740 LEES-MILNE, JAMES: *The Age of Inigo Jones* (1953).

S–741 LEES-MILNE, JAMES: *Baroque in Italy* (1959).

S–742 LEVEY, MICHAEL: *Early Renaissance* (1967) and *High Renaissance* (1975).

S–743 LEVEY, MICHAEL: *Painting at Court* (1971).

S–744 LOWRY, BATES: 'Notes on the *Speculum Romanae Magnificentiae* and Related Publications', *Art Bulletin*, XXXIV (1952), 46–50.

S–745 LOWRY, BATES: *Renaissance Architecture* (1962).

S–746 LYNCH, J. B.: 'Lomazzo's Allegory of Painting', *Gazette des Beaux Arts*, CX (1968), i, 325–9.

S–747 MACDOUGALL, ELIZABETH B., and F. H. HAZLEHURST (eds.): *The French Formal Gardens* (Washington, D.C., 1974).

S–748 MAHON, D.: *Studies in Seicento Art and Theory* (1947).

S–749 MANDER, CAREL VAN: *Dutch and Flemish Painters*, trans. C. van de Wall (1936).

S–750 MASSON, GEORGINA: *Italian Gardens* (1961).

S–751 MAUGHAM, H. NEVILLE: *The Book of Italian Travel, 1580–1900* (1903).

S–752 MCCLUNG, WILLIAM A.: *The English Country House in Renaissance Poetry* (Berkeley, 1977).

S–753 MEISS, MILLARD, *et al.* (ed.): 'Recent Concepts of Mannerism', in *Renaissance and Mannerism: Studies in Western Art*, Acts of the 20th International Congress of the History of Art, Vol. II (Princeton, 1963).

S–754 MERCER, ERIC: *English Art, 1553–1625* (Oxford, 1962).

S–755 MERRIFIELD, MARY P.: *Original Treatises, dating from the 12th–18th Centuries on the Arts of Painting* (1849).

S–756 MILLAR, OLIVER: *The Age of Charles I: Painting in England 1620–1649* (1972).

S–757 MILLAR, OLIVER: *Rubens: The Whitehall Ceiling* (1958).

S–758 MILLON, HENRY A.: *Baroque and Rococo Architecture* (1961).

S–759 MITCHELL, CHARLES: 'Archaeology and Romance in Renaissance Italy', in *Italian Renaissance Studies*, ed. E. F. Jacob (1960), pp. 455–83.

S–760 MURRAY, LINDA: *The High Renaissance* (1967) and *High Renaissance and Mannerism* (1977).

S–761 MURRAY, PETER: *Architecture of the Italian Renaissance* (1963).

S–762 MURRAY, PETER and LINDA: *The Art of the Renaissance* (1963).

S–763 NASH, J. M. (ed.): *The Age of Rembrandt and Vermeer* (1972).

S–764 NORBERG-SCHULZ, CHRISTIAN: *Baroque Architecture* (1972) and *Late Baroque and*

Rococo Architecture (1974).

S–765 OGDEN, H. V. S. and M. S.: 'A Bibliography of Seventeenth-Century Writings on the Pictorial Arts in English', *Art Bulletin*, XXIX (1947), 196–201.

S–766 OGDEN, H. V. S. and M. S.: *English Taste in Landscape in the Seventeenth Century* (Ann Arbor, 1955).

S–767 ORGEL, STEPHEN: *The Jonsonian Masque* (Cambridge, Mass., 1965).

S–768 PALME, PER: *Triumph of Peace: A Study of the Whitehall Banqueting House* (Stockholm, 1956).

S–769 PALME, PER: 'Ut architectura poesis', in *Idea and Form*, Acta Universitatis Upsaliensis: Figura Nova series, I (Stockholm, 1959), 95–107.

S–770 PARKS, GEORGE B.: *The English Traveller to Italy* (Rome, 1954).

S–771 PANOFSKY, ERWIN: *Galileo as a Critic of the Arts* (The Hague, 1954).

S–722 PANOFSKY, ERWIN: *Idea: A concept in Art Theory*, trans. Joseph Peake (Columbia, S.C., 1968).

S–773 PANOFSKY, ERWIN: *The Life and Art of Albrecht Dürer* (Princeton, 1955).

S–774 PANOFSKY, ERWIN: *Renaissance and Renascences in Western Art* (Stockholm, 1960; repr. 1970), 2 vols.

S–775 PANOFSKY, ERWIN: *Studies in Iconology: Humanistic Themes in the Art of the Renaissance* (1939).

S–776 PETERSSON, ROBERT T.: *The Art of Ecstasy: Teresa, Bernini and Crashaw* (1970).

S–777 PEVSNER, NIKOLAUS: *Academies of Art: Past and Present* (Cambridge, 1940).

S–778 PEVSNER, NIKOLAUS: 'The Architecture of Mannerism', in *The Mint*, ed. Geoffrey Grigson (1946); 'Renaissance and Mannerism', in his *Outline of European Architecture*, 6th ed. (1960); and 'Mannerism and Elizabethan Architecture', *The Listener*, 27 February, 5 and 19 March, 1964.

S–779 PHILLIPS, JOHN: *The Reformation of Images: Destruction of Art in England, 1535–1660* (Berkeley, 1973).

S–780 PINE-COFFIN, R. S.: *Bibliography of British and American Travel in Italy to 1860* (Florence, 1974).

S–781 POPE-HENNESSY, JOHN: *An Introduction to Italian Sculpture*, Part II: *Italian Renaissance Sculpture* (1958), and Part III: *Italian High Renaissance and Baroque Sculpture*, 2nd ed. (1970).

S–782 POPE-HENNESSY, JOHN: *Raphael* (1970).

S–783 PORTOGHESI, PAOLO: *Rome of the Renaissance*, trans. Pearl Sanders (1972).

S–784 PRAZ, MARIO: 'Baroque in England', *Modern Philology*, LXI (1964), 169–79.

S–785 PUPPI, LIONELLO: *Andrea Palladio*, trans. Pearl Sanders (1975).

S–786 RHYS, HEADLEY H. (ed.): *Seventeenth Century Science and the Arts* (Princeton, 1961).

S–787 RICHARDSON, JOHNATHAN: *An Essay on the Theory of Painting* (1715).

S–788 ROBINSON, FRANKLIN W., and STEPHEN G, NICHOLS, JR. (eds.): *The Meaning of Mannerism* (Hanover, N.H., 1972).

S–789 ROSENBERG, JACOB: *Rembrandt: Life and Work*, 3rd ed. (1968).

S–790 ROSENBERG, JACOB, and SEYMOUR SLIVE and E. H. ter KUILE: *Dutch Art and Architecture, 1600–1800* (Harmondsworth, 1966).

S–791 ROSKILL, MARK W.: *Dolce's 'Aretino' and Venetian Art Theory of the Cinquecento* (1968).

S–792 SALERNO, LUIGI: 'Seventeenth Century English Literature on Painting', *Journal of the Warburg and Courtauld Institutes*, XIV (1951), 234–58.

S–793 SAXL, FRITZ: *Lectures* (1957).

S–794 SAXL, FRITZ, and RUDOLF WITTKOWER: *British Art and the Mediterranean* (1948).

S–795 SCOTT, GEOFFREY: *The Architecture of Humanism* (1954).

S–796 SEZNEC, JEAN: *The Survival of the Pagan Gods: The Mythological Tradition and its*

       Place in Renaissance Humanism and Art, trans. B. F. Sessions (1953).

S–797   SINGLETON, CHARLES S. (ed.): *Art, Science, and History in the Renaissance* (Baltimore, 1967).

S–798   SLIVE, SEYMOUR: *Rembrandt and his Critics* (The Hague, 1953).

S–799   SMART, ALASTAIR: *The Renaissance and Mannerism in Italy* (1972) and *The Renaissance and Mannerism outside Italy* (1972).

S–800   SMITH, LOGAN P.: *The Life and Letters of Henry Wotton* (Oxford, 1966).

S–801   SPENCER, JOHN R.: 'Ut rhetorica pictura', *Journal of the Warburg and Courtauld Institutes*, XX (1957), 26–44.

S–802   SPRINGELL, FRANCIS D.: *Connoisseur and Diplomat* (1963).

S–803   STECHOW, WOLFGANG: *Rubens and the Classical Tradition* (Cambridge, Mass., 1968).

S–804   STEINBERG, LEO: *Michelangelo's Last Paintings: The Conversion of St. Paul and the Crucifixion of St. Peter in the Capella Paolina, Vatican Palace* (1975).

S–805   STEWART, STANLEY: *The Enclosed Garden: The Tradition and the Image in Seventeenth Century Poetry* (Madison, 1966).

S–806   STRONG, ROY: *The English Icon: Elizabethan and Jacobean Portraiture* (1969), and *The Cult of Elizabeth* (1977). Also his collections of *Portraits of Queen Elizabeth I* (Oxford, 1963) and *Tudor and Jacobean Portraits* (1969), 3 vols.

S–807   SUMMERSON, JOHN: *Architecture in Britain, 1530–1830*, 4th rev. ed. (1963).

S–808   SUMMERSON, JOHN: *The Classical Language of Architecture* (1964).

S–809   SUMMERSON, JOHN: *Inigo Jones* (Harmondsworth, 1966).

S–810   SYPHER, WYLIE: *Four Stages of Renaissance Style: Transformations in Art and Literature, 1400–1700* (1955).

S–811   TAPIÉ, VICTOR-L.: *The Age of Grandeur: Baroque Art and Architecture*, trans. A. R. Williamson (1960).

S–812   TRAPP, J. B.: 'The Iconography of the Fall of Man', in *Approaches to 'Paradise Lost'*, ed. C.A. Patrides (1968), pp. 223–65.

S–813   TURNER, A. R.: *The Vision of Landscape in Renaissance Italy* (Princeton, 1966).

S–814   WARREN, AUSTIN: *Richard Crashaw: A Study in Baroque Sensibility* (Ann Arbor, 1939).

S–815   WATERHOUSE, ELLIS K.: *Italian Baroque Painting*, 2nd ed. (1969).

S–816   WATERHOUSE, ELLIS K.: *Painting in Britain, 1530–1790* (1953).

S–817   WEISS, ROBERTO: *The Renaissance Discovery of Classical Antiquity* (1969).

S–818   WELLEK, RENÉ, et al.: ten studies on the baroque, in *Journal of Aesthetics and Art Criticism*, V (1946), 77–128; XII (1954), 421–37; XIV (1955), 152–74; and XIX (1961), 275–87. One of these ('The Concept of Baroque in Literary Criticism') is reprinted in *Concepts of Criticism*, ed. Stephen J. Nichols, Jr. (New Haven, 1963), pp. 69–127.

S–819   WELSFORD, ENID: *The Court Masque: A Study in the Relationship between Poetry and the Revels* (1927).

S–820   WHIFFEN, MARCUS: *An Introduction to Elizabethan and Jacobean Architecture* (1952).

S–821   WHINNEY, MARGARET: *Sculpture in Britain, 1530–1830* (Baltimore, 1964).

S–822   WHINNEY, MARGARET, and OLIVER MILLAR: *English Art 1625–1714* (Oxford, 1957).

S–823   WHITE, JOHN: *The Birth and Rebirth of Pictorial Space* (1957).

S–824   WIESNER, HERBERT: *Master Painters of Holland: Dutch Painting in the Seventeenth Century* (1976).

S–825   WIND, EDGAR: *Pagan Mysteries in the Renaissance*, rev. ed. (1968).

S–826   WITTKOWER, RUDOLF: *Architectural Principles in the Age of Humanism*, 2nd ed. (1952).

S–827   WITTKOWER, RUDOLF: *Art and Architecture in Italy, 1600–1750* (Harmondsworth,

1958).
S–828 WITTKOWER, RUDOLF: *The Artist and the Liberal Arts* (1952).
S–829 WITTKOWER, RUDOLF: *Gian Lorenzo Bernini: The Sculptor of the Roman Baroque*, 2nd ed. (1966).
S–830 WITTKOWER, RUDOLF: *Gothic vs. Classic: Architectural Projects in Seventeenth Century Italy* (1974).
S–831 WITTKOWER, RUDOLF: 'Inigo Jones, Architect and Man of Letters', *Journal of the Royal Institute of British Architects*, LX (1953), 83–90.
S–832 WITTKOWER, RUDOLF: *Palladio and English Palladianism* (1974).
S–833 WITTKOWER, RUDOLF and MARGOT: *Born under Saturn: The Character and Conduct of Artists* (1963).
S–834 WÖLFFLIN, HEINRICH: *Classic Art: An Introduction to the Italian Renaissance*, trans. Peter and Linda Murray (1952).
S–835 WÖLFFLIN, HEINRICH: *Renaissance and Baroque*, trans. K. Simon (1964).
S–836 WOODWARD, J.: *Tudor and Stuart Drawings* (1951).
S–837 YATES, FRANCES: *John Florio* (Cambridge, 1934).
S–838 YATES, FRANCES: *The Valois Tapestries* (1959).

See also §§S–173, 391, 428, 611, 920, 959, 967, 995.

Studies in languages other than English are particularly indispensable in relation to the fine arts—for example, *Il mondo antico del Rinascimento, Acti del V convegno internazionale di studi sul Rinascimento* (Florence, 1956; 1958); C. Hülsen, *Römische Antikengartendes XVI Jahnhunderts* (Heidelberg, 1977); Emile Male, *L'Art religieux apres le Concile de Trente* (Paris, 1932); R. Pallucchini, *La critica d'arte a Venezia nel Cinquecento* (Venice, 1943); Ludwig Schudt, *Italienreisen im 17. und 18. Jahrhundert* (Vienna and Munich, 1959); Aby Warburg, *Gesammelte Schriften* (Leipzig, 1932); etc.

LOGIC, RHETORIC AND LITERARY CRITICISM

S–839 ATKINS, J. W. H.: *English Literary Criticism: The Renascence*, 2nd ed. (1951).
S–840 CROLL, MORRIS W.: *Style, Rhetoric, and Rhythm*, ed. J. Max Patrick *et al.* (Princeton, 1966). On Renaissance Prose and Rhetoric.
S–841 CURTIUS, ERNST R.: *European Literature and the Latin Middle Ages*, trans. W. R. Trask (1953).
S–842 DUHAMEL, P. ALBERT: 'Milton's Alleged Ramism', *Publications of the Modern Language Association*, LXVII (1952), 1035–53.
S–843 EISENSTEIN, ELIZABETH L.: (a) 'The Advent of Printing and the Problem of the Renaissance', *Past and Present*, XLV (1969), 19–89; (b) 'Some Conjectures about the Impact of Printing on Western Society and Thought: A Preliminary Report', *Journal of Modern History*, XL (1968), 1–56.
S–844 EISENSTEIN, ELIZABETH L.: *The Printing Press as an Agent of Change* (1978), 2 vols.
S–845 EMMA, RONALD D.: *Milton's Grammar* (The Hague, 1964).
S–846 EMMA, RONALD D., and JOHN T. SHAWCROSS (eds.): *Language and Style in Milton* (1967).
S–847 FLOWER, ANNETTE C.: 'The Critical Context of the Preface to *Samson Agonistes*', *Studies in English Literature*, X (1970), 409–23.
S–848 GILBERT, NEAL W.: *Renaissance Concepts of Method* (1960).
S–849 GROSE, CHRISTOPHER: 'Milton on Ramist Similitude', in *Seventeenth Century Imagery*, ed. Earl Miner (Berkeley, 1971), Ch. VI.
S–850 HARDISON, O. B., JR. (ed.): *English Literary Criticism: The Renaissance* (1961).
S–851 HARRISON, J. L.: 'Bacon's View of Rhetoric, Poetry and the Imagination', *Huntington Library Quarterly*, XX (1957), 107–25.

S–852 HATHAWAY, BAXTER: *Marvels and Commonplaces: Renaissance Literary Criticism* (1968).

S–853 HOWELL, WILBUR S.: 'The Arts of Literary Criticism in Renaissance Britain', in his *Poetics, Rhetoric and Logic* (Ithaca, N.Y., 1975), Ch. II.

S–854 HOWELL, WILBUR S.: *Logic and Rhetoric in England, 1500–1700* (Princeton, 1956).

S–855 JARDINE, LISA: *Francis Bacon: Discovery and the Art of Discourse* (Cambridge, 1974).

S–856 JOHNSON, W. R.: 'Isocrates Flowering: The Rhetoric of Augustine', *Philosophy and Rhetoric*, IX (1976), 215–31.

S–857 JONES, RICHARD F.: 'Science and Language in England in the mid-Seventeenth Century', in §S–378; also 'The Rhetoric of Science in England of the mid-Seventeenth Century', in *Restoration and Eighteenth-Century Literature*, ed. Carroll Camden (Chicago, 1963), pp. 5–24.

S–858 KNOWLSON, JAMES: *Universal Language Schemes in England and France, 1600–1800* (Toronto, 1975).

S–859 LANHAM, RICHARD A.: *The Motives of Eloquence: Literary Rhetoric in the Renaissance* (New Haven, 1976).

S–860 LAWRENCE, NATALIE G., and J. A. REYNOLDS (eds.): *Sweet Smoke of Rhetoric: A Collection of Renaissance Essays* (Coral Gables, Fla., 1964).

S–861 LESHNER, SISTER JOAN MARIE: *Renaissance Concepts of the Commonplaces* (1962).

S–862 MAJOR, JOHN M.: 'Milton's View of Rhetoric', *Studies in Philology*, LXIV (1967), 685–711.

S–863 MIRIAM JOSEPH, SISTER, C.S.C.: *Rhetoric in Shakespeare's Time: Literary Theory of Renaissance Europe* (1962); abridged from *Shakespeare's Use of the Arts of Language* (1947).

S–864 MOHL, RUTH: *John Milton and his Commonplace Book* (1969).

S–865 MURRIN, MICHAEL: *The Veil of Allegory: Some Notes Towards a Theory of Allegorical Rhetoric in the English Renaissance* (Chicago, 1969).

S–866 MORKAN, JOEL: 'Wrath and Laughter: Milton's Ideas on Satire', *Studies in Philology*, LXIX (1972), 475–95.

S–867 NADEAU, RAY: 'A Renaissance Schoolmaster on Practice', *Speech Monographs*, XVII (1950), 171–79.

S–868 NELSON, NORMAN: *Peter Ramus and the Confusion of Logic, Rhetoric and Poetry* (Ann Arbor, 1947).

S–869 ONG, WALTER J.: *Ramus: Method, and the Decay of Dialogue* (Cambridge, Mass., 1958).

S–870 ONG, WALTER J.: 'Tudor Writings on Rhetoric, Poetic, and Literary Theory', in his *Rhetoric, Romance, and Technology* (Ithaca, N.Y., 1971), Ch. III.

S–871 PATTERSON, ANNABEL M.: *Hermogenes and the Renaissance: Seven Ideas of Style* (Princeton, 1970).

S–872 SACKTON, ALEXANDER H.: *Rhetoric as a Dramatic Language in Ben Jonson* (1948).

S–873 SEIGEL, JERROLD E.: *Rhetoric and Philosophy in Renaissance Humanism: The Union of Eloquence and Wisdom, Petrarch to Valla* (Princeton, 1968).

S–874 SHAWCROSS, JOHN.: 'The Rhetor as Creator in *Paradise Lost*', *Milton Studies*, VIII (1975), 209–20.

S–875 SHERRY, BEVERLY: 'Speech in *Paradise Lost*', *Milton Studies*, VIII (1975), 247–66.

S–876 SONNINO, LEE A.: *A Handbook to Sixteenth-Century Rhetoric* (1968).

S–877 SLOAN, THOMAS O.: 'Rhetoric and Meditation: Three Case Studies', *Journal of Medieval and Renaissance Studies*, I (1971), 451–58.

S–878 SLOAN, THOMAS O., and RAYMOND B. WADDINGTON (eds.): *The Rhetoric of Renaissance Poetry from Wyatt to Milton* (Berkeley, 1974).

S–879 SMITH, G. GREGORY (ed.): *Elizabethan Critical Essays* (1904). Primary Sources.

S–880 SPINGARN, JOEL E.: *A History of Literary Criticism in the Renaissance*, 2nd ed. (1908).

S–881 SPINGARN, JOEL E. (ed.): *Critical Essays of the Seventeenth Century* (Oxford, 1908–9), 3 vols.

S–882 STEADMAN, JOHN M.: *The Lamb and the Elephant: Ideal Imitation and the Context of Renaissance Allegory* (San Marino, Calif., 1974).

S–853 STEADMAN, JOHN M.: ' "Passions Well Imitated": Rhetoric and Poetics in the Preface to *Samson Agonistes'*, in *Calm of Mind*, ed. J. A. Wittreich (Cleveland, 1971), pp. 175–207.

S–884 TAYLER, EDWARD W. (ed.): *Literary Criticism of Seventeenth Century England* (1967). Primary sources.

S–885 WALLACE, KARL: *Francis Bacon on the Nature of Man* (Urbana, Ill., 1967).

S–886 WEINBERG, BERNARD: *A History of Literary Criticism in the Italian Renaissance* (Chicago, 1961), 2 vols.

S–887 WITTREICH, JOSEPH A., JR.: 'Milton's *Areopagitica*: its Isocratean and Ironic Contexts', *Milton Studies*, IV (1972), 101–15.

S–888 WITTREICH, JOSEPH A., JR.: ' "The Crown of Eloquence": The Figure of the Orator in Milton's Prose Works', in §S–947: pp. 3–54.

S–889 YATES, FRANCES: *The Art of Memory* (Chicago, 1966).

See also §§S–208, 290, 295, 477, 611, 893, 987, 988, 1003.

THE LITERARY BACKGROUND

S–890 ALLEN, DON C.: *Image and Meaning: Metaphoric Traditions in Renaissance Poetry*, rev. ed. (Baltimore, 1968).

S–891 ARNOTT, PETER D.: *An Introduction to the French Theatre* (1977). On the period to the late seventeenth century.

S–892 BABB, LAWRENCE: *The Elizabethan Malady: A Study of Melancholia in English Literature from 1580 to 1642* (East Lansing, Mich., 1951).

S–893 BARISH, JONAS: *Ben Jonson and the Language of Prose Comedy* (Cambridge, Mass., 1960).

S–894 BAROWAY, ISRAEL: 'The Bible as Poetry in the English Renaissance: An Introduction', *Journal of English and Germanic Philology*, XXXII (1933), 447–80; and three related studies in *Journal of English Literary History*: II (1935), 66 91; VIII (1941), 119–42; and XVII (1950), 115–35.

S–895 BENTLEY, GERALD E. (ed.): *The Seventeenth-Century Stage* (Chicago, 1968). See also his *The Jacobean and Caroline Stage: Dramatic Companies and Players* (Oxford, 1941–68), 7 vols.

S–896 BLACKBURN, RUTH H.: *Biblical Drama under the Tudors* (The Hague, 1971).

S–897 BOWRA, C. M.: *From Virgil to Milton* (1948). Essays on Virgil, Camões, Tasso and Milton.

S–898 BRADNER, LEICESTER: *Musae Anglicanae: A History of Anglo-Latin Poetry* (1940), Ch. I–VI.

S–899 BRERETON, GEOFFREY: *French Tragic Drama in the Sixteenth and Seventeenth Centuries* (1973).

S–900 BUSH, DOUGLAS: *English Literature in the Earlier Seventeenth Century*, 2nd rev. ed. (Oxford, 1962). With indispensable bibliographies.

S–901 BUSH, DOUGLAS: *Mythology and the Renaissance Tradition in English Poetry*, rev. ed. (1963).

S–902 CAMPBELL, LILY B.: 'The Christian Muse', *Huntington Library Bulletin*, VIII (1935), 29–70. The history of Urania's christianisation.

S–903   CAMPBELL, LILY B.: *Divine Poetry and Drama in Sixteenth Century England* (Cambridge, 1959).

S–904   CAVE, TERENCE C.: *Devotional Poetry in France c. 1570–1613* (Cambridge, 1969).

S–905   CHAMBERS, A. B.: 'Christmas: The Liturgy of the Church and English Verse of the Renaissance', *Literary Monographs*, VI (1975), 111–53.

S–906   COHEN, J. M.: *The Baroque Lyric* (1963).

S–907   COLIE, ROSALIE L.: *Paradoxia Epidemica: The Renaissance Tradition of Paradox* (Princeton, 1966).

S–908   COLIE, ROSALIE L.: *The Resources of Kind: Genre-Theory in the Renaissance* (Berkeley, 1973).

S–909   CONLEY, C. H.: *The First English Translations of the Classics* (1927).

S–910   COPE, JACKSON I.: *The Theater and the Dream: From Metaphor to Form in Renaissance Drama* (Baltimore, 1973).

S–911   CRUTTWELL, PATRICK: *The Shakespearean Moment and its Place in the Poetry of the Seventeenth Century* (1960). But see H. M. Richmond, 'Donne's Master: The Young Shakespeare', *Criticism*, XV (1973), 126–44.

S–912   DAVIDSON, PETER (ed.): *Critics and Apologists of the English Theatre* (1972).

S–913   DELANY, PAUL: *British Autobiography in the Seventeenth Century* (1969).

S–914   ELLIS-FERMOR, UNA: *The Jacobean Drama: An Interpretation*, 5th rev. ed. (1965).

S–915   ELLRODT, ROBERT: *L'Inspiration personelle et l'esprit du temps chez les poètes métaphysiques anglais* (Paris, 1960), 2 vols.

S–916   FISCH, HAROLD: *Jerusalem and Albion: The Hebraic Factor in Seventeenth-Century Literature* (1964).

S–917   FISH, STANLEY: *Self-Consuming Artifacts: The Experience of Seventeenth Century Literature* (Berkeley, 1972).

S–918   FISH, STANLEY (ed.): *Seventeenth-Century Prose: Modern Essays in Criticism* (1971).

S–919   FLETCHER, ANGUS: *The Transcendental Masque: An Essay on Milton's 'Comus'* (Ithaca, N.Y., 1971).

S–920   FREEMAN, ROSEMARY: *English Emblem Books* (1948). The emblem can now be studied through the collection edited by Arthur Henkel and Albrecht Schöne, *Emblemata* (Stuttgart, 1967). See also the bibliographical supplement in *Renaissance Quarterly*, XXIII (1970), 66–80.

S–921   FROST, DAVID L.: *The School of Shakespeare: The Influence of Shakespeare on English Drama, 1600–42* (Cambridge, 1968).

S–922   GRIERSON, SIR HERBERT: *Cross-Currents in English Literature of the XVIIth Century* (1929).

S–923   HALEWOOD, WILLIAM H.: *The Poetry of Grace: Reformation Themes and Structures in English Seventeenth-Century Poetry* (New Haven, 1970).

S–924   HAMILTON, G. K.: *The Two Harmonies: Poetry and Prose in the Seventeenth Century* (Oxford, 1963).

S–925   HARDING, DAVIS P.: *Milton and the Renaissance Ovid* (Urbana, 1946).

S–926   HARDISON, O. B., JR.: *The Enduring Monument: A Study of the Idea of Praise in Renaissance Literary Theory and Practice* (Chapel Hill, 1962).

S–927   HERRICK, MARVIN T.: *The Poetics of Aristotle in England* (New Haven, 1930). With a chapter on seventeenth-century interpretations.

S–928   HERRICK, MARVIN T.: *Italian Tragedy in the Renaissance* (Urbana, 1965).

S–929   HIRST, DÉSIRÉE: *Hidden Riches: Traditional Symbolism from the Renaissance to Blake* (1964).

S–930   JONAS, LEAH: *The Divine Science: The Aesthetic of Some Representative Seventeenth-Century English Poets* (1940).

S–931   JONES, RICHARD F.: *The Seventeenth Century* (Stanford, 1951), pp. 75–160. Studies of the period's prose styles.

S–932 JONES, R. C.: *A Literary History of Spain: The Golden Age: Prose and Poetry, the Sixteenth and Seventeenth Centuries* (1971).

S–933 KANE, ELISHA K.: *Gongorism and the Golden Age: A Study of Exuberance and Unrestraint in the Arts* (Chapel Hill, 1928).

S–934 KAUFMANN, U. MILO: *The Pilgrim's Progress and Traditions in Puritan Meditation* (New Haven, 1966).

S–935 KEAST, WILLIAM R. (ed.): *Seventeenth-Century English Poetry: Modern Essays in Criticism* (1962; extensively revised, 1971).

S–936 KERMODE, FRANK: 'Dissociation of Sensibility', *Kenyon Review*, XIX (1957), 169–94; repr. in *Essential Articles for the Study of John Donne's Poetry*, ed. John R. Roberts (Hamden, Conn., 1975), pp. 66–82.

S–937 KRANIDAS, THOMAS: *The Fierce Equation: A Study of Milton's Decorum* (The Hague, 1965). Also, 'Milton and the Rhetoric of Zeal', *Texas Studies in Literature and Language*, VI (1965), 423–32.

S–938 KURTH, BURTON O.: *Milton and Christian Heroism: Biblical Epic Themes and Forms in Seventeenth-Century England* (Berkeley, 1959).

S–939 LANCASTER, HENRY C.: *A History of French Dramatic Literature in the Seventeenth Century* (Baltimore and Paris, 1929–42), 9 vols.

S–940 LANGDON, IDA: *Milton's Theory of Poetry and Fine Art* (New Haven, 1924; repr. 1965).

S–941 LATHROP, HENRY B.: *Translations from the Classics into English from Caxton to Chapman*, University of Wisconsin Studies in Language and Literature, XXXV (1933).

S–942 LEE, SIR SIDNEY: *The French Renaissance in England* (1910).

S–943 LEWALSKI, BARBARA K.: *Donne's 'Anniversaries' and the Poetry of Praise* (Princeton, 1973).

S–944 LEWALSKI, BARBARA K.: *Milton's Brief Epic: The Genre, Meaning, and Art of 'Paradise Regained'* (Providence, R.I., 1966).

S–945 LEWALSKI, BARBARA K.: *Protestant Poetics and the Seventeenth-Century Religious Lyric* (Princeton, 1979).

S–946 LEWIS, C. S.: *The Discarded Image: An Introduction to Medieval and Renaissance Literature* (Cambridge, 1964).

S–947 LIEB, MICHAEL, and JOHN T. SHAWCROSS (eds.): *Achievements of the Left Hand: Essays on the Prose of John Milton* (Amherst, Mass., 1974).

S–948 LOW, ANTHONY: *Love's Architecture: Devotional Modes in Seventeenth-Century English Poetry* (1978).

S–949 MADDISON, CAROL: *Apollo and the Nine: A History of the Ode* (Baltimore, 1960).

S–950 MARTZ, LOUIS L.: *The Poetry of Meditation: A Study in English Religious Literature of the Seventeenth Century* (New Haven, 1954).

S 951 MAZZARO, JEROME: *Transformations in the Renaissance English Lyric* (Ithaca, N.Y., (1970)).

S–952 MILES, JOSEPHINE: *The Primary Language of Poetry in the 1640s* (Berkeley, 1948), being Part I of *The Continuity of Poetic Language* (Berkeley, 1951).

S–953 MINER, EARL: (a) *The Metaphysical Mode from Donne to Cowley*, and (b) *The Cavalier Mode from Jonson to Cotton* (Princeton, 1969 and 1971).

S–954 MOURGUES, ODETTE DE: *Metaphysical, Baroque and Précieux Poetry* (Oxford, 1953). On French poetry of the late Renaissance.

S–955 NELSON, LOWRY, JR.: *Baroque Lyric Poetry* (New Haven, 1961).

S–956 NICOLSON, MARJORIE H.: *The Breaking of the Circle: Studies in the Effect of the 'New Science' upon Seventeenth-Century Poetry*, rev. ed. (1960).

S–957 NICOLSON, MARJORIE H.: 'The Discovery of Space', in *Medieval and Renaissance Studies*, ed. O. B. Hardison (Chapel Hill, 1966), pp. 40–59.

S–958 NICOLSON, MARJORIE H.: *Mountain Gloom and Mountain Glory: The Development of the Aesthetics of the Infinite* (Ithaca, N.Y., 1959).

S–959 ORGEL, STEPHEN: *The Illusion of Power: Political Theater in the English Renaissance* (Berkeley, 1975).

S–960 ORNSTEIN, ROBERT: *The Moral Vision of Jacobean Tragedy* (Madison, 1960).

S–961 PALMER, HENRIETTA R.: *List of English Editions and Translations of Greek and Latin Classics printed before 1641* (1911).

S–962 PATRIDES, C. A. (ed.): *Approaches to Marvell* (1978).

S–963 PATRIDES, C. A. (Ed.): *Milton's 'Lycidas': The Tradition and the Poem* (1961).

S–964 PETERSON, DOUGLAS L.: *The English Lyric from Wyatt to Donne: A History of the Plain and Eloquent Styles* (Princeton, 1967).

S–965 PRINCE, F. T.: *The Italian Element in Milton's Verse* (Oxford, 1954).

S–966 PRAZ, MARIO: *The Flaming Heart: Essays on Crashaw, Machiavelli, and Other Studies in the Relations between Italian and English Literature* . . . (1958).

S–967 PRAZ, MARIO: *Studies in Seventeenth Century Imagery*, 2nd rev. ed. (Rome, 1964).

S–968 RAJAN, BALACHANDRA: *'Paradise Lost' and the Seventeenth Century Reader* (1947).

S–969 RICHMOND, H. M.: 'Ronsard and the English Renaissance', *Comparative Literature Studies*, VII (1970), 141–60.

S–970 RØSTVIG, MAREN-SOFIE: 'Ars Aeterna: Renaissance Poetics and Theories of Divine Creation', *Mosaic*, III (1970), 40–61.

S–971 ROSENMEYER, THOMAS G.: *The Green Cabinet: Theocritus and the European Pastoral Lyric* (Berkeley, 1973).

S–972 SASEK, LAWRENCE: *The Literary Temper of the English Puritans* (Baton Rouge, 1961).

S–973 SCOTT, IZORA: *Controversies over the Imitation of Cicero* (1910).

S–974 SCOULAR, KITTY W.: *Natural Magic: Studies in the Presentation of Nature in English Poetry from Spenser to Marvell* (Oxford, 1965).

S–975 SEATON, ETHEL: *Literary Relations of England and Scandinavia in the Seventeenth Century* (Oxford, 1935).

S–976 SHARP, R. L.: *From Donne to Dryden* (Durham, N.C., 1940).

S–977 SHERGOLD, N. D.: *A History of the Spanish Stage:* . . . *until the End of the Seventeenth Century* (Oxford, 1967).

S–978 SPARROW, JOHN: 'Latin Verse of the High Renaissance', in *Italian Renaissance Studies*, ed. E. F. Jacob (1960), pp. 354–409.

S–979 SPROTT, SAMUEL E.: *Milton's Art of Prosody* (Oxford, 1953).

S–980 STAUFFER, DONALD A.: *English Biography before 1700* (Cambridge, Mass., 1930).

S–981 STEADMAN, JOHN M.: *Milton and the Renaissance Hero* (Oxford, 1967).

S–982 STEIN, ARNOLD: 'On Elizabethan Wit', *Studies in English Literature*, I (1961), 75–91.

S–983 SUMMERS, JOSEPH H.: *George Herbert: his Religion and Art* (Cambridge, Mass., 1954).

S–984 SUMMERS, JOSEPH H. (ed.): *The Lyric and Dramatic Milton* (1965).

S–985 TAYLER, EDWARD W.: *Nature and Art in Renaissance Literature* (1964).

S–986 TILLYARD, E. M. W.: *The English Epic and its Background* (1954).

S–987 TRIMPI, WESLEY: *Ben Jonson's Poems: A Study of the Plain Style* (Stanford, 1962).

S–988 TUVE, ROSEMOND: *Elizabethan and Metaphysical Imagery: Renaissance Poetic and Twentieth-Century Critics* (Chicago, 1947).

S–989 TUVE, ROSEMOND: *Images and Themes in Five Poems by Milton* (Cambridge, Mass., 1957).

S–990 VICKERS, BRIAN: *Francis Bacon and Renaissance Prose* (Cambridge, 1968).

S–991 WADDINGTON, RAYMOND B.: *The Mind's Empire: Myth and Form in George Chapman's Narrative Poems* (Baltimore, 1974).

S–992 WALLERSTEIN, RUTH: *Studies in Seventeenth-Century Poetic* (Madison, 1950).

S–993 WALTON, GEOFFREY: *Metaphysical to Augustan* (1955).

S 994 WARNKE, FRANK J.: 'Marino and the English Metaphysicals', *Studies in the Renaissance*, II (1955), 160–75.

S–995 WARNKE, FRANK J.: *Versions of Baroque: European Literature in the Seventeenth Century* (New Haven, 1972).

S–996 WARNKE, FRANK J. (ed.): *European Metaphysical Poetry* (New Haven, 1961). Texts with translations.

S–997 WASSERMAN, EARL R.: *The Subtler Language* (Baltimore, 1959).

S–998 WATKINS, WALTER B. C.: *An Anatomy of Milton's Verse* (Baton Rouge, 1955).

S–999 WEBBER, JOAN: *The Eloquent 'I': Style and Self in Seventeenth-Century Prose* (Madison, 1968).

S–1000 WHIPPLE, THOMAS K.: *Martial and the English Epigram from Sir Thomas Wyatt to Ben Jonson* (Berkeley, 1925).

S–1001 WHITE, HELEN C.: *English Devotional Literature, Prose, 1600–1640* (Madison, 1931).

S–1002 WILLIAMSON, GEORGE: *The Donne Tradition* (Cambridge, Mass., 1930).

S–1003 WILLIAMSON, GEORGE: *The Senecan Amble: A Study in Prose Form from Bacon to Collier* (1951).

S–1004 WILSON, EDWARD N.: 'Spanish and English Religious Poetry of the Seventeenth Century', *Journal of Ecclesiastical History*, IX (1958), 30–53.

S–1005 WILSON, EDWARD M., and DUNCAN MOIR: *A Literary History of Spain: The Golden Age: Drama, 1492–1700* (1971).

S–1006 WILSON, ELKIN C.: *Prince Henry and English Literature* (Ithaca, N.Y., 1946).

S–1007 WILSON, F. P.: *Elizabethan and Jacobean* (Oxford, 1945).

S–1008 WILSON, F. P.: *Seventeenth Century Prose: Five Lectures* (Berkeley, 1960). On Burton, Browne, biographies, and sermons.

S–1009 WITTREICH, JOSEPH A., JR. (ed.): *Milton and the Line of Vision* (Madison, 1975).

S–1010 YARROW, P. J.: *The Seventeenth Century 1600–1715* (1967), in *A Literary History of France*, ed. P. E. Charvet, Vol. II.

See also §§S–96, 109, 157, 315, 342, 358, 372, 374, 477, 518, 549, 558, 610, 612, 691, 697, 699, 767, 805, 814, 819, 840, 846, 852, 878.

Index of names

The index includes individuals born before 1700. It also includes select mythological figures, but excludes biblical personalities, the individuals named only in the chronological outline (above, pp. 365–9), and the authors of all *STC* items unless mentioned in the preceding chapters (pp. 373–92: §P–1 to §P–686).

Index of names

Index of subjects

n this book respected authorities
n non-literary disciplines make
heir expert knowledge accessible
o students of literature. Each has
ndeavoured to provide not just a
rvey of his own field, but to offer
a coherent and incisive overview
from the perspective of his own
scholarly contributions.

While primarily intended to
provide necessary background
contexts and inter-disciplinary
perspectives to illuminate the
terature of the period, *The Age of
Milton* will also be highly valuable
to students of the historical
disciplines, music and the arts. It
should be as useful to the teacher
ishing to review the current state
f scholarship in adjacent fields as
o the student seeking to grasp the
broader dimensions of the age.

C.A. PATRIDES
is Professor of English at the University
of Michigan at Ann Arbor

RAYMOND B. WADDINGTON
Professor of English at the University of
Wisconsin

---

jacket picture
Gerrit van Honthorst, *Apollo and Diana*,
Hampton Court (see Chapter 9).
Crown copyright reserved; reproduced
by gracious permission of H.M.
the Queen

ISBN 0-389-20051-4 (hardcover)
ISBN 0-389-20052-2 (paperback)

**BARNES
& NOBLE
BOOKS**

81 Adams Drive, Totowa
New Jersey 07512